BOOKS BY ALEXANDER KENDRICK

———————

PRIME TIME
The Life of Edward R. Murrow

THE WOUND WITHIN
America in the Vietnam Years, 1945–1974

THE WOUND WITHIN

THE WOUND WITHIN

America in the Vietnam Years, 1945–1974

BY ALEXANDER KENDRICK

Little, Brown and Company — Boston — Toronto

PRINTING A

The author is grateful to Macmillan Publishing Co., Inc., for permission to reprint
lines from "The Second Coming" by William Butler Yeats from *Collected Poems*.
Copyright 1924 by Macmillan Publishing Co., Inc., renewed 1952 by Bertha
Georgie Yeats.

LIBRARY OF CONGRESS CATALOGING IN PUBLICATION DATA

Kendrick, Alexander
    The Vietnamization of America

    Bibliography: p.
    1. Vietnamese Conflict, 1961–   —United States
2. United States—History—1945–   I. Title.
DS557. A63K45   959.704'3373   74-4076
ISBN 0-316-48841-0

Published simultaneously in Canada by Little, Brown & Company (Canada) Limited

PRINTED IN THE UNITED STATES OF AMERICA

For Sarah

The wound that bleedeth inward is most dangerous.
—JOHN LYLY, *Euphues*

PREFACE

HISTORY IS HINDSIGHT. According to Senator Sam Ervin's Lightning Bug Theorem human beings, too, carry their illumination behind them. During the Vietnam War many Americans invoked their sacred right Not to Know, extenuated by presidential refusal to tell. Even now it is widely felt that Vietnam and Watergate are best forgotten as quickly as possible; they are still too close for comfort.

History is customarily written years later, when the full facts have been assembled, when perspectives can be applied, when, frankly, the scars have healed. But in our times the historiographic process has been speeded up in consonance with other social acceleration, and facts now become known and can be appraised more quickly than before. "Instant analysis" may be complained of, especially by those subjected to it, but it is not too early for judgments to be made about decisions and actions in the Vietnam-Watergate era. They are of course amenable to future modification. Every attempt is made here to report and assess events in their own context, both those known and those undisclosed at the time. But this is not only the history of 1946, and 1954, and 1965, and 1968. It is also that history as seen in 1974. The 20/20 vision of hindsight is obtained through bifocals, looking at things as and when they happened, and then in closer current prospect.

This book is less about Vietnam than about what Vietnam has done to America and Americans. It does not seek to "prove" anything, but rather to explain. It does not believe in the conspiracy theory of history, now much in vogue, at least not in conspiracy as a guiding force, but it does premise that in the interplay of human affairs, as in ecology, "everything is connected to everything else," if only coevally. It strives to follow the rule used in the author's forty years of news reporting and interpretation, that while objectivity in its dictionary definition is not possible — "uninfluenced by emotion, surmise or personal prejudice" — fairness is.

A climate of fear, suspicion, uncertainty, political demagogy and public spectacle bred the virus that Vietnamized America. It grew through indifference, ignorance, moral righteousness, unwillingness to confess error, and other human faults, notably arrogance.

Many Americans may still not want to know anything more about Vietnam and what it did to them, including Watergate. The day will come when they will, and must. For the words of de Tocqueville, written in the first half of the last century, retain their pertinence: "A democracy can obtain truth only as the result of experience, and many nations may perish while awaiting the consequences of their errors. The great privilege of the Americans does not consist in being more enlightened than other nations, but in being able to repair the faults they may commit."

CONTENTS

THE WOUND WITHIN

I

"NO BIG DEAL"

"THINGS FALL APART; THE CENTER CANNOT HOLD." Yeats's line has been among the most quoted of the past decade. In its full context his dream prophecy "The Second Coming" may be even more pertinent:

> Turning and turning in the widening gyre
> The falcon cannot hear the falconer;
> Things fall apart; the center cannot hold;
> Mere anarchy is loosed upon the world,
> The blood-dimmed tide is loosed, and everywhere
> The ceremony of innocence is drowned;
> The best lack all conviction, while the worst
> Are full of passionate intensity.
> Surely some revelation is at hand . . .

The Irish poet and playwright had his apocalyptic vision a half-century ago, in the time of his country's fight for independence against the Black-and-Tans. It marked a step in his own turn against all political systems because of "the cruelty of governments" of whatever variety. His words might have been written yesterday, to describe the Vietnam era and what it has done to the American nation. The revelation, if any, is to be determined. Might it have been Watergate that brought home from Vietnam the abuse of presidential power, shattered the Nixon administration with indictments, trials and jail sentences, raised a "firestorm" of public clamor that led to congressional consideration of impeachment of the President, and caused the ancillary resignation of the Vice-President?

For more than a decade the Vietnam War was a central issue in American policy. For many young Americans of draft age it was in fact the central issue of their lives, and for nearly fifty thousand of them a mortal one.

Some have pointed out, as President Johnson did when the first casualty lists came in, that more than fifty thousand Americans die every year in highway accidents and for no principle higher than that of the right-of-way. But the fifty thousand who died in Vietnam were there in the name of their country's power and prestige, indeed righteousness, and as the war progressed many of them became increasingly dubious about their role and purpose and even about their country's wisdom and morality.

Beyond the dead and wounded, moreover, beyond the monies spent that might have gone instead for the improvement of welfare, internal cohesion and understanding — or in the interest of world cooperation and order — the Vietnam War was disruptive and destructive of the fiber of American life and society. It helped create the amoral climate that nurtured Watergate. It brought into question the quality of national leadership, the uses of national power, the validity of national aims and values, the order of national priorities, the processes of decision-making, the nature of the American governmental structure, the pretensions of American world "leadership," the constitutional freedoms of press and assemblage, the effectiveness of political democracy, the consequences of technology, even the sacrosanct rule of law.

All these things were already undergoing scrutiny and metamorphosis as part of the inevitable machinery of change. Many of the events of the Sixties would have occurred in the normal course. The Vietnam War, however, sharpened issues, and intensified political and social conflict. Both a cause and a symptom of national dislocation, rebellion and alienation, and of course, their countereffects, the war almost sundered the nation. It may not be too much for history to say that the American Century, promulgated by Henry Luce in 1941, ended thirty years later in the jungles of Vietnam.

The war created an open and suppurating wound which has not yet healed, and if it does, it may leave a permanent scar on the American body politic. In tropical Indochina wounds often go bad and gangrene sets in. Parts of the body in effect die, and an atrophy of feeling results.

Lyndon Johnson came to believe that the wound, which he called "self-inflicted," was caused not by the war but by the bitter domestic dissension it aroused. This, he said, "encouraged our enemies, disheartened our friends, and weakened us as a nation." Defeated commanders are prone to blame lost wars on the stab-in-the-back at home. In Vietnam the stab was from the front, hara-kiri fashion. The grievous blow was dealt by the war itself, with its miasmic quality, its shifting sands of justification, the deviousness and secrecy of the decision-makers, their stubbornness and self-delusion.

Yet in the phrase used by Lieutenant William L. Calley, Jr., to describe the mass murders at My Lai for which he was tried and convicted — the overseas equivalent of the prototypical "Battle" of Wounded Knee — the war began as "no big deal" for the American people. If the English slept in the Thirties while the Germans armed, the Americans nodded before their television sets in the Sixties, as their leaders took the United States more and more deeply into an Asian commitment that grew by feeding on itself.

When the war finally broke into the American living room it seemed as unreal as the rest of television fare. It had to vie with the other war still being portrayed on the screen in *Combat, Twelve O'Clock High* and *Hogan's Heroes* (could anyone in 1944 have possibly imagined that a Nazi prisoner-of-war camp would ever be a subject for slapstick comedy?). In the shank of the evening, receiving the highest audience ratings, were seen the film epics of World War II: *The Bridge on the River Kwai, The Longest Day, Anzio* and *The Sands of Iwo Jima*. Which was the real war and which was the movie?

The time came when the actuality of Vietnam painfully asserted itself: when the Marines set fire to native huts with their cigarette lighters; when the severed ears of "Viet Cong" dead were proudly displayed for the camera by young Americans; when a Marine major's leg was cut off between commercials, and the police chief of South Vietnam executed a bound prisoner in open view; when Presidents appeared suddenly in the place of favorite programs, to promise peace while increasing war, and the Secretary of State warned of the Yellow Peril — "a billion Communist Chinese armed with nuclear weapons"; when the reassurances of generals and ambassadors were no longer believed; when Christmas after Christmas passed without the boys coming home, and the light at the end of the tunnel went out.

Not only for those at home but for many in combat in Vietnam the war had a feeling of fantasy about it. Young conscripts risked their lives daily in a kind of trance and one of them won the Medal of Honor for valor while under the influence of drugs.

"What are we doing in Vietnam?" was not only a political and diplomatic question but one of life-and-death for the young soldiers who perished in dubious battle, were wounded in meaningless combat, and measured achievement only by the body count, since terrain, cities, rivers and other normal war objectives had no significance. "We're here because we're here" was sung in World War II but was really written for Vietnam.

On the other hand Vietnam was the essence of practical experience for the professionals. Generals used it as a laboratory and proving ground for new weapons and theories, and created missions to fit their machines instead of the other way around. For officers and NCO "lifers" in the Army, Vietnam was the road to promotion, the place where their tickets were punched.

Though it brought many, perhaps too many, decorations and citations, it was a war without true heroes. Those who fought it were not able to win it; they tried only not to lose it.

A generation ago Americans were horrified by Guernica and Lidice. Vietnam has known hundreds of Guernicas and Lidices and when the records are added up, scores of Hiroshimas (at least in bombing tonnage). The B-52 bombers, built as the ultimate weapon of their time to carry nuclear devastation to the homeland of an equally armed and powerful adversary, were used in Vietnam to destroy the barnyards, as well as the bridges, supply trucks and military emplacements of a small, largely agricultural and, until the war itself changed things, obscure state.

The same trait that made American workers in 1940 respond to Franklin D. Roosevelt's demand for fifty thousand planes a year with remarks like "That's impossible. Now, how shall we do it?" led administration problem-solvers to apply themselves to the how and how much of Vietnam without asking why. Whether something ought to be done was subordinate to whether it could be done. The conduct of American foreign policy came to be so strongly influenced by military thinking that every President was his own Clausewitz.

Perhaps the most gangrenous aspect of the Vietnam involvement was that it was accepted for so long and so phlegmatically by so many people. For with it was accepted the weakening of Congress before the Executive, and other impairment of the delicately balanced American system of government. Accepted with the war were inroads into traditional freedoms, actions against the news media, conspiracy trials, preventive detention in the nation's very capital, and the Kent State shootings, in which the victims were the ones to be indicted. Accepted were the indiscriminate killing of Vietnamese, Laotian and Cambodian civilians — many died from "friendly fire" and what were officially called "friendly wounds" — the torture and execution of prisoners and bombing to a degree amounting to presumptive violation of the rule of war that there must be a reasonable proportionality between objectives and means.

Accepted with a shrug was the miming of democracy in Saigon under American aegis, and in the end was accepted the continuation of the war by massive American air power after American ground troops had been stood down, and the infliction of unprecedented amounts of bombing on both parts of Vietnam to insure "respect for the Office of the President of the United States."

In what began as a booby-trap war Vietnam itself became the biggest booby trap of all for American pride and power. The war accentuated the negative in the theses and antitheses of American life, and as Vietnam became increasingly Americanized, so America became increasingly Vietnamized.

Americanization of the war meant not only the use of American troops, weapons and supplies, but also the application of American methods under a self-assumed personal, collective, cultural and even racial superiority. It meant American control of Vietnamese economic life, American choice of the form and personnel of the government, American training of the Vietnamese army, American military policy, and the use of American-written textbooks in the schools, and elevation of the American worship of consumerism above the values of a four-thousand-year-old society that worshipped ancestors. In the slaughter many of South Vietnam's dead were left unburied, in violation of religious tradition. Their disturbed ghosts were released, it was believed, to bring about a massive perpetual haunting of the shattered land.

The war fragmentized, demoralized, dispersed, corrupted and terrorized Vietnamese life and social structure far beyond the death, suffering and physical damage it caused. The United States, spared the bombing that so many other countries have experienced, spared warfare on its own soil, received the impact of the faraway conflict as a recoil upon itself, also in the form of fragmentation, demoralization, corruption, alienation and self-doubt. In both countries government became less responsible to those who had elected it.

In America, as in Vietnam, attempts were made to repress opposition. In both countries students, intellectuals, war veterans and religious groups were most prominent among the dissenters, and charges of disloyalty, conspiracy, and even treason were freely uttered. Draft evasion was large-scale and in both the American and South Vietnamese conscript armies disintegration of morale was expressed by desertion, sometimes mutiny. The American Army had its "fragging" and the Navy its "fodding" — Foreign Object Damage to carriers and planes, meaning sabotage.

The war coincided with and helped bring about a reordering of American values. The Affluent Society was beginning to receive the bills incurred on its credit cards. They included the weakening of the family, the breaking of cultural customs, the insurgency of minorities, the growth of drug addiction and crime, the acceptance of violence as a means of achieving ends, rebellion against "noncreative" jobs, disenthrallment from education, the pollution of the environment, and the aggrandizement and concentration of business, labor and government.

In perspective it can be seen that the age of cultural "permissiveness" was an age of political submissiveness — to the war and presidential dominion, to governmental surveillance and political hollowness. A kind of moral insensibility, perhaps numbness, settled over human relationships in the spiritual twilight zone where opportunism was called timing, ambiguity called tact, cynicism called realism, and the greatest freedom was freedom from principle.

Alienation was the catchword for the discontents of American civilization. The Harris Poll devised an "alienation index." "Do you feel: The rich get richer and the poor get poorer? What you think doesn't count very much? The people running the country don't really care what happens to you? People who have the power are out to take advantage of you? Left out of things around you?" This may sound more like a paranoia index, but in 1972, with inflation and unemployment both high, it registered 47 percent.

One facet of the social change in America was an increased rootlessness, which was due to increased mobility, mechanical as well as social. Its effects were both physical and spiritual, entailing loss of security, loss of identity, and with the footlessness a kind of mindlessness. Not only farm workers but skilled technicians and corporation executives could be called migrant labor.

At the same time, the United States was imposing upon the Vietnamese a similar loss in their identification with past and place, by making so many of them refugees and destroying their Antaean contact with the earth. The ancestral village, focal point of Vietnamese life, was replaced by the refugee camp, made of tin and American packing cases. In 1972 the number of refugees reached five million in a population of eighteen million. Between 40 and 50 percent of Vietnamese lived in and around towns, against a prewar figure of 15 percent. This enforced urbanization was that of an industrial economy, but there was no industry.

The small distant country became a mirror of the larger American society, as it used to be of the French, and for centuries before that, of the Chinese. It was not a simple mirror, however. It magnified, and the reflection it returned set fires in the United States as if by a burning glass.

The American command in Vietnam damaged not only its own spirit but that of the Vietnamese people by condoning the widespread corruption of Vietnamese government officials and the military. This included graft, theft and embezzlement on a grand scale, black marketing, trading or collusion with the "Viet Cong," the sale of army commissions and government posts, nepotism, the political protection of inefficiency, kickbacks on contracts, customs' fraud, and not least, trafficking in drugs.

Corruption has existed in all societies, but not often in the integral way in which it permeated Vietnam, as a mixture of Asian cumshaw, French *débrouillage*, and American wealth, waste and wild oats. It defiled everything, including the South Vietnamese presidential election of 1971, when the United States in its manipulations to contrive a pretense of democracy, offered funds to other candidates to "oppose" the incumbent, General Thieu, and then dropped even the pretense and sanctioned Thieu's solo candidacy. The egregiousness of the American Embassy surpassed its own precedent of 1955 and the rigged plebiscite of Ngo Dinh Diem, which enabled the United States to replace France as the protector of his uncertain future.

After his election Thieu also exceeded Diem in the sweeping nature of his rule by decree, his imprisonment of alleged opponents of his regime, and his censorship of the press. As in 1956, the United States decided it could not interfere in South Vietnam's "internal affairs." To many Americans it seemed as if the United States had two Presidents making policy, one in Washington, the other in Saigon.

When Thieu received 91.5 percent of the vote in 1971 it was explained in Washington that even some American elections have been dishonest. The presidential campaign of 1972 proved the point. By that time Vietnamization had eaten its way well into the core of American democracy. Mayors of large cities were being indicted for corruption and political bosses jailed. One of the nation's most respected federal judges, Otto Kerner, was sent to prison for bribery, conspiracy and tax evasion while he was governor of Illinois. But the Kerner case and other such individual venality as Harry Vaughn's deepfreeze in the Truman administration, Sherman Adams's vicuna coat in the Eisenhower administration, and the Bobby Baker influence-peddling scandal in the Johnson administration, were sinisterly overshadowed by the political apocalypse of Watergate under Nixon.

Watergate differed from the previous scandals not only in degree but in kind. It could not be called simply campaign skulduggery or "dirty tricks," as the President's defenders held. On the surface — when the surface came to be exposed — it involved the use of lavish Republican funds, some secretly contributed, to carry out the burglary and "bugging" of Democratic national headquarters, and the infiltration and bedevilment of the 1972 Democratic primaries. Beneath the surface lay the accumulation of power, political and personal, which the Nixon administration had extended beyond all precedent and used in the furtherance of a presidential system of government.

Like Vietnam, Watergate was not an aberration but the logical extension of authority, indeed the political form of Vietnam. The unaccountable exercise of power in the war was meshed with the power being exerted at home to give the White House control of the cabinet departments, to place the "President's men" in federal agencies, to dictate the budget by veto or impoundment of funds. The concentration of power would have become cancerous with a proposed, admittedly illegal program of "internal security" in 1970, which would have advanced Orwell's ominous date by fourteen years. The "Gestapo mentality" that the chairman of the Senate committee investigating Watergate discerned behind this domestic counter-insurgency plan was possessed by men "who almost stole America," in the words of another committee senator. Howard Hunt, the former CIA agent arrested in the Watergate burglary, summed up matters through his fictional hero, the CIA agent Peter Ward: "We became lawless in a struggle for the rule of law."

In Watergate, the "law and order" administration, which used conspiracy charges like a broadax against suspected subversives, was involved in the darkest conspiracy of all, the subversion of the fundamental political processes. Richard Nixon, who may be known in American history as the Great Impugner — as Lincoln was the Great Emancipator, Clay the Great Compromiser and Bryan the Great Commoner — was in the end himself impugned as no other President has been, widely found by public opinion to have violated the democratic ethos that power is not only transferred but is used under constitutional rules. Nixon's Vice-President, Spiro Agnew, maintained the links with more traditional political practice by being brought into an investigation of state contracts in Maryland. The result was the first vice-presidential removal from office for criminal cause, though effected by resignation.

The Watergate inquiry, the rarely summoned Grand Inquest, conducted jointly by Senate committee and special prosecutor — with its dismissals from office and its indictments of once powerful figures, its guilty pleas, turning of state's evidence, and taking of the Fifth Amendment by men who had previously regarded its use as tantamount to conviction — was seen by some as proof that the "System" was decadent, by others that it "worked." In concentration on the morality of the administration it may have been overlooked how closely entwined had government and business become, not only as to interests but as to ethics.

The giant multinational conglomerate, International Telephone and Telegraph, did not stop at an antitrust settlement with the Justice Department, made following a financial pledge to the Republican convention, but solicited the clandestine intervention of the American government to protect its corporate interests in Chile. Other corporations contributed to the 1972 presidential campaign in willful illegality, and the government approved an increase in milk support prices following donations from the dairy interests. Cost overruns were ordinary in defense contracts, and the Lockheed Aircraft Corporation was bailed out of its own mistakes by a government-endorsed loan. The cost of consumer fraud was estimated at $200 billion a year in the form of overpricing, inferior quality, surcharges, deception, violation of standards, and monopoly. Fraud has indeed grown into an institutionalized corporate crime.

The blurring of American values, always present to some degree in the realm of Making It, had apparently been widened as never before, with the help of mass media acting upon mass audiences. The decade that began with John F. Kennedy's ringing inaugural speech closed with a measurable loss of national confidence and hope. "Ask not what your country can do for you," the new young President had declared in 1961. In May 1972 his only surviving brother wrote the era's epitaph. How often, asked Senator Edward Kennedy, has the average American been failed by his country?

Within the decade the torch John Kennedy accepted for a new generation of Americans had been lowered and the trumpet calling the nation into a "long twilight struggle" muted. The domestic concerns which had not intruded at all upon his inaugural rhetoric had become the most important for the legatee generation. That men walked on the moon was less important to many Americans than that they still knew social and economic inequality, that even among the more favored, jobs for the mere sake of jobs were not enough; that the problems of racial and ethnic minorities, the cities, the environment, "law and order," had been compounded by the obsessive, never-ending war.

Even education, the American Holy Grail, became tarnished as students rebelled, not only against the war and the government's connections with the university but against the inadequacies, disappointments and misconstruing of education itself. Universality of schooling, it had become evident, did not mean equality of economic opportunity. Other controlling factors were at work. Equality required legal and social sanctions, and this meant "socialism." Unhappily socialism had not functioned too well in the countries where it was statutorily practiced.

The country's apparent moral exhaustion was deepened by Vietnam. It was a decade of war, assassinations, everyday violence, economic uncertainties, embittered domestic relationships — American troops were sent not only to Indochina, the Dominican Republic, Thailand and the Tonkin Gulf, but to Mississippi, Alabama, Detroit and Washington — environmental impairment, and flight from reality. The American capacity to learn from mistakes was somehow no longer functioning, as the mistakes continued to be repeated.

Other countries also fought wars during the decade, in the Middle East, in southern Asia and northern Africa, and countered insurgencies in eastern Europe and the Western Hemisphere. Youthful rebellion was as much a fact in war-free Sweden and Germany as in the United States. Racial hostilities were no less acute in South Africa or the Sudan. Barriers of color, caste, religion and language provoked strife from Quebec to Northern Ireland to East Pakistan. Still, it was upon America, raised to believe it was born in revolution for equality and opportunity, that much of the hope of the world's future had rested, if only by force of example. Now the hope was diminished, as principle and precept were abandoned for prestige in Vietnam.

It could be seen, if not by Americans then by others, that what the American system had come to offer was freedom without power to the great majority. Seventy-three percent of the people might make it plain that they wanted the war to end and the United States to withdraw from Vietnam completely, but the President was able to make it equally plain this would not happen until he himself had decided upon it.

The resultant conflict, embroiled with all the other issues of the decade, was one of radical challenge and conservative counterchallenge. The young faced their elders, the poor their more affluent neighbors, students faced their teachers, blacks faced whites, women faced men, and homosexual "gays" defied the "straights." At the same time, orthodoxy made its own confrontation with heterodoxy, the puritan with the hedonistic, ruralism with urbanism. Would some sort of Hegelian synthesis ultimately create itself between the "two nations" that unlike Disraeli's England were more than merely "rich" and "poor"? They might better be called the still enchanted and the disenchanted. Or might they even be, as Richard Nixon suggested in his 1972 nomination acceptance speech, American and un-American?

The liberal credo, above all, was in the cross-fire between the opposing sides. It had been used to justify the intervention in Vietnam, which it variously called action again aggression, containment of Communism, support of self-determination, limitation of war aims, restraint upon war conduct. When all the cherished formulas were mocked by the actuality of Vietnam, leading to the devastation of another society, the liberal credo was inevitably challenged also, as the dominant force in American thought.

Vietnam was the liberals' war, the liberals including politicians and even some generals. Their values had been transferred, like a Japanese decalcomania, to Southeast Asia. The intellectuals of the Kennedy and Johnson administrations — "the best and the brightest," David Halberstam called them — came to be identified with the carnage and cruelty of the war. Even Richard Nixon called himself a Wilsonian as he continued it for four years more.

Vice-President Spiro Agnew could assail the "eastern liberal establishment" from the Right, especially news media that he thought could not understand that criticism of a President's words and actions constituted treasonable defamation of the very institution of the Presidency. The thunder from the New Left, however, was more damaging to the pretensions of the liberals than the anti-intellectual salvoes of the new Know-Nothings. Pericles once remarked: "In Athens we think that silent men are useless." In Agnew's and Nixon's America the "silent majority" was provided with purpose. Yet the government continued to treat not only its critics but its supporters with suspicion, and its "silent majority" became those who received, and did not seem to mind, silence about many governmental actions, intentions, and reasons.

The "new American revolution" of the Sixties — which Nixon upon entering office sought to preempt as a mere reshuffling of bureaucracy, administrative controls, and federal financial dealings with the states — consisted of a number of interlocking revolutions, against various institutions, traditions and relationships. All were quickened, dramatized, personalized and otherwise enhanced by the communications revolution that was taking place simultaneously.

Telstar and Early Bird, followed by Comsat, the earth satellites, made it possible to see things as they happened virtually anywhere in the world. Thereby all men became part of the same time as well as of the same space, in the United States, in Vietnam, in the Congo, New Guinea and the Matto Grosso. Change could be seen taking place everywhere at once, though of different degree or pace. Problems, because omnipresent, became greater than ever before, qualitatively as well as quantitatively. Not only was Lake Erie polluted but also Lake Baikal, and Lake Tanganyika and Lake Titicaca were becoming so.

Vietnam, as the radical student leader Carl Oglesby saw it, was the first American war "to be so big, so protracted, and above all so well observed: a whole nation beholds itself in the act. . . . We can scarcely return unchanged from this spectacle to dream the old dreams, take comfort in the old verities. . . . With this war history becomes the intimate affair of each of us, a private act for which each of us has to account personally."

If the United States was a racist society, as the Kerner Commission report on the urban riots of the decade forthrightly found, in the minds of many it was fighting a racist war. The antiwar movement and the civil rights movement became intertwined like the serpents of the caduceus.

In the same way that extremist opponents and extremist supporters of the war could both question the concept of "limited warfare," so extremists on both sides of the racial question, diehard white supremacists and black nationalists, separatists and advocates of "community control," joined in opposing school integration and bussing. Black Power demands further aroused ethnic consciousness among whites. The Jewish Defense League opposed blacks in the mixed neighborhoods of New York City while the Italo-Americans in Newark became vigilantes and made their neighborhoods antiblack fortresses.

The theme "Black Is Beautiful," a compensation for inequality, was linked with the belief by some, like Malcolm X, that America was a "prison" for blacks. This made "political prisoners" of those in confinement for robbery, rape and other crimes. Radicalization of the prisons with their growing numbers of blacks and Puerto Ricans came to a climax in the bloody Attica insurrection and the San Quentin killing of the black activist and self-taught revolutionary George Jackson, who had made the prison a university for others also.

In these years many American blacks saw in their own country the Heart of Darkness that Joseph Conrad had found in Africa. The increase in the numbers of blacks in prison did not, however, mean that only blacks were committing more crimes. Lawbreaking in general increased, most noticeably among white middle-class suburban youth. The fact remained that the blacks, the poor and the uneducated made up the largest part of the prison population. They often had inadequate legal representation. They received harsher sentences and were less readily paroled.

Their rebellions and the reasons for them were not addressable as a political problem. The economic and social justice they sought was not in the power of wardens or parole boards to grant. The demand to be "treated like human beings," moreover, though not to be gainsaid, came too often from those who had scarcely treated their victims as such. To aggravate matters of "law and order," administration officials and other authorities often preferred to find scapegoats rather than solutions, and these included the news media, war dissenters, college "bums" and the courts.

The American "revolution" had its own internal conflict also. The traditional or "Old" Left in politics, it seemed to younger activists, merely promised more technology, more formulas, more bureaucracy, even though in different hands. The New Left held itself to be interested in subjective impulses rather than in the objectivity of dialectical materialism — in consciousness, feeling, identity and individualism. The New Left therefore assaulted the Old, and the principal combat area was the universities. Like the Old Left, the New was soon riven by its own factionalism. A section of it became acutely radicalized by the lack of accommodation it found, and was drawn to violence by the often violent methods used to still it. This in turn conservatized other parts of the New Left. By 1972 students were no longer fighting police but seeking the protection of the onetime "pigs" against the nonpolitical facts of campus robbery, theft and drug trafficking.

The "revolution" of the Sixties was less Marxist than Proudhonian. The French utopian socialist had declared, "Property is theft," and in urban rioting but no less in everyday circumstances "countertheft" was widely practiced as a form of social protest, or a pretext for it. Self-appointed youth leaders advocated the "rip-off," or "instant socialism," as the only means of survival in a predatory civilization. Just as some blacks considered themselves "political prisoners," many young whites professed to regard shoplifting, burglary, and bilking the telephone company by electronic methods as political protest.

Some "revolution" was also "for the hell of it," as the "Yippie" leader Abbie Hoffman phrased it, the consequence of boredom. Social and political pressures affected the nature of the theater, art, music, even religious practices. The theater — Living Theater, Open Theater, Guerrilla Theater — was for many a mystical experience while the church became a theatrical one. God was not dead, after all; indeed Jesus Christ was Superstar.

During the Sixties youth became a class, almost a separate race, instead of merely an age-span, and a key word in the sorrows of young Werthers was "irrelevance," a concept that led to the curt dismissal of much of the stockpile of custom and social behavior. The "relevance" of technology was especially questioned. Even working-class youth, secure in union jobs, revolted against the repetitiveness of "noncreative" work and halted the assembly lines at the world's most modern auto plant, disrupting the American myth that Henry Ford had emancipated the workingman. The assembly-line rebellion of "blue-collar" youth, by strikes, absenteeism and large turnover, followed by a few years the campus rebellion of middle-class youth, but in both cases more than specific working or schooling conditions were involved. The acts acquired political meaning because they were against "something wrong" with the "quality" of life. As the cup of sullen dissent was brimmed, the American feeling of guilt for not being able to "make it," the Willy Loman disease, the blaming of oneself for the inability to adjust to society, was inverted into the criticism of society for having become so difficult to adjust to.

Many of the rebels of the Sixties, having proclaimed their own "counter"-culture, formed "families," groups, collectives and communes, rural, suburban and urban. They engaged in neighborhood law practice, arts and crafts, medical clinics, farming, teaching, architecture, and local politics. Having learned that to change the world might take a long time, they were willing to try to change their block or barnyard first. Some also changed their minds and "dropped back in."

Dissidents who shook their fists and fought the police outside the Democratic convention of 1968 raised their hands for recognition and fought for platform planks inside the Democratic convention of 1972. The Black Panthers, who had chilled the marrow of white society by brandishing rifles and threatening to "off the pigs," came to dispute Chairman Mao's thought that "power springs from the barrel of a gun" and ran for local office within the system they had talked of overthrowing. When "Black Power" was achieved in some northern cities it proved chimerical. Mayor Kenneth Gibson found that he could not solve bankrupt Newark's problems any better than his white predecessors could. Mayor Carl Stokes of Cleveland stepped out and became a news broadcaster in New York City. But it had become easier for other blacks to seek and win office, even in the South.

In the colleges blacks, having achieved more entry, more choice of courses and new teachers, became part of a new status quo and mounted guard against any threat to their position, including the open admission of "brothers" of lower income. College blacks remained apart from ghetto blacks or southern tenant farmers and field hands. They had at least established that racial militancy was not always to be equated with political radicalism.

Vietnam served as the label on the bottle of tumult, alienation and readjustment that represented the decade. Though catalytic in its essence, the war in a larger sense was also antithetical to much of the renewal and change that the Sixties are now seen to have represented. It was a kind of last gasp of old policies and methods. Still, as a tragic moral experience, it emphasized the profundity of the changes that had to be made because of the graveness of error. How and why did the obsession with Vietnam come about, the war that George F. Kennan, the 1946 apostle of containment, in 1972 called "the most disastrous of all America's undertakings over the whole two hundred years of its history"?

To Walter Lippmann the major mistake was the belief that the undisputed American position at the end of the Second World War was "a permanent arrangement of power in the world." Others, perhaps more moralistic, thought the mistake was made in coming to the succor of a dying colonial system, trying to keep it alive in Indochina after India, Indonesia and Israel had proved it doomed.

As a very young congressman John F. Kennedy condemned the moribund colonialism. As President he became the executor of the deceased's estate. With some tolerance, Lippmann thought that the United States was simply "sucked in" by the vacuum which the breakup of the British, French, Dutch and finally Japanese colonial empires created in the Far East. If this was the fault of political physics, it was made a colossal misjudgment and worse by the failure to acknowledge it, or to correct it without acknowledgment.

Originally in Vietnam, the United States was on the side of the Viet Minh against Japan in World War II, the same Viet Minh which as the National Liberation Front and the People's Army of North Vietnam confronted American troops when they replaced the French expeditionary forces. The change in American policy and attitude was the result of the Cold War against Communism in the postwar years, and the application of the Truman Doctrine to Asia in the Korean War. As in Korea it was deemed necessary in Vietnam to be against Peking and thus on the side of the French. After Dien Bien Phu and the Geneva armistice of 1954, the United States supplanted the French and began its own active role in Indochina, as an adjunct to its complex relations in Europe with the Soviet Union. Vietnam became a third front, as Korea had been a second front, against "world Communism" ruled from the Kremlin. Under Kennan's theory Communism had to be "contained" at all points.

Other reasons have been offered for American entry into Vietnam, for example, as a logical continuation of historical interest in the Pacific, going back to the clippers and the "Open Door" in China; or again, as a capitalist-imperialist venture in the Marxist sense.

Some have seen intervention as idealism, some as an aberration, some as deliberate aggression, and some have resignedly attributed it to the very nature of a Great Power, which must demonstrate its ability to have its will in the world. Some have cited Parkinson's "Law" as sufficient explanation: a military machine will expand to fill the work it has decided it must do, even if the work has to be invented. The Pentagon Papers, it has been argued, merely illustrated contingency planning, but as Parkinson foresaw, after contingencies were planned for they had to be realized so that the plans could be used.

Perhaps something of all these motivations went into Vietnam, though with due deference to historical materialism, the old-fashioned imperialist theory would seem to have less pertinence than the others. If the United States had entered Vietnam for the sake of pecuniary profit — President Eisenhower spoke of the rubber, tin and tungsten there as stakes, and others have seen the prospects of oil — any sagacious investor would have cut his losses long ago and turned to tax-free municipal bonds. Vietnam constituted for the American "ruling class" a political, economic and moral catastrophe.

Even "neo-imperialism," connoting political and ideological domain through alliances and economic aid, has caused gigantic American deficits abroad and a decline in American overseas economic power, with the German mark and Japanese yen becoming firmer and more desirable currencies than the twice-devalued dollar. Neo-imperialism is to some economists less a matter of specific advantage than a sort of crusade to maintain the spirit and climate for a free ingress of American capital wherever it might want to go in the world. If so, the timing has been particularly ill-advised, in the face of a growing consciousness of "something wrong" with the system of free enterprise and an ever-grosser National Product.

There are also those who would place the onus of Vietnam on the particular decision-makers involved, implying that other individuals would have acted otherwise, against the American mythos, against the hubris of Manifest Destiny, against the proud determination to remain "Number One." But Vietnam was not a personal idiosyncracy. It was rooted in history, habit and hauteur.

In whatever way the underlying causes of American intervention may be apportioned, when intervention became in 1954 a deliberate, full-bodied policy, the primary generating force was an intricate interrelationship of fears and misapprehensions about Communism, at home and abroad. It may be concluded in retrospect that these fears were not justified or that they could have been ministered to by other means. In the immediate post-war period they were painfully understandable. The United States had rapidly demobilized across the Atlantic and Pacific, while Soviet forces, though also much decreased, not only remained in Europe but imposed their pattern on its eastern states. Soviet diplomacy was rude and overbearing, though this may have been to conceal weakness and uncertainty rather than to prove strength, and Soviet propaganda was strident and pervasive.

There was, in fact, a Stalinist menace, though not an actual military threat from a war-devastated country in the form of a "march" to the English Channel. Doubt about Soviet intentions had existed in the war itself, despite the nominal alliance against Hitler, and entered into the very founding of the United Nations, and into continuing mutual suspicion and rivalry.

Whatever its causes, the postwar Soviet malignity cannot be discounted. It has not been forgotten by those who lived in the period of the building of a separate Germany on the ruins of Hitler's chancellery, of the Communist coup in Czechoslovakia, the Berlin blockade and airlift, the founding of the Cominform, Yugoslavia's secession from the Communist "bloc," the ten-year occupation of Austria, the triumph of the Chinese Communists, the Korean War, Soviet acquisition of the nuclear "equalizer," and Foreign Minister Molotov's declaration that "all roads lead to Communism." It can be perceived now that Moscow's postwar interests lay within what had been defined, in one way or another, as the Soviet sphere of influence. Its consolidation should not perhaps have been taken as an intention of further expansion. The plain fact is that in the context of the times it was.

This assumption, fed upon by domestic events — the "Soviet spy" cases of Alger Hiss and the Rosenbergs, the disloyalty accusations against the atomic scientist J. Robert Oppenheimer, Senator Joseph R. McCarthy's charge that "Communists" in the State Department had "lost China" — made it impossible for any administration, Democratic or Republican, to contemplate the "loss" of Indochina as well.

The American decision to intervene in Vietnam, by supporting the creation of an American-financed and American-directed South Vietnamese "republic" there in violation of the Geneva agreement, reflected the prevailing judgment and the "historical and political truth" of 1954. The virus of McCarthyism, however, maintained the anti-Communist fever after the basic illness had begun to wane.

For by 1954 Stalin was dead. His Communist suzerainty had begun to weaken, thawing at home and bending to the forces of nationalism in the satellite countries, nationalism which the war against Hitler had stimulated in the Soviet Union as well. Moscow's wards — Romanian, Polish, Hungarian, Czech, Albanian and above all Chinese — were exhibiting growing anti-Russian sentiments, whatever the nature and degree of their own authoritarianism. Even in the Soviet citadel of East Berlin workers had rebelled, pointing the way to Poznan, Budapest and Prague. Western Europe had been held and restored, and was being made prosperous. The Third World was establishing itself, and its neutralism meant that if it would accept no American neo-colonialism it would accept no Russian neo-colonialism, either. Stalin's successors were seeking detente with the West after years of animosity. The Communist adventure in Korea had ended not in victory but at best in stalemate. The Chinese were back beyond the Yalu, and the principal question concerning them was not where they would intervene next but how long before they would challenge Moscow openly.

The Cold War against the Soviet Union had in short been "won," if such confrontations are ever won. Communism had been contained and without resort to nuclear arms. America's power and international prestige could be accepted as categorical and it could be recalled that the stated purpose of containment was not mutual destruction but coexistence.

Then the great democracy of the West succumbed to its inbred doubts. It not only remained in Vietnam but enlarged its commitment there, beyond the rational demands of the situation, at great cost, and finally with mounting humiliation and the diminution of the honor and prestige it said it sought to preserve.

Primarily the United States made the celebrated miscalculation that Communist China was a "Slavic Manchukuo," a "colonial Russian government," as Assistant Secretary of State Dean Rusk had phrased it in 1951, and thus part of a Sino-Soviet "bloc" engaged in a worldwide conspiracy for aggression and expansion. The pronouncement was self-fulfilling. By entering Vietnam, the United States compelled both Russia and China to support a "war of national liberation," which at Geneva they had clearly showed themselves anxious to be rid of by persuading Hanoi to accept a settlement it regarded as unfair and insufficient.

Another dubious American conviction was that it was important, in Kipling's "Great Game" of Big Power conflict, whether poor rural societies like Vietnam were "Communist-dominated" or not. Like nuclear weapons, capitalism and Communism have meaning only to advanced industrial societies. John Kenneth Galbraith has noted that "capitalism is not an issue in a country that has yet to experience capitalism and neither is Communism as an alternative." The Vietnamese, moreover, have never been given more of a chance than between Communism and some authoritarian form of anti-Communism — French colonial rule, Japanese occupation, the repressive Diem regime, and a series of American-installed military dictatorships leading to President Thieu's one-man "election."

Yet beyond the substantive there was another mistake made by Americans in Vietnam, perhaps the most serious and costly of all. It was the inability, despite all the Games Theory practiced in the Pentagon and at MIT, to see things from "the other side of the hill," in Liddell Hart's phrase, to appreciate an opposite point of view. This is a failure not of intelligence but of imagination. Lack of imagination has always been an American weakness, perhaps because the country has never experienced bombardment (except briefly at Pearl Harbor), invasion or occupation. Americans have flown around the dark side of the moon, but the other side in Vietnam has remained dark to American understanding. Only years later did former Secretary of State Rusk, who had participated in escalation from its beginning to its peak, confess how dismally the United States leadership had underestimated the purpose, determination and ability of "the enemy."

North Vietnamese troops in South Vietnam, for all their dedication and courage to the point of mortal foolhardiness, had over the years suffered hunger, fatigue, discomfort and fear, like any other soldiers, as their diaries, notebooks, letters and poems revealed. They were kept under discipline by indoctrination and the constant tutelage of their political officers. Many deserted from among the 100,000 who went down the Ho Chi Minh trail each year. American Intelligence reported the bad morale, shortages, poor leadership and dissatisfaction. It failed to report that all these things had been brought into the open for purposes of self-criticism and to seek solutions. They did not mean that the North Vietnamese army was falling apart. For all its skills, American Intelligence could not get inside Vietnamese minds.

In "containing" Communism the United States forsook many of its boasted principles. Any other declared foe of "the Sino-Soviet bloc" became its friend, including military regimes in Greece, fascism in Spain, feudalism in Saudi Arabia, dictatorships in Latin America, Communism itself in Yugoslavia. An American global chain was forged of forty-four treaties against Communist "aggression." It was not important whom they were with or for what restrictive internal purposes they could be used.

Another forsaken principle was a constitutional one. The virtual abdication of Congress from its proper functions enabled the Chief Executive to act not only as the commander-in-chief of declared war, but as the declarer.

"Strong" Presidents in American history have been those popularly so regarded as much for their forceful personalities as for their willingness to extend the presidential power to its stated limit. With Franklin D. Roosevelt the assumption of unstated powers was undertaken in domestic affairs, requiring adjudication by the Supreme Court. Roosevelt also pressed beyond previous limits the use of executive authority vis-à-vis previously responsible cabinet departments, especially the State Department. With respect to war, Roosevelt withheld information and practiced deceptions, such as "neutrality," because he evidently did not believe the American people were prepared to enter into another European conflict no matter how strongly they might feel about the domestic excesses or territorial conquests of the Nazis. A vociferous "America First" movement at any rate said so. Since the war when it came, as the result of direct attack on American soil, was accepted as a just and necessary one, the deceptions which preceded it were in effect legitimated. Roosevelt could be said to have taught his successors, the most worshipful of whom was Lyndon Johnson, that lying succeeded and could be for the "public good."

As commander-in-chief Roosevelt directed a global war, and though some accused him of making American participation in it inevitable — by an embargo on Japanese trade and the exchange of American destroyers for American bases in British territories — it seems safe to say that Hitler's conquest of Europe was not a White House plot but a development rooted in European history and the First World War.

Strong Presidents are so now, not by force of character, but by virtue of the extent of their assumed, or as some have called them, usurped powers. Responsibility for policy-making, carrying with it the means of changing international relations, is cushioned by the claim of Executive Privilege, extended to presidential advisers, notably to Nixon's assistant for national security, Henry Kissinger. The uninformed Secretary of State could be questioned by congressional committees, but for Kissinger immunity was argued until he himself became Secretary of State. Even then his continuing role as presidential assistant created potential conflict. When the White House was implicated in the Watergate inquiry Nixon tried to extend immunity to all government employees, past as well as present, and to make all White House documents "presidential papers." The question was whether Executive Privilege covered politically partisan or even criminal activity, as well as presidential.

The Tonkin Gulf Resolution of 1964 launched the controversy over presidential war powers toward its eventual climax in Cambodia in 1973. The President's continuing use, or as some senators saw it, misuse of powers they presumed to be temporarily granted to meet an emergency caused a belated congressional attempt at reassertion by various "end the war" amendments, and a definition of presidential limitations. All these efforts were fought by the White House. Congress learned that restorations seldom follow voluntary abdications.

Plain reality in fact militates against any binding restriction on presidential war-making powers. One reason a President is able to involve the United States overseas without congressional declaration is that he has at his disposal the troops and machines to do so. A standing army of two million, deployed in bases around the world, takes care of the logistics. All that is really required is the will to act. After commitment Congress must automatically support, finance and reinforce "our boys."

Failing effectiveness on the issue of presidential powers, critics of the Vietnam policy as implemented under the broad terms of the Tonkin Gulf Resolution turned to an assault on presidential "credibility." It is no new jousting point in American history, either. The Mexican War was begun by Polk's proclamation that American forces had been attacked on American soil, though in truth they were in disputed border territory. McKinley's fervently stated belief, in a turn-of-the-century preview of Vietnam, was that the United States was "Christianizing" Filipinos by putting down their nationalistic aspirations for independence. The illness of Woodrow Wilson created doubt as to who was in fact acting as President. Franklin Roosevelt's promise that "your boys are not going to be sent into any foreign war" was fortuitously vacated by Pearl Harbor. Eisenhower lost "credibility" with the U-2 affair, and Kennedy with the Bay of Pigs.

Lyndon Johnson's "credibility" was put into question by his use of the Tonkin Gulf Resolution and then became a constant of controversy in successive stages of escalation, though it must be said that Johnson could believe that he was responding to "consensus" in favor of an American "obligation" to intervene in Vietnam.

With consummate stagecraft, which history may decide exceeded his statecraft, Johnson's successor, Richard Nixon, raised the credibility issue to new levels as he reversed all the public positions of his political career to seek an end to the war. He linked it to new relationships with the former partners of the awesome "Sino-Soviet bloc," now become mutual adversaries. On the domestic front the Nixon deals with corporate business, after Roosevelt's New Deal and Truman's Square Deal, further strained presidential credibility.

It should have been evident from the beginning in Vietnam that whatever their own differences, Communist China and the Soviet Union were not going to allow North Vietnam to be defeated, much less conquered or occupied, by Americans any more than by the French. This might be called "Communist aggression" on Capitol Hill or in Foggy Bottom, but for the Chinese the presence of large American military forces in Southeast Asia was a matter of national security because of common borders with Vietnam and Laos. Security was the more involved because the United States, by its defense treaty with Taiwan, had intervened in the Chinese civil war, put American troops and planes on the island to which Chiang Kai-shek had fled, and interposed the Seventh Fleet between Taiwan and the mainland.

For the Russians, support of North Vietnam was a matter of both ideological and Great Power necessity. A "sister Socialist state" could not be permitted to succumb to a rival "imperialism," whether American, by military defeat, or Chinese, by dependence.

Though it defined its own objectives and methods as "limited," the United States did not comprehend that for the National Liberation Front and the North Vietnamese the war could not be limited; survival was the imperative. "Victory" is not a limited aim, and it was victory that both sides sought. American policy-makers were in their confidence oblivious to Wellington's conclusion that "there is no such thing as a little war for a great nation." But at Vietnam's cost the United States learned that the power to destroy was not inevitably the power to control.

Beyond the question of why the United States went to war was the equally troubling one of how the war was fought. The American psyche has had a long-term mutual assistance treaty with violence, cruelty, and nationalistic and racial supremacy. All American Presidents who have intervened, no matter where, felt they "had to," from Johnson in the Dominican Republic, back to Eisenhower in Lebanon, Kennedy in Cuba, Truman in Greece, Hoover in Haiti, Wilson at Archangel, McKinley in the Philippines, Polk in Mexico, indeed Jefferson on the Barbary coast. The intervention in Vietnam, however, had tragic dimensions far larger than those of any previous American adventure, in their effect not only upon Vietnam but upon the entire American nation, if it should ever stop to think about it.

Whatever the United States intervened on behalf of, it intervened against the moral and historical verities of Vietnam. Independence was being achieved there after eighty years of French colonial rule. A nation was in the process of formation when the United States imposed its own ideas of "nation-building." Yet how could a nation be built by bombing, defoliation, population dispersal, political uncertainty, enforced urbanization, and the end of village cultural custom?

Besides those who believe for these and other reasons that Vietnam was an "immoral" war, many Americans regard it as an unconstitutional one, violating the requirement of the separation of powers. Most earlier presidential military interventions could be regarded as reactions, properly speaking, to ad hoc situations called emergencies. Vietnam was a deliberate, persistent and long-term calculation, as the Pentagon Papers have amply confirmed, though it began in understandable circumstances.

If in 1954 the finite reasons for American concern over Southeast Asia had begun to disappear, there lingered enough political and psychological reason, even in 1961, to provide cognizable if not entirely adequate compulsion for the Kennedy decision to send troops to Vietnam in the guise of "military advisers" to superintend exercises in "counterinsurgency." The Kennedy intervention was engaged not only with real power and prestige but also with "image," "style," and the advertising-world concept of "posture." Provocation could be argued, however. Though Stalin's successor, Khrushchev, had embarked on "destalinization," he had continued to build and rattle nuclear rockets and to proclaim his intention to "bury" the United States. After Kennedy's election Khrushchev announced his support of "wars of national liberation," called Berlin the "bone" in his throat, and having received the fealty of the new revolutionary leader Fidel Castro, proceeded to introduce nuclear weapons into Cuba to point at the United States.

However, when Lyndon Johnson began to turn Vietnam into a full-scale war in 1965, Khrushchev was gone from office, and though China had displayed nuclear potential in its first test explosion, it was in the throes of a great internal convulsion. Cuba was again only an island off the Florida Keys, Austria was long since sovereign and independent again, nuclear rivalry had been stabilized and a nontesting agreement signed. There had been two postwar "summits" and the End of Ideology seemed a growing reality in international relations. By 1965, in fact, Vietnam was largely irrelevant to the true and pressing problems of the world, economic, environmental, social and cultural: the problems of human survival.

As the human body renews itself, so does the world in each accelerated generation. Escalation in Vietnam was in obeisance to the old world, the call of the old skin. If the Truman Doctrine had not been wrong to begin with, certainly after eighteen years (by 1965) it had served its purpose and had to be replaced.

The United States had somehow lost perspective. Vietnam had become the lone active confrontation point with Communism, and should have been assessed as not very important, given the global possibilities. The President's advisers instead chose to regard it as supremely important, overriding all other considerations. The United States put all its contingency plans in one basket.

Some American officials, especially Pentagon civilians, have come to believe that while the original American commitment of 10,000 men and $500 million a year was justified, it was followed by overcommitment in terms of the American national interest. The point is made that while the United States as a Great Power had interests practically everywhere, it had no special interest in Southeast Asia warranting massive military intervention. No moral factor enters into this conclusion.

In this view it was not American "nerve" or "will and character," as Walt Rostow put it, that were tested in Vietnam so much as American judgment and wisdom. American prestige was less at stake than American common sense. Not American but North Vietnamese staying power became the determinant, and the Vietnamese had had many centuries of practice at it.

Other American officials, especially of the Kennedy entourage, who initially supported the exciting game of counterinsurgency as a kind of extension of touch football, came to see Vietnam as a "tragedy without villains" brought about by "the politics of inadvertence." Those who began the new game failed to realize the truth about counterinsurgency: "pacification" cannot be an end in itself and insurgency can only be extinguished by responding in some fashion to the needs that caused it. Counterinsurgency must thus serve at least some of the aims of insurgency. Not a few Americans in Vietnam recognized this fact and called for a social revolution that could challenge the Communist-promised one, but Vietnamese rulers like Diem, Ky and Thieu could not envision such an idea. Under the theory of the "lost revolution," it can be argued that the United States, by supporting the French colonial regime and its "sovereign" successors, by failing to guide the desire for social change along nationalist, even socialist lines, in the end encouraged the growth of Communism in the very act of fighting it.

A principal charge from "revisionist" historians is that the United States did not enter Vietnam as into a quagmire, marching blindly, but that it acted with computed intention of aggressiveness as each commander-in-chief in turn refused to become "the first President to lose a war." The Pentagon Papers show how much ignorance, misjudgment and ordinary obtuseness were to blame, rather than nefarious purpose. The only conspiracy that could be charged, according to Air Force Under Secretary Townsend Hoopes, who became an opponent of escalation, was "the conspiracy of optimism."

Each step in escalation was taken by men of presumed probity, perception, even enlightenment. By character, function, and familiarity with the uses and limitations of power, they should have represented an island of rationality in a surrounding sea of emotionalism, aggressive instinct, undefined terms, semantics and wishful thinking making up the body of public opinion. To judge by results, the rational could not be distinguished from the irrational, as the sea swallowed up the island.

At every stage of escalation there existed the option to reduce or indeed end it. No choice made was inevitable. Each President did what he thought minimally necessary to prevent a Communist victory in Vietnam without seeking "total victory" for the United States. Many a mickle made a muckle. Such a war might be halted by a military cease-fire but it could never be ended by political compromise. The power in Saigon was not negotiable.

In the planning, as was natural, first attention was given to decisions which the United States could best carry out. In 1965 these were predominantly military. Even political problems were believed subject to military solutions. The long Cold War, with its global vigilantism and nuclear arms rivalry, had given the United States a war machine big and unmanageable enough to frighten its commander-in-chief, President Eisenhower. The Vietnam War provided the machine with a new *place d'armes*, and an example of the commitment to which the United States had continued to pledge itself.

Increased military influence in affairs of state had come about in part because after the Second World War, which they so decisively won, American military men had assumed an unprecedented role in the formation and implementation of political policy. They served in the State Department, one even as Secretary, and as ambassadors, presidential advisers and Intelligence chiefs, in the face of the widespread liberal tenet that it was unwise, even dangerous, for the soldier to engage in politics; he could become the man on the white horse.

In Vietnam, where political and military distinctions crossed each other,

American soldier-statesmen exercised power on behalf of the statesmen-soldiers at home. The generals did what they were called on to do; they planned, sought and undertook more and more military action. It was their civilian superiors, the liberals in the government and the "Whiz Kids" in the Pentagon, who let the war continue by feeding on its own mistakes.

One step led to another in the escalation of the Vietnam War, each error to a greater one. They all seemed logical and reasonable at the time, based on computer-programmed response to a given situation as algebra is based on axioms. Behind the "Whiz Kids" in the Pentagon sat the elite of American policy-making, the Council on Foreign Relations, the bankers, economists, academicians, corporation executives and retired generals, admirals and diplomats who have supplied the plans and people for a myriad government decisions and top jobs, and the constancy and continuity of American political philosophy behind its apparent zigzags.

When by supreme irony the war which had begun as a countermove to Chinese "aggression" drew to a close with the friendly visit to Peking of an American President who had built his career on assailing those he found "soft on Communism," the explanation was that China had changed. The Council on Foreign Relations knew better. It was the United States which had changed, back to an original concept of the 400 million, now become nearly 800 million, "customers."

In 1972 a Columbia University survey was made of the American "leadership class": 450 of the wealthiest and most influential individuals in the United States, including multimillionaires, corporate chief executives, congressional and political-party leaders, high-ranking civil servants, trade union chiefs, widely read and listened-to figures in the communications media, and spokesmen for minority groups and civic and social associations. In every category but one — Republican officeholders and politicians — a considerable majority was "dovish" on the Vietnam War and large defense spending. Two-thirds of the business leaders and a larger proportion of other groups agreed with the statement "The United States has sometimes contributed to the escalation of the Cold War by overreacting to Soviet moves or military developments." When questioned on social issues, a majority in every category endorsed Keynesian economics and the welfare state in some form, and agreed that "the rebellious ideas of youth contribute to the progress of society."

Such sentiments can be compared with those prevailing when the United States challenged the "Sino-Soviet bloc" in the Fifties, when it repudiated the Geneva Agreement of 1954, when it undertook "counterinsurgency" in Southeast Asia in the Sixties, when escalation began in 1964, when the campuses erupted in 1968. By 1972 something had apparently been learned from it all. Yet there have been, and always will be, some Americans who believe that the United States did not intervene drastically enough in

Vietnam if it really wanted to achieve the purposes it set forth. Such an attitude assumes the American right to dispose of Asia. Since many of its proponents also opposed involvement in an Asian land war, it evidently supposes that "the Bomb" should have been dropped on China, and on Russia too if needs be. That such a hypothesis has been entertained at all, where no provable security was at stake, is evidence of a lack of tenability in American policy in Southeast Asia.

It will remain an open question whether cumulative public opposition to the war, creating a national reversal of opinion, came about because it was a mistaken war or only a lost one. Since pragmatism rules politics, it can fairly be said that if it had succeeded Lyndon Johnson might have been acclaimed the ablest of political leaders instead of one of the most inept and unlucky.

More than success was involved, however. The French had already demonstrated that Vietnam could not be won. If all that was required was not to "lose" Indochina to Communism as China was "lost," then the Vietnam policy of Truman, Eisenhower, Kennedy, Johnson and Nixon has been vindicated. A non-Communist South Vietnam was maintained for two decades and may be for a "decent interval" in the future. There then arises the question of cost.

For years the war could not be ended because American leaders were not really looking for a way out of Vietnam. Despite all the talk and supposed effort to the contrary, it was as if the mere act of negotiation with a minor power like North Vietnam would itself be a humiliation. All the Presidents concerned believed that American prestige required "victory" in Vietnam if only through the avoidance of defeat. For five years every prospect of negotiation merely brought larger military involvement. In its turn the escalation thus applied to end the war only widened it. Each administration, failing to reassess the assumptions of its predecessors, passed Vietnam on to its successors in worse shape than received. At the end "peace with honor" was proclaimed on terms that might have been had years before.

The engineers of Vietnam policy have not been wrong to say they did what most Americans wanted them to do there. They also continued doing it after most Americans wanted them to stop. Always the question could be asked whether anti-Communism was enough of a policy in Vietnam, and especially when the President contracted friendlier relations with North Vietnam's two principal protectors and suppliers. In mid-1971, as Richard Nixon announced his intention of visiting Peking, 55 percent of the American people accepted the risk of a Communist take-over in Saigon if the war could be ended. Much had been learned and unlearned since 1954.

The war was bizarre in many ways. Never has an "enemy" been more fraternized with, or more openly supported by Americans. Correspondents were permitted to visit North Vietnam and report from there, instead of being interned as in Berlin or Tokyo. Americans individually and in groups found their way to Hanoi in a steady stream, witnessed the damage caused by American planes, talked to American war prisoners, and carried letters to and from them. Some even escorted prisoners home, released for Hanoi's purposes, presumably as an incentive to an acceptable settlement which would free all captive Americans. Other prisoners were shown on American television, appealing for an end to the war over their commander-in-chief's head. Visitors to Hanoi made antiwar statements which were broadcast to American troops south of the 17th parallel. An American Catholic priest from Minneapolis celebrated mass in Hanoi in the midst of the most intensive bombing campaign in the history of warfare, and thousands of "Communists" flocked to the Church of Saint Dominic to receive the sacrament. A senator's wife went to Hanoi with two American women poets in the name of cultural exchange, and they were shown around by the Committee for Solidarity with the American People.

At antiwar demonstrations in the United States the National Liberation Front or "Viet Cong" flag was often carried, though also frequently wrested away and trampled upon. Most Americans for long favored "victory" if only to "get it over with," but not a few wanted the NLF to win. Some actually declared themselves to be "pleased" when B-52 bombers were shot down over Hanoi in the final air offensive of Christmas 1972. Even in the Third Reich there had been some who wished the Wehrmacht and Luftwaffe bad cess.

In the American antiwar movement, as it waxed and waned with the fortunes of conflict, the Catholic factor was an important one, just as it had been in the original American interest in Vietnam. Catholic antiwar activism, doctrinally based on the distinction between "just" and "unjust" war, was part of a larger context of church-state relationship. It may be coincidence that the first draft-card burner, David Miller, was a Catholic, but the Catholic Ultra-Resistance, centered about the Berrigan brothers, both priests, was certainly part of the *aggiornamento* of the Church begun by Pope John XXIII.

Though John in his famous last encyclical, *Pacem in Terris*, had rejected war as "contrary to reason" and inconceivable as an "instrument of justice," his views, like those of Augustine and Aquinas on the moral theology of war, were not signally honored by most of the American hierarchy. Unlike nearly all other national hierarchies, it assumed the justice of the Vietnam War, and thus added to the disaffection of many Catholic communicants, a disaffection caused by other failures to implement the Second Vatican Council. That convocation had condemned immoral means of war, though without precisely defining them.

To many American Catholics their bishops were lamentably remiss in providing spiritual guidance in judgment of the war, as the German bishops had been in World War II. The Berrigans and other clergy and laity thereupon acted as individuals to "bear witness," and tried to move Catholic action for peace from the theology books to secular politics. "Is a Christian Christ's man or the State's?" asked Father Philip Berrigan.

Besides opposing Vietnam the forces for Church renewal joined with the civil rights movement, the campus rebellion, the women's movement, and political radicalism, to present a challenge to authority, spiritual as well as temporal. Nuns played a significant role in the emancipation campaign. The secularization that began with "Sister" Ingrid Bergman playing baseball in a Hollywood movie came to civil disobedience, in the process of modernizing the convent.

Proclamation by succeeding Presidents that Vietnam was indeed a just war and necessary was another formulation of the moralism that has always tinged American foreign policy and been criticized by professional diplomats like Kennan, scholars like Hans Morgenthau, and political observers like Lippmann. Such American moralism has customarily been onesided, that is to say anti-Communist and not anti-Fascist or antimilitarist, except passingly in World War II. Right-wing authoritarianism, as in Greece, Spain or Brazil, is reckoned to be autonomous and an example of self-determination, while left-wing authoritarianism is subversive and an example of "outside aggression."

There is one easy test of the "just" nature of the Vietnam War: suppose that its motives and methods had been applied to Europe rather than to the small southeastern corner of Asia. Imagine then what would have been done to the people and terrain of the "Mother Continent" by the unrestricted bombardment of undefended populations, the massive destruction of crops and forests, the forcible removal of whole villages and provinces of civilians, search-and-destroy missions under "Free Fire Zone" rules, and the Phoenix program to destroy by kidnapping and murder the political leadership and cadres of insurgent organizations. In truth such things have been done in Europe, which has known bloody war for centuries, but those who did them in World War II were brought to book at Nuremberg.

If it is argued, as it frequently is, that Asia is not as "civilized" as Europe, that life there is somehow less worthy or desirable, it can be pointed out that even the Japanese conquerors of Asia, not to mention the Mongols, did not go so far in systematic wholesale carnage as the American liberators of Indochina.

In any event, as the Vietnam era came to an end, it was evident that all the things done in the name of national security — war abroad, inroads against civil rights and civil liberties at home — had brought only a great national insecurity. Presidents found it necessary to pledge that they would keep the United States always "Number One." It was also plain, despite this promise, that America no longer had a formula for the rest of the world. If the Battle of Waterloo was won on the playing fields of Eton, the play of American example and moral suasion had been lost on the battle-fields, the Hamburger Hills, of Vietnam. The American continuation of the war as a means of insuring the world's respect was to most of the world so wrong as to be unbelievable. Whereas Nixon, like many other Americans, professed to regard Vietnam as "our finest hour" — an affront to the British people of 1940 — his 1972 presidential campaign opponent McGovern spoke for perhaps not so many others when he called it "the saddest chapter in our national history."

Though the 1972 campaign was fought to "keep America Number One," as the incumbent saw it, at least in the field of armament, earlier that year the President, about to visit Peking and Moscow, had in the state-of-Henry-Kissinger's-world message acknowledged the end of the Age of Containment. After twenty-five years, despite continuing record defense spending, the Truman Doctrine ended with the proverbial whimper. The Cold War had been won years before through the internal contradictions of Communism, which Marx had never contemplated. Now it was finally accepted as won. It would not be necessary to take on Moscow and Peking, only to play them off against each other.

Responsible not only for Vietnam but also for many other geopolitical and military adventures in its quarter-century of confrontation with Communism, the United States had perhaps become a bit tired of super-power. Not a few Americans yearned for what others derogated as "neo-isolationism," or at least a more limited view of undertakings and priorities around the world. Neo-isolationism was a 1972 campaign issue, nurtured by McGovern's acceptance speech with its theme "Come home, America." The matter could be debated in its political meaning. The truth was that in the more precise sense of the term, the United States by its actions in Vietnam had isolated itself from a considerable part of the world.

As at the beginning, so in the end Big Power considerations prevailed over Vietnam's own intrinsic significance, as Nixon used his new friends in Peking and Moscow to exert their influence on Hanoi for a cease-fire, signed a week after his second inaugural, and followed by the release of prisoners and American military withdrawal, at least from South Vietnam. Kissinger in fact called Vietnam a "mere footnote" to the great achievement of a new relationship with China.

To help history judge Vietnam, three basic views of the American involvement can be offered in summation, as McGeorge Bundy offered options to Lyndon Johnson:

One is that it was an equivocal success. It achieved limited ends with limited means, but it did not solve the fundamental problems which brought it about; no war does. It may have deterred other insurgencies; in any case North Vietnam, the enemy presumptive, was dealt heavy blows which will affect its future thought and conduct.

Another view is that Vietnam was a failure of proportion. It became a mistake when it ceased to be worth the cost. Intervention was proper but became unwise when it persisted beyond the point of adequate return. The war also diverted resources from more useful domestic pursuits, teaching the lesson of the limits of American power.

The third view is that it was a failure of tactics. This leads to the so-called Nixon Doctrine. The American "mission" in Asia is not changed, only the methods, or as Ambassador Ellsworth Bunker stated, "the colors of the bodies." The new rationale honors treaty commitments and gives aid to allied regimes, but does so on a more sparing basis of selectivity, and is wary of military involvement except where "vital" American interests are concerned. Vietnam was itself regarded as a vital interest, however. The Nixon Doctrine offers no clarifying definition and does not specify who is to provide it.

All three of these views share the assumption that American counter-policy — "containment" of Asian political conflict and change — remains justified.

History may opt for another judgment, not offered by the Bundys. It is that American policy in Vietnam was both pragmatically and morally wrong and has therefore failed, not only in itself but as a warning for the future.

The Vietnam experience showed that the requirements of realpolitik can come into conflict with democratic processes. A "popular" war must be rooted in something besides diplomatic formulations such as "state interests" or the balance of power. It must arise from a general personal sense that justice, social as well as statutory, has somehow been acutely violated. As William Bundy remarked, it was extremely difficult to carry out war plans under the "klieg lights" of democracy. The lights had to be dimmed. The same was true with Watergate, which as Clausewitz might have said, was an extension of Vietnam by other means. In history's judgment, taken together at home and overseas, Vietnam and Watergate may mark the turning point in presidential power, allowing for a return to checks and balances.

The end of the war does not mean the end of American commitment, but different forms of commitment. It should also mean less simplism in national attitude toward situations more complex than ever before — not only the intricacies and intertwinement of global relations but of social relations at home, and the knottiness of political leadership, authority and purpose in the operation of democratic processes in an open society.

As GI's in Vietnam became accustomed to speak of "the world" which was everywhere else, as POW's came back on flights "to the world," so in a larger sense the United States was able with the end of the war to return to "the world" from which it had for so long alienated itself. It returned with its prestige and leadership devalued, like the dollar, and its democracy debased by the excesses that had made Vietnam and Watergate possible. But it could, if it would, strive to repossess itself of that "decent Respect to the Opinions of Mankind" which it assumed in its original Declaration of July 4, 1776.

2

THE ELEPHANT AND THE TIGER

THE FRAIL GRAYING FIGURE with ascetic features and a wisp of beard returned to the familiar surroundings of Paris amid a chorus of cheers at Le Bourget airfield from many other small brown men who in their enthusiasm tried to break through police barriers.

To them he was a national hero, the attainer of Vietnamese independence, worthy to be ranked with the peasant warrior Le Loi, who had freed the country from the Chinese. To the Minister of Overseas France, meeting him with an official handshake and more important things on his mind, the self-styled President of the so-called Democratic Republic of Vietnam was only another colonial suppliant, come to accept the new French Union in place of the old French Empire. It was June 22, 1946, and the postwar world was in the process of reconstruction.

Ho Chi Minh was not a delegate to the Fontainebleau conference on Indochina. The official party from Hanoi was led by the imperial mandarin's son Pham Van Dong, Ho's scholarly longtime comrade-in-revolution. The President of Vietnam was on a mission of good will, to ease the climate of readjustment between France and her Far Eastern outpost, to recall old associations, talk to journalists, and most of all to meet the Americans gathered in Paris on Europe's business and their own, the business of peace-making.

The canny veteran of international politics already divined — he did not know how well — that his destiny and his country's would somehow come to depend on the United States. By the same token it would befall that the great democracy across the Atlantic from France, across the Pacific from Vietnam, would involve its own destiny in the rice fields and jungles of his small land.

It was not the first time Ho Chi Minh had looked to the United States for help in obtaining the same kind of freedom it had won in revolution. The meeting of twenty-one nations which had brought the American Secretary of State to Paris in 1946, and would be held simultaneously with his own small affair with the French, was his second Paris peace conference. In 1918 he and two other Vietnamese had addressed the Big Four of the First World War with a petition for limited independence. Their memorandum, *Notes on the Revindications of the Annamese People,* protested the artificial division of Indochina under French rule. At Versailles Ho singled out Woodrow Wilson as his best hope for national deliverance and submitted several requests for a hearing. But the United States had not made the world safe for democracy in order to deprive an ally of its colonies. Self-determination was for Europe.

Ho's seeming confidence in the United States rested on his knowledge of American history, gained in his omnivorous reading, though he had a passing acquaintance with the country itself. As a mess attendant on French passenger liners before the war, he had made shore visits to Boston and New York, including a tour of Black Harlem. He acquired a taste for American cigarettes which never left him. He added English to the five other foreign languages and several Chinese dialects he could converse in. He admired the Statue of Liberty while sardonically pointing out that it came from the France that held his own land subservient.

Ho's awareness of Lincoln preceded his awareness of Lenin, whom he did not read until the question arose in 1920 of the French Socialist party's joining the Third International. In later writings for the French Communist press he paid tribute to John Brown and Harriet Beecher Stowe, and saw a parallel between American slavery and French colonialism. By then, after reading Zola, Victor Hugo, Shakespeare and Dickens, and delving into Buddhism, Confucianism and Christianity, he had chosen Marxism as his faith. As a founding member of the French Communist party and an Asian, he thus became dedicated to the use of Western-originated doctrine against the West. Yet if Vietnam had been granted independence in 1918, and he had returned to take part in its democratic rule, instead of becoming an exile obsessed with the colonial question and a Comintern functionary, the whole history of Southeast Asia, and its impingement upon the United States, would obviously have been different.

Between the two world wars Ho lived the life of a professional international revolutionary, as a bureaucrat in Moscow, an interpreter for the famous but unsuccessful Soviet mission to China of Michael Borodin, and a secret agent in China. In 1930 in Hong Kong he organized the Indochina Communist party.

The long-sought "war of national liberation" was provided by and within the Second World War. Ho was in a Chinese Nationalist jail as a "French spy" when he was released by Chiang Kai-shek's regime in 1942, after Pearl Harbor, to set up a guerrilla movement in Indochina against the common enemy, Imperial Japan. He called it the Viet Minh, an abbreviation for the League for Vietnamese Independence, and it was financed by the Chinese and thus indirectly by the United States.

So again Ho Chi Minh and Indochina came into the American ken. Into the jungles parachuted downed American pilots, who were rescued by the Viet Minh guerrillas and helped out of the country into China. Other American parachutists were OSS men sent from General Albert Wedemeyer's command in Kunming to make contact with the anti-Japanese irregulars. They helped train Ho's forces, treated the gaunt and ailing Ho himself for malaria, dysentery and other tropical illnesses, and even supplied weapons, though in limited quantity, since Ho would not promise that they would not be used against the French as well as the Japanese. Some five thousand American rifles were dropped, with their ammunition, converting Ho's guerrillas into an organized army with standardized equipment. The United States in effect created the Viet Minh.

The OSS detachment in Kunming included a twenty-seven-year-old "Air Corps lieutenant" named E. Howard Hunt, Jr., who was fiercely anti-Communist. But most of the OSS officers who made contact with the jungle fighters were sympathetic to the anticolonial cause, and so were bitterly resented by the French, their nominal allies. While President Roosevelt at Teheran was proposing a trusteeship for Indochina after the war, General Charles de Gaulle in Algiers was envisioning a "French community" as the restored colonial domain. In Brazzaville, on the Congo, de Gaulle's French Committee of National Liberation denied any similar liberation to French colonies by declaring them barred from self-government "even in the most distant future." The reason given was France's civilizing role overseas.

In the French Far East, as in half of France, authority was held by the Vichy regime, though it included some resistants, also as in France. The Japanese occupied and ruled Indochina while their French collaborators administered it and the few Free French engaged in sabotage.

Then the day came in March 1945, with the imminent defeat of their Berlin Axis "partner," when the Japanese dismissed their French collaborators, interned French troops, crushed the Free French underground, and in a final Asian gesture against the white West commanded the last of the Annam emperors, Bao Dai, to proclaim Vietnamese "independence" under Japanese auspices.

It lasted as long as the Japanese did, five months. Two days after the Japanese surrender in August, Ho Chi Minh emerged from the jungle to promulgate a provisional government and a "free Vietnam." His Viet Minh controlled six northern provinces. Emperor Bao Dai in Hue at once offered Ho his sanction, abdicated in favor of a republic, and became a privy councillor, under his personal name and with the new republican title, as Citizen Vinh Thuy. The ex-emperor accompanied Ho Chi Minh when he received or visited the French, to signalize the fact that the Mandate of Heaven had been transferred. Thus in Vietnamese eyes was Annamite rule given continuity.

Ho continued to address the former emperor as "my lord," at least in public, and with his approval was able to broaden the government to include non-Communists and even Catholics, who had historically centered themselves in the North. He won at least silent support from priests and congregations, but Ho's efforts at conciliation failed with the most important Catholic political figure in the country, Ngo Dinh Diem, who had previously refused to become Prime Minister under the Japanese, and who refused Ho's offer of the same post. Diem had personal as well as political and religious reasons. He had been captured by the Viet Minh and held for five months, becoming perilously ill, while his elder brother Khoi, the Governor of Quang Nam province, had been killed. Released when Ho decided he needed him, Diem told the President he could never serve a godless regime.

Ho's assumption of power in Hanoi was ignored by the French, and de Gaulle had named Admiral Georges Thierry d'Argenlieu High Commissioner for Indochina and had dispatched General Jacques Leclerc, the "liberator" of Paris, to repossess the Southeast Asia territories.

Ho's eyes were turned not to France, however, but to the United States. He and Vo Nguyen Giap, the former Hanoi schoolteacher who had done the guerrillas' military planning, were accompanied into the capital by American OSS officers. On the seventy-five-mile march from their headquarters they were cheered by crowds of peasants, and so were the Americans. Through the OSS Ho sent a message to the United States for the newly created United Nations, "If the UN forget their solemn promise and do not grant Indochina full independence, we will continue fighting until we get it."

The men from the jungle were met in Hanoi by Americans already there, flown in from Kunming. The American detachment, led by Major Archimedes L. A. Patti, in civilian life a New York lawyer, was accompanied by a small group of French, headed by Jean Sainteny, who before the war had been a banker in Hanoi. Viet Minh flags, red with a gold star, waved in the capital and banners in English read "Vietnam for Vietnamese" and "Independence or Death." In Theater Square Ho Chi Minh proclaimed the new republic in the familiar words of the American Declaration of Independence: "All men are created equal. They are endowed by their Creator with certain inalienable rights; among these are life, liberty and the pursuit of happiness." He had talked to the OSS officers about the Declaration. "He knew more about it than I did," said an American lieutenant.

At Ho's side in the inaugural ceremonies stood Major Patti and other obviously approving Americans, and two American planes which flew overhead were cheered by the Vietnamese. As Viet Minh units passed in review American officers saluted, while Giap raised his clenched fist, Communist-style. The Americans were so close to Ho, in a city that had become unfriendly to the French, that it was they who arranged the first contacts for the latter with the provisional government, introducing de Gaulle's emissary Sainteny to Giap, who had been designated Minister of the Interior.

The amity between the Americans and the Viet Minh was short-lived. The death of Franklin Roosevelt had brought a change in Washington's attitude toward Indochina. The President's idea of a United States trusteeship under four powers — the United States, the Soviet Union, Great Britain and China (note the exclusion of France) — had been rejected by Winston Churchill, who feared to set a precedent that might affect Burma and other parts of the British Empire. Roosevelt persisted in the idea that Indochina should eventually become independent. At Yalta shortly before his death he told Stalin that de Gaulle had asked for American ships to carry a French expeditionary force back to Saigon. "We have been unable to find any ships," he smiled. If Roosevelt had lived, the history of Southeast Asia might have been different.

However, as Ho Chi Minh raised the red flag with gold star in Hanoi, General de Gaulle had already received from the new American President the assurance that no obstacle would be raised to French reclamation of Indochina. Visiting the White House a week after Japan's surrender, de Gaulle was told by Truman that he could have the ships denied him by Roosevelt, and was further gratified to hear that France would be included in receiving the formal capitulation of Japan. On the same day that Ho Chi Minh announced the Democratic Republic of Vietnam, September 2, General Leclerc took part in the ceremony aboard the battleship *Missouri* in Tokyo harbor. The Viet Minh were absent, though it was they and not the French who had fought the Japanese.

The United States swiftly made it possible for the French to reenter Indochina, furnishing not only the ships but even the uniforms for an expeditionary force, which grew to 70,000. It also sold the French $160 million in war equipment with which to fight the Viet Minh. American intervention had begun.

The British, meanwhile, given the assignment of disarming the Japanese in the south of Vietnam while the Chinese did so in the north, turned the administration in Saigon back to the French whom they released from Japanese internment and rearmed. French troops joined the British in putting down riots by "fanatics," and the British commander, General Douglas Gracey, went so far as to enlist the Japanese to fight the Viet Minh. Watching from Tokyo, General Douglas MacArthur was moved to call this reconquest of "the little people we promised to liberate . . . the most ignoble kind of betrayal."

Considerable ambiguity, perhaps duplicity, must be ascribed to the American attitude on Indochina. At the same time that it aided French colonial restoration, the United States was prodding the Dutch to give up their rule in the East Indies, and there was no doubt about American approval of the independence of India and Ceylon from Britain. Ho Chi Minh, moreover, was no longer a mere suppliant for independence. He had already established it and now sought American help in having it accepted and recognized. No fewer than eight times, in the five months between October 1945 and February 1946, he addressed President Truman or Secretary of State James F. Byrnes, asking American support at the United Nations for the same free status that the United States was giving the Philippines, after almost as long a rule as the French had enjoyed in Indochina. In the last of his representations, three weeks before he signed an agreement accepting French Union, he appealed to the Americans as "guardians and champions of world justice" to endorse Vietnamese independence. He received no reply. Washington in fact never revealed the existence of any such messages until the Pentagon Papers were published twenty-five years later.

American foreign policy in 1946 admittedly was occupied with larger matters. With Germany's defeat wartime cooperation with the Soviet Union had ended, if it had ever honestly existed at all, and had been succeeded by a policy of confrontation, at first over Germany but then on a worldwide front. Truman made it plain that his first priority was to check the spread of Communism, and in this context Vietnamese independence was dismissed by the new Secretary of State, General George C. Marshall, with the words, "We are not interested in seeing colonial empire administrations supplanted by a philosophy and political organization directed from and controlled by the Kremlin." The Cold War in Europe was thus linked to a small parcel of Asian land well before the emergence of China as a Communist state, and America's traditional anticolonial role was altered to the needs of anti-Communism.

There was in truth ample connection between Europe and Asia in what Wendell Willkie had called "one world." In 1941, when Japan moved from northern Indochina into southern Indochina, the United States imposed an oil embargo and froze Japanese assets. In the diplomatic-economic struggle that followed, Japan demanded an American pledge to stop aiding China, and the United States counterdemanded that Japan evacuate all of China, and Indochina as well. The embargo remained, Pearl Harbor followed, and Germany's declaration of war involved the United States in battle across the Atlantic as well as the Pacific.

After the war Indochina and Europe were joined again, through France.

The Soviet army, hailed as it reached the Elbe, was now suspected of planning to march to the English Channel. The four-power occupation of defeated Germany bred new conflicts as the Russians communized their zone after separating it from the rest of the country. As in Germany, so in Austria. The Red Army continued to stand on the Danube, in quadripartite occupation, without any sign of a peace settlement. Communist guerrillas fought in Greece. The Kremlin demanded bases on the Dardanelles from Turkey and the return of the provinces of Kars and Ardahan, ceded in 1918. In Iran the Russians were not leaving as pledged but had suddenly recognized an "autonomous" republic there.

From the American Embassy in Moscow, opposite the Kremlin, came the American plan to meet "the challenge of Communism." On Washington's birthday 1946 the chargé d'affaires, George Frost Kennan, sent the State Department a lengthy memorandum on "the sources of Soviet conduct." It called for an American policy which Kennan defined as "containment."

As early as 1944, when Soviet armies after halting the Germans in the Ukraine and Byelorussia were moving west, Kennan had proposed that American military and economic aid to Moscow be cut off, on the ground that the Red Army was now engaged in a war of aggression, instead of liberation, in East Europe. For obvious reasons, such as the continued existence of German armies and the agreements Roosevelt had made at Teheran, his recommendations were not carried out. Now there was another President.

"Containment" was quickly interpreted, to Kennan's expressed dismay, in terms such as those used by Clark Clifford, Truman's counselor. "The language of force is the only language which disciples of power politics understand. Compromise and concessions are considered by the Soviets to be evidence of weakness, and they are encouraged by our 'retreats' to make new and greater demands." It was the consensual wisdom of the time. Two weeks after the Kennan memorandum from Moscow, British Prime Minister Churchill, in the approving presence of the American President, spoke resoundingly at Fulton, Missouri, of the "iron curtain" that had clanged down across Europe.

The next day the French and Viet Minh in Hanoi, halfway around the world, arrived at a preliminary accord calling for autonomy in Indochina, though not independence. De Gaulle had abruptly left office for "retirement" because of Communist opposition within his coalition government, but the plan he had proposed for Southeast Asia was carried through by his successors. It recognized Ho's republic as "a free state with its own government, parliament, army and finances, forming part of the Indochinese Federation and French Union." The federation would consist of the three "associated states" of Vietnam, Cambodia and Laos, but Vietnam would include only Annam and Tonkin, the two prewar French protectorates, making up the northern and central portions of the country. Cochin China, in the south, with Saigon as its capital, would decide whether to join the federation by referendum. Under French supervision, the obvious answer would be "No."

By the Hanoi accord General Leclerc, languishing in Saigon, was permitted to land French troops in Haiphong, including elements of his Second Armored Division which had entered Paris. The tall, thin, austere officer, leaning on his familiar cane, had held back his entry for formal permission. He agreed with Sainteny that if force of arms was attempted, "we must be prepared to meet with powerful resistance."

Discarding his previous views during his months of enforced waiting in Saigon, Leclerc had come to believe that Indochina should have some form of independence, and may have been the first French official to contemplate the idea seriously, though Paul Mus, the French scholar who had been raised in Hanoi, made the case for it in his sociological-historical writings, unheeded in Paris. Leclerc advised what he called "a peace of the brave" — a partnership instead of a protectorate — because the only alternative would be the bogging down of French troops in hostile terrain seventy-five hundred miles from home. He was called an appeaser by many, in Paris and Saigon.

Though the March 6 agreement, allowing French troops to return to Indochina, was far from what they had hoped for, the Viet Minh had decided upon patience for several reasons. One was that as the result of elections in the Democratic Republic, in which Ho had won 98 percent of the votes, a new provisional government had been formed in which the Communists held only four cabinet posts, the others going to old-line political parties, joined in broad coalition. Ho needed time for consolidation before venturing a showdown with the French.

Another reason for delay derived from the postwar coalition in Paris. It also included Communists, and Ho felt he could depend on them to support his aims, especially after they had forced de Gaulle's departure. The French Communists, however, were as much French nationalists as Ho's Communists were Vietnamese nationalists. The "party line" in Paris was that the tricolor could not be hauled down in Hanoi. Some day, *naturellement*, the French colonies would become Communist in orderly fashion, just as France surely would. Equally important, French-Soviet relations in Europe would be embarrassed by Communist-led insurgency in French overseas territories.

After the March 6 accord Sainteny was told by Vice-Premier Maurice Thorez, "If the Vietnamese do not respect its terms we will take the necessary measures and let the guns speak for us, if need be." Thorez was the leader of the French Communist party, which he and Ho Chi Minh had helped found, and his words constituted the first of three betrayals, as the Vietnamese revolutionaries would see it, by the world Communist movement. The second came in 1954 at Geneva, and the third in 1972, when President Nixon was feted in the Kremlin while American bombs fell on Hanoi, and the port of Haiphong was blockaded by American mines.

The French-Vietnamese agreement of 1946 required fleshing out, and to that end a meeting was held in April at Dalat, in the Vietnamese highlands. It resulted in a further specification of autonomy, but not enough to satisfy the Viet Minh, and still another meeting was called, for July in Paris, or more accurately Fontainebleau. As he had gone fruitlessly to one symbol of past French empire, Versailles, in 1918, Ho in 1946 came equally fruitlessly to another, the palace of Francis I and Henry IV, where Napoleon had signed his first abdication.

The Fontainebleau Conference was foredoomed. Ho was in midflight to France when the news came that the "Republic" of Cochin China had been proclaimed. This ended the hope of Vietnamese unity, as Ho conceived it, but it also repudiated the understanding arrived at in Dalat. Ho wanted to turn back without proceeding to Paris, to consult with his fellow revolutionaries about their next course of action, but Jean Sainteny, who met his plane at Biarritz, persuaded him to continue the talks.

Ho arrived in Paris on the first day of an exquisite summer, with a sadness and foreboding out of keeping with his own normal buoyancy of spirit, and the general vivacity that greeted him. Despite the lingering evidences of war and occupation, such as bread and gasoline rationing and the clatter of women's wooden shoes, Paris in the two years since liberation had become once again the City of Light, and the capital, as the French believed, of Western culture. The 1945 vintages were superb, and café terraces were crowded.

Political activity had reattained its prewar intensity after de Gaulle's "retirement," but within a new postwar structure. By its ballots, the electorate had divided itself into three equal major groupings — the Catholic M.R.P., the Socialists and the Communists — and ferociously partisan newspapers spurred their rivalry.

The reflowering of French political life was part of the phenomenon of a reawakened Europe. At Marie de Medici's Luxembourg Palace, turned into an edifice for peace-making, the men of the New Europe met for the first time and conversed animatedly, as they walked in the Hall of Lost Footsteps. Molotov was there, and Jimmy Byrnes, and Britain's Ernie Bevin, and the new French Premier, Georges Bidault, who had been leader of the French Resistance. Other Resistance figures from East and West, war heroes, guerrilla commanders, trade unionists, and former political prisoners, were delegates to the Conference of the Twenty-One, called to sign treaties of peace with Hitler's former satellites, Italy, Finland, Romania, Hungary and Bulgaria.

The Europe that was being restored, however, was in two parts, divided by the Iron Curtain. The end of the war had also ended common endeavor and purpose. Among the "victors" at the Luxembourg were countries that Hitler had occupied, and now the Russians did: Poland, Czechoslovakia and Yugoslavia. The Soviet Union, though perhaps acting less from menacing intent than from weakness and suspicion, preferred its own satellites as buffer states to the twenty-five-year Four-Power treaty on Germany offered by the West. These were the political realities, foretelling long years of the Cold War. Still, there was adaptation in Paris, as war spoils were given up, boundaries fixed, and new regimes dealt with, in the meticulous processes of peace.

For the men of the New Asia, at Fontainebleau, there was no accommodation. The French were not taking Vietnam very seriously, regarding Indochina as a purely domestic matter, and the Americans did likewise when Ho Chi Minh again pressed his case in person to embassy officials.

The Fontainebleau Conference opened two days after the Philippines, on the carefully chosen Fourth of July, received its independence from the United States in the manner that the Vietnamese sought from the French. Already compromised by the creation of the phantom Republic of Cochin China, and by the insistence of the French on continued control in Hanoi through a High Commissioner, the negotiations were further jeopardized when French troops occupied public buildings in Hanoi and took over the customs in the name of the Indochinese Federation.

Publicly Ho displayed good spirits and his customary animation. At the Royal Monceau Hotel, where a red carpet covered the sidewalk, he met other petitioning colonials: Ben-Gurion of British Palestine and Ferhat Abbas of French Algeria. On Bastille Day he laid a wreath at the tomb of the Unknown Soldier and as a crowd quickly gathered he told an aide lightly, "Everyone wants to see the Vietnamese version of Charlot [Chaplin]." At a reception at the Hôtel de Ville, the Paris city hall, he refused food and drink but stuffed an apple into the pocket of his tunic. Outside he, like Charlot, presented it to a small girl.

He was disappointed not to meet de Gaulle, whom he much admired if only as one resistant admires another. The general had publicly renounced politics, though he came to Paris weekly and received many visitors at the Legion of Honor offices, building a new movement he called the Rally of the French People. Ho was also avoided by General Leclerc, who had been under some criticism for his "softness" on Vietnam.

The man from Hanoi made up for the lack of political success at Fontainebleau with considerable social and personal success in Paris. He went to the Opéra, attended receptions, visited Lourdes, held press conferences, gave roses to girl reporters, and signed wartime "short snorter" dollar bills for American male reporters. One of these described him as "part Buddha, part Lenin."

Among Ho Chi Minh's engagements that fateful summer was a small dinner party with American correspondents at the home of David Schoenbrun of CBS News, in the quiet suburb of Saint-Cloud. Four or five of us were in the living room with aperitifs when the Schoenbruns' maid Louise came in clearly frightened, and whispered most sibilantly, "Assassins!" Several armed men in cloth caps had silently materialized around the house, and were poking about the garden. Suddenly Ho was there. He too wore a cloth cap, and his gray tunic was open at the neck, for he buttoned it only at white-tie dinners and other formal occasions. His goatee was brown, his eyebrows bushy, and his cheeks were drawn.

As everyone who has met him has remarked, the first impact was from his dark eyes, alert and burning. Even with his chipper ways, mobile features, and gestures, which facilely expressed amazement, doubt or scorn in Gallic fashion, the overriding impression he gave was rather of calmness, even serenity. The longtime revolutionary was soft-spoken and there was a kind of awkwardness about him which those who were not charmed said was assumed, to give him a common touch. He spoke French but often lapsed into English that was almost as good, as he recalled the Paris of the early Twenties where he earned a living as a photo-retoucher and attended radical meetings.

The meal prepared by the Schoenbruns' cook, Roger, was a triumph of French cuisine, but though Ho had once in London served in the kitchen of the great Escoffier — like Roger, he had specialized in patisserie — he paid no heed to what he ate, and was more appreciative of the American cigarettes he chain-smoked. He had brought his own French brand but eagerly switched to the American packs offered him, courtesy of the embassy commissary, and indeed left with one of them.

His most deeply felt remarks came at the end of the lavish, uncherished meal. He said he felt he had been slighted by the French, since he was willing to compromise much sovereignty for the sake of Vietnamese unity, but the French formula called for neither unity nor independence.

"If the French do not give you some form of independence, Monsieur le Président, what will you do?" asked Schoenbrun.

"Why, we will fight, of course."

"But they are powerful. They have airplanes and tanks and modern weapons. You have no weapons, not even uniforms. You are peasants. How can you fight them?"

He answered from what was evidently a Vietnamese fable. "We will be like the elephant and the tiger. If the tiger ever pauses, the elephant will impale him on his mighty tusks. But the tiger will not pause, and the elephant will die of exhaustion and loss of blood."

Ho was anxious to know what Americans thought of the situation in Indochina and was told that it was hardly part of their postwar consciousness. On the other hand, they were in general opposed to Communism, because of the apprehensions raised by Soviet conduct.

The President of the Democratic Republic of Vietnam invoked the memory of the late President of the United States, Franklin D. Roosevelt, and said he thought Americans to be by nature anticolonial. As he had done in his unanswered messages to the American government, he cited the liberation of the Philippines as an example of American purpose, and a model for the settlement in Indochina. He also noted that the United States had considerable influence on France and could act persuasively.

Ho asked those present not to be blinded by the Communist issue. "If the people called Communists are the only ones to fight for independence, or those who fight for independence are called Communists, then Vietnam will be Communist." However, he declared, "Independence is the motivating force, not Communism." His "secret weapon" was Vietnamese nationalism.

Ho evidently believed that his talk with American correspondents would get back to their government, and that perhaps it might be conveyed to the French that they risked war, something they did not seem to comprehend at Fontainebleau. He himself kept warning them not to send him back to his own extremists empty-handed. Was he sincere, or only being wily and devious? It did not much matter. France refused to yield.

The Fontainebleau Conference was suspended in less than a month by the news from Saigon that the French High Commissioner — Admiral Thierry d'Argenlieu, a former Carmelite monk who like de Gaulle was a visionary of French *grandeur* — was holding another meeting in Dalat with representatives not only of the new "state" of Cochin China but of another invention he called South Annam. Vietnam's unity was thus even further prejudiced.

On September 2, the first anniversary of Ho's republic, Fontainebleau finally broke down, without agreement on independence or unity. France would continue to operate Indochina as a federation of "associated states."

"I have just signed my death warrant," Ho told the French Overseas Minister, Marius Moutet. He went on: "If we must fight, we will fight. You will kill ten of my men, while we kill one of yours. But you will be the ones exhausted in the end."

He was clearly reluctant to hurry back to Hanoi and the disappointment and perhaps anger of his militants. He, Pham Van Dong and the others who had thus far gone along with the French had done so against the counsel of more radical Viet Minh members, both in the Paris delegation and at home in Hanoi. Instead of flying, as he had come, he chose the month-long sea journey. Arriving in Marseilles to embark, he told a Vietnamese gathering of the modus vivendi he had signed with the French, and shouts of "Viet-gian!" ("Traitor!") broke out.

In Vietnam, meanwhile, sporadic anti-French incidents had occurred, the most serious in August when some Viet Minh troops in the South, angered by the rump Dalat Conference, clashed with a French unit. It was a customs dispute that led to war, however, beginning in an exchange of French–Viet Minh fire when French patrol boats stopped a Nationalist Chinese barge bringing gasoline into Haiphong.

Against the advice of the French in Hanoi, the authorities in Saigon ordered Viet Minh troops to leave Haiphong and backed up the order with an artillery barrage and a heavy naval bombardment from the cruiser *Suffern*, shattering the Vietnamese quarter of the port city. The estimate of dead ranged from 6,000 to 20,000.

In Paris the government had changed to hands friendlier than Bidault's. Léon Blum, the old Socialist whom Ho had known from his Paris days — Blum led the anti-Comintern forces at the 1920 Tours conference at which Ho and other Socialists joined the Third International — was a liberal on colonial questions, and as Premier he expressed support of Vietnamese independence. Ho Chi Minh at once proposed a return to the status quo ante, before the shooting started. His message, passing through hostile French offices in Saigon, was "delayed in transit" for nearly a month, until December 26. By then it was too late; more incidents had occurred. Barricades were put up in Hanoi by the Viet Minh and torn down by the French as they prepared to drive the insurgents out of the capital.

General Giap struck first. On December 19 Hanoi was blacked out by an explosion at the main power plant. The next day Ho issued a proclamation accusing the French of bad faith and ordering armed combat "to save the fatherland." The Viet Minh, in both the northern and southern parts of the country, took to the fields, jungles and hills. Ho and Giap established their headquarters amid the limestone slopes of Thai Nguyen province, eighty miles from Hanoi.

The tiger and the elephant had joined in mortal conflict.

As the war began, clearly a colonial struggle, the United States made its sentiments known, revealing why it had never responded to Ho's numerous appeals. The American consul in Hanoi received a message signed by Under Secretary of State Dean Acheson. "Keep in mind Ho's clear record as agent [of] international Communism."

A few days later John Carter Vincent, head of the Far Eastern section of the State Department, noted in a memorandum to Acheson that the French had made concessions on paper toward Vietnamese autonomy but had not acted to honor them. With an inadequate force, a divided public opinion and unstable governments, the French were trying to do in Indochina, he said, what Britain found it unwise to do in neighboring Burma. So, concluded Vincent, "guerrilla warfare may continue indefinitely." For his prescience in Asian affairs, Vincent, who had similarly forecast the turn of events in China, would become a victim, with other State Department experts, of the anti-Communist wave that was already beginning to sweep the United States.

In California, for example, a newly returned naval officer — who had served in a noncombat capacity and played winning poker in the Solomon Islands — had been elected to Congress against a five-term liberal incumbent, Jerry Voorhis, by identifying him with alleged Communist causes. He declared untruthfully that Voorhis was endorsed by the "Communist-supported" Political Action Committee of the CIO, and the report was spread by a telephone "whispering" campaign. The victor, beginning a political career to be based largely on the same anti-Communist foundation, was named Richard Nixon. On his arrival in Washington he announced, "I was sent here to fight the Communists." Elected at the same time in Massachusetts, another new congressman, John F. Kennedy, was also strongly hostile to the "Communist conspiracy." His and Nixon's speeches on the subject could not be told apart. Communism was everywhere, in their thesis, and Nixon soon became a member of the House Un-American Activities Committee, to combat it.

"Everywhere" included Southeast Asia as the Kremlin's province, and colonial war or not, the State Department blamed Ho Chi Minh's "direct Communist connections" for the outbreak of hostilities in Indochina.

Ho never concealed his ideology, but his regime included many non-Communists. After the proclamation of the republic, in fact, the Indochina Communist party had voluntarily dissolved itself, an action unique in revolutionary annals, in order to stress the nationalist basis of independence and win wider support. The dissolution was condemned by the Kremlin.

Communism had been fostered in Indochina, in truth, not by ideological conviction or the appeal of "scientific Socialism," but by France's prewar policy of tolerating no legal nationalist activity. With nationalism made illegal, the Communists became not only outlaws but patriots. Lenin was a legend to most of them, however, and Stalin but a name. When rebels died — "fanatics," the French called them — more than one did so uttering the forbidden word "Vietnam!"

If the French had honored the Dalat agreement of 1946, the non-Communists in Ho's regime might have tempered, even prevented, completely authoritarian rule in Hanoi. On the other hand, the Indochina war was not only an anticolonial, anti-French war for independence, but a class war as well, against those, generally the middle and upper classes, who had supported or collaborated with the French. It was thus a civil war in the fullest sense of the word, and when it began many in the North fled to the South, among them the Catholic leader Ngo Dinh Diem. He had been in hiding, often disguised as a monk, but now he went to Saigon. There he was known as an active nationalist, but one with little following in the Buddhist population.

The struggle that broke out in Indochina at the end of 1946 was a prototype for all Asia, as other insurgencies arose and were met by counterinsurgencies which did not resolve the causes. It was convenient to ascribe it to a Communist conspiracy, especially since it coincided with the undertaking of the new American policy of global "containment."

Symbolically, Europe's golden summer had been succeeded by the harshest winter in a half-century. Blizzards blew across the continent. Ports were frozen solid. Power failures and other economic distress paralyzed Britain and brought her to the brink of collapse. Heavy snows in Moscow congealed into thick layers of ice, and in this apt physical setting for the Conference of Foreign Ministers in the Soviet capital, the Cold War began.

Britain's strains caused her to give up her commitments in southeastern Europe and appeal to the United States to relieve her. London notified President Truman it was necessary to withdraw the 40,000 British troops stationed in Greece. Washington was receptive to the idea, proposing to help not only Greece but Turkey, the direct neighbor of the Soviet Union.

On March 12, 1947, President Truman addressed Congress and enunciated the doctrine which was thenceforth to bear his name. "I believe it must be the policy of the United States to support free peoples who are resisting attempted subjugation by armed minorities or by outside pressures."

The Moscow "ice-box" conference of the Big Four was the visible turning point in East-West relations, which even during the war had been less a cooperative arrangement than one of mutual convenience. The new American Ambassador in Moscow, succeeding the veteran diplomat Averell Harriman, was a military man, General Walter Bedell Smith, who had been Eisenhower's chief of staff through the war. He was chosen for the post, he himself explained, because Secretary of State Byrnes felt that Stalin preferred soldiers to diplomats. Byrnes and President Truman also believed that the Soviet war commanders had and would continue to have strong influence on Kremlin policies, though prewar evidence was to the contrary. Not only was the new Ambassador a soldier but the new Secretary of State who came to the Moscow conference, General Marshall, had been the nation's top war strategist, and he brought with him other high officers, including Lieutenant General Mark W. Clark.

As the foreign ministers argued futilely, American generals in their Metropol Hotel rooms declaimed loudly upon the repressions of the Soviet state, hoping to be heard over the microphones they were sure were hidden in the old-fashioned chandeliers and air vents. While they were slanging the Russians army style, Secretary Marshall received from Washington "radio message after radio message to give the Russians hell." He commented: "That is quite a proposition when you deal with somebody with over 260 divisions, and you have one and a third."

Marshall sent several objections to the State Department about the text of the Truman declaration, received in Moscow before it was delivered, because he felt it to be "overstating" the Communist factor in postwar change. Washington's reply was that this was the only basis on which Congress would approve it. Senator Arthur Vandenberg, the Republican chairman of the Foreign Relations Committee, had indeed told Truman that it was necessary to "scare hell out of the American people" if he wanted public support.

The key questions at Moscow were disarmament and German unity, in short the future of Europe. Stalin refused a European settlement under which, he suspected, the United States would rebuild Germany. The United States for its part decided that "never again" would it negotiate "without strength," or even better, superiority.

The Truman Doctrine, which wrecked not only the Moscow Conference but whatever was left of Soviet-American amenity, was economically implemented by the Marshall Plan for the reconstruction of western Europe. Hailed as a great act of American generosity, it was also a powerful political weapon. Benefits under it "will come to an abrupt end in any country that votes Communism into power," Secretary Marshall sternly declared. The Italians took heed and in their next election voted against what was regarded as the threat of Communist-shared power.

The Truman Doctrine had its immediate domestic consequences. Ten days after his congressional appearance the President issued a sweeping order to investigate 2,300,000 employees of the executive branch of the federal government and eliminate the "disloyal or subversive," without, however, defining those terms. "Whereas each employee of the Government of the United States is endowed with a measure of trusteeship over the democratic processes which are the heart and sinew of the United States . . ." the order began, as it braided together the strands of official anti-Communism at home and abroad.

The rationale for the foreign phase of the policy of "containment" was explicated by an article in July 1947 in the chapbook of the so-called Establishment, *Foreign Affairs*. Its author, who signed himself X, was the same George Kennan who had written brilliant essays on Soviet behavior from the Embassy in Moscow. He was now back from the field as head of the State Department policy planning staff, and his proposal was that all Soviet moves to expand political, economic and ideological influence should be met by "the adroit and vigilant application of counter-force at a series of constantly shifting geographical and political points, corresponding to the shifts and maneuvers of Soviet policy."

Kennan later complained that he had been misunderstood, that he had not meant military containment but only political and economic, and not everywhere but only where "American interest" required it. His words, however, were plain enough for all to read. Increased American pressures, he said, would increase Soviet internal stresses, "force" moderation and circumspection upon the Kremlin, and thus "promote tendencies which must eventually find their outlet in either the break-up or the gradual mellowing of Soviet power." The President, the State Department and the chiefs of staff, who defined "American interest," were only too ready, not only to carry out "containment" in their own way but to hasten its realization. Kennan seems to have been cast as the Sorcerer's Apprentice, who could say the magic words to set things in motion but did not know how to stop them. After the promulgation of the Truman Doctrine he wrote and spoke publicly against the open-end anti-Communist commitment it implied, and on behalf of "limitationism." By then the game was out of the hands of the theorists.

Though he was regarded by others in the diplomatic service as one of the principal moralists of American policy — he disapproved of the Soviet regime as "wrong, deeply wrong" — Kennan continued to consider himself the pragmatist and antimoralist. Even two decades later, when he appeared before the Senate Foreign Relations Committee as a critic of Vietnam policy, he acknowledged he might have felt differently about American intervention there if it had been successful.

The Truman Doctrine was directed against the Soviet Union because, despite the devastation it had suffered in war and its lack of the atomic bomb, it was seen as a global threat to "the free world." Moscow's shadow was cast over Indochina, in the American view, by Ho Chi Minh's presumed fealty to the Kremlin, even after Tito in Yugoslavia would demonstrate the primacy of nationalism by breaking with the Russians. It was, however, recognized by some in Washington that Indochina's undoubted colonial status made anti-Communism less simple as a policy.

After the Viet Minh began their war against the French, Secretary Marshall pledged to Paris that the United States would keep hands off, but pointed out that the conflict "is playing into the hands of the Communists in all areas" and that its continuation could "lead to the very eventualities of which we are most apprehensive." He urged a generous settlement "recognizing the legitimate desires of the Vietnamese" and especially warned against "creation of an impotent puppet government" or the restoration of Emperor Bao Dai, "implying that the democracies are reduced to resorting to monarchies as a weapon against Communism."

France was already engaged in exactly what Marshall was afraid of. Bao Dai was being solicited to accept the terms which Ho Chi Minh had refused — French control of Vietnam's foreign and military affairs — and to receive what the French had refused to give Ho — the return of Cochin China as part of "the Vietnam state," under French control.

The reality was perceived by Ngo Dinh Diem, the Catholic leader who had refused to serve either Bao Dai or Ho Chi Minh as Premier. To protest Bao Dai's failure to demand real independence, Diem left his native land and went into exile. He journeyed to Rome to visit his brother, Bishop Ngo Dinh Thuc, for Holy Year, but spent a month in the United States en route. Then he returned to the United States in January 1951, to live there for three years and become eligible to prosecute the American experiment in "Diemocracy" in Vietnam. His entry and residence, under university sponsorship, were arranged by Professor Wesley Fishel, who taught political science at Michigan State University and whom Diem had met in Tokyo.

The Soviet threat that had inspired the Truman Doctrine became the "Sino-Soviet threat," which would shape American foreign policy for more than two decades, when Mao Tse-tung's Communist forces won victory on the Chinese mainland and Chiang Kai-shek and what was left of his army and governmental apparatus fled to the island of Formosa, or Taiwan.

The reaction of Republican Senator Wherry of Nebraska to the Communist victory was one of Christian charity, and therefore hardly typical. "With God's help," he declared, "we will lift Shanghai up and up, ever up, until it is just like Kansas City." Nearly everyone else on Capitol Hill was critical of the "loss of China," including the freshman congressman John F. Kennedy, who called it a "disaster." The thirty-two-year-old Democrat, a supporter of the anti-Communist "crusade" of Republican Senator Joseph McCarthy of Wisconsin, blamed not only the Democratic incumbents of the White House and State Department for "the onrushing tide of Communism" in Asia, but went back to the Roosevelt days for the origins of "the tragic story of China," and mentioned especially General Marshall, who had tried to mediate between Mao and Chiang after the Japanese defeat. Marshall, now stigmatized as "a living lie," had been succeeded as Secretary of State at the start of Truman's second term by former Under Secretary Dean Acheson. The latter too would be assailed as "soft on Communism," particularly by Richard Nixon in future campaigns, but as he assumed office Acheson yielded to no man in his belief that strong and firm policies were required against the "Sino-Soviet bloc."

Within a month of Mao's assumption of power Truman's National Security Council defined the American purpose as "to block further Communist expansion in Asia," with "particular attention . . . given to the problem of French Indochina." Soon it was made more specific — "to prevent the countries of Southeast Asia from passing into the Communist orbit." The implication seemed to be that if China intervened the United States should, unilaterally if necessary, defend Indochina.

For all the perturbation in Washington, the Communist Chinese triumph was presumably received with mixed feelings by Ho Chi Minh in Hanoi. He may have been pleased as a Communist but hardly as a Vietnamese nationalist, whom history had schooled to be wary of a strong, united and purposeful giant neighbor.

When Peking and Moscow recognized Ho Chi Minh's Republic of Vietnam in February 1950, the United States recognized Bao Dai's "State of Vietnam," though it was clearly a make-believe regime, a recognition which meant that for Washington the country had in effect been partitioned, four years before the Geneva Conference.

The announced American policy toward China after Mao's victory was that of wait-and-see, to "let the dust settle," as Secretary Acheson put it, but it did not take very long to decide that this had happened. Soviet achievement of the atomic bomb had spurred the United States into rapid development of the even more terrifying hydrogen bomb, and presumably by no coincidence, President Truman's announcement that the Atomic Energy Commission had been authorized to proceed with the H-bomb came as the Communist leaders of the Soviet Union and China, Stalin and Mao Tse-tung, were conferring in the Kremlin. The result of their meeting was a thirty-year mutual assistance treaty and a Russian grant to China of $300 million in credits. The military and economic aid enabled China to intervene in Korea in force before the year was out.

The Soviet aid was not free. It carried a capitalistic interest rate, and it made the Chinese debtors subject to the "suggestions" of their Russian bankers in the formulation of the Chinese First Five-Year Plan beginning in 1953. The seeds of dissension were already being sown.

For Washington it was enough that its belief in a Sino-Soviet "bloc" had been amply confirmed, though this did not mean the partners were equal. As the Assistant Secretary of State for Far Eastern Affairs, Dean Rusk, saw it, vast China had become "a Slavic Manchukuo," recalling the establishment of a puppet state in Manchuria by the Japanese in 1932.

The Sino-Soviet treaty was signed as the reality of Soviet possession of the atomic bomb spread alarm through the United States, heightened by controversy over the need for bomb shelters. Civilian Defense units were set up in cities and rural townships. Many people responded to real estate offers of home sites "outside bomb and radiation areas." If they did not move themselves, many transferred their assets from city to country banks.

Alger Hiss, the State Department official who had stood behind Franklin D. Roosevelt's chair at the Yalta Conference, was convicted of perjury, due largely to the efforts of the California congressman Richard Nixon, but the larger implied charge was that of passing official papers to the Russians. Senator Joe McCarthy accused the leading sinologist, Owen Lattimore, of being also the "top Russian espionage agent" in the United States. In Britain the scientist Klaus Fuchs, who had worked at the American wartime atomic laboratories at Los Alamos, confessed to giving "atomic secrets" to the Russians and his arrest was followed by that of Julius and Ethel Rosenberg on the same charge in this country.

The Communist spy scare coincided with the outbreak of the Korean War. On June 25, 1950, the armed forces of North Korea crossed the 38th parallel into South Korea and swiftly moved upon Seoul, the capital. The invasion was in Washington's eyes clearly the work of the Russians, further evidence of Communist aggressive intentions. The wartime demarcation line in Korea put Russian troops in the north and American troops in the south for the initial purpose of disarming the Japanese, and the Russians had seized upon the opportunity to forge a strong Communist satellite in Pyongyang. Secretary Acheson, moreover, in defining the American area of vital interest in the far Pacific, had somehow omitted Korea from the chain of American security, and the Russians may have taken the omission as an invitation. Some historians later theorized that as in Europe, the Russians were inspired by weakness and suspicion. The United States was negotiating a peace treaty with Japan, to formalize continued occupation, and the Russians had several times protested at the American exclusivity of domain over Japan while the West was at the same time trying to interfere, as they saw it, with their suzerainty in eastern Europe. By crossing the 38th parallel, it may have been Moscow's intention to create a Korean counterweight to the American presence in Japan. The Communists also charged provocative border actions by South Korea to forestall national reunification.

Whatever the reasons, and they are all conjecture, as is indeed the degree of Russian complicity in the invasion, the United States reacted quickly upon its own inferences. The opportunity was provided by the convenient absence of the Russians from the United Nations Security Council, one reason for believing they may have been taken by surprise by events in Korea, since otherwise they would have made sure to be present to exercise a veto over any proposed sanctions. In any event the United States emerged as the authorized agent of the "Free World" in Korea, and soon a dozen other United Nations members, though more or less reluctantly, were sending forces there. The brunt of the fighting was borne by Americans, with President Truman explaining that "we are not at war" but engaged in a "police action," which he deemed not to require congressional approval. It was war, however, and dirty, frustrating war. It was also larger than Korea. "You can't win anywhere if you don't win this one," declared the former Supreme Allied Commander in Europe, General Eisenhower. Before long, President Eisenhower would be conceding that the United States had not won that one.

As a troublesome, confusing, and inglorious passage of arms, which had not formally ended twenty years later, the conflict in Korea was a foretaste and presage of Vietnam, even though Korea was not an "instant" war delivered by television into the living room.

But even before Korea, the United States had begun to intervene in Indochina, following the signing of the Sino-Soviet treaty. No special provocation was required. When Mao's Communists reached the Indochina border they could easily have crossed over and aided the Viet Minh, but this would have meant conflict with the French and perhaps led to complications with France's friend and well-wisher, the United States. So they stayed on their own side, apparently confident that the end of French colonialism could be achieved by the Vietnamese themselves, if given sufficient equipment and training. Ho Chi Minh visited Peking to ask for such aid and it was readily granted. The border was opened. Some of Giap's troops crossed over into China, received training and arms, and went back to fight. Chinese experts and instructors visited Vietnam to make sure the new arms were being used properly. Chinese rifles and artillery pieces replaced those which had been seized from the French and Japanese or bought from the Chinese Nationalists.

For all the material aid, North Vietnam's principal bond with China was not military or economic, but came from the affinity of two similar revolutions. One condition of Chinese aid was revival of the Indochina Communist party, which had been dissolved by Ho to get a broader national front. Both Chinese and Indochinese Communism were based on masses of peasants and the countryside, rather than the industrial proletariat of original Marxist belief. The China hands in the American State Department were "purged" by McCarthyism because they had called Mao's Communists agrarian reformers, but that is what they primarily were, and so were the Viet Minh.

The revolutionary tie between Peking and Hanoi had to put aside, and did not quite succeed in doing so, centuries of Vietnamese mistrust and fear of the Chinese Empire. Vietnam had suffered fifteen Chinese invasions in two thousand years and spent one of those two millennia under Chinese occupation.

The French comforted themselves with the thought that at least the Chinese had not intervened openly by crossing the border, and felt confident they would get enough help from the leader of the "Free World," the United States, to put down the Viet Minh insurgency.

They were right. The Sino-Soviet treaty and Peking's support of Hanoi, taken in conjunction with developments in Europe — Soviet consolidation of a Communist bloc, the 1948 Communist coup in Czechoslovakia, the Berlin blockade and Allied airlift, the formation of the rival NATO and Warsaw Treaty organizations — helped transform the French colonial war in Indochina, a war of guilt and shame to many in France, into a salient of the worldwide anti-Communist deployment of the United States. It became not only justified, for the sake of "Western civilization," but even moral.

As soon as Mao achieved power he asked the United Nations for admission. It was refused, at the behest of the United States, and Chou En-lai formally protested the refusal on January 8, 1950. If Peking had been granted entry at the time, hindsight declares, both the Korean and Vietnam wars might well have been avoided.

Though acknowledging there were "two Chinas," one in Peking and one in Taipei, the United States continued to deal only with Chiang Kai-shek because, in Assistant Secretary Rusk's words, "he more authentically represents the views of the great body of the people of China." This did not mean, President Truman explained, that the United States would "get involved militarily in any way on the island of Formosa." With the Korean War, however, the United States did get involved. The American Seventh Fleet was ordered to the Formosa Strait "to prevent any Communist attack," to continue its patrol there for nineteen years.

The Korean War, not very popular in the United States at its beginning and soon to become less so, reinstituted the traditional American controversy over presidential and congressional powers. The war was never constitutionally declared. The authorization of the UN Security Council took the place of congressional action, and the UN Charter that of any treaty. To those who challenged this state of affairs, Secretary Acheson replied, "The argument as to who has the power to do this, that, or the other thing, is not exactly what is called for from Americans in this critical juncture." His actual reference was to President Truman's decision to keep troops in Europe indefinitely, but it also applied to Korea.

The conflict over powers was outweighed, however, by that between the President and his supreme commander in the Far East, General Douglas MacArthur. Defiant of any limitations on his authority, opposed to negotiation, announcing that the Truman Doctrine had to meet its major test in Asia rather than in Europe, and prepared to use atomic weapons in China — which Truman indeed had threatened, only to retract when British Prime Minister Attlee arrived panic-stricken at the White House — MacArthur was relieved of his command by the President for being "unable to give his wholehearted support to the policies of the United States Government and of the United Nations in matters pertaining to his official duties." MacArthur had in effect called on the Chinese to surrender, under threat of invasion and aerial attack, while the White House was seeking a negotiated settlement.

"There is no substitute for victory," MacArthur had declared, and his dismissal caused a traumatic shock in the nation. The people had been taken into war by presidential fiat, it was said, the war had gone badly and now the hope of "victory" was ended by the abrupt removal of the military hero who advocated it. It was easy to suspect "appeasement," or worse. Protest demonstrations were held, and senators made demands for the President's impeachment.

MacArthur came home, still the peerless leader to many Americans, was bade fond farewell by Congress when he addressed it in joint session, was cheered by the greatest crowds in New York City's history, and was warmly greeted on the steps of St. Patrick's Cathedral by Francis Cardinal Spellman. Among the general's staunchest supporters was Richard Nixon, the newly elected senator from California, who continued to call for victory in Korea and directed contumely against Acheson as "Dean of the Cowardly College of Communist Containment."

Eisenhower would in all probability have been elected President in 1952 in any event, but his victory was certainly aided by his promise to "go to Korea" and end the war. He chose as his Vice-President the man who, believing with MacArthur that there was "no substitute," was still for "victory" in Asia, Richard Nixon.

As the Chinese entered Korea, they were also able to continue their aid to the Viet Minh in Indochina. Ho's guerrillas in 1950 had inflicted a series of small disasters on the French along the northern frontier, and American aid began to arrive soon after, before the start of the Korean War. Secretary of State Acheson, visiting Paris on May 8, 1950, agreed with the French on the "urgency of the situation" in Indochina and "the necessity for remedial action." He promised American help in "the restoration of security" in this "area dominated by Soviet imperialism." An initial grant of $10 million was explained as an expenditure on behalf of "self-determination and independence" and was followed by a mutual defense agreement between the United States and Bao Dai as "chief of state" of Vietnam. A more tangible quid pro quo was also involved. In exchange for American aid, French Foreign Minister Robert Schuman told Acheson, the Schuman Plan would remove postwar restrictions on German coal and steel production, in order to strengthen western Europe and NATO against any Soviet encroachment.

Much more quickly than usually occurs, the first American aid reached Saigon, preceded by an American economic mission to supervise it. When the Korean War broke out, an American military mission was sent, and soon the U.S. Military Assistance Advisory Group, MAAG, thirty-five strong, was teaching Vietnamese the use of American weapons.

The United States began its involvement in Vietnam from scratch. Americans knew nothing about the country except what the French chose to tell. There were no experts in Vietnam studies in the United States. Washington accepted Indochina as a French internal concern, and Indochina affairs, principally economic, were handled by the State Department's French desk. Acheson's instructions to Ambassador Donald Heath in Saigon declared that the United States must assist France "to defend the territorial integrity of Indochina and to prevent the incorporation of the Associated States within the Commie [sic]–dominated bloc of slave states."

Two decades later in his memoirs Acheson wrote of the beginning of American aid, "I could not then or later think of a better course." Walter Lippmann at the time characterized Acheson as one who had "persuaded himself to believe that a government could be conducted without the support of the people." Acheson's policy would continue not only with Bao Dai, but with Diem, Minh, Khanh, Quat, Ky, Thieu and all the others who succeeded the playboy emperor–chief of state.

The Korean War, for its duration, shifted the focus of American attention from Europe to Asia. It was widely believed that the Communists might have deliberately staged a diversionary action in order to carry through some purpose in Europe. To that end, American policy dictated a new large buildup on the continent, and since this was possible only with German participation, Acheson in the fall of 1950 called for Germany's rearmament and membership in NATO. Again, Europe and Asia were interlocked.

The reality of the Sino-Soviet alliance did not match the assumptions of State Department policy planners. Though Stalin and Mao had signed a thirty-year treaty of friendship, the historic relationship of animosity between Czarist Russia and Imperial China dictated continued suspicion even between two Communist states, as did the history of China and Vietnam. During the Chinese civil war Stalin had constantly favored Chiang's Nationalists. He tried to dissuade Mao from combat in 1946 and clearly was not enthralled by the prospect of a unified Communist China if only because it would represent a center of rivalry to his own leadership. Mao had made his Long March and fought his long war without Soviet aid, and therefore like Tito had come to relish independence of Moscow. The entry of China into Korea added to the strain between the two Communist giants. The Chinese had to pay with loss of international standing, debarment from the United Nations, condemnation as aggressors, and the loss of men and materials, to redeem an adventure presumptively inspired by Moscow that would end only in stalemate.

In 1950 American aid to the French in Indochina was overlooked in the drama of American military action in Korea, but it was equally fateful. The humiliating American retreat from the Yalu firmly established in American minds the picture of China as the inevitable aggressor and enemy, though in fact the Chinese did not enter the war until American troops approached their border, and after several public warnings that Peking would indeed intervene if the 38th parallel were crossed.

If the United States regarded the Korean invasion as a part of Communist global aggression, the Chinese regarded American military action in Korea as part of America's containment of themselves. Even with the Korean War ended, Indochina was held to justify continued anti-Communist action by the West in Asia. While the United States continued to hold the line against the Chinese northern flank on the 38th parallel, French troops supported by American aid held it on the southern flank in Vietnam.

The first American aid to Vietnam reached Saigon in June, two weeks before the start of the Korean War. A few old DC-3's were handed over to the French at Tan Son Nhut, the small landing strip which would become the busiest airfield in the world before the United States was through with it. There were no ceremonies. The white star of the U.S. Air Force was painted over with the red-white-and-blue circles of France. Then came the Liberty ship *Steelrover* fifty miles up the Saigon River with military supplies. She was accompanied by French patrol boats, a minesweeper and planes overhead, while armed French troops lined both banks. American generals, visiting senators, journalists and CIA agents sprouted everywhere in Saigon.

American aid ranged from planes and artillery to DDT and canned K-ration cheese, which the Vietnamese thought was a new kind of soap and disgustedly threw away when it did not clean. They were, after all, accustomed to the four hundred cheeses of France. Unlike the French, who took money out of Vietnam and spread corruption by their currency manipulation, export-import deals and other financial shadiness, the Americans brought money to Vietnam and spread corruption by affluence, gradually creating a motorcycle society on underpinnings of black marketing. Though it brought much, the American presence was therefore not entirely welcome. Crowds demonstrated in Saigon against the unloading of the first supplies, and it was believed they were Communist-inspired, though their leader was a fervent nationalist, a lawyer, Nguyen Huu Tho, who would become chairman of the National Liberation Front when it was formed ten years later. Communists were certainly involved in the protests, for back in Paris, finally, the French Communist party, having thought things over, had dropped its insistence that Indochina remain in the French Union. Now Thorez demanded negotiations with Ho Chi Minh, and called strikes and ordered demonstrations against the "filthy" war which for four years he had supported. It was too late. The United States had arrived in Southeast Asia to combat "Sino-Soviet aggression."

As Chinese troops fought Americans in Korea, American aid in Vietnam, on China's other flank, grew so rapidly that by February 1951 Ho Chi Minh declared the Americans to be the real enemies of the Vietnamese revolution and the French their mercenaries. Though the United States paid the bills, it was still the French, and some "loyal" Vietnamese forces, who did the fighting. They made all the mistakes that the United States would repeat in the subsequent decade. One was the falsified body count. "What is a Viet Minh?" a French officer asked, and answered himself, "A Viet Minh is a dead Vietnamese." For Viet Minh, the Americans would say

"Viet Cong." The French used tactics of "hit and run," "mopping up" and "raking over," which the Americans would call "search and destroy," "seize and hold," and "free fire." Both French and Americans tried to combine military action with civil action, under the label of pacification. Both employed Vietnamese troops against Vietnamese, as well as subsidized foreign forces.

Even "Vietnamization" was a French idea. When Paul Reynaud became Vice-Premier in June 1953, late in the day for the French cause in Indochina, he declared, "This war must stop being a French war supported by Vietnam and become a Vietnamese war supported by France."

The French in 1950 began to fight a war of attrition in Indochina as the United States would in 1965. They quickly learned attrition could cut both ways. French officers were killed off faster than Saint-Cyr could turn them out. France spent a billion dollars a year of her own in Vietnam, plus the increasing funds the United States supplied. French commanders frequently announced that they could see the light *au fond du tunnel*.

In the United States the "loss" of China and fear of the "loss" of Indochina were woven into the political events of the year 1950. Republican charges that they had been "soft on Communism" injured the Democrats in the midterm congressional elections, in which the Republican hero of the Alger Hiss case, Richard Nixon, was elected to the Senate in a campaign based on alleged Truman administration failure in Asia, and the impugning of the loyalty of his opponent, Representative Helen Gahagan Douglas, whom he called "the pink lady." Nixon's principal tactic was to distribute pink-colored leaflets showing that Mrs. Douglas's voting record "followed the Communist line" because Vito Marcantonio, the "Red Congressman" from New York, often voted the same way.

In his 1950 Christmas message to the nation, President Truman proclaimed a national emergency as the result of the Chinese attack across the Yalu, an increase in the size of the armed forces by a million men, up to 3,500,000, and the creation of the Office of Defense Mobilization. Soon thereafter the French commander-in-chief in the Far East, General Jean de Lattre de Tassigny, visited Washington to consult on Indochina, and expounded a sort of super Domino Theory which combined metaphysical and geopolitical elements. First, he explained, the loss of Tonkin would mean "the loss of Asia." That in turn would lead to "the end of Islam," the consequence of which would be "upheavals in North Africa, jeopardizing the strategic European defense bases situated there." The result, by implication, was the "end" of Europe.

Not all Democrats agreed with the Truman-Acheson belief that there was no alternative to American intervention in Indochina. Though Representative John F. Kennedy, of Massachusetts, had with Joe McCarthy assailed the "loss of China," he returned from a trip around the world with his brother Robert, during which they visited Indochina, with a less simplistic view. In his first remarks on the subject, as he decided to seek election to the Senate, he declared: "In Indochina we have allied ourselves to the desperate effort of the French regime to hang on to the remnants of empire. There is no broad general support of the native Vietnamese [Bao Dai] government among the people of that area."

During his visit to Saigon the young Congressman asked General de Lattre de Tassigny why Vietnamese should be expected to fight other Vietnamese to keep their country French. The commander entered formal complaint of Kennedy's remarks with the American Embassy, which had arranged the meeting. On his return to Washington Kennedy suggested that the United States rely on Asian nationalism rather than the French military to check Communism and urged the administration to press the French for Indochinese independence. "Otherwise the guerrilla war is going to spread and grow, and we're going to finally get driven out of Southeast Asia."

Kennedy, among others, was already grooming a candidate to provide the "democratic alternative" to either French colonialism or Communism in Vietnam. The Catholic leader Ngo Dinh Diem, who had left his country in protest against the tinsel Bao Dai regime, was living at the Catholic Maryknoll seminaries at Ossining, New York, and Lakewood, New Jersey, lecturing at various universities, and lobbying for his cause — in New York with the helping hand of Cardinal Spellman, the good friend of his brother, now the Bishop of Vinh Long in the Mekong Delta; in Washington under the patronage of other fellow Catholics, Senator Mike Mansfield of Montana, and the young Massachusetts Congressman's father, former Ambassador Joseph P. Kennedy. Others who joined an organization called the American Friends of Vietnam included Supreme Court Justice William O. Douglas, and the liberal historian Arthur Schlesinger, Jr., as well as Henry Luce, the publisher of *Time* and *Life* and a walking companion of Cardinal Spellman's.

The 1952 elections made Congressman Kennedy a senator, and Senator Richard Nixon the Vice-President, on the Republican ticket headed by General Eisenhower. The young Californian had come to the point of being dropped, following disclosure of an $18,000 secret fund formed by businessmen to aid his campaign, but in an emotional and memorable use of television, Nixon cited his wife's "Republican cloth coat" and the pet dog Checkers, a gift he refused to give back, as evidences of his probity, and explained that the money had supported his efforts "against Communism and corruption." Eisenhower, who had declared that Nixon had to be "as clean as a hound's tooth," was sufficiently relieved of embarrassment to declare, "That's my boy!" As for Nixon, the Checkers speech, as it came to be known, which he employed to overcome press opposition and "to tell my story directly to the people," set the mold for his views on the news media and how they could be managed to his advantage.

President-elect Eisenhower did visit Korea, as pledged, and the war there waned into a cease-fire and armistice, with American troops remaining in force. But the new Republican Secretary of State, John Foster Dulles, made it clear that the armistice did not end "American concern" so long as "a single Communist Chinese aggressive front extends from Korea in the north to Indochina in the south." The war in Indochina would have to continue.

The French were beginning to have different ideas. After the Korean armistice they saw no reason why there should not be a similar cease-fire in Indochina, Premier Joseph Laniel told Eisenhower and Churchill when the three met at Bermuda. Public pressure against the war was steadily rising at home in France.

The United States insisted that France should not and could not negotiate. There were those in Washington who saw the Korean armistice as "appeasement" in Indochina. The French were persuaded to fight on, but to appease French opinion, and more particularly to win French adherence to the European Defense Community, the United States agreed to conversations on Indochina with the Russians, within the Big Four context. The French were the more eager since Ho Chi Minh, answering questions put by a Swedish newspaper, professed himself ready for an armistice. Laniel's Foreign Minister, Georges Bidault, snorted that "diplomacy is not conducted by means of classified advertisements," but the way to Geneva had been opened.

At the Council of Foreign Ministers meeting in Berlin in February 1954, called to discuss the German question and the Austrian treaty, disagreement was quickly reached on a Soviet proposal for a fifty-year European security treaty. On Asia, on the other hand, there might be accommodation. The Russians were willing to discuss not only Indochina but Korea, though in addition to the Big Four they insisted that Communist China participate. Foreign Minister Molotov was even ready to talk about Formosa, but Dulles refused.

To better their position for the Geneva negotiations, the Viet Minh with Chinese aid began the military buildup for what they hoped would be a decisive battle against the French, in a North Vietnamese valley near the Laotian border called Dien Bien Phu.

With Dulles in Berlin, the Acting Secretary of State was Walter Bedell Smith — Eisenhower's chief of staff during the war, former Ambassador to Moscow, and director of the Central Intelligence Agency after the invasion of South Korea, until Dulles brought him into the State Department — and he told the Senate Foreign Relations Committee that the Viet Minh had petered out as a military force and had won "only real estate victories," which were given up to French counterattack. Meanwhile 105 U.S. Air Force technicians were arriving in Indochina dressed as civilians, to join 125 previously sent to maintain American-supplied planes. President Eisenhower, responding to congressional criticism because the technicians were sent without consultation, said he bitterly opposed American active intervention in Indochina and rejected any possibility that the Air Force mechanics could provoke such intervention by being caught up in combat. The Secretary of Defense, Charles Wilson, scoffed at the idea that Indochina could become another Korea, when Senator John Stennis of Mississippi expressed fears of Chinese intervention, as in Korea, because of increased American aid.

All that the United States proposed to do, as Secretary Dulles stated it, was to give the French whatever they needed to defeat the Communists. Washington was already paying 78 percent of the cost of the war, the French National Assembly was informed, and Harold Stassen, director of U.S. Foreign Operations, was in Saigon to oversee the diversion of $300 million in supplies from Korea to Indochina. This addition to $800 million already directly allotted made a total of $1,160 million for the fiscal year.

With mounting American aid the French military were resolved, after more than seven years of guerrilla combat, to win a decisive victory and then "negotiate" with the beaten Viet Minh. General Henri-Eugène Navarre, the French commander-in-chief, was drawing up plans to bring this about. The American MAAG mission in Saigon gave him advice as well as ammunition, and now, to help formulate the Navarre Plan, came a special American mission led by Lieutenant General John "Iron Mike" O'Daniel, chief of Army forces in the Pacific.

The O'Daniel task force included Colonel Edward Lansdale, who wore an Air Force uniform but specialized in warfare more unconventional than bombing. In the Philippines Lansdale had helped Defense Minister Ramón Magsaysay put down the Huk Communist rebellion, and he gave the French the benefit of his experience; in fact he horrified General Navarre by telling him there could be no victory unless the Vietnamese were given full rein for their nationalism. Like the good CIA operative he was, Lansdale played both ends of the Indochina game. While advising the French he also quietly made contact in Vietnam and Laos with local political groups, cults and factions, and filed what he learned for future reference.

Despite all its disavowals of any intention to intervene in Indochina, the Eisenhower administration continued to make the case for doing so, if only to justify the increasing expenditures there. The commander-in-chief, in his inimitable fashion, told a conference of state governors the reason for concern. "Now let us assume that we lost Indochina. If Indochina goes, several things happen right away. The peninsula, the last little bit of land hanging on down there, would be scarcely defensible. The tin and tungsten that we so greatly value from that area would cease coming. . . . All India would be outflanked. Burma would be in no position for defense." Eisenhower's National Security Council at the same time decided that "the loss of Indochina would be critical to the security of the United States." Congress added to the commodity list. Not only tin and tungsten were at stake, but zinc, manganese, coal and lumber in the North; rubber, tea, pepper and cattle in the South.

Eisenhower's Vice-President was also concerned over Vietnam. Touring Asia, he visited Hanoi to avow in person his support of the French effort, promising more American arms but opposing any negotiations. He pleased the French brass exceedingly. Years later the first American correspondent in North Vietnam saw at the Hanoi War Museum a photograph of Richard Nixon with General Navarre, preserved as evidence of American hostile intentions from the beginning.

As the Navarre Plan was put into effect in the fall of 1953, the French had an army of 517,000 in Vietnam, almost as large as the American army of sixteen years later. It included 369,000 Indochinese, 48,000 North African troops, 20,000 Foreign Legion, and 80,000 French, who were the officers, NCO's and specialists. To gain his decisive victory, General Navarre sought to lure the Viet Minh into a set-piece battle on the most favorable terrain he could find. He chose the valley of Dien Bien Phu, meaning "seat of the border county prefecture," guarding the Laotian border eight miles away. The small village of 112 houses, which grew rice and processed opium brought in by the Meo tribesmen from the surrounding slopes, had been in Viet Minh hands for a year.

On November 20, 1953, a French airdrop of two battalions put 1,800 men into the valley, and after a brief skirmish the Viet Minh — now officially called the Vietnamese People's Army — fled to the hills. The airdrop had an American flavor. The squadron commander's code name was Texas, his planes were American. More airdrops by American planes followed the first, and soon American helicopters were brought in.

By March 13, 1954, when the Battle of Dien Bien Phu began, the French garrison numbered 10,814. It was surrounded by 50,000 Vietnamese combat troops, with 55,000 more in support. Dien Bien Phu was supplied by American planes, which also flew in French paratroop reinforcements halfway around the world, from Paris. The New York Times lauded the American ferry service and declared that Dien Bien Phu must not be lost, since it was the "first open battle Communists have dared to fight in seven years of war."

More than American arms and aircraft were involved at Dien Bien Phu. French gun emplacements were made on suggestions based on the American experience in Korea, as a steady stream of American officers and planners visited the garrison during the buildup. A week after the initial airdrop the MAAG chief in Saigon, Major General Thomas Trapnell, came with General Navarre on an inspection visit. He returned three weeks later with his staff and expressed admiration for the way things were progressing. So frequently did he reappear thereafter that Bernard Fall, historian of the battle, wrote of Trapnell that he "beamingly hovered over the French military enterprise like a mother hen." Three American officers remained at Dien Bien Phu to keep an eye on things. Not one of the many American visitors ever noted, apparently, that the French, instead of being brilliantly emplaced, had dug themselves into a hopeless position. Above all, the garrison at Dien Bien Phu was not only isolated militarily, but isolated from the history and politics of the twentieth century.

As the battle began, American aid to the French for Indochina had reached the $2 billion mark, supplemented by a special grant of $385 million for the Navarre Plan. Since 1950 the United States had supplied 400,000 tons of war material, including 1,400 tanks, 340 planes, 350 patrol boats, 150,000 weapons, 240,000 rounds of small arms, 15 million cartridges, and 15,000 radio sets. The American equipment at Dien Bien Phu totaled well over $10 million.

The battle was indeed decisive, but not in the way General Navarre had envisaged. Because of the valley location, ringed by hills in which the Viet Minh mounted artillery in an aggregate which French Intelligence was never aware of, because of failure to calculate the effect of monsoon weather on air operations, because of stubbornness and pedantic thinking, but principally because it represented a grievous miscorrelation of French resources and risk with French objectives, Dien Bien Phu, a fifty-six-day siege, ended with the overwhelming in the mud of the garrison of 10,000. It was a military defeat, and a political and psychological debacle.

The plain truth about it, moreover, was that though fought by the French, Dien Bien Phu was essentially an American battle. It was not a military action to accomplish the defeat and surrender of insurgent nationalist forces in a colonial campaign, so much as a political and ideological action to defend the "Free World" and repulse Communism everywhere. At least that is what it had been made by the United States, and such a commitment required unlimited support, and not merely supplies, advice and good wishes. Vice-President Nixon, Secretary Dulles, Admiral Arthur Radford, chairman of the Joint Chiefs of Staff, and others who wanted an American air strike, some even an atom bomb, were logically correct if their assumptions were accepted.

As it was, Dien Bien Phu became a small lost battle in a continuing war, a temporary setback on the "Free World" road to destined triumph. It was even called a "victory" because while the fortress fell it did not surrender. No white flag was shown to Communism. As the last shots were being fired at Dien Bien Phu, symbolically the grave of French colonialism in

Southeast Asia, a new instrument of the will and determination of the "Free World" was being commissioned. From the Boeing production line in Seattle rolled the first B-52 Stratofortress strategic bomber, hailed by the Air Force chief of staff as "the long rifle of the air age," designed to strike nuclear blows "deep behind any aggressor frontier." Expanded production swiftly began, but the B-52 would never be used for its intended purpose. It would smash North and South Vietnam and Cambodia instead.

Dien Bien Phu did not fall without last desperate efforts by the French to obtain more American help, and even American participation. The Congress and most of the people, recently relieved of the Korean millstone, were in no mood to assume another "police action" in the Orient, while America's European allies, who faced Soviet divisions and medium-range missiles across their continental divide, feared a conflagration that might eventually engulf them. Yet though the effort to bring direct American action into the French Indochina war failed, it laid the groundwork for future intervention.

Eisenhower had set up a special committee on Indochina, consisting of Under Secretary of State Smith, the Joint Chiefs of Staff, Deputy Defense Secretary Roger Keyes, and the director of the CIA, Allen Dulles, brother of the Secretary of State. The French had requested twenty-two B-26 bombers, and the committee agreed on ten, with more possible. The French also asked for four hundred Air Force mechanics, and Bedell Smith favored sending the full number, but in face of Keyes's doubts reduced it by half. Keyes, the civilian, then raised the question whether even two hundred Americans would not so commit the United States as to make combat intervention ultimately certain. Smith thought not, but felt that the importance of winning was so great that if worst came to worst he would favor air and naval intervention, though he would not sanction ground troops. Admiral Radford agreed with Smith, and when the question of air intervention arose acutely a few days later, favored air strikes at Dien Bien Phu and reportedly even the use of the atomic bomb. Allen Dulles got what he wanted, which was that Colonel Lansdale, the Intelligence operative, be sent as a liaison officer with General Navarre.

President Eisenhower dispatched not only the Air Force technicians but forty B-26's, nearly twice as many as the French had asked. He had not consulted Congress, and Senator John Stennis of Mississippi rose to declare, "It proves my contention that step by step, we are moving into the war in Indochina, and I am afraid that we will move to a point from which there will be no return. . . . We are going to war inch by inch." Stennis continued to hold private objections but when he became chairman of the Armed Services Committee he provided even more than the Pentagon asked for Vietnam.

As America's Vietnam role began to change from supplier and instigator to participant, a key position was held by Under Secretary "Beetle" Smith, of the postwar crop of soldier-statesmen typified by General Marshall, and for that matter the President himself. Smith, valued as much by Eisenhower during the war for his ever-ready bridge partnership as for his administrative ability, was Ambassador in Moscow when the Cold War began, and returned home to become head of the CIA. As such he ordered the integration of intelligence-gathering with covert operations. An agent trying to evaluate foreign developments could at the same time be engaged in trying to influence the developments he was reporting on. Nowhere would this be truer than in Vietnam.

Smith succeeded Admiral Roscoe Hillenkoetter as CIA director soon after the Korean War began. In spite of announced intentions, as well as substantive reports, the CIA discounted the possibility of Chinese intervention. When it took place, just as Peking said it would, both the CIA and its chief suffered obvious injury to their reputations, so when Smith was named Under Secretary of State by Eisenhower he was a prominent casualty of the war. As the head of the American delegation to the Geneva Conference, after Dulles's opening appearance, Smith aptly personalized America's sullen obstinacy as it progressed toward full involvement in Vietnam.

The American bombers and ground crews were sent off to Saigon, as the Battle of Dien Bien Phu intensified, but the French wanted more. General Paul Ely, the French chief of staff, came to Washington to press for it and Admiral Radford, instructed by Eisenhower to do all he could, offered American tactical air support. Specifically, sixty giant B-29's, predecessors of the B-52's, from Clark Field, Manila, would drop 450 tons of bombs during each of several night raids, escorted by 150 fighters from the Seventh Fleet carriers.

This operation, morbidly called Vulture, was calculated to smash the Viet Minh cordon tightening about Dien Bien Phu. It was gratefully accepted by General Navarre, though the French and Viet Minh positions were so proximate that Vulture might also devastate the former. The French plight had steadily become worse. The landing strip was under artillery attack and the planes dropping supplies had to do so against heavy antiaircraft fire.

The contemplated American air strikes never occurred. Operation Vulture was grounded by violent objections from congressional leaders. Even the President, for all his willingness to help the French, believed, or so he later wrote, that despite the well-known American "willingness to fight for freedom anywhere," under the conditions existing in Indochina American unilateral intervention, such as by air strikes, would be nothing less than "sheer folly."

Among the voices publicly raised against intervention was that of Senator

Kennedy of Massachusetts. "I am frankly of the belief that no amount of American military assistance in Indochina can conquer an enemy which is everywhere and at the same time nowhere, 'an enemy of the people' which has the sympathy and covert support of the people." The young Senator in passing blamed former Assistant Secretary of State Rusk for having absolved French colonialism with assurances that Vietnamese independence "has or will be granted." Seven years later Kennedy would be sending American troops to Vietnam and his Secretary of State would be Dean Rusk.

Kennedy did not permit his anticolonialism to prejudice his anti-Communism. He had campaigned for the Senate against the Republican incumbent, Henry Cabot Lodge, on charges that the bipartisan foreign policy was not anti-Communist enough in the Far East. He subscribed fully to the Domino Theory, believing it essential to defeat Communism in Vietnam before it spread, and thought the French had confused the issue by being so persistently colonial; as the world knew, the United States was different. But if he assailed French rule he spoke equally against negotiations which would allow Ho Chi Minh any legitimate role in Vietnam.

The Kennedy view embodied the inherent contradictions that would for so long plague American foreign policy, holding American intentions to be so pure that "police" functions against Communism could be undertaken while traditional forms of colonialism were ostensibly opposed.

Whether Secretary Dulles was genuinely disappointed in the decision not to intervene directly at Dien Bien Phu, or secretly welcomed the congressional veto — to which had been added a British one — so that his policy of "massive retaliation" would not have to be put to the test, can never be known. The nimble legal mind had already been casting about for an alternative. Calling for "united international action" against Communism, Dulles began the formation of the Southeast Asia Treaty Organization to signify to the "Sino-Soviet bloc" that the defeat of the French in Indochina could not mean the final victory of Communism there.

The consciousness of Communist threat from both without and within had been steadily rising in the United States. Attorney General Herbert Brownell asked for new laws to destroy the American Communist party, providing for loss of citizenship for advocating the overthrow of the government by force. Senator Kennedy's brother Robert had joined Joe McCarthy's committee, which was holding hearings on alleged Communist penetration of governmental departments and the armed forces. Dr. J. Robert Oppenheimer, head of the wartime atomic laboratories, was suspended as a security risk by the Atomic Energy Commission. Ethel and Julius Rosenberg had been executed as "atomic spies" for the Soviet Union, the judge who sentenced them for a crime he called "worse than murder" having blamed them for causing the Korean War. Down Under, the defection of a Soviet Embassy third secretary, Vladimir Petrov, revealed a Communist espionage ring in Australia. In the Soviet Union itself, however, the new oath for Communist youth dropped its pledge of allegiance to the teachings of the dead Stalin, and a new party Secretary, Nikita Khrushchev, thus began the process of destalinization.

In this climate of apprehension, and despite congressional doubts and the President's wariness, some American voices continued to demand more decisive intervention in Indochina, as the new front against world Communism. A "high Administration source" who told the American Society of Newspaper Editors that American troops might have to be sent there was quickly revealed as Vice-President Richard Nixon.

"The United States as a leader of the free world cannot afford further retreat in Asia," he declared. "It is hoped the United States will not have to send troops there, but if this government cannot avoid it the Administration must face up to the situation and dispatch forces." If "unified action by the free world" could not be obtained, he added, the United States "will have to take on the problem alone." Nixon opposed negotiation because Korea, he said, had demonstrated its "futility."

The Vice-President made it clear he was speaking for himself and not for the administration, thus indicating some internal disagreement. President Eisenhower in effect confirmed this by declaring "there is no plausible reason for the United States to intervene" and "we could not even be sure that the Vietnamese population wanted us to do so."

As for the population closer to home, the one thing that seemed to emerge clearly from the controversy over Dien Bien Phu was that whatever else Congress and the American people might want in Indochina, if indeed they wanted anything, they did not want another Korea, with its 33,629 American combat dead.

Nixon's interventionist remarks roiled Washington and caused widespread protest through the nation. In the Senate the Democratic minority leader, Lyndon Johnson of Texas, attacked what he called "the Nixon war," declaring, "I am against sending American GI's into the mud and muck of Indochina on a bloodletting spree to perpetuate colonialism and white man's exploitation in Asia. The Monroe Doctrine and Asia for the Asians should be the foundation of our foreign policy."

The criticism Vice-President Nixon received for his speech to the editors did not still his voice. He followed it with another, declaring the Indochina conflict to be not colonial or civil war but a war of aggression directed and controlled by Communist China.

Even though the United States did not intervene more directly, for one reason or another, even though there were differences on tactics and timing, ambiguity was in fact the basic tool of the Eisenhower-Nixon-Dulles administration. While limiting its belligerence in Indochina to rhetoric and airdrops, it was also building up the bases around China, on Chiang Kai-shek's Taiwan, in Korea, Japan and Okinawa, plus the mobile striking power of the multicarrier Seventh Fleet. If it did not commit any more troops to Asia, it kept those it had in Korea. And in Indochina, it was charting the course by which troops would be sent there also.

The air strikes at Dien Bien Phu might be vetoed but the administration's new foreign-aid program submitted to Congress listed as its largest single item $1.133 billion more for Indochina, including $500 million for direct support of military forces there, through the French, and $300 million for equipment. Even if the French should decide to leave, a considerable American "investment" would have been introduced. Nor was it only in money and goods; it was beginning to be in lives. American "civilian" pilots of the CIA-operated Civil Air Transport — the postwar version of the "Flying Tigers" over China — and some Air Force pilots in civilian garb, sent to "get acquainted" with Indochina's skies and terrain, were among those dropping supplies to doomed Dien Bien Phu. Several were shot down. Five of the Air Force mechanics who serviced American planes at the Danang air base were captured by the Viet Minh while swimming at an off-limits beach, the first American war prisoners in Vietnam. They were released with the French taken at Dien Bien Phu.

As the Battle of Dien Bien Phu was being waged, another of Eisenhower's numerous special committees, this one on the Threat of Communism, made its recommendations for the Geneva Conference the United States was preparing reluctantly to attend. It was American policy, declared the committee, to accept nothing short of military victory in Indochina. Failing French support for this view, the United States must actively oppose any negotiated settlement. If this had no effect, the United States must insure with the three "associated states" of Vietnam, Laos and Cambodia that the war continue, without the French and with active American participation, which was left unspecified.

Despite any statements it would make to the contrary in Geneva, including its pledge not to use force to upset any agreements, the American delegation, led by John Foster Dulles and then by Walter Bedell Smith, therefore went to the conference resolved to reject, and if necessary sabotage and subvert whatever settlement was arrived at.

The Geneva Conference was held under the shadow of the French defeat at Dien Bien Phu, which made the settlement possible. The French simply walked away from this consequential event and then set about divesting themselves of the rest of their colonial possessions, as the British and the Dutch were doing.

But Dien Bien Phu created a trauma from which American Presidents and generals would long suffer. It made impossible, in their minds, any withdrawal from Vietnam, for that would discredit the judgment and sully the prestige and even "honor" of the United States. It forged the determination to make up for Dien Bien Phu by staying in Vietnam, to achieve not only victory but vindication. In such a context, negotiations were held to be inconceivable in Vietnam. Too much was at stake there, and the least of that stake was Vietnam itself.

Being vividly illustrated was one of the fundamental defects of American foreign policy, as noted by Hans Morgenthau, that of drawing large generalizations and deriving broad principles from specific local problems and situations. At Geneva, as the United States saw it, the issue was not Vietnam, not Indochina, not Southeast Asia, but the world.

3

"THINGS ARE IN THE SADDLE"

THE FLAGS OF THE WORLD flew in the international city of Geneva, as always, and among them for the first time was the red banner of Communist China, with its large gold star crescented by four smaller ones.

The visitors from Peking, headed by Premier Chou En-lai, were making their formal bow to the West after nearly five years of their revolutionary regime. They had come to Geneva because the subject of the 1954 conference at the Palace of Nations was Korea, then Indochina, and the Chinese had fought against the "United Nations" in Korea, and were supplying arms, equipment and training to the Viet Minh in Indochina. Chinese advisers and experts were said to be taking part in the battle being fiercely fought, as the Geneva Conference opened, in the North Vietnamese valley of Dien Bien Phu.

The cold mountain wind from the Alps, called *Die Schwarze Bise*, had blown bitterly for nine days, through Easter, but now had relented, and spring sunshine had come to Calvin's city, where by some law of the Protestant ethic the churches and the banks could be mistaken for each other. The green lawns along Lake Leman bloomed with spring flowers, and the public gardens were carefully planted with tulips and rhododendrons. The famous *jet d'eau* shot up from the lake to its 470-foot height, the swans glided about the islet named for Jean-Jacques Rousseau, and the lake steamers criss-crossing between Switzerland and France paddled their way to Lausanne and Montreux, sailboats ducking before them. The tourists thronged the antique shops and fondue restaurants of the old city on the hill, lunched at the Perle du Lac on perch and white wine, drank beer at the Restaurant Bavaria with its caricatures from the original League of Nations, and idled on the café terraces of the Quai du Mont Blanc, or in the smaller neighborhood cafés where Lenin wrote messages to Russia and James Joyce sipped fendant. Excursion parties from all parts of the world swarmed through the halls of the Palace of Nations, shopped for chocolates and Persian rugs in the rue du Rhône, and appraised Swiss watches in the city in which they were made.

The crowded North Atlantic sea-lanes, with four American, ten British, three French, four Italian and five Dutch liners in regular service, brought more travelers each day to Europe. As in 1946, it was a spring of relaxation there, though the vital question of Germany was still unsettled nine years after the war and the troops of East and West confronted each other along the barbed wire and minefields between them. The main thing was that Stalin was dead, his successors were seeking detente with the West, and a "thaw" had begun in the Soviet Union as the "anti-Titoist" purges in the satrapies of eastern Europe ended. With Moscow's iron fist unclenched, workers had actually rebelled in East Berlin, an ill augury for the Communist future, while western Europe, on the other hand, was coming closer together in an economic community which it was hoped would eventually also be political.

Even in Asia, where the Korean War had at least ceased to be a shooting war, it was apparent that the eight-year conflict in Indochina would soon come to a halt. That at any rate was the anticipation of the gathering Geneva Conference. Most Frenchmen were tired of a war that had dragged on so long, aggravated disunity, distracted from problems at home, and would cost 170,000 casualties in dead and wounded. French political leaders sought some way out "with honor."

Three of the four other major Geneva conferees — Britain, the Soviet Union and China — were similarly relieved by the prospects of an Indochina settlement, the two Communist nations because they could account it a victory over colonialism, the British because they were no longer able to play the global role they had once enjoyed, and saw an easement of tensions in Asia contributing to more easement in Europe.

The fifth Geneva power had another perception of things. For the United States this was not a ceremony to end a dirty, insignificant and outdated war in a small and remote land of paddies and water buffalo. It was a principal point for the containment of Communism in a global chain of such points, another engagement in the crusade against the conspiracy which sought to undermine Western civilization and replace it with atheistic and expansionist Bolshevism.

The first intention of the United States at Geneva was to prevail upon the French not to negotiate a peace with Ho Chi Minh, behind whom stood Peking and the Kremlin. For four years, since the Communists had driven Chiang Kai-shek out of China, the United States had supplied increasing amounts of aid to the French in Indochina, in common cause. It was prepared to supply more.

As Geneva opened, the Americans stated their position candidly and did not mind threatening France in the process. President Eisenhower's National Security Council urged him to inform Premier Joseph Laniel that "acquiescence in a Communist take-over of Indochina would bear on France's status as one of the Big Three"; in fact "American aid to France would automatically cease." If France participated in a Geneva settlement anyway, the United States would maintain its own goal of nothing short of "a military victory."

Secretary of State Dulles saw a French withdrawal from Indochina, like the British withdrawal from Greece in 1947, as creating a vacuum into which Communist power would swiftly flow unless the United States prevented it. Southeast Asia had become the logical extension of the Truman Doctrine. "In 1954 the French knew they could transfer the problem of Southeast Asia's security to our shoulders," Lyndon Johnson recalled in his 1971 memoirs. Southeast Asia, however, was no longer France's for the mere handing-over.

Because of its agenda — Korea, then Indochina — the Geneva Conference naturally revolved about China, the U.N.-branded outlaw and aggressor, but though the Americans had agreed to meet with the Chinese at Geneva, as they had at Panmunjom, this did not imply recognition, diplomatic or otherwise. Dulles was cautioned against any such implication by senators of both parties, and among the Democrats not only the conservative Russell of Georgia but the liberal Mansfield of Montana actually opposed the holding of the conference at all because of China's presence. Nonrecognition of China was not intended to imply intervention in Indochina, and even Dulles's journalistic supporters, the Alsop brothers, conceded that the Secretary would be gambling with the risk of general war by intervening, while noting that he had similarly resorted to "brinkmanship" in Iran and Korea, and "won."

The Chinese arrived for the conference first, in a khaki-colored two-engine Soviet plane of American design, flown in from Moscow via Berlin by a Russian pilot and an American navigator. On the Saturday after Easter a large crowd of diplomats and journalists was waiting at Cointrin airport to greet Chou En-lai and his entourage, all in blue tunics, on their first visit to the West.

As the initial delegation, the Chinese were officially welcomed only by the Swiss. Federal troops with machine pistols stood on guard duty at the airport and throughout the city. Russian ZIM limousines were waiting to drive Chou to the sumptuous villa of Grand Mont-Fleuri in suburban Versoix, converted by furniture and carpets borrowed from China's art treasures into a sort of national museum overseas. During the conference the villa served not only as Chou's headquarters but as China's Embassy to all Europe, receiving callers from every part of the continent.

Chou deposited his baggage, changed from military cap to fedora, and returned to meet Soviet Foreign Minister Vyacheslav Molotov that evening. The crowd of two thousand now included 150 Russian plainclothesmen. A second Soviet plane brought caviar, sturgeon, vodka and kitchen facilities to be installed at the Russians' cavernous downtown hotel, the Metropol — within forty-eight hours it became the spiritual twin of the grim hostelry of the same name in Moscow — while Molotov was sped to the villa of Les Chatillons, one of the two leased for the large Moscow delegation. In contrast to Chou's resplendent residence, with its large sun balcony, Les Chatillons looked like a technical high school.

The British Foreign Secretary, Sir Anthony Eden, who flew in the following day, was settled in the Swiss idea of a British country home at Pregny, while French Foreign Minister Bidault, arriving by overnight train from Paris, was installed in a Loire-like château at Versoix. It stood adjacent to another, rented for Pham Van Dong, head of the Viet Minh delegation, who was coming for the second part of the conference.

The American Secretary of State wanted no villa, château, or technical high school. The traveling salesman of foreign policy, not intending to stay very long, was comfortable on the sixth floor of the Hôtel du Rhône, on the riverbank, which also conveniently housed the American Consulate General and the United States Information Services offices. Unlike the others, Dulles arrived with a prepared statement for American television cameras expressing the wish that "the aggressors come here in a mood to purge themselves of their aggression." In Calvin's city his pastoral message was, "Sinner, repent ye."

On his hotel floor, guarded by U.S. Marines, the Secretary had a staff of forty diplomats and eighty administrative assistants, a large allotment of manpower for a conference the United States had already kissed off. Each day fifty thousand words went in and out of the Rhône code room with the most urgent messages coded, transmitted, decoded and acknowledged by Washington all within seventeen minutes.

Since Geneva, contrary to the belief of American tourists, is not the capital of Switzerland, its diplomatic establishment consists of prosaic consulates in office buildings. The lakeside villas for which it is known take the place of the embassies that foreign ministers usually reside in during international conferences. The embassies are in Berne, two hours away.

The Geneva Conference opened with 1,150 newsmen and cameramen accredited to it. The Maison de la Presse, a seven-story converted department store, was equipped with 220 telephone lines and the cost-conscious

Swiss reported that they had spent 300,000 francs, at four to the dollar, to provide news facilities, plus 700,000 francs for renovating the official villas and 150,000 francs for extra police. The troops of the Seventh Schüt-zen-battalion, on guard duty in the city, were listed as on spring maneuvers.

The start of the conference was delayed because of difficulties about the shape of the table. The United States objected to a round table, square table, or any other kind of table at which it would have to sit with Communist China, so a kind of Gothic arch was made of two touching tables to separate them. The American Secretary of State honored his promise to the folks back home to have no truck with the Chinese. At the opening ceremony he ignored both Communists when Molotov introduced Chou En-lai to Eden. In the anteroom, after the first session, Chou started toward Dulles, but the tall gray-haired American, son of a Presbyterian minister, turned his back on evil and walked away, his facial tic working in disapproval. The top-level snub would not be repaired until Richard Nixon eighteen years later vigorously shook hands with and offered toasts of friendship to Chou En-lai in the Forbidden City in Peking. Dulles's 1954 behavior still rankled, Chou said, when he received American congressmen after the Nixon visit.

If the Chinese leader felt humiliated at the time, or if he remembered the two occasions when Dulles, in Eisenhower's name, had transmitted nuclear threats to Peking to hasten the Korean armistice, he was inscrutable. His opening conference speech made his feelings about the United States plain enough. For too long, he declared, "Asia for the Asians" had really meant Asia for the Japanese and for Chiang Kai-shek, both of whom he regarded as American "running dogs." Now, demanding the withdrawal of all foreign troops, the closing of all American bases and the end of aid to Indochina, Chou made manifest his desire that Asia be for the Communists, confirming the darkest American suspicions. He spoke, said the New York *Times*, "with the arrogance of a conqueror laying down his terms."

The first phase of the Geneva Conference was the Korean. The North Koreans, also making their first appearance in the West, had arrived in baggy trousers and topcoats of almost ankle length, looking like the Russians of a decade before in Berlin and Vienna. The meetings of seventeen delegations, including all the countries which had fought in Korea, even Luxembourg, quickly spread like lava all over the Geneva landscape, into private discussions at the villas and occasional tête-à-têtes in embassies in Berne. Despite the abundance of diplomatic exchange, the results were negligible. The Communists refused all-Korean elections for the same reason they had refused all-German elections; they knew they would lose them. In Vietnam they wanted elections because the reverse was true, and though the Korean sessions lasted two weeks and ratified the Panmunjom armistice — a political settlement was never contemplated — everyone knew the real business at Geneva was Indochina.

At first it seemed there might be no Indochina conference. Bao Dai, ensconced at Evian — one of his favorite watering places, which was not only on the other side of the lake but in another country — vetoed the seating of the "North Vietnamese," as they were called to avoid the official name, the Democratic Republic of Vietnam. The United States also wanted the Viet Minh kept out of the conference, in order to avoid "recognition." Then it was remembered that this, after all, was the successful adversary. How could any talks be held without it?

The Viet Minh came to Geneva directly from the limestone caves above Hanoi, where Ho Chi Minh and General Giap had directed the war. Unlike the Chinese, the North Vietnamese were culturally Westernized. Pham Van Dong, the former history teacher, could quote from Montaigne and the acerbic Voltaire, who two centuries before had lived outside Geneva at Ferney. The North Vietnamese were guerrillas but they were also men of learning and wit, riposting and often confounding their French opposites in repartee. They had no opportunity to charm John Foster Dulles. Having attended five plenary sessions and a private one without speaking a word to Chou En-lai or acknowledging his presence, the Secretary of State left Geneva before the Viet Minh arrived. Departing, he told the French to prepare for the "coming counterattack" by the "Free World" within two years' time, and meanwhile to hold the Red River and Mekong deltas after the inevitable outcome at Dien Bien Phu.

Dulles returned to the United States in the midst of the garish television spectacle programmed as "the Army-McCarthy hearings." Despite all the Secretary's efforts to keep Indochina a matter of vital American concern, as he and the President held news conferences and gave speeches, it was the domestic aspects of the great anti-Communist crusade that commanded the major public attention. The Republicans did their best to connect the two salients. As explained by Vice-President Nixon in the 1954 midterm election campaign, the "loss" of 600 million people to Communism in China had been realized by treason, committed by "Communists in government," in Joe McCarthy's phrase.

Before turning upon the Army for allegedly harboring subversives, the Senator had decimated the State Department and its propaganda arm, the Voice of America, with Dulles's compliance, and had induced the Department of Defense to prohibit "known Communists" from the armed services.

The Alger Hiss and Rosenberg cases fortified the Republican cause and the Supreme Court helped by upholding a compulsory testimony law to circumvent the Fifth Amendment. While McCarthy of Wisconsin looked into "subversion in government," Jenner of Indiana and his Senate Internal Security subcommittee sought it in Academe, investigating university faculties. McCarthy was further reinforced by Eisenhower's extension of the Truman "loyalty" test for federal employees to the broader category of "security risk." In short order, twenty-two hundred government workers were discharged.

There was enough Red-hunting for all to share. In its first term the new Republican Congress elected with Eisenhower actually worked out an apportionment plan among various committees to obtain coordination, instead of competition, for the news headlines. While the Army-McCarthy hearings were held, the House Un-American Activities Committee was also in action in a dozen cities, investigating unions, churches, and other organizations allegedly infiltrated by Communists. The New York and Hollywood entertainment worlds were under scrutiny for radicalism, the movie industry blacklist was expanded, and the American Federation of Television and Radio Artists, which included not only actors but broadcast newsmen, voted to expel any member declining to answer the committee's questions, thus depriving him of employment.

Domestic American anti-Communism included anti-Communism in the Western Hemisphere, Uncle Sam's backyard, and the government was keeping a wary eye on the small Central American republic of Guatemala, where the "anti-Americanism" of President Jacobo Arbenz Guzmán, demonstrated by expropriation of United Fruit Company land, was equated with pro-Communism. Arbenz had been elected three years before, largely by labor union support, and the trade unions in Guatemala were Communist-led. On his return from Geneva, Dulles, at a cabinet meeting, deplored the inability of others to appreciate the American view that a Communist regime in any nation, no matter how brought about, was destructive of that nation. Such a view was at variance with public American statements that if a Communist government was legitimately elected it would have to be accepted. The leftist regime in Guatemala, elected with the aid of a small Communist vote, had been marked by the CIA for overthrow, while at Geneva the United States sought to avoid an election in Vietnam that would inevitably bestow legitimacy on a nationalist-revolutionary system.

The Army-McCarthy hearings began four days before the Geneva Conference, as a thousand GI's of the Forty-fifth Infantry Division, back from Korea, paraded up Broadway in New York City to the cheers of sidewalk crowds. In Korea the commander of the Eighth Army, General Maxwell Taylor, announced the Fortieth Division would soon be leaving for home also, but fifty thousand Americans would remain.

The hearings on Capitol Hill opened with Secretary of the Army Robert Stevens testifying that Senator McCarthy had lied in ascribing "easy on Communism" attitudes to Army officers and that he had done so only after failing to get preferential treatment for his protégé Private G. David Schine. When the Geneva Conference got under way, it was overshadowed by two mysteries, one a photograph purportedly showing Private Schine and Secretary Stevens in friendly association, the other the disclosure that an American "Pilots Employment Agency" was hiring Americans to fly bombers and fighters in Indochina. The photograph had been doctored. The "Pilots Employment Agency" was the CIA.

Though Bao Dai in his Evian retreat finally agreed to admit the "North Vietnamese" three days after the conference began, Dulles through President Eisenhower warned that a Communist "conquest" of Southeast Asia was "unacceptable." Nevertheless, a modus vivendi was required with the Communists in Asia as in Europe. In New Delhi, China and India were signing a nonaggression pact. In London, Winston Churchill urged the Russians to join in "links" for peace, while in Hanoi thousands demonstrated against any partition of Vietnam. They carried signs in English, "Independence or Death." Ho Chi Minh was still trying to get through to the Americans.

Like the Viet Minh, the United States at Geneva opposed partition as well as any sort of coalition government, and preferred a simple cease-fire to a more formal settlement. These were the instructions of the President and the Joint Chiefs of Staff given to Under Secretary Smith as he left for the Palace of Nations to replace Dulles. If the United States could not keep France from making a settlement, Smith was ordered to be prepared to withdraw from the conference, or at best to limit the American role to that of observer. He was to sign nothing. Thus the United States would not be associated with any move which saw Vietnam "amalgamated into the Communist bloc of imperialistic dictatorship."

"Beetle" Smith was the right man for the assignment. He was fresh from an appearance as a witness at the Senate hearings, and had taken part in Dulles's purge of some of the "subversives" McCarthy said lurked in the State Department. Eisenhower's former chief of staff arrived in Geneva on May Day, which was celebrated in New York City by an anti-Communist parade of 210,000; in Moscow by the unveiling of a new intercontinental nuclear bomber — photographs showed Malenkov, the nominal leader, solemn and subdued while at his side the new party Secretary, Nikita Khrushchev, waved his hat and smiled at the passing marchers — and in Belgrade by a parade featuring American tanks and jet planes, supplied to Marshal Tito after his break with the Kremlin.

In Guatemala City, President Arbenz and Communist labor leaders marked May Day with speeches against "American imperialism," and rejected the American demand for a $15 million indemnity to the United Fruit Company for 225,000 acres of land. The payment, said Arbenz, would be based on the land's tax valuation, which United Fruit had been able to keep quite low. United Fruit wages were also low. Its banana workers received $1.36 a day, and were receptive to Communist recruitment.

At Geneva peacocks paraded across the lawns of the Palace of Nations and sightseers trooped through the halls, as the agenda moved from Korea to Indochina. Outside the gates, in a small tent, the leader of Vietnam's militant Buddhists, the Venerable Tri Quang, fasted and kept vigil as the fate of his country was decided. The monk received visitors and in his good English spoke unpiously of French colonialism. His role in Vietnamese politics was destined to be an important one, but there were no experts on Vietnamese Buddhism in the American delegation at the conference.

The Chinese marked the opening of the Indochina phase of the Geneva Conference with their first cocktail party for Western newsmen at their downtown headquarters, the rambling Hôtel Beau Rivage, which they shared with the British, the flags of both nations flying in front side by side. The party was exactly like any other except that it offered Chinese wine. Though they stayed largely to themselves, dined in their hotel and avoided Geneva's four Chinese restaurants, and were not seen in public except to gaze at wristwatches in the jewelry store windows — the Russians had done the same at the Paris peace conference in 1946 — the Peking delegation of two hundred, the largest present, had quickly learned the ways of Western public relations. Like the Western delegations, they gave a cocktail party but no real news.

Their hotel pressroom was stacked with brochures and leaflets about the New China, in several languages, and these constituted the only information available. The room was decorated by objets d'art from Peking, not only red lacquer boxes and cloisonné vases but photographs of the Great Wall and of children with doves. Not all the propaganda leaflets were by Mao Tse-tung; some bore the name of Dr. Sun Yat-sen, the "bourgeois" revolutionary of 1910, whose widow still lived in Peking.

The Chinese senior delegate, Huang Hua, who had taken part in the Panmunjom armistice talks, was regarded as an anti-American "hardliner." When he talked about American bases in Asia he became agitated, his hand shook, and he had difficulty with his excellent English, learned at American-supported Yenching University. In 1971 Huang Hua, all smiles, would welcome Henry Kissinger to Peking and become China's first Ambassador to Canada, and the head of the finally admitted Peking delegation at the United Nations.

The fall of Dien Bien Phu came on a Friday promptly dubbed "black" in Paris. It was responded to in Washington by Secretary of State Dulles, still proclaiming the possibility of American intervention in Indochina, though not without congressional approval, he explained, and in association with other states. The means would be the Southeast Asia Treaty

Organization, toward which the first step had already been taken by the offer of "Free World" bases made by the military dictatorship in Thailand, against further "Communist advance" in Asia.

French heroism at Dien Bien Phu was the dominant theme in American headlines and editorials — "They Fight for Us," declared the Alsop brothers — rather than French obtuseness and error. The French had blundered not only by concentrating such a large force in a vulnerable position, but by underestimating Viet Minh tenacity and resources. Dien Bien Phu was considered safe because the Viet Minh had a 350-mile-long supply line, but they did not need trucks to bring up artillery and supplies. They used human backs, their primary power, and were able to undertake a set-piece major conventional battle as successfully as they had waged ambush and booby-trap warfare.

While the French lost 10,000 at Dien Bien Phu they still had an army of 500,000 in Indochina, and could fight on. "Submerged, not conquered," explained the New York *Times,* and its foreign affairs commentator, Anne O'Hare McCormick, in the first of what would be a long series of such conclusions by Americans, found that the Viet Minh had taken "unacceptable loss."

Though its fall had been anticipated, the psychological shock of Dien Bien Phu upon the French was profound. Foreign Minister Bidault at Geneva at once asked for a truce, to be followed by political talks. The Viet Minh refused and offered a peace plan of their own which the New York *Times* found "arrogant." Ho Chi Minh declared he wanted to negotiate with the French for a cease-fire and peace agreement but that "United States ruling circles are trying to frustrate a peaceful settlement."

The news of the fall of Dien Bien Phu came to Paris on V-E Day, transforming it into an occasion of mourning. Solemn mass for the dead was said at Notre-Dame. French television canceled all its programs. In fear of anti-Communist demonstrations, the Opéra called off the appearance of the Moscow-Leningrad ballet company, tickets for the first performance of which had brought $100 each from scalpers. There was a demonstration nevertheless by ticket purchasers unable to get back from the box office what they had paid the speculators.

V-E Day ceremonies at the Arc de Triomphe were interrupted by shouts at government leaders, "Send them to Dien Bien Phu!" When the "exiled" General de Gaulle appeared to lay his private wreath, after the official ritual, the shouts became *"Vive de Gaulle!"* and *"De Gaulle au pouvoir!"* It was forgotten, if indeed it was ever realized, that de Gaulle had put France on the road to Dien Bien Phu nine years before. Despite the shattering military defeat Premier Laniel won a vote of confidence, though by a mere two votes, to continue his Indochina policy of maintaining a French presence there.

Bedell Smith in Geneva received new instructions from Dulles to make the American role that "of an interested nation which however is neither a belligerent nor a principal in the negotiations." After that the soldier-statesman, a dyspeptic, frequently went fishing on the lake instead of taking part in staff meetings and briefings. At the conference sessions, however, unlike Dulles he at least acknowledged the existence of Chou En-lai. As the Chinese leader recalled it years later, Smith did not shake hands either, conveniently holding a teapot in his right hand when they first met, but he used his left hand to grasp Chou's arm.

In the arguments in the Pentagon about American intervention during the Battle of Dien Bien Phu, the Army chief of staff, General Matthew Ridgeway, had opposed the other members of the Joint Chiefs on air strikes and warned against any American thought of a future land war. After the fall of the fortress Ridgeway and Lieutenant General James Gavin, the Army chief of plans and development, made a full study of the feasibility of war in Indochina, and concluded that modern military forces could not fight there without "tremendous engineering and logistical effort," and that this effort and its cost would be greater than in Korea. The Ridgeway-Gavin report, from men he had confidence in, apparently resolved President Eisenhower's equivocations on the matter, and confirmed his opposition to intervention. His Vice-President was not dissuaded.

The long-expected fall of Dien Bien Phu was reported on the third page of the New York *Times* while the front page told of Senator McCarthy's challenge of the Chief Executive's claimed right to keep secrets from Congress. The daily television spectacular had become a source of jaded amusement. Overexposure is a hazard politicians never seem to be aware of. McCarthy, with his unshaven jowls, had become the subject of take-offs. His phrase "Point of order" was used by TV comedians. Familiarity made him no longer untouchable but subject to derision, hence vulnerable.

At this point the crusade against Communism at home and abroad was abruptly punctuated by a domestic Dien Bien Phu, as many Americans saw it, a blow against their own particular form of "colonialism." Unanimously the Supreme Court of the United States, reversing the "separate but equal" ruling of 1896, ordered the end of racial segregation in the public schools of twenty-one states and the District of Columbia, where it had been the law.

The decision did not settle the matter. Segregation had been bred in the American bone, and not only in the South. The courts, it was said, could not "change human nature." Instead of ending a century of struggle for explicit civil rights, the Supreme Court thus opened a new era of struggle for not only more explicit but many implicit rights. White racism reacted to *Brown v. Board of Education of Topeka* with White Citizens Councils and other forms of "backlash." Injunctions would be sought, new statutes passed, local conflicts take place between school boards and outraged white supremacists, campus confrontations arise in colleges, private "academies" supplant public schools. Even violence would erupt, as a way of life lashed itself to its dictated end.

The high court's ruling, delivered by Chief Justice Earl Warren, former Governor of California and Thomas Dewey's Republican running mate in the 1948 presidential election, negated the fifty-eight-year-old *Plessy* v. *Ferguson* decision that "legislation is powerless to eradicate racial instincts or abolish distinction based on physical differences." "Separate but equal" was the law, but southern schools, though separate, were hardly equal between black and white. Even if school facilities and educational expenditures had been equal, the Warren Court found, blacks would still be deprived of equal educational opportunity. Powerful intangible considerations were also involved, and separation for racial reasons generated a feeling of inferiority among blacks. And though its immediate impact was upon the agitated South, the Supreme Court decision had potential application to some areas of the North as well, where school segregation, if not lawful, existed de facto by reason of residential patterns, as in the black ghettos of the big cities.

As the shattering decision reverberated through the South, a twenty-five-year-old Negro preacher, three years out of the seminary and still working on his doctorate, delivered his first sermon, at the Dexter Avenue Memorial Baptist Church in sight of the Alabama State capitol in Montgomery, where the Confederate flag still flew. Martin Luther King, ordained at seventeen while still a junior at Morehouse College, by his father and in his father's church in Atlanta, had served as the elder King's co-pastor before going to Montgomery. Soon he would help organize a bus boycott, the beginning of the active civil rights movement in the South.

Congress was more distressed by the Supreme Court's action than by Dien Bien Phu, or what was happening in Geneva, or for that matter in Guatemala. The United States, in exercise of the Monroe Doctrine, had established a naval blockade of that small republic after the CIA reported that two thousand tons of "optical glass" arriving there aboard the Swedish ship *Alfhem* from Sczeczin, Poland, were actually arms from Czechoslovakia. The State Department demanded a hemisphere inquiry, and meanwhile, exiled Guatemalans opposed to the Arbenz regime had set up bases in adjacent Honduras and Nicaragua and were broadcasting charges of Communist "plots" against Latin America.

Just as it had airlifted French paratroops and arms to Dien Bien Phu, the United States flew arms to Honduras and Nicaragua because of the "threat" from Guatemala. Opportunely the State Department had signed "mutual defense" pacts with the two Central American states just before the arms shipments began. Secretary Dulles explained that the guns spotted arriving in Guatemala menaced the Panama Canal "only" eight hundred miles away. In truth the Arbenz regime was trying to equip itself against the attack and invasion that were so clearly in the making. It was not the first time, and would not be the last, that cause and effect were transposed in Washington. While his brother, the CIA director, drew up the plans for scheduled events in Guatemala, Secretary Dulles was busy with larger considerations. He was putting together the Southeast Asia Treaty Organization. The Geneva Conference had settled down to private meetings about cease-fire terms, for after Dien Bien Phu the fighting had continued in other regions and the Viet Minh pressed its gains, moving closer to Hanoi. The Russians now proposed an armistice supervised by four Communist and four non-Communist nations, as in Korea, but the United States stirred out of its somnolence as an "observer" to enter objections. It did not wish to be reminded of Panmunjom. British Foreign Secretary Eden suggested that the best way to get a cease-fire was to call in military representatives of both sides for that specific purpose. American delegates denounced this as "the Molotov proposal," calculated to give the Viet Minh "recognition."

French realism took over. Dien Bien Phu had compelled Bidault to change his view that the Viet Minh were merely auxiliaries of the Soviet Union and China and did not have to be dealt with directly. If only to obtain the evacuation of the wounded of Dien Bien Phu and the exchange of ailing prisoners, it was necessary to talk to the victors. French and Viet Minh military men were brought face to face and began a more fruitful phase of the conference. Meanwhile the military had also emerged to "resolve" the "dangerous" situation in Central America. In Honduras, the leadership of Guatemala's anti-Communist exiles had been taken over by Lieutenant Colonel Carlos Castillo Armas, who like so many other Latin-American officers had received his training at Fort Leavenworth, in Kansas. The colonel's "movement" was superintended by the CIA. Its representative in Honduras was E. Howard Hunt, Jr., on temporary duty from Mexico City.

In Washington the Army-McCarthy hearings approached a climax. The Army, striking back, questioned the authenticity of documents used by the Senator to make his charges. Senator Ralph Flanders, Vermont Republican, likened McCarthy to Adolf Hitler and said he had helped, not harmed, the Communist cause. McCarthyism still rolled on. The General Federation of Women's Clubs unanimously supported the outlawing of the Communist party. Numerous college teachers were discharged or suspended as suspected Communists. Even at West Point and Annapolis all seniors were investigated for "loyalty, integrity and reputation" before being graduated; three at the Naval Academy were not cleared. In New York City thirty-one teachers in the public schools were dismissed for refusing to answer questions about alleged membership in alleged subversive organizations.

McCarthy's focus was on "Communists in government." While still in combat with the Army he charged there were "Reds" in the CIA and in atomic weapons plants, but President Eisenhower was able to defend his administration's record in rooting out subversives, and by due process. In an early civilian version of the Vietnam body count, he cited one treason conviction, two espionage convictions, denials of entry to 127 "subversive aliens," and the deportation of 84 others. He had also been able to add 62 names to the Attorney General's list of "subversive organizations," making a total of 255, while 41 Communist party leaders had been convicted and all other un-American suspects were being kept under "constant surveillance, 24 hours seven days a week, 52 weeks a year." There was to be no cease-fire on the domestic front against Communism, though the shooting was about to stop in Indochina.

During this period in 1954, anti-Communist feeling in the United States, displayed in its countless ways, was recognized as hysteria by some, and was naturally opposed by its victims, their friends, and civil liberties groups. It was supported, or at the least tolerated, by the great majority of Americans. The New York *Times* and other representatives of the "liberal" viewpoint caviled at some of the methods used and would have preferred the Justice Department or the FBI to do the Red-hunting rather than Joe McCarthy, thus providing Eisenhower's "due process." Most "liberals" nevertheless approved of McCarthy's purpose, to frustrate what the *Times* now called "creeping Communist aggression."

Colonel Castillo Armas, meanwhile, from his insurrectionary headquarters in Honduras declared that President Arbenz of Guatemala, under Communist direction, was arming a "popular militia" to march against the "democratic" Latin American governments. An American Air Force major who had resigned as deputy chief of the U.S. Air Mission in Guatemala to take up "farming" in the countryside, hurriedly departed when his new occupation was publicized as a CIA cover. The Arbenz government declared a national emergency and discontinued constitutional guarantees. Attorney General Brownell in Washington urged the suspension of the Fifth Amendment to compel testimony to learn "which leaders are plotting the country's destruction." He did not mean Guatemala.

The Army-McCarthy hearings crested when Joseph Welch, the Army's special counsel, turned upon the Senator and assailed him for "recklessness" and "cruelty" in questioning the patriotism of Welch's young aide, a former member of the blacklisted National Lawyers Guild. In a scene worthy of daytime television at its most melodramatic, Welch, in what appeared to be genuine tears, won the nation's sentimental sympathy, and at that moment, in the bosom of the American living room, McCarthy's inquisitorial career arrived at a dead end. Senator Flanders at long last introduced a motion to find McCarthy in contempt of the Senate and to strip him of his committee chairmanship unless he could purge himself.

The climax in Washington detracted from the twin climaxes in Geneva, where France agreed to accept an Indochina cease-fire, and in Paris, where the National Assembly's foreign affairs committee voted against French membership in the European Defense Community. The two French actions were linked, not only by the fact that many in the Assembly favored both withdrawal from Indochina and abstention from the EDC, but also in the plans of the American Secretary of State. For John Foster Dulles the game now was to play off Indochina against Europe, to switch to American acceptance of a Geneva settlement in exchange for French adherence to what amounted to German rearmament. It was not a bona fide nor a redeemable offer. The SEATO Treaty was meant to insure a continuing American role in "protection" of Indochina. A settlement at Geneva, in addition, depended not on the French but on the Viet Minh, who held extensive territory and were increasing it daily. The only outside influence the Democratic Republic of Vietnam was susceptible to was that of its sister Communist states, the Soviet Union and China, and they, like the United States, were more interested in the interplay of Great Powers than in Vietnam with its small circumferences.

The Geneva settlement was in the end achieved by an understanding between the Russians and the French. "Peace" in Indochina, the cessation of hostilities by the Viet Minh, would be bought by French rejection of the European Defense Community treaty. More than anything else in Europe, Moscow feared the rearmament of Germany.

The attainment of the peace required other Frenchmen than those who had waged the war. The Laniel-Bidault government had exhausted any confidence that remained in it, defeated by a National Assembly vote repudiating Bidault's (and Dulles's) plan to remain in Indochina with American aid, by agreeing to an armistice but no political settlement. The Assembly voted it was time to get out.

The new Premier named by President René Coty had led the opposition and above all others stood for an immediate Indochina settlement, eventual French withdrawal, and the end of American intervention. He was the brilliant, some thought saturnine, Pierre Mendès-France, a lawyer-economist, a Radical-Socialist and thus anti-Gaullist, a wartime Free French pilot and escapee from a Nazi prison, and what many Frenchmen were willing to overlook, a Jew.

Mendès-France proposed to be his own Foreign Minister, and on the promise to end the war within thirty days he was voted into the premiership by an overwhelming 419 to 47. He also pledged to seek a "compromise" on EDC.

Vietnam underwent an abrupt change of government also. Bao Dai, still in Evian and having received certain Americans among his other visitors from nearby Geneva, announced the appointment of Ngo Dinh Diem as Premier, replacing the Emperor's cousin Prince Buu Loc. Diem's patriotic record was indisputable, going back to the Thirties. He had been anti-French, anti-Japanese, and anti–Viet Minh. Now he was ready to work with the Americans for a program of "social reforms, austerity, anti-Communist mobilization," and to form "the new defense line of the non-Communist world," as Washington saw it.

Diem's government was "essentially a creation of the United States," as the Pentagon Papers put it, but after nearly twenty years there remains considerable uncertainty as to exactly how he became Premier. Colonel Lansdale of the CIA was in Saigon already, nominally as an assistant air attaché, under orders to prepare for the inevitable partition of the country, and then to save what was left of Vietnam from Communism. Next door to Indochina, General William J. Donovan, head of the CIA's wartime predecessor the OSS, arrived as Ambassador to Thailand, which the Pentagon planned to make an anti-Communist bastion with military aid, troop-training and road-building.

By Lansdale's account Diem was chosen by Bao Dai on the recommendation of not merely the French "Colonial Office" but the "French Government." Behind this CIA cover story the United States had notified the Quai d'Orsay that French acceptance of Diem was a condition of continued American aid to France. Mendès-France later expressed regret at French compliance, but at the time thought he was already in enough disfavor with the United States over his opposition to the EDC treaty. Moreover, since France was going to be leaving Indochina soon, it could not matter too much who ruled in Saigon so long as French interests were not nationalized.

Lansdale himself played a significant role in the choice of Diem. Among the Vietnamese politicians with whom he had established contact was Ngo Dinh Nhu, a prominent Catholic, who had founded the Movement of National Union for Independence and Peace, composed of Catholics, the Dai Viet nationalist party, and the Cao Dai and Hoa Hao religious sects. Nhu demanded a new regime for the express purpose of fighting Communism, and proposed as its head his brother Diem, who had been living abroad. As soon as this had been agreed to, Lansdale went to work to make Diem not merely Bao Dai's Premier but his successor as chief of state.

Diem arrived in Saigon on June 25, while the Geneva Conference was still in progress. At the airport he told government and church dignitaries he was "destined" to lead the way to "national salvation." While most of the capital's population, largely Buddhist, stayed at home and seemed indifferent, Diem received an enthusiastic welcome from the Catholics, who lined the streets as his heavily guarded black limousine whizzed past with closed windows. They were, however, disappointed that few got a glimpse of the new leader. Diem's arrival was symbolic of his entire regime, arousing great expectations with few results, marked by detachment from the mass of people but with pious words for the chosen few. The new Prime Minister moved into his small official "palace," really an office, near the Saigon Zoo. Norodom Palace, the main government building, was occupied by the French High Commissioner, but soon Diem was allowed to take it over and he renamed it Dac Lop, or Independence Palace. Meanwhile fifty American military men arrived in Saigon to join the MAAG. They had been trained for "dirty tricks," and Lansdale found speedy use for them, though he did not believe they were up to "real" political warfare.

The "anti-Communist mobilization" that Diem intended for Vietnam had already materialized in Central America. The New York Stock Exchange reached a twenty-four-year high as the Guatemalan opposition forces launched the most widely anticipated, best-publicized, and probably best-financed coup in history, an invasion by land, sea and air from Honduras and Nicaragua. The American State Department explained it as a "revolt of Guatemalans against the government," and denied American bombing of the capital, as President Arbenz charged, but acknowledged that three "old" B-26 bombers, of the kind sent to the French in Indochina, had somehow been acquired by Castillo Armas. Guatemalan government forces counterattacked, but the rebels set up a rival regime under Castillo Armas and called on Arbenz to surrender. The New York *Times* could not, it said, "conceal our satisfaction."

The overthrow of the Arbenz regime, later matter-of-factly accepted as an enterprise engineered by the CIA, was accomplished as Mendès-France in Geneva set about liquidating eighty years of French rule in Indochina — rubber planting, pleasant afternoons at the Cercle Sportif in Saigon and Hue, and "petites Tonkinoises" mistresses.

The Premier–Foreign Minister's first move was to confer with Chou En-lai, asking him to bring influence to bear on the Viet Minh for acceptable terms. Ho Chi Minh's emissaries had proposed a political settlement to include a cease-fire, a formal armistice, elections, and independence for all three Indochina states — Vietnam, Laos and Cambodia. The proposals were regarded as moderate by most Europeans, indeed long overdue, but the New York *Times*, presenting the American view, found them "completely unacceptable."

During a recess necessitated by Mendès-France's private talks, the chief American delegate, General Smith, returned to Washington to report that the conference had failed. From the American viewpoint this was true. For the first time since the war the United States had been unable to keep France and Britain from negotiating with the Communists on their own. The Western disarray at Geneva, in fact, brought Churchill and Eden, the latter directly from the Palace of Nations, to discuss Allied unity at the White House. The British Prime Minister, soon to retire, urged patience and forbearance. "To jaw-jaw," he declared, "is always better than to war-war." Churchill thought the Russians would not "throw away" any opportunity for peaceful coexistence. It was eight years since his Fulton, Missouri, speech, and Stalin was a year dead.

There was considerable doubt about the return of the United States to Geneva, since it was clear the outcome would be displeasing. Vice-President Nixon was continuing to make activist speeches urging American "firmness." He was critical of the British for differing with the United States, and kept asking "Who lost China?" That "loss" by the Truman administration, he said, had caused both the war in Korea and the latest setback in Southeast Asia.

Nixon's speeches clearly seemed to annoy Eisenhower. Whoever had "lost" China, it would be embarrassing for him to be charged with having "lost" even part of Indochina. Partition was inescapable in Vietnam and members of the China Lobby already declared that ten million Vietnamese in the Red River Delta would "pass under Communist control." With Geneva and Guatemala occupying American attention, as well as the developing senatorial drama in which Joe McCarthy had been transformed from prosecutor into defendant, a prediction by Soviet scientists passed unnoticed except by American scientists. Within ten years, or by 1964, it was forecast, the Soviet Union would have an artificial earth satellite; by 1975 it would be flying manned spacecraft around the earth; between 1980 and 1990 a spaceship with two or three men aboard would fly around the moon. Flights to the moon and back would be made within the century. The Americans marveled at the excellence of Soviet science-fiction.

If things were not going well for American "interests" at Geneva, a clear victory over Communism could be pointed to in Guatemala City, and without the use of American troops. President Arbenz, under armed attack from all sides, had agreed to step down in favor of a military junta. The formula was that the junta would mediate between the Arbenz forces and those of Castillo Armas to strike an agreement. American Ambassador John Peurifoy was not happy, though the junta had immediately outlawed the Communist party. There could be no settlement, he said; Arbenz had to go. Peurifoy, who had been in charge of State Department security before becoming a "diplomat," who carried a pistol and was of distinct CIA complexion, was given an even more sensitive assignment after his success in Guatemala. He went to another major CIA theater of operations, as ambassador to Thailand. Arbenz fled to Mexico.

The overthrow in Guatemala was swift, decisive and relatively bloodless, but it did not win total acclaim in the hemisphere, even though "Communism" had been beaten down. The American role was regarded in Latin America as a violation of the Organization of American States agreements which had supposedly replaced the Monroe Doctrine, and who could say against what other hemisphere country the CIA would next intervene? Senator Lyndon Johnson provided reassurance. It was the Soviet Union against which intervention was aimed, he said, warning Moscow that no further interference in the hemisphere would be tolerated. Secretary of State Dulles announced that "world Communism" had been defeated in Guatemala. Both George Meany, president of the American Federation of Labor, and Fulgencio Batista, president of Cuba, hailed the counter-revolution. It was plain what had happened in Guatemala, but at the United Nations American Ambassador Henry Cabot Lodge denied any American involvement.

The new military regime pledged itself to reform, for even the New York Times allowed that 70 percent of the land in the country was owned by 2.2 percent of the population. The junta's first action was to cancel Arbenz's nationalization measures, especially nationalization of United Fruit land. Then it abolished the income tax as Communist, which was how many in the United States had regarded it when it was introduced in 1913. Several regimes later, in 1972, reform was still being awaited in Guatemala, and scores of American youth volunteers and priests and nuns had become radicalized by the experience of the striking contrast between rich and poor there. Castillo Armas was assassinated by his own palace guard in 1957.

The victory over "world Communism" in Central America carried an ironic footnote. The Czech arms shipment, which had given the United States its reason for underwriting the coup, was found to be made up of obsolete and useless German weapons from World War II apparently abandoned in the retreat of Hitler's wehrmacht from eastern Europe.

The cease-fire in Guatemala was followed by a cease-fire in Indochina, where during the haggling over terms the Viet Minh had taken Nam Dinh province south of Hanoi. They also controlled considerable territory below that, in fact had held Qui Nonh, between the 13th and 14th parallels, since the beginning of the war. That was why, Pham Van Dong argued, the partition of Vietnam, by whatever name it was called, should be along the line of Qui Nonh, giving the Viet Minh command of the full length of the Laotian border.

The French insisted on the 18th parallel as the demarcation line, since Qui Nonh was only an enclave. Pham agreed to give up Qui Nonh for the

14th parallel, but France held to the 18th. After two weeks of discussion, and presumably under Chinese and Russian prodding, Pham offered the 16th parallel, which would have given the Viet Minh both Danang, Vietnam's second city, and Hue, the former imperial capital. Premier Diem, barely settled in Saigon, told American Ambassador Heath that without Danang and Hue he would not only refuse a settlement, but also renounce all obligation to France, thus creating political chaos. It was up to the French to make sure this did not happen.

The final decision on the demarcation line was taken at the French villa at Versoix, with the reassembled ministers — Mendès-France, Chou En-lai, Molotov, Eden and Pham Van Dong — poring over a map. Both the United States and the South Vietnamese were absent, to denote their opposition to what they considered capitulation, no matter what the terms. The deadlock was broken when Molotov proposed the 17th parallel and then persuaded Chou En-lai to help him persuade the Viet Minh, who would be giving up considerable territory they had won by force of arms. The latter considered they had been used by their Communist kin for Great Power purposes, and indeed they had been, for Molotov now expected the French to kill the European Defense Community treaty.

The agreement declared the demarcation line to be merely temporary, for the regrouping of troops, French on the southern side, Viet Minh on the northern, and specifically not a political boundary. The amount of dispute that went into its designation, however, made it plain that to all intents and purposes, and until something removed it — reunification either by political process or by future war — the 17th parallel would be a permanent fixture.

Bedell Smith, who had been sent back to Geneva despite Dulles's reluctance — and because the British thought the United States would be defaulting both power and responsibility by remaining outside such an occasion — saw Molotov privately after the 17th parallel agreement. He knew the Foreign Minister well from his three years as Ambassador in Moscow, and he complained about the partition, which from the American viewpoint had "lost" part of Indochina to the Communists. Molotov answered that this could be quickly remedied by holding elections to decide which side would control a unified country.

Dulles had no doubt which way elections would end. Eisenhower later wrote that nobody he knew or talked to ever thought otherwise than that Ho Chi Minh would easily win "possibly 80 percent of the population" in an election against Bao Dai. The Secretary of State ordered the American delegation to stave off such a test for as long as possible after a cease-fire; he preferred in fact that no date at all be set at Geneva. Mendès-France told Smith that would suit him also.

Pham Van Dong proposed a six-month interval between cease-fire and elections, which would still mean an assured Viet Minh victory. The French and British, finally conceding that some date would have to be fixed, wanted a term long enough to allow the Diem regime to consolidate itself, with American aid. Despite North Vietnam's obvious desire for the speedy confirmation of its battlefield gains by the ballot, Molotov was more interested in pleasing France and keeping Germany disarmed. He must have stunned Pham Van Dong by increasing the six months to sixteen. The French and British countered with eighteen. The logical compromise might have been seventeen months. Utterly unexpectedly, instead, the Kremlin's Foreign Minister changed his own proposal to a round two years, fixing elections in July 1956. Mendès-France and Eden hastened to accept.

The Russians were clearly acting for their own interests in Europe, whatever Ho Chi Minh's might be in Indochina. They were at the same time pressing for a European security conference, seeking recognition of the status quo in eastern Europe and ratification of the new German border, which the other members of the Big Four had rejected at their Berlin meeting. They had now given Britain and France a quid for the quo of reconsideration.

The two-year hiatus before elections was the Geneva Conference's most decisive, and as it turned out most ill-fraught agreement, hardening the temporary military demarcation line into a permanent political boundary.

The final formalities came quickly in the Palace of Nations. With the aid of a halted clock to meet the thirty-day deadline Mendès-France had set for himself to end the war, the Accords were adopted and became part of history. All that was actually signed, however, were three cease-fire documents covering Vietnam, Cambodia and Laos, by the military men concerned.

The agreement on elections and for an interim modus vivendi was an instrument without any signature, something of a precedent after centuries of diplomacy based on treaties, protocols and seals. Even the final declaration at Geneva was unsigned, when the United States refused to bear witness to it in the traditional formal way. Mendès-France was much put out and Eden also perturbed by what they considered an American evasion of duty and propriety. Premier Diem ordered his delegation not to sign either. So nobody did. At the final plenary session, instead, Bedell Smith read a separate American declaration of intention not to disturb the agreement by the threat or use of force.

Saigon's representatives protested the entire proceedings: the armistice, the demarcation line, and the elections. Diem was thus able to declare, when he unilaterally abrogated the voting agreement, that he was not bound by anything that happened at Geneva. His position would have been more valid if Bao Dai's regime had been the duly constituted government of a sovereign state. This was a matter of some doubt. Not only was South Vietnam still part of the French Union, but Geneva gave the responsibility for insuring elections in 1956 not to the South Vietnamese but to the French. Even though they soon departed, the cease-fire document they had signed bound their successors.

It was not difficult to understand why the French should leave. When the armistice came their Indochina war had lasted seven years, seven months and two days; longer than World War I and twice as long as Korea. The French Union forces had suffered 45,000 dead, 48,000 missing and presumed dead, and 75,000 wounded. The cost of the war had been $5 billion, which included $2 billion from the United States. In the Geneva settlement the Viet Minh had won 77,000 square miles of territory with a population of twelve million.

Two decades later there are as many interpretations of Geneva as there were participants. The French lost their Asian colonial empire after nearly eighty years. What had begun as a gallant "civilizing" adventure, spreading culture and Catholicism, ended in bloody humiliation and defeat. At least one Frenchman principally involved, the defeated commander General Navarre, blamed what happened on the lack of a clear policy. No one, he said, "knew just why we were fighting."

For the Chinese Geneva was hardly a triumph except that it established their place in the category of Big Powers and introduced them in the West. Chou En-lai later confessed that "we were very badly taken in" by the Russians in being persuaded to let Hanoi yield more than it need have, and by the Americans in accepting their oral pledge not to interfere. Geneva was the Chinese leader's first international conference and he laid it to his inexperience that "we made a mistake." In any event it had become evident, despite outward appearances, that Chinese and Russian interests were not necessarily always the same.

As Chou explained it to Mendès-France, China was less interested in the reunification of Vietnam than in an assurance that the United States would not move in if the war continued after Dien Bien Phu. Peking had evidently believed the United States would not intervene in Korea, but it had, and its drive northward had compelled the Chinese to send their own forces in. Thus, while the United States feared Chinese aggression, on "the other side of the hill" the Chinese were apprehensive of American intentions.

There were still ample substantive reasons for Chou to support Molotov in imposing a settlement upon Hanoi. It would presumably close out one Western colonial presence in Asia and debar another. Moreover, association with Moscow had its advantages: the thirty-year mutual assistance treaty; the trade agreement under which Peking received credits for equipment and materials, later to include even atomic equipment; joint arrangements for developing Sinkiang; cooperation in civil aviation.

To Americans these things confirmed China's position as Russia's Asiatic partner in advancing the Communist cause. With its Asian flank secure, and possessed of the hydrogen bomb, the Soviet Union under Khrushchev could plan a new world role, not merely a Eurasian one.

On the other hand, Sino-Soviet relations in 1954 were already producing their disagreements. The Chinese objected to the joint stock companies Moscow formed in 1950, on the eastern European model, and demanded to do their own economic planning. After Geneva the Russians had to dissolve their share in these enterprises. In the political-ideological sphere Moscow's new coexistence policy was at odds with Mao's theory of permanent revolution. Following Stalin's death the Chinese leader claimed doctrinal leadership for himself in the Communist world. China's entry into Korea, even if only defensive, as well as costly, had had the effect of creating rivalry in what had been a Soviet area of interest. China's very presence at Geneva increased Peking's influence in a way that could not be altogether pleasurable to its historical Muscovite adversaries in Asia. Geneva, in fact, led China to seek for itself, not for Moscow, the guidance of the Asian and African "Third World" at the twenty-nine-nation Bandung Conference in Indonesia, from which the Soviet Union, though unmistakably an Asian power, was pointedly excluded.

For the Russians the Geneva Conference fitted into much larger considerations in Europe, as has been seen, but it had ideological implications also. The Communists of North Vietnam, like those of Yugoslavia, had come to power without the aid of Soviet forces and Moscow did not joyously contemplate another Tito. It had enough Communist nationalism on its hands in eastern Europe, and hoped to keep concessions to it within bounds, there as well as in Asia.

The North Vietnamese at Geneva believed that if the fighting had gone on they could have won all Tonkin, and most of Annam, Cochin China, Laos and Cambodia within a year. They gave up more territory than they thought they had to, and agreed on an election date far later than they wished, but they decided to accept the settlement as a victory. Ho Chi Minh issued party and government directives to observe the armistice terms, and taking the agreement at face value, depended on the French to police the interim period until 1956. The Viet Minh's southern cadres were instructed to begin "political struggle" with Diem's governmental structure for the 1956 elections, which Hanoi expected to win despite the delay.

Whatever they may have been in each specific instance, the calculations of all the other conferees at Geneva were based on the assumption that the United States, as it promised, would not upset the agreement. The United States was already in the process of doing so, through its two arms in Saigon, Prime Minister Diem and Colonel Lansdale of the CIA. Diem at once abrogated the Geneva agreement's provision for free trade between the two zones, thus depriving the North of the South's rice surplus it had always depended on for sustenance, and ended the right of movement between the zones. The United States contributed to Diem's divisive purposes by suspending all export licenses for the North. The Prime Minister then cut off all other relations with Hanoi, even those of ordinary postal service, forbade Viet Minh graves registration teams from entering his domain, and ordered Viet Minh cemeteries in the South torn up, a violation of the cease-fire agreement. Hanoi retaliated by excluding French graves registration teams from the North. The dead of Dien Bien Phu, if honored in Paris, rotted unmarked where they lay.

The Eisenhower-Dulles administration crossed its Southeast Asian Rubicon with the President's celebrated letter of support to Diem. It fell short of a hard-and-fast commitment, and was in any case an offer to the Prime Minister personally, not all his heirs, legatees and assignees in perpetuity. It was also a breach of the implicit pledge of "no more Koreas" that Eisenhower had made.

By aiding the Diem regime and cutting off the North, the United States altered the pattern of Vietnam's economy and constrained Hanoi to more dependence on Peking and Moscow. North Vietnam became, in fact, part of the "world Communist conspiracy" that the United States had engaged itself against, a classic example of the creation of a condition which, if it did not exist, had to be invented.

At Geneva the chairman at the closing session, Foreign Secretary Eden, summarized the results as not completely satisfactory to all, though they were "the best our hands could devise," and at least had ended a war which had brought hardship to millions. It was quickly evident that the war was by no means over. The United States thought Vietnam could still be saved from Communism. The first thing was to make sure the election would be won by the "Free World" and to that end, the New York *Times* advised, to build up "some real personality to offset the leadership quality of the adversary," Ho Chi Minh. Believing that the Geneva agreement would be honored, the *Times* pointed out that while no more American military aid could be sent, under its terms, increased economic and technical aid should be given the Diem regime to make it a better electoral choice than the North. "We cannot wash our hands of responsibility simply because we dislike some aspects of the truce," the *Times* told Secretary Dulles, who needed no telling. Within two weeks of Geneva the Joint Chiefs of Staff in the Pentagon called for French withdrawal from Vietnam, as a precondition for direct American aid to Diem.

The general reaction to Geneva in the United States was one of relief that the dangerous Indochina situation had been resolved without the American military intervention that some officials had called for. Only the Republican right wing saw Geneva as a complete Communist triumph, though George Meany expressed the fear that the Eisenhower administration was moving from "massive retaliation" to "massive appeasement." General Bedell Smith, returning, pointed out the difference between Geneva and a previous conference to which some had compared it. "At Munich things were given away when there was no fighting. This was a war." Dr. Norman Vincent Peale's The Power of Positive Thinking reached its ninetieth week on the best-seller list, and the Angel of Dien Bien Phu, Nurse Geneviève de Galard Terraube, rode up Broadway in open car and cotton frock, waving to the crowds.

Politics interfered with sober judgment about Geneva in the midterm election year. Adlai Stevenson assailed the Republican administration because "Communist China has staked out another menacing salient into free Asia and enveloped thirteen million people and one of the richest rice-growing areas in the Orient." He attributed the American setback in part to enchantment with stock phrases like "the liberation of the enslaved nations," "unleashing Chiang Kai-shek," "seizing the initiative," "massive retaliation," and "no more little wars." It was difficult to understand what he was arguing for, and what against.

A glimpse of what could have been instead of a Geneva settlement was offered when President Syngman Rhee of South Korea addressed the American Congress. He declared that the Geneva deadlock on Korea had invalidated the Panmunjom armistice, and he called for Korean unification by force, the overthrow of the Peking government, and if Moscow interfered, the nuclear bombing of the Soviet Union. Congress blinked, shuddered, and drew back in horror.

The Geneva disappointment was heightened for American policy planners when Mendès-France delivered his part of the bargain with the Russians, and the French Assembly rejected the European Defense Community treaty, discarding four years of Allied effort. The Mendès pledge, however, did not go beyond the defeat of EDC. When the British produced a new plan, to bring Germany into a six-nation Western European Union, the French Premier supported it, working with Chancellor Konrad Adenauer to Moscow's distinct dissatisfaction.

The creation of a new European community, seeking concert and stability, brought to mind an earlier European arrangement. In the year of Geneva a young academic, Henry Kissinger, who had come to the United States as a refugee from prewar Germany, was added to the Harvard University faculty in the Department of Government. He was writing his doctoral thesis on Metternich's Balance of Power.

The United States, Britain and Canada joined the European Six in the plan to rearm Germany and bring her into NATO, and at the same time the United States and France agreed that French forces were to be withdrawn from Southeast Asia and that direct American aid would be given to the three Indochina states: South Vietnam, Laos and Cambodia.

With the East-West conflict in Europe sharpened by new developments — for West Germany's inclusion in NATO was followed by Moscow's creation of the Warsaw Treaty Organization, and the new Soviet leader, Khrushchev, threatened a separate peace with East Germany if the question of Berlin were not settled — it might have seemed an overextension of American commitment to assume deeper involvement in Asia. The commitment was nevertheless made. Postwar globalism was formalized. If Germany could be divided, in violation of Potsdam, why could not Vietnam be, in violation of Geneva?

The first giant step was to conclude the SEATO agreement, the chosen instrument for continued American involvement in Asia. It was signed at Manila six weeks after Geneva, by eight nations agreeing to act, each in accordance with its constitutional processes, in the event of aggression by armed attack. "Indirect" aggression was to bring consultation. Of the signatories only three nations could be called Asian — Pakistan, the Philippines and Thailand — and only Thailand represented the area covered by the treaty. The other SEATO members were Australia, New Zealand and the Western "Big Three."

Implicitly SEATO was directed against China, and the Chinese obligingly furnished it with a baptism by fire. It was signed as Mao's forces, perhaps flexing their muscles after Geneva, perhaps merely reacting to SEATO, began to bombard Quemoy and Little Quemoy, the Chinese offshore islands. The American Seventh Fleet at once received orders to give "full logistic support" to Quemoy's Chinese Nationalist defenders. The Quemoy incident led to an American defense treaty with Chiang Kai-shek, and both Houses of Congress passed the Formosa Resolution authorizing the President to use American forces to protect that island.

Since the SEATO treaty called for action only in the case of direct aggression, Vietnam would have to be labeled such to justify any American intervention in what under the Geneva agreement would be a civil war. In its consideration of the treaty the Senate Foreign Relations Committee eliminated the requirement of a congressional declaration of war, to authorize the use of American forces, after Secretary Dulles testified that "we do not intend to dedicate any major element of the American military establishment to form an army of defense in this area," and the White House declared it would seek congressional consent if that intention changed. Taken with the Tonkin Gulf Resolution of ten years later, the treaty constituted all the authority President Johnson needed, as he saw it, to escalate the war, begin bombing North Vietnam, and send ground combat forces to Southeast Asia. Congress thus relinquished its own powers as early as 1954, though it could later claim it had been misled about the possibility of war.

SEATO in hand, the United States moved to shore up Diem's regime.

After Geneva the CIA's National Intelligence Estimate, the first of many on Vietnam to be ignored over many years, warned that even with American support it was unlikely that a strong government could be established in Saigon and predicted that "the situation would probably continue to deteriorate." But policy-makers regarded that as only another problem to be solved and the National Security Council, which had described Geneva as a "disaster," recommended further military and economic aid. The President offered it in his fateful letter to Diem, though it is usually forgotten that the proposal was contingent on the carrying out of social reforms, in order to help build and maintain "a strong viable state." During the Eisenhower administration aid to Vietnam amounted to one-fourth of all American foreign aid, but only in 1960 was the Geneva-fixed limit to American military personnel in Vietnam increased from 327 to 685 men.

Since the United States had embarked upon the comprehensive mission of defeating Communism in Southeast Asia, however, the Eisenhower offer was the thin edge of an open-ended commitment, putting the United States into the morass the French had barely succeeded in getting out of. That the action held the seeds of calamity was foreseen by some in Congress. After the Democrats had recaptured both Houses in 1954 the new chairman of the Senate Armed Services Committee, Richard Russell of Georgia, who opposed American involvement, told the President he would rue the day he began sending aid to South Vietnam. Russell further informed Secretary Dulles he was "weary of seeing American soldiers being sent as gladiators, to be thrown into every arena around the world." Not long before his farewell to arms, by retirement, General Douglas MacArthur similarly opposed intervention and the policy which fostered it. War was obsolete, he told the American Legion, and the Cold War and the arms race were fueled by "two great illusions," the Soviet fear that the United States was preparing an attack, and the American fear of Soviet attack.

The domestic crusade against Communism had meanwhile come to something of a culmination. Whatever other breaches of conduct or political process Joe McCarthy might or might not be guilty of, his senatorial colleagues could at least hold him contemptuous of their amour-propre, by his personal abuse during the tortuous debates and hearings. On these grounds solely, and not because of his arrogation of power, his encouragement of "loyal" government employees to give him secret documents, his unfounded charges against many citizens, his violation of standards of decency and politesse, or his demagogy, censure was recommended by a special Senate committee. The citation was akin to the indictment of Al Capone on a charge of evading income taxes.

McCarthy's supporters in the Senate, defending him against the censure motion, held that he was being "persecuted" for his anti-Communist views, which some who knew him said he was really not a votary of. Barry Goldwater, Arizona Republican, explained that the Communists had as usual cleverly arranged matters so that sincere anti-Communists were violating their own principles by acting against McCarthy. A letterhead styled *Ten Million Americans Mobilizing for Justice* sought that number of signatures against censure, but failed to report how many were actually obtained.

The Senate finally voted to "condemn" McCarthy for contempt but did not deprive him of his committee posts. The 67 who voted for censure were 44 Democrats, 22 Republicans and 1 Independent. The only Democrat not to support censure was John F. Kennedy of Massachusetts, marked down as not present and not recorded. McCarthy was politically finished by the Senate's action, and it was said to have contributed to his death three years later. An ample McCarthy legacy lived on, of doubt, suspicion, fear and malice.

In Vietnam, where the Geneva agreement had already been broken by the South's economic rupture with the North, there was one kind of zonal passage Diem was most anxious to see successful. Five days after he arrived in Saigon and a month before the demarcation line was fixed, he had flown to Hanoi to set up the Committee for the Defense of the North, and to persuade the Catholics to leave. "Christ has gone to the South," the faithful were told. "The Virgin Mary has departed from the North."

The resultant exodus of refugees, mainly Catholic, which the United States aided with shipping and medical supervision, can be likened to the flight of the Arabs from Palestine at the behest of their leaders, in the 1948 war with Israel, or that of the Moslems from India to Pakistan a year earlier. The Catholics of North Vietnam had a purpose larger than that of ideology, or even personal safety and welfare. Diem needed them to give him his political base in the Buddhist South. They were a zealot breed. The two bishoprics of Phat Diem and Bui Chu were in effect theocracies, functioning politically as well as ecclesiastically; at Phat Diem indeed Bishop Le Huu Thu had his own Catholic militia. The two bishoprics in the Red River Delta lived a virtually feudal existence. The church was the castle, the curé, the local lord, and the parishioners were his serfs, while Annamese priests and nuns were the overseers and bailiffs. The bishops collected taxes and held their own law courts.

Under the French the Catholic minority had received favored treatment throughout Vietnam, constituting almost a separate class. Their villages were given special aid. They got land grants for schools and colleges, priority for loans, export-import licenses, the best land for development, educational opportunities, wealth, and even French citizenship. In the North the Church owned an estimated 30 percent of all the land.

When Ho Chi Minh declared the Democratic Republic in 1945, he allowed the Catholic system to continue, as evidence of national unity and

purpose. With the consolidation of Communism in the North, and the spread of atheistic and anticlerical propaganda by the regime, Bishop Le fostered anti-Communist, anti-Ho organizations of Catholic youth, women and peasants. The Catholic militia, headed by the redoubtable Father Quyinh, clashed frequently with the regime's militia before the eruption of war in 1946 sent Ho Chi Minh and his forces into the hills and jungles.

When the war ended and the victorious Ho Chi Minh returned to Hanoi in 1954, the white-clad Trappist Bishop Le, who was also Apostolic Vicar, led the exodus to the South in support of the Catholic Prime Minister there and his new government. The favored treatment given Catholics by the French would be continued in Saigon. Diem's own brother was, after all, a prince of the Church.

Yet not all Catholics left. Many remained north of the 17th parallel, and by 1972 more than a million lived there and continued worship. They were no longer favored, but they were not persecuted either, as Catholics had been earlier in Vietnamese history.

Originally converted by Italian and Portuguese Jesuit missionaries in the eighteenth century — who among other things transliterated the Vietnamese alphabet from Chinese to modified Latin characters — Catholics had at the hands of the Annam emperors suffered the largest single persecution of Christians since Nero, 130,000 of them being murdered, according to Catholic statistics, in the thirty years before the French arrived in 1856.

The French first landed at Danang to protect the local Catholics from repression. They had been preceded by Americans, however, similarly intervening because of the "wholesale massacre" of Christians. On May 10, 1845, the USS *Constitution* put Marines ashore at Danang to rescue the Bishop of Hue, condemned to be executed. The landing was made on the initiative of the *Constitution*'s skipper, and when the news arrived in Washington the State Department in the Polk administration professed to be appalled and sent the American consul at Singapore to the Imperial Vietnamese court at Hue to apologize.

American Marines would land again at Danang 120 years later, with no apologies deemed necessary. In the North the Phat Diem cathedral, largest in all Vietnam, would be destroyed not by Communists but by American bombs.

4

WHILE PRACTICALLY NOBODY
WAS LOOKING

As Ngo Dinh Diem installed himself in Saigon in July 1954,
Ho Chi Minh reinstalled himself in Hanoi. After eight years of war the
Viet Minh, now the North Vietnamese People's Army, entered the capital
again, including the 308th Division, which had triumphed at Dien Bien
Phu. They were heroes. The victorious battle had become a glorious chapter in Vietnamese history, and given its name to a brand of state-made
cigarettes.

Ho's immediate problem was to persuade the French to keep their in-
vestments and commercial enterprises in the Democratic Republic. He
received his old friend Jean Sainteny, head of a French mission, and proposed they work together. "How do you say it? Fifty-fifty," Sainteny quoted
him. Ho also asked diplomatic recognition from the French, pending the
expected reunification of the country.

Sainteny recommended the establishment of formal relations with the
DRV as an independent state. The French government refused. Sainteny
explained to Ho that American support of Saigon precluded the recognition of Hanoi, and that the French "had neither the material nor the
morale to risk aggravating the United States." They also did not want to
imperil French interests in Diem's South Vietnam. Hanoi had to be content with merely a "commercial attaché" in Paris until de Gaulle finally
extended full recognition in 1966.

The United States, though refusing to recognize Hanoi, sought to keep
its consulate there on the ground that Vietnam was a single state, as the
Geneva Accords made clear, and that American representation in Saigon
included that in Hanoi. Since Washington was at the same time supporting

Diem as he turned the demarcation line into a political boundary, the North Vietnamese called the American position inconsistent if not arrogant, cordoned off the consulate, and then shut it down.

With the American flag gone from Hanoi the Russians and Chinese, representing Ko Rut Sop — as Khrushchev was called in Vietnamese — and Mao Trach Dong respectively, dominated the small diplomatic corps. Ho's capital provided the first open sign of the Sino-Soviet breach as both countries vied for influence there.

Ho Chi Minh himself was torn by the rivalry. As a longtime Cominternist and frequent visitor to Moscow he was generally regarded as pro-Russian, the more so since the Vietnamese are historically hostile to Chinese neighborliness. He was nevertheless an Asian, and his veneer of French culture covered a deep Chinese vein. He had mastery of the Chinese language, in several dialects, and had studied the Chinese philosophies. He also knew that Mao was not Chiang, and believed that as Communists he and Mao had been chosen by history to confront Western imperialism together. In his last testament, fifteen years later, he would still be calling on China and Russia for comradely reconciliation.

If the United States had no longer any open link with Hanoi, there were other means of contact. Since one of the ways to strengthen Diem in Saigon was to weaken Ho in Hanoi, the CIA's "department of dirty tricks" was at work in the northern capital. Within days of Diem's arrival in Saigon, Colonel Lansdale was reinforced by a team of "unconventional warfare" experts, trained for guerrilla combat, sabotage, terrorism, and the gathering of intelligence. Their initial operation was to spread rumors in the South that Chinese Communist troops in the North were taking reprisals against villages which had protested their wholesale raping of women. There were no Chinese Communist troops in the North, but this was what Chinese Nationalist troops had done in 1945. A Vietnamese psychological warfare unit in civilian clothes was dispatched to Hanoi by Lansdale to spread the same story in the North, but it deserted in a body to the People's Army and failed to return.

Lansdale's functions were not limited to rumor-mongering. American-trained saboteurs were busy in Hanoi even before Ho returned, led by Lansdale's second-in-command, "Army Major" Lucien Conein, a paratrooper who had served with the French Foreign Legion in 1940, then with the OSS in the ranks of the French Resistance. He had also been a teammate of Howard Hunt's in the OSS at Kunming, and had jumped into Vietnam in 1945 to make contact with Ho's guerrillas. Conein was one of the Americans present when Ho declared the republic. But now he passed for French in Hanoi. His CIA squad damaged railroad equipment, contaminated the oil supply of the municipal bus system, and distributed leaflets declaring falsely that the Communists intended to seize property and change the currency. As a result, registration of refugees to go south tripled and North Vietnamese money lost half its value. The CIA men also bribed astrologers to predict good luck for Diem and bad luck for Ho. To keep the Pentagon happy they made notes for future military reference in North Vietnam.

One of the principal CIA assignments was in fact to stimulate the flow of refugees to the South. American shipping, transit facilities and medical care were provided at the port of Haiphong for those wishing to leave, and in August mass evacuation by sea began. Lieutenant Tom Dooley, a young Navy doctor from St. Louis, was among the Americans engaged in this open endeavor, which combined the political with the humanitarian. He took his work seriously enough not only to expedite it but to create it. On All Saints Day at the cathedral of Phat Diem he helped organize a gathering of 35,000 of his fellow Catholics to demand evacuation. Tom Dooley for several years personified for many Americans their country's role in Southeast Asia. Colonel Lansdale and Major Conein came closer to the heart of the matter.

The CIA's pranks were minor, even puerile, left over from OSS days. The Lansdale team did not undertake truly significant sabotage like that of power plants, water facilities, harbors and bridges, or the country's vital dike system. In the Pentagon Papers the reason given for forbearance was adherence to the Geneva Accords. If so, it was the only such.

In truth, Lansdale's purpose was considerably larger and more significant than "dirty tricks" against the North. He was expected to be to Diem the same kind of adviser and confidant he had been to Magsaysay in the Philippines. However, the Huks, the "People's Liberation Army" in the islands, had numbered fifteen thousand at most, and Magsaysay subdued them less by force of arms than by offering them rehabilitation, land distribution, economic development and rural credit. This would never be true in Vietnam, and if Lansdale expected in Diem another Magsaysay, standing for relatively clean government and efficient administration, he was speedily disillusioned.

The CIA operative was officially listed in Saigon as an assistant American air attaché. It was in a "personal" capacity that he served as consultant to Diem, becoming in effect the Prime Minister's public relations counselor, and the coach in social reforms that the United States asked in return for its aid. Lansdale also had the job of integrating all military and paramilitary forces in the country, which meant establishing a central authority against the private armies of the various sects, both religious like the Cao Dai and Hoa Hao, and political-criminal like the Binh Xuyen. Led by a veritable warlord, General Le Van Vien, the Binh Xuyen were river pirates and controlled the rice trade, gambling and prostitution, and above all opium, concessions given them by the French in exchange for information and other help against "fanatics." As always, the criminal elements were among the most "patriotic" in the society.

The Lansdale-Diem relationship was not an easy one because of the peculiarities of the Prime Minister, whom the American described after their first meeting as "the eldest of the Seven Dwarfs deciding what to do about Snow White." When Diem returned to his native land after his years in the United States it was to rejoin four of his five remaining brothers, the eldest having been killed by the Viet Minh. Nhu, who had prepared the way for him, became his right arm, in charge of police and politics. Can, in Hue, was the political boss of central Vietnam. Thuc, Bishop of Vinh Long, would soon be made Archbishop of Hue. Thuan was Diem's Secretary of State. The fifth Ngo brother Luyen, who was abroad, was named Ambassador to London.

As Annamese and strong Catholics besides, the Ngos had little support among the Buddhists of the South, so the masses of Catholics Diem brought from the North provided him with not only a constituency but an administrative bureaucracy. Hanoi had tried to halt the drain of Catholics from its territory, which by the time it was ended was calculated at about 800,000 persons. Some violence attended the attempt but since the transfer of population was completely legal under the Geneva agreement, nothing like a "blood bath" took place, such as would be cited by Presidents Johnson and Nixon as a reason for opposing a "Communist takeover" in Saigon. Just as they had done in the North the resettled Catholics in the South flew the yellow-and-white Vatican flag in their villages beside the yellow-and-red nationalist one.

Ngo Dinh Diem's undoubted nationalism and burning anti-Communism were his principal strengths, in American eyes, as he began with their help the task of "nation-building." His strengths would be distorted into his fatal weaknesses. His nationalism was of the old style, seeking to adopt the French system to indigenous forms, with the same class and social relationships, in contrast to Ho Chi Minh's brand of nationalism, which demanded abolition of the French colonial system even if it meant more authoritarianism. Diem had not been in Vietnam during the war against the French, the period which changed everything, achieved independence (at least in the North), and ended collaboration and mandarinism. He was simply out of date.

Diem has been called the "last mandarin" and he consciously tried to live up to the appellation. He claimed four hundred years of noble lineage, which was somewhat exaggerated. His father was Grand Chamberlain to the Emperor Thanh Thai, but when the latter was deposed by the French in 1908 and exiled to Reunion Island — for having too many concubines, among other gaucheries — the Grand Chamberlain retired from the imperial court and turned to rice-growing as he raised his sons. Diem wanted to study for the priesthood like his brother Thuc, but entered the civil service instead and rose in it rapidly.

By all accounts the fifty-three-year-old man who had come to inhabit Independence Palace with his American advisers was one of the colossal bores of all time, a compulsive talker whose conferences were monologues often lasting for hours. His conversation, which he presumed to be philosophical and profound, was a droning compendium of trivialities and clichés. He was suspicious, stubborn, sensitive, a perfectionist, messianic, and serenely confident of his uniqueness and indispensability. His communication with Lansdale was hampered by his scanty English — he always carried a small French-English dictionary with him — while the American, knowing not only no Vietnamese but no French, talked, or rather listened, through an interpreter. Despite Diem's volubility it was Bishop Thuc, his older brother, who as Lansdale recalled it "usually had the final word on any subject."

The CIA operative's tour of duty was not a successful one. Lansdale confessed in his memoirs that the "social revolution" he had come to Saigon to promote consisted more of palace bull sessions than of any serious plans for reform. The small moon-faced Diem in his white linen suit, a bachelor who was prim and fussy in the manner of a spinster, did not have the vision, temperament or capacity to construct a "viable nation," as Eisenhower had hoped. Though he was undoubtedly the Americans' man he was also a Vietnamese nationalist, a fact that Americans tended to overlook. Instead of being used by the United States, he believed he was using the United States for his own Vietnamese purposes. If he had lived, it is possible he would not have allowed the war to become so large by American increment. He was certainly becoming less and less the Americans' man when he died in an American-supported coup in 1963.

At the time the partnership began, in 1954, Colonel Lansdale was not the only American gray eminence in Saigon. Another Diem adviser was Wesley Fishel of Michigan State University, who had sponsored his residence in the United States and who now lived in the palace and breakfasted with the Prime Minister three times weekly. In American magazines the professor lauded Diem's "democratic one-man rule" and called the Saigon regime "one of the most stable" in Asia.

Michigan State's specialty was supplying expertise to new nations which needed it, as colonialism was ended around the world. The university was headed by the forceful John A. Hanna, who used the campus as springboard to become Assistant Secretary of Defense, chairman of the Chicago Federal Reserve Bank, a director of utility companies, chairman of the American Council on Education, and director of the American overseas development program, AID.

This new-style Renaissance man represented in his own person the interlocking of government, business and the university that the next decade of college students rebelled against. Michigan State in 1954 was almost an extension of the United States government. Its Center for International Programs conducted on profitable contract terms "educational projects" in a dozen countries, embracing such activities as fingerprinting, police training and administration, budgets and bookkeeping, civil service and the writing of textbooks and national constitutions. In Vietnam the Michigan State project, which began in May 1955 under a seven-year contract, included a heavy CIA representation, and among the activities carried out were the training of the presidential security guard in revolver shooting, the distribution of handcuffs, and the lamination of identity cards for Vietnamese civilians to prevent forgery, since the "Communists" were not believed to possess a "capability" in advanced gadgetry. The CIA helped train the police and created the VBI, the counterpart of the FBI. CIA station chiefs who followed Lansdale were extremely close to Diem's brother Nhu, who commanded the secret police apparatus and his own Special Forces in Saigon. Nhu was also in charge of the Ngo brothers' personal political party the Can Lao, to which army officers and civil servants had to belong under penalty of losing their jobs and possibly even being arrested for "disloyalty."

American feelings about the Can Lao were divided. It was supported by the Embassy as a means of welding a single strong nationalist force against the numerous squabbling and divisive factions which had always plagued Vietnamese politics. It was opposed by Lansdale, who could not envision it as an instrument of social revolution. He may also have regarded it as a rival to the CIA's control of secret power.

As American experts in Saigon drew up land and other reforms which never came about, VIP's came from the United States on frequent visits of inspection. One was Diem's old friend Senator Mike Mansfield of Montana. He strongly supported the regime but with the proviso that if Diem were ever ousted the United States should at once cut off aid to South Vietnam. Another early visitor was Cardinal Spellman of New York, who had done so much for Diem in the States. The prelate bore a sizable check for refugees from the North, sent by the Catholic Relief Agency, and came fresh from an address to the American Legion convention in which he declared that the Geneva Conference meant "taps for the buried hopes of freedom in Southeast Asia, taps for newly betrayed millions of Indochinese who must now learn the awful facts of slavery from their eager Communist masters."

The most demonstrative of all the American bishops in his anti-Communism, the Cardinal was thereby the Church's strongest partisan of American intervention in Vietnam. Since 1939, as Military Vicar of the Armed Forces, that is, Bishop of Army and Navy Chaplains — as a young priest he had originally tried to become a chaplain himself — it had been his duty and indeed pleasure to visit American troops in all parts of the world. If they were not yet in Vietnam, he would be happy to assist in getting them there.

Cardinal Spellman's first acquaintance with Saigon was in 1948, when he stopped off en route to Australia and helped demonstrate against the "massacre" of eight priests by the Viet Minh, but he already knew Diem's brother well; they had studied together at the Collegium Augustinium in Rome. As Military Vicar, wearing an officer's uniform, the Cardinal visited American troops in Korea at Christmas in 1951, 1952 and 1953, and actively opposed the Panmunjom armistice negotiations.

The New Yorker was not only more military-minded but more politically active and more concerned with American policy abroad than any other Catholic prelate. He conducted himself, some thought, as a temporal rather than a spiritual leader, from his ecclesiastical "powerhouse" behind St. Patrick's Cathedral, "plugged in" to banks, boardrooms and other inner circles of command. To be a chaplain, giving comfort to troops, was one thing. To be a touring hierarch, greeted by chiefs of state, foreign ministers, ambassadors, generals and admirals, shuttling between Masses and military ceremonies around the world, was distinctly something else.

Ngo Dinh Diem had potent support in the United States in the person of His Eminence, it could not be doubted, but despite all the American aid and advice he was getting, the Prime Minister quickly proved that he lacked the essential ingredient for nation-building, popular endorsement. The Mandate of Heaven was not his. Bao Dai continued to be absentee emperor, usually to be found at Cannes, and Diem was challenged by the numerous sects and political factions. He tried to make his own deals with them, reshuffling his cabinet to accommodate them, but to no avail. Even his army was disputed by the paramilitary forces of the sects, creating disaffection among army officers.

With the United States oozing in to replace the French, it was necessary to do something in South Vietnam to establish a firmer operating base than Diem offered. General J. Lawton Collins, "Lightnin' Joe" of World War II fame, and former Army chief of staff, named by Eisenhower as his personal representative in Saigon to oversee the transition, signed a secret agreement with the French commander-in-chief, General Ely, taking over all military training. It had to be secret because it violated Geneva, as did the French withdrawal itself. On Lincoln's Birthday in 1955 the first American "advisers" arrived to train the new indigenous South Vietnamese army.

Collins, in his quick judgment of the situation, recommended Diem's removal. Secretary of State Dulles replied that the United States was committed. "No other choice," he cabled. "Sink or swim with Ngo Dinh Diem" became the cynical password in Washington.

Fighting broke out in the streets of Saigon as various groups combined against Diem, and the French told Washington that its man was "mad" and "hopeless." General Collins returned home to urge Diem's removal again and Dulles was eventually convinced that he had to be dropped, less than a year after he had been instated, and cabled the Embassy to find someone else.

The CIA determined on a last effort to save him and through him itself. Colonel Lansdale, made aware of a coup being planned against the Ngo brothers, helped Diem frustrate it by exiling several key plotters in American-provided planes. The agency from its secret funds then matter-of-factly bought off Diem's lesser opponents. Lansdale also persuaded the reluctant Prime Minister to order an armed attack on the Binh Xuyen forces and was so confident of the outcome that suspicion must arise that the CIA had gone so far, and had enough money at its disposal, as to buy out the Vietnamese version of the Mafia. In what passed for fighting, the Binh Xuyen were defeated by government troops led by General Duong Van Minh, popularly called "Big" Minh, who was embraced by Diem at the victory parade. Diem and Nhu then simply took over the rackets, piracy, exchange manipulation, extortion, gambling, commercial graft and opium trade that the gangs had thrived on. Their own Can Lao replaced the sects and political parties they had disposed of. Thenceforth, leaders of the ultra-nationalist Dai Viet (Greater Vietnam) and VNQDD (Vietnam Quoc Dan Dang, the equivalent of the Chinese Kuo-min-tang) lived in exile in Europe and the United States.

Diem the puritan wanted to end the lucrative opium traffic which originated in Laos, but instead his practical brother used its profits to pay his numerous agents and informers, while the CIA paid for his police and Special Forces.

As for the army, though its training had passed into American hands, its corruption remained Vietnamese. Bribery or political influence continued to be a principal method of obtaining promotions and commissions. Generals dealt in opium or rice, and their wives in real estate. Ordinary soldiers, paid only a few piasters a months, stole and raped.

It could soon be said that Diem's forces, supported by the United States, were in occupation of their own country. Secretary Dulles revoked the decision to change the nominal leadership and the Prime Minister was emboldened to accomplish what he and the CIA had planned from the first, to replace the absent Emperor as chief of state. The conversion of South Vietnam to a republic with Diem as its first President came about through a plebiscite which he won against Bao Dai with 98.2 percent of the vote. In Saigon, which had 450,000 registered voters, Diem's total was 605,025 votes. Some Americans suggested that 60 percent would have been "convincing" enough, and others shrugged their shoulders and said that even American elections were not completely honest. Lansdale told Diem that as the first President he could be a new George Washington.

Among other things, the American adviser had devised the color scheme of the plebiscite, the Diem ballots being printed on red sheets signifying happiness, while the Bao Dai ballots were a less propitious green. The Diem ballots also identified the Prime Minister as the creator of "a democratic regime" based on the "deposition" of Bao Dai. Under the circumstances, the Emperor was hardly a real candidate.

Diem's victory was not only manipulated but strictly speaking the plebiscite was illegal. Only a fortnight's notice was given, and when Bao Dai learned of it he dismissed the Prime Minister, by cable. Diem ignored the message and so did his American advisers. The date of his election, October 24, became South Vietnam's National Day.

While Diem in Saigon cemented his reign, Ho Chi Minh in Hanoi was enduring assorted misfortunes. Though some French business firms remained in North Vietnam the French military and administrative structure had finally been disbanded. The port of Haiphong, declared a free zone for three hundred days after Geneva to allow orderly French withdrawal and the evacuation of emigrants and refugees, saw the last 3,600 of these depart on May 16. With them went Dr. Tom Dooley, who had been engaged in the evacuation. CIA agents stayed on, secretly, and Dooley himself was suspected of covert activities, for before he left he was taken into police custody and was intensively questioned. The walkie-talkie conversations he was discovered to be holding with American vessels offshore might have seemed perfectly normal in the evacuation procedure, but the voluble young man was uncharacteristically silent about his interrogation in his later numerous books and lectures.

The government in Hanoi had in its early stages maintained a "popular front" formula embracing non-Communists, deeming it necessary to consolidate itself before proceeding to socialization. Saigon's economic boycott compounded its problems, chief among them hunger. Any timetable Ho Chi Minh might have had for systematic development of a planned economy was short-circuited by emergency. He tried to institute agrarian reform, industrialization and resettlement all at the same time.

The permanence of partition was accepted on both sides of the 17th parallel. Even before becoming President, Diem had declared he would not carry out the July 1956 elections fixed at Geneva. From Hanoi Jean Sainteny sent Paris a warning based on Ho's reaction: "Any policy tending to confirm the partition of Vietnam by opposing free elections carries with it the seeds of a new conflict." France's departure from the South would make it certain the elections would not be held.

One strong reason for the French withdrawal was that another colonial rebellion had broken out. As they were extricating themselves from Asia, following insurgency, they were confronted by insurgency in North Africa. In some respects the Algerian war was the direct consequence of the Indochina war, though it had its own pressing reasons. Many of the French

Union troops in Vietnam were Algerians and Moroccans, and they went back to their own countries well schooled in revolutionary warfare. Some of the prisoners of Dien Bien Phu were in no hurry to be released but stayed on in the Democratic Republic learning tactics from the Viet Minh and the Chinese. For that matter, after Dien Bien Phu, French officers also began to read Mao and Giap, as they were transferred to Algeria to try to do again what they had failed to do in Vietnam, "pacify" a consuming nationalism.

North Vietnam's economic ills were aggravated by the fact that while Ho's government wanted French capital and enterprise to stay on in profitable coexistence, its sensitive and militant nationalism required dictation instead. French industry leaving the North did so from fear of expropriation. Those companies that remained found themselves harassed, ensnarled in red tape, and baffled by bureaucracy. The former colonial rulers encountered difficulty in getting visas either to enter or leave the country. They were continuously subjected to anticolonial propaganda amounting to threat. Other French companies gradually left, and in some cases American instigation was involved. Businessmen in France who persisted in trading with Hanoi found themselves suddenly unable to trade in the United States.

Ho Chi Minh clearly was in trouble, yet in Saigon, following General Collins's arrival, the American press was being treated to stories from the CIA and other "reliable" sources of the growing military strength of North Vietnam through massive Chinese help. The French saw no evidence of such aid, but the new "Communist threat" spurred American military and economic support of South Vietnam. A three hundred-man American training mission was soon in being there, and it organized seven full-size Vietnamese divisions, to replace the small units of the mobile French-trained national army. The new troops were equipped with American weapons, in the conventional pattern used in Korea, and for antiguerrilla purposes units of Marines, Rangers and paratroops were also formed.

Backing up ARVN, the Army of Vietnam, was the might of the United States. Vice-President Nixon told the Executive Club in Chicago that in the event of war in the Far East, "tactical atomic explosives are now conventional and will be used . . . against the military targets of any aggressive force." All that ARVN was intended to do, under American plans, was to withstand an attack from the North, as in Korea, long enough for SEATO allies to get there.

While Vietnamese troops were being trained by methods the Pentagon said had been successful in Greece and Korea, while Vietnamese police were being trained by former American policemen and FBI agents, Americans had begun to place their mark upon Saigon in numerous other ways. The American Embassy grew steadily into one of the largest in the Foreign Service, with all varieties of overt and covert operations under its wing.

The terrace of the Continental Hotel, which had served Frenchmen a *fine à l'eau* or a vermouth-cassis or Vietnamese beer — the palatable "Bamiba" or "33" — converted to bourbon-and-soda, Coca-Cola, and American canned beer. French commissaries gave way to American PX's. Three English-language newspapers sprang up where one in French had long sufficed. American MP's replaced Foreign Legionnaires as building guards. American menthol cigarettes not only supplanted the French Gauloise but became a substitute currency and a means of barter, as in American-occupied territories in World War II.

Despite the increasing number of Americans in Vietnam candid diplomatic reporting on the Diem regime was inhibited, not only by lack of American experience in Indochina but by memories of what had been done to the State Department's China experts of the Forties for their account of Chiang Kai-shek's weaknesses. Not all the Americans who came officially to Vietnam saw eye to eye on the Diem regime or Pentagon policy, but it was left to the American news media to do the objective factual reporting, even when it hurt back home.

Outside the small corner of Southeast Asia the Geneva Conference had been followed by other international maneuverings, some of them illustrative of the increasing Sino-Soviet rupture. The Soviet party leader Khrushchev, soon to become Premier also, visited Peking and was met by Mao's demand for "the return" of Outer Mongolia, despite earlier Chinese recognition of its "independence" as the Mongolian People's Republic. It was the first of Peking's claims to former Chinese territory.

The United States was more interested in other aspects of the Peking encounter. Khrushchev's agreement to help China's Five-Year Plan was read as confirmation of Sino-Soviet unity, Communist monolithism and "world conspiracy," though it was actually a Soviet attempt to buy Chinese fealty, which failed. Mao rid himself of unilateral Soviet supervision of its aid programs and received formal agreement of equality in scientific and technological cooperation. The Russians were enormously irritated by Chinese political independence in contrast to their economic dependence. From this point relations steadily grew worse, especially as Mao tried to establish himself as Lenin's true successor, the new Communist Dalai Lama.

Sino-Soviet incompatibility at least had a geographical and historical foundation. American relations with China derived from lack of comprehension. From America's beginnings it could be said that there was misunderstanding, misperception, misjudgment and mistreatment of China, whether as decaying Confucian empire, nominal democratic republic, or Communist state. The misperception was deepened by the myth of a special American guardianship, created by kindly missionaries, the Chinese who went to Yale, the number of Chinese in the United States, and the number of Americans in China, many of them born there. The myth was politicized by the Open Door policy, which sounded free, broad and friendly, but was exploitative. The Door was not held open by the Chinese; it was kicked open by the Westerners.

A year after the conference of 1954, which had seen the emergence of Mao's China in the West, Geneva also welcomed the new Soviet rulers, Khrushchev and Nikolai Bulganin, the nominal Premier. They rode in an open car, something which had not been done by Russian leaders since the Czars, while President Eisenhower shopped for Swiss toys for his grandchildren. But behind the "spirit of Geneva" lay the achievement of Soviet nuclear power to challenge the American, a fact that would govern their relations ever after.

The Chinese were at the same time making their own soundings with the United States, with diplomatic meetings first at Geneva, then Warsaw. Handshakes were not reported by either side and the sessions were not under any diplomatic protocol, the two ambassadors being accredited to each other, rather than the respective governments. While the Russians basked in the "spirit of Geneva," the Chinese then created the "spirit of Bandung." That Asian-African conference marked a major advance in Sino-Soviet competition, extended to India. The two Asian giants, China and India, went to Bandung under the banner of coexistence. It would not last long, in friendship, but it nettled the Russians.

The struggle within China between Mao and Chiang had been more a contest for power than combat between Lucifer and Gabriel. The American diplomats who foresaw Mao's victory did not predicate it on any ideological superiority, but saw it as historically inevitable change from a politically weak and corrupt regime to a new and forceful one. But it was not possible for an Iowa Republican senator like Bourke Hickenlooper, or a Californian like William Knowland, raised on a China policy of moralism, wishful thinking and the vision of "four million customers," to accept that the forces of darkness could overcome the Christian, American-supported Generalissimo, and his charming, clever American-educated wife.

In the same manner, though on a smaller scale, the United States had entered upon a similar error of judgment in Vietnam. As the dissension under Diem was broadened by refusal of social reform, to include students, intellectuals, professional men, and merchants, as well as the political-minded Buddhist monks and not least the ideological opposition represented by the Viet Minh, the small man in the white suit found it easier to use repression against his critics by calling them Communists. He was simply echoing the Americans.

This is not to say there were no Communists in South Vietnam. They were among the most active in mobilizing and expressing opposition. On the other hand, those who were not Communists to begin with, or Communist sympathizers, were in many cases made so by Diem's actions. Widespread arrests, especially of Buddhists; press censorship, even the assassination of dissidents, including governors, mayors and army officers, were carried out by Nhu's American-trained goon squads.

The civil war that now began in the newly created Republic of Vietnam was not between Communists and anti-Communists, as the State Department professed to believe, but between Ngo Dinh Diem's armed forces and those who opposed "Diemocracy," although many Vietnamese, perhaps a majority, might be neutral, or at least passive. In its beginning the insurgency was a southern one. The Viet Minh was a national entity and had its supporters everywhere.

There had always been a North and a South in Vietnam, as there are cultural and regional differences in any country. Under the French the capital was Hanoi, with its deep national roots, while Saigon with its cosmopolitan ways and large Chinese population was the market and principal seaport of the country. The northerners made the best civil servants and academics; they were more politically aware than their southern cousins; they understood French ideas and philosophy. Above all the people of Annam and Tonkin — both Diem and Ho were Annamese — were more nationalistic than the colonials of Cochin China. Now, with Ho commanding the tough, flinted, ardent soil of the North and Diem the loose political loam of the South, the war was joined between North and South, between city and countryside, between Asia and Europe, between the new and the old.

If the Vietnamese internal struggle had been left to play itself out, it would have been decided one way or another, perhaps by a Communist military victory, perhaps by a coalition in Saigon or a Vietnamese federation, or international guarantees of independence and neutrality. American intervention turned the small Vietnamese affair into a Great Power confrontation involving international prestige, even "honor." The Cold War was converted into a shooting one, and escalation and counterescalation followed until both halves of the country were ravaged, hundreds of thousands were killed and millions made homeless, and land and other vital resources destroyed.

The lack of knowledge about Vietnam told against the Americans from the first. Colonel Lansdale, busy with a score of facets of "nation-building," was completely unaware of Diem's most serious blunder. The abrogation of the 1956 elections surprised no one, but at the same time Diem abolished the centuries-old Vietnamese political organism created by the villages and village elections. Thus he centralized the Saigon government on the pattern of the French government, though the French themselves had not thought it wise to alter the traditional structure.

Diem replaced elected village elders with appointed village chiefs, who held office at the pleasure of Saigon. This not only disrupted time-honored patterns and relationships but placed a heavy burden on the central government, which was unequipped to bear it. The abolition of the village system provided both a further reason for rebellion and a visible target for the rebels. The kidnapping and murder of Diem's village satraps were called terrorism by the State Department but many in Vietnam saw only a necessary weapon in the insurrection against the assumption of authoritarian power.

Lansdale, who had made his reputation in the Philippines by his rapport with the countryside and his acute awareness of the requirements of "pacification," declared later that he had learned about Diem's action "only long after I had left Vietnam." He added that "the disbelievers of this world may find it incredible." Indeed so, but no more than many other things in Vietnam.

When the CIA man did leave in 1956, with him went the social reforms he had hoped to bring about — the building of schools and roads, campaigns for hygiene and against illiteracy, and most of all what had ended the Philippine insurgency, the rehabilitation and useful employment of people from politically contested or dissident areas. The remedy applied by Diem and his brother was instead the imprisonment of dissidents, or at the least their exclusion from the "nation-building" process.

With Lansdale gone the United States also lost some of its control over the utilization of American aid. Diem's and Nhu's spending of American funds on various kinds of repression contributed directly to the rise of rebellion, and the anti-American flavor it acquired.

The brothers had set out to suppress the Viet Minh and its sympathizers. This meant that nearly all Vietnamese who had actively opposed French rule lived under the threat of being declared enemies of the state. Under the broad "anti-Communist" purposes of the regime tens of thousands of Diem's opponents, many of them merely grumblers, were rounded up and sent to "reeducation" camps. More than 50,000 were reported imprisoned and whole villages were purged of former Viet Minh members, as many as 75,000 persons being killed, according to some accounts, in a "blood bath" that the State Department somehow overlooked. All "individuals considered dangerous to national defense and common security" risked what amounted to preventive detention. This could mean anyone Diem and Nhu disfavored in any way. They were the State.

Diem did go through one form of electoral process at Lansdale's urging. A constituent assembly was chosen to draft a new strong-man constitution. The voting was entirely financed and controlled by the government, and there was no organized opposition, though numerous independent candidates were listed. The chamber that was elected was filled with Diem's supporters and included his brother Nhu and the latter's termagant of a wife, who was more than consort or in-law in the power center at Independence Palace. The assembly's first act was to repudiate Geneva again and confirm the nullification of the scheduled July 20 elections.

The new steps taken in the name of "Diemocracy" were hailed by Vice-President Richard Nixon in person. He journeyed to Saigon to address the new assembly and declare that "the militant march of Communism has been halted." He also invited President Diem to visit the United States, while the Pentagon, again violating Geneva, slipped 350 more military men into Saigon on the pretext of helping the Vietnamese recover equipment left by the French. They stayed on as part of the MAAG, to aid in administration and intelligence.

Cardinal Spellman also helped celebrate the flowering of "Diemocracy," spending three days in Saigon to underline his special interest in Vietnam. He was greeted at the airport by ten thousand Catholic refugees from the North. In the city he got out of his car and, bestowing his blessing on the crowds, walked to the cathedral to celebrate a special Mass. He also visited Hue and President Diem's brother, the new Archbishop.

The North was likewise experiencing significant developments. Hanoi took no action beyond filing a formal protest when the July 20 election date passed unhonored. General Giap accepted partition by speaking of North-South "competition" as if it were like that between socialism and capitalism in Europe. Moscow also made a complaint to the International Control Commission for the record, but soon after accepted the idea of two Vietnams by proposing the admission of both to the United Nations. The Russians were, moreover, busy with their restive "people's democracies," Poland and Hungary, after Khrushchev's secret party speech denouncing Stalin's despotism. Widespread open defiance of Communist authority — counterrevolution to the Kremlin — broke out in Budapest, and Russian tanks and troops came in to put it down in a week of fighting and turmoil that saw thousands of Hungarians fleeing to the West.

Military action in the Middle East, the Suez War which followed President Gamal Abdel Nasser's seizure of the Suez Canal and a coordinated British-French-Israeli invasion of Egypt, coincided with the Budapest uprising and similarly held the world's breathless attention.

So, like South Vietnam, North Vietnam passed through a vital change that went virtually unnoticed by the outside world. If the 1956 elections had been held as scheduled, there is a distinct possibility that Hanoi would not have won them, for excesses reminiscent of the forced collectivization of agriculture in Russia during the Stalin era had provoked a full-scale uprising against a regime based on the peasantry.

During the North Vietnamese land reform, which gave peasants about an acre of soil apiece, their former landlords were liquidated as a class either by imprisonment or outright execution, while richer peasants were deprived of their holdings, though in many cases they were listed as capable of "redemption." The poorer peasants who received tiny allotments then unhappily found themselves paying as much to the government in taxes as they had paid to the landlords in rent. They rebelled, and the ensuing repression, in which land reform tribunals meted out capital punishment for what was considered political opposition, resulted in some 50,000 deaths, according to American accounts based on the data of a ranking North Vietnamese defector. Later examination and analysis reduced the figure to considerably less, perhaps to 2,500, but American statements continued to use the original estimate, and Richard Nixon, as President, put the number at 500,000 when he responded to end-the-war demands by warning of "another blood bath."

It is all the same true that disaffection, open rebellion and relentless punishment seared the vital fabric of the Democratic Republic of the North. Communist officials led by Ho Chi Minh himself were forced to be publicly "self-critical," and in acknowledgment that things had gone grievously wrong they carried out a program of Rectification of Errors. Many party functionaries who had purged others were themselves purged.

President Diem in Saigon failed to take the opportunity offered for contrast, and continued his own harsh measures against dissidents. *Life* magazine, otherwise steadfast in its support of the regime, noted that "behind a façade of photographs, flags and slogans there is a grim structure of decree, political prisons, concentration camps, the milder 'reeducation centers,' secret police."

Those who called themselves the American Friends of Vietnam were less censorious. Their cochairmen were two generals, "Wild Bill" Donovan and "Iron Mike" O'Daniel, who had trailblazed the American entry into Southeast Asia. Prominent members of the Friends included Senators John F. Kennedy and Richard Neuberger, the academic liberals Max Lerner and Arthur Schlesinger, Jr., even the Socialist Norman Thomas. Behind them stood Leo Cherne, head of the International Rescue Committee, which had been formed to aid refugees from Hitler and was now aiding refugees from Communism. Diem hired an American publicity firm, received favorable mention in magazines and newspapers, and prepared for his visit to the United States.

Senator Kennedy in a speech to the Friends urged that the United States "never give its approval" to elections which the Communists might win, but instead, in the new South Vietnam, "what we must offer is a revolution, a political and social revolution far superior to anything the Communists can offer." It was on this occasion that the man who four years later was elected President went beyond the notion of simply helping Vietnam and urged acceptance of American responsibility for its future. "If we are not the parents of little Vietnam, then surely we are the godparents," he declared. He saw Vietnam as a "proving ground of democracy" in Asia, "the cornerstone of the Free World . . . the keystone in the arch, the finger in the dike," and "a test of American . . . determination." He sounded exactly like John Foster Dulles.

If the experience of the French in Indochina did not instruct the Americans succeeding them there, neither did the French experience in North Africa following the disastrous adventure of Suez. Misled by Dulles's tough talk toward Nasser, for his attempt to play off the United States against the Soviet Union in seeking aid, the British and the French who invaded Egypt to recover the Suez Canal had been forced to withdraw by American threats of ending financial assistance. It was extremely painful for the former British Empire to be given an ultimatum — "called to account by one's bank-manager," a disgruntled M.P. said — and Prime Minister Eden, Churchill's successor, was forced to resign. The French for their part lost whatever influence they had left in the Arab world. Involuntarily they were being phased out, as the Algerian war daily demonstrated.

On North African ground that was nominally part of the French homeland, with even more troops than they had had in Indochina — 500,000 regulars and 300,000 militia and police — with the support of a million armed white settlers in a population of ten million, they were being held down by a mere 35,000 guerrillas.

For the French, Algeria was Indochina all over again, with added refinements. They carried out psychological warfare, resettled two million Algerians in regroupment centers, napalmed villages, used torture on captured rebels, and erected electric fences to halt infiltration across the Tunisian border. The Algerian population sheltered the guerrillas, as anti-Diem insurgents were sheltered in Vietnam. The Algerians, using Ho Chi Minh's "war of national liberation" as an example, formed the National Liberation Front, in French called the FLN, which in turn served as an example for the NLF in Vietnam.

Of all the unlearned lessons of Algeria for the Americans in Vietnam, the most important was that while the French could not be militarily defeated, on the other hand they could never win.

As the preserver of peace, its champion against even traditional allies in the Suez crisis — though this strengthened the Soviet position in the Middle East and Mediterranean — Eisenhower was renamed President in 1956 by the largest electoral vote in twenty years. In the campaign Adlai Stevenson, again the Democratic nominee, charged the administration with not doing enough to stop the Communists and called the United States a "paper tiger" for allowing half of Indochina to become a "new Communist satellite." Both political parties adhered to their firm belief in Sino-Soviet joint intentions and action. When Edward R. Murrow interviewed Chou En-lai in Rangoon, the Premier called any antagonism between China and the Soviet Union "impossible" because their "friendly systems" precluded antagonism or rivalry. Chou knew better and so did Khrushchev.

For all the campaign talk, Indochina was of less interest to most Americans than some other things, one of them President Eisenhower's health, another the state of racial relations in the wake of the Supreme Court's school desegregation decision of 1954. An ever-darkening cloud hung over the land. Dulles's threat of "massive retaliation" abroad was of less moment to Congress than the massive resistance proclaimed by southerners in both Houses to the Supreme Court decision, as 101 members from the eleven original Confederate states signed a Southern Manifesto of opposition to school desegregation. "Louisiana is not going to integrate," shouted one irate congressman. "I do not care what kind of a law you pass here."

Though the Court's order to desegregate with "all deliberate speed" was taken by the southerners to emphasize the deliberateness rather than the speed, it provided incentive for other action on what had come to be called the civil rights front. Blacks had begun to push for desegregation beyond the schoolroom.

In the birthplace of the Confederacy, Montgomery, Alabama, on December 1, 1955, Mrs. Rosa Parks, a seamstress, decided not to move to the back of the bus, as usual, or yield her seat to a white man. She was arrested and fined $10, and the Montgomery bus boycott began, to last for a year. Every day during that time thousands of blacks — who made up 75 percent of the city's bus passengers — were driven to work by volunteers from church and social organizations, while thousands more walked, and many were given lifts by white sympathizers.

As union strikes for recognition had done in the Thirties, the boycott produced its own new leadership, a movement of young southern blacks, autonomous and thus not dependent on funds from white northern liberals, like the National Association for the Advancement of Colored People and other traditional groups. The principal new figure to emerge was Reverend Martin Luther King, Jr., the twenty-seven-year-old pastor of the Dexter Avenue Memorial Baptist Church. He was a follower of Gandhi, believing in nonviolence, and he clung to that belief despite considerable provocation. The boycott led to the indictment for conspiracy of 115 blacks, and King, the first to be tried, was found guilty of transgressing various local ordinances and fined $500. Then the Supreme Court desegregated public transportation and recreational facilities, as it had desegrated schools.

After the boycott Martin Luther King organized the Southern Christian Leadership Conference in Atlanta, and it was inevitably pronounced Slick, to rhyme as well as to vie with the more militant SNICK, or Student Nonviolent Coordinating Committee.

The Supreme Court school decision was invoked meanwhile to admit the first Negro to the University of Alabama, Autherine Lucy, but campus demonstrations, including the burning of Ku Klux Klan crosses, led to her suspension by university trustees "for her own safety." She was reinstated by court order and then promptly expelled for making "false defamatory charges." Whites rioted in Clinton, Tennessee, to stop the enrollment of twelve Negroes in the high school, the National Guard was called, and the FBI sent in to arrest white leaders. The students solved the problem themselves. The seventeen-year-old president of the school council called for compliance with court orders, and in municipal elections all segregationist candidates were defeated. For a long time Clinton, population 4,000, remained the only town in Tennessee with integrated schools.

The black rebellion in the United States was evolving concurrently with the anti-Diem rebellion in Vietnam, and Communism was blamed by many Americans for both, according to what they had been taught. In the Thirties the Communist party had made a special appeal to American Negroes, and who knew what it had been up to since then? The Supreme Court was in fact held to be part of the Communist conspiracy. It had expunged some of the legislation of the McCarthy period, and the cry was widely raised, especially in the South, "Impeach Earl Warren!"

Opponents of desegregation were stirred to further fury by the events at the Little Rock, Arkansas, Central High School. Governor Orval Faubus called out the National Guard to bar nine Negro children from enrolling with two thousand whites. As the six girls in bobby-socks and three small frightened boys in open shirts appeared, under the protection of a federal court order, a large crowd of whites descended on the school and the black children had to be taken away by police. President Eisenhower then sent a thousand paratroopers into Little Rock, in the first use of federal troops to protect Negro rights since Reconstruction. They were compared to "Hitler's Storm Troopers" by the eminent Senator Russell of Georgia, chairman of the Armed Services Committee.

The children did go to school, under military protection, but obstructionist moves by city and state, and the closing of all Little Rock high schools for the term delayed for two years the eventual token admission of three Negro students, while police held down the permanent hostile crowds outside.

In view of such events it was small wonder that insurgency in South Vietnam was passing unnoticed. President Diem was still entrenched in American favor, and it was displayed when he arrived in the United States in the plane of the American President and was welcomed by him at the airport. Diem addressed a joint session of Congress, touched base with his other protector, Cardinal Spellman, at breakfast, and was feted by the American Friends of Vietnam and the International Rescue Committee. Symbolically, he was photographed between His Eminence and Henry Luce.

Diem's American friends could not help him in Vietnam, where rebellion was spreading, occasioned by specific grievances. The village, district and province chiefs, all now appointed by Saigon, had been too often chosen without qualification and by political favoritism or the payment of bribes, and they expected to be repaid not only by power but by whatever pecuniary profit they could turn. Diem had also returned to the landlords the land redistributed by the Viet Minh in the areas they held at the time of the Geneva Conference and had been compelled to give up by the partition agreement. The countryside was now so aroused, and kidnapping, assassination and other terrorism was so common, that 80 percent of all American aid had to be spent on security instead of agriculture, education and transportation as originally intended. If this was pacification it was by the police rather than by politics.

The insurgency in the South was reinforced by southerners who had gone to the North after Geneva, received training, and were being infiltrated back to assume leadership roles among the guerrillas. The insurgents were not all Communists, as Diem and Nhu charged, but Communists were the most active, articulate and able among them.

The full extent and meaning of the rising revolution were minimized by the Ngos for their American advisers. The American administrative apparatus concerned itself with the surface operations of the state without much awareness of the shaking at the roots. USOM, the United States Operations Mission, furnished technical aid. USMAAG continued to train troops. Michigan State University ran civil service schools. American educators wrote textbooks. The CIA "coordinated" security. AID supplied the funds. In the United States the Vietnam lobby trumpeted Diem's virtues. Supreme Court Justice Douglas, after a trip to Saigon, reported that Diem was "revered by the Vietnamese." Ambassador Eldridge Durbrow, General Samuel T. Williams of the MAAG, and other Americans in Saigon publicly voiced their confidence that Diem could hold against all opposition, and that the United States could look forward to withdrawing from a safe, secure and stable "nation" by 1961. Their private reports were less optimistic.

Another pressing matter of public concern had, however, been added to civil rights to guarantee that not very much attention be paid to Vietnam. A 184-pound spheroid had chirped its cheerful way around the earth, the first man-made satellite, or as the Russians who launched it called it, "Sputnik," fellowtraveler. Small as the satellite was, it heralded the achievement of a threatening new nuclear challenge to the United States, giving the Russians the capacity to fire intercontinental missiles armed with atomic warheads.

Some in high office ridiculed Sputnik at first as a mere "basketball" in space, but its portent was only too clear to policy-makers and indeed to a public which came close to panic as the first attempt to launch a tiny American satellite failed. To still fears and controversy the Eisenhower administration had to suppress the Gaither Report calling for a $22 billion fallout-shelter program and preparation for "limited" nuclear war.

Sputnik opened the space and missile race that would dominate the Sixties in the relationship of the two superpowers, the United States and the Soviet Union. The Russians had taken three years instead of ten to make good their forecast of an earth satellite. Subsequent stages of space science — manned space flights, orbits around the moon, eventually moon landings — could also be expected to become reality more quickly than had been anticipated.

The United States joined the space contest with its own visions of satellites, space stations, and not only ballistic missiles but antiballistic missiles, even control of the surface of the moon for military or any other purposes. Any true scientific program to fulfill such ambitions had to go beyond mere space technology, however. American education, it was decided, with its easy courses, lavish credits and Dewey progressivism had become too lax and permissive, too "irrelevant" for the Spartan requirements of the Space Age. An acute new emphasis was placed on science. Laboratories, research centers, "think tanks" and campuses were requisitioned to constitute what President Eisenhower soon called "the scientific-technological elite."

The competition with the Russians, which was based on missiles, created the psychology of the "missile gap" as a political issue in the next presidential election campaign. Sputnik also contributed to Sino-Soviet differences, as Mao Tse-tung posited against the peril of nuclear war the plain fact of so many Chinese. In any conflict between Communist and anti-Communist missiles, the Russians realized, hundreds of millions of Chinese would be the principal survivors. Moscow, therefore, was entertaining doubts about the atomic "access" it had recently promised Peking, especially since Mao Tse-tung had increased the decibel level of his dissatisfaction with the Soviet leadership. Journeying to Moscow to help celebrate the fortieth anniversary of the Bolshevik Revolution, he demanded major changes in the political and economic strategy of world Communism. "The East Wind prevails over the West Wind," he declared, and by West he did not mean Europe or America but the Soviet Union.

By perhaps no coincidence Mao's essay on international aggrandizement came during mounting domestic troubles. "Let a hundred flowers bloom," he had proclaimed, to encourage freer cultural activity, but the flowers were trampled down when his ukase was taken too broadly. Then he made China's Great Leap Forward, seeking to achieve Communism at one giant stride instead of following Moscow's theoretical path through "socialism" first. The Chinese converted all their agricultural cooperatives into communes, thus obtaining Communism at least semantically, retrieved for the state land previously given the peasants, and at the same time began "industrialization" by setting up backyard iron furnaces and other lilliputian enterprises.

The Great Leap Forward proved to be a gigantic stumble, causing widespread economic dislocation and political confusion. Mao stepped down as chief of state, in favor of Liu Shao-chi, but he remained party chairman and made his longtime friend Lin Piao Defense Minister, thus holding control of the army as well as the party machine.

The Chinese rivalry with the Russians was linked with the internal power struggle, both revolving about the question whether China would depend on junior partnership with the Soviet Union, deriving benefit from more advanced technology, weaponry and industrial aptitude, or would set its own course.

The Sino-Soviet relationship was further embittered when in the Quemoy-Matsu incident of 1958 — intensive Communist shelling of the offshore islands — Khrushchev refused to back whatever plans Mao might have against Taiwan, which the American Seventh Fleet was guarding. The Soviet leader was moving from the "spirit of Geneva" to the "spirit of Camp David" in his quest for detente with the United States, but he also had deep misgivings about the Chinese, which he did not hide. He had barely assumed Stalin's mantle, indeed, when he told German Chancellor Adenauer, who was visiting Moscow, of the Chinese "leeches" who "suck us dry," and of his fears of the ever-increasing Chinese population. "Where will it end?" he asked. "These are people who live on a handful of rice. Therefore help us!"

As the failure of the Great Leap Forward indicated, China had by 1958 clearly entered on a defensive, introspective period, and just as clearly was at increasingly bitter odds with the Soviet Union. Yet to American decision-makers — the State Department, the National Security Council, the Congress, the news media and many academic experts — Asian Communism, meaning China, was still aggressive and expansionist. When Khrushchev called the signals, it was believed, as for "wars of national liberation," Mao obeyed. The growing civil war in South Vietnam was therefore being directed from Hanoi, the seat of Vietnamese Communism, and behind Ho Chi Minh stood Moscow and Peking with clasped hands.

In contingency planning, which is often done by games theory, the principle of the Worst Possible Case is followed. The most adverse and unlikely sets of circumstances are imagined, on the premise that a solution applicable to them will cover anything short of them. This sort of reasoning may be a test of ingenuity but it is not necessarily a sound basis for foreign policy, since the Worst Possible Case has so frequently failed to materialize.

A corollary of the Worst Possible Case, the Lesser Evil, also came into play again and again in Vietnam. This may be defined as the undertaking of action in the knowledge that it is wrong, misdirected or "counterproductive" for the reason that some alternative might turn out to be worse.

With respect to North Vietnamese direction of the South Vietnamese insurgency, it was not until May 1959 that the Central Committee of the Lao Dong or Workers Party in Hanoi decided it could no longer, without dereliction, avoid the insistent demands of the southern comrades for more help than slogans. From 1954 the Viet Minh had pursued in the South, through its cadres there, a policy of "political struggle." As the Diem regime's strong repressive measures depleted the opposition ranks, the People's Revolutionary party, the southern wing of the Lao Dong, insisted on a change to "armed struggle." Reluctantly Hanoi sent organizers and leaders southward. There can be no doubt that the National Liberation Front was created from the North but the demand and inspiration for it came from the South, after five years of rebellion. When formed, the NLF was actually more southern in its make-up than Diem's Saigon regime. It was also largely non-Communist, a "popular front."

Diem and after him the Americans, especially the news media, refused to give the rebels the recognition implied by the term National Liberation Front, but instead derisively called them "Viet Cong," meaning Vietnamese Communists.

The new NLF was encouraged by the success of the model which it followed, the FLN in Algeria. The insurgency there had become so widespread, without effective action by Paris, that the army had seized power from French civilian authority and demanded that Charles de Gaulle return to insure that *Algérie* remain *Française*. By a historical irony Mendès-France, who had ended the Indochina war, had been voted out of office for proposing self-rule in Algeria. For more than eight years de Gaulle had been in the political wings building up his own party. To achieve his return mobs marched on the Assembly in Paris, and parachute seizure of the capital by the Algerian-based generals was not deemed impossible.

In Vietnam, having been asked for help from the South, Hanoi had to act, however hesitantly, to keep alive the promise of unification made at Geneva. This was not the simple matter it might have seemed. North Vietnam had become a sovereign state, with international relations, trade agreements, and an army, while the rebel movement in the South was only that, unable even to call itself a provisional revolutionary government. Hanoi had also by now moved from its own popular front period to that of Communist doctrine and its implementation. As in the Soviet Union and China, not to mention the eastern European countries, government and party commingled. When the call for help came from the South Vietnam Liberation Front, Hanoi had for some time been critical of it for distorting Marxist-Leninist theories in its broadcasts, and for refusing party guidance.

While North Vietnam undoubtedly wanted reunification, it also clearly preferred a political, not a military strategy for accomplishing it. On the other hand the blunt fact was that no unity with the South was possible without removal of the principal obstacle to it, Ngo Dinh Diem. The aid Hanoi gave to the southern brotherhood had to be for the achievement of Diem's downfall.

The American response to the involvement of the North in the affairs of the South came from President Eisenhower in a Fourth of July speech at Gettysburg, a site of some North-South significance. The offer he had made to Diem five years before, American economic assistance in "nation-building" in return for social reforms, had grown into something quite different. Now he linked America's "national interest" not only to Diem but to the survival of any non-Communist regime in Saigon. Four days later two American casualties were recorded in Vietnam, the first since the United States took over from the French. Two U.S. Army officers died from a bomb thrown into a camp at Bien Hoa where they were watching a movie with the Vietnamese soldiers they were training.

Richard Nixon, the Vice-President Eisenhower had been curiously ambiguous about in both the 1952 and 1956 campaigns, was the Republican presidential candidate in 1960 against the Senator from Massachusetts and founding member of the American Friends of Vietnam, John F. Kennedy. Into the electoral campaign two other campaigns were woven, the one for civil rights for blacks, the other the American campaign for world leadership in the face of the Russian nuclear challenge.

Moscow and Peking came to the cataclysmic parting of their ways during the presidential electioneering. On the occasion of Lenin's birthday in April an anti-Soviet diatribe in the Chinese press, headlined "Long live Leninism!" bared to public view the Sino-Soviet dispute in unmistakable terms, which amounted to Mao's proclamation of himself as Lenin's true heir against anyone in the Kremlin. At a Communist twelve-party meeting in Bucharest the Chinese delegation then denounced Khrushchev in person, and on all possible occasions afterward there were bitter polemics and Chinese walkouts amid charges of "revisionism" against the Russians. The Chinese took especially hard Khrushchev's two visits to the United States in 1959 and 1960.

The Russian answer to Mao's pretensions was the abrupt ending of technical aid to China and the withdrawal of the corps of fourteen hundred Soviet experts, as well as of machinery and equipment, as had been done in Yugoslavia in 1948. Instead of sister state, China was now hostile neighbor. At the Communist eighty-one-party Congress in Moscow in November, after Kennedy's election, each Communist giant went its own way. There was no longer a Sino-Soviet bloc, if indeed there had ever been one.

In the American election campaign, notwithstanding, "Sino-Soviet aggression" had still been the main policy theme. Kennedy several times assailed Nixon for having proposed that American troops be sent to Vietnam in 1954 in "an unpopular colonialist cause." At the same time he demanded American intervention against a Communist threat much closer to American shores: Cuba, where a revolutionary regime had ousted the American-supported military dictator, Fulgencio Batista. This embarrassed Nixon, who knew only too well, as a member of the National Security Council, of a plan to invade Cuba by CIA-trained exiles hostile to the new Castro regime, though he was obviously unable to speak of it. The situation was made more devious by the fact that Kennedy too knew what was afoot, having been given the customary White House briefing of the opposition candidate. Among other things, Kennedy called "too little and too late" the Eisenhower administration's imposition of a trade embargo and suspension of the American sugar quota on which Cuba's life depended. Yet these actions helped put Fidel Castro into Moscow's waiting arms.

Three days after the sugar quotas were ended Khrushchev, pledging full support of Castro, declared that the Soviet Union would answer with rockets any American military intervention in Cuba. Eisenhower reacted equally quickly, warned the Russians not to meddle in the Caribbean, and declared the United States would "never" allow a Communist Cuba. In reply to Khrushchev's rocket-rattling, an American submarine fired two Polaris missiles from beneath the ocean surface, hitting a target 1,150 miles away in fourteen minutes.

American rivalry with the Russians also furnished the "missile gap" issue to the 1960 campaign, the Democratic candidate charging that the United States had fallen behind the Russians during the Eisenhower years, for all the Dulles rodomontade. But with due regard for the global contest with Communism that both presidential candidates paid obeisance to, it was the surging movement of the American domestic uprising that dominated 1960 and as some thought actually elected Kennedy.

After the blooding of the nonviolent black leadership in Montgomery and Little Rock, a new echelon of young black militants filled the civil rights ranks. They staked their claim at the lunch counter of the five-and-ten-cent store in Greensboro, North Carolina, where four students at the North Carolina Agricultural and Technical University asked for coffee and were refused and ejected. Day after day young blacks from Greensboro's several colleges — the tranquil city, birthplace of O. Henry and Edward R. Murrow, had pioneered in black education — sat at the counters, too numerous for eviction, their requests for food ignored, while others picketed outside in Elm Street, where whites flicked cigarettes at them and waved Confederate flags.

A continent away on the Berkeley campus of the University of California another sort of student demonstration was sowing more seeds for the Sixties. Students there like Abbie Hoffman marched on behalf of Caryl Chessman, a convicted murderer who had apparently rehabilitated himself in prison through the long ordeal of eight stays of execution in twelve years. When he finally went to the gas chamber in May 1960, he left behind a regiment of campus protesters, ready for dissent against other supposed injustices.

The Greensboro food-counter sit-ins spread to other North Carolina cities, then to all other southern states except hidebound Mississippi. Gradually under the pressure of nationwide publicity and of a surge of white Freedom Riders from the North, the lunch counters of the South surrendered. By August blacks were being served in sixty-nine southern cities.

The sit-ins were, like boycotts and picketing, illegal in many places. They violated local and state segregation, disorderly conduct, loitering, vagrancy and trespass ordinances. They were undertaken in the name of higher laws. Within the civil rights movement the Student Nonviolent Coordinating Committee was formed, to concentrate on voter registration in the South. It entered the white fortress of Mississippi and created the Freedom Democratic party in opposition to the whites-only political organization of planters, businessmen and public officials. SNCC members were arrested, beaten and shot.

In the fall the sit-ins spread to Atlanta, held to be the most modern city in the South, where Martin Luther King had established his SCLC. The young pastor was arrested when he sought service in a department store lunchroom, and a "hanging judge," citing a previous arrest on an auto-license charge — though a Georgia resident, King drove on an Alabama registration — decided he had violated probation and sent him to state prison.

The Kennedy campaign managers knew an opportunity when they saw one. At the suggestion of a Kennedy brother-in-law, Sargent Shriver, the candidate called Mrs. King and promised his aid while Robert Kennedy telephoned the Georgia authorities and won King's release on bail. Grateful blacks, it was said, then gave Kennedy enough votes to win his scant victory over Nixon. It was true at any rate that a week before the election the Kennedy forces distributed two million pamphlets on the

King case, 250,000 of them in Chicago, and Kennedy took the essential state of Illinois by fewer than 9,000 votes in a total of 4,750,000 cast. The more skeptical attributed the Illinois result to Chicago Mayor Richard Daley's control of the ballot boxes.

The black student activism in the South, the white student activism at Berkeley, and the merger of the two in the Freedom Rides and other civil rights causes prompted Professor C. Wright Mills of Columbia University to deny in a "Letter to the New Left" the conclusion of another sociologist, Daniel Bell, that American students were not interested in politics and that the time had therefore arrived to observe "the end of ideology." Mills, to the contrary, while rejecting Old Left theories of a revolutionary "working class," foresaw an intelligentsia of college radicals leading the way to non-Communist if not anti-Communist socialism. Echoing his ideas, a small group calling itself Students for a Democratic Society was formed within the venerable League for Industrial Democracy, which had been created as an educational bridge between worker and intellectual in the American labor movement of the Twenties and Thirties.

The Sixties began, then, with a new political awareness among youth, as the "beat generation" faded away. With their detached and amused view of society, the beatniks — a publisher's catchword to enhance the sales appeal of numerous works of prose and poetry — regarded themselves as the American version of the existentialists of Europe, sloughing off the values of the past, as they thought, to Live for the Moment. Their bohemian and revolutionary-romantic movement was given intensity by the threat of "instant doom" from the Bomb. In the embrace of Zen Buddhism and "Dharma consciousness," the beats did not seek change so much as readaptation to the pains and stresses of life, for them the Great Anxiety.

What C. Wright Mills called the New Left was based less on any actual political theory than on an outraged innocence, real or pretended; outrage at the asserted lack of freedom, equality, justice and peace. John Kennedy, though the youngest President ever elected, was not quite representative of a generation in which many did not "trust anyone over thirty," the seething generation which had succeeded the complacent campuses of the Eisenhower years. Kennedy's campaign pledge to "get this country moving again" was stirring to youthful emotions but on analysis seemed far from precise as to direction or goal.

One of the directions in which the country was steadily moving was into Vietnam. Three days after Kennedy's election President Diem's own troops encircled his palace in Saigon, and their leaders, charging "interference" with the army, demanded the removal of Diem's brother Nhu and Madame Nhu. At the same time the "Caravelle group" of politicians — named for the hotel in which they met — called for sweeping political reforms, in a letter to Diem. Having surrounded the palace with five howitzers, the mutinous officers asked American Ambassador Durbrow to carry their demands to Diem. Durbrow instead warned them that a coup would result in the immediate cutoff of American aid. The military rebels did not belong to the true insurgency that required Diem's removal at any price, and backed down, satisfied with another promise of "sweeping reforms."

The Saigon putsch had been brought on by two military blows to the Diem regime. In September 1959 the guerrillas had made their first sizable commitment against South Vietnamese regular forces, unlike their previous village raids and skirmishes with local gendarmerie. They engaged two ARVN companies in battle and won — exposing the military inefficiency and lack of plan, organization and leadership of Diem's troops, despite all the American training. Four months later in Tay Ninh province, a rebel stronghold, an ARVN outpost was overrun and overwhelmed, with the direct cooperation of the residents in the area.

The setbacks turned some army leaders, aware of the corruption in their military establishment, against the Ngo brothers. The first coup attempt would be followed by others. Diem's fall came to be regarded as a matter of time, and to speed it the National Liberation Front received formal public endorsement from Hanoi and announced a ten-point program calling for Diem's overthrow in favor of a "broad national democratic coalition" replacing "foreign occupation." It was thus as much anti-American as anti-Diem.

In the last days of the Eisenhower administration Colonel Lansdale, the old Saigon hand now serving in the Pentagon as aide to Defense Secretary Thomas Gates, visited Vietnam again and found the situation slipping badly. He advocated an active American program of "counterinsurgency." Gates passed the idea on to the incoming Defense Secretary, Robert McNamara. President-elect Kennedy quickly "bought it." The Lansdale plan was intended to obviate the need for American ground forces, by increasing ARVN and the Civil Guard. It was still basically "political warfare." It was also unworkable.

For just as he inherited the Cuban invasion plan and the identification of America's "national interest" with the unstable and unpopular regime in Saigon, Kennedy inherited something more quintessential from the Eisenhower administration. The Dulles policy of "massive retaliation," though largely bluff as a political or diplomatic weapon, had transformed the military establishment. Based on nuclear missiles, "massive retaliation" connoted strategic deployment of a precise and substantial sort, and thereby it created "a new breed" of military Organization Men, soldier-technicians and soldier-bureaucrats to replace the soldier-statesmen who had come out of World War II.

The army's new men were exemplified by General Maxwell Taylor, the key military figure in the Kennedy administration, who had as chief of staff already introduced the corporate structure and spirit. Ambition, promotion, organization and expansion were the computerized elements of a military conglomerate cutting across regimental and service lines.

But as the youthful President-elect prepared for his inaugural the skies were bright and new horizons beckoned. The realities of the Far East were so removed from popular awareness that as the year ended the Freedoms Foundation awarded its medals for 1960 to the three "Democratic leaders of Asia": Chiang Kai-shek, Syngman Rhee and Ngo Dinh Diem.

5

THE SPLENDID, QUIET, UGLY AND
HIP AMERICANS

THE FIRST AMERICAN PRESIDENT born in the twentieth century took office as the problems of the twentieth century began to merge, forming a mighty torrent. The converging streams were many and they flowed together into a symbolic Mekong Delta of danger, dissatisfaction, disunity and doubt.

There was the Vietnam War, leading to political and social upheaval. There was the other war for civil rights, leading to emancipation efforts in the South and heightened black sensibilities in the North, to white "backlash" and ethnic conflict within class conflict. There was the increasing monopoly in industry, eliminating competition and the traditional motivation of "free enterprise." There was the transition from production to services as the source for jobs, constricting the "work ethic." There was affluence with its easy credit, causing the "revolution of rising expectations" and underlining the contradiction of poverty. There was the increase of crime, not always due to economic deprivation but often to relative social deprivation in a widening Open Society. There was growing ecological apprehension because of growing environmental pollution. There was the population increase, and especially that of youth. There was campus unrest and protest against the size and impersonality of the "multiversity." There was cultural change, a more tolerant attitude toward drugs and sex, the pervasiveness of rock music, and the commercialization of sports. There was accreted presidential power, bringing conflict between Executive and Legislature. There was church reform, stimulated by the Vatican Council and ecumenicalism. There was mass communication, with "instant" news and its analysis. There was the spread of euphemism, evasion and exaggeration in public and political life.

Any one of these national tendencies and manifestations required adaptation and adjustment on a grand scale, including resistance to it. Taken all together they constituted a social cataclysm, which began to make its effects felt as the Eisenhower era was succeeded by Kennedy's "thousand days." Yet history may record that the presidential inauguration of January 20, 1961, did not mark the opening of a new American chapter so much as the closing of the old one of global hegemony.

Not long before he entered office the young President himself had declared that the United States must face the fact that it is "neither omnipotent nor omniscient," and that it could not always impose its will on the rest of the world, "right every wrong or reverse each adversity." Therefore "there cannot be an American solution for every world problem." The perception was acute enough, but Kennedy's actions as President would belie his words, as he changed American policy from the messianic of Dulles to the managerial of McNamara, Rostow and Bundy.

The inaugural speech served notice on "friend and foe alike" that the United States would "pay any price, bear any burden, meet any hardship, in order to assure the survival and the success of liberty." His generation, Kennedy said, was one of the few in history "granted the role of defending freedom in its hour of maximum danger." After taking his oath the new President affirmed, "I do not shrink from this responsibility. I welcome it."

The speech could just as easily have been delivered by the narrowly defeated Republican candidate, Richard Nixon, though in the campaign Kennedy intellectuals like the historian Arthur Schlesinger, Jr., had gone to great lengths to demonstrate that it made a considerable difference which was elected. Kennedy's most-quoted words, "Ask not what your country can do for you, ask what you can do for your country," were in fact recalled by Senator Barry Goldwater, of the Republican party's right wing, at the 1972 convention which renominated President Nixon.

On that cold, snowy, innocent new St. Crispin's Day, however, the speech was moving, warming and intense. It sounded young and therefore idealistic, seeking to banish the country's doubts about itself raised by the Soviet Sputnik of 1957 and the "missile gap" of the 1960 campaign.

A decade of experience revealed the oration to have been in truth not only rhetorical, but jingoistic, if not arrogant. Any doubts about American omnipotence that Kennedy may have recognized were not moral but pragmatic ones. In the new Augustan "golden age of poetry and power" hailed by Robert Frost at the inaugural, primacy of place was held by power. The poet struck his lyre more truly than he perhaps knew in his invocation. Though Augustus gave his times peace, prosperity and cultivation of the arts, he also made Rome into an imperial dictatorship while observing republican forms. The state became all-important and the ruler's opponents became enemies of the state. Law and order prevailed at the cost of liberties; civic virtue and democracy paled, and those who believed in the republic were accounted conspirators.

Whatever misjudgments the new administration embarked upon, including the basic one of American combat involvement in Vietnam, it could not be denied that in its first flush it engendered a national spirit of optimism. Youth was indeed ready, it seemed, to respond to the call of the new President and receive with him the passed torch. The failure of the expectations aroused by the inaugural undoubtedly contributed to young Americans' loss of belief in the Sixties. For some the Bay of Pigs — not the repulse but the very attempt — quickly shattered the Kennedy dream. Those who had crystallized their romantic radicalism around Fidel Castro and his companion-in-guerrilla-arms Che Guevara, formed the Fair Play for Cuba Committee. One of its members in New Orleans was Lee Harvey Oswald. As the Pentagon Papers showed, on the other hand, most Americans were not appalled but merely frustrated by the Bay of Pigs, and could view with equanimity increasing American involvement in Vietnam.

In nearly all respects President Eisenhower's "farewell address" was a clearer crystal ball for the decade ahead than the Kennedy inaugural speech three days later. In it the retiring soldier, whose Presidency somehow had not dimmed his luster as national hero, had finally freed himself from the exigencies of politics, or at least his speech writer had done so for him. His parting service was to warn his country not only of the "military-industrial complex," with its "potential for the disastrous rise of misplaced power," but also that "public policy could itself become the captive of a scientific technological elite." Eisenhower envisioned the subversion, no less, "of the nation's scholars by federal employment, project allocations, and the power of money." Massachusetts Highway 128 had already in fact become the symbolic route, lined with defense plants and research laboratories, that linked Harvard and the Massachusetts Institute of Technology with the Pentagon.

The leave-taking President cautioned his fellow Americans against the temptations of embarking on "spectacular and costly" actions as "the miraculous solution" to all difficulties. The nation's course had to be balanced "between actions of the moment and the national welfare of the future." He even had some words to say for ecology: "We must avoid the impulse to live only for today, plundering for our own ease and convenience the previous resources of tomorrow." Eisenhower concluded that "America's leadership and prestige depend, not merely upon our unmatched material progress, riches and military strength, but on how we use our power in the interests of world peace and human betterment."

His younger successors were not listening. Eisenhower himself in office had not paid much heed to what he was now saying. Malcolm Moos might write the President's speeches but John Foster Dulles and the National Security Council had formulated his policies. When the outgoing and incoming tenants of the White House met on the day before the inauguration, Kennedy was startled to learn that the United States had 700 soldiers in Laos, Vietnam's neighbor state, and that on the other side 500 Soviet troops were reportedly giving logistical support to the Communist-led Pathet Lao.

The Green Berets, as the Army Special Forces were called, and the CIA had entered Laos in 1959 to enlist Meo hill tribesmen in an intelligence-gathering mission against Chinese and North Vietnamese "plans for conquest" in Southeast Asia. They proceeded to build a secret army of Meos south of the Plain of Jars to keep the Pathet Lao bottled up there. Like the Viet Minh, the revolutionary Pathet Lao had been formed against the French, had come to power in an election victory, and were now engaged in a civil war as the result of a coup against them. The Meo tribesmen, on the other hand, had been used by the French against the Viet Minh in the years before Dien Bien Phu, in return for the right to carry on the opium trade. The CIA took over on the same terms.

As he handed the problem to his successor, Eisenhower with considerable emotion called Laos the key to Southeast Asia. American policy-makers regarded it as the crossroads of the area, the corridor from North Vietnam and China to South Vietnam, Cambodia, Thailand, even Burma and Malaya, if not to Indonesia. By the Domino Theory, if the United States permitted Laos to "fall," it would mean the "loss" of the entire region. It was therefore imperative that "Laos be defended."

Echoing Eisenhower, the new President, with the aid of maps showing Communist gains, told a televised news conference that "the security of all Southeast Asia would be endangered if Laos loses its neutral independence. Its own safety runs with the safety of us all." Kennedy's first instinct about Laos was to solve the problem by disengagement. "Let us never negotiate out of fear," he had said at the inaugural, "but let us never fear to negotiate." Laos was his first piece of business with Nikita Khrushchev.

The Soviet leader had joined in the general enthusiasm which had greeted Kennedy's election abroad, sent his congratulations and expressed the hope that the new President would return to the Roosevelt pattern of Soviet-American mutual tolerance. He thought Kennedy's election had repudiated "the Cold War and the arms race," despite the election campaign against a nonexistent "missile gap." Even Castro in Cuba, with whom the Eisenhower administration in its last weeks had broken off relations, sent a message to Kennedy asking that the two countries "begin anew" in amity.

Peking had different views from Moscow's about the American election. Disagreeing with Arthur Schlesinger as well as Khrushchev, the Chinese assailed Kennedy as "no different from Nixon" in "pursuing aims of the aggressive and reactionary policies of American military circles." In Saigon President Diem was disappointed by the election of one of his American Friends, believing, as the New York *Times* reported, that Kennedy was "more inclined to seek compromise solutions with the Communists than would Mr. Nixon."

Since the election, however, the National Liberation Front had emerged in South Vietnam and Hanoi had endorsed its program of "armed struggle." Two weeks before Kennedy's inaugural Khrushchev made a speech pledging Moscow's support of "wars of national liberation." This seemed to the Kennedy crisis-managers in the White House basement and the Pentagon to be the signal for Communist-supported insurgencies around the globe, and it had to be quickly met — especially after the dismal failure at the Bay of Pigs — by elaborate plans for counterinsurgency, likewise global if need be. Walt Rostow in the White House basement foresaw "virtually total power exercised from Moscow" as dominating the world in ten years unless it was somehow halted.

Counterinsurgency was at once the watchword of the new administration. The President read Mao and Che Guevara as well as the handbook of the Irish Republican Army. He circulated Khrushchev's speech to all government departments. Counterinsurgency planning was assigned to CIA-sponsored research in universities and "think tanks." One of the texts was the Rockefeller Brothers Fund report on "international security" prepared under the direction of a Harvard professor and Rockefeller adviser, Dr. Henry Kissinger. It called for a military establishment diversified enough to be able to fight "concealed wars" and "nonovert aggression" which "may appear as internal revolution or civil war." The Kissinger report specifically cited Vietnam as an example, but not without an awareness of risk. American security could depend, it said, on willingness to act against the new kinds of aggression, including "willingness to engage in nuclear war when necessary." In this grandiose setting Laos, the remote, tiny, opium-wreathed land of the lotus-eaters, was deemed pivotal to the world balance of power. And after Laos there was Vietnam.

As was so often the case, Khrushchev's speech was misread by the political analysts of Foggy Bottom. It really had to do with Sino-Soviet relations. Some months before, Chou En-lai had declared while visiting Hanoi that China and the Democratic Republic of Vietnam were socialist "brothers sharing the common weal and woe" who had formed a military friendship. The implication was that Peking, which regarded itself as the world's only truly revolutionary power, would back Hanoi in any eventuality created by involvement in South Vietnam.

Khrushchev's speech was the return volley. He denied that he had sold out to American imperialism, as Peking charged, by pledging Soviet support also, if only moral support, to "liberation" movements. This meant not collaboration with the Chinese in Hanoi but rivalry, though both might furnish aid, and the rivalry in fact would extend to other "Third World" states in which the Chinese might be interested.

Kennedy's advisers were not looking for evidence of the Sino-Soviet breach and therefore did not find any in Khrushchev's speech. At his inaugural Kennedy still spoke as if a united Communist movement was on the offensive against the West. He cited the "ambitions for world domination" which had been "forcefully restated only a short time ago" — meaning Khrushchev's speech — when it seemed apparent that all the Soviet leader had been talking about was local Communist involvement in rebellions such as in Greece, Malaya and the Philippines, all of which had failed.

Since the immediate problem was Southeast Asia, Colonel Lansdale's ideas for a counterinsurgency program there blossomed into forty separate projects of social reform by paramilitary means. The Mekong Valley would become part of the New Frontier as the Tennessee Valley had been part of the New Deal. Vietnam was, moreover, only the beginning. Kennedy pledged that counterinsurgency would be taken wherever required, "beyond traditional military needs." In the visions of liberals it was another "do good" enterprise like the Peace Corps and the Alliance for Progress. In Vietnam it would be the fruition of the good intentions already applied by such Americans as Dr. Tom Dooley, whom Kennedy had cited as the prototype for the Peace Corps, in announcing its formation.

The citation was also a eulogy. Only two days before Kennedy was inaugurated the former Navy doctor, whose books and lectures contained all that millions of Americans knew about Vietnam, had died, aged only thirty-four. He had been associated with Indochina since he helped carry out the evacuation of refugees from North to South Vietnam after the Geneva Conference of 1954.

To Dooley, with his penchant for vivid prose, the mainly Catholic resettlers were making "the epic Passage to Freedom" from "terror-ridden North Vietnam." The American presence in Vietnam as he saw it was based on "gentleness." "We had come late to Vietnam but we had come," he wrote, "and we brought not bombs and guns but help and love." In contrast to American generosity and friendship were "the godless cruelties of Communism." Dooley's tales of disemboweling and other Communist atrocities were told with a relish for minutiae that made undoubted good reading.

His first book, *And Deliver Us from Evil*, went into twenty-one printings, sold 90,000 copies and 500,000 more in paperback, and carried a foreword by Admiral Arleigh Burke, chief of Naval Operations. As late as 1972 it was still read as an authoritative account of Vietnamese events, and the numerous Communist cruelties Dooley recounted were regarded by many Americans as reason enough for sending troops to Vietnam and bombing.

It was not in Vietnam, however, that the Dooley saga acquired its principal significance, especially in retrospect. After completion of the Catholic evacuation from Haiphong to Saigon, and his sudden resignation from the Navy despite a promotion, Dooley had gone into Laos, which he called "this underbelly of China," as a kind of medical missionary, a "white witch doctor," with the intention of "trying to practice medicine and do some public relations for America." The auspices under which he went to Laos were those of the International Rescue Committee.

Dooley professed to be nonpolitical. His horror-struck anti-Communism might have been of the moral variety, but his anti-Communist letters from Indochina, his lecture tours when he returned, his books and appearances on radio and television, all produced their share of revenue for the intensely political IRC.

From Laos, where he reported that he was known as "Dr. America," Dooley's letters about his hungry, precarious, close-to-nature existence, his appeals for funds and Kelly-green sweaters, his life without deepfreezes, air conditioning, flush toilets and chromium auto fins, softened American eyes with the thoughts of the Brotherhood of Man and loosened American pockets for the healer of the sick and the saver of souls, with his Irish charm, courage and high humor. Supported by volunteers and fan clubs, by students of parochial schools, by the Maryknoll Fathers and Cardinal Spellman, Dooley represented another link in the Catholic chain of concern for, and implication in, Indochina.

That was the least of it. His presence and activity in Laos coincided with the awakening American political and military interest there, leading to the secret introduction of American forces and intelligence gatherers. In the light of later knowledge about covert operations in Laos it may be wondered whether not the IRC but the more familiar initials CIA represented Dooley's first obligation. The Chinese certainly believed so.

Dooley's stated purpose was to go to northern Laos, near the Chinese and Burmese borders, a place of obvious prime interest to American intelligence. It was where the Pathet Lao had been formed and had its strength. To avoid any suspicion of espionage, as he himself acknowledged, he based himself 120 miles north of the capital, Vientiane, among the Meo, Yao and Kha mountain tribes the CIA would enlist as mercenaries. He wrote frequently in his letters of an expected Chinese invasion in that area. In a few months' time he moved closer to the Chinese border, and then, after another best-seller, *The Edge of Tomorrow*, based on his experiences there, he established his newest mission only six miles from China and the same distance from Burma, in the strategic extreme northwestern tip of Laos, guarded by a fortress at Muong Sing, in a bend of the Mekong River. Later, he built another hospital conveniently located at the Thai border.

The suspicious Chinese assailed Dooley's close presence over Radio Peking, and Communist cartoons showed an American doctor with the germs of imperialism dropping from his hypodermic needle. The doctor was by now making excursions along the Chinese border, ostensibly in the interest of medical research. On one of these he fell heavily down a riverside slope and badly bruised the chest wall below his right shoulder. It did not heal. Pain continued to trouble him, and eventually surgery revealed malignancy instead of what he had believed to be a cyst.

Dooley's subsequent operation was carried out in the full glare of the publicity he had come to command in the United States. The three-hour procedure was filmed by CBS cameras and hospital visitors were surprised to see him being made up with grease-paint for a television program *Biography of a Cancer*, in order to induce more sympathy and financial support for what had become a worldwide enterprise. After the operation he continued to lecture, raising nearly a million dollars with forty-nine speeches in thirty-seven cities. He wrote his third book, *The Night They Burned the Mountain*, and was listed in a Gallup Poll with Churchill, Eisenhower and Pope John among "the world's ten most admired men." Mrs. Agnes Dooley was chosen "Mother of the Year."

The Dooley interests had prospered, establishing hospitals and clinics in such politically as well as medically intriguing places as Cambodia, Malaya, Afghanistan, Kenya, Tanganyika, Jordan, Gabon and Peru. They received drugs and surgical supplies donated by American pharmaceutical houses, money from American citizens, largely through Catholic schools and charities, and the volunteer services of doctors and nurses. The personable young bachelor had a large and devoted following. And whatever other purposes he might have served, Tom Dooley did bring help and easement of pain to primitive areas that needed them. An ABC television program about him was entitled *The Splendid American*.

There was also the Quiet American, in Vietnam in the Fifties. Graham Greene's novel of that title told of Saigon when the Americans were replacing the French, and U.S. agents came as part of the "package" of U.S. aid. The Quiet American was a young crew-cut naif named Alden Pyle, engaged in the mission of finding a "dependable" American viceroy for South Vietnam.

"I never knew a man who had better motives for all the trouble he caused," the British correspondent in the book, Fowler, said about Pyle, a man he found "as incapable of imagining pain or danger to himself as he was incapable of conceiving the pain he might cause others," a man who was "impregnably armored by his good intentions and his ignorance."

Alden Pyle, oblivious to Vietnamese history, culture or language, who brought his plastique explosives into Saigon under diplomatic immunity and with a cover story of setting up a local toy industry, who caused "incidents" or property damage to be blamed on "the Communists," was an amateur compared with the real CIA agents, Edward Lansdale and Lucien Conein. Their feats of sabotage were incidental to the political fixing, bribery and coercion that helped keep Diem in power until he had outlived his usefulness to the United States.

Pyle had finally to be disposed of in Greene's book in order to stop him from provoking more Vietnamese deaths even though "in the right cause," as he explained it. The British novel was ridiculed by numerous American literary critics and thought to be anti-American. The New York *Herald Tribune* suspected Greene of "elaborate leg-pulling." At best, according to the *Christian Science Monitor*, it was "a political parable" that he related.

After *The Quiet American* vicarious interest in Southeast Asia was stimulated by Burdick and Lederer's *The Ugly American* in 1958. This series of short narratives, describing much of what had happened since American entry there and foretelling a good deal of the rest, was on the best-seller list for seventy-eight weeks; more than three million copies were sold and in Britain ten printings were needed to keep up with the demand. Ostensibly fiction, it depicted the three salient elements of the American presence. There was the military, which like the French before it and despite its counterinsurgency slogans, tried to fight a conventional war against guerrilla forces. There was the Ugly American of the title — not the villain of the piece but the hero, contrary to the wide misuse of the term — the homespun technician who descended to the local level to help villagers solve their small problems; his metier was water pumps and brick kilns, not military highways or strategic hamlets. Finally there was the intelligence agent, a politico-psychological warrior and troubleshooter. In the Burdick-Lederer book he was Colonel Edwin B. Hillendale, for whom read Colonel Edward G. Lansdale. *The Ugly American* left no doubt that clandestine activity was one of the principal levers of American policy in Southeast Asia. It also portrayed some of the inept American diplomats let loose on the scene and a senator who was led about by the nose in a way to confirm the charge of a presidential candidate a few years later that he had been "brainwashed" in Vietnam.

The various roots of American involvement in Vietnam were already planted when John F. Kennedy took office, and in the White House basement offices of McGeorge Bundy, the Harvard University dean who had been named presidential adviser for national security affairs, they were watered by Bundy's assistant, an economist from the Massachusetts Institute of Technology. He was Walt Whitman Rostow, who with his brothers named for Eugene Victor Debs and Ralph Waldo Emerson, obviously came from an idealistic father. Rostow was a specialist in his own theory of the stages of economic growth. His belief that economic development was the way to stave off Communism, and that Keynesian economics was the answer to Marxism, led him to the logical conclusion, when the time came, that since North Vietnam had labored so hard to build up its economic capacity it would go to any lengths to preserve it. Thus it would yield readily to bombing, and if not, then to more bombing. Like his book, the Vietnam War was an academic exercise to Rostow, the application of library-stack postulates without reference to real situations or human beings, with scant heed to methods or consequences. Because he was judged too theoretical in his concepts, Rostow was soon sent to the State Department by the Kennedys. But the transfer did not entail his exclusion from Vietnam planning.

The fiasco at the Bay of Pigs — a key CIA figure in it was Howard Hunt — is credited with influencing President Kennedy to take more forceful measures than he might otherwise have done in Vietnam, in order to avoid another encouragement to Khrushchev. On the other hand, the first escalation in Vietnam was begun three days before the Bay of Pigs, when Rostow, nursing his little domain, recommended that Vice-President Lyndon Johnson visit Saigon and that meanwhile the number of Americans in the MAAG be increased from 685 to 785. This, said the professor, "involves some diplomacy," since it would be a breach of the Geneva limit on foreign military personnel. The President agreed to the increase but kept it secret. The pattern was being established for American actions in Vietnam.

Soon after the Bay of Pigs, Kennedy in an address to the nation's newspaper editors — recalling Nixon's similar appearance at the time of Dien Bien Phu — linked the two theaters of conflict. Cuba was an example, he said, of the new type of warfare by subversion and infiltration, where victory could be won "without the firing of a single missile or the crossing of a single border." The United States would not abandon Cuba even if it meant military intervention unilaterally. "The message of Cuba, of Laos . . . are the same. We dare not fail to grasp the new concept, the new tools, the new sense of urgency we will need to combat it, whether in Cuba or South Vietnam. . . . We face a relentless struggle in every corner of the globe that goes far beyond the clash of armies or even nuclear armaments." Called to the White House for consultation, Kennedy's campaign opponent, former Vice-President Nixon, pledged his support "to the hilt" of "positive action."

A week after the Bay of Pigs a Vietnam task force headed by Deputy Defense Secretary Roswell Gilpatric with the ubiquitous Colonel Lansdale as operations officer suggested that more American aid be furnished South Vietnam to permit an increase in Diem's forces, in fact "a modest commitment" of American ground combat forces, "with the nominal mission" of establishing two more training centers. The Joint Chiefs of Staff supported the request for a combat force — four years before one was actually sent —

on the ground that NLF fighting strength had grown to 12,000, though Diem's troops and reserves outnumbered the insurgents many times over.

The Gilpatric recommendation allowed the National Security Council in its Action Memorandum 52 to restate the American objective as being to "prevent Communist domination of South Vietnam." The troops sent to Vietnam, it was reasoned, would avert a recurrence there of what was happening in Laos, where the Communist-led Pathet Lao were steadily making gains against the American-supported forces of Phoumi Nosavan.

Again, without any announcement, Kennedy ordered more Americans to Vietnam, this time 400 Special Forces, nominally for training purposes. Since they were financed by the CIA and not the Pentagon, there could be no congressional scrutiny of this action. The President also increased covert operations in North Vietnam by CIA-directed South Vietnamese agents.

None of this sounded like very much, then or now, and it was nowhere near a formal decision to commit regular ground forces. Psychologically it was a quantum jump nevertheless, for NSAM-52 removed any limit from Eisenhower's limited-risk, mainly economic project. Small as it was, French President de Gaulle told Kennedy in Paris a few weeks later, it was an unwise thing to do; it could bring "entanglement without end," since "once a nation has been aroused no foreign power, however strong, can impose its will upon it.

"The more you commit yourself there against Communism," de Gaulle explained to the younger man, "the more the Communists will appear to be the champions of national independence." He concluded: "I predict to you that you will, step by step, become sucked into a bottomless military and political quagmire, despite the losses and expenditure that you may squander." The warning came from the man responsible for the decision to retake Indochina by force, but also from one nearing another moment of truth in Algeria. A few days later he opened negotiations with the rebels of the FLN.

De Gaulle's advice fell on deaf ears. Vice-President Lyndon Johnson, on the trip to Saigon recommended by Walt Rostow, further increased the American commitment there and decided that Ngo Dinh Diem was "the Churchill of Southeast Asia." At an embassy reception the ebullient Texan declared the United States was ready to stand "shoulder to shoulder" with South Vietnam against Communism. The Vice-President's journey also included Manila, Bangkok and Karachi, and he pledged American support against Communism everywhere he went, returning home to urge an American "major effort" that could require "major American forces" to be sent to Asia. Next day President Kennedy delivered a special message to Congress in person requesting $100 million for aid to Southeast Asia, as part of his new global "freedom doctrine." The aim, as stated by Johnson, was no less than to "banish the curse of poverty, illness and illiteracy" in Asia.

The trumpet had sounded. It also called for increased civil defense funds, fallout shelters, food stockpiles, warning systems, reorganization of the Army, and more Marines for "brush fire" situations. Stirring imaginations, the President then announced the latest race with the Russians, in space, to land on the moon "before the decade is out," and thus help win the battle "between freedom and tyranny."

Just before the Bay of Pigs man's first space flight had been achieved when Yuri Gagarin made a single orbit of the earth and returned safely. It followed numerous other successful Soviet space ventures since Sputnik, including the landing of a rocket on the moon and lunar circumnavigation with the first photographs of the legendary "dark side."

"Do we have a chance of beating the Soviets by putting a laboratory in space, or by a trip around the moon, or by a rocket to go to the moon and back with a man?" Kennedy asked Johnson, who was also chairman of the National Aeronautical and Space Council. "Is there any other space program which promises dramatic results in which we could win?" The President wanted a reply "at the earliest possible moment." Johnson recommended a moon landing. On the day Alan Shepard, Jr., made the first American suborbital flight, the President announced that the Vice-President was going to Vietnam to discuss the future American role there.

In the Senate Lyndon Johnson had opposed American intervention in Vietnam by the Republican administration. Now he saw things differently. On his return from Saigon, in an unusual joint declaration with Kennedy, he spoke of the American "responsibility" and "duty" to aid against "Communist terror," and cited a "deep sense of common cause" and "recognition of mutual objectives." The commitment was not only large but seemed emotional.

The Johnson visit to Vietnam was followed by an eleven-man White House mission there headed by Walt Rostow and General Maxwell Taylor. The latter, after a brilliant career as wartime commander of the 101st Airborne, chief of staff of the postwar European command, American Commander in Berlin, Eighth Army commander in Korea, and Far Eastern commander-in-chief, had retired as Army chief of staff. In that position he had had his doubts about the Dulles "massive retaliation" policy, if for no other reason than that, with its emphasis on Air Force nuclear bombers and the Navy's Polaris missile submarines, it left not much of a role for the Army.

Taylor, a personal friend of the Kennedys, was recalled from private life to discover what went wrong at the Bay of Pigs, and reported that the landing had failed because of a lack of communications. No suggestion of moral inadequacy or even political error came from the inquiry, in which

Taylor was joined by Allen Dulles, director of the agency in charge of the operation. The CIA thus investigated itself, and its findings having been accepted by the White House, Taylor remained as the President's military adviser.

The Rostow-Taylor expedition was sent to Vietnam because the Churchill of Southeast Asia was under rising pressure from the NLF, now being assisted from the North. Kennedy wrote Diem that the increased insurgent "terror" was a tribute to his success, since South Vietnam was economically fast outstripping North Vietnam, as West Germany was outstripping East Germany. Since the NLF step-up was in fact a response to Diem's obvious failures, the White House was engaged in self-deception. Diem knew better. He asked for a 100,000-man increase in the size of his army, plus some American troops.

Departing for Saigon, General Taylor declared that "any American" would be reluctant to send troops to South Vietnam "unless absolutely necessary." Thus all contingencies were covered for the next ten years. On the general's return the White House let it be known that troops would not be sent "except as a last resort." For Taylor and Rostow that was already the case. They recommended a 10,000-man American task force for "self-defense" operations, to be followed by direct operations against North Vietnam if the infiltration of men and supplies into the South continued. Deception about Vietnam had become easier with practice. Taylor proposed that the American troops be sent in the guise of a "flood control" force.

Faced with the request for 10,000 combat troops, Kennedy "compromised" and settled for a thousand more "advisers," down to battalion level, with support units, helicopters, coastal patrols and air reconnaissance. Sending combat troops, the President explained, was like taking a drink. "The effect wears off and you have to take another," he told Arthur Schlesinger. Instead of drinking he sipped. The only compromise was with more extreme steps. The genuine alternative, to do nothing, even to disengage, had long since ceased being considered. Nor was the American purpose any longer questioned. Even at this early stage Vietnam was not a matter of why but of how and then how much.

Taylor listed the risks in his report. American prestige would be increasingly involved as more troops were sent. There would be more global tension, perhaps even "escalation into a major war in Asia." The retired general nevertheless urged that ground forces be sent without delay. He believed the game was worth the candle, though "any troops coming to Vietnam may expect to take casualties." Walt Rostow, the economist, increased the stakes, urging immediate retaliation for the infiltration by "conventional bombing" against North Vietnam. How else to prove his theory that Hanoi prized its few factories too highly to allow much damage?

Taylor and Rostow were supported by Defense Secretary McNamara's "Whiz Kids," though these Pentagon civilians feared that 10,000 troops would be a mere start and envisioned a "maximum" of six divisions, or 205,000 men. Secretary of State Rusk, ever cautious, was initially dubious. He viewed Diem as another Chiang Kai-shek, defeated by his own intransigence and corruption as much as by the Communists, and told the President he was reluctant to harness American prestige "to a losing horse." Like other racetrack goers, he soon found himself swept up by betting fever.

Rusk and McNamara went to South Vietnam themselves and reported that its "loss" would stimulate bitter domestic controversies in the United States and would be seized upon by extreme elements to divide the country and "embarrass the Administration." They therefore recommended that the United States commit itself "to the clear objective of preventing the fall of South Vietnam" with enough combat troops for the purpose. It was already clear that dissent to policy, and not policy itself, would be blamed for any national disunity.

One of the doubters on the New Frontier, at least with respect to Vietnam, was Under Secretary of State George Ball, a banker-lawyer. When he told Kennedy that the Taylor-Rostow request, if granted, could lead in five years to an involvement of 300,000 men the President exclaimed, "George, you're crazy!" Five years later, in November 1966, there were 358,000 American troops in Vietnam, and 33,000 more in Thailand.

Though Ball acquired something of a reputation as respected dissenter in two administrations, it was difficult to gauge how deeply his doubts ran. Under both Kennedy and Johnson he was a Mr. Facing-both-ways, serving as the latter's token dove to satisfy the principle of exploring all options. Ball spoke, Johnson listened, and policy proceeded as before. While objecting to details or phases of specific actions in Vietnam, Ball subscribed completely to the basic doctrine of Pax Americana, or global guardianship. He was dubious about escalation but not about the assumptions that made escalation inevitable. Whatever skepticism he might express in inner circles, his public utterances exhibited no tremor of hesitation about the administration's course. His explanation for remaining Under Secretary for so long, while disagreeing with Vietnam policy as strenuously as he professed, was that he was only a presidential "hired hand."

In the Kennedy administration the only real dissenters appear to have been two, and they were far removed from Vietnam policy, literally as well as in terms of influence. Chester Bowles, former Governor of Connecticut, former Ambassador to India, was Kennedy's Under Secretary of State to begin with, but he was regarded as "too idealistic" and "too liberal" for Congress, and he expressed unmistakable doubts about intervention in Vietnam. Bowles eventually went back as Ambassador to India, taking over in New Delhi from the other true antibeliever, John Kenneth Galbraith, the economist, who had written Kennedy frequently from the Embassy in protest. The United States was "increasingly replacing the French as the colonial military force," Galbraith declared, and as for sending troops to Vietnam, "a few will mean more and more and more."

The most important source of uneasiness about Vietnam in the Kennedy administration, with access to the President, was the CIA's National Intelligence Estimate. It frankly stated that even if American or other SEATO troops were sent the NLF and Hanoi would not back down. Any American escalation would be matched by the other side. While the National Security Council and the Joint Chiefs of Staff emphasized the need for American troops to "clean up" the "Viet Cong," the intelligence appraisals repeatedly underlined the indigenous strength and resources of the National Liberation Front, and above all its tenacity.

The unheeded warnings given by the CIA illustrated that agency's strange, dual nature. All its intelligence pointed against the success of the American venture in Indochina. At the same time the operational side of the CIA was up to its neck in Laos, managing a war, and already up to its chest in South Vietnam, carrying out "action programs" of sabotage and secret ways. Plainly the CIA's right, or intelligence-and-analysis hand, did not know or did not care what its left, or covert-operations hand, was doing. For all its assertions that overt intelligence was now its major occupation — academic pursuits like studying foreign economic reports or translating foreign scientific journals — the successor to the OSS was heavily involved in clandestineness, as it had been in Iran, Guatemala, Cuba and the Congo.

"The agency" was thickly laced with military, in and out of uniform. By law a military man served as deputy director when indeed he was not the director. The CIA thought of itself predominantly in terms of warfare, in which it was merely carrying out orders and performing its duty, but in reality it had a large say in determining what its orders and duty were, and thus helped formulate policy. In Laos the CIA enlisted and trained mercenaries and operated an airline and a spy network because it decided that was what it had to do there. The "civilian" Air America was no ordinary common carrier. It dropped Meo tribesmen and other secret agents behind North Vietnamese and Pathet Lao lines. It trained mechanics for the aviation arm of the Thai national police. It hauled American AID cargo and ferried VIP's and American civilians and newsmen around South Vietnam, evacuated wounded, lifted Air Force troops from Okinawa to Japan and Korea, engaged in intelligence along the Chinese coast. Some of its cargoes won it the name Air Opium.

The CIA's "action programs" in Indochina became the more important as time went on if only because its intelligence was disregarded. It might not tell Presidents what they wanted to hear, but the intelligence services of the Pentagon and State Department did, and the CIA was left to do whatever it thought required doing. As it went on, ignored in intelligence, it also failed in action. All in all, there was not much for it to take pride in.

While Taylor and Rostow were in Saigon, the Soviet Communist party was holding its Twenty-second Congress in Moscow. Chou En-lai, attending as a "fraternal" delegate, ostentatiously laid a wreath on Stalin's glass coffin, which was in joint occupancy of the Lenin mausoleum, and left Moscow before the congress ended. A few days later the corpse of "the great Marxist-Leninist," as the Chinese wreath called him, was removed unceremoniously overnight and buried near the Kremlin wall, with more ordinary Bolsheviks. Stalin's name was removed from its myriad memorials. Stalingrad became Volgograd.

The Sino-Soviet quarrel had continued at the party congress, and Khrushchev's denunciation there of Albania for its persistent Stalinist course was followed by the break of Soviet relations with China's only European cohort. The progressive disrepair in what had been Stalin's Communist world was compensated for by more bluster from Stalin's successor at the points where the Russians still commanded strength.

Kennedy and Khrushchev had met in June at the Hofburg in Vienna, and the encounter left the young American President much shaken. The Soviet leader threatened a separate peace with East Germany, unless the "bone" of Berlin in his throat was removed. Memories of the Berlin airlift of 1948-1949 must have filled the room where Emperor Franz Josef once sat. After Vienna American and Soviet tanks came into head-on confrontation at Checkpoint Charlie, as the hemorrhaging flow of East Berliners into the western sectors of the city was cut off by the building of the Berlin Wall. Kennedy returned from Vienna in somber mood. Back in Washington, he told James Reston of the New York *Times* about Khrushchev's threats. "Now we have a problem of trying to make our power credible, and Vietnam looks like the place," he said.

At least Kennedy and Khrushchev seemed to be in agreement on Laos, deciding it was not worth making a Big Two issue of, especially since, as the Communist leader no doubt thought, it would eventually fall to the Pathet Lao anyway. Both sides contracted to support Laotian neutrality, but this did not bind the local forces, and the fighting continued as a new coalition was sought. The possibility of further American intervention hung in the air, and in order to exert pressure for a cease-fire Kennedy sent 5,000 Marines and Special Forces to Thailand, the nucleus of what would be a continuing American military establishment there.

The young President had begun to pursue all the policy lines laid out by Dulles in 1954 even though the world had changed considerably since then. By all objective criteria, given the clear evidence of an ever-widening Soviet-Chinese breach, if the United States still believed Peking was behind Hanoi's increasing aid to the South Vietnamese insurrection it could be asked how American intervention in Southeast Asia could block Khrushchev in Berlin, or compensate for the Bay of Pigs. Why did Kennedy not negotiate with Khrushchev and thus encourage him in his conflict with Peking? The answer, in the words of a young ballad singer making his debut in Greenwich Village, was "blowin' in the wind." Policy always suffers from inertial lag and wars are traditionally fought with the motives and methods of preceding wars. The personalities of the two men, Kennedy and Khrushchev, also entered into the situation, and their concern for their public images. Though "cool" on the surface, in keeping with the much publicized "style" which as much as anything else brought him into office, Kennedy's foreign policy was introspective, if not romanticized. Soviet-American relations often seemed to be a clash of temperaments between him and Khrushchev.

There were also the men around Kennedy, who encouraged the idea that they were another court of King Arthur at Camelot. The White House entourage of academic intellectuals and new-fashioned "crisis managers" functioned under Parkinson's Law, the area of their management increasing according to the opportunity available for management. Power created its own new imperatives. The young men thirsted for the power to use power. They did not feel that the why of American involvement in Vietnam, or anywhere else, had to be explained except for the technical purposes of formal diplomacy. It was enough that the United States felt it had to intervene, for whatever reason. Vietnam was only a problem requiring a solution, a technical matter to be decided by the experts.

Under Robert McNamara, the man from Ford — who had been vice-president in charge of the Edsel, among other things — the Pentagon war games became real. While Maxwell Taylor saw American "flood control" troops in Vietnam as a warning and barrier to Hanoi, McNamara was prepared to see them as provoking a larger war, and proposed 205,000 troops. He believed public opinion would respond better to initial large, firm and decisive action than to gradual escalation, and he may well have been right. Kennedy and Johnson decided otherwise. They believed in the theory of increased public tolerance, by degrees.

Vietnam was the board on which the dramatic game of counterinsurgency was to be tested, not merely as governmental policy but as personal pursuit by the Kennedy brothers. The President put the Attorney General in charge of it. The new strategy was articulated by Walt Rostow, at the Green Beret graduation exercises at Fort Bragg, and by the head of the State Department's Intelligence-Research section, Roger Hilsman. The latter had served with the OSS, led guerrilla forces in Burma, and written about counterinsurgency in the Marine Corps *Gazette*. Mao Tse-tung's treatise *On Protracted War* and Che Guevara became texts in American military staff schools, the Foreign Service Institute and the CIA, and 57,000 government officials, many of high rank, were ordered to attend special courses. Even the Chaplains' Corps developed a counterinsurgency program.

The new Kennedy policy of global strategy which replaced "massive retaliation" was one of "flexible and limited response," a formulation of Maxwell Taylor's. It rested on American MAAG groups everywhere, which could muster Green Berets and American "specialists" to the support of local forces. Counterinsurgency appealed instinctively to a Kennedy generation grown up on G-men and Tarzan, of whom the Green Berets were an amalgam. It was greeted appreciatively by many intellectuals, both in the Defense Department and the universities. Kennedy had decided to build a thousand more intercontinental ballistic missiles to repair the nonexistent missile gap, but the smaller vistas of counterinsurgency offered an opportunity to bring back the use of force from inconceivable multi-megaton levels of terror to the more familiar ones of ground, group and individual effort. Such liberation from the nuclear hypothesis made any conventional strategy, even if "unconventional," welcome, in a sense blessed as an alternative to swift annihilation. This was one of the rationalizations of the time. To it was added the glamor of the Special Forces.

Given not only military training but security and intelligence duties, equipped with a sense of mission, the Green Berets became Camelot's knights-errant, global paratroops descended from heaven to fight guerrillas, give medical aid, provide food, speak the language, and combine civilian with military purposes, thus "winning hearts and minds" — in the Washington acronym WHAM! When the perimeters of counterinsurgency were extended, training camps were set up in Panama and Okinawa as well as in Vietnam and Germany. American Green Berets also drilled soldiers from countries which had special need of repressive forces, such as South Africa, Saudi Arabia, Portugal's African colonies, Jordan and Haiti. In Bolivia they helped in the capture and death of the "peerless" Che Guevara.

Despite the multifarious plans, the intricate details, and the zeal with which it was launched, counterinsurgency was from the very start another American misjudgment. What was taking place in South Vietnam was much more than the insurgency that is defined by the dictionary as "a revolt against a government, not reaching the proportions of an organized revolution and not recognized as a belligerency." Vietnam was in fact at the same time a civil war, a social revolution against an existing system, and a nationalist revolution against foreign intervention. It could be seen as such by anyone who had no reason not to see it as such.

As Kennedy instituted counterinsurgency in Vietnam, France was agreeing to leave Algeria after 132 years of rule. The American President gave his blessing to the independence which the Algerians achieved in nearly seven and a half years of war. He had called for it himself from the Senate floor. Though praising the cease-fire as a "historic accomplishment" and lauding President de Gaulle in a personal message, he drew no conclusions from Algeria that might apply to Vietnam. De Gaulle by contrast had come around to seeing that there was no essential difference between the two territories, though extrication from Algeria was more difficult because it was an integral part of France, because of the European settlers and the Secret Army Organization. The French, by liberating Algeria, were in a sense liberating themselves. Americans apparently could not understand that.

One reason for shortsightedness was the secret nature of American intentions. Plans were carried out without congressional or public knowledge by the Special Group, Counterinsurgency, of which Maxwell Taylor and Robert Kennedy were cochairmen. That group interlocked with the 303 Committee, named for the number of the room in which it met in the Executive Office Building next door to the White House. McGeorge Bundy was chairman of 303, and Deputy Defense Secretary Gilpatric, Richard M. Helms, the CIA's deputy director for plans, and Deputy Under Secretary of State U. Alexis Johnson were members.

The 303 Committee's function was to coordinate actions in Indochina. Among the operations it supervised were the training of the montagnards in Laos, South Vietnamese commando raids into North Vietnam, hit-and-run forays designated as 34-Alpha by South Vietnamese patrol boats against the North Vietnam coast, and so-called De Soto patrols by American electronic espionage ships along the coast.

Besides counterinsurgency or as part of it, the defoliation of South Vietnam was begun by the Kennedy administration. It was called Operation Hades at first, a name soon changed to Ranch-hand to soften its impact. Defoliation was ordered to be "selective and carefully controlled." It was euphemistically described as "improvement of visibility in jungle areas," and crop destruction became "resources control" and the destruction of villages "collateral civilian damage."

Though what was happening secretly in Vietnam was already passing out of both physical and moral control, this does not mean that if a full disclosure had been made at the time, with the President appearing every evening on television news programs to keep the public informed, there would have been any noticeable reprehension. The nation that had shrugged off the television quiz scandals, Guatemala, and the Formosa Resolution putting it into the Chinese civil war, was not breaking any new frontier of virtue. The Kennedy term began with the electrical industry price-fixing case. By conspiracy and secret conclave, like the Mafia, some of the pillars of society, it was revealed — corporation executives who were church wardens and the managers of charity drives — had been engaged for a decade in illegal price-fixing, from electric light bulbs to whole power plants. As believers in free enterprise they felt free to engage in restriction of trade. In the conspiracy, in which twenty-nine companies were convicted, more money had been illicitly gained than in all ordinary crime for a year. One of the accused explained that price-fixing "was illegal but it wasn't unethical." Another said that "conspiracy is just as much a way of life in other fields as it was in electrical equipment." Despite the scandal, the chairman of General Electric was named Man of the Year by the National Association of Manufacturers. The twenty-nine companies were permitted to deduct their fines as ordinary and necessary business expenses in their income tax returns.

There was also the case of Billie Sol Estes, a Texas wheeler-dealer who had built up a financial empire on illegality and the wholesale corruption of politicians, farmers, bankers, businessmen and laborers. Estes illicitly transferred federal cotton acreage allotments and leased out imaginary grain-storage and fertilizer tanks. He owned 1,800 tanks but sold mortgages on 30,000.

Even police had become criminals. Graft and corruption in police departments have been an immemorial part of American life, but a new trail was blazed when eight Chicago policemen were convicted of a series of burglaries in company with a professional. The Kennedy administration also saw inaugurated another bold new chapter in outlawry when an eight-passenger plane flying from Miami to Key West was forcibly diverted to Havana. What was marked down as an isolated instance of psychopathological behavior by the instigator, who babbled of an anti-Castro plot, was followed three months later by the first hijacking of an airliner to Cuba. By the end of 1961 there had been five.

The Supreme Court added to the growing controversy about law and order when by a key decision it ruled out evidence obtained by irregular arrest procedures, such as had been used in nearly half the states, especially in vice, gambling and drug cases. It would follow with other decisions redefining the rights of those arrested and, according to many police, making criminal law enforcement more difficult.

The Kennedy administration proposed income tax changes to curtail the expense-account way of life, which allowed businessmen to claim deductions for yachts, hunting lodges, Miami Beach apartments, parties, nightclubbing and sports tickets for their clients. The tax reforms were voted down by Congress. A new revenue bill made entertainment expenses deductible when bona fide "business discussion" took place. Thus a new brand of corporate lie was created.

Why should any American be shocked by anything that happened in Vietnam?

After General Taylor's visit there, with its concomitant request for some modest reforms, such as decentralization of the Saigon administration and the release of political prisoners — by 1962 their number was estimated at 20,000 — Diem and Nhu waged a campaign in their controlled press against American infringement on South Vietnamese sovereignty. It was a popular cause and it served to detract from the battlefield news. Sixty miles north of Saigon 1,500 guerrillas had attacked and burned the capital of Phuoc Vinh province, killed the province chief and Civil Guards, and released a score of "VC" prisoners, in the war's largest assault until then.

Diem's campaign had the desired effect. The United States backed off from its small demands and the brothers tightened their control. They banned all meetings unless specifically authorized; even weddings and funerals required permission. Books were censored, like the newspapers. Madame Nhu, who belied her Saigon press corps nickname of the Dragon Lady by deep-seated prudishness, got the Assembly to pass the Bill for the Protection of Morality, which closed down bars and banned public dancing.

For all its sanctimonious tone the Diem-Nhu regime was steeped in graft and corruption, some taken over from the Binh Xuyen gangs, some fashioned by itself. Complaints against a corrupt province or district chief — who was usually corrupt per se, having bought his office — were regarded as subversive propaganda and punished, even by imprisonment. Once again, as before, dissidence showed itself in the ranks of the military. Two pilots bombed the presidential palace, damaging a wing of it, but Diem was in another wing and escaped unhurt. Talk of overthrow continued. Yet there was the case of South Korea to testify that its result might be not to improve but worsen matters.

In Seoul the dictatorial Syngman Rhee had been driven from power, largely by student protest. The regime of limited reform succeeding him was then also turned out by a military junta, which abolished all representative government and outdid Rhee in authoritarianism. Despite the opposition of many Koreans the United States supported the new military rulers and kept its 50,000 troops in the country.

The repressive and increasingly unpopular Diem regime in South Vietnam was also being held together by American money and advisers, who in effect made up a shadow government, down to district level. All the while, American war equipment poured in. At the end of 1961 the small aircraft carrier USS *Cord* delivered thirty-three helicopters, as well as spotter planes and transport aircraft, accompanied by 400 more uniformed American personnel. Other aircraft supply deliveries followed, intended for bomber units.

As Kennedy's first year in office and in Vietnam ended, the first American combat casualty in South Vietnam was recorded. James T. Davis, twenty-five, specialist fourth grade, of Livingston, Tennessee, was killed ten miles from Saigon in a guerrilla ambush of ARVN troops he was attached to. The Special Forces soldier died of a rifle shot after a land mine blew up the truck in which he was riding. He had gone to Vietnam on a civilian passport, and his father did not know where Vietnam was when he left.

The new year opened with 2,646 American servicemen in Vietnam, two helicopter companies in combat support missions, surveillance flights by F-101 planes from Thailand and the Seventh Fleet, six defoliant aircraft in action, an air-commando unit instructing South Vietnamese, and five Navy minesweepers.

With the American role grew the deception about it. The uniformed Americans operating in battle areas with South Vietnamese troops or carrying them into battle were authorized to fire back if fired upon. When President Kennedy was asked at a news conference if American troops were "now in combat in Vietnam," his answer was "No." Soon American forces were authorized to fire first, and American pilots were permitted to strafe "enemy targets." It was still denied that Americans were in combat when fifteen helicopters took part in an attack on the guerrilla-held village of Hung My in the Mekong Delta, and one was shot down.

With guerrilla activity increasing and the number of Americans growing, the American command structure was altered. The Military Advisory and Assistance Group, MAAG, became the Military Assistance Command Vietnam, MACV, with a complement of 4,000 men, part of a new Vietnam-Thailand command headed by General Paul Harkins. By the spring of 1962 MACV was 6,000 strong, by the end of the year it deployed 11,300 men. Several thousand more Americans supervised economic aid. The new command was visited by Secretary McNamara. "Every quantitative measurement we have shows we are winning the war," declared the master of computerized analysis, but a Washington observer noted he was "trying to quantify the unquantifiable."

A logistical buildup accompanied the military. An American construction combine, largely from Texas, awarded a ten-year contract, began the largest single building enterprise since the Pyramids. It would entail the spending of two billion dollars on public works and military installations — highways, airfields, bases, hospitals, barracks, a new American embassy, a huge port complex at Cam Ranh Bay, deep-water ports at Saigon, Danang and Qui Nonh. Enough asphalt would be laid to pave a highway from Saigon to Paris, enough concrete poured to build a five-foot wall around all South Vietnam.

American ships filled the Saigon River, American uniforms the Continental Hotel terrace and the Caravelle Hotel roof. American men and planes were shot at regularly, and at home questions were raised about American "tactical air support." The New York *Times* remarked that "it is difficult to ascertain whether the people who are being killed by napalm and fragmentation bombs are guerrillas or merely farmers." Most Americans did not seem concerned. Vietnam was a long way off.

Despite public indifference, however, Vietnam was a political issue in the midterm election year. The Republican National Committee charged Kennedy with being "less than candid" about American involvement, and said the people should be told if the United States was "moving toward another Korea" before "casualty lists are posted." It assailed the "pretense" that the United States had only advisers in Vietnam.

The first organized public antiwar declaration also made its appearance in a New York *Times* "open letter" advertisement asking why the United States had sent troops to prevent "the well-deserved overthrow" of Diem, and quoting Kennedy's 1954 remark as senator that "no amount of American military assistance" could bring victory. Attorney General Robert Kennedy brought things up to date. "The solution in Vietnam lies in our winning it. That is what the President intends to do," he said.

One Republican who agreed with the Kennedys and not with the National Committee was former Vice-President Nixon, defeated for the Presidency in 1960 and now seeking the governorship of his native California. "My only question is whether it will be too little and too late," he said of the Vietnam buildup. He favored more. "I support President Kennedy to the hilt and I only hope he will step up the buildup and under no circumstances curtail it because of possible criticism."

The President himself, addressing the West Point graduating class, explained the new kind of war, "war by ambush instead of combat." It could be long and costly, he said, but "if Communism is to be stopped, it is necessary. And we mean to see this job through to the finish."

The new kind of war was political as well as military, and its principal weapon, the Strategic Hamlet program, officially called Operation Sunrise, was designed to win support for Diem in a countryside where it was said the government ruled by day, the "Viet Cong" by night. Whole communities were uprooted and resettled, in violation of the fundamental relationship of the Vietnamese with the soil which provided life, and with the spirits of their ancestors who lay there. Moreover, the political objective of "pacification" became confused with the aims of the military. The ideal of Winning Hearts and Minds was pursued by the steel and machinery of modern warfare.

On the military side the question of the degree of American involvement gradually became academic. "Americans and Vietnamese march together, fight together and die together," noted the New York *Times*, "and it is hard to get much more involved than that." Soon the *Saturday Evening Post* reported that "virtually all the fighting is done by American troops." Americanization of the Vietnam War was thus already beginning in mid-1962, and there were some cheers. Eisenhower, in retirement, thought his successor "did the right thing" in raising the number of "advisers" to 16,000.

Many Americans, however, had their doubts, not only about the war and the decision-making process attached to it, but about other aspects of the national spirit and course. College campuses especially were sensitive to an uneasy stirring, and fifty-nine members of the small group calling itself Students for a Democratic Society, gathered in a trade union summer camp at Port Huron, Michigan, raised the cry for "participatory democracy." Less than eighteen months after Kennedy's inaugural address, which had rhetorically put state above self, at least a portion of American youth responded with skepticism about "the world we inherit," and specified the things it found "too troubling to dismiss."

"First, the permeating and victimizing fact of human degradation, symbolized by the southern struggle against racial bigotry, compelled most of us from silence to activism. Second, the enclosing fact of the Cold War, symbolized by the presence of the Bomb, brought awareness that we ourselves, and our friends, and millions of abstract 'others' we knew more directly because of our common peril, might die at any time . . ."

The SDS, in its hardly Marxist manifesto, looked to "a new Left" to "transform modern complexity into issues that can be understood and felt close up by every human being" and to "give form to the feelings of helplessness and indifference, so that people may see the political, social, and economic sources of their private troubles, and organize to change society." The Port Huron statement spoke specifically for "people of this generation, bred in at least modern comfort, housed now in universities."

The "southern struggle" which had activated them had moved from Alabama to Georgia, then to Mississippi. As the members of the SDS went back to their classrooms in the North, James Meredith, a former Air Force sergeant, sought entrance as the first Negro at the University of Mississippi. His attempt to register was blocked bodily by Governor Ross Barnett, who had won election as an ardent foe of "niggers" and "mongrelization." Meredith obtained a federal court order but was again prevented from registering, this time by the Lieutenant Governor.

When President Kennedy federalized the Mississippi National Guard and sent other troops to nearby Memphis, Governor Barnett yielded, but not the white students of "Ol' Miss" and their friends. Rioting broke out as Meredith, protected by U.S. marshals, tried to enter the college, and Guardsmen had to rescue them. Two persons were killed by snipers, one a French reporter, and other newsmen were beaten or fired upon. After fifteen hours of disorder Meredith was finally registered in clouds of tear gas.

The fledgling SDS numbered an initial two hundred members, none of them at the University of Mississippi. Its original goals lay in community work, notably in Newark, New Jersey, where one of its founders, Tom Hayden, a young Catholic, headed a group concerned with the problems of slum poverty among blacks. SDS was in its beginning a moderate, idealistic movement but gradually it would turn to radicalism and even violence for lack of response to its purpose, as manifested most indefensibly, its members believed, by the widening of the Vietnam War.

The campus was also being "turned on" in another way. Besides the political New Frontier in Washington, in which men from Harvard played a prominent role, besides the scientific New Frontier in which MIT and other institutions were participating, a new frontier of the mind was opening up in Cambridge. Two professors of psychology at Harvard, Timothy Leary and Richard Alpert, were experimenting with hallucinogenic and "mind-blowing" drugs to "liberate" the young. At his home in suburban Newton, Leary, who had begun his experiments after a visit to Mexico for the "sacred mushroom," administered psilocybin and other derivatives to graduate students and faculty members to test their reactions. They tried all manner of drugs, but put them aside for lysergic acid-d, which had been chemically synthesized in England. It induced "trips" into a world of fantasy, distortion and often terror, thus in Leary's phrase "opening the door" of the mind. Alpert coined the word "psychedelic" to describe the results.

LSD began to vie with SDS for the minds of many young Americans, and sometimes to accompany it. Restiveness and rebellion were fermenting on the campus, and before the Vietnam War became the principal explanation for them, the most effective recruitment came, as the Port Huron manifesto made clear, from the fears generated by "the Bomb." These were translated into harrowing experience by the Cuban missile crisis, the "eyeball-to-eyeball" confrontation between Kennedy and Khrushchev over the Soviet emplacement of deadly weapons a hundred miles from American shores.

For two weeks in October the threat of the nuclear devastation of two continents was real, until the Russians finally backed off. The first nuclear test of wills threw many Americans into panic, digging bomb shelters, stocking up on supplies, leaving the cities. In hysterical reaction high school students in Los Angeles sobbed, "I don't want to die." Nor was the United States the only country deeply affected. European governments wondered incredulously what effect a Russian rejection of the Kennedy ultimatum might have on the destiny of their own peoples. Americans in Moscow tried not to think of American missiles striking there.

A decade later at least one historian suggested that Kennedy had actually acted cautiously, not recklessly. He had refused to retaliate for the loss of a U-2 plane and pilot shot down over Cuba by Soviet-supplied fire. He had ordered the defusing of American missiles in Turkey and in effect made a "deal" with Khrushchev to obtain Soviet withdrawal of its Cuban missiles in exchange for an American pledge not to invade Cuba.

The public impression of Kennedy courage and nerve forcing a Soviet capitulation, however, was clearly the impression the administration sought to give at the time. Certainly the effect on Washington was a euphoric one, providing a triumphant feeling of strength, steadfastness and invincibility. The President himself gave off an aura of transcendental accomplishment, in spite of an official posture of salving Soviet sensibilities by not "rubbing it in."

Apart from its potential consequences, what made the confrontation terrifying, by any objective appraisal, was that given the nuclear readiness and targeting of both powers, the addition of missiles in Cuba posed no greater threat to the United States than already existed. They represented no change in the strategic balance. It was in psychological terms that a "victory" and a "defeat" were necessary, a matter of national prestige and public image.

The Chinese, who apparently could not contemplate the reality of the situation, charged Khrushchev first with "adventurism" for putting the missiles in, and then with "capitulation" for taking them out. In the final judgment the Soviet leader, to whose political downfall the episode contributed, could be credited by most of the rest of the world with rationality, when on the American side, if all the implications of the situation were seriously meant, there did not seem to be an oversupply of it.

Eventually the Cuban missile crisis, which had caused the two nuclear superpowers to think about the "unthinkable," led to the first steps in the limitation of strategic armaments. Inside the Soviet Union Khrushchev had been proceeding with the "thaw" of destalinization, with its connotation of detente with the West. The day on which Kennedy revealed the presence of the missiles in Cuba, for instance, *Pravda* appeared with a poem by Yevgeny Yevtushenko, "The Heirs of Stalin," denouncing the recrudescence of Stalinist influences. During the week of the Cuban drama Alexander Solzhenitsyn's *A Day in the Life of Ivan Denisovich* was published, lifting the curtain on the Stalin labor camps in which tens of thousands of Russians, including the author, had been imprisoned. Khrushchev had approved the printing.

If the Russians were thawing, the Chinese were not. After a month of incidents on the disputed border between China and India, fighting broke out on both the Tibetan and Kashmir fronts in response to Chinese incursions. The armed conflict, coinciding with the Cuban missile crisis, was Peking's first such move since Korea, and the United States saw it as renewed evidence of Maoist aggression and expansionism. Other diplomats were reporting that India was at fault and had provoked the clash, and that once the border was adjusted that would be the end of it. In Washington the Chinese were seen as trying to destroy Indian democracy in order to win the ideological battle for Asia. Ambassador Galbraith in New Delhi contributed to American suspicions by keeping his assumptions "on the dismal side" and crediting Peking with notions of territorial aggrandizement despite initial reservations.

By the Chinese action and by American default, the Soviet Union became India's friend and ally, the last nail having been driven into the Nehru-Chou compact of "brotherhood." New Delhi appealed to the United States for aid during the border war, but though Peking was the common adversary Washington refused to give "too much help" to India lest it disturb the SEATO ally, Pakistan. It was deemed useful, moreover, for India to learn that neutrality, if not "immoral" as Dulles had thought, could be risky.

Galbraith, incidentally, told the President that the 1962 election results, generally favorable to the Democrats — they included the election of the President's youngest brother, Edward, as senator from Massachusetts, the election of Galbraith's friend George McGovern as senator from South Dakota, and the defeat and presumed retirement from politics of Richard Nixon, who had sought the governorship of California — constituted a strong endorsement among other things of "your Cuban policy."

Whatever else, the missile crisis also encouraged those who, as the result of increasing commitment in Vietnam without any appreciable improvement there, had begun to charge the administration with a "no-win" purpose. If Communism could be so dramatically repelled in Cuba why could it not be in in Indochina? Conservative Republicans like Senator Barry Goldwater of Arizona, an Air Force Reserve general, were openly critical of "no-win" and so were some of the top military.

The public fears that the Cuban missile crisis had aroused of the possibility of nuclear exchange, including the danger of radioactive fallout, were deepened by the strontium-90 scare, in which contaminated material drifted down from the sky after several large test explosions, and was discovered in cows' milk. Americans had already been made aware of environmental pollution and its slower, though no less specific, dangers to life on the planet Earth. Rachel Carson, biologist and teacher, employed by the U.S. Fish and Wildlife Service as writer and editor, had stirred their forebodings with her book *Silent Spring*.

The book was not science fiction, as some readers evidently believed, but the guilty truth, giving the first wide public notice that all existence on the planet is interrelated and dependent upon an ecological chain. One decayed or shattered link in it could end the whole process, and the break in the chain had already been started, Miss Carson reported, by the indiscriminate use of the pesticide DDT and its accumulation in the tissues of living creatures including human beings. Over the years of use of DDT — originally called a "savior of mankind" — and similar chemical agents, the government and the medical associations had become as heedless of their effects as the industry which made them.

As some Americans viewed things, increasing contamination was not limited to the natural environment. There was also Pop Art. It was introduced by an advertising illustrator and former window decorator, Andy Warhol, with an exhibition of paintings of giant soup cans in stark detail and other commercial products, and silk-screen portraits of Marilyn Monroe, the film star. She had died that summer from an overdose of sleeping drugs, as something of a symbol in American life though no one knew precisely of what.

Warhol was followed by others. Roy Lichtenstein's Pop Art ran to the reproduction of comic strips and household appliances, Jim Dine's to neckties and tools, Jim Rosenquist's to auto parts, Claes Oldenburg's to hamburgers and ice cream cones. All were presumed to be reacting against the abstract expressionist trend that had dominated the Fifties.

Treated at best as a huge joke at first, at worst as a surrender to American mass-product materialism, Pop Art was not the popular cultural revolution it might seem to be, but a cross-current to sharpening political, social and cultural dissension, not only acceptance but glorification of the status quo in its most concrete forms. Its practitioners were soon called New Realists, and Pop Art ceased being a joke when they scored financial success with galleries, dealers and buyers.

Pop music was no less commercial than Pop Art, but it had countercultural pretensions. At boîtes like Folk City and the Bitter End in Greenwich Village a small, thin, pale-skinned guitarist from Duluth had given up his imitations of the revered Woody Guthrie to become a folksong prophet in his own right of youthful rebellion against the indifference of Life and Society. Bob Dylan, at the age of twenty-one, was writing what he called "finger-pointin' songs" for himself and others to sing. His best-know ballad "Blowin' in the Wind" was followed by "A Hard Rain's A-gonna Fall," "Masters of War," and "The American Nightmare." They helped recruit many young Americans into the antiwar movement.

By now there was much more war in Vietnam to be against. Maxwell Taylor had become Kennedy's personal chairman of the Joint Chiefs of Staff and was back in uniform. As 1962 ended forty-two Americans had been killed in Vietnam, twenty-two American generals were serving there, and one of the most significant occurrences of the war took place, the Battle of Ap Bac. A guerrilla battalion was quartered in the Mekong Delta village of that name, and it was the South Vietnamese army's plan to land a battalion by American helicopter and use two battalions of the Civil Guard to encircle Ap Bac on the ground. A company of armored personnel carriers with machine guns and bazookas was also put into action.

Though outnumbered, the NLF decided to stand and fight, presumably to test the mettle of their American-trained foe. They shot down five helicopters, killing three Americans and numerous South Vietnamese. The

Vietnamese commander refused to take the armored vehicles into the battle. The Civil Guard commander refused to attack. The American adviser at Ap Bac, Lieutenant Colonel John Vann, rallied some cooks and radio operators and led the personnel carriers toward the village. His men took a few prisoners but the battle was lost, indeed had not really been fought by ARVN. The guerrillas escaped, leaving sixty-one South Vietnamese dead and more than a hundred wounded. The stunning defeat corroborated the doubts about the fighting qualities of ARVN that American reporters and some advisers like Vann had been expressing.

Diem's government and General Harkins called Ap Bac a victory — the village had been "taken" after the "VC" left — but Vann spread the true story far and wide and wrote a report that "pacification" was failing because of Saigon's lack of initiative and the corruption of the regime, evident throughout the army. His outspoken criticism brought him into official disfavor; it was in conflict with the authorized optimism, and Colonel Vann returned home and resigned his commission. He would go back to Vietnam as a civilian, become the senior American adviser in the central highlands, and be killed in a helicopter crash at Kontum, in the last days of the war, almost a legendary figure, still unhappy at the end that the United States had not fought a more political and social war.

After Ap Bac, Senator Mike Mansfield, an original supporter of Diem but no longer quite sure, visited Vietnam and, questioning the increasing amount of American aid, called for more of a South Vietnamese effort. The United States had no conceivable interest to justify converting the situation "primarily into an American war to be fought primarily with American lives," the member of the Senate Foreign Relations Committee declared. The President's reply was that the United States must continue to "meet what I think are very clear national needs." In a special message to Congress Kennedy related the American involvement to "the political economic and military challenge of Communist China's relentless efforts to dominate the Continent."

Amid the shibboleths of weltpolitik the lesson of Ap Bac was easily overlooked. It was not merely a small military defeat inflicted by determined insurgents upon unenthusiastic and frightened counterinsurgents, but went to the very heart of the Vietnam problem, which was no open heart for American decision-makers. The defeat at Ap Bac derived in effect from the Diem regime's abolition of the village electoral system in 1956. That a guerrilla battalion could shelter in the village was not entirely due to the intimidation of the villagers. More than other elements of the society, Vietnam's peasants were nationalist, to the point of folk tradition. To a rice farmer a paddy on one side of the 17th parallel was like a paddy on the other side, so long as his ancestors lay nearby. Diem's failure to provide land reforms, his favoritism toward the landlords, his mass resettlement of villages, his pacification by force, were all anti-peasant moves carried out by the urban, elitist, mercantile "establishment" in Saigon.

American civil policy in South Vietnam was concentrated on economic development in its broadest aspects, to fulfill the aim of "nation-building." American economists made studies of productivity, compiled statistics of employment, examined the institutional foundations of distribution. Under Walt Rostow's theory of economic growth a quickened process of development would form the relationships, social classes and values to support the new nation. Urbanization and modernization were the channels. The peasants, the core of the nation, received a low priority. What was wanted in South Vietnam was a Little America, to prevent a Little China.

Rostovism failed to reckon with the power of nationalism and independence when these were put ahead of economic growth, as Hanoi and the NLF put them. It also failed to reckon with Ngo Dinh Diem. The American plan for urbanization was to him a plan for population control. In addition to selecting village chiefs and council members he reorganized the villages into five-family units, each with its appointed elder. All movement by the peasants was under close scrutiny. They were fingerprinted and given identity cards. Many were arrested and detained. Diem's controls were as authoritarian as anything that went on in North Vietnam, but they did not instill in village dwellers any sense of identification with national purpose, such as the NLF did provide.

The anti-Diem rebellion was not confined to the countryside where it originated. Segments of the urban population were also in active dissent, including members of the former old-line political parties, intellectuals, students, and especially the Buddhists, who were not only a religious force but a political one. The same Thich Tri Quang who had sat in his tent outside the Palace of Nations during the 1954 Geneva Conference, to oversee Vietnamese independence, furnished the Buddhist spearhead by which Diem was finally overthrown.

The climactic event of the Buddhist uprising, the rioting at Hue on May 8, 1963, and its subjugation by rifle fire and tear gas, had both religious and political origins. Two weeks before, President Diem's brother Ngo Dinh Thuc, Archbishop of Hue, had celebrated the twenty-fifth anniversary of his consecration as bishop with a parade in which Catholic banners were carried. On the occasion of Buddha's 2,527th birthday, which followed, the Buddhists also sought to parade in Hue. Their banners were forbidden, the government explaining that the standing order against all religious flags was now being enforced precisely because it had been violated by the Catholics. The effect was to discriminate against the Buddhists, who felt that they had had discrimination enough — both in the general sense that French laws in Vietnam had recognized Catholicism as a religion while Buddhism was merely an "association," and in the specific sense that Hue was a political as well as religious fiefdom of the Catholics, held by Diem's two brothers, the archbishop Thuc and the political boss Can.

On Buddha's birthday, as thousands of angry citizens demonstrated outside the Hue radio station against the government ban, they were fired upon by police and Vietnamese Special Forces. By order of the assistant province chief, an ARVN major, American grenades were thrown into the crowd. Eight persons were killed. Diem's supporters charged that the Buddhists were themselves responsible for the killings, by the deliberate use of plastique explosives. The grenades, they said, could produce only shock and concussion. In the light of subsequent Buddhist acts of self-immolation either version of the events was plausible. It made no difference. The Buddhist uprising moved into its decisive stage.

The incident at Hue inaugurated a summer of open warfare between the Buddhists and the Saigon government. On June 11, in the capital, a seventy-year-old monk, the Venerable Quang Duc, saturated himself with gasoline and burned himself to death. He was the first of seven monks to do so. Pictures of the small funeral pyres shocked the conscience of the United States, the more so when the gracious Madame Nhu ridiculed the suicides as "barbecues" and suggested that American newsmen should follow the example of the monks.

The conflict between Diem and the Buddhists, capped by the invasion of pagodas by Nhu's Special Forces and the arrest of many monks, made the fall of the Saigon regime inevitable. Yet the trouble in Hue came as a complete surprise to the Kennedy administration, according to Michael Forrestal, a White House adviser. The United States had been counseling Diem for nine years, but Forrestal believed there was no one in the entire American government who knew anything about Buddhism in Vietnam. A Catholic American President was now presented with the problem of a Catholic South Vietnamese President putting down dissension by non-Catholics, thus subordinating the political nature of the conflict to the religious. If there was anything worse than a religious majority persecuting a religious minority, in American eyes, it could only be a minority trying to repress a majority.

The news stories and photographs from Vietnam were undoubtedly galling to an American President who had succeeded in removing the religious issue from politics, but who knew of the special interest in the fortunes of Diem held by Cardinal Spellman and prominent Catholic laymen, including his own father and many friends. On the front pages and television screens every day religious discrimination at the hands of a regime kept in power by the United States was seen to be taking place. Outside the White House for the first time demonstrators carried banners reading "Down with Diem." In inner-circle discussions of the Buddhist crisis Robert Kennedy raised the question whether the United States should take this opportunity to withdraw from Vietnam. Alternatively, he went on to say, if Diem was the obstacle to "winning the war" the United States should get rid of him.

Though it was not particularly remarked at the time, the events in Vietnam were paralleled by events in America's own internal crisis. In the national subconsciousness, at least, the Vietnam War was joined with the American civil rights war as the dramas of Hue and Birmingham, Alabama, were simultaneously played out. In both cases religious leadership — in Hue, Thich Tri Quang; in Birmingham, Martin Luther King, Jr. — undertook political action against discrimination. Both causes had their martyrs to violence and suffered desecration of their places of worship. Both used the same tactics against the authorities: mass demonstrations, civil disobedience and passive resistance. In both causes many prayed publicly; against both causes official assaults were deliberately provoked, the authorities thought.

On May 6, two days before the Hue riots, a thousand persons were arrested in Birmingham in demonstrations for the desegregation of public places. The Birmingham public library not only enforced separate facilities for whites and blacks but had taken from the shelves a children's book containing pictures of white and black rabbits together. Many clergymen besides Dr. King took part in the demonstration and 40 percent of the demonstrators were under twenty-one. Two days later in Hue many students similarly marched.

Birmingham erupted with fires and explosions on May 12, following two dynamite blasts in the Negro section, one aimed at Dr. King's brother, the other at a motel where the black leadership was gathered. The sending of troops to Hue was followed by the sending of federal troops to the Birmingham area. The use of grenades and tear gas against the Hue demonstrators was followed by the use of fire hoses and police dogs against those in Birmingham. Like the television pictures from Hue and Saigon, those from Birmingham appalled and stirred the nation.

To some Americans the similarity between Hue and Birmingham was more than coincidental. Southerners especially saw their troubles with the niggers and white liberals as part of the same Communist conspiracy that South Vietnam was the victim of, at the hands of radicals from the North.

In both countries the confrontation widened. As the Buddhist rebellion spread, Governor George Wallace stood in the doorway of the University of Alabama at Tuscaloosa to bar the admission of the first two black students, and to repeat the slogan he had campaigned on, "Segregation now, segregation tomorrow, segregation forever." But when President Kennedy called out the federalized National Guard, Wallace having made his promised gesture stood aside, and the two blacks registered. That evening the President on television, in one of his notable speeches, called the situation in Alabama "a moral crisis," which could not "be met by repressive police action," and made a fervent plea "for this nation to fulfill its promise" of racial equality and "no second-class citizens." The next day Medgar W. Evers, the NAACP field secretary in Mississippi, was shot in the back as he entered his home in Jackson. Civil rights demonstrations there became riots in protest against murder.

In his address Kennedy drew a particularized connection between Vietnam and civil rights in America. "Today we are committed to a worldwide struggle to promote and protect the rights of all who wish to be free," he declared. "When Americans are sent to Vietnam or West Berlin we do not ask for whites only." In actuality Vietnam had reached the same point of moral crisis that he recognized in Alabama. Diem continued to use the kind of repressive action that Kennedy saw as no solution, and in August, after a declaration of martial law, Nhu's Special Forces, wearing army uniforms as a disguise, attacked Buddhist pagodas in various cities, and killed several monks and arrested many. Thich Tri Quang and two other leaders found sanctuary in the American Embassy.

In September four teen-age Negro girls were killed and eighteen persons injured in the bombing of the Sixteenth Street Baptist Church and civil rights advocates began calling the Alabama city Bombingham. Two more blacks were killed by police as they poured into the streets to protest. The violence occurred after President Kennedy, acting to redress the patent grievances of blacks, had sent Congress the most sweeping civil rights bill in history, banning discrimination in public places. It came also after Martin Luther King, at the head of 200,000 people, about 50,000 of them white, "marched" on Washington, and spoke there of the Dream he had of a transformed United States, practicing freedom and justice. At the same time, civil rights pickets marched at construction sites in New York City seeking jobs for blacks and Puerto Ricans and membership in the "hard hat" unions which led all others in the application of racial discrimination.

The massive March on Washington combined the two themes of civil rights and economic opportunity, and was organized despite the President's trepidation, personally expressed to black leaders, that it might impede the passage of his proposed legislation, and despite also the opposition of the AFL-CIO majority led by George Meany.

The orator of the Washington demonstration and the seer of the Dream, Martin Luther King, had become the undoubted leader of the new mainstream black movement formed under the clubs and fire hoses of Birmingham. He took his stand between the complacent and ever-hopeful "Uncle Toms" on the one side, and the bitter Black Muslims and diverse nationalists on the other. The middle course, though primarily concerned with civil rights and jobs, was also a search for group and individual identity. Was the conscious member of the movement a Negro American, an

Afro-American, or an African-American? "Black" was somehow still deroga-
tory. The movement had not yet found it possible to proclaim black
"beautiful" or to demand Black Power, Black Studies or Black Art.

Identification with Africa was not new in America. Marcus Garvey be-
spoke it in the Twenties, complete with a return to the ancestral continent.
But Africa, except as a symbol of cultural heritage, was not the answer, as
black Americans who went there quickly discovered. They might take
African names, adopt Islam, wear African garb and the most extreme
African hair styles, but their problems and the solutions to them lay in
America. As Vice-President Johnson stated it, on the centennial of the
Emancipation Proclamation, what was required was the translation of
emancipation into a fact.

In Vietnam Ngo Dinh Diem, unlike Kennedy or Johnson, did not
articulate such thoughts to his dissidents. Their number had further increased. By Nhu's use of Special Forces in army uniforms to attack the
Buddhist pagodas, so that the military was at first blamed, the coup sentiment among the generals had been pushed to the stage of an active plot
to overthrow the brothers.

The new American Ambassador, Henry Cabot Lodge, arrived in Saigon
the day after the attack on the pagodas. It was deemed a political master
stroke for the Democratic President to send a leading Republican as his
envoy — the man Kennedy had beaten for the Senate in 1952 and again
as Nixon's running mate in 1960 — to nail down the bipartisanship of
Vietnam policy. Lodge succeeded Ambassador Frederick Nolting, for whom
Diem, whatever he did, had always been right. As he departed Nolting
declared that he had seen no evidence of any religious persecution in
Vietnam, and that the Buddhist question was extraneous to the winning
of the war. The brothers Diem and Nhu were overjoyed by his remarks,
but Nolting represented the old American policy, Lodge the new.

The generals' plot quickly became an American-encouraged affair. Following the pagoda attack two of the uniformed conspirators asked Lodge
how the United States would react to a military coup. Lodge in turn asked
Washington. Swiftly, on August 24, came back one of the most controversial documents in American diplomacy.

The President was at Cape Cod for the summer weekend. In the capital
Averell Harriman, the Assistant Secretary of State for Far Eastern Affairs,
Under Secretary Ball, Roger Hilsman, the State Department's Intelligence
chief, and Michael Forrestal drafted the cable of reply. The United States,
they said, would find it hard to continue support of Diem unless somehow
the Buddhists were mollified. Washington therefore was prepared to support "an interim, anti-Communist military government," though any actual coup decision had to be made by the generals. The Eisenhower offer
of aid to Diem thus became an advance promise of aid to his successors,
another fateful and completely conscious step into the Vietnam morass.

By telephone from Hyannisport the President approved the message Pontius Pilate could have been proud of. Secretary Rusk, the CIA and the Joint Chiefs of Staff concurred. It is not clear whether Vice-President Johnson was made privy to the cable to Lodge, but in his memoirs he later described it as "hasty and ill-advised," and "a green light to those who wanted Diem's downfall."

When the President returned to Washington and the National Security Council met, there were some second thoughts. McNamara, General Taylor and the CIA director, John A. McCone, all expressed misgivings about the cable. Upset and angered, Kennedy began to hedge on his original approval of it. More meetings were held, and at one of them Paul Kattenburg, of the Vietnam interdepartmental task force, raised the larger question of continued American intervention after Diem. He did not think it possible to "win" in Vietnam under any circumstances. Secretary of State Rusk's reply was that American policy stood on "the firm basis of two things: that we will not pull out of Vietnam until the war is won, and that we will not run a coup." Vice-President Johnson averred that the war was being won and it would be a "disaster to pull out."

The United States in any case was running a coup. Lodge passed on the message of August 24 to the generals and in so doing bestowed on them all the blessing they required. Despite continued denials for many years, there is on record a message from Lodge to Rusk dated August 29. "We are launched on a course from which there is no respectable turning back: the overthrow of the Diem government," reported the Boston Brahmin. "We should proceed to make all-out effort to get generals to move promptly." Hilsman also, in a memo to Rusk, recommended that the generals be encouraged to act.

A date had been fixed for the coup, August 31, but it came and went without incident. The generals had for so long been warned by successive American ambassadors not to impede or complicate the war effort they could not quite believe the United States had actually sanctioned Diem's removal. The coup was postponed, as it turned out, for two months.

In public the Kennedy administration was being detached and matter-of-fact about Vietnam. Without mentioning what was afoot in Saigon, the President, inaugurating CBS's expansion of its evening television news program from fifteen minutes to a half-hour in September, told Walter Cronkite that "in the final analysis it is their war. They are the ones who have to win it or lose it . . . and unless greater effort is made by Saigon to get popular support, it can't be won. The government [in Saigon] has been out of touch," as the repression of Buddhists showed. "A change of policy and personnel" was required. The intimation was that the sacrifice of Nhu, who had tried to dishonor the army, was the essential. Secretary Rusk also believed that Diem and Nhu could be separated. Lodge did not. "The best chance of doing it is by the generals taking over the government lock, stock and barrel," he cabled. Then they could decide whether to put back Diem without Nhu, or dismiss both.

Kennedy's remarks were later cited as evidence that he was prepared to leave Vietnam to the Vietnamese, and at some future date might actually have done so. Against the Cronkite interview, however, stood another, opening NBC's rival half-hour news program. "We don't want a repetition of China," said the President on that occasion, "the most damaging event of the century to us, when it passed into the hands of the Communists." Then at a news conference he said about Vietnam that "we are not there to see a war lost," and added the pledge to continue "advancing those causes and issues which help win the war."

One witness has testified that as early as the spring of 1963, before the Buddhist rebellion peaked, the President had decided to pull out of Vietnam after the 1964 election. According to Kenneth O'Donnell, the White House appointments aide, Kennedy told this to Senator Mansfield, and the latter corroborated it.

"In 1965 I'll be damned everywhere as a Communist appeaser," Kennedy reportedly declared, "but I don't care. If I tried to pull out now we'd have another Joe McCarthy Red scare on our hands, but I can do it after I'm reelected. So we had better make damned sure I am reelected." This example of the cynicism of practical politics, from one who had not judged the McCarthy period too harshly when he himself was a supporter of the Wisconsin Senator, still leaves in doubt what Kennedy would actually have done if he had lived. All those who were counseling him to stay in Vietnam continued to do so, and gave his successor the same advice.

Two of them, McNamara and Taylor, returning from another journey to Saigon and with their eyes fixed on the 1964 election also, as well as the light at the end of the tunnel, foresaw the withdrawal of a thousand American troops by the end of 1963, and the completion of the "major part of the American military task" by the end of 1965. The White House added the assurance that large-scale American aid would not be required for long.

There was at any rate no immediate thought of leaving Vietnam. "That would be a great mistake," Kennedy declared in his CBS interview, even though "people don't like Americans to be engaged in this kind of effort." He was right. The winds of dissension were increasing in force. The Young Democrats of California adopted a policy statement calling for the recognition of Communist China and East Germany, and the withdrawal of American forces from Vietnam. "I don't know what's happening with the Young Democrats or the Young Republicans," declared the young President, "but time is on our side."

A few days later the first antiwar resolution, though somewhat qualified, went before the Senate. Frank Church of Idaho proposed that the United States end its aid to Saigon and withdraw troops if Diem continued his "cruel repressions." George McGovern of South Dakota also criticized the continuing use of American funds and arms "to suppress the very liberties we went in to defend." He denounced the American policy as "a moral debacle and a political defeat."

One factor in the administration's ambivalence about Vietnam was, as Robert Kennedy suggested during the interminable discussions, that it never got enough "facts" to determine what it should do. The facts it did get were contradictory to boot. On the return of still another presidential mission to Saigon, one of its two members, Marine General Victor Krulak, reported that the war could be won despite Diem. The other, Joseph Mendenhall of the State Department, said it could not be won with Diem. Not altogether jocosely, Kennedy asked the two men if they had been to the same country.

Ambassador Lodge in Saigon may have been dusting off the headsman's block for Diem, but at least one American agency remained loyal to the regime it had infiltrated, if not created, nine years before. The CIA had invested too much prestige and too many "action programs" in Diem and Nhu to do otherwise. Suddenly the CIA station chief, John Richardson, was recalled to Washington, and a member of the CIA's original Saigon cast became an integral part of the plot to dispose of Diem. Lucien Conein, with the rank of "lieutenant colonel," began to serve as intermediary between the American Embassy and the council of generals, actually sitting in at the latter's meetings. The plot was headed by General Duong Van Minh, called "Big" Minh because he was six feet tall, and soon Conein was reporting to Washington, with true CIA relish, that the Buddhist question was no longer important and that Diem was being deposed because he was "negotiating" with Hanoi.

Madame Nhu later explained that it was her husband who was in contact with the North, but the purpose of such a move, if indeed it had been made, was obscure. Was Diem, considered by the United States the last Vietnamese to have any truck with Hanoi, trying to impose a peace on Ho Chi Minh with the threat of growing American aid? Was he sounding out Hanoi on President de Gaulle's latest call for a Vietnam solution based on neutrality? Was he, in the face of the coup rumors, seeking to save what he could in Saigon? Or was he only pretending to negotiate and thus trying to communicate to the Americans what he could do if they persisted in trying to bring him down?

To increase the confusion, one of Nhu's newspapers, the English-language Saigon *Times*, in large front-page headlines charged "CIA Financing Planned Coup d'Etat," while among the many rumors in Saigon was one that Diem and Nhu were plotting a false coup against themselves in order to bring to the surface the real coup, which they could then put down. The plotters should not have been difficult to identify. They consisted of virtually the entire military council, and held numerous meetings, working on a plan to kill Nhu and exile Diem. Conein advised Washington he was prepared to fly Diem out of the country.

The CIA was playing both sides in Saigon, a tactic not unknown in covert operations. It had established Nhu's Special Forces and now it revealed their disposition to the generals. The double game also worked against the CIA. The use of the disguised Special Forces in the pagoda raids instilled some suspicion of double-dealing in the generals' minds. The CIA took pains to remove it. A week before the coup Lodge cabled McGeorge Bundy: "CIA has been punctilious in carrying out my instructions. I have personally approved each meeting between General [Tran Van] Don [the coordinator of the plot] and Conein." The former Senator, UN Ambassador and vice-presidential candidate explained that "we should remember that this is the only way in which the people in Vietnam can possibly get a change in government."

Four days before the coup Conein met General Don again and was told that the details of the plan might be available to the Ambassador four hours before it was executed. The general also suggested that Lodge go through with his announced intention of returning to Washington October 31, since any change "would tip off the palace." Completely immersed in the plot, Lodge remained in Saigon.

The overthrow came on November 1, All Saints Day. Diem was killed as well as Nhu, by General Minh's bodyguard, Major Nguyen Van Nhung. Gia Long Palace, to which Diem had moved after the bombing of Independence Palace, was surrounded by the tanks of the Fifth (called the "anticoup") Division, commanded by General Nguyen Van Thieu, implicitly trusted by Diem. Thieu thereby won his place in all future governments. The brothers, having fled the palace by an underground passage and sought refuge with a merchant friend in the Chinese quarter of Cholon, gave themselves up when found there, and were presumably being taken back to the palace to face its new occupants when the double murder took place. Later, when his master had been displaced by another general, Minh's aide was taken into "protective custody" and was found hanged in his cell by his own parachute cords.

Diem had made a final effort to avert the coup. "Tell me what you want me to do and I will do it," he said to Ambassador Lodge. The capitulation came too late. Lodge had already taken the last necessary action making the coup possible, announcing that the American Embassy would no longer pay for Nhu's Special Forces unless they were sent into combat. They were moved out of Saigon October 30, and Diem and Nhu thus deprived of their protection.

The day after Diem's overthrow and death, the State Department spokesman, Richard Phillips, declared in Washington: "I can categorically state that the United States Government was not in any way involved." Lodge also denied any American complicity, as he had done about Guatemala in 1954, and would continue to do so. The United States "never participated in the planning, never gave any advice, had nothing whatever to do with it," he said on one occasion a year later. Subsequently he amended his version of events. The United States did "not thwart" the Saigon coup and this, he explained, was quite different from supporting it.

Diem and Nhu were buried in a corner of the military headquarters compound near Tan Son Nhut airport, but later they were reburied in a midtown cemetery, assertedly because the generals, animists like most Vietnamese, feared their ghosts would haunt the headquarters.

After the coup their brother Can, political boss of central Vietnam, sought American asylum in Hue. He was flown to Saigon but was arrested there, and eventually he was executed by a firing squad. The clerical brother, Archbishop Thuc, who had taken to riding about his diocese in an armored car, was recalled to Rome when he received threats that he would be burned at the stake. Luyen, the brother who was Ambassador in London, remained abroad. Madame Nhu, visiting the United States and having been feted by Henry Luce and his editors, was in Beverly Hills when she heard of the coup, on her return from All Saints Day Mass. She charged that the United States had incited and backed it.

President Kennedy was shaken by the gory events in Saigon — he was awakened by the news at 3 A.M. — for Diem's murder, at least, was not part of any American plan. According to Arthur Schlesinger, Kennedy had not been so depressed since the Bay of Pigs, and had tears in his eyes. "No doubt he realized Vietnam was his greatest failure in foreign policy." But though the President ordered a speedy reassessment of the situation in Saigon, his conclusion was to continue support of the new nominal rulers, General Minh's twelve-man military junta. The recognition of failure had once again not been enough to bring about any change in policy.

The New York Times, in an editorial headed "Opportunity in Vietnam," went to the heart of the matter. "Fortunately the new Vietnamese rulers are dedicated anti-Communists, who reject any idea of neutralism and pledge themselves to stand with the free world." The American Friends of Vietnam, founded on the endorsement and support of Diem, sent congratulations to those who had deposed him. Professor Wesley Fishel, who had lauded "democratic one-man rule," now found the Diem system to have been "peasant-based revolutionary fascism."

"Dedicated anti-Communists" the generals might be but they were not effective political leaders. Their high rank did not erase the fact that most of them had served as NCO's with the French, and the intrigue, maneuvers and infighting that followed Diem's overthrow, leading to further coups and countercoups, were on the level of the sergeants' mess. Governmental action was made difficult by a unanimity rule within the junta and by the absence of any administrative plan except to stay in office. The nightclubs and bars closed by Madame Nhu were reopened and prostitution returned, but the war was prosecuted no better by the military than it had been by Diem, and the NLF was able to step up its offensive against the disorganized army.

The ouster of Diem was obviously a major gain for the insurgents. For one thing, General Minh's bourgeois Cochin Chinese–Buddhist new order did the NLF the favor of purging the old aristocratic Annamese-Catholic order. The civil service, secret police, province and district chiefs, and trade union leadership were all shaken up. When Minh declared that inhabitants of the remaining Strategic Hamlets in the Mekong Delta could leave the barbed wire if they chose, there was mass desertion. But the NLF's principal hope was vain. The collapse expected in Saigon did not come about. The insurgents had reckoned without the United States. Washington had virtually given up the notion of "nation-building," and did not press for the return of the old political parties, or any appreciable reforms. It chose to back the army, in whatever form of administration the generals desired.

A week after Diem's death the NLF in radio broadcasts called for cease-fire negotiations by "interested groups," general elections, and a national coalition of "all forces, parties, tendencies and strata of South Vietnamese people." Pointedly it made no mention of North Vietnam or of reunification, but on an all-southern basis appealed to the Minh junta to "separate themselves from the control of the American imperialists" and join in replanning "a future which will be brilliant, which will have no more nightmares."

No one in Saigon was listening. When it received no answer the NLF held a national congress in secret to decide its future course of action. At that time, according to Douglas Pike, an American expert on the "Viet Cong," "perhaps half the population of South Vietnam at least tacitly supported the NLF." The decision was to intensify the tactics of "armed struggle," since "political struggle" had been rejected. Within a year the NLF in effect won the civil war, only to have the victory denied by the United States.

For whatever John F. Kennedy might have done to repair, redeem or renounce "his greatest failure in foreign policy" was made an academic question when he himself died of an assassin's bullet three weeks after Diem and Nhu. Madame Nhu, in Paris at the time, declared, "Anything that happens in Vietnam will find its counterpart in the United States." The Cassandra from Saigon was presciently speaking of more than the two presidential assassinations. Kennedy's last public words on the subject of Vietnam were uttered the morning of his death when he breakfasted with the Fort Worth Chamber of Commerce before proceeding to Dallas. He noted that he had increased the "counterinsurgency" forces in Vietnam by 600 percent during his term, and said, "I hope those who want a stronger America and place it on some signs, will also place those figures next to it."

At the same time it was later said, he had already ordered the pullout of 1,300 Americans from Vietnam by the end of 1963, in pursuance of his supposed plan for full withdrawal after reelection. How would he do it without injuring American prestige? According to O'Donnell, "Easy. Put a government in there that will ask us to withdraw." Yet Diem had been overthrown, in part at least, because of his independence and supposed willingness to deal with Hanoi. In the face of O'Donnell's belated revelation, moreover, Walt Rostow declared that Kennedy's "painful judgment" had been that "a failure to hold in Southeast Asia" would lead to a larger war.

Two days before Dallas, in fact, Kennedy's top civilian and military advisers met in Honolulu to plan increased clandestine warfare against North Vietnam. Ambassador Lodge, on his way to Washington to report to the President after the Diem coup, stopped off in Hawaii to confer with Secretaries McNamara and Rusk, Generals Taylor and Harkins, and McGeorge Bundy. They certified the administration's support for the new Minh regime. Then came the news from Dallas.

Even before the funeral the new President received Lodge, endorsed the Honolulu decisions, and pledged himself to carry on the Kennedy policy in Vietnam as he knew it. Lodge had given him a pessimistic report on "Big" Minh's prospects. It would take hard decisions to save Vietnam, the Ambassador said. "I am not going to lose Vietnam," replied Lyndon Johnson. "I am not going to be the President who saw Southeast Asia go the way China went."

There were 16,600 American "advisers" in South Vietnam at the time. "Only" 109 Americans had died and 486 been wounded in the Kennedy "thousand days," but it was estimated that Vietnamese casualties, including civilians, were already about 500,000 dead in the long war that had begun under the French.

Johnson's intention not to be "the first President to lose a war" would be often expressed. Since he believed Diem's ouster a basic error he was presumably therefore committed to redressing it by "victory," and to furnishing support and more support, whatever the regime in Saigon. For the record Washington remained expectant that too much American involvement would not be needed. As Eisenhower had done to Diem, Johnson wrote to Minh, to promise support of the latter's "revolutionary government" against forces "directed and supported by the Communist regime in Hanoi . . . the forces of enslavement, brutality and material misery." Then came the wishful thought, "as the forces of your government become increasingly capable of dealing with the aggressors, United States military personnel in South Vietnam can be progressively withdrawn."

Meanwhile, American escalation was already being contemplated, following Secretary McNamara's latest trip to Vietnam just before Christmas. Contrary to his public cheerfulness, he told the White House that the situation was "very disturbing" and unless remedied would lead to neutralization or "more likely, to a Communist-controlled state."

Johnson's Vietnam Working Group, as he called it, was headed by William H. Sullivan of the State Department, who believed that Hanoi must be "punished" by direct American force. General Curtis Le May, the Air Force chief of staff, urged the bombing of North Vietnam, as he later would phrase it, "back to the Stone Age." General Thomas S. Power, chief of the Strategic Air Command, encouraged the use of the mighty B-52's, not only to "pulverize" North Vietnam with nonnuclear weapons but to hit guerrilla bases in South Vietnam also. Walt Rostow argued for the bombing of North Vietnam by stages, thus reversing the stages of economic growth. The Pentagon and the CIA wanted more air action over Laos.

In Saigon General Minh, tall and round-faced, had been quickly replaced by General Nguyen Khanh, who was short and had a goatee, in a second coup by the younger generals of the junta. Khanh pledged his obeisance in turn to the commander-in-chief in Washington and demanded the invasion of North Vietnam. He also rechristened Diem's Strategic Hamlets as New Rural Life Hamlets. Military and political factionalism continued to prevent the creation of a popular government, however, and the NLF continued to prosper in the countryside and win battles.

Since Khanh was regarded in Washington as pro-American, unlike Minh who had been thought a bit too pro-French, the slogan "Sink or Swim with Ngo Dinh Diem" gave way to "It's Khanh or Chaos." When McNamara and Taylor journeyed to Vietnam again in March and reported that conditions had "unquestionably been growing worse," more American military and civilian personnel were sent. Soon Maxwell Taylor was back in Saigon, and this time not merely to survey but to stay, as he replaced Ambassador Lodge, while General William C. Westmoreland, one of Taylor's "new breed" of soldier-technocrats, took over from General Paul Harkins, whose deputy he had been. Now there were 23,000 American "advisers" in South Vietnam.

The "small picture" of war was symbolized by the Mekong Delta story of two American helicopters which left Can Tho for Saigon, each carrying eight prisoners, and arrived with one and three prisoners respectively. A Vietnamese captain explained that the other twelve had "tried to escape" from the aircraft in midflight. They had in fact been pushed out, with the forbearance of the American door-gunners, to make the other four talk.

The war's "big picture" was in Lyndon Johnson's hands, in the White House "situation room." As Vice-President he had advocated escalation and as President he pursued it. He was also very much the personal commander-in-chief, unlike Kennedy. He sought quick results in North Vietnam through increased covert operations, and ordered the development of a list of bombing targets there. He told visitors "Vietnam is the only war we've got." He obviously believed it would soon be ended in a military victory, though General Taylor frankly envisioned it lasting up to ten years, at "whatever level of activity may be required."

Kennedy had done some escalating, he had equivocated, misjudged, and feared being charged with another "loss" to Communism, but he was probably more annoyed with Vietnam than absorbed in it because it interfered with his "Grand Design" for Europe. De Gaulle had decided after Dien Bien Phu that the United States would not risk its own security for the sake of an ally, and the Cuban missile crisis had demonstrated that the United States was prepared to go to the nuclear extreme for a dubious definition of that security. The American refusal to consider de Gaulle's advice that Southeast Asia be neutralized was added to these other elements in France's increasing resistance to any American plans for Europe.

Kennedy had seen Vietnam in paramilitary terms with political underpinnings. Undeniably he wanted to keep the war limited and American policy flexible and manageable. For Johnson the limits of "limited war" were larger, and as they grew into masses of men and materials, flexibility diminished and unmanageability took over.

A month before his death John Kennedy in high spirits had dedicated the Robert Frost Library at Amherst College. He recalled the poet's phrase about "poetry and power" at his inauguration. "The men who create power make an indispensable contribution to the nation's greatness," he said, "but the men who question power make a contribution just as indispensable. For they determine whether we use power or power uses us."

Kennedy's successor, the new President of the United States, exulting in the use of power in Vietnam, was already being used by power instead.

6

THE WAR OF JOHNSON'S FACE

If the Tonkin Gulf "incidents" of August 2 and 4, 1964, had not taken place they would have had to be invented to meet the demands of American policy in Southeast Asia. And indeed most of their supposed substance was invented, imagined or presumed.

On those dark murky nights in the choppy waters off the North Vietnamese coast, in action of war even though against a relatively negligible power, and in large dependence on mechanical devices, human tensions and errors were perhaps inevitable. It was the use of the Tonkin Gulf "incidents" to justify the introduction of American military might into Southeast Asia that cannot escape historical judgment.

Tonkin Gulf's unmistakable convenience was the consequence of the admittedly worsening military and political circumstances in Vietnam. "Khanh or Chaos" had become Khanh and Chaos, made up of ARVN's incompetence, laziness and lack of courage; of political favoritism in the army, red tape, waste, loss of equipment and desertion. A congressional group headed by Representative Gerald Ford, Republican of Michigan, had recommended that the United States take over control of the war. Tonkin Gulf provided the opportunity to do so.

The "crisis" that broke water in the Tonkin Gulf in August had been laid there, like a mine, by President Johnson's approval on February 1 of the plans worked out for Operation 34-A by the 303 Committee. They called for covert action against North Vietnam, including South Vietnamese commando raids, sabotage, coastal bombardment and air reconnaissance, supplemented by the so-called De Soto patrols of American destroyers making electronic probes along the North Vietnamese coast.

Johnson's Vietnam Working Group had also mapped out more considerable courses of action, such as South Vietnamese army attacks on the Ho Chi Minh trail in Laos, "hot pursuit" into Cambodia, aerial mining of North Vietnamese ports, air strikes on North Vietnam by unmarked planes manned by South Vietnamese, and not least, sustained American bombing of North Vietnam from Japan.

Congress was not apprised of these plans, listed as "contingencies." By mid-February of 1964, however, the State Department was talking of a formal congressional resolution to wage war, and William Bundy, the new Assistant Secretary for Far Eastern Affairs, drafted such a document in May. Roger Hilsman had resigned as Assistant Secretary in protest at the plans to bomb the North, and McGeorge Bundy's elder brother had come over from the Pentagon to replace him. From May until it was passed three months later in a less precise version, the President, it was said, walked around with the Tonkin Gulf Resolution in his pocket.

The Tonkin Gulf affair occurred at a time when the international barometer indicated clearing weather. The Soviet elder, Anastas Mikoyan, a member of the Politburo, had declared that the Russians were ready to help the United States find a solution in Vietnam. Hanoi had joined Moscow in calling for still another Geneva Conference to consider the war in Laos, where the Pathet Lao had been halted by American air strikes and the infusion of large amounts of American material. Cambodia, the NLF, and even the Chinese supported the call of the Soviet co-chairman for a third Geneva, and so did President de Gaulle and UN Secretary General U Thant.

President Johnson rejected the idea. To his mind two Genevas had been enough. "We do not believe in conferences to ratify terror," he declared. Instead he ordered 5,000 more Americans to Vietnam. But 1964 was an election year. Johnson was seeking to become President in his own right, and American military involvement abroad, with prospects for more, was a shaky reelection platform. He therefore spoke against it while proceeding with it. No less straightforward conclusion can be drawn.

Kennedy in 1963 had said that the Vietnamese must win their own war, while sending more American men and weapons to help them. The Johnson version in 1964 was that "American boys" would not be sent to do "what Asian boys should be doing." Even if things went "very badly," Defense Secretary McNamara told the House Armed Services Committee, American forces would not be shipped across the Pacific. "I don't believe that pouring in hundreds of thousands of troops is the solution to the problem of Vietnam." The new chairman of the Joint Chiefs of Staff, General Earle Wheeler, declared, "I would oppose the use of American troops as the direct means of suppressing the guerrillas in South Vietnam."

No President had ever assumed office with more public support and sympathy than Lyndon Johnson, because of the tragic circumstances, or had so quickly won confidence. His 1964 election theme was that peace must be restored in Vietnam, and Senator J. William Fulbright, chairman of the Foreign Relations Committee, bestowed a congressional blessing on all efforts, including military ones, to bring about negotiations with Hanoi. The President sent a "peace feeler" to North Vietnam through friendly channels, assuring Ho Chi Minh that the United States desired peace, did not seek to overthrow his regime despite all Khanh's talk in Saigon, and had no wish to retain bases or a military position in South Vietnam. Hanoi was required only to abide by the Geneva agreements, keeping its troops inside its borders and sending no military supplies south. In return the United States would give economic aid to both Vietnams, indeed create a new TVA in the Mekong and Red River deltas. Within the velvet glove was the iron fist. If Hanoi did not stop the NLF, the United States would retaliate with "the greatest devastation" against North Vietnam.

The Johnson proposals failed to touch upon what Hanoi regarded as the three essentials for any settlement. The President did not refer to the NLF, which was doing the fighting, as a participant in negotiations. He did not specify American withdrawal. He did not mention a political settlement to establish a new government in Saigon. "They slammed the door shut on our peace offer," Johnson complained about Hanoi's reply, which was that North Vietnam "will not provoke the United States," but on the other hand would continue supporting the NLF.

At Nam Dong, west of Danang, an American Special Forces camp was attacked by hundreds of guerrillas in an eight-hour siege, and three of the Green Beret team of twelve were killed. Captain Roger Donlon, of Saugerties, New York, wounded four times in the engagement, became the first Congressional Medal of Honor winner in Vietnam, while the other eight survivors were awarded two Distinguished Service Crosses, three Silver Stars and ten Purple Hearts among them. In Quang Tri, meanwhile, Major Floyd Thompson, also of Special Forces, had become the first American war prisoner when the South Vietnamese plane in which he was an observer was shot down below the Demilitarized Zone.

American plans to escalate the war, if it became necessary, continued to be made in Washington, stimulated by a larger development. Though Moscow and Peking might agree to attend a new Geneva Conference to discuss a matter of peripheral importance to them, their own hostile confrontation had passed beyond the hope of any political settlement. Premier Chou En-lai was therefore seeking alternatives. Through several channels — Pakistan, Romania, Canada, Japan and Indonesia — he let President Johnson know that Peking would like to explore the possibility of some sort of rapprochement. The Chinese were obviously worried by the ever-increasing number of Soviet troops on their long border. Chou emphasized that the only problem between China and the United States was the American role in Taiwan. He would welcome an American emissary. None was sent.

The Chinese proposal was instead taken in Washington as evidence that Peking was too preoccupied with the Russians to intervene in Vietnam if the United States escalated there. Vietnam would not be another Korea. When escalation did begin and the question arose publicly whether China would enter, it was because of Chou's secret overtures that Secretary Rusk was able to say confidently that she would not. In addition to China's worries about the Soviet Union, her internal problems, both economic and political, further diminished the possibility of intervention in Vietnam.

Though some in Congress and the news media were vigorously counseling "Americanization" of the war, other voices at home and abroad were raised against it. Walter Lippmann wrote that the United States should frankly admit its involvement was a mistake and "go to a conference." John S. Knight, in his chain of newspapers, declared editorially, "Vietnam: It Isn't Worth the Cost," explaining that "the white man is through in Asia, and there is nothing we can do to turn the rising tide of nationalism." De Gaulle again called for an end to all foreign intervention in Vietnam. In Saigon, however, General Khanh repeated his cry for the "liberation" of North Vietnam by invasion, and since he had no army good enough to try it he clearly meant an American invasion.

President Johnson's contingency planners changed their operative word from If to When. Daniel Ellsberg, a special assistant in the Pentagon to Deputy Defense Secretary John McNaughton, was shocked to discover "that there existed in our armed services people capable of writing on demand plans for the Nazi general staff, in fact writing plans for the genocide of entire nations." Ellsberg himself had been engaged in planning for nuclear war, which also entailed a certain degree of genocide, but his thinking had been brought down to more conventional levels by the growing strategic belief that the Russians might not be pursuing a first-strike capability after all. At any rate his shock evidently soon wore off, for he helped draw up plans for the invasion of North Vietnam, though he objected to bombing, and continued to serve the administration's Vietnam policy.

Counterinsurgency in Vietnam had died with Kennedy, if only because it had proved unsuccessful. The Johnson method was to seek the same end with a limited number of conventional American forces and the "restrained" use of the mightiest air power in the world. Once again the unwelcome advice of the CIA's National Intelligence Estimate intruded. This time it challenged the hallowed Domino Theory, which the President, an inveterate domino player himself, completely believed in, though if his brother Sam Houston Johnson is to be credited, he cheated at it.

With the possible exception of Cambodia, said the CIA, no other nation would "succumb" to Communism if both South Vietnam and Laos did. The President decided otherwise. "From all the evidence available to me," he wrote later, it seemed likely that "all of Southeast Asia would pass under Communist control" if the United States "let South Vietnam fall to Hanoi."

The contingency plans for war became reality on the night of August 2, when, according to the official account, the U.S. destroyer *Maddox* "on routine patrol in international waters" met "unprovoked" attack by torpedoes and gunfire from three North Vietnamese PT boats. The *Maddox* countered with her own gunfire, aided by the rockets and strafing attacks of four fighter planes called in from a nearby carrier.

In a twenty-one-minute engagement all three PT boats were damaged, one of them floundering dead in the water, the others retreating. No damage was taken by the *Maddox* except a half-inch bullet hole found later in the outside bulkhead of the after gun-director.

The news of the faraway encounter did not strike Washington as much to get excited about on a quiet August Sunday afternoon. The Pentagon's first reaction, as quoted by the New York *Times,* was that it was not "especially serious, certainly no major crisis." President Johnson in his memoirs said it was regarded as a possible local miscalculation by an "overeager" North Vietnamese commander. Who indeed would dare attack an American warship with full deliberation?

Aboard the *Maddox,* however, Captain John J. Herrick regarded continuation of his patrol "an unacceptable risk" and so advised Washington. He received orders to "make passes" at the North Vietnamese shore by daylight, then retreat at night. At the Tonkin Gulf maritime location called Yankee Station the *Maddox* was joined by another destroyer, the *C. Turner Joy.* They resumed the patrol together, Herrick informing the *Joy*'s skipper that North Vietnam "has thrown down the gauntlet and now considers itself at war with the United States. It is felt they will attack U.S. forces on sight, with no regard for cost."

What happened next, according to the official version, was that while "cruising in company on routine patrol in international waters about sixty-five miles from nearest land" the two American warships were set upon by an "undetermined number of North Vietnamese PT boats" in "a second deliberate attack." The Pentagon reported "at least two sunk" of the attacking craft and two others damaged by fire from the destroyers and assisting carrier-launched planes.

Even before the new attack was authenticated, and in the face of serious reason to doubt it had ever taken place, the President told Secretaries Rusk and McNamara and McGeorge Bundy at a White House meeting that Hanoi must be punished. It only remained to decide how and how much.

The Pentagon's National Military Command Center was activated. The Joint Chiefs of Staff met, and so did the National Security Council. The President also called in sixteen key congressmen to tell them an air attack on North Vietnam had been decided upon. As soon as he received confirmation of it he appeared suddenly on the nation's television screens at 11:37 P.M. to declare solemnly that "air action is now in execution." American planes were striking at five targets in North Vietnam. As later reported, in sixty-four sorties against four PT-boat bases and an oil storage depot, twenty-five boats were damaged and two American planes lost and two damaged.

The President in his remarks mentioned the support of his Republican opponent in the campaign, Senator Barry Goldwater, nominated three weeks before. Then Secretary McNamara came on the television screen to give a Pentagon midnight news conference the details of the Tonkin Gulf battle, with pointer and charts. He described what had happened as "continuous torpedo attack."

Captain Herrick of the *Maddox* had already in effect denied what the President and Defense Secretary stated as fact. After his first flashed report of an attack the destroyer's skipper radioed that "many reported contacts and torpedoes fired appear doubtful." He blamed "freak weather effects and overeager sonar-man." There had been "no visual sighting" of any hostile craft, and unlike the August 2 incident no interception of any messages. Herrick suggested "complete evaluation before any further action."

The order for action had already gone out. Washington bristled with the feeling, "Hell, they're shooting at the American Flag. They can't get away with this." Planes from the carriers *Ticonderoga* and *Constellation* put North Vietnam under direct American fire for the first time. Naval Lieutenant Everett Alvarez, Jr., of San Jose, California, became the first of nearly six hundred American war prisoners in North Vietnam — Major Thompson was held by the NLF in South Vietnam — when he was shot down in the raids. Another pilot, also downed, was presumed dead.

Even if error had been made in the Tonkin Gulf it could not be admitted. At the start of a political campaign in which the President's opponent would be depicted as "trigger-happy" because, for one thing, he had casually spoken of defoliation by atomic weapons, how could the commander-in-chief be revealed as having panicked over the equivalent of a flock of geese on radar? So the Tonkin Gulf incident, if not a Pearl Harbor, became the battleship *Maine* of the longest war in American history.

More contingency plans were executed as Secretary Rusk the next day spoke of North Vietnam's "lack of rationality." McNamara told the joint Senate Foreign Relations and Armed Services committees of a quick American buildup. An attack carrier group was on the way to the Western

Pacific. Fighter-bombers and interceptors were flying to Vietnam, bombers to Thailand, bombers and interceptors to Pacific advance bases, an anti-submarine force was going to the South China Sea. Army and Marine units were being alerted. At the Pentagon Daniel Ellsberg, waiting for further reports from the Tonkin Gulf, was struck by "a readiness, a strong eagerness" of the American command for reprisals.

Radio Hanoi, which had admitted a sea encounter on August 2, and claimed victory in it, denied any further combat as "a sheer fabrication." And in truth, aboard the *Maddox* and *Joy* it had become increasingly evident that the tense expectation of an attack had created the belief it was actually taking place. The destroyers had fired at invisible targets as the *Maddox* rookie sonar-man reported torpedo after torpedo, twenty-two in all, coming out of the darkness from all sides. The *Joy*'s veteran sonar-man heard no torpedoes, though he was supposedly in the midst of them. What the *Maddox* really recorded were the sudden sharp turns of her own rudder.

The two destroyers not only fought a battle with ghosts but came to the point of fighting each other. Toward dawn, *Maddox*'s radarscope gun control received orders from the bridge to fire at a radar contact, "a nice fat blip." He was about to do so when a dread thought came to him and he held fire to ascertain the location of *Joy*. The *Maddox* bridge asked the sister ship to turn on her lights. There, fifteen hundred yards from *Maddox*'s guns and right in their cross-hairs, was the target, *Joy*, herself. She would have been blown out of the water.

The tension eased. *Maddox* crewmen began asking, "What are we shooting at? What is going on?" First light showed no evidence that a desperately joined battle had taken place. There was no debris, no oil slick, no life preservers, no survivors, only water, water everywhere.

In the eighteenth century England fought the War of Jenkins' Ear against Spain, provoked in commercial rivalry when Spanish coast guards boarded a British merchantman off Havana in search of contraband and allegedly tore off the ear of its captain. Jenkins himself displayed a bottle with an ear in it in the House of Commons, and though some members called it a hoax and said removal of his wig would have shown that Jenkins had never lost his own ear, eagerness for revenge and trade aroused Britons to a conflict which they carried into the much more important War of the Austrian Succession.

In the Tonkin Gulf the United States began a war against North Vietnam over an unsubstantiated attack and actual damage of one scarred bulkhead. Even that became suspect when the caliber of the bullet indicated that it came not from a North Vietnamese patrol boat but from one of the American strafing planes of the *Ticonderoga*. Senator Goldwater, an ardent hawk, seemed privately to regard the entire Tonkin Gulf affair as suspect, though he never said so publicly. What might have been called the War of *Maddox*'s Bullet Hole, carried into the much larger war of the South Vietnamese Succession, was in dismal truth the War of Johnson's Face.

Still, even if there had been no attack on August 4, there was no doubt of the incident of August 2. Hanoi boasted of it. Had the North Vietnamese really lost their rationality, as Secretary Rusk said, to seek combat with the world's greatest power, and open "unprovoked attack" in "international waters" on an American ship cruising on "routine patrol"?

It was not a routine patrol in international waters. The *Maddox* was not an ordinary destroyer but an electronic intelligence ship, the first of several American espionage craft to run into trouble. Her mission was to conduct surveillance of North Vietnamese coastal activity and installations, monitor radar transmitters, and provide navigational information about channels, buoys and tides. Further orders were to "stimulate North Vietnamese and Chicom [Chinese Communist] electronic reaction." The destroyer came as close to the North Vietnamese coast as was deemed safe, and in what Hanoi claimed as territorial waters.

Most pertinent to the Tonkin Gulf affair, the attack on the *Maddox* was not unprovoked. A 34-A operation had begun July 31 and a De Soto patrol August 1, and as the two came together the North Vietnamese acted against the latter in the belief it was connected with the former. They had good reason to draw this conclusion. North Vietnamese islands had been bombarded on the night of July 31 by South Vietnamese craft, as Hanoi complained to the International Control Commission. South Vietnamese gunboats leaving the scene passed the *Maddox* going in the other direction. Discovered in the vicinity of the attack, *Maddox* could be drawing North Vietnamese patrol boats away from the fleeing South Vietnamese craft. The destroyer was obviously held to be a legitimate target. Confirmation came from Captain Herrick. *Maddox*'s interception of North Vietnamese messages on August 2 prompted his report to Washington that "DRV considers patrol directly involved with 34-A ops."

It is not quite fair to say that the Tonkin Gulf incident was entirely manufactured, though it came to be seen as the epitome of the deception that many Americans believed had been systematically practiced by their government. The most dispassionate assessment must be that while it could not be proved that the second attack on the *Maddox* and C. *Turner Joy* had not been made, neither was it proved that it had been, and the burden of proof lay on the administration.

Lyndon Johnson, in any case, was at last able to take the draft of Bill Bundy's Tonkin Gulf Resolution out of his pocket. It was reworded, and on August 7 the Senate passed by a vote of 88 to 2 — Morse of Oregon and Gruening of Alaska opposing; such future critics of Vietnam policy as Church, Mansfield, McGovern and Gore supporting — a measure which Fulbright, its floor manager, agreed gave the President "advance authority to take whatever action he deems necessary." The Arkansan denied there had been any American provocation, though Morse had disclosed the fact of the South Vietnamese strike against North Vietnamese islands, and said that *Maddox* had come "within six to eleven miles offshore." Morse further declared that the American reprisal bombing of North Vietnam was "an act of war, not an act of self-defense."

The Tonkin Gulf Resolution read: "Congress approves and supports the determination of the President as commander-in-chief to take all necessary measures to repel any armed attack against the forces of the United States and to prevent further aggression." Fulbright acknowledged that this could mean the landing of large American armies "in Vietnam or in China" and that he did not know "what the limits are." The air strikes against North Vietnam, he declared, were "appropriate as policy as well as justified in law," especially against a regime "which has been engaged in consistent and repeated aggression against its neighbor states." The chairman of the Foreign Relations Committee calmed the doubts of those who feared the authority being given the President was too sweeping, or that the man who had served so long on Capitol Hill himself might fail to consult with Congress on future steps.

August 7, 1964, was the day J. William Fulbright would forever rue. Later he led senatorial criticism of the Tonkin Gulf Resolution and ascribed his own advocacy of it to "the emotions that naturally arose." Support for the President's leadership jumped after Tonkin Gulf from 42 to 72 percent in the Harris Poll, while 85 percent approved of the air strikes against North Vietnam, and 66 percent favored taking the war into the North on the ground. Other opinion polls showed that the President had the American public's overwhelming support for virtually any Vietnam policy he thought correct. The reprisal raids brought praise for Johnson from his campaign opponent Goldwater, from the returned Ambassador Lodge, and from Richard Nixon, who had not retired from politics after all.

Whether, instead of the Tonkin Gulf Resolution expressing the "sense" of the Senate, Johnson could have obtained a congressional declaration of war, enabling him to mobilize the Reserve and National Guard, to increase taxes and impose economic controls, cannot be adjudged. One certain factor was the fear that going to war against North Vietnam might also have been taken as a declaration of war against China, and even the nuclear-armed Soviet Union. There were other reasons for avoiding the constitutional path. A formal war, with mobilization, would have meant the curtailment of the "Great Society" so often spoken of by the man who considered himself Franklin D. Roosevelt's heir. Declared war against North Vietnam would have meant the end of the "War on Poverty" announced in the first Johnson State of the Union message in January, and jeopardized medical insurance, aid to education, and the Civil Rights and Voting Rights acts.

Already, in less than a year in office, Johnson had been able to achieve in domestic legislation what Kennedy could not. A month before the Tonkin Gulf Resolution he signed the Civil Rights Act of 1964, passed by the Senate after an eighty-three-day debate which included a sixty-seven-day filibuster by southern opponents. Not only racial but sex equality was written into the act, and though the latter was intended as a joke by southern congressmen and another delaying tactic, it became a foundation of what would be called the women's liberation movement, already given its Bible, a book called *The Feminine Mystique*, by Betty Friedan, magazine writer and mother of three.

The day after the Tonkin Gulf Resolution the Economic Opportunity Act was passed and the War on Poverty begun. The United States went into two incompatible wars at the same time, under the banners of its affluence and with the promise of both "guns and butter."

Poverty had not passed entirely unnoticed in the Kennedy administration, but there were stirring things in prospect like going to the moon and building more missiles. Though it was no news to the millions who endured it in rural slums, migrant labor camps and mountain valleys, as well as in the big cities, the knowledge of its full dimensions had come as a shock in 1962, when disclosed by Michael Harrington in his book *The Other America*.

Harrington wrote with a sense of outrage. Though poverty could be regarded as a relative matter — the poor in America were well-off compared with the millions of India or the Bantustans of South Africa — yet in terms of American resources, living standards, technology, aspirations and needs, poverty was not only an affliction, he felt, but a social evil.

Now, with considerable fanfare, the War on Poverty had been opened. The Great Society it was intended to help bring about "rests on abundance and liberty for all," the President declared. "It demands an end to poverty and racial injustice, to which we are totally committed in our time."

It also depended on peace and on confidence in the national leadership. There was the matter, for example, of the President's own protégé, whom he regarded almost as an adopted son: "Bobby" Baker, the Senate majority's secretary, who had taken advantage of economic opportunity and had conquered poverty by accumulating in nine years a fortune of $2,000,000 on a salary of less than $20,000. Baker served as concierge and private eye for the Senate Democrats, solicited campaign funds, shuffled committee assignments, and gave legislators, lobbyists and Army brass surcease from care at his hideaway club. The President himself was involved in the scandal that eventually sent Baker to prison after he loyally refused to answer questions about his connections. As senator, Johnson had received gifts of hi-fi sets from an insurance man, who also gave him a rebate on his policies by buying advertising on the Johnson broadcasting stations in Austin. Like the vicuña coat of the Eisenhower administration and the deepfreeze of the Truman administration, the Johnson hi-fi was an example of petty favors sullying high office.

Much more ominous were the portents for civil rights. Barely was the ink dry on the President's signature of the Civil Rights Act when Harlem, the prototype of northern black ghettos, erupted with rioting. The trouble began from a white police lieutenant's killing of a Harlem youth who allegedly drew a knife against him, but it ran much deeper. The rioting followed a street rally held by the Progressive Labor party calling for "revolution" at which the black speaker proclaimed that "we're going to have to kill a lot of these cops, a lot of these judges, and we'll have to go up against their army. We'll organize our own militia and our own army."

The Harlem riots of 1964 brought the Negro protest movement home to roost in the North, where there was as much racial discrimination as in the South, though not in the form of statutes and ordinances. The riots also joined civil rights with the Vietnam War, and not merely by the simultaneity of events, as in Birmingham and Hue the year before. The Maoist-influenced Progressive Labor party, active in urban matters, had also organized the May 2 Movement, named after antiwar demonstrations in New York City on that date, which had been broken up by mounted police and nightsticks. M2M issued the first "We Won't Go" statement, and looking about at the burgeoning New Left scene, the PLP set about trying to capture the campus dissidents who had joined the Students for a Democratic Society.

After Harlem there were outbreaks in Brooklyn, Jersey City, Chicago and Philadelphia, touched off by similar incidents but with their roots in job discrimination and lack of social opportunity. The problems of the northern cities had been increased by migration from the South, which made them increasingly black. But despite its new focus on the North the civil rights movement was possessed of continuing explosive force in the South: 1964 was another "Mississippi Summer," called "Freedom Summer" by SNCC, which led a registration drive in that state.

Three young civil rights workers, two of them northern whites, the third a southern black, were murdered in Mississippi, with the apparent complicity of local police authorities, since they had been turned over by deputy sheriffs to a mob, in old-style lynch fashion. The FBI found their bodies six weeks later buried in an earthen and concrete bridge, on the night the United States made its reprisal strikes for the Tonkin Gulf incident.

While young whites from the North helped to register blacks and poor whites in Mississippi, blacks in Alabama entered the electoral lists. In Lowndes County, with an 80 percent black population, they campaigned for local offices under the ballot symbol of a black panther, entered in opposition to the symbol of George Wallace's segregationist forces, the peculiarly apt white bantam rooster. The black panther had been the insignia of a Negro combat unit in the First World War.

Civil rights, poverty and the Vietnam War all were themes and issues in the 1964 presidential election campaign. College students returned to their campuses after their Mississippi "Freedom Summer" and took up antiwar and other causes, chief among them a group from the University of California at Berkeley. The Johnson administration moved from the Tonkin Gulf to the Atlantic City convention hall for the ceremony of nominating the President and Senator Hubert Humphrey of Minnesota as his running mate, in a hall where forty-foot-high portraits of Lyndon Johnson flanked the stage on both sides. Though Johnson received the delegates' votes, it was Robert Kennedy who received the cheers of the convention, if only out of sentiment for his dead brother.

The synthetic convention drama, the huge portraits, the overwhelming confidence in the President expressed by the Tonkin Gulf Resolution added up to a public image of forceful, resolute and righteous American leadership. Yet by his own account Johnson had in a fit of self-doubt before Atlantic City written out an announcement that he could not provide the grasp the country needed and was therefore withdrawing, allowing the convention to select its own nominee. Mrs. Johnson, he said, prevailed on him to stay on, until he carried out his intention four years later. No one at the Atlantic City convention, or outside it, would have been able to imagine such a withdrawal, or the President's disclaimer of personal ambition as he began a vigorous campaign against Barry Goldwater.

On the hustings, the Republican nominee sought the votes of those who opposed further attempts toward equality for the blacks. "In your heart you know he's right," read Goldwater billboards and television ads. The Arizonan, who had voted against the Civil Rights Act, spoke in the code words of the segregationists: "Law and Order," "Safety in the Streets," and "States' Rights." At the Republican convention in San Francisco he had thrilled his admirers and chilled many other Americans by his pronouncement that "extremism in the defense of liberty is no vice! . . . Moderation in the pursuit of justice is no virtue!"

"In your heart you know he's right" also appealed to those who thought North Vietnam could be "taken care of" on any Wednesday afternoon by the Strategic Air Command armed with nuclear weapons, though of course "small ones." The Republican platform of 1964 charged the Johnson administration with encouraging aggression "by appearing to set limits on America's willingness to act." Reprisals against North Vietnam were not enough for the Goldwaterites. Years later the Republican candidate declared that if elected he would have "ended the war in a month. I would have made North Vietnam look like a mud puddle."

In his acceptance speech Goldwater, besides extenuating extremism, held that "failure in the jungles of Vietnam . . . proclaims lost leadership, obscure purpose, weakening wills, and the risk of inciting our sworn enemies to new aggressions and to new excesses." Despite the lack of any declaration, "We are at war," he asserted unequivocally.

Johnson for his part conducted a "he is keeping us out of war" campaign that was not much different, in either content or deception, from Wilson's in 1916 and Roosevelt's in 1940. Escalation of the Vietnam War in order to win "victory" and save Lyndon Johnson from being "the first President to lose a war" was in the advanced planning stage, even as he time after time asserted, "We seek no wider war."

One of the television commercials used against Goldwater by the Democrats showed a small girl picking the petals from a daisy, in a kind of countdown which ended with a mushroom-shaped explosion. The voice of Lyndon Johnson was heard saying, "These are the stakes." The commercial was used only once, as Republicans protested its implications, though for these Goldwater himself was responsible. His disingenuous ways and vague manner of speaking had encouraged belief that he favored the use of nuclear defoliation; he did say it was a method that could be feasible against North Vietnamese supply lines in Laos, and while he declared he did not subscribe to it, he added that "times might change."

As passage of the Tonkin Gulf Resolution showed, Vietnam was not a true campaign issue, despite the rhetoric expended on it, because neither political party was thinking in any terms but those of continuing the intervention, though differing as to its extent and the methods used. While denouncing those who would "supply American boys to do the job that Asian boys should do," Johnson added, "Nor have I chosen to retreat and turn it [South Vietnam] over to the Communists." He explained to Bill Moyers, his press secretary, that people listened to only half of what he said.

"I did not mean that we were not going to do any fighting, for we had already lost many good men in Vietnam," he later elucidated in his memoirs. "We were not going to rush in and take over, but we were going to live up to the commitments we had made. . . . The American people knew what they were voting for in 1964. They knew Lyndon Johnson was not going to pull up stakes and run."

They could not know that he would send a total of 2,500,000 "American boys" to Vietnam during the four years of his second term. Neither could the President know. His authority and contingency plans allowed him virtually anything. His planners were ready at any time after the Tonkin

Gulf incident, or for that matter before it, to undertake Operation Rolling Thunder, the continuous bombing of North Vietnam. The CIA pointed out that Rolling Thunder would increase the insurgency, that North Vietnam would meet escalation with counterescalation, and fight on instead of yielding, but Walt Rostow thought Hanoi would have to succumb to a process of "slow squeeze."

McNamara's Assistant Secretary for International Security Affairs, John McNaughton, suggested that North Vietnam be provoked, as it had been in the Tonkin Gulf, into another attack so that "serious" retaliation could be taken, including the mining of harbors, and air strikes at industrial as well as military targets. The United States must demonstrate to the world, McNaughton said in one of his innumerable memoranda, that it would not be restrained by anything — "fear of illegality, of UN or neutral reaction, of domestic pressures, of American losses, of deploying U.S. ground forces in Asia, or war with China or Russia; of the use of nuclear weapons, etc." The "etc." was regarded by friends as a deft McNaughton touch. He was accounted a brilliant scenarist. Meanwhile, Ambassador Taylor and General Westmoreland in Saigon kept recommending air strikes against North Vietnam because of an approaching Communist victory in South Vietnam.

Two days before the election the American air base at Bien Hoa, fifteen miles from Saigon, was hit by guerrilla mortar attack. Four American soldiers were killed and five big B-57 bombers were destroyed on the ground and eight damaged. The blow was considerably more severe than that in the Tonkin Gulf, but the candidate of reason and restraint did not respond in November as he had in August, despite the urging of his advisers.

As a result of the attack on Bien Hoa the Joint Chiefs of Staff, who did not have to be reelected, recommended a three-day air blitz of North Vietnam with night bombing by the new B-52's from Guam, followed by day bombing by carrier-based planes. They also wanted air strikes in Laos, the landing of Marines at Danang, an airlift of troops from Okinawa to Saigon, South Vietnamese air force action in the South, and the evacuation of American dependents. It was "the works." The Pentagon was saying, "We have all these contingency plans in this drawer. Now's the time to use them."

The time was not yet. On Election Day Lyndon Johnson, as the man of both peace and determination, following the middle course of moderation between "all-out" and "pull-out," won the greatest popular majority in American history: 61 percent of the vote. Senator Goldwater carried only five southern states and his own Arizona.

As Kennedy told Mike Mansfield he would have done after winning reelection, Johnson had the ostensible option after receiving his huge mandate of cutting American losses in Vietnam — 1964 recorded 146 more

American dead and 1,038 wounded — and ending the involvement. The disintegrating situation in South Vietnam could conceivably have provided the opportunity for departure. He saw it instead as not in the nature of the American Presidency to "cut and run," incurring the inevitable backlash of the Goldwater-minded, and charges of the "loss of Vietnam." Elected in his own right, Lyndon Johnson more than ever was not going to be "the first American President to lose a war."

The bold guerrilla foray against Bien Hoa demonstrated two things, the inadequacy of the Saigon government's control of territory, and the acknowledgment that since the Americans were increasingly taking over the war they also had to take the consequences.

The American reaction to the Tonkin Gulf affair briefly shored up the Khanh regime, encouraging the general to declaim "To the North!" even more loudly, but in trying to strengthen his position Khanh succeeded only in overreaching himself. He declared a national emergency, with press censorship and stricter government controls, and set aside the draft for a new and more liberal constitution to replace Diem's, proposing his own authoritarian one. He too called himself President; his opponents called him dictator. Buddhists and students again joined in protest demonstrations. Khanh gave way and formed a triumvirate composed of himself, the same "Big" Minh he had displaced, and General Tran Thien Khiem, the Defense Minister. The dissidents were not satisfied, and street fighting broke out in Saigon and Danang, with Buddhist youth groups battling young Catholics, while others evidently in the services of the NLF provoked both sides into clashes with the police. In two days of violence seventeen persons were killed and fifty injured.

The other generals then attempted a coup against Khanh and troops under their various commands held some parts of the capital. The flashy young commander of the air force, Nguyen Cao Ky, who for three years had led missions over North Vietnam, sent his planes over Saigon instead in support of Khanh and threatened to bomb the rival generals' positions. Ky thereby emerged as a political factor in South Vietnam.

After the failure of the coup and as Lyndon Johnson was being elected, another gambit was tried in Saigon. Khanh stepped down for a nominal civilian regime headed by Tran Van Huong, former schoolteacher, ex-Viet Minh soldier and mayor of the city. Behind the scenes the generals retained their power and Khanh continued as commander-in-chief. Premier Huong did no better than his predecessors in uniform, though Washington increased its aid to $45 million monthly and financed another enlargement of ARVN from 615,000 to 715,000. The "hard-core" NLF, including those returned from the North, were meanwhile estimated at 30,000 to 40,000 combatants.

The National Security Council had recommended, and President Johnson approved, "slow-squeeze" bombing to "hurt Hanoi," Rostow's formula seeking to answer Ambassador Taylor's plea "to change the tide which is running against us." The options presented to the NSC by McGeorge Bundy were three: reprisal air strikes plus destroyer patrols and coastal raids, as before; uninterrupted bombing until Hanoi agreed to "negotiate"; and the aerial "slow-squeeze." As always, any suggestion of a fourth course, de-escalation or disengagement, was excluded. Under Secretary George Ball, the "official" dove of the administration, was the only one to vote for the first option, not being moved by moral or legalistic qualms, he explained, but only by practical doubts about the efficiency of bombing. He had been a director of the Strategic Bombing Survey made after World War II and was familiar with exaggerated claims for air power. In the end the President approved the first option for thirty days, then the third. It was estimated that the "slow-squeeze" air war would last two to six months, by which time Hanoi would yield.

Another step taken by Johnson to widen the war while publicly reiterating that he advocated "no wider war" was to seek allies in the Indochina venture. "We want your flag" in Vietnam to prove it was not an American colonial war, he told two British correspondents in anticipation of the Washington visit of the new Prime Minister, Laborite Harold Wilson. There should be 300 to 400 Britons in Vietnam and "an aircraft squadron or two," the President declared. A few days later he told Wilson he would even settle for "a company of bagpipers." The British leader, with a parliamentary majority of a bare three votes, provided only moral support, but Australia and New Zealand, closer to the scene, later sent small contingents to Vietnam.

Hanoi's Prime Minister, Pham Van Dong, had meanwhile been visiting Moscow, attending the Bolshevik November 7 celebration. Nikita Khrushchev had been replaced by Leonid Brezhnev as party leader and Alexei Kosygin as Premier, but all the same, after the Tonkin Gulf reprisal, Moscow could not stand idly by and had to provide aid to North Vietnam if only in rivalry with Peking. Before long, American pilots were being shot down by Soviet-supplied antiaircraft weapons. The sundered Sino-Soviet bloc was thus in a sense re-created for the ad hoc purpose of helping North Vietnam. At this point history may have decided that the war would not be won by the United States because the two big Communist powers, despite their mutual enmity, would not let it be won.

The Huong "civilian" regime in Saigon lasted three months, until new riots by the Buddhists broke out against it. Then the military forced the Premier to bring into his government both Ky and Thieu, and two other uniformed "young Turks." The situation in Saigon was reported so pessimistically by two RAND Corporation analysts, who had interviewed captured guerrillas and found in them a deep commitment, that John

McNaughton in the Pentagon declared, whether seriously or in jest (one never knew), "If what you say is true, we're fighting on the wrong side." McNaughton was the enigmatic one on McNamara's staff. A former Harvard Law School professor, he had on the one hand been general counsel of the Defense Department, and on the other Averell Harriman's aide in the 1963 nuclear test ban negotiations in Moscow. He had a wry wit, but, as happens in bureaucracy, it was largely lost on his superiors.

A few days before Christmas Ambassador Taylor met with American correspondents in Saigon for a year-end summation. "The fighting is going on, on four fronts — the government versus the generals, the Buddhists versus the government, the generals versus the ambassador, and I hope the generals versus the VC." On Christmas Eve the American billet called Brinks Hotel was blown up by guerrillas in the heart of Saigon, and two GI's were killed and fifty-eight injured. Taylor and the Pentagon urged a strong response. The President refused again. No one except himself could know whether he was indecisive, fearful or merely being patient. In the week after Christmas the South Vietnamese army and marines suffered heavy casualties in recapturing the village of Binh Gia, southeast of Saigon, and five Americans were killed and three taken prisoner.

Johnson proceeded with the plans for the air war on the evident assumption it would be generally accepted as less repugnant than ground war, but he surrounded his intentions with secrecy. When he was asked at press conferences about the new decisions which had become the subject of thick rumors, he fended questions off. He refused the NSC suggestion that he make a television report, and chose also not to brief any congressional leaders. It was all very different from August 4 and the Tonkin Gulf. Untypically, Johnson had become uncertain. The only administration consensus he had was on the principle of wider action. The chiefs of staff frankly did not think the President's bombing plan went far enough; they would never think so, even as the bombing increased. Richard Nixon was among those urging that the Air Force and Navy be sent against North Vietnam to destroy staging areas and installations. The President hesitated. He was resolved and at the same time cautious, committed and at the same time equivocal. He was a man prepared to embark on something he felt he had to do, without exactly knowing why.

George Ball, in a lengthy memorandum to Rusk, McNamara and Bundy, had in October expanded his pragmatic arguments against escalation. "Once on the tiger's back," he wrote, "we cannot be sure of picking the place to dismount." Ball opposed American ground action, fearing the "heavy loss of American lives in the rice paddies and jungles." He also foresaw home-front opposition to the war. "The frustrations and anxieties that marked the latter phase of the Korean struggle would be recalled and revived — and multiplied in intensity." Ball proposed a peaceful settlement without bombing North Vietnam "to the conference table," preferably through an international meeting, and pleaded that Southeast Asia policy be looked at in the light of "our total world situation."

There was no mention of the alternative that was always ignored, American disengagement. Still, Ball had spoken up, even though he did not resign, as a British Under Secretary might have done. His warning was withheld from the President by Secretary Rusk because of the elections. It reached Johnson's desk in January. By that time the sands of indecision had run out.

After his overwhelming election victory Johnson was able to sever the sentimental cord that in the public eye bound him to the Kennedys; in actuality it had never been more than an uncomfortable relationship of political expediency on both sides. Robert Kennedy, rejected by Johnson for the vice-presidential nomination, had left the administration and been elected senator, a separate and rival political command. Kennedy retainers departed from the White House. Though painfully aware of the invidious comparisons made between him and the Kennedys, Johnson had done what John Kennedy had not been able to do, achieved the passage of important social legislation. Now he could outdo his predecessor on the world stage. Kennedy had backed down the Russians in the Cuban missile crisis. Johnson, having been given the opportunity, would back down both China and the Soviet Union in Vietnam. He would end the Vietnam War, by winning it.

The NLF attack on the American base at Pleiku in February brought into operation the secret war plans nurtured over so many months. At Pleiku in the central highlands the United States suffered its sharpest blow since the intervention began, losing 9 dead and 140 wounded. The time had come to end a situation, the President said, in which Americans fought with one hand tied behind their backs.

"They are killing our men while they sleep in the night," he said to the congressional leaders he finally called in to announce retaliatory air attacks. Over several days these numbered 267 sorties which hit 491 targets, including staging areas, barracks and military buildings in North Vietnam. The bombing was done not only by forty-five American planes from the carriers *Coral Sea* and *Hancock*, but by South Vietnamese planes led by Air Force Marshal Ky.

Operation Flaming Dart, as it was called, destroyed only 47 of its 491 targets and damaged 22, not a very good record, but the military action was dwarfed by its political implications. Despite his professed feelings about bombing, George Ball appeared in a news conference with Secretary McNamara to defend it. "It's very important they understand the strength of the American purpose," he explained. Richard Nixon hailed the bombing and called for bipartisan support of it. Antibombing feeling was also mobilizing. A protest demonstration was held at the United Nations building in New York and students at Rutgers University gathered on the campus to express their opposition.

The attack on Pleiku was from all indications a local action by the NLF, a military tactic involving a mere ten mortars and less than a company of men. General Giap in Hanoi may not even have been aware of it. Both McNamara and UN Ambassador Adlai Stevenson charged North Vietnam with direct responsibility, however, and there was no doubt in the White House that the Pleiku attack, the third in three months on American installations, was a deliberate political decision "directed probably from Hanoi," perhaps from Peking, to frighten the United States out of South Vietnam. It had to be met by another political decision, to institute not retaliatory but methodical and continuing air bombardment of North Vietnam. Operation Rolling Thunder was mounted, to begin in two weeks' time.

Presidential adviser McGeorge Bundy was in Saigon when the Pleiku attack came. With General Westmoreland and the South Vietnamese commander-in-chief, General Khanh, he flew to the scene and got his first bloody sight of American war casualties, visiting the wounded in the field hospital at Nhatrang. The White House aide was described in a news dispatch as "hatless, tense and pale," and he viewed the attack as a defiance which could not pass unmet. When he returned to Washington he was less presidential option-keeper and more protagonist than ever. The administration described the Pleiku raid as an "additional affront" because it took place during Bundy's visit to South Vietnam.

The Russians also had an "additional affront" to complain of. Kosygin, the new Soviet Premier, was in Hanoi when bombs from Operation Flaming Dart dropped nearby. As part of the sober new Kremlin leadership which succeeded the theatrical Khrushchev, he was hoping to meet the American President, and two days before the bombing Johnson said he would like to go to Moscow. Kosygin may have been in Hanoi asserting Soviet influence against the Chinese, for he came with a large delegation weighted on the economic side. He may have been there, as UN Secretary U Thant said, to try to mediate an end to a dangerous situation which had spread from the Tonkin Gulf to Communist soil and could grow into a Great Power confrontation. If Soviet mediation was the aim, it was ended by the American bombing. Moscow and Hanoi signed a mutual aid treaty.

A few days after Pleiku the American barracks at Qui Nonh were blown up with twenty-three dead, and 160 American planes were sent over North Vietnam in further retribution.

The flare-up of unmistakable war action raised some apprehension in the Senate of the perennial nightmare: mass engagement in a ground conflict on the Asian continent. Some newspapers called for negotiations, keyed to the supposed Soviet mediation effort, but Republican Senators like Dirksen of Illinois and Saltonstall of Massachusetts declared negotiations would be tantamount to "the white flag." The State Department rejected a French offer to aid in arranging talks. Secretary McNamara told a House committee that the United States could not leave Vietnam because China was making that country the "decisive" test in the rivalry with the Soviet Union, to prove the efficacy of violence. The situation in Vietnam, he declared, was "grave but not hopeless."

The well-informed Hanson Baldwin, military affairs expert of the New York *Times*, anticipated the need for American ground forces of "perhaps 200,000 to one million" in South Vietnam, to fight a war and not merely advise, to provide security for American installations, to make more and heavier continuous air and sea attacks on North Vietnam, and to hold territory as well as clear it. Baldwin gave the stereotyped reason why. It was better to fight the Communists in Vietnam, "on China's doorstep," than a few years later in Hawaii, "on our own frontiers." Other hawks were in full cry. Richard Nixon, perhaps already campaigning for 1968, said the United States was "losing the war" and would be "thrown out" of Southeast Asia unless air and naval action was increased despite any risk of conflict with China. Any negotiation, he added, would be "surrendering on the installment plan."

Not all Americans were for war. The day after Baldwin's views appeared Walter Lippmann, in a television interview, described the bombings of North Vietnam as "political" and "public relations jobs" rather than military, with no evidence that "they killed anybody, because what we bomb is wooden sheds." If sustained heavy bombing was ordered, Lippmann thought, the North Vietnamese army would move into South Vietnam, and this would lead to demands for American ground troops to meet them. What then? he was asked. "At first, if the war hawks prevail and we become involved in a big war, they will rejoice, but in the end the people will weep."

From the Pentagon itself came one unconventional statement of American objectives. Assistant Secretary McNaughton saw the aim as 70 percent to avoid a humiliating defeat, 20 percent to keep South Vietnam from Chinese hands, 10 percent to permit the people of South Vietnam to enjoy a better life. Also, he thought, "to emerge from crisis without unacceptable taint from methods used."

Before Operation Rolling Thunder was unleashed U Thant made a final appeal for negotiations. "I am sure that the American people, if only they knew the true facts and the background of the development in South Vietnam, would agree with me that further bloodshed is unnecessary. . . . As you know, in times of war and hostilities, the first casualty is truth." His reference was to the Soviet mediation efforts, aborted by bombing, and to his own attempts to get an American–North Vietnamese meeting in Rangoon, which Johnson had rejected. George Ball answered for the administration, telling the Secretary General that he was "naive."

The official case for large-scale American air war against "aggression from the North" was made in a State Department White Paper, which declared that North Vietnamese regular forces were in South Vietnam in estimated regimental strength. Senator Mansfield later set the total figure at 400, in the South Vietnamese insurgency force of 140,000.

Whatever other reasons there were or that might be provided for the bombing of North Vietnam, perhaps it all came down in the end to the fact, as the Pentagon Papers disclosed, that it had not been tried yet, and there was a "lack of alternative proposals." Even those who believed it would not succeed thought it at least worth trying.

It was time for the Air Force to take over. The first day of Operation Rolling Thunder, scheduled for February 20, had to be postponed at the last moment by political turmoil in South Vietnam. The generals were still fighting the government in Saigon, though four of them had been added to Premier Huong's cabinet, and anti-Huong, anti-general and anti-American demonstrations led by the Buddhists demanded "Vietnam for the Vietnamese!" Trade unions went on strike in Hue and Danang. The U.S. Information Services library in Hue was sacked and burned, while 200 protesters were arrested at the American Embassy in Saigon and 30 wounded in street fighting there. To satisfy the Buddhists General Khanh was reseated as Premier by the Armed Forces Council in place of Huong. Khanh no longer satisfied the American Embassy, however, from fear that under Buddhist influence even he might seek peace with the NLF, and he was in turn made to step down in favor of Phan Huy Quat, a medical doctor and leader of the Dai Viet nationalist party. But the generals still controlled. They named Nguyen Van Thieu not only Defense Minister but Deputy Premier.

Because of the continuing confusion in Saigon, Ambassador Taylor asked that the bombing of North Vietnam be postponed a week. Then bad weather set in. On March 2, with a first strike by 104 U.S. Air Force planes, Rolling Thunder finally began.

It was a failure from the start. In an aerial parallel to the "body count" of ground combat, the emphasis in Rolling Thunder was arithmetical. The number of sorties was in effect its own objective, so pilots used the shortest routes in order to be able to drop their bombs and return for second loads. These regular routes were quickly lined by North Vietnamese anti-aircraft guns, resulting in a high loss of American planes and the capture of many pilots. Though the sortie totals pleased both the Pentagon and the pilots, who won service ratings and promotions based upon them, the "hurry-up" tactics also led to extremely poor accuracy. Japanese correspondents in Hanoi reported civilian targets hit in daylight raids, including schools, churches and hospitals. Their accounts shocked Japan, which had also experienced American bombs dropped on Asians, up to the ultimate two. The State Department was in turn furious at the Japanese reaction.

The Japanese had raised the question of American "image" rather than American intentions. As John McNaughton put it, the United States must be seen in Southeast Asia as a "good doctor." "We must have kept promises, been tough, taken risks, gotten bloodied, and hurt the enemy badly." No doubt could ever be given to any nation "regarding American policy, power, resolve and competence." That was the image the United States had now begun to pursue. The cost would be enormous.

A few weeks before Rolling Thunder began, the twentieth century's most familiar symbol of empire had passed into history. Winston Churchill had known, possessed and relished the appurtenances of imperial power in the long span from Tommy Atkins and the Fuzzy-Wuzzies to nuclear missiles. His state funeral was symbolic of imperial sunset. Britain had gone from East of Suez. But the United States had now fully embarked on Asiatic adventure.

7

THE YEARS OF THE HAWK

As the forces of war went into combat in Vietnam, so did the antiwar forces in the United States. Even before Operation Rolling Thunder hundreds of college teachers signed an open letter on behalf of a negotiated settlement. A demonstration in New York led by the Reverend A. J. Muste, a veteran pacifist, resulted in the arrest of fourteen persons, and a few days later thirteen more were arrested in another New York protest. The same day students picketed the White House. It was not the first sign of student unrest and activism.

The American campus was seeded with revolt when those who had spent the "Freedom Summer" of 1964 in Mississippi returned to their colleges and looked about for other causes. The University of California at Berkeley led the way with the Free Speech movement, triggered by rules against campus enlistment in off-campus matters, such as racial job discrimination in San Francisco across the bay.

The Free Speech sit-in and resulting melee, in which 814 Berkeley students were arrested, were not really concerned with a four-letter Anglo-Saxon word which was known to practically everyone above the age of six and could not have shocked the university chancellor or the state's regents, not to mention the police.

Beneath the Free Speech waves deep currents ran. Clark Kerr, the Berkeley president, had stated the issue in the Godkin Lectures at Harvard the year before, when he deplored the replacement of the university by the "multiversity." The Berkeley students, taking him at his word, and assailing the bureaucratization of education, complained of loss of individual identity, assembly-line teaching, computerized curricula, overcrowded classrooms, overconcentration on research, and "diploma-ism." They carried signs reading "I am a human being. Do not fold, bend, spindle or mutilate." Mario Savio, the twenty-two-year-old philosophy student who emerged as spokesman, explained matters. "There's a time when the operation of the machine becomes so odious, makes you so sick at heart, that you can't take part. You can't even tacitly take part. And you've got to put your bodies upon the gears and upon the wheels, upon the levers, upon all the apparatus, and you've got to make it stop." One of Savio's followers was a brilliant young student named Jerry Rubin.

The rebellion was dramatic, it was emotional, and it may have been the first notable public example of group therapy. It was nonetheless a clear challenge, not only to the "knowledge factory" but to the "military-industrial complex" that American colleges had come increasingly to serve in the nuclear age, and thus to the "System" and to the war in which the System was engaging itself. Rusk, McNamara, Bundy and Rostow, the President's war council, it was remarked, were all former college teachers.

The 1964 election campaign had left its impress on the campus. What happened at Berkeley was clearly not to Barry Goldwater's liking, but his campaign issues of the War, the Flag, and Crime in the Streets conveyed the message that the United States was in a moral crisis. While not translated into votes because of fears where "extremism" might lead, the Goldwater themes reflected a growing feeling by many Americans that their affluent society had somehow gone astray. The young especially were affected, those who had grown up with "the Bomb" and responded to the manifesto of the SDS. They did not seek a return to the Good Old Days, as Goldwater did. They listened to the philosopher Herbert Marcuse instead. When the Free Speech movement at Berkeley found itself accused of violating the principles of free speech in its opposition to Navy enlisting booths, the ROTC, and campus recruitment by defense contractors, there was Marcuse to give reply, teaching that one's intolerance of opposition views had nothing to do with the demand for tolerance of one's own views. Free Speech was intended for those with whom you agreed.

Other influences swelled the malcontent tide on the campus. Pop Culture continued to enunciate political protest. Bob Dylan, Tom Paxton and others who sang about the state of affairs were no longer satisfied to lament but asked the reasons why. The Beatles, emerging from their Liverpool cellar, had been launched on their Midas-like careers of music and money-making with songs that at first said "I Want to Hold Your Hand" and "She Loves You, Yeah-yeah-yeah," and turned into "Give Peace a Chance" and a supposed paean to the drug LSD, "Lucy in the Sky with Diamonds."

Drugs were not only sung about but widely used. Dr. Timothy Leary, dismissed from Harvard for his hallucinogenic drug experiments, "set up a scene" in New York State, a commune of the young where his League for Spiritual Discovery, with its significant initials, created "good, laughing people" who were "turned on." Leary's colleague at Harvard, Dr. Richard Alpert, solicited youth in another way. Having experienced the numerous varieties of chemical elevation, he embraced metaphysics. Soon he called himself Baba Ram Dass.

The revulsion of a large part of American middle-class youth toward the Vietnam War may have come in some degree because it offended their idealism and moral sense. As it continued and widened, it also, and perhaps more germanely, became a personal threat. To be drafted now could mean to fight, and perhaps die or be wounded.

The continuous bombing of North Vietnam was widely condemned in the college press, from Berkeley on the left to the University of Texas on the right. Not all of those going to school, however, opposed the war. So anxious to enter upon military careers leading to Vietnam were 105 cadets at the Air Force Academy that they cheated in their exams and were dismissed. The cadets had been reckoned the best of American youth by many who compared them with the students at Berkeley, and the *National Observer*, published by Dow Jones of Wall Street, said they should not be blamed, considering the example of their elders. Crime statistics showed a phenomenal growth in shoplifting by "respectable" people and teenagers in affluent suburbs, in embezzlement and other "white-collar" offenses, and in police and municipal corruption.

Escalation of the war in Vietnam was matched by escalation of the civil rights conflict at home. Martin Luther King, after his return from Oslo where he had received the Nobel Peace Prize for his earlier activities, entered Alabama with his Southern Christian Leadership Conference to join a voting registration drive begun by the young enthusiasts of the Student Nonviolent Coordinating Committee, under their black panther sign from the Lowndes County election campaign. The focal point was the small city of Selma, a cotton center of earlier days. There civil rights groups assembled to march the fifty-four miles to Montgomery, the state capital, where Governor George Wallace held sway. King and other black clergymen were joined by white clergy of all denominations, including Roman Catholic priests and nuns.

The march to Montgomery was seized by history. Deputy sheriffs and mounted state troopers set upon it with clubs and tear gas as it crossed the Selma city line. Shown on television as a clear picture of peaceableness assailed by unprovoked brutality, the incident at Pettus Bridge was widely viewed as another Concord. Though Sheriff Jim Clark, whose deputies had beaten up the marchers, said they were "one-quarter Communist and one-half pro-Communist," thousands of protesters, black and white and of every political stripe, streamed into Selma from all parts of the country, and under the protection of federalized and obviously reluctant National

Guardsmen — and with full live coverage by network television cameras — the two-day march to Montgomery was successfully completed. It had been transformed by police violence from a small local occurrence into something of an armageddon, as the New York *Times* saw it, between "a reactionary racist cause" and the southern Negro's struggle for "rights by legal peaceful means." Governor Wallace kept himself inside the Capitol, beneath his Confederate flag, while speeches were made and songs sung outside, particularly a quiet but powerful hymn "We Shall Overcome," which resounded throughout the nation, by television. Selma was the direct cause of another notable piece of Great Society legislation, the Voting Rights Act of 1965, and when President Johnson proposed it in person to a joint session of Congress he feelingly exclaimed, "And we *shall* overcome."

He meant not only in Alabama but in Southeast Asia. Johnson provided troops to protect civil rights at the same time that he sent troops to Vietnam. To him the two actions were part of the same whole; he was fostering self-determination for American blacks and Asian yellows alike.

On the same day that violence broke out in Selma, undisguised American combat troops arrived in Vietnam. On the same beach at Danang, where Marines had landed 120 years before to rescue persecuted Catholics, the Ninth Marine Expeditionary Brigade from Okinawa came ashore, to succor the hard-pressed regime in Saigon. Operation Rolling Thunder had not prevented continuing NLF gains on South Vietnamese soil.

The Americans already in place, though some had known combat, were still officially advisers and trainers. They included the green-bereted Special Forces, military police, engineers, psychological warfare experts, civil affairs officers, helicopter pilots, and supply, transport and communications units. The Marines who joined them came to fight.

Deception is part of standard operating procedure, but the official dissimulation of policy and intentions, to lull and mislead public opinion, is not quite the same as tactical security to mislead the adversary. The 3,500 Marines who landed at Danang were sent for "defensive purposes only," declared Ambassador Taylor; they would protect the American air base and free ARVN units for combat. Secretary Rusk said the Marines were to provide "local close-in security." Secretary McNamara said they would merely "patrol within narrow limits" and "should not tangle with the enemy." The Pentagon Papers published six years later showed that the arrival of the Marines had instead consciously marked a "pivotal" change in American policy, from the defensive to the offensive. President Johnson sought to avoid the "appearance of sudden changes in policy," McGeorge Bundy informed the National Security Council, and therefore desired no "premature publicity." As the NSC well knew, the change had been long contemplated.

To dispel rumors about a decisive turn in policy, the State Department had explained why it was not a good idea to commit combat troops to Vietnam: "The VC uses terrorism and armed attacks, as well as propaganda. The Government forces must respond decisively on all appropriate levels, tasks that can best be handled by the Vietnamese. American combat units would face several obvious disadvantages in a guerrilla-war situation of this type, in which knowledge of terrain, language and local customs is especially important. In addition, their introduction would provide ammunition for Communist propaganda which falsely proclaims that the United States is conducting a 'white man's war' against Asians."

The reasons having been given for not sending the Marines, the Marines were sent. When they arrived, just ten years after the last French combat forces had left, their belief was that they were going to help a friendly population repel a foreign enemy. They found instead that a large part of the South Vietnamese population, especially in the central and northern provinces, regarded the United States as the invader, and supported or at least accepted the supposed alien foe.

Once the American flag had been put into the conflict by ground forces, it became no longer possible simply to walk away from the war. To withdraw now without "victory" would be an American defeat. The battle plan was to increase American pressure until, as Secretary Rusk put it, Hanoi "stops doing what it is doing." Not until well after the landing of the Marines, however, could the CIA report as a fact that an identifiable North Vietnamese battalion of the 325th Division was at Kontum in the highlands, with 400 men.

By then 3,000 more Marines had arrived and other American forces were on the way. Except for an occasional newspaper leak, the troop movement was secret. Two days after the NLF had struck again at the American presence, blowing up part of the Embassy in Saigon with heavy damage from a bomb in a parked car — 2 Americans and 15 Vietnamese employees were killed, and 54 Americans and 129 Vietnamese passers-by were injured — the President told a news conference in answer to pointed questions that "no great decision" was being taken, and he knew of "no far-reaching strategy that is being suggested or promulgated." It was April Fool's Day and he had just ordered paratroops to Vietnam, a brigade of the 173rd Airborne, who unlike the Marines could not be passed off as defensive. Within three weeks Johnson authorized a troop level of 100,000. This step up the ladder of commitment followed another visit to Saigon by Secretary McNamara, who at General Westmoreland's request had recommended a sharp rise in combat forces: to 185,000 by the end of 1965, and 380,000 by the end of 1966.

Critics of the Vietnam policy have suggested that if troop figures such as were being contemplated had been generally known, they might have caused a traumatic national shock. Actually the popular feeling of the time seems to have been in favor of doing whatever was necessary to get the embarrassing distant involvement over with. To many Americans it was as simple as to a Marine who landed with the First Amphibian Brigade in July. He and his companions had been taught, he said, to believe that "if South Vietnam fell that would be the end of Asia, and Communism would take over everywhere. We were the good guys, they were the bad guys."

Beyond what a declaration of war and mobilization would do to his Great Society, the President evidently feared the creation of a war spirit that would have demanded much more extreme military measures. "Bomb Hanoi" was one of the war's earliest slogans, and even the Red River dikes were seen as legitimate targets by some. Johnson believed that the mighty power of the United States did not have to be fully unleashed in order to win "victory." A declaration of war, moreover, could bring into play Hanoi's alliances with the Russians and Chinese, with unforeseen consequences.

In the absence of a formal declaration of war, on the other hand, with its controls and restrictions, the economy could be seriously overheated. When the Marines landed, the level of American unemployment was a "normal" 4.5 percent, inflation was modestly increasing by 2 percent annually, prices were stable, corporate profits were rising. Five years of uninterrupted prosperity had been recorded. All could now be threatened. War costs piled on top of domestic spending, without a tax increase, spelled large budget deficits. With monetary and credit expansion proceeding on a large scale, the result would be a huge increase in total spending, both governmental and private. As prices rose and wages followed, the classic inflationary spiral uncoiled.

As it turned out, all the things it was feared a declared war might do — curtail social progress, set back civil rights, increase urban pressures, cause inflation, create dissension — would be done by the undeclared, and unexpectedly protracted war.

The war may have been generally supported when it began precisely because so little was known about it, the reasons for it, or the possible effects. American newsmen in Vietnam had found that only the "positive" side of reporting was encouraged — the official version of events. The American press was divided on Vietnam, and made some criticism of intervention, but virtually no debate was held in Congress on the subject as increased military appropriations were voted. A few senators, like Gore of Tennessee, salved their consciences by distinguishing between "support" and "approval" of the war. Morse of Oregon continued to speak against it, but he also believed there was a threat of Chinese Communist expansion in Southeast Asia. Other critics were quieted by the means Johnson had learned as Senate leader. When the chairman of the Armed Services Committee, Russell of Georgia, recalled the warnings of MacArthur and other generals against a land war on the Asian mainland, the President informed him that the biggest war contract on record was earmarked for his state, $3.4 billion for the giant C-5A transport plane at Lockheed's Marietta plant. Whatever doubts the Senator thereafter entertained he kept to himself. Other defense contracts were also farmed out where they would do the most legislative, as well as economic, good.

By now the casualty lists had begun arriving. The NLF and North Vietnamese had counterescalated, as the CIA had predicted, and struck back at American troops faring into "VC country" to "search and destroy." Guerrillas were so bold as to attack the Danang air base, after penetrating a defense perimeter guarded by 9,000 Marines. Another NLF attack on Song Be, capital of Phuoc Long province, overran the town and the American advisers' compound.

The President did his best to avoid the questions inevitably raised. In recommending an increase to 380,000 troops, McNamara had also suggested that Johnson "explain" the war in a television appearance, and that he call up the Reserves and increase taxes, to make the seriousness of American intentions clear not only to Americans but to Hanoi. The President refused all such proposals, and Congress was generally pleased not to have to consider a tax increase; the year before it had reduced taxes. Though his Council of Economic Advisers recommended higher levies on personal income and corporate profits as soon as possible after January 1966, Johnson decided that a tax increase was "impossible until the spring of 1968" because Congress would not approve. But the principal reason Congress would not approve was the administration's concealment of the proposed troop levels, hence of the cost of the war.

Among the expenses of the undeclared war were those for the support of the "Free World" forces, as MACV communiqués put it. The Vietnam intervention lacked the UN cloak of the Korean War, but the United States was able to obtain the participation of 50,000 South Korean troops and 12,000 from Thailand. Neither force was exactly voluntary and both were munificently paid for. As was now Washington habit, the Korean entry was covered by deception. Secretary Rusk said the ROK troops were not intended for combat, only "engineering tasks here and there." The Koreans proved to be the cruelest of American "allies," behaving as conquerors rather than friends, and the South Vietnamese loathed them. McNamara opposed the use of the auxiliaries if only because of their "cost-ineffectiveness." Rusk explained that sometimes irrational moves had to be made for political reasons. At least some "Asian boys" had been found to help "American boys" do what the President said they should not have to do.

General Westmoreland, having started with the 16,500 "advisers" of the Kennedy administration, was now commander of a rapidly swelling military enterprise. The handsome West Pointer and former paratroop leader was obviously destined for great things, perhaps even a political future such as a former commander in Asia had envisioned but not attained, though the former commander in Europe had indeed become President.

One of the Westmoreland improvements to the science of war was the body count, described by another general as an attempt to overcome the Vietnamese birthrate. According to the commander himself it was instituted to correct and give credibility to the habitually wildly inaccurate reports of the South Vietnamese about their military actions. Intended as a sort of American monitoring device, it came instead to be the greatest single factor of unbelievability about the war, and clear proof of the Vietnamization of the American army. Even more perniciously, the body count made its victims impersonal by turning them into statistics. They were only "gooks," "slopes," or at most "Oriental human beings."

In order to establish the "positive" results of combat, field reports of guerrilla casualties were routinely magnified at each successive upward stage of command. Each rank was under pressure from each higher rank to "produce." Not only were unarmed civilians counted as "VC dead," of whatever minor age, but often their bodies were counted more than once to add to the figures. Some units buried their "kills" on the way out, after reporting the number, and dug them up for recounting on the way in from an engagement. Bodies, more bodies, were urged upon all American units by their officers circling overhead in helicopters. Charts hung in company, battalion and regimental headquarters, registering the competition in body count. Prizes were awarded for the best numbers, in the form of three-day passes, rest-and-rehabilitation furloughs, and cases of beer and soda. Who will ever know how many American medals were awarded for killing unarmed civilians? Asked once about the incredibly large NLF and North Vietnamese casualties, Westmoreland replied that any exaggeration compensated for the unrecorded casualties from artillery fire and air strikes, which needless to say were mostly civilian also. The body count, becoming an end in itself, the only achievement that could be measured, was the bloody symbol of wantonness that adhered to the war from its beginning to its end.

Westmoreland executed the directives of the Joint Chiefs, but as the flow of American troops and supplies to Vietnam increased, the President increasingly became commander-in-chief in person as well as by constitutional designation. The Tuesday luncheons of his "war cabinet," it was said not entirely in jest, began with prayer and ended with the selection of bombing targets. A popular story was of the man who said, "They told me if I voted for Goldwater we would be bombing North Vietnam and fighting a land war in Asia within a year. I did, and we are." But as more and more American troops were sent to Vietnam, a Gallup Poll showed that only 24 percent of Americans felt that involvement there was a mistake, while 61 percent said it was not.

In Washington the Voting Rights Act had been passed and signed in less than five months. It became law as even the early stages of the war were already impeding previous measures for the alleviation of the condition of blacks and other minorities. The War on Poverty was not waged with the same intensity of purpose and application as the War on Communism in Southeast Asia. The Office of Economic Opportunity became a massive failure of implementation, mired in local and state politics. The "maximum feasible participation" of the poor themselves, which the law called for, somehow was converted into control by "representatives of the poor." Politicians, social workers, bureaucrats, and not a few grafters and thieves fastened themselves upon the apparatus, and the War on Poverty soon proved itself simply an extension of welfare.

Two reasons were the Vietnam War and the lack of domestic funds. A third was that a true war on poverty could only mean a social revolution, including a redistribution of wealth. Lyndon Johnson's Great Society was not prepared for that. The War on Poverty, finally, was complicated and for many Americans soured by the fact that after the Selma-to-Montgomery march many younger members of the black movement challenged Martin Luther King's nonviolent leadership and demanded more militancy, and counterviolence against violence. They cited the "white backlash" in Mississippi and Alabama, and the formation of White Citizens Councils. They said southern leaders like the two ministers, King and Ralph Abernathy, were not the ones to win the blacks of the northern big cities, and attached the label "Uncle Tom" to the members of the Southern Christian Leadership Conference, the NAACP and other traditional Negro organizations with their white liberal support. Young black nationalists were as much opposed to racial integration as white supremacists were.

The most articulate of the nationalists, Malcolm Little, who called himself Malcolm X, had as a Black Muslim visited Mecca and become aware of the worldwide embrace of Islam. Before that, as a follower of Elijah Mohammed, he had indoctrinated a handsome young black boxer from Louisville, Kentucky, Cassius Clay, and helped him thereby to achieve his unexpected knockout of the black heavyweight champion Sonny Liston. Clay's behavior at the weighing-in, taunting and scornful, apparently so "psyched" the slow lumbering champion that some took it as an example of the new tactics of "confrontation." The day after he won the title Clay joined the Black Muslims and became Mohammed Ali. Malcolm X saw Clay's triumph as that of a hero of Islam over Western and white Christianity, but his pilgrimage to Mecca had taught him that brotherhood was not dependent on skin pigmentation. He broke with the Black Muslims, formed the Organization of Afro-American Unity, and set up his own mosque in Harlem, where whites were also welcome. He now believed that the solution of racial problems required a unified effort. Not long after, while speaking in a crowded Harlem auditorium, Malcolm X was shot and killed by several black gunmen. Whatever the motive, the murder illustrated the differences among blacks themselves.

One of these concerned the war in Vietnam. For many young blacks in both North and South the war was a challenge more important and more immediate than voting rights in Mississippi. As American troops poured into Vietnam the proportion of black soldiers exceeded the proportion of blacks in the general population. Poor and less well-educated blacks were the first to be drafted, unable to claim exemption or deferment. Many who went to war to obtain "freedom" for the South Vietnamese could not vote in their own hometowns, let alone acquire an education or a decent job. The war emphasized the unequal status of blacks and deprived them of social and political ameliorations long overdue. On the other hand, as individuals, the war could improve their lot, by offering them careers, income status, identity and purpose. There was much room for argument pro and con.

The Student Nonviolent Coordinating Committee took an active position against the draft, the first black organization to oppose the war publicly. In Dr. King's headquarters city, Atlanta, SNCC members demonstrated daily at the Army induction center chanting "Hell, no, we won't go!" Stokely Carmichael, the SNCC chairman, declared he preferred prison to serving in the Army. Seventeen SNCC members were soon under indictment for draft resistance. The case of Julian Bond, a SNCC member, intensified the organization's antiwar stand. The young Georgian was elected to the state legislature but was denied his seat because of his open opposition to the war. He was elected again and again unseated. Eventually he was upheld by the Supreme Court but meanwhile he had become another symbol of white injustice.

Martin Luther King had received the Nobel Peace Prize for his efforts on behalf of racial equality and not against the war, but now his Southern Christian Leadership Conference, if only not to lose its supporters to the militants, was compelled to risk its "respectability" by joining the anti-Vietnam cause. King was authorized to "turn the full resources" of SCLC to the ending of the war. He called on President Johnson to seek unconditional peace talks.

The commander-in-chief had made what he regarded as a conciliatory speech — "Peace without Conquest" was its theme — at Johns Hopkins University, offering "unconditional discussions" with Hanoi and, to bring them about, a "Marshall Plan" for the Mekong Valley with a billion-dollar backing. He also restated the Domino Theory, and declared, "We will not be defeated. We will not grow tired. We will not withdraw, either openly or under the cloak of a meaningless agreement."

Though it offered "unconditional discussions" the Johns Hopkins speech made conditions, rejecting in advance Hanoi's Four Points, which envisioned a political settlement, based on the cessation of bombing, eventual American withdrawal of troops, and a new provisional regime in Saigon. At this juncture, it was estimated, the NLF controlled about two-thirds of South Vietnam.

Instead of aiding peace the Johns Hopkins speech showed it to be unattainable, given the attitude of the opposing sides, who were talking past each other. Escalation proceeded; so did domestic dissent. After the first landing of Marines forty-nine members of the University of Michigan faculty signed a call to a "teach-in," a one-day moratorium on classes in favor of a forum on the historical, political, military and moral aspects of the war. Three thousand students attended, of whom only about seventy-five said they were in favor of the war. Next day came a teach-in at Columbia, then Michigan State, and the universities of Buffalo, Chicago and Pennsylvania. Campus and off-campus rallies followed in numerous colleges. In a full-page advertisement in the New York *Times*, 2,700 ministers, priests and rabbis pleaded, "Mr. President: In the name of God, stop it!"

It had only really begun, and indeed another American intervention was also already in progress, to stir controversy and discord. In April, to "prevent another Cuba" and combat Communism in the Caribbean as in Southeast Asia, Marines were landed in the Dominican Republic, the first of 24,000 American troops to be sent there.

Two years before, President Juan Bosch, elected after the assassination of the dictator Trujillo, had been overthrown by an army coup and forced into exile in New York. His supporters had arisen to demand his return and a return to the constitution, a familiar Latin-American situation connoting no outside "aggression," no threat of invasion, no Soviet missiles, no appeal for assistance by either side. Dominicans proposed to settle matters in their own way.

But the Caribbean was the jealously guarded swimming pool of the Yanqui hacienda. The United States stepped into the Dominican Republic, at first "to protect the lives and property of Americans," then because "Communist conspirators" were at work.

When a military junta took over the government and began hostilities with the pro-Bosch forces, the generals turned to the United States to "help restore peace." Ambassador Tapley Bennett recommended armed intervention.

At the Council of the Organization of American States, which vigorously debated the North American intervention, the United States was represented by Ambassador Ellsworth Bunker, a businessman-diplomat with sugar interests in the Dominican Republic. He put together a new provisional regime, leading to "free elections" in which Trujillo's last Premier was chosen President, under the protection of American arms.

Bunker had been called in after an earlier peace plan by McGeorge Bundy was rejected by the President, apparently because it was considered too liberal. This rebuff to the presidential adviser marked the beginning of a change in Bundy's fortunes. He was on his way out of the White House. He was still prepared to argue the merits of the Vietnam intervention, however, and had agreed to do so at what was called the National Teach-in, in Washington. Detained in Santo Domingo, he sent his regrets, while reiterating that the administration's "purpose is peace" and that "all of us want a decent settlement."

The college teach-ins were a new instrument of antiwar feeling, though a limited one, since they were primarily intellectual in tone. They collectivized an opposition which had been largely individual, and helped join faculty members with students. They supplied the impetus and the information by which the college generation, no longer quiescent, was able to demand reconsideration not only of the intervention in Vietnam, but reassessment of the Cold War itself, reexamination of the values by which the nation acted, and reassumption of academic independence.

The Dominican crisis, though eventually it arrived at an uneasy "solution," had several bearings on the Vietnam War. For Ellsworth Bunker it was a rehearsal for similar government management and manipulation in Saigon. For Lyndon Johnson it was added proof of Communist aggression; he so informed Congress in asking supplemental funds for both the Dominican Republic and South Vietnam. For Senator Fulbright it began his disillusion with the Johnson administration and the war policy.

The Foreign Relations Committee chairman had taken the lead in obtaining the Tonkin Gulf Resolution, had remained silent when the bombing of North Vietnam began, had voted for war appropriations, all with the President's assurances that he sought only a negotiated settlement. Fulbright now broke the senatorial tradition that the Foreign Relations chairman does not criticize the President's foreign policy. Charging Johnson with "lack of candor," he declared that military victory in Vietnam was not possible, and opposed further escalation. As he spoke, new American bases were being built in South Vietnam and the draft was being doubled.

A similar change was being experienced somewhat more slowly by another senator. After his brother's death Robert F. Kennedy had continued in support of the counterinsurgency doctrine, though sprinkling it with appeals to youth and calls for a broader foreign policy, not based on maintaining the status quo for unpopular regimes. He offered his services as ambassador in Saigon or "in any capacity" there. As a senator his first major speech was in support of the supplemental appropriations the President asked for Vietnam and the Dominican Republic. He thought the administration's Vietnam policy one of "honorable negotiation" and said Hanoi was being shown "that it cannot win the war."

The first clue to a change in Kennedy's thinking came with a speech before the International Police Academy. When his advance text prompted newsmen to ask if he would campaign against administration policies, he omitted the key paragraph stating that "victory in a revolutionary war is not won by escalation but by deescalation," and that "air attacks by a government on its own villages" were worse than "selective terrorism of an insurgent movement." As delivered, the speech vaguely urged political as well as military action in Vietnam, but it was what had been left out that made the headlines.

The young Senator, highly popular with youth, was absorbing some of the arguments he heard from them and soon he was publicly expressing approval to University of Southern California students who wanted to send their blood to North Vietnam as well as South Vietnam. Senator Goldwater termed such a position "close to treason." Kennedy said he still supported the President "basically," including the idea of bombing to obtain negotiations, but he warned of "internal conflagration" as well, resulting from disunity, and of a society so riven that "no war will be worth fighting." He was still no "dove" but he was moving away from the hawks.

The youth and minorities to which he addressed himself were in effect pulling him along with them. The SDS, returning from Newark and other urban centers where they had entered community work, made antiwar protest their principal activity instead. Their first mass demonstration brought 20,000 persons to the Washington Monument. Then a Declaration of Conscience Against the War arrived at the White House with 4,800 signatures collected by pacifists. Being against the war, it was also against the draft.

On some campuses students burned their draft cards, and Congress promptly made such action punishable by five years in prison and $5,000 fine. The new law was quickly defied. David Miller, a young Catholic, burned the first card in violation of it, in New York City. He had been influenced by the Reverend Daniel Berrigan, his teacher at Le Moyne College. Outside the Pentagon a thirty-two-year-old Quaker, Norman Morrison, father of three, burned himself to death in protest against the war, as Buddhist monks had done in Saigon. Demonstrations inspired counterdemonstrations. In New York a prowar rally — or it may have been an anti-antiwar rally — in Union Square, a traditional site for radical expression, carried signs reading, "Burn Yourself Instead of Your Card" and paraders shouted, "Drop dead, Red!" and "Give us joy, bomb Hanoi!" Roger La Porte, a young Catholic, burned himself to death outside the United Nations building. The Attorney General who had succeeded Robert Kennedy, Nicholas Katzenbach, announced an investigation of SDS for its antiwar activities.

With the first SDS-sponsored protest at the Washington Monument the peace movement began to take clearer shape. It was composed of three main elements: the original pacifists, who acted in moral indignation; those who sought to end the war by political means; and those who saw it as proof of an unjust society, against which they were prepared to take revolutionary action.

Antiwar sentiments were hardly new in American history. The War of 1812 bred a large secession movement in New England. In the Mexican War battalions of American deserters fought on the Mexican side. The Civil War had its Draft Riots in New York and other cities. A large Socialist vote went hand in hand with an antidraft movement in the First World War.

Against the war in Vietnam tens of thousands of Americans would regularly take to the streets of scores of cities to register their feelings. Yet for all the passion and the numbers, none of the antiwar manifestations equaled in intensity, bitterness, violence, and destruction what happened in six hot August days of 1965 in the black Los Angeles suburb of Watts.

Whether the Watts riots had any tenable connection with Vietnam is difficult to establish. There was certainly a symbolic one. American Marines in Vietnam had been shown on living room television screens, setting fires to village huts with their lighters, and like the riots in Birmingham and Hue two years earlier, the burning of Cam Ne came simultaneously with the burning of Watts. The Los Angeles police chief said of Watts with its guerrilla street fighting that it was "very much like Vietnam."

Only two weeks after the ceremony at which the President signed the new Voting Rights Act, Watts exploded into a confusion of riot, arson, shooting and looting that seemed to fulfill novelist James Baldwin's prophecy of "the fire next time." In the violence 36 Americans were killed, 33 of them black, and 1,000 were injured; 4,000 arrests were made; 744 buildings burned down with $45 million property damage; and 50,000 stolen articles were later recovered. On the day that 6,400 more Marines arrived in Danang and Chulai, 20,000 National Guardsmen were ordered into Watts to put down the riots, which in fact were not so much put down as self-exhausted. Helicopters with cameras fed live coverage of the holocaust to home screens.

Sociologists could point out that property was not respected in Watts because those destroying it did not have any of their own. Behind the riots also lay many incidents of what blacks deemed unfair police treatment, and exploitation by white storekeepers. Like all black ghettos with their poverty, Watts was a high-crime and high-unemployment area. It also paid relatively higher taxes than nearby white suburbs.

The true tragedy of Watts, however, may have been epitomized by the fact that the Los Angeles *Times,* one of the nation's notable newspapers, discovered when the riots began that its abundant "morgue" of clippings and documents contained not a single pertinent story about the black suburb that went beyond the police blotter. Watts was known in Los Angeles primarily for its ziggurat called the Watts Towers, a labor of love by an immigrant tilesetter who for thirty-three years had patiently erected a crazy edifice of rail ties, steel rods, tiles, bottles, seashells, broken pottery and chicken wire. The Towers survived the riots, no doubt because they were completely valueless in any terms.

Whatever the immediate causes of the outbreak, the underlying human condition in Watts had simply not been part of the consciousness of the white media, and if Watts did not exist for the Los Angeles *Times* it obviously had not existed for the rest of the country. Now it did. Though it was a setback to the orderly struggle for civil rights, Watts gave ghetto blacks a new sense of power, and pride in identity. "Black is beautiful," they said; while the fires raged they had said "Burn, baby, burn." The net result of the Watts riots was a physical rebuilding, long needed and long ignored. It was remarked that Watts had achieved "instant urban relocation." In the ashes of Watts was born Budd Schulberg's Black Writers' Workshop.

From one extreme the balance scale shifted to the other. Black, if not always Beautiful, was undeniably News, covering the irresponsible aspects of color awareness as well as the responsible, the imagined grievances as well as the real. The news media were soon being accused of having "created" fire-eaters like Stokely Carmichael and Hubert "Rap" Brown, and it could not be denied that their existence and activities were magnified, especially by television, the handmaiden of drama, while the more moderate leaders of the black communities were disregarded. The Watts riots were followed by four days of similar frenzy in Chicago, widely regarded as the best governed of the big cities, though with its large population of "ethnic" whites it was also the most segregated, and racial friction has been a constant in its history.

Watts and Chicago seemed to offer evidence that the Civil Rights and Voting Rights acts had sharpened racial differences instead of reducing them. The misunderstanding between blacks and whites, product of three hundred years of unequal life together, could not be dissolved by mere statute.

One of the consequences of the Watts riots which was out of key with any concept of a Great Society was the beginning of civilian surveillance by the military. After the revelation in 1963 that a sergeant in a "sensitive" post had been a Soviet agent, the Army Intelligence Command at Fort Holabird, Maryland, had interested itself in what it chose to regard as "internal security." Under the broad aim of gathering information in the event that troops would have to be used in civil disturbances, the Army had taken to using infiltration, surveillance and provocation, and the accumulation of photographs and dossiers of participants in urban demonstrations, including antiwar protests. A "domestic war room" was set up in the Pentagon. The chief of Army Intelligence, Major General William P. Yarborough, did not conceal his belief that campus and urban demonstrators were "insurgents" either consciously or unconsciously aiding "the Communists." John F. Kennedy's counterinsurgency in Vietnam came home to roost in Lyndon Johnson's America.

In the war it could be seen by all that Operation Rolling Thunder had failed. The administration had promised that bombing would bring negotiations in six weeks. "What if it didn't?" some congressmen asked. "Then we'll give them four weeks more. That'll do it," was the reply. The bombing had instead made negotiations impossible, nor did it help when air action was briefly suspended, for Hanoi refused discussions so long as the United States insisted that they be "unconditional," a term that sounded too much like surrender.

It was deemed necessary to raise the American ground-troop level again. Secretary McNamara appeared before the Senate Appropriations Committee to ask that a total of 125,000 be authorized "to back up the hard-pressed army of South Vietnam," though ARVN, he acknowledged, was 545,000 men strong, while against it and the Americans were arrayed an estimated 70,000 rebel troops, plus 90,000 irregulars and 30,000 political cadres. Despite reinforcement a mere three battalions, 3,000 men, of the North Vietnamese regular army were in the field in the South. The Pentagon thought it would need a 10-to-1 ratio for counter–guerrilla warfare; its 4-to-1 ratio was not enough.

The new American escalation was made more palatable by what was reported as political improvement in Saigon. A new government was in power, and once again the United States believed it had found the men who could insure stability, build an effective Vietnamese fighting force, and perhaps command some popular support. They were military men, it went without saying. The nominal civilian regime of Premier Quat had been forced out and a new National Leadership Council formed, headed by General Thieu, while the head of the new Executive Council and Premier was the flashy Air Force commander, Nguyen Cao Ky, widely called "Captain Midnight" for the black jumpsuit he affected. Ky soon dismayed the Americans by remarking that what South Vietnam needed was an Adolf Hitler, his personal hero. The new Premier was a northerner and nominal Buddhist who had enlisted with the French to fight the Viet Minh in 1951, who loathed the Hanoi regime and had led the South Vietnamese air attacks against it. Unlike the preceding regimes of Quat, Huong, General Minh, even General Khanh, Ky's ascent seemed to foreclose any possibility of a coalition or neutralist government in Saigon. The new chief of state, General Thieu, was even more adamant on the question. He was especially trusted by the Americans. He had received training in the United States, at Fort Leavenworth, Kansas, and Fort Bliss, Texas, as he climbed the military ladder.

Ambassador Taylor, though himself a military man, did not much care for the new Premier, the playboyish Ky, and was opposed to his selection. Ky stayed and it was Taylor who left, replaced at the Embassy by Henry Cabot Lodge, easily persuaded to make his second tour of duty there.

In the controversy over the bombing of the North an equally significant move had escaped attention, the bombing below the Demilitarized Zone. The two air offenses, North and South, were begun simultaneously before the arrival of American ground troops, and by June, B-52's flown three thousand miles from Guam were in use in the South. To some expert observers, notably Bernard Fall, the giant aircraft, originally intended for strategic bombing with nuclear weapons, changed the whole character of the war, not only militarily but morally. According to Fall unlimited aerial warfare by the B-52's denied all the political aims of American interven-tion — to "prevent aggression," to insure South Vietnamese "indepen-dence," to "maintain South Vietnamese morale," to aid an ally, to "contain Communism" — for the sake of the military objective of victory by de-struction.

The B-52's had been built to annihilate the Soviet Union, if needs be, by the deadliest force known. They were now being flown from Guam, as well as Thailand and Okinawa, for tactical purposes, enforcing "pacifi-cation" from thirty thousand feet, hitting unseen targets which included trucks, bicycles, dirt roads, small infantry units, and jungle hideouts. When NLF adherents tossed grenades into Saigon restaurants or American billets they were regarded as terrorists, but American planners viewed the dropping of fifty 750-pound bombs by each B-52 as not only legitimate but effective warfare. Bombing was the "American way," since it was also the "cheapest" way, the true product of technological superiority. The bombing of North Vietnam continued to receive the headlines, but by the end of 1965, while 10,570 tactical air strikes had been made above the 17th parallel, 37,940 strikes by American fighter-bombers had been carried out south of the parallel, with 23,700 more by the South Vietnamese air force. The B-52's added 10,000 sorties of their own against targets in South Vietnam.

On July 28, 1965, a Wednesday, President Johnson suddenly appeared on television at midday. He muffled his latest decision in Vietnam with his announcement that Supreme Court Justice Arthur Goldberg would become the American Ambassador to the United Nations, replacing Adlai Stevenson, who had died suddenly in London. Goldberg, who was being succeeded on the bench by Abe Fortas, the President's lawyer and confidant, had been told of the golden opportunity he was being given to help bring about peace in Vietnam. His assignment was foredoomed by the rest of the President's announcement: that the war was again being widened. "We did not choose to be the guardians at the gate," Johnson declared, "but there is no one else." Therefore "I have today ordered to Vietnam the First Cavalry (Air-mobile) and certain other forces which will raise our fighting strength from 75,000 to 125,000 men almost immediately. Additional forces will be needed later and they will be sent as requested." The "limited" war had begun to lose its limits.

The announcement stirred public anxiety but also brought a kind of relief. For weeks Washington had been filled with rumors that 300,000 troops were to be sent to Vietnam, that the Reserves would be called up and new taxes imposed. Many secret consultations had taken place in the White House. The upshot was to leave the troop level "open-ended," but the 125,000 figure was both specific and lower than had been expected, dispelling some of the uncertainty. What Americans did not know was that not 50,000 but 100,000 more men had already been ordered into action and that the President had concealed the fact, in short, had lied. Mobilization indeed had been recommended by the Pentagon, and Daniel Ellsberg, McNaughton's assistant in the Pentagon, had written a presidential speech to explain it. The President chose not to mobilize, for the sake of his Great Society. Instead of increasing taxes to meet the new costs, as his economic advisers urged, he planned to continue the boom by tax cuts, he let it be known.

The concealed jump from 75,000 to 175,000 troops, more than doubling the American ground forces in Vietnam, still fell far short of what the Pentagon wanted. Premier Ky's first move in office was to impress upon Secretary McNamara, paying his usual Welcome Wagon visit, that "at least" 200,000 Americans would be needed in order to "win." The Secretary was not disturbed. His own plans called for a level of 380,000 in 1966. Meanwhile the body count for July was 3,000 "VC" dead, the highest monthly figure yet reached.

The swift troop increase confirmed that the generals were running things both in Saigon and Washington, and that the civilians gave assent. George Ball's advice that the United States cut its losses and negotiate a withdrawal, rather than try to win a protracted Asian war against guerrillas, was met by Secretary Rusk's reply that this would compromise American "credibility" and encourage "Communists everywhere." The President agreed with Rusk. If the United States pulled out of Vietnam, he said, the result would be a third world war. He outlined five options — nuclear attack, "cut and run," continuation of a "limited" policy, full mobilization, and "giving the generals what they ask" — and chose the last one. He did not mention negotiation. Ball as usual gave his public support to a policy he disagreed with.

The Joint Chiefs of Staff would continue to get most of what they wanted in Vietnam, though not all of it, such as the invasion of North Vietnam or the bombing of China; and not as quickly or as readily as they might have wanted, perhaps even reluctantly. Gradually the various purposes of the American military effort — to break North Vietnam's will, to strengthen the Saigon regime, to stop infiltration, to punish "liberation" wars, interdict supplies, honor commitments — were wrapped in a dual purpose, to prevent an American defeat and to "save American lives," naturally including the safe return of American war prisoners.

The hawks were not all military. Walt Rostow kept prodding for more effort, to redeem the effort he had already recommended which had failed. Now he proposed that American ground troops be sent into Laos, "across the Ho Chi Minh trail," and into North Vietnam, to prevent a "long, uncertain attritional struggle" which would also wear down public support. Abe Fortas, lightly overlooking the notion that a Supreme Court Justice should remain independent of the other two branches of government, continued to give Johnson his hard-line advice. One of the famed "Washington lawyers," Clark Clifford, chairman of the President's Foreign Intelligence Advisory Board, expressed doubts about American success in Vietnam, as George Ball had, but at National Security Council meetings Clifford always approved the increasing American commitment.

There were some in the Pentagon, like Air Force Under Secretary Townsend Hoopes, who opposed escalation on the ground that American power and prestige were being dissipated in Vietnam, away from more important concerns throughout the world — Germany, NATO, the Middle East, and the Indian subcontinent.

The last-mentioned area was a sore case in point. As the United States put more men into Southeast Asia, war broke out in South Asia between the two always-antagonistic neighbors, India and Pakistan. Both sides used American tanks and other weapons, originally furnished against a supposed Communist threat from either Russia or China. Secretary Rusk saw things writ large. The Communist powers, he declared, were seeking to win control of Asia, Africa and Latin America and thus encircle and strangle the "Atlantic world." He believed that "successful defense of South Vietnam will change this judgment."

What was at work, however, was not Sino-Soviet conspiracy but more Sino-Soviet rivalry. As a result of the ambiguous American position, the Russians were able to step in to mediate the conflict, and by a settlement the Pakistanis complained of, they further increased their influence in India. Pakistan promptly turned to China, even though Peking had been set back by events in Indonesia. There, after President Sukarno had quit the United Nations and joined a fanciful Jakarta–Hanoi–Phnom Penh–Pyongyang–Peking Axis, a Communist coup attempt was overwhelmed by the Indonesian military, Sukarno was made a figurehead, and hundreds of thousands of Chinese were killed as "Communists."

Except in North Vietnam, where American intervention in the war had compelled them both to give aid to Hanoi, Russia and China widened their breach further after the India-Pakistan War. Nineteen Communist parties met in Moscow, with Peking pointedly absent, and demanded American withdrawal from Vietnam. Peking for its part assailed "Khrushchevism without Khrushchev."

By the middle of September the number of American troops in South Vietnam reached 128,000 and by the end of October 150,000. Legal justification for their presence was questioned by the Lawyers Committee on American Policy toward Vietnam, which pointed out that it was not sanctioned by the SEATO treaty no matter how many times Secretary Rusk said it was. The President's lawyers, Fortas and Clifford, did not belong to the committee, and another lawyer took the occasion, in a letter to the New York *Times*, to urge the restriction of speech and press freedom "when necessary" in "wartime." An NLF victory, he declared, "would mean ultimately the destruction of freedom of speech for all men for all time, not only in Asia but in the United States as well," indeed "the right of free speech will be extinguished throughout the world." This agitated member of the bar was former Vice-President Richard Nixon, who had never forgiven the press for causing, as he believed, his defeat in California in 1962.

It was difficult to invoke press censorship in an undeclared war, as Nixon wanted, but the Johnson administration tried. The Pentagon's public affairs chief, Arthur Sylvester, a veteran Washington correspondent in the righteous position of poacher turned game warden, told American newsmen in Saigon that their patriotic duty was to report only "what made the United States look good." When the veracity of the American Embassy and of MACV briefers was impugned, Sylvester said, "Look, if you think any American official is going to tell you the truth, then you're stupid." George Ball, too, thought that public lying, if necessary, was a proper function of any government official.

To help correspondents in Vietnam report only "what made the United States look good," the Administration created the Joint U.S. Public Affairs Office, JUSPAO, in Saigon, and put the U.S. Information Agency in charge of all psychological operations, civilian and military, as well as the release of all news. JUSPAO with its numerous activities was spread thin. Too often, also, it failed to distinguish between American interests and the interests of the Saigon military junta, notably in election campaigns which USIA helped organize and which were carried out with widespread fraud and corruption by the Vietnamese. At the end, just as the military complained it had not been given enough "to win," USIA officials like Thomas Sorensen declared that the agency had not been allowed "to do the job properly." Sufficient evidence indicated that no number of men or amount of money could do something that Edward R. Murrow as USIA director thought impossible. "Propaganda cannot make bad policy succeed," he had said.

In any case how much was "enough"? As the number of troops increased in South Vietnam, so did the supporting system, and with it representation by news media. Saigon and the provinces were chock-a-block with RAND experts, computer analysts, interrogators, specialists in captured documents, map readers, sociologists, producers of USIA films, writers of leaflets, "voices" for loudspeaker planes, and many other cogs in the gigantic effort to "educate" the Vietnamese and preserve their nation for them. Colonel Lansdale, who dated back to the earliest days of the American effort, returned to Saigon to advise Premier Ky on "rural reconstruction" as he had advised President Diem on social reforms. The result was approximately the same. Ky made numerous public utterances about correcting injustices, but after all, there was a war to fight.

One of those who went to Vietnam with Lansdale was Daniel Ellsberg, transferred from the Pentagon to the State Department. He had volunteered for a mission which he saw as winning hearts and minds "without bombing." He was still enthusiastic about American intentions, but by his own testimony, during the two years he spent there he was converted from hawk to dove, not only because of the apparent senselessness of much of the military action but because of a lack of inspiration and commitment on the part of the South Vietnamese.

Most other Americans in Vietnam simply reconfirmed their original beliefs. American expertise, fed on optimism, engaged in an abundance of wishful thinking. The NLF could not possibly stand up against American arms and ability, it was reasoned, therefore its morale had to be reported as deficient. If NLF influence over the peasants could not be got rid of in many areas, then move the peasants. RAND thinkers advised the creation of more civilian refugees as a strategic loss to the NLF, and advocated more bombing, defoliation and resettlement. That was why B-52's had to be used against chicken yards.

Originally the RAND Corporation's "VC Motivation and Morale Project," sponsored by John McNaughton's department in the Pentagon, had found the NLF to be an authentic liberation movement, and evaluated the war as a class conflict in part, with the wealthy landowners fleeing to Saigon or Paris and the peasant poor in the countryside coming under guerrilla control. It was on the basis of this report that McNaughton, whether jocularly or not, declared that "we have joined the wrong side." To prevent further misguidance the RAND study was placed in other hands. Technologists took over from academics, political scientists and

Vietnamologists, and from the special Air Force vantage point of six miles of altitude they quickly reported that air power was the principal destroyer of guerrilla morale, thus providing the rationale for increased bombing. Prisoners and defectors were interrogated not about motivation and morale but about the physical effects of various kinds of bombing. When they praised the NLF it was ascribed to fear rather than conviction.

The war's inner realities were too formidable and too gross to be so easily finessed. The burning of the huts at Cam Ne by Marines with lighters undid six months of JUSPAO briefings and official handouts. Ellsberg and others like him, who went to Vietnam supporting American policy but trained in objective analysis, learned to doubt when their superiors disregarded their reports and continued preconceived programs wrongfully assumed to be succeeding.

The war as it entered the American living room was oversimplified, overdramatized, and immediate in its aspect; such is the nature of the medium. Television could not impart the whole story. Newsmen in Saigon could go to almost any battlefield and accompany troops, but they were not, after all, accredited to the NLF. American reporters and cameras could record the killing, maiming and dislocation on their side of the war only. The death and destruction caused by NLF mortars, "incoming mail," could be witnessed but not the effect of American bombing on the other side. Occasional NLF dead and wounded were shown, and guerrilla prisoners being interrogated and sometimes tortured by South Vietnamese, with American officers standing by. The war that the American people saw and read about could not be what Arthur Sylvester wanted, only "what made the United States look good." By 1966 Paul-Henri Spaak, the Belgian statesman, who with all other Europeans had also "viewed" events with fascination and horror, could say that the United States "has completely lost the information war in Vietnam."

China helped the administration retain support in the information war at home. Mao Tse-tung's Defense Minister and designated successor, Marshal Lin Piao, had taken up where Nikita Khrushchev left off, and gave Peking's encouragement to "people's war." His speech, described in Washington as a Far Eastern *Mein Kampf*, was as misread as Khrushchev's remarks on "wars of national liberation" had been. What Lin Piao said was the opposite of what he was interpreted as saying. He was telling guerrilla movements that they were essentially on their own, and that no victory could be won "entirely" with outside aid. Such aid did not exclude Chinese-made weapons of Soviet type, furnished to North Vietnam. It did not exclude the use of Chinese troops as railroad labor in North Vietnam, just as they were used in China. It assuredly did exclude any real Chinese military intervention.

To the extent that Chinese weapons and other supplies were carried down the Ho Chi Minh trail through Laos to South Vietnam the war had been intensified by Peking. Lin Piao was not posing any actual threat to the United States, however. China was never weaker internally or less influential internationally than when he spoke. Rather than attacking the United States in Vietnam as in Korea, the Chinese seemed to fear invasion by the United States as more American ground troops poured into South Vietnam. Large areas of South China were evacuated and civilian defense organized. Peking printed maps showing China surrounded by forty-two American bases, a dozen of them in Southeast Asia.

If American troops ran no danger of encountering Chinese "volunteers" in Vietnam, they did encounter North Vietnamese regulars with increasing frequency in conventional battle, and no longer the small jungle units of the NLF with their snipers, boobytraps and ambushes. The Ia Drang Valley was the scene of the first fierce combat between the North Vietnamese and the newly arrived U.S. First Air Cavalry. There, south of Pleiku and near the Cambodian border, the North Vietnamese decided to stand against the Americans and threw 2,000 troops of the Sixty-sixth Regiment into battle, begun by a 500-man North Vietnamese ambush attack. During the fighting Hanoi established its readiness to reinforce its troops and to match American ground power with its own. Without air power the Air Cavalry might have suffered another Dien Bien Phu. The fighting was broken off when American planes, including B-52's from Guam, pounded North Vietnamese positions. As it was, the American force took casualties of 300 dead and 1,000 wounded, its military effectiveness being destroyed, but it claimed 1,186 North Vietnamese dead. The American losses at Ia Drang were added to the 678 dead of the preceding seven weeks, to confirm that the war had been joined in earnest.

The Air Cavalry came from Fort Benning, Georgia, and the Battle of the Ia Drang Valley gave the nearby Army town of Columbus a bleak Thanksgiving as Department of the Army telegrams began arriving, announcing combat deaths, even before news of the fighting was received. On the first day, eighty-eight Pentagon "regrets" were delivered to unsuspecting families.

In the Ia Drang Valley, where the North Vietnamese People's Army stood and fought, the United States prevailed when the latter withdrew under aerial bombardment. At that point, perhaps, the revolutionary forces stopped winning the war. That did not mean they had begun to lose it.

During one of his appearances on Capitol Hill Secretary McNamara was asked by a senator about "Johnson grass," higher than a man's head, which impeded military tactics. There is such a weed, *Sorghum malepense*, named for an American agriculturist, but in the Vietnam context it seemed peculiarly apt also as a description of the American plight. A popular song was sung about the "captain" who was knee-deep, then waist-deep, then shoulder-deep in "the big Muddy" but ordered his troops to "push on."

The antiwar movement meanwhile was appositely experiencing weed-like growth. The first nationwide demonstrations, organized by the student-run National Coordinating Committee to End the War in Vietnam, mustered 70,000 persons in forty cities from Berkeley to New York calling for a halt to the bombing. Thousands beset the Army base in Oakland and were turned back by police. Antiwar crowds took over Boston Common, while 10,000 marched in New York City, and Joan Baez advised young men in her audience, between songs, "don't cooperate with the Draft." As the Battle of Ia Drang was fought, 25,000 persons converged on the White House in a March for Peace.

A plea for peace at a more exalted level came from Pope Paul VI, who in the first pontifical visit ever made to the United States held religious services in Yankee Stadium in New York City and addressed the United Nations. His words, not relished by Cardinal Spellman, gave added impetus to the antiwar movement in the lower ranks of the Church, part of the renewal that Paul's predecessor John XXIII had invoked with the Second Vatican Council. This assemblage and John's encyclical *Pacem in Terris* set into motion forces which in combination with other pressures and problems of the temporal estate were causing upheaval in the Church, not least in connection with the war in Vietnam. The Council, intended to exemplify a reawakening of faith and to institute a search for new meaning, opened the way to broader concepts of the individual and his society. Priestly celibacy was called into question. Nuns unveiled themselves. Liturgy was vernacularized. Pentecostalism was revived. Parish missions were redefined as more than preaching, administering the sacraments, caring for the sick, and teaching school. As for the war, the Council had uttered "the unequivocal and unhesitating condemnation" of "any act of war aimed indiscriminately at the destruction of entire cities or of extensive areas, along with their populations," finding it to be a "crime against God and man himself."

The theological controversy over whether "God is dead" developed into new forms of social activity by Catholic clergymen to demonstrate that at least conscience was not. Many priests joined the Freedom Riders into the South and marched from Selma to Montgomery. Father James Groppi in Milwaukee went to jail in the cause of unsegregated housing. Above all, clerical activism found expression in the antiwar movement. At one end of the spectrum of Church sentiment on Vietnam was Cardinal Spellman, who was able to bless the war as a struggle for civilization. "My most satisfying moments as a priest," he wrote, "were spent on war fronts." At the other end of the spectrum were the Berrigan brothers, Daniel the Jesuit and Philip the Josephite. Their Catholic Ultra-Resistance was directed not only against the war itself but against the Catholic bishops and archbishops who sanctioned it. While Cardinal Spellman visited the troops, Daniel Berrigan and two other priests, with several scores of students from Fordham University, picketed his chancery.

The Pope's was not the only plea for "peace." The seventy-year-old Spiritual Master, His Divine Grace A. C. Bhaktivedanta Srila Prabhupad, arrived in New York from India to spread Krishna consciousness in the West. He rented a storefront in the East Village, a former "psychedelic" souvenir shop, and sat in the middle of the floor chanting. The local hippies began to drop into the first Vedic temple, and then to "tune in" by reading Hindu scriptures. Within weeks saffron-robed, scalp-shaved youths and sari-clad girls, who were brought up in Great Neck, Long Island, and Davenport, Iowa, were tinkling bells and intoning "Hare Krishna" in Tompkins Square, begging alms and selling incense sticks on Fifth Avenue and even in Wall Street. The Spiritual Master was plainly a more satisfying father figure than their own parents, and the International Society for Krishna Consciousness multiplied into twenty-seven temples in America and thirty-five in Europe, and became proprietor of the largest incense company in the United States.

The Beatles, symbols of Pop, for a while were devotees of the Maharishi Mehesh Yoga, though in the main they were occupied with other devotions in which they themselves were the venerated objects. They appeared in Shea Stadium in New York and sixty thousand adolescents made their distraught affection so loudly known that hardly a note of the concert could be heard. For adults it was "an experience of pure terror," one of them declared. On the heels of the Beatles arrived another British import of cultural significance, the mini-skirt. American minis blossomed everywhere but they never reached the uttermost mini-ness of the British.

Some American youth avoided drugs in austere deference to Krishna but other youth reached after them at the behest of their "spiritual" mentor, the self-styled "high priest" of the "psychedelic brotherhood," Timothy Leary. Seeking to "recondition society" by opening the Doors of Perception, Leary called on them to "turn on, tune in, drop out." Drugs may have "freed" some young minds, but many tragic cases of pain, grief and death from "bad trips" were reported, and Leary himself soon ran afoul of the society he had shocked. Driving with his family to Mexico, he was arrested at the border in possession of a small amount of marijuana, and on conviction by a Texas jury which could not "tune in," he was sentenced to thirty years in prison. The case began its way through the appeals courts.

An American walked in space, Major Edward White, after a Russian had done so, but while American eyes were fastened aloft, more than one commentator pointed out, American boots slogged through the mud of

Vietnam. As the Joint Chiefs of Staff had planned, 200,000 American troops were in place there at the end of 1965, and in the first not quite complete year of "real war," 1,365 Americans had been killed, to bring the total to 1,631. South Vietnam acknowledged 11,000 dead for the year, but the "body count" certified that 35,000 "Viet Cong" had been killed.

The bombing of North Vietnam, at first aimed at military targets in the border areas, had gradually spread farther north to cover most of the country and hit the approaches to heavily populated Hanoi. Congress had appropriated $2.4 billion specifically for the war and anticipated the need for $12 billion for 1966. The administration was said to feel that the Communists had been "stopped," but the rebels nevertheless held as much territory and controlled as many people as they had a year before.

Despite the casualties, the appropriations and the spreading dissension at home, the first year had established in congressional speeches, public forums, television programs, and in the subliminal ways in which public impressions are created, a widespread belief that the Vietnam hawks were truer to American tradition, more patriotic, more candid and more manly than the doves, who were apologetic, devious, and divided as to how to accomplish what they said they wanted, peace. Of course, "everybody" would like to have peace, said the hawks. Former Vice-President Nixon, appearing on a television program, urged the bombing of Hanoi and the mining of the port of Haiphong as sure ways "to win the war in Vietnam, and to end it."

Yet so much had been made of bombing Hanoi into negotiations that when ten months of it proved futile, an opinion poll showed that 73 percent of Americans favored a bombing pause instead. If not blasted, the North Vietnamese could perhaps be coaxed into discussions. To see the old year out and the new year in, President Johnson extended the normal Christmas cease-fire through the customary Tet Lunar New Year cease-fire, to make a thirty-seven-day bombing halt during which he engaged in a worldwide "peace offensive." In music stores the new song hit was "Ballad of the Green Berets."

The peace effort was proposed by Secretary McNamara before taking the military escalation to the next inevitable level. The President was skeptical about Hanoi's acceptance; so was McGeorge Bundy, and most of all Rusk, who saw the proposal a sign of weakness. It was in truth the beginning of a wavering by the Defense Secretary.

The President's peace envoys winged their way around the world, Vice-President Humphrey to the Philippines and India, Ambassador Harriman to Warsaw and Belgrade, Arthur Goldberg to Paris, London and Rome; Assistant Secretaries of State Mennen Williams to Africa and Tom Mann to Latin America. To make mere motion appear to be action is a device of all governments. In reply to Hanoi's Four Points the United

States offered Fourteen Points of its own, accepting the principle of eventual American withdrawal but still finding no place for the NLF in any American peace plan. Hanoi stood on its own proposals, including a coalition in Saigon, and Ho Chi Minh himself demanded a return to the Geneva agreements of 1954.

When the "peace offensive" failed and the question arose of resuming the bombing, twenty-five senators said they favored it, but twenty-five others were opposed, among them Robert F. Kennedy. Under Fulbright's leadership some members of the Foreign Relations Committee took the unprecedented, if belated, action of openly challenging the legality of the American involvement. They demanded more explanation. Instead came the order to renew the bombing. Fulbright then announced public hearings on Vietnam, to "educate" the American public. As the bombs began to fall again, Senator Kennedy neither endorsed nor opposed the action, but said it was "not the answer." Behind the scenes Senator Mike Mansfield, returned from a visit to Vietnam, where MACV was asking for more troop reinforcements, reported to Johnson that continuing escalation would lead eventually to the need for "upwards of 700,000" men. Johnson kept the Mansfield report secret. It was declassified six years later.

During the bombing pause the President reiterated his belief in the Great Society and held that the United States could easily manage both guns and butter. His budget message two weeks later told a different story. The Great Society program was cut back to put it "at a pace which reflects the claims of our commitment in Southeast Asia." It could not have been stated more clearly. A school milk program was the first to go. Funds for education were reduced, as were those for school buildings and libraries. At the same time $12.76 billion in supplemental funds was requested for Vietnam. Senator Kennedy asked why so much should be spent on a questionable war when there were so many pressing domestic needs. But the bill passed 94 to 2 and neither of the negative votes was his.

Fulbright's decision to hold his hearings indicated that the line between doves and hawks was becoming clearer and the confrontation more open. The dispute was not only over right and wrong in Vietnam, or over how much, but also over presidential power. The Senate's function of "advice and consent," which the Chief Executive believed to be embodied in the Tonkin Gulf Resolution, was seen by some senators as having rather been abrogated by the resolution. War funds were still voted but the consensus Lyndon Johnson cherished seemed to be slipping away.

The President's riposte to the Fulbright hearings was an attempt to capture the headlines from them by flying to Honolulu to meet with South Vietnamese Premier Ky and the chief of state, General Thieu, to put his arm around Ky's shoulder and with him pledge "social revolution." At the same time he approved an American troop level of 383,500 by the end of the year and a goal of 425,000 by the middle of 1967. By designating Premier Ky "our man in Saigon" — no South Vietnamese leader since Diem, visiting Washington in 1957, had ever shaken hands with an American President — and by pledging still more aid, Johnson had acknowledged the American assumption of responsibility for all aspects of South Vietnamese life. In a pep talk to American officials summoned from Saigon to Honolulu he explained that it was necessary to quantify their "democracy-building" in Vietnam's rural areas. "How much of it [i.e., democracy] have you built, when and where? Give the dates, times and numbers," he instructed them. The civilian equivalent of the body count ranged from new roads constructed to toilet paper supplied. Ky meanwhile confined himself to public demands for more bombing and public refusal to negotiate with the NLF.

The Fulbright hearings, seen on television for six full days, displayed the familiar administration spokesmen Secretary Rusk and General Maxwell Taylor, but high-level disagreement was for the first time given equal opportunity to air its views to a nationwide audience. Against Taylor appeared a "soldier-statesman" of equal standing, retired Lieutenant General James A. Gavin, former head of Army Plans and Development. Like Taylor, Gavin had disputed the Dulles strategy of "massive retaliation," like Taylor he had served as an ambassador. He was the first top military man to oppose the conduct of the war, not merely question it, and to condemn the bombing. Against Rusk appeared the former State Department policy planner and Ambassador to Moscow, the articulator of the "containment of Communism" doctrine himself, George F. Kennan.

The President was visibly displeased by the "equal-time" rule which the television networks applied, though it was not quite as equal as it seemed. CBS, for example, decided to forgo the Kennan testimony for another rerun of the popular program I Love Lucy, on the ground that housewives were not interested in Vietnam. This brought about the resignation of the president of CBS News, Fred W. Friendly, who then joined McGeorge Bundy in the more agreeable environment of the Ford Foundation.

The Secretary of State presented the Fulbright committee with a Catch-22 in his testimony: American troops would not be in South Vietnam if it had not been for infiltration from North Vietnam, but infiltration from North Vietnam was taking place because American troops were in South Vietnam. Rusk conceded that Hanoi had put its first regulars below the 17th parallel only after the Tonkin Gulf reprisal strikes.

The Kennan testimony, of which CBS deprived "housewives," discounted the decisive importance of Vietnam as an American interest even if South Vietnam passed under Communism. The veteran diplomat described himself as "bewildered" by the American commitment, not only to defend South Vietnam's frontiers but to insure the internal security of a government which could not insure its own. He feared that the American attempt to root out the NLF would cause a degree of damage and civilian suffering in South Vietnam "for which I would not like to see this country responsible."

General Taylor's belief was that it was necessary to demonstrate the failure of "wars of liberation" everywhere except presumably in the American colonies in 1776. He also took exception to the use of the term "escalation," preferring "extension" since in military parlance escalation would mean resort to nuclear weapons. Senator Morse challenged the witness. "It isn't going to be too long before the American people as a people will repudiate our war in Southeast Asia," he remarked.

"That of course is good news to Hanoi, Senator," Taylor said icily.

"I know that is the smear that you militarists give to those of us who have honest differences of opinion with you," returned the Senator from Oregon, but "in my judgment the President of the United States is already losing the people of this country by the millions in connection with this war in Southeast Asia."

After the hearings the Foreign Relations Committee received twenty thousand letters and telegrams pro and con on the subject of Vietnam. Most of them expressed thanks for the exploration of the American commitment, about which it was evidently widely felt that the administration had misinformed, uninformed or underinformed the public. Senator Fulbright himself openly admitted his error in pushing for the Tonkin Gulf Resolution. "I guess I'll have to keep saying it from now on," he declared, and he said it again a few days later when Morse introduced a bill to repeal the resolution. The vote was less a test of sentiment on the war than on the repudiation of the commander-in-chief in time of war, and though Fulbright voted for repeal the measure was defeated 92 to 5. Then the $12 billion military appropriations bill for Vietnam was approved. Dissent in the Senate had still only a slippery foothold, and despite Morse's prophecy a new poll showed 53 percent of Americans favoring "more offensive ground war."

As the Fulbright hearings ended Senator Robert Kennedy caused a flurry on Capitol Hill with the proposal that the NLF be allowed into a Saigon coalition, recalling President Kennedy's acceptance of a coalition in Laos in 1962. Vice-President Humphrey, just returned from Saigon, where he had declared the NLF to be "unfit" to participate in any government, said Kennedy would be "putting the fox in the chicken coop" and "an arsonist in the fire department." The administration's official dove, George Ball, also attacked Kennedy's statement. The Senator then "clarified" it and said he meant a coalition after elections. The White House could find no disagreement with that, since no elections were contemplated besides those of Ky and Thieu. Kennedy was still pursuing a course of supporting the war "basically" — any withdrawal would be "catastrophic for American interests," he said — without endorsing the bombing of North Vietnam.

The President had meanwhile assailed the "nervous Nellies" who opposed him on the war, and those "who break ranks under the strain, and turn on their leaders, their own country, and their own fighting men." He had closed the White House ranks by bringing back Walt Rostow from the State Department when McGeorge Bundy left. By the economics of growth, in fact, Johnson now had two Rostows to advise him, as Walt's brother Eugene, of the Yale Law School, became Under Secretary of State for Political Affairs. Like their Tolstoyan namesakes, the Rostows were deeply concerned with matters of war and peace. The younger brother's contribution to political philosophy was the complement to Rusk's. The Secretary believed that other nations should be kept uncertain as to what the Americans might do, thus capitalizing on fears of irrational American behavior. The new Under Secretary's attitude was to expect irrationality from other nations. Taken together the two casts of mind had their effect not only on the Vietnam War but on the world's opinion of American policy and practices.

As he departed the White House, McGeorge Bundy told the National Press Club that it was "a great error" to conclude from words spoken on Capitol Hill or on college campuses that either Congress or the academic community was opposed to the deepening Vietnam involvement. John Kenneth Galbraith for his part found the growing revolt against the war and increased armaments "the most remarkable political phenomenon of our time." The truth was a combination of the two facts. As the mood of dissent hovered between doubt and wishful thinking, differences sharpened among Americans. Antiwar marches were broken up in Boston and Oklahoma City, and in New York City demonstrators were pelted with stones. Admittedly there was provocation in the latter case, caused by the carrying of the "Viet Cong" flag, a gesture no less simplistic than the rival one of waving the American. Four young men who were burning their draft cards outside a Boston courthouse were set upon by indignant bystanders and beaten, while police stood by approvingly and television cameras ground.

Dissent and disturbance were equally in the ascendant in Vietnam, as Ky and Thieu found when they returned from Honolulu. The Buddhists, led by Thich Tri Quang, were calling for the overthrow of the "rotten" military regime despite if not because of the warm embrace of the American President, and Father Hoang Quyn, chairman of the Catholic Greater Unity Force, joined in the attack, terming the Ky-Thieu junta "worse than the dictatorial government of Ngo Dinh Diem." Protest demonstrations, strikes and school boycotts, all with a strong anti-American flavor, in

Danang and Hue followed Ky's dismissal of the popular, to Buddhists, commander of the northern military region, General Nguyen Chang Thi, whom the Premier considered a serious political rival. When Ky flew South Vietnamese Marines to the two cities, Thi's troops fought pitched battles with them until subdued. The Buddhists meanwhile turned their pagodas into citadels, and as monks and nuns resorted again to self-immolation by burning, Ky put down the new insurrection by capturing the pagodas and the Buddhist Secular Affairs Institute in Saigon.

The State Department, the Pentagon Papers disclosed, reacted to the Vietnamese internal discord with "unrestrained fury." "This may require tough talk but the United States cannot accept this insane bickering," read the cable sent to Ambassador Lodge. "The American people are fed up with the games they are playing while Americans are being asked to sustain such major burdens." The Embassy was instructed to threaten total American withdrawal unless the strife ended. George Ball, as administration spokesman, declared that the United States supported "the people of South Vietnam whatever form of government they happen to choose," and denied that the Honolulu meeting constituted President Johnson's personal endorsement of Premier Ky. The fact was that Ambassador Lodge did support Ky, and the Embassy provided the planes in which Ky's troops were flown to Danang when the Premier said they were needed to "liberate" the city "already controlled by the Communists." The coalition opposing the military regime protested to Lodge that the United States was "directly protecting" Ky and Thieu and "giving them means and advice to suppress and wipe out the Vietnamese people." In Washington Senator Fulbright declared, "I think we are . . . intervening in a civil war, and our announced objectives are not attainable."

Since Lodge had been privy to the generals' plot against Diem three years before and President Johnson regarded Diem's overthrow as the paramount American mistake in Vietnam, it was perhaps to be expected that the anti-Ky uprising should have a different outcome. After its suppression elections were embarked upon, under the American aegis, as well as under rules prohibiting "neutralists" and "pro-Communists" from being candidates for the Constituent Assembly.

Despite the restrictions, the regime's complete control of the voting, and strict censorship, the United States called the election fair. It could not be regarded as representative, since it was boycotted by the NLF, excluded areas under insurgent influence, and was opposed as "antidemocratic" by the Buddhists, Father Quyn's Catholics, and the Cao Dai and Hoa Hao religious sects. The regime nevertheless reported that 81 percent of the 5,290,000 registered voters had turned out, and it was true that many Vietnamese feared reprisals if they did not vote — their identity cards noted the fact — while large numbers of soldiers voted twice.

The Assembly, dominated by Ky adherents, insured a similarly restricted presidential election for the following year. The new or "American" constitution declared opposition to "Communism in every form" and prohibited "every activity designed to propagandize or carry out Communism." Under it were passed laws against "all plots and actions under the false name of peace and neutrality, according to a Communist policy." On these foundations the Second Republic was created in Vietnam.

The Assembly refused to make the province chiefs and the mayors of the six largest cities elected rather than appointed officials, but did restore the village elections which Diem had abolished in his First Republic in 1956. It was the price grudgingly paid by the generals for the ever-increasing infusion of American troops and financial aid, and limited as it was, it became the high-water mark of American democratic influence in South Vietnam.

Increased American influence in Southeast Asia was paid for by loss of American cohesion at home. Racial violence spread as black militants came to the fore in the civil rights movement. A "March Against Fear" into Mississippi, to register new voters, acted as a catalyst for the new combativeness. A small procession was led by James Meredith, who had been the first black student at the University of Mississippi, and as it crossed the state line from Tennessee, Meredith was wounded by shots from a lurking sniper. As at Selma the year before, the disrupted march was resumed by black leaders summoned to the scene of confrontation, Martin Luther King and Stokely Carmichael among them. It reached Jackson without further hindrance but on the way it amply demonstrated the internal strains in the black movement, as King preached his moderation and nonviolence while Carmichael and his young firebrands cried out for "Black Power!" The chairman of SNCC had by now excluded whites from his organization and cut it loose from any connection with the "Uncle Toms."

As communicated by demonstrations and demands, on the nation's television screens, Black Power was a stirring, strident, and to many Americans a frightening thought. Its threat, as well as its weakness, was that it meant all things to all black men. King saw it as an expression of black nationalism, others as merely equal voting power or economic opportunity. Floyd McKissick of CORE supported it, but Roy Wilkins of NAACP denounced it as "a reverse Mississippi, a reverse Hitler, a reverse Ku Klux Klan," in short, black racism. To that definition another fearsome conjecture was added as Carmichael changed the N in SNCC to mean National and no longer Nonviolent. He explained that nonviolence could not be accepted as a valid concept while the United States practiced violence in Vietnam.

The "long hot summer" ensued. Rioting broke out in the crowded black slums on the West Side of Chicago in a quarrel over a turned-on fire hydrant, and the National Guard was summoned against rooftop sniping and the looting of stores. Mayor Richard Daley blamed King for the trouble instead of his city's segregationism, but negotiated a settlement with the black leader providing for portable swimming pools in Negro neighborhoods. The Chicago outbreak was followed by rioting in the black sections of Brooklyn, Cleveland, Omaha, Baltimore, San Francisco, Jacksonville and Atlanta, mostly against police but in some instances involving roving bands of whites. The scene of conflict moved to a white residential area when King returned to Chicago on behalf of open housing. The city still smarted from the earlier disorders, and now his marchers were mocked and jeered and he himself was hit by a rock as angered white "ethnics" fought with Black Power advocates. King called the incident the "ugliest" he had ever known.

Black Power was not exclusively a black cause. Broad and vague as its demands were, they won the approval of the SDS, which added its own call for Student Power as a means of radicalizing campuses. The college antiwar movement, primarily an antidraft movement, grew with the number of American troops in Vietnam, though those who protested the draft the most were also most favored by it. They could be deferred during their school years, and after that receive graduate-study deferments and deferments for "essential service" in laboratories and research centers. Many were commissioned from ROTC and were therefore not draftees. Notwithstanding their preferred status, a large number of student dissenters had moral doubts about the war itself, as a previous generation had not had about the Second World War.

Whatever the anomalies, the campus was the heart of the antiwar cause. It was led, typically, by such as the student president at Stanford, David Harris, a lawyer's son studying on a scholarship and majoring in Social Thought. Like many others he had been conditioned by the Mississippi "Freedom Summer" of 1964, when he was threatened by "white citizens" and one of his group kidnapped and beaten. Now he saw Mississippi, the draft, the Vietnam War and the educational system as "all one thing" called "Peace." The formulation was a common one.

Besides the war, other strands of disaffection were being spun into the national fabric. Senate hearings on automobile safety came to drama with the disclosure that General Motors, the world's largest and richest corporation, had been investigating the personal life of a self-appointed "consumer advocate," Ralph Nader, after his allegations that the cars rolling off the assembly line were "unsafe at any speed." The young lawyer sued for damages, received a jury award of $280,000 and was thus enabled to establish research and study centers to inquire into other aspects of American corporate institutionalism. Mining safety, radiation hazards, pollution, union corruption, corporate responsibility, tax inequities, governmental inadequacy in consumer-protection became the broad province of Nader's Raiders. Their consumer campaigns were not ideological but contained deep political significance, since many of the reforms sought would mean drastic political and economic change, and they became a channel for the discontents of the Sixties.

There were other outlets. Pop Music had entered a state of "moral crisis," as some called it, because of an increasing number of songs about drugs, drink, suicide and prostitution. Bob Dylan's "Rainy Day Woman" hymned a drug party. Ray Charles sang "Let's All Get Stoned," and "The Needle of Death." Timothy Leary, out on appeal of his Texas drug conviction, arrived "where the action is," in the East Village in New York, to give "psychedelic celebrations." In San Francisco, where "topless" waitresses and singers had been succeeded by "bottomless," a "topless-bottomless" girl on a swing in a cabaret was ruled not indecent by a local court. Ministers of all religious denominations worked among big-city youth, establishing their own coffeehouses and helping drug addicts.

All the while, the Vietnam War was, in Maxwell Taylor's term, undergoing "extension." Walt Rostow's first move, back in the White House basement, was in support of the request from the Joint Chiefs of Staff to bomb oil facilities above the 17th parallel, because once again it was something that had not yet been tried. The CIA once again was opposed, deeming such action not worth the effort in view of Hanoi's continuing supply of fuel from the Soviet Union, but the Air Force called the bombings "the most important strike of the war." In one month, it said, 70 percent of North Vietnam's oil-storage capacity was destroyed. Premier Ky predicted the "fall" of North Vietnam within three months.

Jean Sainteny, sent from Paris to prepare for a visit by de Gaulle to Cambodia, saw his friend Ho Chi Minh for the last time as American bombs fell on their new targets. "We know the power of our enemies," the frail old man told him. "We know that the Americans, if they like, can wipe out this city as they can wipe out all the principal towns of Tonkin — Haiphong, Nam Dinh, Bac Ninh, all the others. We expect it and we are prepared for it, but that does not weaken our determination to fight to the very end."

The CIA was right about the bombing of the oil installations in the Hanoi-Haiphong area. It did not seem to hamper North Vietnam's war effort. The air operation was a careful one, "surgical" was the word used. Only the most experienced American pilots were given the assignment. Visual identification of targets was ordered, when possible. The patterns of attack avoided populated areas. Maximum electronic countermeasures were taken against antiaircraft fire. High-precision weapons, the first "smart" bombs, were used. It was a magnificent training exercise, but as in the case of the Light Brigade at Balaklava, it was futile.

The lesson was not lost on some in Washington. George Ball finally left the administration, though almost imperceptibly, being replaced by Attorney General Nicholas Katzenbach. John McNaughton was represented as being "fed up." McNamara, or as some called him "the other McNamara," in a speech in Montreal declared that the United States "has no mandate from on high to police the world," and looked to the day "when no single nation, however powerful, can undertake by itself to keep the peace outside its own borders." Bill Moyers, the President's press secretary, regarded by Johnson as almost an adopted son, also left.

Not only the massive air strikes at oil installations but all the bombing of North Vietnam had proved to be in vain; there had been very little there worth bombing. Besides obvious military targets of immediate though small significance — encampments and supply and munitions depots — the Joint Chiefs of Staff could find "only eight industrial installations worth listing" as objectives. After sixteen months of it both the CIA and the Defense Intelligence Agency reported that the bombing had had "no measurable direct effect on Hanoi's ability to mount and support military operations in the South." A secret seminar of weapons scientists held at Wellesley College discounted all varieties of bombing and wondered if the United States could achieve its purposes in Vietnam by any kind or degree of effort.

Something the strikes at the fuel depots did accomplish was to increase the number of American war prisoners in North Vietnam. One pilot in every forty sorties was lost in the attack, and captured airmen, many of them wounded, were soon being paraded abjectly through Hanoi.

The Pentagon's frustration was painfully visible. The Joint Chiefs had done everything military planners could be expected to do — short of dropping "the Bomb" — and their orders had been executed well, but they had not produced the desired results. Again the war demanded "extension." Again General Westmoreland asked for more troops. The Joint Chiefs wanted a new level of 543,000 in 1967, while a "final level" with no date attached was set at 671,000. The Joint Chiefs also once again asked for mobilization of the Reserves, 688,500 strong, as well as more air war and the invasion of Cambodia, Laos and finally North Vietnam.

McNamara made another weary trip to Saigon, but this time, for the first time, he recommended the rejection of a troop request. In the air war, he pressed for the return of bombing back below the 20th parallel to reduce plane and pilot losses, and coupled with that, a serious new initiative for a political settlement. The once-optimistic Defense Secretary was now gravely doubting that the war could be successfully concluded, having come to share the skepticism of his close friend Robert Kennedy, as well as of John McNaughton. Only 84 of 454 members of Congress opposed the President's course, a poll showed, but away from Capitol Hill public protest had risen further. McNamara found out for himself when on a visit to Harvard he was booed and shoved by students. The incident shook him and corroborated his sense of an American loss of will and patience toward the war. He found himself being frequently overruled on bombing targets by the commander-in-chief, and more and more opposed by the Joint Chiefs. He was approaching the frame of mind to leave.

Not only at Harvard but on other campuses the antiwar cries had become more shrill. Student editors and leaders representing college moderates warned the President in a letter that "unless this conflict can be eased, the United States will find some of her most loyal and courageous young people choosing to go to jail rather than to bear the country's arms."

The disaffection reached those already in uniform. Three draftees at Fort Hood, Texas, refused their orders to go to Vietnam and launched the GI Movement, which soon took the form of desertion, stockade rebellions, formation of the American Servicemen's Union, the printing of underground papers and pamphlets, gatherings in offpost coffeehouses and participation in antiwar parades. The civilian minority opposed to the war grew and in some unlikely directions. A Baltimore insurance man organized Business Executives Move for Vietnam Peace, representing small businessmen, factory owners, real estate operators, department store officials and insurance agents. They sent a letter to the White House in the name of "the new patriotism" urging negotiations and an end to bombing, and at stockholders' meetings they demanded that large corporations also oppose the war and remove banking and other interests from Vietnam.

Not only military, moral and patriotic arguments were made against the war, but an anthropological one. Robert Ardrey, playwright become ethologist, in his widely read book *The Territorial Imperative*, predicted an American defeat, though on political grounds he enthusiastically supported the intervention and its professed goal of checking Communist "expansionism." Still, he pointed out: "The intruder's motives may be superior morally, politically, ideologically; the defender's motives may be parochial, contemptible, justifiably intolerable on the part of world opinion; or relative merits may be reversed: it is all one, since our sympathies are meaningless." His conclusion was that "intrusion will not only fail but will accomplish, in all probability, the opposite of its objectives," that is, it would foster the spread of Communism.

As it happened, Communism was containing itself. The Great Proletarian Cultural Revolution had taken possession of China, a cataclysmic purge to reestablish "revolutionary purity." Youthful Red Guards physically assaulted those considered to be lacking in dedication to the Thoughts of Mao, which in a Little Red Book were waved as the symbol of the cleansing. A thousand wall posters bloomed with slogans and denunciations. Schools and colleges were closed down for two years. President Liu

Shao-chi and other "revisionists" were held in house arrest for alleged Soviet sympathies. Marshal Lin Piao's army helped carry out the great purge; then the power of the military, politically unloosed, confronted the party.

The American political process still favored the status quo. The midterm elections of 1966 by and large gave President Johnson and his war policy a vote of confidence, though not an overwhelming one. Some "peace" candidates were defeated and some moderates hardened their positions in order to get reelected. Ronald Reagan, the former film actor still to be seen on television in late-night movies, was elected Governor of California, to a large degree on the platform of quelling student insurgency. Massachusetts sent to Washington the first black senator since Reconstruction, Edward Brooke, a Republican. The minority party won three Senate seats in all, forty-seven seats in the House, and eight governorships, and the new Congress was even more conservative than the old. Most of its members subscribed to the world view of the President, as stated before the balloting. "There are three billion people in the world and we have only two hundred million of them. We are outnumbered fifteen-to-one. If might did make right they would sweep over the United States and take what we have. We have what they want."

Lyndon Johnson's remarks were no more fanciful than some being made on the war. Before a House committee, Professor David N. Rowe, director of graduate studies in international relations at Yale, proposed that the United States buy all surplus Canadian and Australian wheat, to cause mass starvation in China. Another academic, indeed a clerical one, the Reverend R. J. de Jaegher, regent of the Institute of Far Eastern Studies at Seton Hall University, testified that the North Vietnamese "would be perfectly happy to be bombed to be free."

Edward Lansdale, now a general, back from Vietnam, conceived of a Freedom Studies Center, or "Cold War College," to put anti-Communist vigilance to practical use. His plan was to send psycho-political "combat teams" to foreign countries at the request of their rulers or "acceptable third parties," to give "advice on how to resolve problems of concern to freedom." Reminiscent of the CIA in Laos, or the Russians being "invited" to Budapest in 1956, the Lansdale idea was rejected by Congress as "too competitive" with its own House Un-American Activities Committee, but defense contractors and other interested parties promptly supplied the necessary funds. The Center had on its advisory board in 1971 the Vice-President, three cabinet members, nine senators, twenty-eight congressmen, and six governors, and the Army chief of staff, who had been the commander in Vietnam, spoke at one of its dinners.

The horizon of American "patriotism" was not entirely unclouded. Not much attention had been paid, at least in the United States, when a war crimes tribunal convoked by the British philosopher Bertrand Russell sat in judgment on American actions in Vietnam. Not much credence, either, was given to Hanoi's charge that American planes had bombed the center of the city instead of the "industrial" periphery. The Pentagon flatly denied it. The State Department spokesman said he did not know what "city limits" meant. The explanation offered of the damage was that Soviet antiaircraft missiles had misfired. McGeorge Bundy wrote that the bombing of North Vietnam was "the most accurate and the most restrained in modern warfare."

Evidence in refutation of all such asseveration was at hand. After a long wait and many applications, Harrison Salisbury, veteran correspondent of the New York *Times*, was suddenly granted the first newsman's visa to Hanoi. From there he reported that the capital and other cities had indeed been hit, widespread civilian areas damaged, and many civilians killed and injured. Even if the bombing was not deliberate, even if American pilots had taken evasive action from antiaircraft guns and dropped their bombs off-target, even if the houses destroyed were rickety, the damage not monumental, the casualties not staggering, it was plain that Hanoi had been bombed and that the United States had at best dissembled.

The Pentagon was distinctly perturbed by Salisbury's dispatches and belittled his veracity and intentions, charging he had merely reported unverified North Vietnamese statements and statistics, as incidentally Pentagon and MACV reporters did every day with unverified American statements and statistics. The Defense Department's reply to the Salisbury reports was a standard, all-purpose explanation that would endure for the next six years, as bombing waxed and waned, was halted and resumed, and new targets were found over both North and South Vietnam. If civilian bombing had been intended, it was held, casualties would have been far greater. Hanoi was not an "authorized" target, so it could only be bombed inadvertently. Finally, said the Pentagon, bombing "legitimate" military objectives "at Hanoi" was not the same as bombing "the capital" itself; it all came back to intentions, and also, it was obvious, to semantics. The elaborate defense served only to strengthen the impression of official deceit about Vietnam, though in fairness the problem was, as one military man put it, that the Air Force was describing how things looked from thirty thousand feet while Salisbury was reporting "from the ground."

While Salisbury was in Hanoi, Cardinal Spellman was spending Christmas in Saigon, praying for victory, for the war in Vietnam "is I believe a war for civilization." On his way home he told American troops, returned from Vietnam to the Philippines, "I believe that . . . you are not only serving your country but you are serving God." The Pope's Christmas message called not for victory but for a negotiated peace.

The year ended with 5,008 more Americans dead in Vietnam, bringing the total to 6,644 since counterinsurgency began in 1961. In the new year, 1967, the Pentagon intended to take the offensive and "win the war." North Vietnam would be blasted again and again, and since there were no military targets as such left, the President approved "industrial" targets, like power plants, in populated areas.

What 1967 produced instead of victory was the beginning of a national reevaluation of the war. The first indication of a change of mind came from McGeorge Bundy as he discerned "The End of Either/Or." American policy, he wrote, was now refined and perceptive enough to realize it could not choose simply between black and white. No longer was it necessary to decide between isolation and intervention, between Henry Wallace and Jimmy Byrnes, between Europe and Asia, between the Marshall Plan and European collapse, between SEATO and neutralism, between the UN and power politics, in short between anti-Communism and accommodation. Even Vietnam, Bundy conceded after a dozen years of American involvement, was a case of both aggression and civil war; it was not either/or. A victory by the NLF and North Vietnam would not mean the Communization of all Asia, nor would their defeat end China's natural regional domination. Bundy still upheld the American entry into Vietnam, but concluded that even the United States could not solve all the world's problems or settle all its disputes. Bundy's discovery had no bearing on operating procedures in either the White House or Vietnam. His successor, Walt Rostow, and the President were still playing Either/Or. The bomb loads became heavier, the ground troops more numerous, chance of negotiations more unlikely. During the bombing recess for the Lunar New Year Soviet Premier Kosygin, visiting London, surprised his British hosts by expressing interest in a renewed mediation. Prime Minister Wilson informed the President and was authorized to propose, according to Wilson, that the United States would end the bombing if Hanoi gave assurances, which could be secret, of an end to infiltration. As Kosygin departed a phone call from Rostow changed the text of the American proposal: Hanoi must close its borders before the bombing could be stopped. After Tet, the B-52's began striking again.

Senator Robert Kennedy, visiting the French Foreign Office while touring Europe, became involved in this diplomatic "misunderstanding," as the White House termed it. News reports that a "peace signal" from Hanoi had been made known to Kennedy were taken by the President as an attempt to embarrass him. The Senator went to the White House on his return, to explain, and encountered vehement resentment. "We are going to win this war, and in six months all you doves will be finished," Johnson fumed. Reportedly Kennedy called his brother's successor "you son of a bitch."

The Senator still nominally supported the administration but he now for the first time questioned the American commitment and its "sweeping moral principles" in the face of pragmatic policy. American youth, he said, was disillusioned by the sight of the United States fighting "the war for freedom" in Vietnam, but not in Mississippi, Alabama or the northern ghettos. He told the Senate, in his first clear antiwar speech, that he himself and his late brother were to be blamed for making the wrong decisions about Vietnam. The admission was the first such to be made by anyone in the Kennedy or Johnson administrations.

Kennedy was widely criticized, especially by former Vice-President Nixon. "Johnson is right and Kennedy is wrong," he said, and the Senator's proposal of a bombing halt to encourage negotiations only prolonged the war by "encouraging the enemy. They are led to believe there is a division in the United States, and they can win."

A division there was, and to Nixon it seemed already that in 1968 Kennedy might be a likelier and stronger candidate against him than Johnson. The former Vice-President was at this point clearly preparing to run against an end-the-war campaign by not only continuing but further expanding the war, in accord with his public pronouncements for more than a decade. Expansion was certainly what the military wanted. General Westmoreland had notified the Joint Chiefs of his need for 200,000 more troops, seeking to bring the authorized level to 671,616 by the middle of 1968. For all their American training, the South Vietnamese were not living up to expectations. While American units were engaged in Tay Ninh province near the Cambodian border, "cleaning up" the NLF, ARVN could not even hold fixed positions. North Vietnamese forces had overrun Quang Tri city, capital of the border province, freed 250 guerrillas from prison, and attacked two regimental headquarters of South Vietnam's best division, the First. Both the army and the national police had fled.

Like Kennedy, his friend Robert McNamara had also come to a decision about Vietnam. The Defense Secretary not only opposed Westmoreland's request for more troops, but at a White House meeting he read a memorandum from John McNaughton citing the "fatal flaw" of raising the level of forces without knowing what their use or purpose would be. In order not to repudiate the military entirely, McNaughton accepted the principle of an increase, suggesting 80,000 reinforcements as a compromise with Westmoreland's 200,000 figure.

Then the memorandum ventured into territory the White House preferred to avoid. McNaughton reported that among youth "a feeling is widely and strongly held that 'the Establishment' is out of its mind. The feeling is that we are trying to impose some American image on distant people we cannot understand (any more than we can the younger generation here at home) and that we are carrying the thing to absurd lengths. Related to this feeling is the increased polarization that is taking place in the United States, with seeds of the worst split in our people in more than a century."

This was the same McNaughton who not long before had authorized secret bombing raids in Laos and suggested that the administration consider the destruction of North Vietnam's dam-and-lock system, to flood the rice fields. "Such destruction does not kill or drown people," he explained. "By shallow-flooding the rice it leads after a time to widespread starvation of more than a million, unless food is provided." McNaughton may have been goading his superiors with satire. As an expert in international law he must have known that at Nuremberg the destruction of the Dutch dikes was held cause for the hanging of the Nazi occupation chief Seyss-Inquart.

McNaughton's new mood matched McNamara's. The Secretary found even 80,000 more troops too much, and his own recommendation was that they be held to 30,000. He also advocated a deflation of American aims in South Vietnam. They should be reduced to a promise, with no guarantees, of self-determination. This sounded like the formula for a coalition government in Saigon, with the NLF included. The President peremptorily rejected it.

Increasingly disillusioned by the war, and pondering the decision-making process that lay behind it, McNamara then ordered a study to determine what had gone wrong, between the good intentions and the lamentable results. One of the thirty analysts chosen for the formidable task was Daniel Ellsberg, who had returned from Vietnam similarly distressed about the war he had once so ardently supported, and had joined RAND. The forty-seven volumes of the study would come to be called the Pentagon Papers.

McNamara, engaged now in a prolonged swan song, finally settled on 55,000 more troops for Westmoreland, to bring the level up to 524,000 "maximum" for 1968. But the Senate Preparedness subcommittee, all hawks, opposed any reduction in the air war, and the President ordered it extended to the buffer zone along the Chinese border of North Vietnam. Each escalation brought him a boost in popularity in the opinion polls. The majority sentiment was unmistakable; it was also unreliable. After MiG airfields in North Vietnam were bombed, the President's support reached 72 percent, and 59 percent wanted more escalation. The entry of American troops into the Demilitarized Zone brought hurrahs. As "quick fix" succeeded "quick fix" and each escalation failed to achieve its purpose and contributed to the casualties, the President's popularity dipped.

Following the opinion "returns" as avidly as he had ever followed any election returns, Richard Nixon was shaping his "plan" to bring the war to an "honorable" end, one that could pass for victory. Since every bombing increase was popular, he would increase bombing. Since combat failures and casualties were unpopular, he would withdraw American ground forces. He would call the plan "Vietnamization." The Battle of Con Thien confirmed his judgment. At the Marine base south of the DMZ 200 Americans were killed and 2,000 wounded when the North Vietnamese laid down an intensive artillery barrage, and the garrison had to be supplied by parachute drop. After Con Thien even *Time* came to doubt the war, now that Henry Luce had died, and after Con Thien also came the Battle for Hill 876 near Kontum, in which 80 Americans were killed and 974 wounded.

Larger implications than those of battles lost and won had begun to dawn upon the Senate. The President found authority for all his actions in the Tonkin Gulf Resolution, and Senator Fulbright, who now regarded that exercise of power as steeped in deception, sought to clarify the form and nature of "national commitments," so that they could be made a matter of joint executive-legislative action. Under Secretary of State Katzenbach gave the President's answer. "The expression of declaring a war is one that has become outmoded in the international arena." One member of Fulbright's committee, Eugene McCarthy of Minnesota, could not believe what he heard. If Katzenbach was right, he explained to students at Harvard, the United States was under a kind of "constitutional totalitarianism . . . a four-year dictatorship," and he was resolved to take the only means available, the next election, to oppose it. The "Dump Johnson" movement was emerging.

With McNamara frankly looking for another job, McNaughton also tried to leave the government, but was persuaded by his unhappy superior to remain as Secretary of the Navy. A few days after his designation, McNaughton, his wife and their eleven-year-old son were killed when their passenger liner collided in midair with a private plane. As the Pentagon Papers showed four years later, though little known outside his milieu, McNaughton had been the most fertile mind in the administration in contingency planning, war scenarios, political angles, explanations, and cynicism. He assuredly baffled the archivists, as he may have intended, by stuffing his files with his imaginative, sometimes whimsical, frequently contradictory memoranda. They touched all bases and hedged all bets. They were made for Vietnam, and Vietnam for them.

To Bundy, Kennedy, McNamara and McNaughton had been added the name of Martin Luther King as one whose thoughts about the war had modified. SNCC and CORE were part of the antidraft movement, and in the face of dissuasion by many who believed it would detract from his leadership in the civil rights cause, the Nobel Peace laureate took the pulpit in the liberal Riverside Church in New York to make a "Declaration of Independence" from the Vietnam War. It was, he said, "time to break silence."

Ten days later when the Spring Mobilization in New York City brought huge antiwar crowds into Central Park, and 150 young men burned their draft cards, King led a parade of more than 100,000 and linked Vietnam to civil rights in a speech outside the United Nations. Sharing the platform was Stokely Carmichael. On their way the marchers had been set upon by city and mounted police on Forty-second Street, and outside the UN counterdemonstrations demanded the invasion of Cuba, the freeing of the "Captive Nations" of eastern Europe, and the bombing of Hanoi. In the parade six Vietnam veterans found themselves marching together amid the other civilians, and formed the Vietnam Veterans Against the War. The White House announced that the FBI was checking "Communist influence" in the antiwar mobilization.

Another prominent black figure followed King in making an important personal judgment on Vietnam. The heavyweight boxing champion of the world, Mohammed Ali, refused to be drafted, opposing the war, he said, as a Muslim "minister." Boxing officials patriotically stripped him of his title, although baseball players, black and white, evaded the draft by joining the National Guard for a few weeks of military training each year, and football players were deferred because of bad knees which did not seem to interfere with their game. Ali, regarded by fellow blacks as another victim of racial discrimination, began a four-year court fight for vindication, which he eventually won.

Martin Luther King carried his antiwar gospel to a Geneva meeting of groups seeking to implement Pope John's *Pacem in Terris* encyclical. "I criticize America because I love her," he said, "and because I want to see her stand as the moral example of the world." Shortly before, Lord Russell's war crimes tribunal, sitting in Stockholm with two American members, had "convicted" the moral example of the world of "atrocities" in Vietnam. The first American to admit publicly to participating in war crimes did so before the Russell tribunal. Peter Martinsen, who had enlisted after a year at Berkeley, admitted the beating and torturing of prisoners and Vietnamese civilians as an Army interrogator; he had won a medal for his successful use of an electric field telephone applied to prisoners' genitals.

Amid the talk of war atrocities, their "prevention" became a *cause célèbre* in the Army itself. Captain Howard B. Levy, a doctor, was court-martialed at Fort Jackson, South Carolina, for refusing to train Green Berets in dermatology, on the ground that they murdered women and children. He invoked the Nuremberg principle to disobey what he regarded as an illegal order. The court ruled that his argument would be valid if atrocities could be proved. They could not be and Captain Levy, in handcuffs, was led off to prison and served twenty-six months. Three years after his release an appeals court not only questioned the verdict but found that the rules of the Military Code relating to "unbecoming conduct" were "void for vagueness." Captain Levy derived at least moral satisfaction.

As 1964 had been "Freedom Summer" in the name of civil rights, 1967 was declared "Vietnam Summer" by the coalescing antiwar movement. It was also the "Summer of Love," an experience in personal freedom entered upon by tens of thousands of young Americans, suddenly broken away from their middle-class homes in suburbs and small towns by the lure of the Haight-Ashbury section of San Francisco and by the East Village in New York, both slum areas transformed by psychedelic magic into places where dreams came true.

Haight-Ashbury, in the six blocks between Buena Vista and Golden Gate parks, west of the black ghetto, meant rock music, drugs, sex, peace rallies, guerrilla theater, astrology, long hair, beads, the underground press, and "crash pads" open to all seeking shelter. It also meant drug-pushers, thieves, pimps, prostitutes, rapists and racial problems. Haight-Ashbury had free concerts, free clinics, free marijuana and LSD, and free sustenance and clothing furnished by the Diggers, who took their name from a similar communal group in the English civil war. The modern Diggers, economic dropouts who burned money and sought to break the "possession syndrome," stole most of the food they handed on. Nobody minded.

Haight-Ashbury, offering new "families" to those alienated from their own, was filled with "Flower Children" and had two free nurseries for their children. Huckleberry House opened its doors to runaways under eighteen. In the numerous communes inhabiting the seedy dwellings instruction was available in guitar-playing, cooking, printing, the use of drugs and confrontation with the police. The neighborhood's own "law" was upheld by the Hell's Angels motorcycle gang. The fanciful clothing of the Hippies was a masquerade less proclaiming their identity than protecting it.

The Summer of Love had begun in January when after sit-ins, teach-ins and sing-ins the first Human Be-in was held in Golden Gate Park, and twenty thousand gathered to listen to rock music and "communicate" with one another by their "vibrations." The publicity provided by television and mass magazines brought hordes of teen-agers to the city, as well as those who planned to batten on them, and thousands of tourists and curiosity-seekers. Haight-Ashbury became "the scene," where "the action" was, a garish spectacle, the Lower Depths taken outdoors.

San Francisco's Summer of Love ended when the leaves began to fall, with the mock funeral in Buena Vista Park of "Hippie, devoted son of Mass Media." The Haight-Ashbury medical clinic, which had treated free 13,000 cases of drug overdose, venereal disease, intoxication, hysteria, pneumonia, hepatitis, stomach ache, fractures and poison ivy, closed down. The Digger Free Store was in debt and the landlord, who had not abolished money, demanded back rent. The Switchboard, which provided legal services and crash-pad information, was disconnected. Following the funeral of Hippie, many from Haight-Ashbury joined 4,000 demonstrators at the

Oakland Army Induction Center, where 2,000 police with clubs smashed up the occasion.

The East Village in New York City, the Atlantic seaboard version of Haight-Ashbury, enjoyed a similar carnival of freedom. Properly speaking the East Village was the Lower East Side, populated by poorer immigrants — blacks and Puerto Ricans displacing the earlier Jews, Hungarians, Irish and Italians — but its name was changed when Greenwich Village, the onetime Bohemia, was taken over by high-rise and high-rent apartment houses.

Haight-Ashbury and the East Village were emancipated and untrammeled, the pleasure pilgrims thought, but they were also completely commercial. A new bonanza had been found in discothèques, clothing shops, book and record stores, and psychedelic "souvenirs." As long as they made money, their entrepreneurs did not really care what thoughts were uttered, words written, plays acted or songs sung in the intimate nightclubs, tiny theaters, and underground newspapers of the "counterculture." The Free Speech movement was transplanted to recording studios, book publishing houses, and folk-song cafés. From Mario Savio the torch was passed to Bob Dylan, Lenny Bruce and the Rolling Stones. They all bit the hand that so lavishly fed them, and the hand returned for more. In the end the social and lyrical revolutionaries became part of the "System" they inveighed against. A revolution was harder to make than to sing or write about. A revolutionary "life-style" within the context of an affluent consumer society was merely outlandish, not outlawry.

The East Village's Summer of Love ended with the sadistic murder in a slum-building furnace room of Linda Fitzpatrick, a pretty art student from the other "bourgeois" Greenwich, in Connecticut, and her friend James "Groovy" Hutchinson from the Long Island middle-class suburbs. The two Flower Children had tried to reform drug addicts. They were stomped to death by a man crazed by drugs or drink, in an Avenue B cellar. The double murder added two more young victims of illusions to the long list of those fallen prey to mugging, beating and rape in the downfallen neighborhood which no amount of psychedelic color and loud discothèque music could disguise. The inhabitants of the Lower East Side hated the newcomers, who called it the East Village. "They really bug us," one young black told a reporter, "because we know they can come down here and play their games for a while and then escape. And we can't, man."

Vietnam Summer and the Summer of Love were also another "long hot summer" in the sweltering mixed cities of the North. More than 150 riots broke out during a six-month period, climaxed by those in Detroit and Newark, each in its own way a symbol of deep social ailment that had not been healed by unprecedented liberal legislation and expression, and unprecedented economic expansion. Detroit especially was not to be easily understood. Unlike Chicago, with its patterned segregation, unlike Watts in its virtual oblivion, Detroit had one of the most liberal and successful administrations in the country. Through labor unions like the United Auto Workers the Negro occupied a social and economic position regarded as the best in the nation. Yet the worst American riots in a century seized and shook Detroit for a week, causing forty-three deaths, injuring 2,000 persons and making 5,000 homeless, inflicting $50 million in property damage from arson and looting. Nearly 5,000 paratroopers and 8,000 National Guardsmen brought vain endeavor to the Dantean scene. Sociologists finally hit upon the explanation that a "commodity riot" had occurred; blacks did not fight whites but instead pillaged their stores.

If Detroit represented an outbreak of raging fever, Newark was a case of chronic municipal deterioration with paroxysms of frustration. The New Jersey metropolis was the first northern city with a black majority. It was also the first American city, according to sociologists, which had become a community of the poor. Not only had middle-class whites moved to the suburbs but also middle-class blacks. The poor who remained in the inner city were unable to pay for necessary municipal services through taxes. In intense economic competition with the whites, blacks could not get bank loans, mortgages or jobs. Construction unions barred them. Newark had the highest percentage of bad housing in the nation, the highest maternal mortality rate, the second highest infant mortality rate. Unemployment in the black ghetto stood at more than 15 percent. Aided by SDS and other liberal white groups, Newark's blacks entered into a political struggle for the school board, for federal funds, finally for the control of the city government, and their efforts fostered white vigilantism. The riots in a sense seemed inevitable. They resulted in the deaths of twenty-three persons, twenty-one of them black, and wrought $10 million property damage, as whole sections of the city were burned out.

Among the many arrested in Newark was the black poet and playwright Le Roi Jones, tried for carrying concealed weapons. The judge saw proof of his guilt in some of Jones's poems apotheosizing Black Power, and though His Honor's reasoning and the case against the poet were thrown out by a higher court, this did not satisfy Jones about justice under the "System." As many other young blacks were doing, he assumed an alien, supposedly ethnic name, became Imamu Amiri Baraka, and rejoined the fight to "redeem" Newark. Another black militant, "Rap" Brown of SNCC, traveled to the Eastern Shore of Maryland and was wounded by a shotgun pellet at Cambridge as he urged black demonstrators to "burn this town down."

Not only blacks enlisted in protest by violence, however much Martin Luther King might preach nonviolence. Puerto Ricans in New York, where their numbers were greater than in San Juan, were as the last arrivals rated even below the blacks in East Harlem and the South Bronx, in terms of housing and economic opportunity. Militants among them formed the Young Lords and "organized" the barrios. The Chicano movement of Mexican-Americans sprang up in East Los Angeles and the cities of Texas, after the spark had been ignited by Rey Tejerina's courthouse raid against ancient land grants in New Mexico. Previously the term Chicano had been a racial slur. It became a badge of honor. In East Los Angeles the Brown Berets emulated the Black Panthers, opposed police mistreatment, and took part in antiwar protests.

The electoral symbol from Alabama had been adopted by a group of young militants in Oakland, and the Black Panthers catapulted from local to shocked national attention as television and newspaper photographs showed them marching with loaded rifles and shotguns into the California Legislature at Sacramento. All they had done, the Panthers said, was dramatize their right to bear arms in "self-defense." Their ghetto organization was soon designated a "political party" by its cofounders at Merritt College, Huey P. Newton and Bobby Seale, though it possessed no political or social program, and operated on "instinct" and racial identity to express black grievances against white authority. In the first instance this was the police, whom the Panthers had taken to trailing on their rounds as self-appointed monitors of conduct. There were frequent set-tos in the Oakland streets and in one of these, in which a policeman was shot and killed, Newton was arrested for murder.

Overnight the nation became Black Panther–conscious. A "Free Huey" campaign recruited new members across the country, eight thousand being signed up in New York City in one month alone. A Huey Newton poster, widely displayed, showed him in leather jacket and black beret, the Panther garb, seated sternly in a thronelike chair with upright spear in one hand and upright rifle in the other.

Gradually the Panthers did form a political grouping of sorts. They called themselves revolutionaries, for their enemy was not merely Whitey but the white ruling class. They put economic struggle higher than racial struggle and fashioned a neo-Marxist ideology based on urban, "anti-colonial" guerrilla warfare, borrowing from Mao Tse-tung, Che Guevara, Frantz Fanon and the Tupemaros of Uruguay. They produced new leaders, one of them Eldridge Cleaver, who wrote the book *Soul on Ice* resulting from his experiences in jail. Exuding drama, menace and violence, the Black Panthers were a natural commodity for television, and it became fashionable — "radical chic" — for many whites as well as young blacks to be on their side against the police, called "Pigs."

Revolutionary talk, however, frightened the black middle class as much as the white. The Panthers began to take part in community activities, organizing against rent evictions and for more welfare. They fought drug-pushers, ran schools, provided free breakfasts to children, opened health clinics, and visited the black inmates of prisons and detention centers. Many black radicals were created behind bars by the intensive study of revolutionary literature.

The Panther image inevitably was overblown, if only by overexposure, and then deflated, by police action, by internal strife, most of all by the hard truth that revolution could not come from a nonrevolutionary situation, despite all the seething rebellion and the violence. The fate of Che Guevara, one of the Panthers' principal heroes, bore witness. The peerless guerrilla had encountered disaster and died, not gloriously. Fidel Castro's *compañero* had left Cuba to begin the "Continental Revolution," taking a guerrilla contingent to Bolivia. There he did everything wrong. He had no tangible objectives, no knowledge of the terrain, no peasant support for his alien forces, and no sympathy from the Bolivian Communist party, which like others in Latin America sought to win or share power legally by parliamentary process. American Green Berets may not have done very well as nation-builders in Indochina but in Bolivia they succeeded in the purpose for which they had originally been created. A Special Forces team trained a Bolivian Ranger battalion in antiguerrilla tactics, and in short order, apparently betrayed by the peasants he had come to "liberate," Che Guevara was tracked down and killed. In his martyrdom he remained a romantic figure to many young Americans, who repeated his prophecy that the United States would be undone by "one, two — many Vietnams."

The war in the first Vietnam, despite continued optimism from the "Pentagon East" in Saigon, looked as if it would continue indefinitely. A message to that effect came to the American people from Hanoi, brought by two French scientists serving as unofficial mediators at the behest of Henry Kissinger, the Harvard professor who was a consultant on "peace" to President Johnson. Xion-Son, as the name was transliterated in Vietnamese, was "suffering from a pain, and this pain is called South Vietnam," Premier Pham Van Dong explained to the two emissaries. The Premier did not believe the United States was ready for a settlement, and said North Vietnam was ready to accept more air attacks, even against the vital Red River dikes. He recalled that the Vietnamese had defeated the Mongols three times. "The American army, strong as it is, is not as terrifying as Genghis Khan."

Pham Van Dong had the same intelligence for David Schoenbrun, the veteran correspondent who was the first broadcast newsman to receive a visa for Hanoi. Schoenbrun had known Ho Chi Minh in 1946, when the failure of the Fontainebleau Conference made the war with the French — "the elephant and the tiger" — inevitable, and now Ho's Premier told him that negotiations could not be held until the American bombing was ended unconditionally. "No reciprocity, no bargaining, no blackmail, no ransom" were the Four No's from Hanoi.

The "enemy" capital was being visited by more and more Americans, who like many at home did not accept the term "enemy." "No Viet Cong ever called me nigger," one prominent black declared. Delegations of students, pacifists, lawyers and other "fact-finders" were afforded glimpses of life under American air assault. Some brought back mail from the increasing number of American pilot prisoners, and indeed obtained the release of a few of them. The American visitors undoubtedly served North Vietnamese propaganda purposes and their reports helped make more abrasive the internal conflict in the United States, where many regarded them as treasonous.

No less than Hanoi had Saigon settled down for a long war. A new American ambassador arrived, Ellsworth Bunker, Vermont Gothic in visage and mien, succeeding the other breed of New Englander, the Boston Brahmin Henry Cabot Lodge. As he had done in the Dominican Republic two years before, Bunker applied himself to "democratizing" the Ky-Thieu regime. The first step was to make it the Thieu-Ky regime, in presidential elections completing the establishing of the Second Republic.

A prodigious amount of American overlordship went into South Vietnam's "democratic" election of 1967. The Voice of America broadcast to the Vietnamese in their own language six-and-a-half hours daily, and the USIS disseminated its "information" by radio, television, films, loudspeakers, and magazines, in a gigantic propaganda effort. An American team of twenty-two observers headed by former Ambassador Lodge pronounced the proceedings "reasonably honest," but they would have been judged clearly fraudulent under most electoral standards.

Both Air Marshal Ky, the Premier, and General Thieu, the chief of state, were presidential candidates, but they refused to resign their military positions, as required under the new constitution. The Assembly, though packed with government supporters, had to exclude both of them, while approving as candidates the retired general Duong Van "Big" Minh, in exile in Thailand, and Au Trong Thanh, the Minister of Economy. Premier Ky then announced that Minh would not be allowed to return to Saigon and declared Thanh to be a "Communist." The Assembly met again, and under the guns of the national police in the balcony, reversed itself, put Thieu and Ky on the ballot, and excluded Minh and Thanh.

Thieu had fought with the Viet Minh for a few months in 1945 against the Japanese and then had joined the French-Vietnamese army against the Viet Minh. He had received training in the United States. He was stolid and single-minded in his anti-Communism, and he was favored by Ambassador Bunker over the showy and less sagacious Ky. In order to avoid a split in the decisive military vote, the Ambassador proposed that the two high-ranking officers be running mates instead of rivals, and persuaded the reluctant Ky, by undisclosed means, to yield to the older man and join him as the vice-presidential candidate. Against the Thieu-Ky ticket were pitted no fewer than ten others, some of them entered by the military men in order to divide the civilian vote.

The election machinery was in the hands of Ky's province chiefs and the national police of General Nguyen Ngoc Loan, but despite many false arrests, strong-arm tactics, the harassment of opposition candidates, widespread fears of reprisal for not voting, exclusion of entire villages from the balloting as "insecure," and the fact that Thieu and Ky campaigned in uniform, they received only 34.8 percent of the total vote. They failed to carry Saigon, Danang and Hue, the principal cities, and six provinces. Under the new electoral law, their small plurality was enough, and since no run-off was permissible the candidate who had received the second largest number of votes and thereby became the potential opposition leader, Truong Dinh Dzu, was instead sent to prison for five years for "talking" about peace. The Thieu-Ky election platform was Saigon's Four No's — no coalition, no neutralization, no territorial concession, no open Communist activities — in reply to Hanoi's.

In the new Vietnamese "democracy" all government functions had American overseers, and all American civilian operations were put under the military. A second full ambassador "coordinated" the "pacification" program, which included the relocation of whole villages, after destruction of their original sites from the air; the killing of crops by defoliation and herbicides, and the arrest and interrogation of suspected members of the "Viet Cong infrastructure." Trained under CIA auspices, "Revolutionary Development" teams of Vietnamese were sent to villages to "reeducate" them.

Not all Americans were as gratified as Johnson, Bunker and Lodge by the advent of "democracy" in South Vietnam in its second incarnation. Senator Robert Kennedy declared the elections "a fraud and a farce," and they provided another issue for the antiwar movement. Still expanding, it now for the first time engaged in direct "confrontation" with the federal government, when a hundred thousand protest marchers converged upon the Pentagon itself. Among them were many Flower Children, who tried to put daisies into the barrels of the rifles held by military police. Students displayed banners reading "End the War," "Support Our Boys in Vietnam — Bring Them Home," and "Hell No, We Won't Go." Veterans of the Abraham Lincoln Brigade, who had fought in Spain thirty years before and now opposed intervention in another civil war, chanted "No More Guernicas," as if anyone remembered. Perhaps some did. In addition to the students and the Hippies the Pentagon marchers included many middle-aged and some elderly Americans.

The daisies were not effective. Tear gas routed the demonstrators when they tried to enter the enormous building, and federal marshals arrested 660 persons. They included Dr. Benjamin Spock, the "baby doctor" who had influenced a generation of child-rearing, the novelist Norman Mailer, and Father Daniel Berrigan. For Spock it was his second encounter with the law. He had previously been indicted for conspiracy with the Reverend William Sloane Coffin, Jr., the chaplain of Yale University, and three other persons, as the result of an antidraft meeting on Boston Common. Though students at Harvard, MIT and other schools enjoyed draft deferment, they were protesting the striking fact that more Americans than South Vietnamese were being conscripted for war.

The Battle of the Pentagon, as it was called, brought together the not entirely smoothly fitted components of the active Resistance — students, Hippies, pacifists, Zen Buddhists, Catholics, Communists, both Moscow and Maoist; Trotskyites, black militants, Chicanos, even some anarchists. Their only point of agreement was opposition to the war.

The two most disparate elements of the Resistance were the blacks from urban ghettos and the young, white, often-pampered college students. The nucleus of the latter, the SDS, was essentially elitist, and in its intolerance of those with whom it disagreed was not much different from right-wing extremists. The blacks came to the antiwar movement by a lower road. The Kerner Commission in its investigation of urban rioting collected a dozen black grievances: unemployment, inadequate housing, inferior education, poor recreation facilities, white disrespect, police attitudes and behavior, a double standard of justice, the inadequacy and mismanagement of federal aid programs, inadequate welfare, double standards in business and credit. These complaints had long existed but they were fused together by the war, and found new expression in new political awareness.

Shortly after the Pentagon march, in which Daniel Berrigan had participated, his brother Philip and three others, in the first public action of the Catholic Ultra-Resistance, entered Selective Service offices in Baltimore and poured ox blood on the draft files as a symbol of those being killed and wounded in Vietnam. Baltimore was the headquarters of the Josephite Order, to which Philip Berrigan belonged.

The President continued to score his critics, and he and his supporters charged that the war was being prolonged by dissent. He lumped all the opposition together, as Thieu and Ky did in Vietnam, and included within it the senatorial disapproval of Fulbright, the remarks of Robert Kennedy — who was speaking like a rival candidate — and the activities of Martin Luther King, Dr. Spock, Stokely Carmichael, the Berrigans, the Quakers, pacifists, draft card burners, campus radicals, peace marchers and flag desecraters. Being thus brought together the dissidents, despite their differences, acted together. Carmichael's cry, "Hell no, we won't go!" was increasingly heard on television. Legislation was introduced to make flag-burning a federal offense and Representative F. Edward Hebert of

Louisiana declared, "Let's forget about the First Amendment." Further dissent stirred further counterdissent. Many Americans linked antiwar demonstrators with racial disturbance and the increase in crime statistics. But doubts were increasingly spreading through the body politic, if not about the necessity for American intervention, at least about the conduct of the war, and certainly about political conditions in South Vietnam. Confidence in the President's war management sank to a new low of 23 percent, in an opinion poll. Secretary Rusk had to enter a New York hotel by a side door to avoid a hostile demonstration in front.

Suddenly the President announced that Defense Secretary McNamara would be leaving the administration, to head the World Bank. The appointment was as much a surprise to McNamara as to anyone else. Johnson's action reflected the fact that for all his defiance of public criticism, he could no longer in his own councils tolerate the most muted dissent, or even equivocation. The ablest man in the Kennedy administration, as he had originally thought McNamara, had become not only a doubter but a troubled one, and such men to Johnson were expendable. If McNamara had left the Pentagon on his own initiative he would have been in effect repudiating the President and his policies, as George Ball had done, though presumably with more impact. By acting first, Johnson made it plain that McNamara was not quitting, he had been fired.

McNamara's friend Senator Kennedy could not be so easily dismissed. Speaking at Marymount, a Catholic girls' college, he called the bombing of North Vietnam immoral. The assembled students and teachers disagreed, and a majority declared itself in favor of more, not less air war. The young Senator was plainly shocked. "Don't you understand that what we are doing to the Vietnamese is not very different from what Hitler did to the Jews?" he asked. Kennedy was still not certain where his criticism of the war was leading him. When asked, as he frequently was, he said that he had no presidential plans and would support the expected 1968 ticket of Johnson and Humphrey for reelection. On the other hand he believed the presidential candidacy of Humphrey's fellow Minnesotan, Eugene McCarthy, would add interest and excitement to the campaign and allow Americans "to take out their frustration in talk instead of violence."

McCarthy had a larger concept of his own intentions. Though reckoned more poet than politician, a man who had once prepared to enter the priesthood, he had been critical in his speeches not only of presidential war policy but of the increased assumption of presidential power. On November 30 he announced he would enter five or six Democratic primaries in 1968, in order to articulate what he believed to be rising sentiment for a negotiated settlement in Vietnam. If this challenge, supported by actual primary votes, did not bring a modification in the administration's line, he intended to seek the nomination seriously, either for himself or for someone else, against the incumbent President. Mc-Carthy said he had told his plans to Kennedy and the latter had neither discouraged him nor pledged to stand aside for him. Press, politicians, and public could perhaps not be blamed for discerning in the McCarthy candidacy the shadowy shape of a Kennedy restoration. The latter was certainly talking more and more like a candidate. The American position in Vietnam, Kennedy said, was no longer based on helping the people of that country. Instead "we're killing South Vietnamese, we're really killing children, we're killing women, we're killing innocent people, because we don't want to have the war fought on American soil, or because 'they' are twelve thousand miles away and 'they' might get to be eleven thousand miles away."

The man in the White House, meanwhile, was not so sure he would seek reelection. He broached the matter to General Westmoreland, asking if such a decision would hurt the morale of the troops, and in what must have been one of the great American understatements was assured it would not. The 475,000 Americans in Vietnam had been learning for themselves that the war was not being prolonged by dissent at home, as the White House and the Washington *Post* asserted after the Pentagon march, but by the fighting qualities and determination of the NLF and North Vietnamese, as well as the inadequacies of the South Vietnamese. The message was delivered this time by the month-long battle of Dakto, in the central highlands, where American troops were engaged by four North Vietnamese regiments, and lost 300 dead and 1,000 wounded, while claiming a North Vietnamese body count of 1,650. During the battle 1,869 tactical air strikes were made — including one by American planes against an American position, with thirty fatalities — 32 B-52 attacks, 1,101 helicopter sorties, and 137,991 artillery shells fired. The result was another empty victory. Westmoreland's attrition policy, it was evident, was ineffective despite the heavy losses it inflicted because the other side held the initiative, deciding when and where engagements took place, and when to stop them. The revolutionary forces also possessed manpower, organization, continuing supplies from the Soviet Union and China, and purpose. Firepower, the chief American reliant, and other technology at best balanced the scale and achieved inconclusive results and military deadlock.

Though they expected to take part in another Kennedy election campaign in 1968, most of those who might be called the Kennedy intellectuals, who had worked with and for the brothers in 1960 against Nixon and gone into the White House as advisers, speech writers, consultants and secretaries, were not clear as to how serious a challenge could be made by Robert Kennedy on the war issue, in view of the presumed wide public support for the Vietnam policy, if not its implementation. Arthur Schlesinger noted that if the United States "wins" in Vietnam "we may all be saluting the wisdom and statesmanship of the United States Government." Like other liberals Schlesinger had not questioned American ends in Vietnam, only the price to be paid for attaining them, and like the President he opposed any withdrawal as "humiliating." Richard Goodwin, another New Frontiersman, similarly condemned the war while justifying it on the ground of American self-interest. He defined that interest as the need "to establish that American military power, once committed to defend another nation, cannot be driven from the field." At the same time Robert Kennedy was asking whether the United States was really defending South Vietnam.

After more than five years of a steadily escalating war, other questions they regarded as more pertinent had impressed themselves on the minds of many young Americans. An increasing number were going to Canada to escape the draft, while others chose prison. An "underground railway" was operated to Canada, as in the Civil War, to assist evaders. The new profession of draft-counseling came into being. Conscientious objectors, draft avoiders and deserters, it need hardly be said, were not all necessarily highly principled or morally outraged. Surely some were unstable, afraid, and maladjusted. It did not matter. They contributed to the cumulative effect of national disunity over the war. So also did the National Security Council's abolition of draft deferments for graduate students. Undergraduates nearing commencement had to make swift decisions. The senior class at Harvard disclosed in a poll that 94 percent disapproved of the war, 59 percent intended to avoid military service, and 22 percent would go to Canada or to prison if necessary rather than to Vietnam. Those already in the Army were deserting in disturbing numbers, some finding refuge in Sweden and starting new lives and families there. Returning veterans seemed anxious only to hide themselves in a population that wanted no reminders of their service.

The war "effort" could hardly be called that in any sense of true national compact. More soldiers and machines were sent to Vietnam, more funds were appropriated, and now after a delay which economists said had caused serious damage to financial stability, taxes were increased. President Johnson pledged solemnly not to devalue the dollar, as it had been rumored he might after the British pound was cut by 14.3 percent. But unlike other wars, no bonds were sold, no metal collected, no goods rationed, no controls imposed. No songs had been sung in praise of Vietnam since "The Ballad of the Green Berets," but Bob Dylan had a mocking new antiwar hit, "God on Our Side."

Whatever defections, whatever doubts there might be about the war, as the election year of 1968 arrived, they were not shared, at least publicly, by the American commander-in-chief. GI's in Vietnam were startled when

President Johnson suddenly appeared, to urge them to "bring the coonskin" home to tack on the wall. He had gone to Australia for the funeral of Prime Minister Harold Holt, who had also divided his country politically by sending troops to Vietnam, and on the way back Johnson stopped not only in South Vietnam and Thailand but in Rome, to visit a baffled Pope. They talked, the President said, about his daughter Lucy's recent conversion to Catholicism.

General Westmoreland and Ambassador Bunker, back in Washington for briefings, declared that all was going well in Vietnam, despite CIA reports to the contrary, and that 67 percent of the country was under Saigon's control. For nearly a year Operation Junction City had been engaged in "search and destroy" activity in Tay Ninh province, the NLF stronghold near the Cambodian border, and had completely incapacitated the foe, it was reported, and made any significant North Vietnamese offensive "impossible."

Despite astrological auguries, military prospects were rated excellent, at least by the military, as the Year of the Sheep ended.

8

"DESTROY . . . TO SAVE . . ."

THE YEAR OF THE MONKEY is inauspicious in Far Eastern astrology but not the most clairvoyant of forecasters could have seen how calamitous 1968 would be for the American effort in the war, the President who so personally superintended it, and the processes and institutions — politics, economics, universities, social and racial relations — affected by it. Things fell apart.

The cause was the turning point of the war, the Tet offensive, a major attack by the revolutionary forces on South Vietnam's major cities — on and within, for it could not have been made without support from guerrillas and their sympathizers inside the urban population. The NLF and the North Vietnamese troops who were "cleaned out" of Tay Ninh province by Operation Junction City had merely been withdrawn and redeployed by General Giap. Their assault against the cities was coordinated with attempted uprisings by the internal "fifth columns" to which another civil war three decades before had given their name. The customary fireworks of the Lunar New Year holiday gave way to the live ammunition of fierce battle everywhere.

The military focal point of the Tet offensive was the desperate combat for Hue, symbolic as the capital of the old Vietnam. It was fought for twenty-eight days and was finally ended by massive American air and artillery attack, and the frontal assault of American Marines with flamethrowers and tank cannon against the ruins of the imperial citadel held by the insurgents. The most vivid and psychologically most shocking impact of the Tet offensive upon American sensibilities came, however, from the bold commando attack on the new American Embassy in the heart of Saigon, some of the action of which was shown on American television screens.

The suicidal lunge of nineteen guerrillas against the embassy compound and their six-hour battle with Marine guards and military police brought death to five Americans, twelve "VC" and four Vietnamese employees of the Embassy, one of whom, a chauffeur, was later discovered to be a "VC." The bodies of the attackers lying sprawled on embassy lawns as members of the staff walked warily about in sports shirts with pistols in hand, conveyed a picture of peril, uncertainty and bewilderment to Americans at home. Equally lurid was the point-blank on-camera killing of a bound sniper suspect by the South Vietnamese national police chief, Nguyen Ngoc Loan.

The attack on the American Embassy was but a small incident in the nationwide pattern of concerted armed action. During the offensive an estimated 32,000 insurgents were killed and 5,800 captured, out of a total force of 84,000. American losses in two months were 4,114 dead, 19,285 wounded and 604 missing. South Vietnamese regular forces counted 2,300 dead and 12,000 captured. In Hue 3,000 persons were reportedly slain, most of them "executed," according to Saigon and Washington, taken from their homes by night singly, in groups and often as whole families, during the month of Communist rule over the city. The NLF undeniably carried out a deliberate policy of assassination of police officials and others regarded as hostile or "pro-American," but in fact most of the casualties in Hue were caused by American and South Vietnamese bombing and artillery in the ferocious block-by-block recapture of the citadel area.

The Tet offensive staggered the Johnson administration and dumbfounded American opinion, wiping out whatever optimism had been created by official statements that the war was going well. Some misgiving had already been occasioned by the *Pueblo* incident a week before Tet, the seizure off North Korea of an American electronic surveillance vessel with its entire crew of eighty-two, and by subsequent clashes along the 38th parallel armistice line. For a few days the White House was transfixed by the thought that the Korean conflict was being reopened as a second front to Vietnam.

What had been happening in Vietnam before Tet had already discredited any belief that the adversary was "finished," as Westmoreland and Bunker had reported. On the rocky terrain of Khe Sanh in the highlands a garrison of 6,000 American Marines had been surrounded by several times that many North Vietnamese regulars. Another Dien Bien Phu seemed to be in the making, but unlike that decisive battle fourteen years before, effective air strikes were made against the North Vietnamese positions in the most intensive air barrage in military history, up to that point. Still, the siege went on for seventy-seven days, through Tet and through the Battle of Hue. When Khe Sanh was eventually relieved by the First Air Cavalry and the casualties were announced — 300 Marines killed and 1,600 wounded — General Westmoreland claimed a "major victory" in "tying down" two North Vietnamese divisions. The North Vietnamese as at Dien Bien Phu could have left at any time they wanted to; it was the Americans who were tied down. To clinch matters and justify incomprehension at home, though officially presented as a proof of American courage and will in a "vital" situation, Khe Sanh was abandoned as of no value shortly after the siege.

Whether or not the Tet offensive was a last-ditch attempt to turn an adverse tide, like the Battle of the Bulge in World War II, which was how American commanders in Vietnam viewed it, the shock it produced in the United States could not be doubted. Not only had Westmoreland declared the NLF to be "eliminated forever," by his "meat grinder" of attrition, but President Johnson, reporting to Congress on the state of the Union, had proclaimed that "the enemy has been defeated in battle after battle." The news of the nationwide attack upon the cities arrived at the White House as Walt Rostow was assuring four correspondents in his basement office that the Communists were "finished."

Pentagon briefing officers based their finding that Tet was a gigantic military defeat for the attackers on the assumption that its purpose had been to take and hold some of the cities and towns, and to establish a provisional government on "liberated territory."

Johnson in his memoirs would call Tet a "military debacle" for the NLF and North Vietnamese, "the most disastrous Communist defeat of the war." It was nullified, he added, "largely because of what we did to ourselves," blaming particularly a "chorus of defeatism" and "emotional and exaggerated reporting." Tet indeed had immediate sharp influence on American opinion. "What's going on here? I thought we were winning," declared Walter Cronkite on CBS News, and his words were echoed by millions. As a result of Tet the graph of American sentiment against the war reached 50 percent for the first time, and as the months passed the opposition increased. The tide had been reversed.

In the strictest of military meanings Tet was authentically a defeat for the Communist-led forces. They took heavy losses, with obvious deterioration of their political organization. Yet by proving that they had merely to continue to exist and fight in order to prevent the United States from "winning" the war, they shattered American hopes and contributed to the pressures for peace. Even the civilian slaughter at Hue, frequently cited as evidence of the "blood bath" an insurgent victory would inflict on South Vietnam, only drove home to many Americans the point that the war was senseless and had gone on too long. After the battle the Saigon troops reentering Hue also executed hundreds of students, teachers and Buddhist priests as "VC" collaborators, also without trial.

Among other consequences the Tet offensive again brought into question the fighting ability of South Vietnamese forces. The attack on the cities was made possible by ARVN's failure to carry out its defense assignments, necessitating the diversion and redeployment of American troops from their positions against North Vietnamese main line units. In many places ARVN simply refused to fight. American air and artillery had come to be so depended upon that in their absence South Vietnamese troops could not function.

During the Tet offensive occurred the battle for Ben Tre, which came to stand for everything that was wrong with the war. At this Mekong Delta group of villages 1,000 Vietnamese civilians were killed and 1,500 wounded in a joint American–South Vietnamese effort to dislodge an estimated 2,500 "VC." Hostile mortar fire from the villages was answered by "friendly" artillery and air strikes. U.S. Air Force Major Chester L. Brown thereupon explained to newsmen that "it became necessary to destroy the town, to save it." Under this formula American firepower caused heavy casualties among people considered pro-Saigon. When driven out, moreover, the revolutionaries returned after the Americans left.

Tet inevitably intensified the national debate on the war. Some in the Pentagon believed its effects could be overcome only by further large additions of American manpower to prove to the NLF that it could not win. But if Tet was really a Communist debacle, as the Pentagon said, and the United States had really won a great victory, why was it necessary, Americans asked, to send 206,000 more troops to Vietnam as General Westmoreland requested? The chairman of the Joint Chiefs, General Earle G. Wheeler, after visiting Saigon, explained that the reinforcements would enable the United States to assume the offensive and follow up its Tet "victory."

The request for 206,000 more troops was revealed by the New York Times two days before the New Hampshire primary election, causing an infuriated President to charge the story had political aims. How much effect the request had on the voting cannot be known, but New Hampshire Democrats contrived a major surprise by a virtual disclaimer of Johnson's renomination, although arithmetically he was given 49.5 percent of the vote by write-in and Senator Eugene McCarthy 42.4 percent.

As the Tet offensive began, the prospects of McCarthy's crusade for "peace" had been reckoned at approximately zero. The aloof, enigmatic poet, full of wise saws and medieval instances, attracted a scattering of idealists, mostly young, but the mundane task of raising funds was beyond them. Instead of providing ready answers McCarthy was with studied casualness asking others to think for themselves about the war. As any professional could see, it was no way to run a campaign.

Within six weeks after the first solid impact of Tet the McCarthy idyll had become a movement with a tenable goal, though it was not clear what the goal was. McCarthy's position did not constitute the clear alternative to administration policy, in terms of the purpose and nature of the war, that many dissidents were seeking. All he said was that the United States was not trying hard enough to find a successful solution and was still seeking military victory instead of a negotiated settlement, a settlement implying North Vietnam's acceptance of defeat. Some in New Hampshire voted for McCarthy because they wanted an end to the bombing. Others, according to the polls, thought that his opposition to Johnson meant that he favored more bombing as the way to end the war. A vote for McCarthy in New Hampshire was not a vote against the war itself, only against its unsuccessful prolongation. To be dissatisfied with the conduct of the war did not mean the war was wrong.

While the Democrats were at odds among themselves in these confused circumstances in traditionally Republican New Hampshire, the expected Republican nominee, Richard Nixon, declared as he would throughout the campaign, "I pledge to you the new leadership will end the war and win the peace in the Pacific." He did not go into details.

However ambiguous the Democratic primary in New Hampshire may have been as to issues there was no mistaking its portent to the man in the White House or to the fortunes of the antiwar movement. The dream of "dump Johnson" advocates had suddenly become realizable. Businessmen, lawyers, teachers, housewives and even industrial workers joined students and pacifists in demonstrations opposing Vietnam. The turn against the war included some of the country's leading newspapers. The Washington *Post,* which had been strong in its endorsement of the Tonkin Gulf Resolution and its condemnation of attempts to repeal it, took a fresh look at things. For the first time it admitted uncertainties about escalation. It was necessary "to begin by acknowledging miscalculation or failure in the strategy which carried us from the Tonkin Gulf Resolution of 1964 . . . to the present involvement of more than 500,000 American combat troops in a struggle with no clearly visible end-result in sight." The *Wall Street Journal,* through the eyes of bankers and brokers, saw continued escalation endangering the whole "free-enterprise system" for the sake of one lonely Asian outpost.

Returning from Vietnam a short while before, Governor George Romney of Michigan, the favorite of many Republicans for the presidential nomination, had booted himself out of consideration by declaring that he had been "brainwashed." After Tet it was realized by many that large-scale deception and self-delusion had indeed taken place. The guided tour of South Vietnam for cabinet officers, congressmen, newspaper columnists and broadcasters, with its Potemkin hamlets, dinner and a helicopter flight with the commanding general, brilliant briefings at "Pentagon East" and mounds of statistics, had like LSD created hallucinations of progress, development and eventual victory. They had dissolved. Now *Time* magazine, long the watchdog of American global guardianship, was in favor of "integrating the Communists into South Vietnamese politics."

The most devastating effect of Tet was upon the administration of Lyndon Johnson itself. Westmoreland's request for 206,000 more troops began the disruption, and it was enlarged by Pentagon recommendations to invade Cambodia, Laos and finally North Vietnam; to increase the bombing around Hanoi and Haiphong, to call up the Reserves, and institute a "semi-war" economy. Clark Clifford, the President's lawyer-adviser, who had been summoned into the breach to succeed McNamara, ordered a review of the entire situation.

A few days before he left office, McNamara lunched with Clifford, Rusk and Rostow. He was on edge, decrying the bombing both in North and South, and remarked that more bombs had fallen on Vietnam than on Germany or Japan. "It's not just that it isn't preventing the supplies from getting down the Trail," he said. "It's destroying the countryside in the South. It's making lasting enemies. And still the damned Air Force wants more." The three others let McNamara talk and did not say much themselves. They were not happy to see the normally sanguine Secretary leave the administration so dejectedly, if only because his going forced them too to wonder about two decades of American policy calculations.

Vietnam had once been called "McNamara's war" by Wayne Morse and McNamara said he did not mind, in fact was "pleased" to be identified with it. As it continued without "victory" his precepts of "cost-effectiveness" created pragmatic warps in his customary smooth certitude. The case of Robert McNamara represented the most traumatic of American eventualities, the failure of logic in problem-solving. The computers had not been able to take everything into account. "Systems analysis" was a method without human equations or historical perspectives.

McNamara's last official act was to reject the Joint Chiefs' request for more troops, and his leaving encouraged the military men to believe that they would get what they wanted from Clifford, generally regarded as a Vietnam "hard-liner." At his Senate confirmation hearing, the counselor who had assured President Truman that the Communists could only understand force, stated firmly that the Vietnam War effort had been successful, and its cost of lives and money justified many times over. American intervention had saved all Southeast Asia, he declared, and would continue to do so.

Clifford had not, however, become one of Washington's most successful lawyers by letting his briefs stand in the way of whatever had to be done when the time for plea-bargaining arrived. As he took over the Secretary's suite in the Pentagon, Clifford discovered an unexpectedly large sentiment among top civilians of the Defense Department against further escalation.

On the very first day, his deputy, Paul Nitze, long accounted an unequivocal hawk though an "enlightened" one, stated flatly that continuing the bombing would not bring negotiations; he would stop it and limit any new troops to 50,000. Paul Warnke, the Assistant Secretary who had taken McNaughton's place, favored a bombing halt or cutback. The Under Secretaries of all three armed services were among the Pentagon's "hidden doves" and so were a number of colonels and younger generals. Even Secretary of State Rusk had come to think a bombing pause might be used as a spur to negotiations, though he felt sure Hanoi would not accept. Neither would Lyndon Johnson accept. He vetoed what he condemned as a policy of "cut and run," and several times spoke of "disloyalty" and "unpatriotic sentiments" in the State Department. Nitze resigned because of the "unsoundness of continuing to reinforce our weakness."

The President had his supporters. Maxwell Taylor opposed any bombing reduction in order to be "consistent" and not "accept needlessly a serious defeat." Secretary of the Air Force Harold Brown favored, instead of a decrease, an increase "without the present scrupulous concern for collateral civilian damages and casualties." Supreme Court Justice Abe Fortas, in his capacity as confidant, was strongly against any sign of "weakness." Forcefully from Vietnam Ambassador Bunker reported that after Tet, which he regarded as a decisive victory, a new peace overture would undermine the Saigon regime and dismay the population.

As Johnson sought within his administration and among his advisers the kind of consensus he had always politically lived by, the nation was moving toward its own great consensus, formed every four years in presidential elections. The returns from Vietnam, as expressed by the Tet offensive, were not read the same optimistic way by most Americans as by the generals, and the returns from New Hampshire, whatever they really meant, could not be construed except as a blow to the President and an encouragement to his critics. Eugene McCarthy's moral victory brought Robert Kennedy into the open. After the primary he went to see Clark Clifford, who he knew was making a reassessment of Vietnam policy, and suggested that instead of the administration's passing judgment upon itself, as it had done after the Bay of Pigs, a special commission be named to explore policy on the basis of a wider peace approach. If this were done, said Kennedy, he would not himself seek the presidential nomination. The thinly veiled ultimatum was rejected out of hand by Johnson, indignant that he of all people should be asked to make a "deal." Four days after the New Hampshire primary Kennedy announced his candidacy.

Inevitably he was seen by many as a "spoiler," and not for the first time, a ruthless opportunist who had not dared openly challenge Johnson before. Kennedy's own story was that he had been deliberating such an action for six months but had feared to split the Democratic party because of what might be seen as a personal vendetta. Once McCarthy had joined the issue in New Hampshire he felt he would not be making matters any worse. Now he asserted it was time to "take a new look at the war" and "tell the truth." Military victory was not in sight and "probably beyond our grasp." The United States must seek a peace settlement based on political compromise. Saigon was an "incompetent military regime" to which the United States should not subordinate its national interest. This was Kennedy's first speech that was not to some degree apologetic or defensive, and he now had his issue. His natural constituency was waiting despite the long period of hesitation and ambivalence.

On the same day that Kennedy announced for the Presidency, March 16, there occurred in Vietnam an event that would not become publicly known for twenty months but that represented the cancer in the war that put it beyond moral recovery. After the Tet offensive the fighting had become fiercer and more relentless than ever. The Battle of Hue, with its civilian slaughter on both sides; Ben Tre, which had to be destroyed to save it; and the siege of Khe Sanh summed up the war's wantonness and futility. Now there was My Lai.

C Company, First Battalion, Twentieth Infantry Regiment of the Twenty-third (Americal) Division, operating as part of a special task force, had left its fire-base, Landing Zone Dottie — sentimentally named for the task force commander's wife — by helicopter to "search and destroy" east of Quang Ngai city on the Batangan peninsula. This was regarded as "VC territory" and the enemy had been identified as the Forty-eighth Local Force battalion of the NLF, tough and experienced. Army Intelligence located the guerrillas at Son My, a hamlet which U.S. Army maps designated as My Lai 4, in the midst of a territory called "Pinkville" and not only because of its color on the map. As a hostile area it had come under periodic air and artillery strikes.

My Lai 4 was the objective as Charlie Company went into battle for its first time, and the company commander, Captain Ernest Medina, anticipated heavy casualties in the three platoons. The first of these, led by Second Lieutenant William L. Calley, Jr., fanned out toward the southern part of the hamlet as the action began. But action in this instance did not mean combat. No "VC" forces were seen at My Lai, only old men, women and children. No shots were fired at the Americans. But from Calley's superiors came questions over his field radio. "What is wrong with your platoon? Why aren't you shooting anybody?" All officers knew that at least two thousand "VC" had to be listed as Killed in Action weekly. When Charlie Company left on the evening of March 16, My Lai 4 had been wiped out, with its four hundred to five hundred inhabitants. No hut was left standing, no animal left alive, no well unpolluted.

Though some in the higher echelon wondered why only three old American rifles had been found for so many supposed guerrillas, My Lai was reported as an important victory and Calley and his superiors received official congratulations. The story of the battle, as told by Lieutenant Colonel Frank Barker, leader of the task force bearing his name, detailed sniper attacks from the village, fierce fighting, booby traps, the killing in action of 128 "VC" and the capture of thirteen "sympathizers." Later he changed his report and said the residents of My Lai had been killed either by artillery or gunship fire. Both versions of events were false, but Barker would not have to answer for them. He died in an air crash soon after My Lai.

The significance of the undoubted massacre, as even President Nixon termed it when the news came out in 1969, was My Lai's illustration of the kind of war American soldiers were fighting, and not only as to method but in the wholesale deception practiced to conceal truth. My Lai was not an aberration, as some would hold, but a typical incident in the war. In the unreality of Vietnam the green, frightened men of Charlie Company, physically and psychologically tense in their vain search for an elusive deadly enemy, reacted at My Lai in an outburst of release as if they had finally found him. In the objective analyses applied when the facts became known, the argument was made that the 347 peasants — the figure finally arrived at — slain at My Lai could not match the 3,000 town and village officials, army officers, civil servants, police, teachers, students, Catholics, foreigners and ordinary civilians reportedly butchered by the "Communists" in Hue less than a month before. Americans had become inured to stories of Communist atrocities — they had been hearing them for years. Now the truth was out that Americans too committed atrocities, though this may have been no news to those who recalled the Filipino insurrection or the wars against the Indians.

Meanwhile, the South Vietnamese, because of the "fifth column" aspects of the Tet offensive, had instituted the Phoenix program, endorsed and supported by the American command and indeed originated by the CIA. It was described as an attempt to "neutralize" the NLF by discovering its "infra-structure" of secret adherents and sympathizers. In practice this would mean the murder of 20,000 suspected opponents of the Thieu regime and the imprisonment of 20,000 others.

A few days after My Lai the Army's "model soldier," Lieutenant Colonel Anthony P. Herbert — one of the most decorated Americans in Korea, a Ranger, Pathfinder, Green Beret, author of a psychological study of General George S. Patton and honor graduate of numerous military schools — arrived in Vietnam for field duty, and in a few months was given a battalion to command. The case history that unfolded confirmed that My Lai was no isolated incident. Herbert declared that he saw atrocities committed by the South Vietnamese, such as the killing of prisoners, both men and women, and that he reported them to his colonel. When told it was "none of his business," he said, he carried the complaint to the brigade commander. As a result Herbert became engaged in his own war with the Army. By his own account he was kept from promotion, relieved of command, and given a bad efficiency rating as undependable, ambitionless, slovenly, uncooperative, lacking in integrity, moral courage and loyalty, and "prone to exaggeration." He was also called unnecessarily cruel in battle himself. Assigned to recruiting service in the United States and then to the "sanitary engineering" on a domestic Army post, Herbert finally resigned his commission, disillusioned, he said, in the service in which he had previously made a brilliant career. The two superior officers involved in his case were meanwhile promoted. They denied that he had made any war-crime charges until after he had lost his command for unfitness.

Herbert saw what had happened to him as a reflection of how the Army had changed: to become motivated by rank, promotion, ambition, personal gain and even comfort, rather than by the qualities of professionalism, purpose and devotion that had won America's previous wars as much as any technology. Whatever the truth about the Herbert case — and it generated continuing controversy — an officer of considerable distinction, undeniably possessed of leadership, had somehow "fouled up" in Vietnam, another symbol — Vietnam is full of symbolism — of what befell the Army as a whole.

In the United States Robert Kennedy had begun the eighty-five days of his primary campaign — the last eighty-five days of his life — with a passion that would help make it politically the most supercharged American experience of the decade of the Sixties. He knew he could not be only an antiwar candidate. Too many Americans still favored continuation of the conflict even after Tet and despite rising demands to end the bombing. Kennedy linked Vietnam to the nation's domestic problems. He would seek new policies, he said, to "end the bloodshed in Vietnam and in our cities, policies to close the gap that now exists between black and white, between rich and poor, between young and old, in this country and around the rest of the world."

Vietnam had in fact caused anti-American demonstrations in some European cities. When the news of Kennedy's declaration of candidacy reached London, thousands of Britons assembled against the war outside the American Embassy, and were forced back by police. In the City of London an assault on another American institution, the dollar, was also repulsed. Like the Marines at Khe Sanh the dollar was under siege in European money markets, and in an attempt to halt the run upon it the seven-nation gold pool in London ended gold sales to private buyers, at the height of which the United States was losing gold at the rate of a million dollars every four minutes. When the Group of Ten, the world's wealthiest nations, created Special Drawing Rights based on gold credits or "paper gold," the international monetary system created at Bretton Woods in 1944 came to an end. The dollar's troubles, however, continued.

Once he had bitten the bullet of open opposition Kennedy did not spare the President, blaming the war not only for draft resistance and other youthful rebelliousness, drug addiction and urban disorders, but attacking Johnson personally for calling upon "the darker impulses of the American spirit" and for setting an example "where integrity, truth, honor . . . seem like words to fill out speeches rather than guiding beliefs."

Secretary of State Rusk, snapping at newsmen's questions, said that criticism of the war raised the question "Whose side are you on?" Kennedy replied, "I am on the side of those who are not afraid to recognize past error, who refuse to blindly pursue bankrupt policies." He seemed to communicate with his audiences subcutaneously and viscerally. There had once been the "bad Bobby" of Joe McCarthy's committee, the Attorney General who authorized wiretapping. Now he was the "good Bobby," who had been tempered not only by his brother's fate but by whatever mass emotions lay behind the social ferment of the times. The murdered President's brother had a dark streak that appealed to other Americans who also had it. Unlike Jack, the shining hard diamond, he was the opaque opal of American politics, made up of materials of different density, emitting an iridescence of changing colors. What he was best able to do, though in a fashion different from his brother's, was to raise expectations. Eugene McCarthy, the antihero who sounded as if he wanted to become the anti-President, consciously lowered them.

College campuses were a natural Kennedy forum. With tousled hair, informal address and spontaneous rejoinder, he could arouse a personal rapport quite different from McCarthy's seminar-like relationship. The antiwar sentiments on the campus were there for the taking. Tiny Cornell College at Mount Vernon, Iowa, was a microcosm of the change that had taken place. In 1967 its student body was generally in favor of the war and had refused Campus Chest funds to send medical supplies to North as well as South Vietnam. In the first three months of 1968 eighty Iowa boys died in Vietnam. After Tet, Iowa students felt differently about the war. Many went into neighboring Wisconsin to work for McCarthy in the primary scheduled for April 2.

After New Hampshire, Lyndon Johnson also had his eye fixed on Wisconsin. He had not yet approved Westmoreland's request for more troops and was preparing a television address to announce his plans for the Sunday evening before the Tuesday balloting. He would reassert his firm attitude despite the cautionary advice of Clifford, UN Ambassador

Arthur Goldberg, and even Rusk, but first he called in a group of senior advisers who had enjoyed preeminence in government or the armed services. Known to the press as the Twelve Wise Men, they included former Secretary of State Dean Acheson and former Under Secretary George Ball; Generals Omar Bradley, Matthew Ridgeway and Maxwell Taylor; McGeorge Bundy and Justice Abe Fortas; former Treasury Secretary Douglas Dillon and John McCloy, presumptive head of the "eastern establishment"; and former Ambassadors Lodge, Arthur Dean and Robert Murphy.

The Wise Men visibly unsettled the President. Virtually all of them were pessimistic about Vietnam, a notable change in their feelings since the previous fall. Several opposed further bombing, including Bundy, while Acheson saw it as more damaging to the administration in Washington than to the administration in Hanoi. Dean, Dillon, Bradley and Ridgeway were of two minds about the bombing, Taylor and Fortas supported it, and Murphy advocated even more. The latter three and Walt Rostow were what the shaken President was left with on his side, and Acheson, whom he respected the most, provided the decisive leadership against him. The war could not be won without the use of unlimited resources and five more years of fighting, the former Secretary said, and in addition the Joint Chiefs were "mad" and the President's speeches were so out of touch with reality that "nobody" could believe them. Vietnam, in short, was a disaster, in Acheson's view.

Despite the advice of his elder statesmen, the President adhered to his plan to "see it through" with more troops — though not as many as the Joint Chiefs wanted — and thus with more casualties. Any doubts he might have, he said, were luxuries he could not afford. Rusk, Rostow and William Bundy worked on his March 31 speech, with the successive drafts being written by Harry McPherson, the White House aide from Texas who had previously served in both the Pentagon and State Department.

Clark Clifford demurred. What was needed was not another war speech but a "peace speech," he said, and predicted national rejection of an uncompromising attitude. Nothing loath, McPherson, long personally opposed to the war, set down an alternative draft announcing the suspension of bombing above the 20th parallel, thus sparing the populous Hanoi-Haiphong area. By making the new draft his working copy the President tacitly accepted a change in his policy. Fumblingly, inchoately, deviously but in the end no less surely, consensus had been realized. McPherson continued to tailor the speech along its more moderate lines but the peroration was still militant, and he was not given time to revise the ending. "Never mind," said the President, "I may have one of my own." He winked at McPherson.

It was an incredulous nation that on the evening of March 31 heard from the commander-in-chief that he would not seek reelection. William H. Lawrence, the politics-steeped correspondent of ABC News, had for some time been predicting Johnson would not run again. In his memoirs the President insisted that he had planned since 1964 not to seek re-election and had told various people so. One reason he gave was that he feared death in office; he had been a cardiac case since 1955. But if it had not been for Tet, the New Hampshire primary, and the Wise Men would he indeed have forborne?

Even after New Hampshire he was behaving like a candidate, naming a campaign manager, holding meetings with fund raisers, recalling a former press secretary. In the opinion polls, however, the President was receiving 63 percent outright disapproval for his handling of the war, with only 26 percent approval. It could fairly be said that when he decided to withdraw there was hardly a place in the United States, except for a "secure" military base, where he could appear in public without facing hostile crowds.

Some historians believe that even without the Vietnam War Johnson would have failed as President because the consensus system of government he favored was not an effective or proper one. What was needed, rather, it was said, was a clear choice of priorities, methods and values. Johnson's one-party Texas background and his Senate career had brought him to believe that leadership consisted in reconciling the competing, often conflicting interests of business, labor, the farmers, the poor, ethnic minorities, the utilities, even ranchers and oil millionaires, by providing a portion for everyone of the giant pizza in the sky he called the Great Society. The only question was who got how much. "To govern is to choose" lost its meaning when everything and everybody were chosen. In his practical political way, Johnson believed that the government was primarily a "delivery system" for education, health, welfare and other benefits. It was his misfortune to be brought down by the failure of the more lethal kinds of delivery systems in Vietnam. Yet some historians have been able to conclude that though he may have gone astray in his conception of American interests and leadership, Johnson at least provided the opportunity to reconsider American global policies, that the only way indeed to get the necessary confrontation with the American past was precisely this hard way.

Any such philosophical considerations aside, there was a quality of mendacity about Johnson's public appearances that marred even the grand renunciatory gesture. His announcement of a partial bombing halt and the acceptance of negotiations was less than the whole truth. For one thing, 13,500 more troops were being sent to Vietnam, including for the first time some reservists. The "partial" bombing halt only altered targeting patterns while in tonnage the attack on North Vietnam was actually increased. Within the thirty-six hours following the stipulation of the new bombing line twelve heavy raids were made far above it, dangerously close to the Chinese border. Then it became known that instead of 13,500 more troops, as announced, 50,000 were being sent. At the same time the joint American–South Vietnamese Operation Total Victory had been launched, involving 100,000 troops in eleven provinces.

The college students and others who poured into the streets the Sunday night of the President's demission were premature in their celebration of "the end of the war" by 30,000 more American dead, hundreds more American prisoners, millions of South Vietnamese refugees and tens of thousands of South Vietnamese casualties, thousands of hectares of destroyed terrain and billions of dollars.

Several Americans heard Johnson's speech in Hanoi, over the Armed Forces Radio from South Vietnam. Harry Ashmore and William Boggs, two visiting journalists, argued with the editor of the official newspaper that North Vietnam could not continue its refusal to negotiate because defiance would strengthen the position of those in America who favored "victory" through increased air power. The Hanoi government split internally on the question, but finally declared itself ready for a preliminary meeting to "discuss" the possibility of negotiations.

The next day, as Johnson prepared to fly to Honolulu to consult with his military commanders and diplomats on the new turn in events, Dr. Martin Luther King, believer in nonviolence, was assassinated by a white man in Memphis. A minor labor dispute, a strike by black garbage collectors — in New York City they were white and were called sanitation men — had brought the thirty-nine-year-old pastor to the Tennessee city. When some of his group objected to his staying in a large downtown "white" hotel, he moved to a small place in the black quarter, and as he stood on a balcony talking he came into the sights of a rifle aimed by James Earl Ray from a shabby rooming house opposite.

King's violent death had its palpable irony. It was seen by black militants as a repudiation of his philosophy, and thus further encouraged violence among them instead of serving, as some hoped it might, as a sobering and pacifying influence. In 168 American cities and towns rioting and arson erupted and forty-three dead were reported, at the news of King's death. Negro charges of a white conspiracy spread a pall of unease throughout the country, intensified by the escape of the assassin in police confusion.

The heart of the maelstrom was the national capital itself, with its large black population, which experienced three days of surging furor. Smoke ascended over the Potomac as whole blocks in the downtown area between the White House and Capitol Hill were burned out after methodical looting. Fifteen thousand troops, more than twice as many as had defended Khe Sanh, patrolled the devastated streets. The seven hundred fires set in the capital recalled what the British had done there in 1814.

Chicago, Detroit, Boston and other large cities were also shaken by riots and National Guardsmen had to be sent in. In Chicago flames destroyed a large black residential area and Mayor Richard Daley ordered his police: "Shoot to kill arsonists, and shoot to maim looters." Eleven persons were killed and 2,900 blacks arrested. A few weeks later the frame of mind which Chicago police had worked themselves up to was indicated when without visible provocation they assaulted an antiwar march to the Civic Center. An atmosphere of apprehension settled upon the making of arrangements for the Democratic national convention, which Daley had won for Chicago for the first time since 1956.

King's funeral in Atlanta was attended by many national leaders, black and white, most conspicuous among them being Robert Kennedy, while the administration was represented by Hubert Humphrey, expected to declare himself a presidential candidate by default. Richard Nixon, in pursuit of the Republican nomination, also decided to come after significant hesitation and even called on Mrs. King, but he felt it to be a political mistake and afterward berated those who had advised him to be present, since it might have antagonized southern voters to whom he looked for support.

King's tombstone, with an eternal flame, recalled his most famous speech at the Lincoln Memorial in 1963, in which he said "I had a dream." The stone carried the engraved words of the Negro spiritual he had quoted, "Free at last, free at last, thank God Almighty I'm free at last." He had often spoken candidly of the possibility of just such a violent death as he had encountered. He thought there might at least in some way be redemption in it for his cause. No immediate evidence supported the hope.

The Year of the Monkey in Vietnam in 1968 was the Year of the Panther in the United States. The militant black group which considered itself revolutionary — "for a black man it is more important to read Marx than to learn Swahili," declared Eldridge Cleaver — had as a "political party" adopted a ten-point program calling for "self-determinism," full employment, the "end of capitalist exploitation," decent housing, exemption from military service, a halt to "police brutality," release of all blacks from confinement, and public education "exposing the true nature of American society." So gorged with doctrine were Panther leaders that inevitably they split into factions. Stokely Carmichael, who had been named "Prime Minister," stood for black separatism, at undoubted odds with the plans of Cleaver to unite all revolutionary forces, including white. Another wing of the Panthers, favoring community action rather than revolution, was represented by Huey Newton.

Whatever their internal political differences, the Panthers symbolized violence, which they preferred to regard as counterviolence. Newton was accused of the shooting of an Oakland policeman. Bobby Hutton and Bobby Seale exchanged gunfire with police, the former being killed, the latter wounded. Cleaver was on parole from a prison sentence for rape, and was arrested again in a police raid in which he was wounded and another Panther killed. Withal, in the perspective of American history, the Panthers were less violent than white minorities had been as they fought their way up the social and economic scale. The Molly Maguires, Irish and Roman Catholic, had waged far more extensive guerrilla warfare a century earlier. Other well-remembered names on the land were the Ku Klux Klan, the Know-Nothings and the Mafia. The tradition which flowed through American history from the first days of settlement — in the Indian wars and the Wild West, in race relations and strikes, in crime and in politics — prompted "Rap" Brown to declare that "violence is as American as cherry pie." Not only did the National Rifle Association advocate the unhindered possession of guns but the *National Guardian,* the left-radical weekly, opposed any weapons restrictions impeding "self-defense while the State itself is abundantly armed."

Black Power advocates had been answered in 1966 by a bill in Congress — called the "Rap" Brown Act — making it a felony to cross a state line "with an intent to incite to riot, or to organize, promote, encourage or carry out a riot, or to commit any act of violence in furtherance of a riot." Besides feeling that this was hardly a solution to historical grievance, civil libertarians were shocked by a statute which would penalize not an act, or even a conspiracy to act, but an "intention." The bill also broadly defined a riot as "a public disturbance involving acts of violence by assemblages of three or more persons." Attorney General Ramsey Clark called the measure unconstitutional and it was not passed. After King's assassination, however, the "Rap" Brown law was made part of the 1968 Civil Rights Act. Its first use was against those — seven whites and one black, Bobby Seale — tried in connection with the disturbances at the Democratic National Convention.

How much influence the King assassination had upon what speedily followed on American college campuses can only be conjectured. The fact was that after it the volcanic force accumulating since the Berkeley Free Speech movement of 1964 and the Vietnam teach-ins of 1965 came to a head. Columbia University in New York City started the violent discharge of social lava when a militant SDS group physically seized and occupied several college buildings.

Like all SDS chapters the one at Columbia was divided between "true" revolutionaries and the romantics who believed the rightness and goodness of their cause would prevail by declamation. There was also in SDS a sprinkling of nihilists, anarchists and garden-variety vandals. In practice the philosophical differences became the differences between demonstration and disruption, resistance and rebellion.

Antiwar feeling was hardly universal among college students, at Columbia or anywhere else. In common with the rest of American society, faculty members and students on every campus were split over Vietnam and the ultimate issue beyond. There were those who believed the "System" could and should be preserved and worked within, and those who saw the war as the proof of an irredeemable and thus disposable society. As Columbia and other campuses spilled over, three thousand self-styled "Yippies" in New York swarmed upon Grand Central Station in academic gowns, feathers and beads. This was more than spring fever. They were rehearsing for Chicago.

When campus rebellion burst into violence many of those involved justified it on the ground that the American government with its armed forces in Vietnam was, as Martin Luther King said shortly before his death, "the major purveyor of violence in the world." Politicization of the campus, it was also pointed out, was not of student origin but began when faculty members and groups of scholars engaged in government research and consultation, thus, as many saw it, compromising academic integrity and independence. How could Michigan State, for example, complain about anti-war activism when it had led the way to academic involvement in Vietnam?

The university in fact was "the surrogate for all the tensions and frustrations of American policy in Vietnam," reported the Committee on Student Disorders headed by Archibald Cox, professor of law at Harvard and former Solicitor General for the Kennedys. In the Columbia uprising campus aspects of the war included research for the CIA, government-financed defense analysis, ROTC training, and recruitment by the military, the CIA and the Dow Chemical Company, which manufactured napalm. Students also objected to the university's furnishing classroom standings to draft boards, leading to possible change in draft status. Since 1965 there had been sporadic protests at Columbia against all these things. But more than Vietnam was involved in the 1968 rebellion.

The battlement-like buildings of Columbia looked down from Morningside Heights on the mean streets of the nation's oldest, best-known and most volatile black ghetto, Harlem. The university represented the pinnacle of white affluent society, remote from urban realities, unattainable to those who looked up at it from Harlem, and supremely indifferent. The relation of the university to its surroundings, an issue to some degree almost everywhere, was made acute at Columbia by a controversy over a new college gymnasium on land which Harlem residents regarded as community property. In addition, as one of the largest and wealthiest of American universities, in permanent and inexorable expansion, Columbia had recently acquired ownership of many neighborhood buildings and had dispossessed the tenants.

In the Columbia riots and others that followed, finally, was the issue of the university itself, as stated at Berkeley in 1964. Students on many campuses had come to feel themselves denied of adequate participation in university affairs, and to resent the impersonality and detachment of college administration. What they sought was a change in the "power structure," that popular sociological deus ex machina of the Sixties.

The desire for change had been slowly developing, for the most part mutely, since the Second World War. It was instilled by the growth of the college population, the broadening of the social spectrum of students, and the growing awareness by the young of the social inadequacies to which the SDS manifesto of 1962 was addressed.

In such educational developments as the haphazard growth of institutionalism, quantity enrollment, the triumph of the elective over the discipline of the required, the value put upon formal success in grades and degrees, the universities reflected the society. They were also evasions of it, as students stayed longer and longer at their books and developed more and more specialized, often abstruse fields of interest. Those who went to college to defer the draft were outnumbered by those forced into "higher" education by their parents and the demands of the success legend. The American campus revolution was the first uprising against authority to be financed by the state through government and foundations grants and scholarships.

For nearly two months in the spring of 1968, between the assassinations of Martin Luther King and Robert F. Kennedy, as the Tet offensive and the President's capitulation changed the political complexion of the country, Columbia University was in a state of insurrection. Two mass sit-ins, both ended by police action, resulted in the arrest of some 800 students and injury to 250 Columbians, students and faculty members, and to a score of police. At Columbia, six years after the Port Huron manifesto, three and a half years after Berkeley, the American student mobilization reached its peak. The SDS, called by some Students for the Destruction of Society, joined with SAS, the Students Afro-American Society, in the forcible possession of five buildings for five days, as the result of which, with faculty support, they obtained their professed objective of promised university reform, starting with a new administration. The blacks, who did not want to tear down the university but asked only for a larger share of its bounty, went their own way, mission accomplished. The young middle-class whites of SDS had other ideas, and organized a second sit-in, giving as the reason the university's intention to discipline the ringleaders of the first. Its real cause lay in the split between the romantics and the revolutionaries. The leader of the latter, Mark Rudd, the SDS chapter chairman, led his followers into a direct clash with the police in the name of revolutionary action, and was arrested for inciting to riot and criminal trespass.

The Columbia outbreak was followed by one at Northwestern University and by arson at Stanford, as well as the bombing of a CIA-affiliated research unit at Michigan State. Later came the prolonged turbulence at San Francisco State University, accompanied by a series of dynamite blasts in the Bay City area.

The Cox Commission Report found the college generation it examined to be "the best informed, the most intelligent and the most idealistic this country has ever known." It was therefore also "the most sensitive to public issues and the most sophisticated in political tactics," with "a higher level of social conscience than preceding generations." Whether they thought of themselves as revolutionaries or reformers, many students had taken seriously the ideals they had been taught, and now they saw them, as they thought, denied or subverted in real life. Having concluded that institutional failings of the society prevented correction by traditional democratic means — the war and racial injustice were the two outstanding examples — they turned to direct action, confrontation, sit-ins and violence. When Dr. Grayson Kirk, president of Columbia, entered his shambles of an office after its five-day occupation, ransacking and defilement, he exclaimed, "My God, how could human beings do a thing like this?" As the students saw matters, greater crimes had been committed against their personalities, identities and ideals, to say nothing of the bloodshed in Vietnam. Some sociologists have made the argument that restraint toward the status quo had in fact been exhibited for too long by American youth.

The use and extent of violence often seemed out of proportion to the aims — which was true also in Vietnam — but valid criticism was invited by the shortcomings of a society which did not use the powerful means it possessed to alleviate poverty, disease and hunger; which had, as youthful dissidents believed, demeaned the quality of life instead of improving it. The small revolutionary cadre within the student movement no doubt sought to destroy the university as a step toward destroying the society, but it would not have been able to win support without the essential grievances, real or imagined.

The new college breed, different from the "silent generation" of the Fifties, raised moral questions as well as economic and political ones. The rebels had a world view. Listening to the rock music of protest, wearing their hair longer, clad in new kinds of old clothes, some smoking marijuana or using drugs, they thought of themselves as representing a counterculture that was not merely alternative but conflictive. As the war continued, students had turned from campus teach-ins to draft board sit-ins, the obstruction of induction centers — in Oakland they tried to halt a troop train by lying on the tracks — draft-card burnings, peace marches and mass demonstrations. Many in the Sixties blamed the actions of youth on a permissive society, but the young themselves responded to what they saw as an oppressive one. They had listened to or read their favorite academic philosopher,

Dr. Herbert Marcuse, who expounded the theory that the American Constitution was not a document promulgating democracy but an instrument of "repressive tolerance" by the government.

The oppressiveness of the society, it was held, and not only by Marcuse's disciples, was magnified by the demands and rigors of technology, by increased state authority and control, by military influence and its academic collaborators, by Big Labor as well as Big Business, by conformism and the narrow aims of consumer satisfaction. Only in the limited confines of sex freedom, drugs, and various "liberation" movements was "permissiveness" to be discovered.

Though led by SDS radicals the Columbia rebellion was not an act of conspiracy, the Cox Report found. "A very few revolutionaries may have been in dead earnest. More, we suspect, were half in dreamland, feverishly discussing romantic tactics but hardly contemplating realistic execution." The Great Un-Proletarian Cultural Revolution had incompatible differences within itself, between activists with political aims, demanding a transfer of power, and those who believed in the "emancipation of sensibility" and for whom the tokens of freedom were flowers, beads, chants and marijuana. To the latter "dropping out" of society meant in some cases adoption of a simpler tribal or communal life, as a return to man's "original intelligence." Others followed Timothy Leary in "opening the door" of consciousness into "the Garden of Eden." The ending of the Vietnam War was a simple matter to Leary. "Let's all drop out and change the American consciousness as quickly as possible." Since his arrest at the Mexican border and conviction for possession of marijuana, the former Harvard professor had experienced some difficulty in his attempts at national regeneration. While his appeal went through the courts, the practice of his "new religion" founded on the use of drugs, at his "shrine" in upstate New York, had been several times interrupted by police raids and arrests, in which the assistant county prosecutor, G. Gordon Liddy, a flamboyant, pistol-carrying "law and order" advocate, received front-page fame. Leary charged "religious persecution." Another channel of spiritual escape had been found by Leary's former Harvard associate, Richard Alpert. As Baba Ram Dass, he had grown a luxuriant beard and gone to India, where he studied Yoga and "surrendered" to the point of "the true death of the ego." On his return Baba Ram Dass wrote, lectured and gave advice to others seeking spiritual comfort.

Of the young rebels with political aims a small minority favored social change by violence; some of these would become the Weathermen. A larger number, as they grew older and the world pressed closer, maintained a belief in change by political process and persuasion. The one thing the students of 1968 of all stripes did have in common, distinguishing them from previous generations, was the breadth and swiftness of the communications by which they lived. Their doings were exposed and overexposed to the inadequacies of the mass media, and through these to the larger society which watched reflections of itself on the living-room screen.

Television does not go beneath the surface. It shows how people act and disseminates what they have to say, and neither deeds nor words are always entirely unstudied. Television could not reveal what lay behind the fears and anxieties of the young, or how genuine they were. One of the truths to be reckoned with was that the universities had become places for prolonging youth. Ponce de Leon's fountain was the postgraduate seminar. The young gentlemen and young ladies of the old college days were the "kids" of the new. They may have been the brightest and most sensitive generation but in many ways they were also the most immature. To a large degree their revolution was a mock affair. It was hard to believe that professional cutups like Abbie Hoffman and Jerry Rubin, who on a Greenwich Village New Year's Eve had founded the Youth International party to explain their exuberant cry of "Yippie!" could speak seriously of social overthrow, especially since in the end they themselves became members of the acquisitive society they professed to deride.

As for the "very few revolutionaries" the Cox Commission found, they disagreed so intrinsically over aims, tactics and almost everything else that a few weeks after SDS had brought Columbia to conflict, concession and reform, it achieved the beginning of self-destruction. At its annual convention SDS split into New Left and Old Left factions. They were told apart by the former's devotion to Marcuse and Camus and the latter's to Marx or Mao; by the New Left's preference for rock over the Old Left's for jazz and blues; by the use of marijuana rather than alcohol; by the wearing of denims and long hair rather than short hair and coats and ties. More to the point, the Old Left, represented by the Progressive Labor party, was disciplined and organized, and ran by "democratic centralism" while the New Left was individualistic and diffused by "democratic participation." SDS factionalism extended to the Vietnam issue. The PLP assailed Hanoi as less than truly revolutionary for agreeing to treat with the United States after Johnson's withdrawal speech and the curtailment of bombing.

Though peace negotiations were now deemed possible, the procedural preliminaries had at once bogged down. After numerous other suggestions — Phnom Penh or Warsaw by the North Vietnamese; Geneva, Vientiane, Rangoon, Jakarta, New Delhi, Colombo, Kabul, Katmandu, Kuala Lumpur, Rawalpindi or Tokyo by the United States — Hanoi proposed the sending of peace delegates to Paris, despite Ho Chi Minh's unhappy memories of 1946, and the United States accepted. President Johnson chose the veteran diplomat Averell Harriman as the chief American negotiator and Ho named a former Foreign Minister, Xuan Thuy. President Thieu of South Vietnam announced, however, that he would not negotiate with those who were trying to overthrow him.

Robert Kennedy took the floor of the Senate to declare that not only had there been no prospect of American victory at any time from 1961, but there was "no light ahead at the end of the tunnel now." That day he won the Democratic primary in Indiana against McCarthy and a favorite son candidate, and then won again in Nebraska a week later, this time with his first clear majority over both McCarthy and Hubert Humphrey. Meanwhile his misgivings about Vietnam had been confirmed. The Paris meeting went into immediate deadlock as Xuan Thuy demanded a specific date for the cessation of bombing, so that substantive negotiations could begin, while Harriman insisted that negotiations start first so that the bombing could be halted.

The fumbling talks were overshadowed by other events in the French capital, student riots far more violent than those in the United States. The Paris uprising had no connection with the American ones though many of the reasons for it were the same, principally overcrowding and student resentment of what was considered depersonalization of the educational process. Pitched battles with gendarmes at barricades in the Latin Quarter quickly had wider effects as several trade unions joined the college rebels in clamor against the government of General de Gaulle. They seized factories and suspended transport and other municipal services, and plunged into a series of nationwide strikes. No appreciable reform, economic or educational, came from the rebellion but it shook de Gaulle perceptibly. He dissolved the National Assembly for new elections and stood ready to call out the army to put down any Leftist coup attempt. Though public reaction to the riots and strikes led to a Gaullist triumph in the elections, the autocrat of France had taken the first step toward political defeat and retirement.

The events in Paris touched off a similar student rampage in West Berlin, also with no apparent connection to Vietnam, though the Tet offensive had had as electric an effect on Western Europe as on the United States, and the French had occasion to remember Dien Bien Phu. Tet's biggest impact, however, was in Asia. The American political scientist Hans Morgenthau, visiting India at the time, reported the feeling of government officials and intellectuals that it was the third great historical landmark in twentieth-century Asian relations with the West. The first had been the Japanese victory over the Russians in 1905, and the second the defeat of the British, French and Dutch by the Japanese in World War II. Tet was to New Delhi evidence that the last colonial war had been lost by a Western power in Asia.

The Western tide was in truth receding in the Far East. Just before Tet, Prime Minister Harold Wilson announced British withdrawal by the end of 1971 from east of Suez — Singapore, Malaysia, and the Persian Gulf. The British decision, though long held inevitable, caused mild consternation in Washington, where some saw it as raising America's own stakes in the Far East. American policy planners still made the argument, after all that had happened between Russia and China, that the Vietnam War was kept going only by the conspiracy of "Communist aggression" by Moscow and Peking. For two years, however, the vast Chinese domain had been in the throes of the Great Proletarian Cultural Revolution. Now, as the Communist party tried to reassume the power it had given the army during the upheaval, Marshal Lin Piao refused to yield the mechanism of state control he commanded. To unsettle matters more, internal Chinese crisis was combined with international insecurity. The army could not be used entirely for Lin's political purposes. It had to hold the long and disputed frontier, and defended itself in numerous armed clashes with the Russians.

In the United States Robert Kennedy, after his primary victories in Indiana and Nebraska, was upset in unpredictable Oregon by Eugene McCarthy, by 45 percent of the vote to 39 percent, the first electoral defeat of a member of his family in thirty consecutive elections over twenty-two years. McCarthy, incensed at what he considered Kennedy's infringement on his antiwar and college student constituency, taunted him with his long ambivalence and late conversion. McCarthy ran against Kennedy, but Kennedy was running against Hubert Humphrey, Johnson's heir apparent and the convention favorite. All roads led to California, and all had come to rest upon that state's primary on June 4. Campaigning, Kennedy said he could see no difference between Humphrey and the Republican Nixon. Still, he would support whomever the Democrats named, Kennedy promised, leaving to McCarthy the intimation of a third-party movement if he failed to win the nomination.

There may not have been much to choose between Humphrey and Nixon, and Kennedy was by no means the only one to think so, but there was not much more to choose between himself and McCarthy. Face to face in a television debate in California three days before the primary, neither was willing to leave Vietnam. McCarthy would de-escalate "while still holding strength" and recognizing there must be a new and broader government in Saigon. Kennedy would pursue negotiations but not "force" a coalition on Saigon, and would gradually let South Vietnam assume the burden of the conflict. This was Robert Kennedy's last important word on the subject of Vietnam. On June 4, with large support from organized labor and various ethnic, racial and cultural minorities, he won the California primary by a 46 percent vote to McCarthy's 42 percent. Flushed with victory, he addressed his cheering supporters that night at the Roosevelt Hotel in Los Angeles, and as he left the rally the assassinated President's brother was himself assassinated by a Palestinian Arab, Sirhan Sirhan, apparently resentful of Kennedy's pro-Israel attitude. He died twenty-six hours after the shooting, and his funeral train drew Americans by the thousands to line the railroad tracks across the continent, in shaken grief and mourning. Many of the college students who had rioted in the spring found Kennedy's death another grievance against the "System." Robert Kennedy, the father of ten children with an eleventh on the way, was a man who had changed much and was still changing when he died. Sorrow and compassion, as many of his youthful followers saw it, had in him apparently become driving forces as powerful as the ambition and competitive spirit originally bred by his father and his brothers.

It was at the Kennedy crest, and by something of an astrological juxtaposition in the week in which the Columbia uprising began, that the Age of Aquarius had dawned in the consciousness of American youth. A song of that name was introduced in the first rock-pot-nude musical *Hair*, which opened on Broadway for a four-year run after seven months in Greenwich Village. Except for its hint of the occult, another popular revival, the Age of Aquarius had no precise meaning, though the Watercarrier's sign is a symbol of friendship. As the Age of Aquarius arrived, the Pop Music scene was given over almost entirely to the Vietnam War and the attendant youth rebellion. Millions of the young played repeatedly the Phil Ochs challenge:

> Call it "peace" or call it "treason,"
> Call it "love" or call it "reason,"
> But I ain't marchin' anymore.

Ochs also sang,

> We're fighting in a war we lost before the war began
> We're the white boots marchin' in a yellow land.

Bob Dylan's "Blowin' in the Wind" ("How many times must the cannon balls fly, before they are forever banned?") had been recorded in sixty versions by as many singers. Dylan now was reporting "The Times They Are A-changin'." Such slogans as "Burn, baby, burn," and "Hell no, we won't go" had become popular songs. Even a "Ballad of Ho Chi Minh" was sung by the Briton, Ewan MacColl. Other popular lyrics were frankly in praise of drugs, of revolt against parents, and of sexual experience, such as Jim Morrison's "Light My Fire." All this led an associate professor of sociology at Pacific Western College to perceive "musical subversion." Rock music was being used to sell dangerous ideas, he charged, and the musical technique of changing rhythm was a form of "mind conditioning." Many who heard the deafening hypnotic beat at the Electric Circus in the East Village and other "psychedelic" discothèques confessed that it "blew the mind, man."

Some of the mind-blowing was also due to marijuana, which had made its mass appearance during the Wild Spring of 1967, in high schools as well as colleges and no matter how far away from Haight-Ashbury. At first it was smoked by campus "freaks" and "oddballs" while most students continued to drink beer, but by the time of the Columbia riots "pot" was being tried by "straight" students as well as Hip. Athletes, cheerleaders and "All-American" types were soon using it freely, and eventually it came to carry no particular cachet, a take-it-or-leave-it experience, the novelty worn off like a Simon and Garfunkel record.

Marijuana also appropriated the scene in Vietnam. GI's had been using it for several years out of boredom, idleness or to make the time pass, and it was largely ignored by sergeants and other disciplinarians. By 1969 it was pandemic among draftees, and the Army's all-out campaign against it, by means of lectures, advice on armed services radio and television programs, the search of barracks and punishment, lessened the use of "pot" but only by increasing the use of less detectable "hard" drugs, especially heroin. Southeast Asia, after all, is one of the world's prime sources of opium, from which heroin is derived, and expansion of the opium traffic was a corollary to American military expansion there.

Though negotiations to end the Vietnam War were nominally in progress, no advance could be discerned. Not only did the bombing of North Vietnam continue, but it had been intensified over Laos. It had also been made more effective, the military boasted, as new technology on the ground aided the delivery of the demolition, high-explosive and anti-personnel charges dropped from the skies. The "electronic battlefield" was blazoned abroad, with its sensory devices, radar, laser beams, infrared devices and "people sniffers," which included both chemical "bugs" and the use of actual bedbugs to detect human presence on distant jungle trails.

The antiwar movement had responded by becoming more radical itself, and the federal government instituted severer antiradical measures. A month after Martin Luther King's death, the riots it produced, and the campus outbreaks, the Pentagon issued new orders to the Army Intelligence network for the civilian surveillance it had been carrying out since the Watts upheaval in 1965. They amounted to contingency planning against "revolution," and dossiers were kept not only on antiwar activists but on elected officials, including senators and governors, who spoke at peace rallies or were interested in civil rights or the problems of Mexican-American farm labor. A thousand military intelligence agents spied on the Black Panthers, the SDS, the Yippies, the John Birch Society, the Ku Klux Klan, and even the NAACP and the Daughters of an earlier American Revolution. Army undercover operatives posed as members of dissident groups or carried false credentials as reporters or photographers for nonexistent news agencies. Some 18,000 civilians were watched, it was later revealed, as the Army ostensibly prepared plans for the use of troops in future urban disorders, and 100,000 dossiers were kept, to become eventually part of numerous federal and state "security" files.

The John Birch Society, the KKK and DAR may have been listed as subjects to demonstrate impartiality, but the principal interest of the gigantic espionage operation lay in blacks and antiwar radicals. From the viewpoint of authority there was increased reason. New elements had entered the peace movement. One was the Catholic Ultra-Resistance. Daniel Berrigan had joined with his brother Philip and seven other Catholics to seize draft files at the Selective Service offices at Catonsville, Maryland, near Washington. They burned the files with homemade napalm as a symbolic antiwar act, using directions given in a Special Forces handbook, and calmly waited to be arrested. All nine were convicted and given two-to three-and-a-half-year prison terms.

The antiwar movement, with all its disparate ideologies, tendencies, elements, factions, "life-styles" and motivations descended upon Chicago in August 1968 for the Democratic national convention.

As the nominators gathered, the official host, Richard Daley, declared that "as long as I am mayor, there will be law and order." The "nondelegates," who vastly outnumbered the delegates, were expected to make trouble. The Yippies announced they planned to disrupt the proceedings, while the SDS and other serious groups said they would protest the war. The sessions began in what visiting newsmen described as a "police city-state." The amphitheater was encircled by chain-link fence topped with barbed wire. Manholes in the vicinity were sealed. City police stood outside the hall in phalanxes and National Guard troops bivouacked in the municipal parks which Daley had forbidden to the rambunctious "nondelegates."

The Chicago newspapers solemnly printed all the hallucinatory threats of Abbie Hoffman and the Yippies, who like King Lear would do things that they could not even imagine, "terrors of the earth." Those they did imagine included "plans" to dump LSD into the city's drinking water supply and to seduce the wives and daughters of convention delegates. Daley came to believe, or said he did, that based on "reports and intelligence on my desk" an assassination plot was afoot against three of the presidential aspirants and "many of the leaders including myself." The Yippies, their minds expanded by marijuana and LSD, held a "Festival of Life" as the counterpart to the "Convention of Death." They presented a live pig as their own presidential candidate, and their derisive theatrics won them the trophy they unabashedly sought, national television time. "TV is not something you watch, it's something you're on," declared Hoffman. Mayor Daley's police tried to counter the Yippie provocations by infiltrating the unkempt groups, tapping the telephones of the leaders, and managing to get their own agent chosen as the unsuspecting Jerry Rubin's bodyguard. If they had not taken the Hoffman-Rubin Theater of the Absurd so seriously it would probably have petered out, swallowed up in the expanses of Chicago's parks, lake front and South Side. The daily television fairy tales of the Yippies instead blew police minds as they frayed police tempers, and created the agitated climate which doomed the convention.

After eight years of Democratic administration the Republicans had already formulated the principal issues of the election campaign. Richard Nixon was easily nominated, as expected, and in his acceptance speech at Miami Beach declared: "When the strongest nation in the world can be tied down for four years, with no end in sight; when the richest nation in the world can't manage its own economy; when the nation with the greatest tradition of the rule of law is plagued by unprecedented lawlessness; when the President of the United States cannot travel abroad, or to any major city, without fear of a hostile demonstration — then it is time for new leadership in America."

On the Vietnam War, which he had done as much as any man to bring about, Nixon declared more specifically: "It is essential that we end this war and end it quickly, but . . . in such a way that we win the peace." Not many Americans asked what that might mean. In another speech Nixon declared: "Those who have had a chance for four years and could not produce peace should not be given another chance."

Nixon's choice for running mate was Spiro T. Agnew, the Governor of Maryland, who had won that office as a comparative liberal, when measured against the stridently segregationist Democratic opponent he defeated. Soon the new Governor was invoking "law and order" at Bowie State College, against demonstrations by black students. When Martin Luther King's murder led to minor rioting in Baltimore, Agnew called in the city's moderate black leaders and stunned them by accusations of condoning extremism. He also summoned television cameras to record the occasion, and told newsmen, "At some point you have to stop leading the people and start following them." The Republican vice-presidential nominee, though little known outside his own state, was important to the domestic aspects of Nixon's campaign. He represented a conscious effort to win votes in the once-Democratic "solid South" and also appealed to "law and order" emotions throughout the nation, a code phrase that to many Americans meant putting blacks in their place. Yet at the very time he was laying down the law, after the Baltimore disorders, the stern, suave Governor was regularly receiving large amounts of graft from engineering firms seeking state contracts, an old Maryland political custom. As a consequence his tax returns for 1967, filed in April 1968, were fraudulent, setting forth $26,099 in income instead of $55,599, and thus evading $13,-551.47 in taxes.

Nixon himself was chiefly interested in foreign affairs, which he regarded himself as expert in — his attraction to them may have been due to the personal power, secrecy and intrigue which they often involved, more than to any true political considerations — and if overseas mileage was the criterion his well-stamped passport bore him out. While the Democrats tore themselves apart at Chicago on the issue of Vietnam and "standing up to Communism," the Republican candidate declared that his longtime views on Communism had changed because it was no longer monolithic, and that he foresaw "an era of negotiation" replacing the "era of confrontation." He thought there should be an American approach to China and improved relations with the Soviet Union, in order to obtain a Great Power settlement of the Vietnam War, and after that the creation of a new world balance. Nixon was speaking under the influence of his foreign policy adviser, Dr. Henry Kissinger, the Harvard professor he had inherited from his onetime political opponent, Governor Nelson Rockefeller of New York.

The Democratic convention, inside the hall as outside, was a Laocoon being strangled by the serpents of Vietnam. On the opening night, Monday, Chicago police cleaned out thousands of demonstrators who had camped in Lincoln Park in defiance of Mayor Daley's prohibition. Some of the police agents among the youth then acted deliberately to provoke the rioting which followed. In the convention hall the key floor battle was over the Vietnam plank in the party platform, with McCarthy and George McGovern backing a minority report of the platform committee which called for an unconditional end to the bombing, a negotiated mutual withdrawal by the United States and North Vietnam, and a Saigon coalition including the NLF. Senator Edward Kennedy, last of the brothers, joined in sponsorship of the minority proposal, but in a turbulent three-hour debate, seen on television, and amid shouts of "Stop the war!" it was defeated by a 3-to-2 vote. The victorious majority plank favored a bombing halt if and when it would "not endanger lives of our troops in the field," American withdrawal after a negotiated settlement, and a postwar government in Saigon chosen by "free elections." This was the policy that the absent Lyndon Johnson favored and still pursued, and its passage cleared the way for the Pyrrhic first-ballot nomination of Vice-President Humphrey.

The tensions of the heated Vietnam debate, the divided passions of the delegates and the public galleries, communicated themselves to the crowds downtown, which had been prevented from marching to the convention hall at the Stockyards. As the nominations began, those on the congested sidewalks outside the hotels on Michigan Avenue surged into action. Helmeted police charged groups of taunting, filth-throwing demonstrators with unrestrained violence, venting their anger. Bags of water and some less neutral substances, dropped from hotel windows, sent police storming into the McCarthy headquarters on the fifteenth floor of the Conrad Hilton Hotel, beating up the Senator's young supporters, dragging some out of bed, and holding them in the lobby until McCarthy himself came to release them. The raiders took the precaution of removing their badges to prevent identification.

In the streets the police, with clubs, tear gas and blinding chemicals struck out at everyone within reach. Their actions constituted "a police riot," "unrestrained and undiscriminate police violence," much of it against persons "who had broken no law, disobeyed no order, made no threat." The words were those of the Walker Report on the disorders, which did not minimize the provocation offered the police but found "overreaction" on their part. Among those deliberately assaulted were sixty-three reporters and cameramen, whose notebooks, tape recorders and cameras were red flags to the police. "The word is out to get newsmen," some detectives told reporter friends. As had become common at antiwar demonstrations, the media which reported the news were blamed for creating it.

The rioting was recorded on tape or film by television cameras outside the hotels. Because of restrictions which limited live cameras to the convention hall — an electricians' strike was Daley's official reason — the riot footage had to be delivered to the South Side convention hall for network transmission, and was therefore delayed at least a half-hour. The result was that American living rooms saw the nomination of Hubert Humphrey interrupted by the scenes of violence. While Humphrey was being seconded by Mayor Carl Stokes of Cleveland to woo black voters — Cleveland and Gary, Indiana, had been the first big northern cities to elect black mayors the previous year — the networks showed young middle-class white Americans being battered to the ground by the law's appointed guardians.

The shock reverberated across America. The constantly simmering controversy about the news media came to a boil. Were they only the messengers of evil tidings or, as the police would put it, perpetrators? The networks were accused of showing police reaction to provocation without showing the provocation itself. The television coverage of the convention fixed in the minds of voters the same kind of indelible image, counting against the Democrats, as the Nuremberg-rally nomination of Barry Goldwater in 1964, which had counted against the Republicans.

Magnified on television, the Chicago convention hastened the process of alienation from party politics under way in the country. Eugene McCarthy's followers, heeding the counsel of their elders to "fight within the System," had helped "dump Johnson" in order to end the war, and the war was continuing. Party lines had been steadily blurring, for intrinsically there was a considerable nondifference between Republicans and

Democrats, as George Wallace, heading a third-party movement, delighted in pointing out. Ticket-splitting was becoming common. Adding to the political confusion, rival convention delegations from Mississippi and other states had claimed to be the only true Democrats. Fusion candidates had won mayoralty elections in various cities, notably John V. Lindsay in New York. The clubhouses of the city bosses were vanishing one by one, and even Mayor Daley's perennial grip weakened after the civic disaster he had brought down.

So from the ruins of the convention came the remaking of the Democratic party, the reform of its structure, an infusion of new blood, vitality and ideas — of blacks, young people, women, and cultural minorities — to confirm that social mobility had found political expression. Some saw in it the beginning of a new kind of populism. Yet if the party's reforms brought new elements in, inevitably it drove some of the old elements out.

For throughout the nation Chicago had also given impetus to Nixon's "law and order" campaign. Besides peace in Vietnam the Republican candidate promised safe streets in America. He blamed the Supreme Court for permissiveness and the increase in crime, and promised stricter law enforcement, with wiretapping and surveillance implied. When President Johnson designated his friend Abe Fortas as the new Chief Justice, following Earl Warren's decision to retire, Nixon, supported by many congressmen, insisted that no appointment be made until after the election. Campaigning, he raised the question of the Warren Court's liberal predilections, as he saw them, and declared himself in favor of judicial "interpretation rather than of breaking through into new areas." In Dutchess County, New York, the Nixon-Agnew campaign manager, G. Gordon Liddy, a fervent "law and order" advocate, promised that a new Republican administration would "fight crime."

The rising graph of crime and violence made a potent impress on the 1968 campaign. A sort of internal arms race was taking place. Suburban housewives formed groups to learn how to use pistols. Police departments acquired new weapons and policemen became political candidates pledging more vigorous legal sanctions. New currents of conflict ran through American relationships. The issue of community control of public schools precipitated a teachers' strike in New York City, as white teachers were dismissed by a black school board in one of the slum districts. The strike not only deprived a million children of classes but fomented the phenomenon of black anti-Semitism: most of the striking teachers were Jewish. Black athletes threatened to boycott the Olympic Games in protest against racism, and then two of them, medal winners at Mexico City, bowed their heads in simulated shame and raised black-gloved fists in clenched salute as the National Anthem was played. In many American minds all these things were linked. Like campus disturbances, black consciousness was a major part of the problem of "law and order" which Richard Nixon daily emphasized in his campaign.

Vietnam remained the principal issue, however, and rising antiwar sentiment, threatening defection from Democratic ranks to Nixon's standard of "peace with honor," required Hubert Humphrey finally to sever, or seem to sever, the silver cord that held him to Johnson. Five weeks before the election, in a speech at Salt Lake City, he advocated an end to the bombing on evidence of Hanoi's willingness to restore and respect the Demilitarized Zone. It was not much of a change, and the Vice-President telephoned the President beforehand to reassure him it was not intended as a major departure from policy, but Johnson called it the speech that lost the Democrats the election. At this point, in fact, Humphrey began to pick up in the polls and many felt that if he had spoken earlier he might have had the time to overcome Nixon's lead.

The best hope for Humphrey's election lay at the Paris peace talks. After nearly six months of deadlock over procedure, Hanoi had agreed to guarantee no crossing of the DMZ and no shelling of South Vietnamese cities in exchange for the end of bombing, and when it further conceded that the NLF should be part of its "side" instead of sitting as a separate entity, Saigon said it would join in the formal discussion of a settlement. Johnson planned to make an announcement of the breakthrough in October, with the negotiations to open on November 2, three days before the election. He had not reckoned fully with President Thieu, who made various excuses; his delegates could not get to Paris in time; he was still dubious about the arrangements.

Johnson's announcement, two days later than planned, had to leave negotiations still in the air. He could say only that South Vietnam was "free to be present." He did announce a complete halt to bombing, based on the "understanding" with Hanoi. General Creighton Abrams, Westmoreland's successor as commander in Vietnam, had assured him that the air war could be ended "without detriment." In Hanoi the aging Ho Chi Minh sent a message to his nation. After four years, he said, North Vietnam had "won a glorious victory" and "defeated the American imperialist war of destruction against the North of our country," but "the sacred duty" remained to "liberate the South" and "proceed toward peaceful national unification." This meant that the terms for a settlement had to include replacement of the Thieu regime and a return to the Geneva agreement of 1954. Uncle Ho would not live to see the end of the war.

On November 5 Richard Nixon was elected thirty-seventh President of the United States, a minority winner like Kennedy, Truman, Wilson, Cleveland and Lincoln, with 43.4 percent of the vote to 42.7 percent for Humphrey and his running mate, Senator Edmund Muskie of Maine. George Wallace, making inroads into the Democratic strength, polled 13.5 percent. Humphrey's "politics of joy," which seemed misplaced to many voters, his identification with the Johnson administration, and Democratic desertions and abstentions were handicaps, but in the end they barely prevented him from beating Nixon after all. Aided by organized labor and by blacks who remembered him as their original civil rights champion, Humphrey had steadily narrowed the gap in the opinion polls, which began with a Nixon lead of 16 percent, and some felt that with another week of campaigning he would have won. The straw that broke his back was the Chicago convention. Mayor Daley, no longer the supreme boss, failed to deliver Illinois to the Democrats, as he had done in 1960 to beat Nixon. The Republican took six of the eleven states of the old Confederacy, Wallace the other five.

The American people, dispirited by events at home and in Vietnam, had chosen for their new leader a man belittled by his own President — in eight years' residence the Eisenhowers had never invited the Nixons to the second-floor living quarters at the White House — rejected in his own first bid for the highest office, and identified with the anti–civil liberties spirit of the Joe McCarthy era and with the most ardent support for the Vietnam War from the start. Five years of Johnson, war, inflation, racial strife and draining self-confidence had apparently stirred up the desire for any kind of change, and Nixon had been heard to promise at least an end to the war, and to "bring the American people together" and maintain an "open administration."

Lyndon Johnson said later that if he had run in 1968, he would have won reelection. Not many would agree. In his post-mortem analysis the retired President blamed not only Humphrey's Salt Lake City speech and Saigon's sabotage of the Paris talks for the Democratic defeat, but also the fact that the party had got too far in front of "the people." Thus, the white artisan felt that his welfare had been traded for that of the black man, blacks themselves demanded their rights faster than most other Americans would yield, white suburbanites resented taxes for antipoverty programs, and the disruptive tactics of radicals had offended many Americans and pushed them toward the right. It was perhaps not a bad thumbnail summation. It also did not say much for his own leadership over five critical years.

Whatever else it meant, Nixon's election offered the opportunity to cut loose from two decades of frustrated and, to judge by its results, deluded foreign policy. But Nixon, like Johnson, was not able to admit that the United States had been mistaken. He was ambivalent between his belief in the rightness of the war and his recognition that it had to be ended. As he entered the White House, vowing dedication to "the cause of peace," 30,991 Americans had been killed in Vietnam and 195,601 wounded.

Hanoi had meanwhile reportedly removed twenty-two of its twenty-five divisions from South Vietnam, and while some thought it was to redeploy them, Ambassador Harriman at the finally joined Paris talks saw it as a bargaining bid. The dejected Lyndon Johnson, in the last days of his administration, paid no heed to Harriman's interpretation. Nixon, instead of taking up the offer, if that was what it was, decided on a new start toward "peace with honor." Senator Fulbright, who saw him soon after his inauguration, received the impression that the new President wanted to end the war expeditiously, and that the United States would be out of Vietnam in six months' time.

Well before he took office Nixon had assigned Henry Kissinger to a review of Vietnam policy. Daniel Ellsberg, on loan from RAND, aided the latter by collecting opinion inside the various governmental departments. He found it divided. The Joint Chiefs of Staff, the American command in Saigon and Ambassador Bunker, as well as some State Department and CIA officials believed that the North Vietnamese and the NLF had exhausted themselves in the Tet offensive and could not continue the war effectively, while Saigon grew steadily stronger. Bunker thought Hanoi would make "significant concessions" at Paris. A more pessimistic view was held by Clark Clifford and his Pentagon civilians, with some State Department and CIA support, namely that North Vietnamese weakness had been exaggerated, as always, and that the South Vietnamese government and its army were not nearly viable. Clifford could see no victory ahead even with "forays into Cambodia and Laos" or "expanded bombing of North Vietnam." Despite their optimism the Joint Chiefs recommended resumption of the suspended bombing plus a naval blockade. The CIA, on the other hand, forecast that the mining of harbors and the bombing of supply routes would not interdict North Vietnam's logistics.

Nixon sided with the Joint Chiefs, evidently determined to show Hanoi he was not bound by Johnson's restraints and that no more than Johnson would he be the first President to lose a war. According to Ellsberg, the President warned the Soviet Union through Ambassador Anatoly Dobrinin that he intended to resume the bombing and continue the war, implicitly invoking Moscow's tacit acceptance. Hanoi's response came in the form of another offensive. A month after Nixon's inauguration several major South Vietnamese cities were shelled and 453 Americans died in the first week of the resumed attack. Ho Chi Minh and General Giap were clearly testing the new President, while Nixon, for his part, regarded the attacks as a violation of the "understanding" his predecessor had claimed to have. Thus his hand was freed for retaliation. Whatever chance for peace might have existed was terminated by a new American "pacification" drive in South Vietnam, with the bombing of villages, destruction of crops and removal of peasants. By April more Americans had lost their lives in Vietnam, 33,641, than in Korea, 33,629.

9

WITHDRAWAL PAINS

JOHNSON'S WAR HAD BECOME NIXON'S WAR. Eisenhower had died, a national hero, and now his former Vice-President confronted the conflict the soldier-President had avoided while creating an American stake in Vietnam.

The man who entered the White House on January 20, 1969, took pride in the claim that he possessed no known tensions, that he had never had a headache, that his blood pressure was a sound 110/80, that he had no allergies and took no medicines or vitamins. He attributed his equanimity to the fortunate circumstance that he did not "take things personally," though in his book *Six Crises* he admitted past symptoms of tension denoting depression during the Alger Hiss case of his early career. He had also consulted a psychotherapist in New York in the interval between the Vice-Presidency and the Presidency. After his defeat for Governor in California in 1962 his angry public outburst, it seemed to some, had verged on the hysterical.

The new President was quickly made acquainted with the reality in Vietnam. As the Tet offensive, the siege of Khe Sanh and the still unrevealed My Lai massacre had typified the vain bloodiness of the war in 1968, so in 1969 its endlessness was symbolized by the Battle of Hamburger Hill, properly Apbia mountain, in the A Shau valley southwest of Hue. In ten days of fighting in May American paratroopers made ten frontal assaults, and were repulsed each time until the last, when they took the height with the loss of 135 dead and 150 wounded. Then they were withdrawn because the position was worthless. The only aim of the battle had been "to kill Communists." That week, in Vietnam, 430 Americans in all were also killed.

The general in charge at Hamburger Hill was quickly promoted for his "victory," despite the battle's disturbing implications. For the first time in the war American soldiers seemed ready to mutiny. Frequently during the battle they questioned their orders. Their attacks, seen on television at home, brought back into the living room the same questions that had been raised by the Tet offensive the year before, emphasized by the fact that the new President had been understood to pledge peace. The battle also renewed congressional debate over Vietnam. Senator Edward Kennedy denounced American military thinking as "senseless and irresponsible," and was himself verbally assailed by such hawks as John Tower of Texas and Margaret Chase Smith of Maine. He was supported by George McGovern of South Dakota. Kennedy then took his criticism to the public platform, calling Vietnam "an unjustified, an immoral war." Veteran Republican Senator George Aiken of Vermont had an idea. "Let's just call the war won and go home," he proposed. The Senate found itself in argument about Saigon coalitions, election arrangements, mutual withdrawal and even "national commitments." Visibly the feeling was growing that the time had arrived for the United States somehow to extricate itself from Vietnam.

Hamburger Hill had its effect on the new President. There was a Nixon plan to end the war, though it could hardly be called novel. From the beginning some American generals and officials had been proposing that the burden of war be shifted to the South Vietnamese, as some French generals and officials had proposed before them. Humphrey had put forward "de-Americanization." Nixon called his plan Vietnamization.

Vietnamization was only part of a larger Nixon concept, devised or at least ratiocinated by Kissinger. The Harvard professor had moved into the White House as foreign policy adviser, in succession to Bundy and Rostow, but instead of being confined to the basement he enjoyed a sumptuous first-floor office near the President who, he had finally decided, needed him. After Nixon's nomination Kissinger told Henry Brandon, a British correspondent in Washington, that he feared Nixon lacked principles, inner security, and confidence in his own leadership, that he was "frozen" to the Cold War and would take undue risks. He "remained distrustful until he actually began to work for him," Brandon reported, his fears dissolving after two meetings.

The two men had in fact much in common, in canniness, assiduousness, self-esteem, and a kind of conspiratorial view of life, Kissinger on the intellectual level, Nixon on the instinctive. If the President was a political creature, the professor was a geopolitical one.

Kissinger entered the Nixon administration to the accompaniment of his published views on Vietnam holding that no decisive American victory was possible because "the guerrilla wins if he does not lose." American prestige was nonetheless involved in Vietnam, he wrote, and American commitments had to be fulfilled in order to maintain it.

Kissinger did not regard Vietnam, for all its perverseness and loss of American prestige, as more than a footnote to the quintessential requirement of the time, a Big Power settlement. To him Peking's "acquisition" of South Vietnam, if that ever came about, would in terms of the world balance of power be infinitely less significant than Chinese acquisition of nuclear weapons. His policy goal for Vietnam, as expressed before he became Nixon's adviser, was that there should be a "decent interval," perhaps two or three years, between American withdrawal and Communist accession in Saigon. In this way the United States could not be blamed for what five successive Presidents had solemnly declared would not be permitted to happen.

Himself from *Mitteleuropa*, Kissinger's concept of world concord went back to the continental Concert of Powers established by Metternich more than a century before, which had brought "a generation of peace," a favorite Nixon phrase. The academician envisioned a global Concert of Powers, including China, Japan and Western Europe as well as the United States and the Soviet Union. Like Metternich, the subject of his Ph.D. thesis at Harvard, Kissinger apparently believed in diplomatic elitism, minimizing the power and influence of legislatures, governmental civil services and even public opinion. One of his original complaints against Nixon had been precisely that he would be too conscious of public pressures and not courageous enough to ignore them.

Kissinger was actually less beholden to Metternich than to another notable Middle European, Bismarck, who acted not in rigid counter-ideology to revolution, but used the balance of power flexibly, as a dynamic, not a static force. Bismarck's diplomacy allowed for changed relations not only with rivals but with allies, and despite its internationalist façade, its purposes were primarily nationalistic. As Bismarck played between France and Russia, to prevent them from alliance against Germany, Kissinger sought to play between the Soviet Union and China, taking advantage of the differences between them, similarly to deter any alliance. With such an end in view and no principles to stand in the way, almost any sort of maneuver was possible for the man in the White House. "Power," Kissinger was fond of saying, "is the ultimate aphrodisiac."

A onetime advocate of limited nuclear war, Kissinger had always displayed bipartisanship in foreign policy. He could at the same time serve as adviser to Republican Governor Rockefeller in his presidential ambitions and write position papers for the Democratic President, Kennedy. As one of the State Department's "outside sources" he helped arrange the secret probings in 1968 which led to Hanoi's agreement to come to Paris. At the same time, through Rockefeller in the 1968 campaign, he advocated overtures to China and the Soviet Union, which in his view were no longer to be regarded as revolutionary. He spoke for David Rockefeller, of the Chase Manhattan Bank, even more than for Nelson, the Governor.

Kissinger had served Johnson as an unofficial Under Secretary of State. With Nixon he was soon being called, not at all humorously, the Over Secretary of State. Besides being adviser he was also chief negotiator. Secretary of State William Rogers, one of the President's oldest friends, ceremonially adorned his offices in Foggy Bottom and attended social functions in the John Quincy Adams room. He even held occasional news conferences. It was in Kissinger's hands that the levers of diplomatic decision-making lay. In his own words he changed the Kennedy-Johnson policy of "malignant altruism" to one of "benign selfishness." No longer could the United States, by promises to fight anybody, anywhere, anytime, buy off the threat of social revolution in other nations, Kissinger believed. The world had changed. The presumptive aggressors had their own problems, including those vis-à-vis each other. The United States should use its power in new and less burdensome ways. Yet Kissinger was fatalistic enough to conceive the possibility of failure and to have a Spenglerian sense of doom for the *Abendlandes* — the West.

From the brows of President and adviser sprang what Nixon himself proudly called the Nixon Doctrine. On the island of Guam, principal base of the B-52 bombers, before proceeding to Midway to meet with Saigon's leaders and inform them they would, at least theoretically, be placed on their own as American troops began to leave, the President shared his thoughts with the numerous newsmen who accompanied him. The latter could not make very much out of them.

Did the Nixon Doctrine mean "Asia for the Asians," as was stated? Yes, but with the United States supporting some Asians against others. Did it mean American disengagement? Yes, of some troops, but not of the American presence, or American interests or concern. American intervention always remained possible. There was nothing in the Nixon Doctrine to prevent "one, two — many Vietnams."

All the same, at least some American troops could be withdrawn from battle and American casualties thus decreased. The force level stood at 543,400, when on June 8 the President announced the first reduction of 25,000 by the end of August. On the day he spoke, the clandestine NLF radio reported the formation of the Provisional Revolutionary Government of South Vietnam.

The beginning of troop withdrawals, which would reach 100,000 by the end of the year, suited the national mood of dissatisfaction with globalism. An opinion poll showed that only 25 percent would favor sending American troops if Thailand were invaded (overlooking the fact that American forces were already there), only 27 percent would intervene in Italy, 26 percent in the onetime "flash point," Berlin, and a mere 9 percent in Israel. Further disillusionment was at hand. A former GI, Ronald Ridenhour, who had not seen service in Vietnam but talked with many who had, reported in letters to the White House, State Department, Pentagon and twenty-four congressmen that "something rather dark and bloody" had occurred there the year before, at a place called My Lai. The Army opened an investigation.

At the Combat Intelligence School at Fort Holabird, Maryland, two lieutenants petitioned a federal court for reclassification as conscientious objectors. They were in training for Operation Phoenix and said they had received lectures on torture methods, and heard of numerous deaths of Vietnamese civilians during interrogation. To the Army's consternation their petition was granted. San Francisco's Presidio was the scene of a "mutiny" by twenty-seven prisoners in the stockade, and it was followed by a riot in the stockade at Fort Dix, New Jersey. The Army was beginning to give under its various strains.

Nixon's troop-withdrawal policy was not the unilateral one it seemed to be. He had hinged it upon a scaling down of combat operations by Hanoi also, and was trying to arrange secret direct talks with the North Vietnamese outside the formal Paris harangues. When a Quaker antiwar vigil set itself up outside the White House its leaders asked to see their fellow-Friend and were referred to Henry Kissinger. The professor beamed at them. He was there, he said, for the purpose of ending the war. What Nixon had intimated to Fulbright, Kissinger promised to his callers. "Give us six months. If we haven't ended the war then you can come back and tear down the fence."

The notion that the war had been "turned around" and would soon be "wound down" served to still campus anxieties, though the draft and casualties continued. Whatever antiwar protests took place were non-violent and did not interrupt college routine. Commencements were frequently the occasion for silent disapproval, such as the turning of backs on Kissinger and other government personages receiving honorary degrees, but the hostility seemed to be directed primarily against campus conditions, not all of them related to the war.

Black students at Cornell University, apparently physically intimidated as the result of a long history of all-white fraternities and discrimination in off-campus housing, formed the Afro-American Society, and demanded more "black studies." They were answered by the burning of a Klan cross on the porch of the black girls' co-op building, and replied in turn by occupying the Student Union. Eventually they marched out in dramatic fashion with rifles in their hands and cartridge belts over their shoulders, and though frightened rather than militant, they accomplished their aims.

Far above Cayuga's waters the restructuring of the Cornell curriculum began. Similarly, the teeming City College of New York was shut down by black and Puerto Rican students for several days with the result that open admission was introduced by that prestigious institution of learning, despite widespread fears that this would make it less prestigious. Berkeley students joined "street people" to "repossess" a block of land owned by the University of California and made a "people's park" of it.

Until the draft was converted into a lottery at the end of the year, resistance to it continued methodically if not as dramatically as before. The New Left did not believe peace lay very soon ahead, despite Kissinger's assurances, and warned against expecting it. Senator Edward Kennedy pointed out that the level of combat had not been reduced and the level of bombing had in truth increased. Skepticism was not enough to summon up very much antiwar activism, however. Easter demonstrations were held, recalling Britain's "ban-the-Bomb" marches, and at a Philadelphia vigil the names of the more than 34,000 American dead were read, one by one, for seventeen hours. But the peace movement had begun to divide into its separate components again, each concerned with its own primary affairs — black studies, women's liberation, homosexual emancipation, increased welfare. In counterarray formed large sections of the Nixon-Agnew "silent majority."

Poll after poll tabulated "Middle America's" complaints, ranging from anger at campus rebels and black militants to frustration about the war, and embracing anxieties about drugs, high prices, unemployment, "too much welfare," a sense of estrangement from God, and the belief that people "don't care for each other any more."

The President who had promised to "bring us together" was not doing so. Psychoanalysts reported a different kind of patient on their couches. Instead of having specific problems of adjustment, tied to experiences, relationships or behavior patterns, these patients exhibited a general malaise, with symptoms of aimlessness, restlessness, dissatisfaction and uncertainty, tinged by depression. The burden of complaint was that the world was changing, and that while "living conditions" in the purely material sense might have improved, "things in general," "the quality of life," had worsened.

One obvious sign was environmental pollution. Four days after the Nixon inaugural the administration faced its first domestic test when an oil company platform in the Santa Barbara Channel off California, from which underwater drilling was being done, blew out and sent 750,000 gallons of crude oil to the surface in a gigantic slick, fouling beaches and destroying marine life. From Nixon's indistinctive cabinet emerged a face, that of Interior Secretary Walter Hickel, former Governor of Alaska. He had been cross-examined by a Senate confirmation committee as a suspected "tool" of the "oil interests" and an anticonservationist, but in the Santa Barbara case and another like it in the Gulf of Mexico he acted not only against the oil companies, who had gone ahead with their drilling despite public protest, but also against pressure from within the administration.

The administration clearly favored business. Attorney General John Mitchell had business on his mind as he took office. The Wall Street lawyer and specialist in municipal bonds, the President's campaign manager and former law partner, pointed out in a cautionary speech that the two hundred leading corporations controlled 58 percent of all American manufacturing assets. "The danger that this super-concentration poses to our economic, political and social structure cannot be overestimated," he said. Mitchell, however, also offered the advice, on behalf of the administration, to "judge us by what we do, not by what we say," and he and the Justice Department were soon negotiating antitrust settlements and lending a sympathetic ear to the same large corporations.

The spreading use of drugs and opiates, high on all public-opinion lists of anxieties, gave Timothy Leary new hallucinations. The Supreme Court reversed his Texas conviction because of faults in the 1937 Marijuana Act, and having resettled in the "freak community" of Laguna Beach, not far from the California White House, he announced his candidacy for governor as the symbol of the "politics of pleasure," promising to legalize drugs, as well as gambling and prostitution. Drug-users had taken to an orange-colored, orange-flavored pill they named Sunshine, with the strongest LSD content yet tried. Its pushers called it "sacramental," to be taken to "see God." Most mind-expansionists were still with "pot." It was in plentiful supply.

Another opiate appeared in movie theaters: John Wayne's version of the Vietnam War, *The Green Berets*. Critics hooted it, but it was highly successful financially, earning $15 million at the box office, and by American logic this spoke for its political soundness also.

The Green Berets in real life were involved in controversy of more import, eight of them accused of "terminating with prejudice," or murdering a Vietnamese espionage agent, or double agent, or possibly triple agent, and throwing his body into the South China Sea. Though dropped by the Army, the case brought to public attention what many in Washington and Indochina had long known, that the Special Forces were running a spy network throughout South Vietnam and along the North Vietnamese, Cambodian and Laotian borders, and had sent sabotage teams into North Vietnam. The once-lauded heroes of counterinsurgency came home, their mission unsuccessful, compromised by "dirty tricks" and the opium traffic of their native mercenaries.

For a brief spell, man's first landing on the moon lifted eyes upward from Vietnam and other earthbound derangements. The promise which had opened the decade of the Sixties had been met before the decade's end. President Nixon termed it the greatest event "since the Creation" and flew to the mid-Pacific to welcome the astronauts back, but the lunar landing proved but another television "spectacular" of ephemeral interest, and in some sense in fact another divisive accomplishment in a sorely divided land. Many Americans, while marveling at the courage and proficiency displayed by the astronauts, felt that the $24 billion being spent on the space program, atop the $31 billion spent annually on Vietnam, might have been better applied to closer and more pressing problems.

While men walked on the moon in a triumph of American technology, telephone service in the nation's largest city was at crisis point. Firms that could not be reached by phone because of some mechanical fault took newspaper ads to announce they were still in business, and invited written correspondence. But the postal service had begun to fall apart also, and so had the unwanted passenger service on the railroads. Commuting to and from New York City touched a new low level of dependability and comfort, and an ordinary heat wave crippled power facilities, halting the many appliances the American consumer had been encouraged to acquire. All the nation's services seemed in disrepair and disrepute.

As the date for the first American troop withdrawal from Vietnam approached, the United States still sat in the Paris peace talks, with three separate sets of Vietnamese and without accomplishment. Henry Cabot Lodge, twice Ambassador to Saigon, had replaced Averell Harriman as the chief American negotiator, but he had no better luck. The formal sessions were in fact a façade behind which the President was engaged in more earnest and less polemic peace endeavors. He had written secretly to Ho Chi Minh asking for "serious" negotiations, and Henry Kissinger had entered upon private conversations in Paris with Le Duc Tho, a member of the Hanoi politburo. Their first meeting was arranged by Jean Sainteny, the French businessman-diplomat who was thus able to reciprocate for his own American introduction to General Giap and Ho a quarter-century earlier. Less than a month after the Kissinger-Tho talks began, Ho Chi Minh died, the war unfinished, national unification unachieved. But regularly, in complete secrecy, the Harvard professor continued to meet with the white-haired Vietnamese revolutionary, and brick by brick they patiently established the structure of an eventual settlement.

The direct talks with Hanoi were not Nixon's only secret undertakings. Shortly after he entered office he also ordered the bombing of Cambodia by B-52's but the fact was concealed from congressional committees by the falsification of Air Force records. Only those in the Pentagon who had "the need to know" were aware that 3,600 sorties carried out over the next fourteen months were in Cambodia, and not in South Vietnam, as fraudulently announced. Those in the know included the Secretary of Defense and the chairman of the Joint Chiefs of Staff, but not the Secretary of the Air Force. The extensive bombing, despite Cambodia's professed neutrality, which the United States professedly observed, was aimed at Communist forces, both Cambodian and North Vietnamese, with the apparent sufferance of Prince Norodom Sihanouk, the chief of state.

When the New York *Times* printed a report on the Cambodian air raids, the White House entered upon other covert action in response. Under the plea of "national security," it instituted wiretapping against thirteen government officials, some of them Kissinger's own aides, and four correspondents, to ferret out news leaks. It also engaged the services of two former New York City police detectives to gather what was later admitted to be political "dirt" against those who were regarded as White House "enemies." The covert surveillance operations would have unforeseen consequences for the Nixon administration. One of the wiretaps overheard Daniel Ellsberg, the RAND analyst who had taken the fateful step of copying the Pentagon Papers and was trying to persuade Fulbright and other senators to make them public.

The secret talks with Hanoi and the secret air war in Cambodia were only part of President Nixon's undisclosed efforts to extricate the United States from Vietnam. He was also wooing the two big Communist powers, the Soviet Union and China, the military and political allies of the North Vietnamese and the NLF, but more than that, the other essential components of any new world balance of power. He did not follow a true navigational course; he never did. Because any detente with the Communist world, even if he was the one who sought it, would displease a large body of his original supporters, he zigzagged his way as ships do in wartime to avoid torpedoes. The strategy was to exploit Moscow's and Peking's weaknesses, and their antagonism to each other.

From his mid-Pacific rendezvous with the lunar astronauts on the aircraft carrier *Hornet* Nixon returned home by continuing around the world, and dropped off for a brief visit to Romania. It seemed on the surface a "showboat" occasion, a President who accumulated "firsts" being "the first to visit a Communist country in peacetime," the first to be cheered by crowds behind the "Iron Curtain." The visit to Bucharest also seemed calculated to annoy the Russians, the nationalist Communist leadership being one of the ideological crosses they bore. One of the striking evidences of Romanian "independence" was the continued amenity with the Chinese. This was the true purpose of the Nixon visit, to enlist the aid of the Romanian leader, Nicolae Ceausescu, in smoothing the way to Peking.

Publicly and for the first time, Nixon also used the term People's Republic of China. The signal may have eluded general notice in America, as at most a matter of protocol, a diplomatic zip code, but it did not escape the vigilant Russians. Ambassador Dobrynin anxiously telephoned Kissinger to ask its meaning. Soviet correspondents from Tass, *Izvestia* and Radio Moscow, embassy third secretaries, UN delegates' assistants, press officers and cultural attachés, called up their American acquaintances in Washington, New York, London and elsewhere, and invited them to lunch in the best places, to ask whether it was conceivable that Nixon was serious. Not many thought it likely.

There had been armed clashes between Soviet and Chinese troops along the Ussuri River frontier in Manchuria, stirring Peking's fears. If the Russians could intervene in Czechoslovakia under the "Brezhnev Doctrine," by which they claimed the right to preserve Communist power in sister states against "counterrevolution," could they not also intervene against "social traitors" in China? Soviet Premier Kosygin visited Peking but was not invited to inspect the underground shelters, like Roman catacombs, with endless tunnels leading to the suburbs, which the Chinese were building, or the early-warning system being set up, against the possibility of a Soviet missile or bomb attack.

So China, it appeared, was receptive to the American President's hints of improved relations. As another quiet signal, the American naval patrol of the Formosa Strait was ended, after fifteen years, ostensibly for "budgetary" reasons.

Since the American soundings were held tightly secret, and the war continued unflaggingly despite the first troop withdrawals, the antiwar forces in the United States gathered themselves for a last mass protest, to be held in November. In Vietnam soldiers of the 196th Light Infantry Brigade repeatedly refused their captain's orders to move down a jungle slope, even when he warned of penal action. "A whiff of mutiny," the New York *Times* called it, and it would not be the last, as officers increasingly found that they had to discuss their plans with the enlisted men instead of merely issuing commands. With withdrawal under way, more and more of the GI's queried the motives and necessity of the war. They were fighting it as a matter of survival, not of principle, ideology or moral commitment, and the fewer chances they had to take the better.

Not all young Americans felt that way. In the copper-mining town of Morenci, Arizona, nine graduates of the high school, five "Anglo," three Mexican-American and one Navajo Indian, who had played football and basketball together, enlisted as a group in the Marine Corps. One of them failed his service aptitude test but the others insisted that the entire group would have to be accepted, or none. All were sent to Vietnam, and six of the nine were killed there. Newer graduates of Morenci High School were eager to replace them.

On the other hand, many of those who came back from Vietnam were bitter, and some politically radicalized. In one sense Vietnam veterans were more fortunate than those of previous wars. They had a higher survival rate. The one-year limitation on Vietnam duty, while it may have impaired Army efficiency, also in the beginning served as a brake on GI discontent. Most of those who returned were inconspicuously reabsorbed into civilian society, even those who were not able to find jobs or had acquired the drug habit. As the number of the returned steadily grew, a sharper light was thrown on the Vietnam veteran, revealing a more difficult readjustment than had been assumed. Fewer took advantage of the GI Bill of Rights than Korean or World War II veterans had. The large proportion of blacks, who too often had been socially conditioned against education, magnified the readjustment problem, and it was further intensified by the indifferent, if not hostile, reception many veterans received when they got back. They were given dead-end jobs in which they earned less than they had as soldiers. Many went on welfare rolls. Stories of drug addiction and "fragging" were added barriers to employment.

The Vietnam Veterans Against the War, organized for political purposes, numbered about twelve thousand members, a tiny fraction of the total who returned. Many others came back as individuals opposed to the war. Thus, in addition to the two basic categories of veterans — those who returned and readjusted, and those who were regarded as maladjusted— Vietnam produced another group, which blamed "society" for the war and for other conditions at home, and believed in the necessity for change. It was not likely that the Vietnam War could produce a revolution at home, but the antiwar veterans, some still wearing uniforms, some in wheelchairs and on crutches, taking part in demonstrations, testifying before congressional committees, appearing as witnesses at kangaroo "war crime trials," were evidence of some of the social disintegration caused.

As the civilian peace movement similarly demobilized, a minority of it had similarly been radicalized. The struggle for control of the SDS, between the original New Left and the Progressive Labor party factions, came to a head at another Chicago convention. The romantic rebels tried to expel the mundane PLP and issued a manifesto proclaiming that the world revolution was already under way in Vietnam and the rest of Asia, as well as in Africa and Latin America. American radicals were urged to forget slums, racism, community action and other "local" issues and join the "anti-imperialist world struggle." The ultra-Leftists, who now called themselves the Revolutionary Youth Movement, had the slogans but the PLP had the votes, the organization and the discipline. Mark Rudd, late of the Columbia uprising, and Bernardine Dohrn led their RYM minority out of the convention, and adopted the new name of Weathermen. It came from Bob Dylan's song "Subterranean Homesick Blues," in which he explained, "You don't need a weatherman to know which way the wind blows."

The Weathermen went into action at once. On the second anniversary of Che Guevara's death they began antiwar demonstrations in Chicago and fought with Mayor Daley's police again, throughout a week in October they referred to as the Days of Rage. The young radicals had confidently predicted that 50,000 to 100,000 persons would join them in their first step toward the violent "seizure of power." As the deadline approached their estimates of support dropped to 10,000, then 5,000, finally 2,500. Greatly outnumbered by reporters and spectators, a sparse group of 300 turned up for the beginning of the revolution. After three days of sporadic skirmishing the Weathermen, routed by the police, retreated to their "subterranean home." They went underground, literally, though only 100 of them arrived at the final stage of clandestineness, the formation of small collectives of three to five in barricaded cellars where society was anathematized and monogamy abolished.

The Weathermen were primarily the children of middle-class and even wealthy homes, where indulgence was their lot, and they evidently believed that the world's oppressed had to be saved in spite of themselves. They rejected a social system which most others in the student movement, including a majority of the blacks, sought to get benefits from. The Czech students who had faced Soviet tanks the year before, the Soviet intellectuals increasingly braving censorship, arrest and confinement in mental institutions, wanted for themselves the kind of political and economic liberties the Weathermen scorned.

The Black Panthers, in whom the Weathermen found allies, had also been playing at revolution and had torn themselves apart in the process, not only in conflict with the police but in internal warfare. Eldridge Cleaver, instead of returning to prison when his parole order was revoked, chose to flee the country. Given sanctuary in Cuba, he was soon in sullen disagreement with the Castro regime, which had troubles enough of its own, and departed for Algiers to set up a Panther "international center." Stokely Carmichael, unable to accept the Panthers' association with white revolutionaries, resigned his premiership in favor of Cleaver and went to live in Guinea, taking lessons in revolution from the first African success and failure at it, the exiled Kwame Nkrumah of Ghana. Huey Newton was serving a prison term for involvement in the killing of an Oakland policeman. Bobby Seale had been indicted for conspiracy and was standing trial as one of the Chicago Eight.

The defendants in that notable juridical process, seen by some Americans as an eight-ring circus, were charged with conspiracy as a result of the Democratic convention riots the year before. They also included the Yippies Abbie Hoffman and Jerry Rubin; a veteran pacifist, David Dellinger; and one of the SDS founders, Tom Hayden. They were not on trial for conspiracy or riot, Hayden declared, but "for our identity . . . long hair, burning draft cards, obscenity." When the Black Panthers' lawyer became ill and could not appear in court, Seale objected so strenuously at this deprivation of counsel and refused other representation so vigorously that he was bound and gagged. But he won judicial separation from the others and the trial became that of the Chicago Seven.

By now antiwar sentiments had become much more respectable, as the nationwide Vietnam Moratorium showed. Those who took part were the spiritual residuals of the college teach-ins, induction center sit-ins, and Pentagon march of the earlier days. At one Moratorium rally even the former Deputy Defense Secretary, Roswell Gilpatric, who had given President Kennedy the first push into troop involvement, joined in reading the long list of war dead. Their total was now 40,028. Vietnam Moratorium activities included antiwar meetings by uniformed soldiers at American bases and ports, though they were then punished by the cancellation of passes, confinement to barracks, and transfers.

One of the largest demonstrations on Moratorium Day, October 15, was on Boston Common, where Edward Kennedy addressed a crowd of 100,000. The Massachusetts Senator had lost some of his national standing as the result of an accident on Chappaquiddick Island. He had apparently panicked after his car hurtled off a bridge into the river below, drowning his young female companion, a former Kennedy secretary who was attending a reunion on the island. The resultant criticism did not deter Kennedy from continued opposition to Nixon's policies as "the road to war, and war, and more war," or to the "corrupt and repressive" Saigon regime. In his Senate subcommittee he focused attention on Vietnamese civilian casualties and refugees. On Boston Common he proposed the complete withdrawal of American forces within a year, and of air and support units within three years, or by the end of 1972.

The President's reply, finally unveiling his plan "to end the war," was delivered between the October 15 Moratorium and another nationwide antiwar demonstration scheduled for November 15. In a television address on November 3 he announced that "in the previous Administration we Americanized the war in Vietnam. In this Administration we are Vietnamizing the search for peace." He rejected any "precipitate withdrawal" as constituting America's "first defeat," but promised "complete withdrawal of ground troops . . . on an orderly scheduled time-table" — which he did not disclose — as South Vietnamese forces took over. ARVN was now a million men strong, in a total population of fourteen million.

Since "Vietnamization" was hardly a new idea, and had in any case begun several months before, the President's speech was significant rather for the rhetoric of polarization it employed. Nixon scorned the antiwar minority and appealed to the "great silent majority of my fellow Americans" to support him as he tried "to end the war in a way that we could win the peace." The calculated words brought tens of thousands of letters and telegrams of concurrence and endorsement into the White House. Many of them, it was soon discovered, had been amassed by Republican state committees and had been sent even before the speech was delivered.

The next day Edward Kennedy on the Senate floor denounced the President's remarks, seeing in them "no new hopes, no new considerations, no new inspiration," and doubting frankly "whether there is in existence any plan to extricate America from this war." Similar criticisms were made by editors and commentators, and it was against this background of doubt and skepticism that ten days later in Des Moines, just before the Vietnam Mobilization with its anticipated record crowds, Vice-President Agnew opened the second phase of the administration's campaign to win the "silent majority." Its purpose was to impeach the organs of news and public opinion, which Nixon inherently disliked and feared, by questioning their credibility and good faith.

Denouncing "instant analysis" of the kind which followed the President's Vietnamization speech on the television networks — as was true of all such speeches and news conferences — Agnew charged that the "tiny enclosed fraternity of privileged men" of broadcast journalism were guilty of misfeasance. The President had the right, he said, "to communicate with the people who elected him without having . . . words and thoughts characterized through the prejudice of hostile critics before they can be digested."

For prejudice, most American journalists would read independence; for hostile, they would read objective. In the small attempt of the television networks at some appraisal of the frequent presidential pronunciamentos and the rare presidential answers to newsmen's questions, the analysis the Vice-President complained of was hardly "instant," since in most cases, as in this one, advance copies of texts were supplied and White House briefings held. More often than not, as the scheduled entertainment programs which the President had preempted were quickly resumed, "analysis" consisted more of summation than evaluation. This did not mean that Agnew's attack, however ill-founded, was not abrasively effective.

On the evening of November 13 all three networks, when they read the advance text from Des Moines, at once dispensed with their regular 7 P.M. news program to give him total command of their air time, and did not allow their news analysts any "instant" judgments on his remarks. Nixon reportedly watched Agnew's Des Moines performance with relish, and telephoned his approval to Pat Buchanan, the White House speech writer he had provided for the occasion. A week later in Montgomery, Alabama, the Vice-President widened his attack to include the critical, assertedly "liberal" press, especially the New York *Times* and the Washington *Post*.

In the historic adversary relationship between Presidents and press few American Chief Executives have not taken umbrage at, parried, or challenged what they felt to be undeserved disapprobation. The Agnew attack went beyond any previous limits of rebuttal and contained, to editorial sensibilities, the threat of censorship or other government reprisal. It also encouraged the divisiveness Nixon seemed to have adopted as a means of governance. As the "silent majority" vented its repressed hostility toward the news media, indignation and resentment poured out against the networks unequaled in vituperation since the days of Joe McCarthy. The American Civil Liberties Union stated its belief that the Agnew speech and what lay behind it put "our entire free democratic society" in peril and threatened the "free trade in ideas" invoked by Justice Holmes.

The President in his Vietnamization speech had declared that "North Vietnam cannot defeat or humiliate the United States. Only Americans can do that." However he may have meant the remark, a few days later came the public revelation of the My Lai massacre of twenty months before. The Army, investigating Ronald Ridenhour's charges, had brought Lieutenant "Rusty" Calley of the first platoon of Charlie Company home from Vietnam shortly before he was to be mustered out and no longer answerable to military justice, like most of the others involved. When he arrived Calley was astounded to learn why he had been summoned. My Lai had long since been forgotten. Any evidence of crime had been obliterated, the victims all buried, the village itself rebuilt, and the residents of "Pinkville" listed as having transferred their allegiance to Saigon. Still, there were the pictures of civilian corpses, taken at the time and now front-page news. There were the printed details of the "incident" from GI sources. There were the stories told on television by men who had taken part in the killings.

The formal charge of murder against Calley sharply intensified the Vietnam controversy. President Nixon called My Lai a massacre and "abhorrent," though he deemed it an aberration. Numerous charges of wrongdoing had previously been brought against individuals or groups of soldiers in Vietnam, including the killing of civilians, rape and torture, and they also had been regarded as what the President thought My Lai was, the exception. Americans did not deliberately commit atrocities. That was for Nazis, at Malmédy, or Japanese, at Manila, or Russians, in the Katyn Forest.

The shocking news of My Lai fueled the antiwar sentiment which the President's Vietnamization speech and Agnew's attack on the news media had not suppressed, if they were intended to do so. The second installment of the Vietnam Moratorium, a month after the first, had brought 250,000 persons to the Washington Monument, drawn record crowds in San Francisco and other cities, and altogether constituted the largest political gathering in American history.

At the Department of Justice in Washington, where some of the demonstrators were dispersed by tear gas, Attorney General John Mitchell watched from the balcony and later told his wife Martha, "It looked like the Russian Revolution." He had forecast major disorders, but for the numbers involved it was a remarkably peaceful occasion. President Nixon, in a White House ringed by a barricade of buses, watched football games on television, ignoring the day's activities. The bus-encircled White House symbolized the administration's spiritual embattlement, under the threat of supposedly subversive elements of the population engaged in dark conspiracies against national security.

How much political import the two huge antiwar extravaganzas had was debatable. Both had in a sense been surpassed by the massive event which preceded them, the Woodstock Festival's weekend of marijuana and music. The Dionysian revel in celebration of the "counterculture" was a study in contradiction, as one observer viewed it, between paradise and concentration camp, between sky and mud, and love and death, since several of the participants succumbed to drugs. Woodstock's connection with the Vietnam War was nominal. Joan Baez, whose husband was on the way to prison for draft resistance, led in the singing of "We Shall Overcome."

At the Chicago conspiracy trial Abbie Hoffman defined "the Woodstock nation" as "a nation of alienated young people" who carried it about with them "as a state of mind, in the same way Sioux Indians carried the Sioux nation around with them." The Woodstock nation was, however, a summer phenomenon at best. Its epitaph was written at another rock festival at Altamont, California, attended by 30,000 young people, so many of whom were so high on drugs that they did not know whether it was real or something they imagined when a fatal stabbing took place on the stage, involving members of the Hell's Angels motorcycle gang.

Rock music itself, which in some ways had represented revolt, had declined, a victim of its own success and excesses. Its idols had been self-sacrificed to pleasures, its high priests tarnished by commercialism, its audiences satiated by surplus sound. Special temples of rock, like Fillmore East in New York City, were closing in a swirl of marijuana smoke, audience vandalism, and triteness. Protest rock had been smoothed out by the shock absorbers of conventionalism. Like other innovations it had broadened the main cultural stream and was no longer "counter," being heard at all hours of day and night from hundreds of radio stations, and accounting for record sales of records. The Beatles had made a great deal of money, quarreled, split up, married, and were otherwise disbanded, though they still appeared occasionally as individuals. Their influence could not be denied, but the Liverpool Sound had become the San Francisco Sound.

Cultural change and absorption were only surface manifestations to the National Commission on the Cause and Prevention of Violence, headed by Dr. Milton S. Eisenhower. It gave warning of grave "internal dangers" to the nation in the form of "haphazard urbanization, racial discrimination, disfiguring of the environment, unprecedented interdependence, the dislocation of human identity, and motivation created by the affluent society." When the war ended, the Eisenhower commission recommended, $20 billion should be spent annually on homes, jobs and welfare.

The war was a long way from ended. Months of congressional inquiry had uncovered evidence of waste, mismanagement, overplanning and profiteering in defense contracts, but Senate and House conferees agreed to spend $20.7 billion not for homes, jobs and welfare, but to give the Pentagon all it had asked and more in the way of military procurement. "No major weapon has been left out of this bill and none has been seriously restricted," proudly declared senior Senator John Stennis. Something was included for every branch of service, an antiballistic missile system, new Army tanks, new Navy vessels and a new fighter plane. Yet ostensibly the United States was trying to reduce both the staggering burden of defense and the risk of nuclear conflict, by beginning negotiations with the Russians for the limitation of strategic arms.

Self-exiled American draft-evaders in Montreal held a "Christmas Dinner in Peace" with their families and sang antiwar songs. Their tree was decorated with tinsel and discarded military ID cards. Among the year's statistics was one from New York City that 210 teen-agers had died in 1969 from overdoses of heroin, among them a twelve-year-old boy.

At noon on March 6, 1970, an explosion tore apart a $200,000 town house off lower Fifth Avenue in New York City and in the wreckage were found the remains of three human beings, as well as SDS leaflets, fifty-seven sticks of dynamite, thirty blasting caps, and some cheap alarm clocks. The Weathermen, who had gone underground a few months before, had inadvertently resurfaced into public prominence. Five of them, it appeared, had been making bombs in the basement of the red-brick, century-old, exquisitely fitted home of an advertising executive, who had gone on holiday leaving it to his eighteen-year-old daughter and her friends. After the blast she and one of the latter, the daughter of a leading labor and civil rights lawyer, fled back to their limbo. Credit cards in the debris established the identity of the dead and of the two girls who had disappeared. All those in the basement had taken part in the Chicago Days of Rage, and then from their underground cells had issued a series of Weathermen "communiqués" declaring a "state of war" against "Amerika" and "Amerikan imperialism."

In Indochina, at the time, doubt had suddenly been created that the actual war "Amerika" was fighting was, as the administration asserted, "winding down." Secretary of State Rogers was called before the Senate Foreign Relations Committee and gave assurances there was "no incentive to escalate." Any move of American ground forces from Vietnam into neighboring Cambodia, he explained, would defeat the purpose of Vietnamization. The American intention was "to be as quiet as possible, to avoid any act which appears to violate the neutrality of Cambodia." That was "one country," Rogers bore witness, "in which our hands are clean and our hearts are pure." In truth, B-52's were at the time regularly bombing Cambodia, as they had been for a year, without notification to Congress, while American ground combat patrols ranged through Cambodia and Laos, and even crossed the border from Tom Dooley country into China and Burma.

The matter of Cambodia and escalation had publicly arisen because of a political overthrow in the small ancient kingdom of the Khmers, which had been a component of the Indochina Federation under the French and received its independence in Geneva in 1954. The North Vietnamese, moving troops and supplies down the Ho Chi Minh trail in Laos, used Cambodia not only for transit but as a staging ground for action in South Vietnam and a sanctuary, and the Cambodian ruler Prince Sihanouk accepted this Communist violation of his territory in order to avoid larger problems with Hanoi, such as invasion or occupation. At the same time he accepted the American bombing of Communist positions and shared in the deception which kept it secret. Sihanouk's neutrality was one of the most delicate balancing acts in Asian history. Now, suddenly he had fallen from the diplomatic high wire.

The prince, who characterized his rule as "Buddhist Socialism" — he had abdicated as hereditary monarch to become the elected chief of state — was in Paris, in quest of both health and foreign aid, when crowds of Cambodians marched upon and destroyed the North Vietnamese Embassy and the NLF Mission in Phnom Penh, the capital, by the obvious design of those Sihanouk had left behind to administrate. After a stop in Moscow, Sihanouk was leaving for Peking, on his way home, when his Prime Minister, General Lon Nol, promulgated his deposition and designated himself the new ruler. Lon Nol ordered all foreign Communist forces to quit Cambodia within forty-eight hours, and thus put his country into the war Sihanouk had for so long dexterously avoided. By the same token this made Sihanouk, in exile, the head of the "Khmer National Resistance." As in South Vietnam and Laos, indigenous revolutionary forces — the Khmer Rouge whom Sihanouk had opposed — joined with the North Vietnamese not against Lon Nol alone but against "United States imperialism" and its allies. American weapons and other help were at once furnished to

Lon Nol, and thousands of ethnic Cambodians were flown in from South Vietnam, where they had been training. Now American planes bombed inside Cambodia without the veil of secrecy, and on April 30 American and South Vietnamese ground forces poured across the border, 25,000 strong.

While withdrawing some of its troops from Vietnam the United States had enlarged the conflict, not only geographically and militarily, but politically and morally, and by adding a Cambodian front to those already engaged in South Vietnam and Laos had created the Second Indochina War. Pham Van Dong was asked to evaluate what had happened. "It makes things very favorable for the success of our revolution," he said.

President Nixon described the Cambodian invasion, which he denied was an invasion, as a bold move to destroy the "main headquarters for the entire Communist military operation in South Vietnam," to rout the North Vietnamese and NLF from their border refuges, and to "shorten the war." The television announcement from the White House was couched in Churchillian prose, to proclaim the grand climax of the entire war.

It also contained the false statement that the United States had observed Cambodian neutrality "for five years." Shortly before, moreover, the President had denied any American deaths in ground combat action in Laos. The official falsification of bombing reports to conceal the Cambodian air strikes would be described by the Pentagon, when discovered, as a "separate channel of reporting," while the families of 121 Americans killed in ground combat in Laos and Cambodia would eventually be notified that they had not died in South Vietnam, as originally deceptively stated.

With the movement of American troops into Cambodia to "shorten the war," Nixon also ended the seventeen-month suspension of bombing against North Vietnam, and thus reactivated another front. Behind the President's stated purpose in Cambodia of destroying the "enemy headquarters," pictured as a sort of Hitler's bunker where all command decisions were made, the American invasion was soon also deemed necessary to save the Lon Nol government. In its six weeks the new regime had engulfed the tranquil and charming country in civil war and chaos. Communist forces were reported approaching Phnom Penh.

The move into Cambodia, increasing American commitments on the Asian mainland, roused Congress as no other development of the conflict had done, especially since, only ten days before, Nixon had announced a further withdrawal from Vietnam of 150,000 troops. He had ordered the invasion without consulting or notifying Capitol Hill, and even some who supported the Vietnam policy were perturbed by the latest use of presidential power. A congressional demand was raised for repeal of the Tonkin

Gulf Resolution, and Senators Frank Church and John Sherman Cooper, and George McGovern and Mark Hatfield, sponsored separate "end the war" resolutions to put a time limit on the American presence in Indochina. Senator Edward Kennedy thought that Nixon had fallen prey to the same "illusions of American victory" that had driven Johnson from office, and said the time had come for the United States to "militarily get out of Southeast Asia lock, stock and barrel." The New York stock market fell precipitately for three days after the invasion began.

An indirect casualty of Cambodia was the President's Family Assistance Plan for welfare reform. Two weeks before the invasion the House had passed a bill providing for $6 billion in direct cash payments to the poor, at a floor of $1,600 annually per family, a step from which Lyndon Johnson had pulled back as too controversial and unlikely of passage. The confrontation which the White House forced with Congress because of Cambodia, intensified by Vice-President Agnew's continued attacks on the news media and other critics, created a mood of no-truck-with-presidential-proposals in the Senate, and the Family Assistance Plan was sent to the deepfreeze of a committee. There it was finally rejected by a coalition of conservatives opposed to its guaranteed income principle, and liberals who either found it inadequate or too much a matter of alms rather than of right.

Three members of Henry Kissinger's staff resigned as a result of Cambodia. Wives and friends of other National Security Council staff members joined demonstrators outside the White House while the members were inside writing official statements justifying it. A dozen Harvard colleagues of Kissinger, led by Thomas Schelling, strategy analyst and game theory expert, called on the presidential adviser to offer rebuke and refused to listen to any explanation when he sought to speak, as he did to the White House press corps, off the record. They virtually broke with him then and there, though he tried to reassure them. "Come back in a year," he said. "You will find your concern unwarranted."

The Lawyers Committee for More Effective Action to End the War assembled twelve hundred barristers from New York City to descend on the Capitol and lobby senators and cabinet officials. "War is too important to be left to the President," declared Francis T. P. Plimpton, the aristocratic head of the New York City Bar Association. "We cannot begin to end poverty, pollution, racial prejudice, inflation and decaying slums until we end our Southeast Asia folly."

Cambodia shook even the inner fortress of the CIA. A large group of younger men, mostly in intelligence analysis, were called to the auditorium by the agency's director and their patriotism appealed to. They had to follow orders, he reminded them, no matter what they felt.

Above all, the Cambodian invasion regalvanized college campuses, which had been lulled by "Vietnamization." The genie was out of the bottle again. Professors resigned as consultants to the National Security Council. Campus protest demonstrations were held throughout the country, and at one of them, Kent State University in Ohio, National Guardsmen, their rifles loaded with live ammunition, their orders unclear, fired into a crowd of youthful dissenters and bystanders, killing four — two youths and two co-eds — and wounding nine. Over the land hung a dark new shadow.

THE NIXON-BREZHNEV-MAO DOCTRINE

COSVN, THE "COMMUNIST PENTAGON" visualized by the President, was a mirage. All that was found were deserted sites where North Vietnamese military staff might have been quartered. The American ground action, moreover, in itself a confession that fourteen months of bombing had failed, drove the Communists out of their border sanctuaries deeply into Cambodia where, installed and entrenched, they became able to recruit and build a large "Cambodian National Resistance."

All that could be said at the time was that, compared with the proclaimed intentions, the immediate military effect of the invasion seemed negligible. On the other hand, the political effect on the American home front was devastating. The embers of dissent leaped into flame again. After Kent State — which a governmental commission would find "unnecessary, unwarranted and inexcusable" on the part of the National Guard — and two more student killings at black Jackson State College in Mississippi, a national student strike, the first of its kind, closed classrooms in four hundred colleges, and nine hundred campuses in effect went into mourning. Unguardedly, President Nixon referred to campus activists as "bums" and seemed to imply that they had got what they deserved. "When dissent turns to violence it invites tragedy," he explained.

Edward Kennedy, speaking of the "strange and tragic fascination of military victory" which had cast a "mad spell over two successive Presidents" — he did not mention the third, his brother — likened Kent State to My Lai: "Can any of us fail to realize now what Vietnam has done to our spirit, our nation, and our sons?" At a memorial service for the four young people killed at Kent State he declared, "Our prayer tonight is a simple one. Dear God, help us. The war must end."

The campus strike protesting Cambodia and Kent State proved to be the last major manifestation of student antiwar expression. College "generations" are short ones, each year bringing its new classes and faces. The leaders of the 1968 rebellion had for the most part gone on. To the newer students, seeing soldiers being recalled from Vietnam, themselves given more chance to escape the draft in its lottery form, opposition to the war was if anything a matter of principle, and principle, like many college courses, was an elective.

Cambodia and Kent State ended the decade which had begun with the Greensboro lunch-counter sit-ins of 1960, a period in which American students had become almost a separate demographic category, like blacks, Chicanos and "ethnic whites." If the purpose of the student movement was to achieve radical change it had failed. The war went on. The corporations became bigger, and by conglomeration acquired even more economic power. Pollution had increased. Government was more centralized. The cities were in deeper debt and desuetude. Congress had grown more unresponsive to those who elected it. The universities had not fallen, and the "System" still stood, though some surface aspects of it had been altered.

Yet the student movement had helped bring into the open, for debate and reappraisal, many subjects besides the war and civil rights which might not otherwise have been considered addressable, such as drugs, sex, the ecology, and the meaning and worth of accepted American values and institutions.

Ecological contamination had in fact become a communal concern. As more oil spills occurred, as dangerous levels of mercury from industrial pollution were discovered in the waters of numerous states, and the American bald eagle was threatened with extinction in his last refuge, Alaska, by DDT, mercury and logging operations, Earth Day was observed across the United States as a kind of environmental late-warning system. As with so many other things in American life, it was itself somehow tainted. The antipollution crusade was joined by some of the nation's principal polluters: oil companies, paper-mill combines, auto manufacturers, soapmakers and public utilities. By identifying themselves with the protest, they helped to neutralize it.

The underground Weathermen punctuated the prevailing state of relative nonviolence by setting off a bomb in New York City police headquarters. They also aided the escape of Timothy Leary from a California prison farm, after he had been "busted" again for drug possession, and put him on his way to Algiers, the new Mecca of American radicals, dissenters and misfits.

The nonviolence was broken in another way. The national response to the Cambodian invasion had by no means been entirely unfavorable. The action in fact encouraged the polarization process which the Nixon-Agnew administration seemed bent on exploiting. When Pace College students in New York City marched peacefully into nearby Wall Street they were physically assaulted by construction workers, who were acting not only in support of the war — though their young were affected the most by it — but also expressing resentment and contempt for the pampered, "rotten," radical youth whom they hated as much as they envied — hated for their mocking of patriotism, for their lack of respect for authority, for their failure to subscribe to the President's work ethic, for questioning American righteousness.

A few days after the attack on the students, twenty thousand "hard-hats" paraded on Broadway with American flags flying, carrying signs reading "God Bless the Establishment." Their leader, Peter Brennan, head of the Building and Construction Trades Council, said of the Wall Street onslaught, "Violence opened the door to some sanity." Vice-President Agnew called the attack on the students "a wave in defense of the country, not a wave to destroy the country."

"Hard hat" is not only a headpiece but a state of mind. Following the Wall Street violence and the patriotic march President Nixon invited a group of construction workers to the White House and was photographed wearing a white hard hat of his own, labeled "commander-in-chief." It was presented by Peter Brennan, who would get his reward by being named Secretary of Labor in the second Nixon administration. The wooing of the organized labor section of the "silent majority" had been begun, by the man who on his first day as a congressman in 1947 told California reporters "I was elected to smash the labor bosses."

The construction workers were possibly less "labor," because of their monopolistic, racially restrictive craft unions and their handsome wages, their cars and suburban homes, than they were "ethnics" — whites of various European stocks who had built up angry aggrievedness against the blacks and other minorities they kept out of their unions. The blacks, they charged, preferred welfare to work and were responsible for street crime, yet were favored by the government.

The American melting pot had, as a result of conscious racism, boiled down to its basic components, as in response to black demands for control of schools in urban communities, for jobs and political representation, the white ethnics became proudly Italian, Irish, Polish and other hyphenated Americans again. In a climate of such social acerbity it was possible to establish a picket line, day after day, in front of the FBI offices in New York City, to demand the end of the use of terms like Mafia and Cosa Nostra as insulting to Italian-Americans.

In the backlash against those who dared deny the American Myth, the flag was the symbol of patriotic virtue. Miniature flags decorated the lapels of politicians from the President down. Love-of-country auto bumper stickers were the equivalent of Chinese wall posters. The flag was displayed as totem on shop windows. Policemen wore flags on their uniforms, and frequent arrests were made for what was deemed improper use. Abbie Hoffman, appearing on a television program in red-white-and-blue costume, was virtually blacked out on the screen, only his disembodied voice being heard. Patriots cut the electric cable which provided the light by which the names of Vietnam fallen were read at one small community's antiwar prayers. Churches suspended pastors who spoke against the war, in one case a Catholic priest who at Mass mentioned the North Vietnamese dead as well as the American. "Trees for peace" planted by day were uprooted by night.

The backlash against dissent, disorder and "disloyalty" came from the highest office in the land. Despite the CIA's assessment that disaffection was native-born-and-bred, and due to obvious social and political causes, the White House was convinced of "foreign Communist" support of the Black Panthers, Weathermen, and other radical groups. While the hardhats reacted to dissent openly, their commander-in-chief called in the various intelligence organizations to undertake a broad covert plan for "domestic security." It included extended surveillance of private citizens, not only by wiretapping, monitoring international communications, and an increased use of campus "informants," but also the admittedly illegal resort to surreptitious entry and the interception of mail. Burglary, while clearly stated to be unlawful, was also held to be a most fruitful method of action by the "law and order" administration.

The White House plans were blocked by the director of the FBI, J. Edgar Hoover, for reasons of his own. They included his unwillingness to allow the FBI to be subordinated to a group effort, and his suspicion of the fact that the President refused to give him the written authorization for illegal acts he had asked for. The White House, dismayed but undeterred, then enlarged the activity of its original secret investigative unit against its "enemies."

All administrations have to some degree, usually through the FBI, engaged in covert practices in the name of "national security," against the "anarchists" of 1919, the gangsters of the Prohibition era, the threat of "Communist subversion" and Nazi spies in the Thirties, against militant minorities, civil rights leaders and labor union bosses, even against political "enemies." To the national heritage of suspicion and fear, however, Richard Nixon had added his own secretive and reclusive sensitivities. Other administrations had indeed used such methods, but to the Nixon administration they were not only an occasional necessary instrument, but seemed a very means of government. The President's "enemies" were accounted enemies of the state and "the people," as under Augustus.

The 1970 midterm election campaign began with the administration making twin points to the voters in the attempt to win control, ideological if not numerical, of the Congress. One was the defense of Vietnamization and of the Cambodian invasion, to "shorten the war." The other was "law and order," for which Attorney General Mitchell soon announced a triumph, the apprehension of the two Berrigan brothers by the FBI. They had gone underground after their conviction for the destruction of draft records in Catonsville, and now they went off to prison. But it was not the end of them for J. Edgar Hoover.

Congressional criticism of the Cambodian invasion resulted in the legislative imposition of a sixty-day limit for the use of the troops, which fitted in with the administration's own apparent intentions, but though American ground units left, the South Vietnamese remained, and American planes continued to fly in their direct support. Cambodia also led to the Senate's repeal of the Tonkin Gulf Resolution, but this did not affect matters much either since Nixon, unlike Johnson, felt he needed no other authority than that which he chose to assume. The Senate's antiwar words in fact never compensated for its prowar deeds. While many senators disapproved of the war or said they did, they recurringly voted the funds for it, and when Senator Charles Goodell of New York offered a bill to set a date for withdrawal from Vietnam and cut off appropriations after that date, he could not find a single cosponsor.

When the draft was extended in 1967, in the midst of wholesale draft-card burning and other organized opposition, an amendment by Gruening of Alaska to forbid the sending of draftees to Asia without their consent received the customary two votes of Gruening and Morse. In 1968 an amendment prohibiting any increase in the B-52 bombing obtained only ten votes, among the seventy-nine opposing it being several notable doves. Voting funds for the training and payment of "local forces" in Laos and Thailand were such doves as Fulbright, McGovern, Cooper, Hatfield and Proxmire. Through the escalation from 1965 to 1969 the Senate voted overwhelmingly for all measures of war, in the name of "not letting our boys down," however mistakenly they might be in Vietnam. It was not politic for politicians to follow any other course.

Congress had the power to reduce or end the war by refusing to approve appropriations, holding up the confirmation of presidential appointees, or cutting off the salaries of White House and other Executive employees. It spent its time in debate over the Cooper-Church amendments, which forbade the use of American ground troops in Laos and Thailand but not of American air power or American mercenaries; and enacted the prohibition of ground troops in Cambodia on the day that they left, after sixty days of fighting.

The Senate was never able to decide how much it was genuinely concerned about the war and how much with its prerogative of "advice and consent," and while at least some senators spoke against the war in the years between 1965 and 1970 the House did not hold a single debate on Vietnam until 1971. The truth seemed to be that while the Senate demanded its rights it shrank from any role in which it could be accused of imposing on the Executive, which in reality had steadily imposed upon it.

By reason of the senatorial record of futility and fustian, the Indochina War, like the Mexican War in 1846 and the Spanish-American War in 1898, had to be debated and examined to a large extent outside legislative halls. While Congress appropriated funds, which now included those for Cambodia as well as for South Vietnam and Laos, a Citizens Committee of Inquiry on U.S. War Crimes held hearings, organized by Vietnam veterans, in a dozen American cities and Toronto. In 1967 the Russell Tribunal had been widely regarded as the crackpot fancy of a senile aristocrat, though some of its members were of high intellectual standing. Witnesses before the Russell panel were held to be radicals, misfits and freaks, but much the same testimony was given at the veterans' hearings in the United States, and the witnesses had good battle records, wore medals, and could display wounds. Most Americans did not want to hear what they had to say, as they had not wanted to hear about My Lai.

There were other things about the war it was better not to know. By the time of Cambodia drug addiction was a serious Army problem in Vietnam. "O.J." there meant not orange juice but opium joint. The American cigarette favored by Vietnamese was a mentholated one, carried in large supply by the PX, but GI's smoked a Vietnamese brand which was opium-tipped. Marijuana, it had been postulated, had no physical or chemical relationship to hard drugs but evidently there was a psychological one. Many who started on marijuana went on to heroin, if only because they established dependence on some form of tension-easement. Dr. Joel H. Kaplan, psychiatrist-in-charge of the Army's antidrug program in Vietnam, reported that 70 percent of all GI outpatients and 50 percent of inpatients in the two northernmost corps areas were users of marijuana, opium-dipped joints, opium, or methedrine, called "opium-speed." Between 10 and 20 percent of all American military personnel, at a conservative estimate, were listed as serious drug users, principally of heroin. During 1969 and 1970 more than 16,000 American servicemen were discharged for drug abuse.

The heroin so abundantly available in Vietnam came from opium grown in Laos. It was refined in Thailand, smuggled into South Vietnam by ARVN officers and civilian officials, customs men and airline pilots and stewardesses, and was sold to GI's not only in the streets of Saigon but in the billets of camps and bases upcountry. It was strong, pure and cheap. It had its obvious effects on combat, slow reaction and mistaken identity, often resulting in the killing of other Americans. Such things were better not mentioned.

Another aspect of the war many at home would rather not be told about was revealed after the Cambodian invasion. A House select committee went to Vietnam to "find facts," its chairman vowing "we will not be led around by the nose . . . this will be a 'no briefings' trip." As usual and despite the disclaimer, the committee was led by the nose, briefed extensively, and given red-carpet treatment everywhere. But Representatives W. R. Anderson of Tennessee, a World War II submarine commander, and Augustus Hawkins, a black Californian, broke away from the tightly controlled delegation and visited Con Son penal island and the "tiger cages" they had heard rumors about.

Con Son, called Poulo Condor by the French, was publicly listed by its American advisers, who were former policemen, as a "correctional institution worthy of higher ratings than some prisons in the United States." One likened it to a "Boy Scout recreation camp" with "supervised swimming . . . canteen . . . vocational training classes." The two congressmen found no Boy Scout camp, and reported inhuman conditions in the "tiger cages," which were concrete cells set in the ground and covered by bars. The inmates were shackled constantly, so that their legs were paralyzed, and the congested cells had no sanitary facilities, no water, and no sunlight. Any who complained were sprinkled with lime dust from above. Most distressing to the Americans was the fact that the "tiger cage" inmates were political prisoners, of whom the island commandant said, "These are very bad people. They won't salute the flag. They won't salute the American flag." The congressional committee did not mention Con Son in its report, but Representative Anderson made the situation known.

The number of political prisoners was a reminder that despite American intervention Vietnam had remained essentially a civil war. A case in point was that of the secretary-general of the South Vietnamese National Assembly, who had met secretly with his brother, a captain in North Vietnamese Intelligence. Despite CIA approval of the meeting, as an exercise in counterintelligence, he was arrested by Thieu's security police, given a military trial, and sentenced to twenty years in prison. The verdict was overruled by the Vietnamese Supreme Court, whereupon he was retried and resentenced to ten years. It was recalled in passing that General "Big" Minh, who remained an important figure in national politics, had a brother who was a high North Vietnamese officer, and a relative of President Thieu himself was said to be a North Vietnamese lieutenant general. The internecine nature of the war made it only the more bitter. The CIA was reporting at this point that thirty thousand persons in the Saigon government machine were "cooperating" with the NLF.

Sir Robert Thompson, the British counterinsurgency expert, acknowledged after an inspection trip for the White House that he was dubious about the success of the Vietnamization program, in marked contrast to his optimistic appraisal given to Nixon a year before. The conclusion to be drawn from his findings was that nothing could stop the NLF after the Americans left. Clearly the United States could not be in any hurry to withdraw. Congress for the most part felt the same way. The Mc-Govern-Hatfield amendment to "end the war," with complete American evacuation by the end of 1971, was defeated in the Senate, 55 to 39.

The long slow haul toward an unfixed conclusion to the war was also under way in American colleges. As the 1970 fall semester began, campus rebellion was definitely dampened. The new freshman class at Columbia, its 705 members from all parts of the country carefully selected from 3,800 applicants, generally expressed itself, two years after the Great Uprising, as ready to settle for "renaissance" rather than revolution. The new freshmen were not interested in personal involvement in political parties or movements. They seemed skeptical of democratic processes and according to the campus newspaper, the *Spectator*, "unusually introspective." These were the same young people who as high school students in 1968 had been thought even more radical than those in college.

Teachers at Columbia found it difficult to get discussions going in the class of 1974. "They want to be taught, lectured at, and are less eager to hear each other talk." A majority still opposed the war and said they would avoid service if drafted but they had no intention of letting antiwar activism or anything else interfere with their studies.

Throughout the nation vocational courses were increasingly chosen in the new college year, with 36 percent more preference for social work as a career, by comparison with the previous year, 27 percent for nursing and 25.8 percent for urban studies. Forestry, biology, architecture, agriculture, business and the fine and performing arts also increased in popularity. Registration declined in engineering courses; in ethnic studies, meaning principally black studies; and in education, history and political science. Graduate schools showed a similar trend toward architecture, business, agriculture, law and medicine, and most striking a 65.8 percent increase in the choice of forestry as a career, perhaps in consequence of the ecological movement and of the appearance of the best-selling *Whole Earth Catalog*, a compendium of methods to change accountants and stockbrokers into a new yeomanry.

All this indicated, if anything, a prevailing desire on the part of the incoming college generation to stay within the "System" and to do any changing from the inside. The professions were the chosen instrument of change; they could be expected to assume new vitality from the fresh blood entering them. Whatever vestiges of college rebellion remained — long hair, informal clothes, drugs, rock music, sexual freedom — were largely divorced of political content or context. Jerry Rubin, the Yippie leader who had denounced "straight" values and "hypocrisy," transformed himself into a foundation to save income taxes on his book royalties and lecture fees. He also embraced physical culture. Abbie Hoffman trimmed his hair, became a father — perhaps derisively, he named his son "america" — urged his followers to vote instead of revolt, and said he would like to host a TV "talk show" as a career.

Not all the young had decided to settle for the "System." Some who had previously opposed it chose to leave it and become members of communes or self-created families, in a search for identity. Such humanistic enterprises, religious, ideological and cultural, are well established in American history from Brook Farm and New Harmony to Oneida, and while some of them flourished most of them had failed, having foundered on human nature. The question the new communes, like their predecessors, raised was whether happiness was any more attainable in counterinstitutions, or whether counterinstitutions were only institutions in another form. Several thousand communes, urban and rural, existed at the peak of the movement, and how permanent they were remained to be seen, since so many were not economically viable and depended on parental remittances or welfare checks. Very few of the farm communes were self-sufficient, their members working at menial or fringe labor in towns or suburbs. In the larger cities commune members tried jewelry crafts, bookbinding, newspaper delivery, factory jobs, baking and barbering, to keep them going. Many communes failed quickly, or moved on, or changed members.

For the most part communes did not attract working-class youth, since these presumably had had enough in reality of the conditions now being simulated, of crowded and intimate existence. Nor were the new communalists necessarily the "best" of their generation. Many were rejects rather than rebels, quitting the "System" before they were fired. Many were playing house, retarded beyond the statutory age of childhood. Nothing in human nature guarantees that unhappy individuals will become less so collectively.

All the same the communes represented a failure of the Affluent Society with its technological nexus, a society which sometimes seemed ashamed of its material goals, values and methods even while striving desperately to attain them. A significant number of young Americans, it was evident, had problems that existing institutions were incapable of accommodating.

Besides those who had become reconciled to the "System" and those who had simply dropped out of it, there remained an irreducible minimum of anti-System militants among youth. The policeman's statue in Chicago's Haymarket, restored after its destruction during the Days of Rage, was blown up again by the Weathermen. Explosions damaged other symbols of "oppression": a courthouse, an ROTC building, a Bank of America branch in a California student community. Just before fall sessions began, a bomb planted in the Army Mathematics Research Center at the University of Wisconsin killed a graduate student at work there. For a decade, weapons development, counterinsurgency operations, and nuclear attack strategy had been studied at the Center, and all its members, whether academics or Army technicians, held faculty status. The target may have seemed as military as anything in Vietnam.

Within the armed services dissension also continued. On bases at home and overseas commission holders of all four branches formed the Concerned Officers Movement to speak against the war as "loyal officers" and without, they said, challenging military authority. They included West Point, Annapolis and Air Force Academy graduates.

In Vietnam refusal to take part in combat had grown more common as the war "wound down." One infantry company's running arguments with its captain, shown in a series of CBS News television reports — not only on, but obviously for, camera — were not entirely atypical. Many units went into the bush to smoke marijuana, "rap" and "sack out." They had decided it was not "worth it" to "search and destroy." Their officers feared that court-martial would only undermine morale further. "Tough" captains and lieutenants and NCO's were frequently "fragged." Career soldiers and officers, the Army's "lifers," were openly ridiculed.

The continuing withdrawal of troops was one reason for a lower casualty rate, but another was the refusal to go into action. Separate companies were soon being set up for those who did refuse. Many soldiers would not put on uniforms, others evaded assignment by indefinitely "visiting" elsewhere. New arrivals in Vietnam were kept from contact with those scheduled to leave soon; they were processed quickly and sent up forward. Some garrisons were almost unarmed as weapons were taken from recalcitrant GI's and locked up. It began to appear as if the soldiers had decided to end the fighting on their own, and troop withdrawal was merely confirmation of the fact.

ARVN was meanwhile being hugely supplied with tanks, helicopters, armored personnel carriers, artillery, planes, patrol boats, rifles, machine guns, grenade-launchers and ammunition. American machines replaced American men on the battlefield. "If they lose the war," it was said of the South Vietnamese, "they can only blame themselves," though by the same token acknowledgment was being made that the United States had failed to win.

The commando raid on Son Tay prison camp in North Vietnam added to the absurd logic of the war. A skillfully mounted airborne assault, covered by intensive bombing from 250 planes, was executed with precision and daring against barracks twenty miles from Hanoi; object, to rescue the American pilots believed imprisoned there. The raid was rehearsed at an

Air Force base in Florida, against a mockup of the prison compound, and rehearsed so often that the techniques of the mission became the mission's most important end. It did not really matter whether the prisoners were at Son Tay or not. As it happened they were not, having been removed three months before. If they had been they would presumably have been rescued, so the leaders of the raid were decorated and the Secretary of Defense praised it as highly successful. In truth it was the swan song of the Pentagon's secret SACSA, the agency created by President Kennedy for "counterinsurgency and special activities."

President Nixon, immersed in the 1970 election campaign, trying to put more of his kind of Republicans into Congress, and regarding Vietnam as more or less behind him, at least as an issue, stood more and more on "law and order." The global policeman was less his symbol than the local one, though crime, it was evident, was no more amenable to Republican than to Democratic application.

How was "law and order" to be achieved, for instance, in Newark? There, in the largest northern city with a black majority, Kenneth Gibson, a civil engineer, was elected mayor in 1970 by a clear majority, 56 percent, through a coalition of his own people and white liberals reacting to years of corrupt rule in City Hall. Newark represented the "worst possible case" of American urban misfortune, as Vietnam did of foreign policy to many Americans. Wasted by economic and ethnic conflict, the city suffered from continuous neglect, white flight to the suburbs, lack of revenue, backward schools, crime and drugs, trigger-happy police, abject poverty in the black ghetto, unsafe housing, rats, massive unemployment, political malfeasance and shattered hopes. As might have been expected in a climate of aroused ethnic consciousness, the outgoing white mayor, indicted for coercion, extortion and tax evasion, made the issue one of anti-Italian defamation. On trial during the election campaign and convicted after the balloting, His Honor was nonetheless sent to prison for ten years.

Gibson, though supported by many whites, was elected on a slogan of Black Power. He found it as empty as the city treasury. The real power in Newark still belonged to the banks, the utilities and the big insurance company which represented the "Rock" of corporatism. Despite his high resolve the new mayor and the other blacks of Newark discovered that the vote does not end, but begins, the quest for equality and dignity.

Newark became a major turning point in the political chronicle of Black America, as Cleveland and Gary with their mayors and even the Black Belt of Alabama had not been. To the cause of local civil endeavor, coalition politics and community affairs, and away from South African apartheid, Portuguese East African colonialism, and other distant considerations, Newark rallied radical figures like the poet-playwright Le Roi Jones, become Imamu Amiri Baraka. "Burn, baby, burn!" blacks had shouted in

1967. In 1970 they said, "Build, baby, build!" and Baraka drew up plans for Kawaida Towers, a middle- and low-income apartment-house complex named in Swahili to signify Tradition, but intended as American "social engineering." As they were narrowed, black objectives became more clearly focused, and in Newark, thus perhaps more controversial. The Italianate whites of the North Ward vowed that Kawaida Towers would never rise.

Black sights were brought down by reality in other ways. Eldridge Cleaver was still in Algiers and Stokely Carmichael in Guinea, but Huey Newton, out of prison and with pending charges against him dropped after three unsuccessful trials — the cry of "Free Huey" thus being answered — broke with the revolutionary wing of the Black Panthers, and announced himself a believer in "black capitalism" and cooperation with black churches. Newton, a minister's son, had untypically apparently been de-radicalized in prison. He had come to believe that the "System" was able to correct itself without being overthrown, and thought it was possible to organize a responsible black liberal party, the only uncertainty being whether the Panthers, with their lurid past, could become its nucleus. A Black Coalition was already taking shape, including not only the Panthers and Imamu Baraka in Newark but Martin Luther King's successors, Dr. Ralph Abernathy in the South and Jesse Jackson in Chicago. As Abernathy viewed "black capitalism," blacks needed boots before they could lift themselves by their bootstraps.

Not all blacks favored improved relations with white America. Panthers who remained faithful to Cleaver formed the Black Liberation Army against the police. A series of outbreaks and attempted breakouts in prisons and detention buildings, where blacks constituted a larger percentage of the inmates than of the general population, reached a bloody climax at San Rafael, California, in an attempted armed courtroom delivery, in which two of the rescued prisoners and the judge were killed, as well as the seventeen-year-old "liberator," Jonathan Jackson. The youth's scheme had been to exchange the kidnapped judge for George Jackson, who had won some fame in prison as a writer, as well as one of the "Soledad Brothers," accused of killing a guard. The elder Jackson, a teacher of revolutionary ideas to other black prisoners, would himself be killed a year later in what was described as a break for freedom at San Quentin.

The suicidal San Rafael courtroom raid, the spate of bombings the Weathermen claimed responsibility for, the first mass demonstrations by Mexican-Americans in East Los Angeles, riots in the Tombs in New York City and other detention centers, taken all together, may have made some Americans fear that the revolution had arrived. Attorney General Mitchell, who had been struck with dread by his view of antiwar marchers from the Department of Justice balcony — the Washington equivalent of the Czar's Winter Palace — acted as if he thought so. In previous administrations the

Civil Rights, Anti-Trust, and Law Enforcement divisions had been the principal arms of the Justice Department. Under Mitchell the emphasis was placed on the reactivated Internal Security Division, ordered to root out radicalism and subversion. Seeking a pattern of revolutionary conspiracy, it set on foot the largest and widest action of its kind since the Palmer "anarchist" raids of 1919.

J. Edgar Hoover, who began his career as Attorney General A. Mitchell Palmer's special assistant in charge of alien deportations, spanned the years between the "sedition" of the post–World War I era and that provoked by Vietnam. The Justice Department's first move against the latter-day "conspiracy," the trial of the "Chicago Seven," had not been entirely successful, for after four and a half bizarre courtroom months the jury had dismissed all conspiracy charges, though it found five of the seven defendants guilty under the "Rap" Brown law of crossing state lines with the intention of creating a riot. Now Hoover appeared before a Senate committee, and in explaining his request for more FBI agents and more money to combat radicalism, he charged a plot by the two imprisoned Berrigan brothers and others to blow up the steam conduits of the Washington heating system and to kidnap Henry Kissinger, the presidential aide. Thus, he said, they expected to force an end to American bombing of North Vietnam.

Hoover was not able to substantiate his charges, and the Justice Department reluctantly found no case. Since the FBI director could not thus be publicly repudiated, a federal grand jury in Harrisburg, Pennsylvania, was thereupon virtually compelled to indict seven persons for conspiracy, headed by Philip Berrigan. A letter which the priest, a prisoner at Lewisburg, received from Sister Elizabeth McAlister in New York City — one of many carried between them by a young inmate with outside school privileges, who was in the pay of the FBI as well as in Berrigan's good graces — was leaked to FBI-favored newspapers, and its affectionate language of fantasy and whim did indeed make speculative mention of the Washington heating system and a "citizen's arrest" of Kissinger. A trial was ordered.

The Justice Department's embarkation upon vaguely defined conspiracy law as its principal weapon against radicalism had been caused by the failure of other means. In a case of more than local significance, Bobby Seale, separated from the Chicago conspiracy trial, had been arraigned in New Haven, Connecticut, with other Black Panthers on the more specific charge of murdering one of their own as a police informer. The president of Yale University, Dr. Kingman Brewster, was moved to remark that a black militant could not get a fair trial in the United States. A jury which could not agree on a verdict brought the dismissal of all those charged in the New Haven case and paved the way for juries in other cities, by disagreements, dismissals and mistrials, to prove Dr. Brewster right in an opposite and unintended sense. Many black defendants did not get truly fair trials because racially mixed juries in large cities in effect leaned over backward to give them the benefit of doubt.

A week before the Harrisburg indictments a comely young black woman, Angela Davis, who had been Professor Marcuse's favorite pupil and was later dismissed from her post of instructor in philosophy at the University of California, Los Angeles, for admitted Communist party membership, was charged with complicity in the San Rafael courtroom raid, in fact supplying the guns used. Those who could believe that all blacks in all penitentiaries were political prisoners believed she was being persecuted for her political views.

With the courts become the testing ground for the concepts of "law and order" held by the Nixon administration, the Justice Department in the Berrigan case and others following it used grand juries, meant originally as a protection against unwarranted prosecution of citizens, in a manner more perverse. Rather than being preoccupied with indictments, the panels became a means of collecting broad general information about radicals — the New Left, the Catholic Ultra-Resistance and antiwar groups — and in effect a surrogate of the FBI, supplying the agency with the subpoena power it lacked. Radicals were called as witnesses in forensic fishing expeditions. They might not know the purpose of their interrogation but if they refused to answer detailed questions about friends and acquaintances, meetings and associations, they could be cited for contempt. Wiretapping and "bugging" were illegally used as the basis for some subpoenas.

Yet the "revolution" against which all measures, legal and extralegal, were held permissible in the name of "national security" had distinctly receded. Not only was the campus quiescent, after its brief reaction to Cambodia and Kent State, but the Weathermen had second thoughts about tactics. A letter from the underground confessed error in reliance on "only bombs," and conceded that "most of our actions have hurt the enemy on about the same military scale as a bee sting." The West Eleventh Street explosion, which had killed the three young people, "forever destroyed our belief that armed struggle is the only real revolutionary struggle." The same decision had been made by most, though not all, the Black Panthers, and by the Young Lords of Puerto Rican Harlem.

The end of 1970 ended a decade of war in Vietnam. The official casualty list, the nation's own body count, kept since January 1, 1961, showed that more than 53,000 Americans had died there, 44,167 in "action by hostile forces," 8,990 from other causes. The peak year had been 1968, the year of Tet, with 14,502 dead. During 1970 Vietnamization had proceeded methodically, and by the end of the year more than 200,000 American troops had been withdrawn. Retired Admiral U. S. Grant Sharp, former Pacific commander and evidently still speaking for the President, made it clear, however, that American air power would continue to be used until the "North Vietnamese aggression is finally concluded."

The new year showed that Nixon's contemplated $1.2 billion budget surplus had somehow become a deficit of $11.6 billion. He thereupon proclaimed "the new American revolution," calling for "power to the people" through increased local government and federal "revenue-sharing." Confronted by recession, unemployment and inflation, he visualized "power to the people" as more purchasing power. The message from a Chief Executive who had amassed and exercised the largest presidential authority since Franklin D. Roosevelt was intended as a heartening one.

The country refused to be heartened. A Gallup survey, financed by several foundations, of the "hopes and fears of the American people" revealed not only a dramatic conversion since 1968 of the prowar into an antiwar majority, but 47 percent of Americans — 57 percent in the 21-29 age group — confessed such apprehension about national unity, political stability and "law and order" as to believe in the likelihood of "a real breakdown" in the national polity from "unrest and ill-feeling between groups." Traditional optimism was absent in the widespread feeling that the United States had "moved backward" in the preceding five years and that the best it could hope for in the next five — arriving at the bicentennial year of 1976 — would be a return to the 1966 standard. The burden of American solicitude had also changed, from improved living standards, aspiration for children, good health, home-owning and a secure old age, to such things as crime, drugs, pollution and political stability. Future hopes were surpassed by present shock.

Among the factors blamed for "unrest and ill-feeling" were the Vietnam War, lack of leadership, mistrust of leaders, youthful alienation, "unreasonable" minority demands, and the feeling that the "System" was "not working." Some Americans still blamed "Communist influence."

The lack of confidence in leadership, the pessimism about the war, the national dissension were all deepened by the invasion of Laos. The secret conflict there became an open one when South Vietnamese troops, supported by American planes, entered to carry out the same stated purpose as in Cambodia a year earlier, to shorten the war and "save American lives." Congress had forbidden American ground troops in Laos, but the invasion was an American initiative and tactic. The South Vietnamese took a drubbing despite American air support, suffering 50 percent casualties in a forty-five-day campaign, to the number of 3,800 dead and 5,200 wounded, while the Ho Chi Minh trail not only remained open but with increased traffic. Within a few months it was necessary for the United States to make more and heavier air strikes against North Vietnam's oil depots, ammunition dumps and supply lines, to protect the American withdrawal from Vietnam — that at least was the official explanation —

because ARVN was unable to offer such protection, being in constant danger of disaster itself.

Perhaps because American ground units were not involved and American casualties had been reduced, perhaps because a kind of political numbness had set in, public reaction to the Laotian incursion never reached the intensity of that caused by Cambodia. Protest demonstrations were held in several cities and on some campuses, and a bomb explosion damaged the Senate wing of the Capitol in Washington, but no Kent State followed Laos and no student strike. College radicals who favored violence had been quietly expelled or dropped away themselves. Most students, like teachers and administrators, had buckled down to the reality of the "academic depression" discovered by the Carnegie Commission on Higher Education.

Economic fears had replaced political conflict on the campus. University deficits were up because of rising costs and declining federal research funds; corporate gifts, endowments and contributions were down, like the stock market. Taxpayers were in revolt everywhere and cities and states reduced their education budgets. At the same time college tuition fees were bigger and harder to pay. Teachers suddenly faced a shortage of jobs. As belts tightened, so did academic communities. Black Studies did not seem important when all studies were threatened with curtailment. The time had come to mark time, and to count the gains and losses of the years of student activism.

The university had not been overthrown as an institution, but it is doubtful if many of the rebels wanted it to be. In any case, considerable change had taken place between Tet in 1968 and Laos in 1971. Quasi-parental authority had been given up in most colleges, co-ed dorms introduced and room-visiting restrictions removed, off-campus residence and student marriages increased. Curricula and grading systems were reformed, and admission policies notably liberalized, especially for blacks and other minorities. Students had been named to college committees and even to boards of trustees. Football games and other traditional interests were popular again. Some students lost themselves in Bogart and other "oldtime movie" festivals. Campus differences in clothing between the "freaks" and the "straights" had become indistinct, like the line drawn for the use of "pot," and the student population was more homogeneous again.

The changes did not mean a retreat to the passivity of the Fifties. Radical rhetoric still came from campuses, but the demand for instant reform had abated, the cries of "hypocrisy" diminished, and group action was replaced by individual participation in politics. Many were skeptical that their votes would make much difference, but students registered widely in preparation for 1972. The presidential campaign had in fact already begun, twenty-two months before Election Day, with George McGovern's announcement of his candidacy. The former history professor was going from campus to campus, speaking for amnesty for draft resisters as well as an end to the war, and urging the newly enfranchised to participate in the peaceful processes of democracy.

Though apathy toward the war was widespread, a peculiar sort of united front formed itself after Laos, a "get-out-of-Vietnam" coalition, which included students and other traditional war opponents, but also many hawks, anti-Communist hard-liners, and right-wing groups, angry that North Vietnam had not been bombed back to the Stone Age but feeling that if the war was not going to be won it should at least be ended.

The "get-out-of-Vietnam" movement received another major stimulus from the court-martial verdict of guilty returned against Lieutenant Calley in the My Lai massacre. Two years and eight months after the "incident" at Pinkville the leader of the first platoon of Charlie Company was put on trial at Fort Benning for the murder of at least 102 "Oriental human beings," names, ages and sex unknown. The racial implication of the charge, though well grounded in American practice in Vietnam, caused the phrase to be changed to "human beings," but the victims still remained abstractions, like all other Vietnamese. Not a single one figured as an individual in the trial. They were distant, depersonalized, truly ghostly figures.

Most of the 105 Americans involved at My Lai were out of the Army when the Calley court-martial began in November 1970, and beyond the reach of military justice, but twenty-five persons had been charged, twelve of them not for participation in the killing but for covering it up.

The Army decided against any sort of group trial, perhaps as too reminiscent of Nuremberg, but also to cushion the total effect. The defendants were tried individually, at different times and on different bases, subject to the final actions of different commanders. The first My Lai trial, a month before Calley's, ended with the acquittal of Staff Sergeant David Mitchell, one of Calley's squad leaders, whose plea was that he was "doing his duty." While Calley's four-month trial ground on, Sergeant Charles Hutto was also separately acquitted. Like Mitchell, he said he was only carrying out orders and would not think of questioning their legality. After the two verdicts all charges were dropped against the other enlisted men, although at Nuremberg and in international law obedience to orders was adjudged not to be a sufficient defense. Cover-up charges were also dropped against all the higher officers named except one, the brigade commander, Colonel O. K. Henderson. Major General Samuel W. Koster, the division commander, was censured, reduced one grade in rank, and lost his Distinguished Service Medal, but he was not tried, the commanding general of the First Army explained, "in the interest of justice."

Calley had emerged as the principal culprit, and as it turned out, the only one to be punished for My Lai, to many Americans a hero, to many others a scapegoat. He also pleaded that he was carrying out his orders, received from his company commander, Captain Ernest Medina, and it had not been his to reason why. On the stand he declared that "there wasn't any big deal" at My Lai. Medina, awaiting court-martial himself, denied as a witness that he had given Calley orders to kill, and said he told the lieutenant to use "common sense" if there was any hostile action by women and children.

The two officers, captain and lieutenant, were in direct contradiction about whether "kill" orders had been issued. The military jury of six combat officers, five of whom had served in Vietnam, chose to believe Medina, making his own acquittal a certainty, and found Calley guilty of "at least twenty-two" murders. In its deliberation over thirteen days the jury minutely reviewed all the testimony and the defendant was apparently given every benefit of doubt. Death by hanging was a possible sentence, but Calley received life imprisonment. His had been the longest court-martial on record, with forty-five days of testimony over a period of four months, 104 witnesses, 700 exhibits and ninety hours of jury deliberation.

As the undersized unheroic "born loser" emerged from the courtroom he was greeted by a crowd, both military and civilian, which cheered him and shouted encouragement. The guilty verdict, a distinct surprise to most Americans, provoked a similar emotional outburst throughout the nation. Thousands of telegrams of protest swept down upon the White House, Congress, the news media and the Fort Benning courtroom. Ever aware of his constituency, and not one to overlook a popular cause however misconceived, President Nixon stepped into the Calley case and allowed the lieutenant to live in his own quarters at Benning instead of going to Leavenworth military prison while his appeal was decided. He also gave public reminder to Calley's superiors in the review process that it was the commander-in-chief who would make final disposition of the case.

The President's words and actions, which Nixon said were to "reassure" the public, stirred as much emotion as the verdict itself. The Army prosecutor, Captain Aubrey W. Daniel — who had undertaken the trial as another routine chore in his four-year Army service and through the evidence came to question the war's morality — sent a personal letter of protest to the commander-in-chief reproaching him for having "damaged the military judicial system." An opinion poll established that 80 percent of those asked opposed the verdict and that therefore "duty" had prevailed over conscience. Calley was held to have committed no crime. Some felt he should not only be freed but decorated.

Supporters of the war and its opponents protested the verdict for their own reasons. Some Vietnam veterans said that if Calley was guilty, so were they, as indeed they may have been. Antiwar veterans saw Calley as the victim of American policy, as they felt they themselves had been. Some critics of the verdict called the entire nation guilty, as "all Germans" had been held to be because of Hitler. For all its larger implications, the Calley case came out in the end as the trial of one man for his actions. When a more equable frame of mind was generally restored — aided by the first review court's reduction of the sentence to twenty years' imprisonment, with other review procedure to follow — it was widely felt that justice had been done. It was not full justice, for it had stopped at Calley. To those like John Kerry, one of the leaders of Vietnam Veterans Against the War, the trial, the principles of military justice, the Pentagon, and the commander-in-chief had failed because they had not distinguished between guilt and responsibility.

Calley's conviction at least made the moral implications of American conduct in Vietnam a more substantive part of the war controversy than ever before. Despite his remark on the stand, My Lai was a "big deal." It stood revealed as just one of the many "free-fire zones" in which Americans had been given hunting licenses for anything that moved. Calley could be defended with the question, "They trained him to kill, didn't they?" On the other hand the verdict reaffirmed that there were laws even in war, and that judgment could be passed on violators. Despite its careful boundaries, therefore, the Calley trial caused many more Americans to face themselves, and even exercise self-judgment. The results may have differed but beneath them was the rising feeling that not only had the United States to get out of Vietnam, but it had to do so to save itself.

The "end the war" sentiment pushed the House of Representatives into its first debate on the subject, ten years after combat officially began, but the cursory nature of the occasion drove antiwar congressmen to their own measures, outside the legislative chambers, including an ad hoc hearing on American war crimes. Moral indignation was the motivation also as thousands of demonstrators descended upon the capital for a long-planned May Day display of "civil disobedience." The banners demanded "Stop the Government to Stop the War," and the intention was to disrupt the massive bureaucracy's functioning by sit-downs at federal office buildings and traffic barriers on roads and bridges leading to the city.

The May Day demonstration's only accomplishment was to provoke the authorities into illegal overreaction. Washington police made more than twelve thousand arrests in a three-day period without the normal charging procedure or other due process, virtually all of them being nullified by the courts. Obstructing traffic but not shortening the working day of government clerks by a half-hour, May Day may have been the worst-planned, worst-executed and most feckless peace action on record, routed in ignominy and skirmishing among trash cans which had been set up as barricades.

It was made the more invidious by contrast with the events of a few days before, when members of the Vietnam Veterans Against the War, some of them crippled, bivouacked in the Mall and threw away their medals in a public ceremony near the Capitol. John Kerry, appearing before the Senate Foreign Relations Committee to press for an end to the war, struck a note that reverberated. "How do you ask a man to be the last man in Vietnam? How do you ask a man to be the last man to die for a mistake?"

Medals had no transferable value in civilian life. While the antiwar veterans demonstrated in Washington, a tall Negro tried to hold up a neighborhood grocery in Detroit and was fatally wounded, shot five times. His wallet contained a membership card in the Congressional Medal of Honor Society, bearing the name of Dwight Johnson. The medal had been awarded at the White House for Sergeant Johnson's action in the Battle of Dakto, when his tank platoon was ambushed and hit by rockets. He rescued a soldier from a burning tank, then killed several guerrillas with a variety of weapons, and fought with a gun stock when he ran out of ammunition.

"Skip" Johnson, raised on welfare in a slum neighborhood, had been an altar boy and a Boy Scout. When he returned from Vietnam he, like many other blacks, could not find a job. He also had psychiatric problems — he suffered from nightmares about Vietnam. The medal, Michigan's only one, did bring job offers, but the Army asked him to serve as a recruiter, for obvious reasons, and he made personal appearances and attended testimonial functions. He married and had a son. Credit was easy to get and when the bills began piling up he wrote a bad check. Black businessmen offered to send him to college but he begged off; it was said he still had a "ghetto mentality" and could not adjust to a wider world. His stomach began to give him trouble, he neglected his recruiting job, missed appointments, and after treatment in an Army hospital went AWOL. His case was diagnosed as depression caused by adjustment difficulties, under the general heading of Post-Vietnam Syndrome. He was found to have guilt feelings about his survival in battle. The disclosure of the My Lai massacre and the trial of Lieutenant Calley apparently further unnerved him but he refused to return to the hospital and his unpaid bills continued to mount. Finally the mortgage on his $16,000 home was foreclosed, and his wife had to undergo an operation. The evening he was killed he had asked to be driven to a friend's house to get another loan; instead, while his companions waited in their car, he went around the corner and entered the grocery with a pistol in his hand. "Skip" Johnson was buried in Arlington National Cemetery with an Army honor squad firing a salute, as was the due of a Medal of Honor winner.

Another sort of case history was revealed, soon after, by the death in an auto crackup of Jackie Robinson, Jr., son of the first black big-league baseball player. Alienated, most probably resentful of his famous father, the younger Robinson enlisted after dropping out of prep school, went to Vietnam, was wounded in action — while "killing kids" younger than he was, he explained — and acquired the heroin habit. Back home he was twice arrested on drug charges. Then he entered a rehabilitation center, and not only freed himself of the habit but became a "drug fighter" in the New York City black slums. He was killed while returning from an evening of therapy with young addicts in a hospital.

American troop withdrawal continued but the United States had not yet been able to kick its Vietnam habit. After more than two years in office it was only in mid-1971 that President Nixon, for all the secret meetings held since 1969 by Henry Kissinger and Le Duc Tho, at last tried in earnest to negotiate a settlement. Presumably the intervening time had been required by "Vietnamization." Equally pertinent, the 1972 campaign, in which he would seek reelection, was fast approaching. George McGovern was still the only declared Democratic candidate but opinion polls revealed that Senator Muskie of Maine was the most strongly supported Democrat and even favored over Nixon, if that were the choice at the time.

The midterm election campaign of 1970 had been an unsatisfying, unsettling and even strident one, with the President stumping for congressional candidates in several states, being heckled in public appearances, and apparently goading youthful dissidents — who may have been provocateurs being used to create "drama" — into "stoning" him at San Jose, in his own California. Apart from the Republican primaries the White House also engaged in a Democratic one, secretly. Some $400,000 of the $1,700,000 left over from the 1968 campaign contributions was put into Alabama by Nixon's personal attorney, Herbert Kalmbach, in an unsuccessful attempt to defeat Governor Wallace for renomination and thus prevent another third-party effort to take votes from Nixon in 1972.

The 1970 national returns in November were inconclusive, though two Senate doves, Goodell of New York and Gore of Tennessee, were defeated by special White House effort. A more definite election result was friction between the Republican party organization, which ran the campaign, and the President, who had cut a poor figure in it. As the polls came in showing him trailing Muskie, Nixon decided to create his own fund-raising and vote-gathering committee to work for his reelection, quite apart from the Republican National Committee, and as his critics put it, to run as "Richard M. President," or as White House aides preferred, "to maximize our incumbency." Another Nixon plan for 1972 was to insure a Vietnam settlement by Election Day.

The way had been opened when, after a long deadlock during which he had demanded the withdrawal of all North Vietnamese troops from South Vietnam as a condition of any cease-fire, Nixon had instructed Kissinger in October 1971 to offer a cease-fire in place. This would allow North Vietnamese units and the Provisional Revolutionary Government to remain in control of any South Vietnamese territory they held, and was obviously unpalatable to President Thieu. But Hanoi persisted in seeking a political settlement, asking no less than that the United States itself replace Thieu in Saigon. To this Nixon and Kissinger continued to say no. The next concession had to be North Vietnam's.

The lack of any apparent progress toward a settlement kept domestic dissent smoldering after the May Day excitement. The Gallup Poll revealed a 61 percent majority opinion that American involvement in Vietnam had been a "mistake," an exact reversal of the figures of August 1965, the change cutting across all political affiliations and age groups. A Harris Poll found that 61 percent would also let other countries defend themselves in the future, and that the only justified American war would be one against actual invasion.

The apparent disillusion with global guardianship, as with the war, provided an appropriate atmosphere for the appearance of the Pentagon Papers, commissioned by Defense Secretary McNamara before he left office. The documents, a chilling though trenchant review of the decision-making of the war that was still in progress, contained no major surprise in their substance. For the most part they confirmed what critics had said during the course of the war and some newspapers had reported, though without complete knowledge or accuracy. The Pentagon Papers did not bare a conspiracy by warmongers or any obvious "imperialistic" intentions. What they revealed were the workings and thought processes of a policy-making elite, increasingly autonomous and self-perpetuating, driven by a Wilsonian sense of historic mission to "make the world safe for democracy" by "defending" it against "Communism." Intervention in Vietnam was not a departure from American history and tradition but a reaffirmation of them, representing a continuity of bipartisan policy that went back beyond the Truman Doctrine to Wilson's intervention in Siberia and Archangel in 1918 in the very first confrontation with Soviet power.

The major Vietnam War decisions, it could be seen, had represented self-deception by the process that George Ball called overintellectualization, caused by a preoccupation with memos, scripts and scenarios, and an absence of reality, relativity and human considerations. The White House and State Department had for years refuted policy criticism by saying that no one who did not read all the diplomatic and departmental telegrams could know what went into decisions. The Pentagon Papers proved the insiders to have no special wisdom and often no more real knowledge of events than could be gained from reading the newspapers. Publication of the documents was nonetheless a momentous example of the not-quite-atrophied democratic process. They had been commissioned in a spirit of self-criticism by McNamara, and after they had been refused as too hot to handle by various senators, including Fulbright and McGovern, they were received by the New York *Times* — itself a notable example of the change in thinking about Vietnam that had taken place in the country — and printed as a journalistic duty, though officially still classified as Secret.

When the federal government, moreover, succeeded in suspending their publication — the Nixon administration thus achieving another "first" in history as the imposer of prior restraint — a 6-to-3 Supreme Court majority ruled against suppression and the printing was resumed. After the *Times* had been enjoined, the Washington *Post* published documents and became involved in the Supreme Court case, and when it was similarly halted other leading newspapers, including the St. Louis *Post-Dispatch*, the Boston *Globe*, the Los Angeles *Times*, and the Chicago *Sun-Times*, challenged the government with further disclosures. John Peter Zenger would have been pleased.

The Supreme Court decision was not a blanket confirmation of constitutional press freedom, and the administration quickly moved to prosecute the two men it charged with responsibility for the publication, but the Pentagon Papers could not be gainsaid. Providing support for those who had criticized the war and something of an accounting from those who had pursued it, they were a major Vietnam landmark.

The *Times* was given the documents by Daniel Ellsberg, the former Marine lieutenant, former RAND think-tank occupant, consultant on nuclear war for the Kennedy and Johnson administrations, researcher for Walt Rostow on "crisis behavior," Defense Department planner, and option-collector for Henry Kissinger and the White House, and now a senior research assistant at MIT. Ellsberg, involved in Vietnam study in one way or another since 1964, had begun as very much a hawk, helping coordinate the ill-starred Tonkin Gulf operations, believing firmly in the American purpose of "containment," and approving the bombing of North Vietnam and the sending of ground troops in 1965. He had thought it "unacceptable" for the United States to "lose" South Vietnam. Then, as a result of two years in Vietnam, he had come to regard the bombing first as "nonproductive" and later as a "disastrous idea," one of "the worst ideas of statecraft of this century," with "elements of absurdity, brutality, criminality and illegitimacy." He was appalled to see that Vietnamese were "hunted like animals" by American helicopter gunships, and distressed by ARVN's ineptitude and the climate of corruption, made possible by lavish American aid, which pervaded Vietnam. He was also convinced that the American government was receiving a distorted picture of events. When he went to work on the Pentagon Papers and read the entire collection of documents he decided that American policy-makers had been ill intentioned as well as ill informed, and that the only way to change policy was to change "the environment of policy," by means of "an informational process and a political process to take place outside the Executive." In RAND language this meant exposing the Pentagon Papers to public view.

Ellsberg believed that if what he did was illegal, as the government said, it was to counter what he considered other illegality. He thought the papers could no longer compromise national security or secret diplomacy — he withheld from publication the volumes concerned with peace negotiations — and that the public had "a right to know." The government charged him with conspiracy and the theft of official documents, but also with espionage, in a new interpretation of that offense which made it clear that the administration regarded the American press as an enemy power. Accused with Ellsberg, because he had helped copy the papers, was a former RAND colleague he had met in Vietnam, Anthony Russo. The latter had been engaged in RAND's Viet Cong Morale and Motivation Project but left after eighteen months when it was converted into a bombing-assessment study exalting the Air Force.

Ellsberg's actions and motives in making the Pentagon Papers known betrayed a dichotomy not to be entirely explained as political change through experience. A great deal of emotion was obviously woven into his apparent conversion. The former zealot for Vietnam policy had turned into an even more zealous condemner of it. He had felt profoundly right about his support of what he unhesitatingly accepted as American interests and became equally positive that they needed to be questioned.

Under orders of the President to investigate news leaks, of which the Pentagon Papers if the most heinous was only the latest example, the White House called in two supposed experts, E. Howard Hunt, Jr., a twenty-year veteran of the CIA, recently retired — his exploits included Guatemala and the Bay of Pigs — and G. Gordon Liddy, the ebullient "law and order" advocate and former FBI agent. The latter had been rewarded for his 1968 Nixon-Agnew campaign activities with an antinarcotics post in the Treasury Department, but left after embarrassing the government in its relations with Mexico by trying to "seal" the border. Now Liddy and Hunt joined the office of "the plumbers," as they were called, in the basement of the Executive Office Building, adjacent to the White House. Their first assignment was to find out what they could about Ellsberg, a task explained as an imperative of "national security," but to a White House going into an election year even more an operation in partisan "political intelligence." The instructions given "the plumbers" from the Oval Office were to regard Ellsberg as another Alger Hiss, whose case had launched Nixon on his political career.

At the same time it investigated Ellsberg the White House set about undermining the candidacy of Senator Muskie as Nixon's leading rival. Edward Kennedy was also a possible Democratic nominee, under surveillance by the White House "special investigations unit" since the Chappaquiddick incident, and Hunt developed "intelligence" on this also. Given access to State Department files, the former CIA operative used them to concoct a diplomatic cable purporting to show that President Kennedy had in 1963 sanctioned Ngo Dinh Diem's murder as well as his overthrow. Even to Hunt the purpose of his forgery was not clear, but it was the kind of thing that was done in the twoscore novels he had written about "cloak and dagger" exploits. As on television so in the CIA, reality and fiction tended to merge. When a CIA "psychological profile" of Ellsberg was found inadequate by the White House — he was described as motivated by "what he deemed a higher order of patriotism" — Hunt and Liddy, with disguises, false identity papers and a camera furnished by the CIA, supervised a burglary by three Cubans from Miami — a CIA stamping ground since the Bay of Pigs — of the Los Angeles office of Ellsberg's psychiatrist. They sought "personal" material.

A long train of singular events, as secret as the Pentagon Papers had previously been, was thus set into motion, leading to political espionage and sabotage, irregular campaign activities, and most of all, a conspiracy of concealment. The order to engage in "political intelligence" was implemented by the total resources of the White House, which was in effect interlocked with the Committee for the Reelection of the President, now formally organized across the street. Liddy was moved over to the committee for the campaign, as general counsel, and Hunt also went to work for it while retaining an office in the Executive Office Building.

As the gigantic and intricate machinery to insure the President's reelection began to turn, and the campaign funds poured in, Richard Nixon set about creating the political basis not only for his reelection but for his place in history. An astonished nation heard his announcement in mid-July of what amounted to recognition of Mao Tse-tung's Peking government after twenty-five years of mutual hostility. It would take two practical forms: a visit by the President to the People's Republic of China, and the end of American opposition to China's admission to the United Nations.

Perhaps the news should not have been as unexpected as it was. No other President would have been able to reverse China policy without risking an accusation of "treason," intimated so often by Richard Nixon himself. This President also was able even more than others to put pragmatism above any previous professions of principle. He had in fact been carefully moving toward this point from the moment he took office, having then already stated his intention. As always, there was ambiguity. A year before his 1968 election he had written of the need for a new relationship with China, and of Peking's eventual UN admission, though such a relationship, he explained, could come only after "detoxification . . . from the Thoughts of Mao." Basically, Nixon made the argument for the continued "containment" of China, but by Asians under Japanese leadership. During the 1968 campaign he defended American intervention in Vietnam as "the cork in the bottle of Chinese expansion." Peking read his speeches, but the oldest civilization on earth had not survived for so long without abundant practicality. A few weeks after Nixon's election the Chinese took the initiative and proposed to Washington the resumption of the suspended Warsaw talks, to discuss the Bandung "Five Principles of Coexistence."

In office, supported by the diligence of Kissinger, Nixon continued to seek the opening in the Great Wall. Not only did the Romanians serve as a conduit to Peking but President Yahya Khan of Pakistan carried a letter there from the American President. Chou En-lai had already told the American writer Edgar Snow that the door was open to a Nixon visit, if the United States were serious about discussing Taiwan, and Mao Tse-tung informed Snow that Nixon would be welcome "either as a tourist or as President."

Nixon found it no longer necessary to wait for "detoxification" from the Thoughts of Mao. He would go and hear them at first hand instead. He had made his first move of detente by suspending the American destroyer patrol of the Formosa Strait. The Chinese responded by resuming the Warsaw meetings. Withdrawal of the Seventh Fleet acknowledged to Peking that after twenty years Taiwan, which both Chinas claimed, was to be a matter between them and no longer the affair of Americans. For the record, the United States sought to keep both Chinas in the United Nations, knowing that the General Assembly, freed of the American restraint upon Peking's entry, would decide otherwise.

With the expected departure before long of the eighty-four-year-old Chiang Kai-shek, and with it the end of the dream of his return to the mainland that the United States had helped keep alive, the change in American policy in 1971 was founded on another dream, that of a global concert of powers, the modern equivalent of Metternich's European policy. As explained by Henry Kissinger, Metternich had sought to avoid major crises requiring an unequivocal commitment and to create "the illusion of intimacy with all major powers," but Kissinger conceded that Metternich's plan was "so intricate that it obscured the fact that none of the fundamental problems had really been resolved."

As Nixon turned to China he ended some of the restrictions on American travel so long ago imposed by John Foster Dulles, relaxed the trade embargo, and allowed the entry for the first time of consumer items which had previously been subject to confiscation when bought by Americans in Hong Kong. Department stores struck a new lode of Chinese porcelain, basketware and clothing. Rough shirts made in Chinese workers' cooperatives became a new and not inexpensive youth fad.

Peking's receptiveness to these American gestures was confirmed by an invitation to the American table tennis team, which had competed in international play in Japan, to tour the mainland. "Ping-Pong diplomacy" at once fired the American imagination, especially since American correspondents were given visas to report the matches, in which the Chinese politely beat the visitors by respectable scores instead of easily overwhelming them. Other American visitors were soon allowed in, and among them, secretly, was Henry Kissinger. He met with Chou En-lai, prepared an agenda, and the President was able to announce he would be going to Peking in February 1972, nine months before the American election, "to seek the normalization of relations between the two countries."

Except for the Republican right wing, which felt betrayed by the President it had regarded as the original Anti-Peking Man, except for the Young Americans for Freedom, who called the President's proposed visit to Peking "morally offensive," the change in policy was accepted calmly by American opinion. There was no rioting in the streets. In the small towns of the American Midwest, Peking and global strategy were less important than the low price of corn, local unemployment, rising school costs, and the use of "pot" by teen-agers.

While playing out the two-China game to the end, the United States now seriously dealt with one China. When the UN vote was taken to replace Chiang Kai-shek's representatives with Mao Tse-tung's, Henry Kissinger was in Peking with Chou En-lai again and Mao himself was once more in undisputed internal control. Lin Piao, who according to Chou had plotted to obtain "sole rule" in a contest of Army versus Party, had — Peking said without offering any evidence — died with eight others in a mysterious plane crash in Mongolia while reportedly fleeing to Moscow for sanctuary. Whatever the truth about Lin's death a few weeks after Kissinger's first visit to Peking, it seemed clear that Mao's chosen successor had opposed detente with the United States.

The Russians eyed with apprehension all the surprising things that had been happening. They had carried out for years the ritual of demanding China's admission to the United Nations, and now Peking had not only a vote but a veto. The bitter Sino-Soviet diatribes formerly exchanged in Communist party congresses were transferred to the world forum as Great Power arguments over rival national interests, between the "social imperialists," as the Chinese called the Russians, and the "social traitors," as the Russians called the Chinese. In the first major debate of the UN's new ecumenical era the animosity between India and Pakistan, over the fighting in and secession of Bangladesh, was no less than that shown by their respective supporters, Moscow and Peking. For the first time the United States found itself on the same side as Communist China, and "tilted" in favor of Pakistan after years spent cultivating India against China.

The Chinese from Peking were received in New York as if they were Martians. At the bourgeois Roosevelt Hotel, where they stayed before buying a midtown motel of their own with rooftop pool and sun deck, the head waiter expressed surprise that they knew how to use knives and forks, and folded their napkins neatly. They were praised by the management for not having loud parties and wrecking furniture. They knew enough to tip, which was not done in China. Their novelty soon passed, in a city filled with Chinese restaurants and laundries. The men from Peking joined the normal stream of diplomatic life. What had all the fuss been about for twenty years?

Moscow's fears of where the Sino-American detente might lead was based on a reading of recent history far removed from the interpretation of American defense "experts." The latter saw the Russians piling up armaments, both conventional and nuclear; enlarging the foothold in the Middle East with a military mission, air fields and pilots in Egypt; reaching a full-time naval presence in the Mediterranean rivaling that of the Sixth Fleet; with a new sea domain in the Indian Ocean and major influence in India; and with new opportunities in Europe as the result of active conciliation with the Germans.

The Moscow view of these things was painfully different. As the underground press of the Soviet "opposition" stated it, the Sixties had seen a series of Soviet setbacks — the break with China, the loss of the race to the moon, the evacuation of missiles from Cuba, the death of Che Guevara, the defeat of the Arabs in the Six-Day War, and worldwide odium as a result of the Czech invasion. The consequences at home had been a larger military budget, in proportion to the Gross National Product, than the American budget; a cutback on consumer goods because of large-scale overseas spending; and the inflation which struck capitalist and socialist societies alike. To cap matters, the American President by going to Peking was giving aid and encouragement to the Chinese in their unrelenting struggle with the Russians.

The result was as Metternich might have foreseen and as Henry Kissinger undoubtedly had. The Russians joined the global balance-of-power calculations to compensate for any American tilt toward Peking, and became hospitable to Soviet-American cooperation of wide range — nuclear arms limitation; scientific, medical and ecological joint enterprises, even some in space; increased trade, indeed encouragement of American investment in the workers' republic. The first American cabinet officer since the immediate postwar period to go to Moscow, the Secretary of Commerce, was followed by advance men for American banks and industrial firms. The President himself was soon able to announce that he would be visiting the Kremlin shortly after visiting the Forbidden City. His declaration that there was no connection between the two events, no attempt to play off one Communist giant against the other, seemed the clearest evidence to the contrary. Simultaneous with the disclosure of the Moscow invitation came the death, almost symbolic, of a principal architect of the Cold War, former Secretary of State Dean Acheson.

Equally in response to the effects of the war, a month after announcing his intention of visiting Peking, President Nixon set forth on a similarly unexpected journey into economic management. Declaring himself a Keynesian, a believer in government supervision of the economy, the onetime clerk in the World War II Office of Price Control who had there formed a fervent opposition to regulation, now imposed a ninety-day wage-price freeze to check inflation, and followed it with loose but nonetheless definite government controls. At the same time he suspended the gold convertibility of the dollar.

The Nixon New Economic Policy began with America's gold supply, once held in the amount of $25 billion, now down to $11 billion, and its international balance-of-payments deficit running at $20 billion a year. The deficit which had been accruing since the Korean War was due to foreign aid, the maintenance of troops abroad, and overseas investment. Globalism carried an expensive price tag, perhaps become too expensive. There had actually been a dollar panic in Europe, the suspension of trading in American currency (to the consternation of tourists brought up in the American belief that only theirs was "real money") and finally new exchange rates. The United States tried to meet the situation through the revaluation of other currencies, but Germany and Japan would be satisfied only with the formal humbling of the once Almighty Dollar. Its devaluation was achieved by raising the official price of gold from $35 to $38 an ounce.

America's economic troubles, aggravated by Lyndon Johnson's refusal to increase taxes while at the same time entering upon extensive ground war in Asia, had finally come home to roost. The domestic aspects were two — inflation, through the ascending spiral of prices and wages, and for the first time in the century a trade deficit in addition to that in international payments. Nixon and his economists laid the deficits to unfair trade competition, especially by Japan. They were more precisely the fault of the continuing drain of Vietnam and defense spending. From 1966 through 1970 the military accounted for 95 percent of the government's foreign expenditures as against an already swollen 77 percent in the five years preceding.

Though the powers by which the Republican Chief Executive changed economic policy had been granted by the nominally Democratic Congress in the 1970 Economic Stabilization Act — which the President had said he did not want and would never use — they added to the continuing congressional debate on presidential authority. Not only Vietnam, to which had been added the Cambodian and Laotian invasions, but also the ordered "tilt" toward Pakistan in the dispute over Bangladesh, and the supply of planes to Israel, reflected the presidential power in foreign policy, employed without congressional consultation and frequently against the advice of the professional diplomats of the State Department. The realization that undeclared wars were no longer emergencies but Clausewitzian extensions of foreign policy, the President's evident belief that powers were made constitutional merely by their exercise, touched sensitive political nerves. Not only Congress but the separate states reacted.

Massachusetts and Minnesota passed bills questioning the constitutionality of the Vietnam War and the ordering of their citizens into combat. From New York to California legislatures sought a Supreme Court ruling on the legality of the Vietnam involvement. The tribunal, like the United Nations, throughout the war evaded direct adjudication of any question arising from it. By refusing to review a lower court finding that Congress had in effect declared war by continuing to vote appropriations, the Supreme Court did at any rate deflate the rationalization of those who had separated their support of the troops from support of the war.

For all its words Congress continued to be as inert as the Supreme Court in any real challenge to presidential war powers. The Senate twice passed an amendment to withdraw all American forces from Vietnam within six months, if American prisoners were returned, and twice the House killed it. When it was finally approved, tacked on to a bill providing for new weapons, the President signed the measure but announced he would not heed the amendment.

By that time, in the two years and nine months since Nixon entered the White House, 2.7 million tons of bombs had been dropped on Indochina, more than on Europe and Asia combined in both World War II and Korea. In North Vietnam the Pentagon no longer bothered to call it bombing. The 184 separate air attacks during this period, some by 250 or more planes, were "protective reaction strikes." The skies over South Vietnam were filled with spotter planes, jet bombers, prop bombers, gunships, flare ships, reconnaissance planes, rescue helicopters, refueling ships, command-and-control planes, and high flying SR-171's which had replaced the U-2's. New "smart" bombs were "delivered," directed by laser and TV. Antipersonnel as well as explosive and incendiary bombs fell.

On the ground things were different. Combat had virtually ceased for Americans. For the week ending October 5, 1971, only five GI's were killed, the lowest figure since 1965. On the other hand Vietnamization meant nearly 400 ARVN dead, a rate even higher than the 300 weekly average Americans had known in 1968. The decrease in battle action encouraged further minor mutinies against combat. More units refused to go on patrol until the captain could satisfy them of the need for the mission. Not only in Vietnam but around the world Army morale and discipline kept sagging. From Long Binh to Darmstadt to Fort Benning, orders were questioned, drugs were used, racial fracases broke out, soldiers stole from one another, and desertions increased. Confused by the visible disintegration, officers compromised, innovated and retreated from tradition. Reveille and bed checks were ended in barracks, and beer vending machines installed. The Army allowed more leave, the Navy longer hair. Many units in Germany, Korea and elsewhere were frankly unfit to go into action if the necessity should arise.

The slackening of combat in Vietnam further diminished antiwar dissent at home, but this made all the more visible the increase in crime, bred in the decay of the cities. The burned-out areas of Washington, Newark, Detroit, Chicago and Watts still stood glaringly empty after three, four, five and six years of further neglect. The black ghettos brooded in their frustration and sullen hatred of the police, and the flight of the white middle class to the suburbs had become a rout. In the cities, stores put iron shutters and grills over their doors and windows, even in fashionable shopping streets like Madison Avenue in New York, and kept their doors locked against holdups in broad daylight. At night, downtown streets were deserted, movie houses were half-empty and restaurants closed early. More murders were committed per year in New York City alone than in Britain, Ireland, the Netherlands, Switzerland, Spain, Sweden, Norway, Denmark and Luxembourg combined. Washington's murder rate, however, in proportion to population, was twice New York's. Crime in the national capital of a law-and-order administration seemed to have become worse than anywhere else.

There may have been something appropriate about what was happening to America. A good part of the world seemed to think so, besides many at home. To them the Vietnam War and the considerable provision of arms to other countries had made Washington the world capital of violence, and the violence had now been turned back upon itself.

Sociological explanations were also available. The high crime areas were the areas of high unemployment, crowded conditions, poverty and squalor. The crime figures and the racial composition of city populations could be correlated. Between the 1960 and the 1970 censuses the proportion of blacks to the total population of Washington had increased from 54 percent to 71 percent; to that of Baltimore from 35 percent to 46 percent; to that of Detroit from 29 percent to 49 percent. The crime rate had gone up in parallel, if only because blacks committed so many crimes against other blacks.

The nation's first and third cities, New York and Los Angeles, despite their huge ghettos, showed only a modest increase in black population over the decade, up from 14 to 21 percent in the former and from 14 to 18 percent in the latter, but they had a special concentration of violence stemming not from ordinary crime alone but from what was left of black militancy. The Black Liberation Army, even more deliberately than the Black Panthers, had declared armed warfare against the police.

The Panthers, for their part, had unexpectedly won a legal victory against constituted authority. A middle-class jury in New York City of six whites, five blacks and one Puerto Rican acquitted thirteen of them on all 156 counts of conspiracy to kill police and to blow up police stations, five department stores, the Penn Central railroad tracks, the Manhattan board of education building and the Botanical Gardens in the Bronx. The longest trial in the city's history, lasting eight months, was ended by a unanimous jury vote on the first ballot, after only ninety minutes of deliberation. The verdict staggered prosecutors and spectators alike, after the solid weeks of testimony by undercover police who had infiltrated Panther ranks and swore they had taken part in the plots. It also set a precedent for other acquittals in what appeared to be a citizens' rebellion against the conspiracy statutes so sweepingly applied by federal and state authorities.

The successive Panther acquittals and dismissals, if they vindicated the jury system in which not all blacks had previously found comfort, came too late to repair the damage done them by imprisonment, flight and factional strife. Whatever appeal they might still have possessed was lost when a prominent Panther, Richard Moore, who had jumped bail to avoid trial with the other thirteen, fell into police hands in the holdup of a black social club in the Bronx. Soon afterward no less a personage than "Rap" Brown, the former chairman of SNCC, was wounded by police and arrested in a similar holdup of a club on the West Side of Manhattan. Moore was convicted and received a life sentence for trying to kill two policemen in an earlier incident. A dozen associates continued to be sought as members of the Black Liberation Army, and one by one, they were killed or captured. "Rap" Brown was convicted and given a five-year minimum prison term.

The Panthers and other black militants would seem to have been eliminated as an overt menace to "law and order," but the issue was carried into the 1972 election campaign, the administration asserting that its efforts had at least reduced the rate of increase in crime. Another emotional campaign issue was furnished by the Supreme Court, headed now by Nixon's appointee, Chief Justice Warren Burger. Seventeen years after the Warren Court's order to desegregate public schools "with all deliberate speed," the Burger Court ruled that school bussing was a proper tool to carry out desegregation where no other method was viable.

The Charlotte-Mecklenburg, North Carolina, decision, though applied to southern states where segregation had been de jure, also caused angry outbursts in the North, especially in the auto cities of Michigan with their many southern migrants, black and white. The President stoked passions by declaring his opposition to bussing despite the Court's ruling. After several violent antibussing incidents, notably at Spartanburg, South Carolina, and Pontiac, Michigan, the issue was seized by George Wallace as his principal talking point for the 1972 campaign, and most of the other Democratic candidates either echoed his antibussing declamations or dissembled, as the political tide swept toward the primaries.

The Democratic "front runner" was Muskie, remembered not only from the 1968 campaign but more recently for the calm contrast he had provided to an overwrought Nixon in the Election Eve broadcasts of 1970. Other Democratic aspirants included Humphrey, Wallace and Mayor John Lindsay of New York, newly turned Democrat; a black woman candidate, Representative Shirley Chisholm of New York; the "Senator from Boeing," Henry M. Jackson of Washington; and George McGovern of South Dakota. Muskie seemed the certain choice, as providing party continuity and middle-of-the-road reassurance.

McGovern had already been campaigning for nearly a year as a "different kind" of politician, in pursuit of a new coalition to replace or at least modernize Roosevelt's original one. McGovern courted minority groups, political, cultural and racial, and paid particular attention to the expected huge new constituency of eighteen-to-twenty-one-year-olds given the vote by the Twenty-sixth Amendment.

The American campus had remained becalmed but the turmoil of earlier years was presumed to have left its mark. Politicians and polltakers believed that if activism had lessened, collegiate awareness had not, as youth arrived at its own consensus, to try to work within the "System." Vietnam was no longer a vibrant issue, and an antiwar moratorium scheduled soon after the 1971 fall term began was a distinct failure. On the college lecture circuit the popular topics were Israel, China, consumerism, and the blacks, and the most popular speakers were Ralph Nader, Julian Bond and Dick Gregory, the black comedian. The Columbia *Spectator*, which had supported all antiwar demonstrations everywhere since they began, for the first time refused an endorsement of the latest one, commenting harshly on "song and dance" methods, and advocating "other means" of hastening peace, though without naming them. Corporate recruiting had been openly resumed at Columbia, and jobs were important again.

The America of 1972 had changed in other striking ways from the Sixties. Begun in antiwar organization, typified by Women Strike for Peace, the "women's liberation" movement had taken on wider and to some males more unnerving implications. On the fiftieth anniversary of the Women's Suffrage Amendment a large parade was held on Fifth Avenue in New York on behalf of a new Equal Rights Amendment, and after it bands of Amazons "freed" bars and other masculine domains, including the city's most venerable saloon, McSorley's Old Ale House, in a shower of suds from its defenders.

A sort of liberation was achieved by the labor movement also. The United Auto Workers won the right of retirement at fifty-eight on $500 a month after thirty years of employment, although of thirty-three thousand eligible for the new emancipation only four thousand were actually able to afford it without fear of the economic future.

The war was old enough and had been absorbed enough to become the subject of successful plays on Broadway as well as off, and to be accepted as part of the plot motivation on television entertainment programs. Standard viewing fare included returned veterans who had failed to readjust or had become drug addicts, or who railed against "all this killing." If Vietnam could be laundered into soap opera it was plain that the war, to all practical intents and purposes, was over. Abortion, venereal disease, homosexuality and other topics previously taboo were also becoming "acceptable" to network censors in popular programs.

For the most part television adhered to its customary levels of violence — the "body count" in police and private-eye dramas was as high some weeks as the actual casualties in Vietnam — though in the world outside the studios a proliferation of mysticism was reported to the American Psychoanalytic Association as an attempt to escape from violence and aggression. The young, especially, were becoming immersed in religious cultism, and the "Jesus people" represented either refuge from or active rebellion against materialism and science. *Jesus Christ Superstar,* a musical spectacular, became the most profitable all-media triumph in show history, with a long Broadway run, two road companies, three million albums of records sold, and a movie filmed in Israel.

A more secular escape from reality was the new eastern version of Disneyland, at Orlando, Florida. One of the first visitors to the $400 million Disney World told reporters, "We need a place like this because of the world situation, a place where we can come and relax, and forget about the bad things." The mammoth amusement center offered retreat to an imaginary past, an ideal America without violence, pain or controversy.

Disney World was created as a tourist attraction, and so was the Florida primary of 1972. The contest would be wide open, with no rules to speak of and embracing all the possible contenders under its Ringling Brothers canopy: three Republicans and ten Democrats, "nominated" by the "news media." The presidential campaign was not opened in Florida, however, or in the traditionally first primary in New Hampshire the week before, but in 1971 in South Vietnam. There Nguyen Van Thieu, in a presidential election of his own that was the opposite of wide open, changed his suspect minority victory of 1967 into an even more suspect majority victory.

Ambassador Ellsworth Bunker had arranged for Thieu's 1967 election by persuading Marshal Ky to run with Thieu for the Vice-Presidency instead of opposing him. The new American slogan became "See It Through with Nguyen Van Thieu," and that was what the United States was prepared to do whatever the consequences. Again Ambassador Bunker was a prime mover.

Two other candidates declared themselves: Vice-President Ky, and General Duong Van "Big" Minh. The South Vietnamese Supreme Court, an adjunct of the presidential palace, ruled Ky ineligible for not receiving the required number of nomination endorsements. Since these had to be made by public officials appointed by Thieu, the Vice-President's difficulty was self-evident. The other challenger, General Minh, then withdrew from the contest, charging it had been rigged. Bunker urged Minh to run and lose, so that he could become "leader of the opposition," and reportedly offered American financing of his campaign, but in a country where Thieu's 1967 runner-up was still in prison the Ambassador's advice did not seem sound.

As the sole candidate Thieu won between 90 and 95 percent of the vote — a measure of the election is this imprecision — which was the equal of anything Ho Chi Minh had ever been able to do. After the voting Ambassador Bunker told a group of American students visiting Saigon, "Well, even after two hundred years we still have gross irregularities in our own elections." Governor Ronald Reagan of California, sent to deliver Nixon's personal congratulations to his co-President, added the observation that George Washington had also been elected without opposition.

The 1971 South Vietnamese election was, like the death of Diem in 1963, another point at which the United States might have ended its part in the war, having done all within its power to insure its small ward security and independence. Such a course was farthest from Richard Nixon's mind. For one thing, he feared, as Henry Kissinger also did, that to "abandon" South Vietnam before his own reelection in 1972 would cause serious disaffection within the Republican right wing.

Thieu's election under American auspices and the war's continuation inspired Hanoi to plan another major military action for 1972, at least the equal of the 1968 Tet offensive, in order to take territory and try to shake the Saigon regime into collapse. By strengthening Thieu's resolve against any sort of settlement, his victory also led Hanoi to break off the secret talks between Kissinger and Le Duc Tho, after eleven meetings in two years.

The election, finally, had a domino effect. With South Vietnam as an example, Lon Nol of Cambodia also ended "the game of democracy and freedom" and installed one-man rule similarly sanctioned by his American friends. In Thailand, with its large American military establishment, the junta which had ruled in one combination or another since the end of the absolute monarchy forty years before, abolished the constitution, closed down the parliament and instituted government by decree. The war which the United States had undertaken to defeat insurgency and contain Communism had created more insurgency and more Communism in Thailand, as in Vietnam, Cambodia and Laos.

For the third time, South Vietnamese troops entered Cambodia, supported by American planes and helicopters, and President Nixon asked Congress for more funds to continue the operation which eighteen months before he had said would shorten the war. Since he refused to disclose how much was already being spent in Cambodia and Laos, he provoked a new clash with the Senate over his powers. Having forced the defeat of another Cooper-Church amendment to limit the further use of funds in Indochina, by threatening to veto the $3.2 billion foreign aid bill to which it was attached, Nixon saw the offended Senate vote to end all foreign aid instead. Begun with the Truman Doctrine, foreign aid had over the years amounted to $143 billion, and the Senate's repudiation of it thus went beyond Vietnam or any other specific dissatisfaction and was almost a revolutionary move, tantamount to a declaration of the end of the Cold War. It was made possible by an unlikely coalition of conservatives, reacting to the new China policy and the weakened world position of the dollar, and of liberals disenchanted by the misuses of overseas spending. Senator Church, delivering the requiem, pointed out that in addition to what foreign aid did do — fostering militarism, rightism and repression — it had failed to contain Communism or promote economic development. The President, distinctly set back, had to ask reconsideration of the defeated bill, and foreign aid was eventually restored on a more limited and more accountable basis. In the future it was bound to be more selective, and probably more technological than military. Uncle Sugar had grown wiser.

Europe was observing its own obsequies for the Cold War. The long struggle had centered on the divided city of Berlin and the existence of two Germanys. Now Chancellor Brandt was laying a mosaic of agreements — between West and East Germany on the access rights to Berlin; between East Germany and West Berlin on border-crossing and other amenities; an agreement on Berlin itself by the four statutory occupying powers; and German-Soviet and German-Polish treaties on the postwar boundaries — to create the elements, if not the form, of a German peace treaty, twenty-seven years after the end of World War II. With Britain joining the Common Market — de Gaulle, who had opposed British entry, had died in retirement after a plebiscitary defeat — Europe could proceed to the long-delayed security conference and mutual reduction of armed forces. Both Germanys entered the United Nations.

A great deal of stubborn history had been written with the Berlin Airlift, the Berlin Wall, Checkpoint Charlie, the Hallstein Doctrine, the

Brezhnev Doctrine, and the Oder-Neisse Line. Yet after more than a quarter-century Europe had wound up just where the war had left it. Nobody had won the Cold War; it may have been unwinnable. That had not prevented it from being waged.

Also unwinnable by either side, the conflict in Vietnam was presumably ending in a similar fashion, at least for Americans. By the close of 1971 their number had been brought under 160,000; by February 1, 1972, it was down to 139,000, and this in turn was halved to 69,000 a few months before the election. The body count had a new meaning. The aim was to keep American deaths down instead of "VC" deaths up. The South Vietnamese, however, were taking many more casualties. During 1971 they suffered 21,500 dead, probably an underestimate, including a good many in Cambodia and Laos. In turn they claimed 97,000 insurgent dead, probably an overestimate.

Americans were not the only foreigners leaving Vietnam. Australia and New Zealand had sent combat troops, under Lyndon Johnson's prodding, and as in the United States at the cost of political divisiveness. The Australians, who had built up a task force of 8,000 backed by their own air support, counted 500 dead and 3,500 disabled. New Zealand's token force of 500 also departed, and so did the 12,000 American-paid Thais. The 50,000 South Koreans began to withdraw after a six-year stay that South Vietnamese charged had produced numerous atrocities on the scale of My Lai.

The ground was being cleared of the various expeditionary forces, but in spite of or because of this the air war continued at a high level in South Vietnam, and increased in Cambodia and Laos. The number of American planes and sorties was reduced from the 1968–1969 peak, but not the tonnage. By the end of 1971 the United States had dropped 6.2 million tons of bombs on Indochina — 3.6 million in South Vietnam, 1.4 million on the Ho Chi Minh trail and 500,000 in the rest of Laos, 500,000 on North Vietnam, 200,000 on Cambodia.

For all the vaunted precision of the "smart" bombs, the Cornell University Air War Study Group found that more than half of them fell outside the intended target areas. By the end of 1971, 150,000 civilian dead and 350,000 injured from bombing were estimated in South Vietnam, all from "friendly action" since Hanoi used no planes. Limitation had from time to time been imposed on the bombing of the North but none had ever been imposed on South Vietnam. Nor did restrictions remain very long for North Vietnam. At the end of 1971, after four American planes were shot down over Laos, 1,000 bombing sorties in five days were sent in retaliation beyond the 17th parallel. The weather was bad. Pilots could not see the ground. The Pentagon nevertheless declared that "only military targets" had been hit, while President Nixon called the raids "very successful." With the increase in "protective reaction" strikes, supposedly to protect the American withdrawal, more planes were lost and more pilots captured.

Even without ground combat, the bombing soon became too much for many Americans. After Thieu's one-man election a Harris Poll showed that 65 percent believed it "morally wrong" for the United States to be fighting in Vietnam, instead of merely a "mistake," as before, and a 3-to-1 majority favored "getting completely out" by May 1972, leaving no residual force and discontinuing the use of air power in support of South Vietnamese troops. For the first time Nixon's rate of withdrawal was found "too slow" by a majority, 53 percent. "Get out" of Vietnam was widely favored over "winding down."

Entering upon the Democratic primaries, Muskie, McGovern and Lindsay seized on the new air strikes for further condemnation of the administration. But public indignation no longer burned as fiercely as it once had, and antiwar demonstrations could no longer be whistled up. The 1972 political campaign had other issues to be concerned with.

After a series of riots in penal institutions, an inmate uprising in the New York State maximum security prison at Attica was put down by state police with the killing of forty-three persons, including ten prison guards being held as hostages. It was a civilian version of My Lai, and again many Americans refused to believe what had happened. Authorities gave out false stories that the guards had been killed by the prisoners, not by the troopers. Governor Nelson Rockefeller, more concerned to crush "revolution," apparently, than to save the hostages by negotiating inmate grievances, explained that "there was the whole rule of law to consider, the whole fabric of our society, in fact." He was lauded by President Nixon. The State Commissioner of Corrections, Russell G. Oswald, called Attica "the swiftest and most skillful revolutionary offensive since the 1968 Tet attack in South Vietnam." The Attica rebels, like the "Viet Cong," were trying "to make the United States look utterly weak and foolish in the eyes of the rest of the world." The official report on the riot found that it sprang from no revolutionary conspiracy or organization, but from spontaneous anger against crowded conditions and racism by prison guards.

In the national clamor for "law and order" some of the reasons for its lack were generally overlooked. Three years after the Kerner Commission's report on local disorders, the National Urban Coalition pronounced its judgment that the cities were in deeper trouble than ever. Schools had not improved. Housing was no less squalid. Welfare rolls had expanded. Crime, drugs and unemployment were more prevalent. Relations between minorities and the police continued to be abrasive. Inequalities and frustrations endured. Worst of all, violence was increasing, especially among the young. Bands of teen-agers roamed New York City streets near the black ghettos, infesting the parks, mugging, stabbing and shooting. Punishment by confinement turned amateur outlaws into professionals. Yet law enforcement could not be put aside while poverty and slums were eliminated and the prisons reformed, if those things were in fact possible.

Against the increasingly lawless state of affairs a new Supreme Court had been made the symbol of remedy and reparation. It was the fruit of President Nixon's oft-stated intention of appointing justices who shared his views of "judicial restraint" and "strict constructionism." The Nixon campaigns, in 1968 for the Presidency and in 1970 on behalf of Republican congressional candidates, had been in large measure against the courts, for their supposed leniency to wrongdoers. The Supreme Court especially he had regarded as too liberal and too "activist," and he had gone so far as to indict it for "weakening the peace forces as against the criminal forces in our society."

Given the opportunity to make four first-term appointments, more than any other President since Harding, Nixon, after a bitter quarrel with the Senate over a successor to Abe Fortas — who had resigned, under the cloud of careless financial conduct — and after the unprecedented rejection of two successive nominees, both southerners, finally established a "conservative" majority with his four appointees and two sitting justices generally regarded as such.

Yet for all their own predilections Supreme Court justices, even more than other jurists, place great store on precedent. Major constitutional interpretations are not easily or quickly discarded. The Court took fifty-eight years to change the original "separate but equal" ruling into the school desegregation decision of 1954. More usual than dramatic reversals as a method of judicial change is the gradual narrowing of broad precepts. In its first year the "Nixon" Court, while acting "liberally" in outlawing the death penalty and prohibiting wiretapping for "national security" without judicial sanction, reduced the protection the Warren Court had given criminal suspects in matters of arrest and interrogation. It allowed non-unanimous jury verdicts to the states in criminal cases, and limited the immunity of witnesses against prosecution. In obscenity cases — a particular interest of the President, who had repudiated what he thought the too-permissive findings of his Obscenity Commission — the Court cast doubt on the previously obtaining test of "redeeming social value." Most perturbing to civil libertarians, in the context of the Nixon administration's suspicions of the press as a hostile foreign power, the Court ruled against the immunity of news reporters before grand juries, regarding the confidential sources of their information, despite the presumed guarantee of the First Amendment.

The tendency of the new Court — asserted in a series of 5-to-4 decisions in which the four Nixon appointees voted together fifty-four out of sixty-six times, and were joined by a "swing" Justice — was to assume, more than its predecessor had, the good faith of the government in its dealings with individuals, thereby enlarging the authority of the state against the private citizen. Unmistakably a new judicial spirit was at work. It could to some degree be accounted another result of the Vietnam War, with its riving of traditional loyalties, and could be the most lasting one.

If it had been supposed that the "other war," which Lyndon Johnson had started against poverty and which had been sidetracked by Vietnam and defense spending, might be reopened as the ground combat in Asia diminished and troops continued to be withdrawn, Richard Nixon ended any such wishful thinking. To keep federal spending down, he vetoed several pieces of social legislation, while giving business tax allowances, as an incentive to expansion. The defense budget remained at a record level. After a three-month freeze of wages and prices, both were put under a loose supervision, but as higher wages generated higher prices and vice versa, the economic machinery institutionalized inflation instead of stemming it.

What had previously been regarded as social and cultural revolution was also coming to be institutionalized. The new restraints of the Nixon administration, economic as well as judicial, and the fading war had their effects on the East Village in New York and the Haight-Ashbury section in San Francisco, and conversely on the rest of the country. The psychedelic boutiques disappeared from St. Mark's Place in the Village, the Electric Circus discothèque followed the Fillmore East palace of rock into oblivion. The special police stations set up to look for runaways closed their doors. The marijuana, LSD and groovy clothes which had drawn youngsters from Iowa and Kansas were now to be found right back home.

The use of drugs was also increasing on college campuses. The Gallup Poll showed that 51 percent of students had "tried" marijuana in 1971; in 1967 it had been 5 percent. The use of LSD had increased from 1 percent to 18 percent in the same period. The more widespread indulgence was also a mark of greater acceptability, even respectability. The youthful taking of drugs was no longer an expression of rebelliousness but a simple means of relaxation, like alcohol in the adult world, to say nothing of the eight to ten billion amphetamine pills of one sort or another lawfully dispensed each year. Thousands of young Americans sought drugs in cheap and easy access abroad, following the "hashish trail" to Amsterdam; to Crete, where they lived in caves; to Katmandu and Kabul. Some of them died abroad. Scores went to prison in Spain and Mexico, where antidrug laws were harsh. At the end of 1972 more than a thousand Americans were in confinement in many countries, awaiting trial or serving sentences. Dr. Timothy Leary found safe haven, as he thought, in Switzerland after his escape from prison and his stopover in Algiers.

There were other reasons for young Americans to exile themselves. By one count, 100,000 were said to have fled their country, refusing to be drafted or deserting after induction. Three thousand draft resisters had served prison sentences and 500 were still doing so. Five thousand were in military stockades for various crimes in Vietnam. Many thousands had been less than honorably discharged. Most of those in Canada were making new lives for themselves, and said they would not return even if amnesty were granted. Some felt it was the expatriates who would have to "forgive" while others would go back, if allowed, to seek changes within the "System." They received no encouragement. George McGovern was in favor of amnesty in exchange for voluntary "public service" but President Nixon gave a flat "No" to any contemplation of amnesty. Even on campuses back home the draft exiles found little support. Without any protest, Princeton University reinstated ROTC as an extracurricular activity after eighteen months of suspension. One reason for lack of opposition was the Pentagon announcement of only 50,000 draftees for 1972, half the 1971 figure.

College administrations were less disturbed by campus activism than by the common practice of buying, instead of writing, term papers and academic theses. The students involved, some of whom were expelled, displayed no particular scruples. Exam questions and papers were regarded as just a service, like the college pants-pressing shop. Some students said it was not they but the colleges which were cheating, by compelling them to take courses they were not interested in. If a college degree was what the world required as a symbol of status, a college degree the world would have.

College youth was only a part of American youth, and changes could be observed in working-class attitudes also. The older generation of factory employees arrived at retirement after thirty years of service, but the new breed was not certain it wanted to put in that much time on the assembly line in screw-turning monotony. A strike at the new $100 million General Motors plant at Lordstown, Ohio, offered convincing proof. Designed as the model for all future auto production, to include a "very intensive motivation program" for the workers, the plant was hailed by the industry press as "an industrial Woodstock." The young workers, whose age averaged twenty-four, were intensely bored. Like their campus cousins of three years before, they demanded changes which would give them more to say in what they did. Management may not have been impressed by the ethos of the walkout but it was clear that something had gone wrong at the heart of American industry. The dulling of senses by routine, the speedup which did not allow adequate command or control of the job, had been translated into great inefficiency. In the previous five years, since 1966, one of every three cars sold had had to be recalled for one reason or another — faulty engine parts, dangerous brakes, loose steering wheels, ill-fitted doors. In all, seven hundred separate recalls brought in 22 million cars. The following year, 1972, saw more than 12 million cars recalled. All through 1973, recall after recall took place.

After the strike at Lordstown 130,000 cars had to be taken back to that industrial Woodstock because of faulty accelerators. Some psychedelic effects were introduced to mitigate workers' boredom, but the legatees of Henry Ford shrank from the kind of heresy that was being committed in Sweden — the abolition of the assembly line by the country's two auto plants, and the introduction of rotating work assignments. Charlie Chaplin's *Modern Times*, portraying the "little fellow" caught up in mindless mechanization, seemed pertinent all over again when revived throughout the United States, especially to the young. In its 1973 contract negotiations the UAW sought to "humanize" industry.

Even in the Soviet Union the first hero of "Socialist labor," Alexei Stakhanov — the Donbas coal miner who had given his name to the movement for increased productivity through more efficient technology in the Stalin years — declared that man had been dehumanized by overmechanization, that not enough attention was being paid to the individual as human being and worker. The voice from the workers' state was like a voice from the grave. Stakhanov had not been mentioned or thought of for years. Most people thought he was long since dead.

II

"PEACE WITH HONOR"

THE YEAR OF THE RAT is an auspicious one in the Oriental calendar, indicating a bountiful harvest. Untowardly, the last Year of the Rat, 1960, with its promise of American vigor and purpose through the election of John F. Kennedy, had seeded an eventual harvest of destruction in Vietnam and internal dissension in the United States. The new Year of the Rat, 1972, presumptively concluding the war, had all the outward appearance of bounty and good fortune for Richard Nixon, the man who had lost in 1960. He would travel with acclaim to Peking and Moscow, and Henry Kissinger would negotiate a cease-fire in Indochina, to lay the foundations of their plan for a world balance of power. The President would be triumphantly reelected, with a mandate to fulfill the further achievements insuring his place in history.

Within the sweet harvest fruit, however, a secret canker had begun to spread, implanted by the same patient enzymes that produced success, and the blight would touch the very rootstock of the American democracy, the relationship of mutual trust between the Presidency and the people. Euripides knew the ancient plot of the drama, and the motivations of its characters.

Two dramas would in fact be played out in 1972, one in public view, to establish Richard Nixon as the bringer of "a generation of peace" and confirm him as the leader of the world's undoubted "Number One" power, and at the same time, behind the scenes, a covert scenario to make "four more years" in the White House inevitable by less worthy means.

The onstage action started with the President's departure for Peking on February 17 for an eight-day visit and tour bridging Washington's

Birthday. With him went Kissinger, the foreign policy adviser from Academe, and H. R. Haldeman, the White House chief of staff from the world of advertising. They represented the opposite poles of the occasion, indeed of the administration — the serious diplomacy on the one hand and the public relations considerations on the other. The White House itself had seen to the emplacement of the television cameras in and about Peking, and the new American-installed ground station beamed the President's moves and words by satellite back home and to the rest of the world. The Chinese were amused that the President went about with facial make-up on, as if he belonged to the Peking opera, but he was "on camera" almost everywhere and at all hours of the day and night in the American living room.

The public drama in the Forbidden City and the Great Hall of the People was the product, in its most obvious form, of what Edward L. Bernays, the pioneer of public relations in America, had named "the engineering of consent." That engineering also had its darker devices, controlled by hidden valves. Nixon, Haldeman and Kissinger left behind them in the White House those concerned with the other scenario of 1972. The New Hampshire and Florida primaries were less than a month away. The Committee for the Reelection of the President was soliciting campaign contributions — it answered its phones with the words "Four more years" — and two days before the President left for Peking, John Mitchell resigned as Attorney General to become its chairman and as in 1968, Nixon's campaign manager. He had already held two meetings in his Department of Justice office with the committee's counsel, Gordon Liddy, and the White House counsel, John W. Dean III, discussing means of obtaining "political intelligence" about the Democrats. Liddy went through an elaborate, advertising-agency kind of "presentation" with detailed charts for the "bugging" of Democratic National Headquarters and other campaign operations. "Bugging, mugging, kidnapping and even a prostitution squad" was how one of those present described them.

The remarkableness of the meetings in Mitchell's office lay in the fact that this brusque, passionless man who listened to the plans for political espionage and disruption was the nation's chief law-enforcement official, so strict in his views that he favored "preventive detention" and had conducted wiretapping on a large scale against those he suspected of endangering "national security," including government figures and newsmen. His special prosecutors had carried out grand jury investigations of radicals and alleged subversives in many cities and his Justice Department had tried for conspiracy the Chicago Seven and the Harrisburg Seven, among other cases.

Mitchell had acquired two impressive reputations before coming to Washington: one as a Wall Street lawyer specializing in municipal bonds and financing, who had joined his own small firm with Nixon's; and the other as manager of the 1968 Nixon campaign, a political novice who had won for his client the highest office in the land, though, as was pointed out, Nixon began the campaign with a gaping lead over Humphrey and wound up with the barest of margins. In Washington Mitchell and the other men around Nixon — they had been advertising and "merchandising" experts and lawyers, without true political experience or sensitivity, and lacking awareness of the public interest — were answerable to no one but the President. And Nixon's expressed view was that only foreign affairs required a Chief Executive's personal attention; the domestic side of America could run itself, with cabinet paternalism. Then he had reduced his cabinet to virtual nullity, leaving the power over policy and programs in the hands of his chosen and trusted few.

Before leaving with the President for China, his chief of staff, Haldeman, publicly condemned administration critics for "consciously aiding and abetting the enemy." The reference was to opponents of "Vietnamization," but its meaning extended far beyond the war. A siege mentality prevailed in the White House. All outside it were the enemy. Those inside were a "law and order" unto themselves. Some of the men now organizing the 1972 campaign had been with Nixon in 1968 also, and the narrow victory then and the unfavorable polls of 1971 had convinced them that "political intelligence" was needed as much as money, to win again in 1972. A few of them harked back to California and 1962, when Nixon was defeated for governor. His manager then had been Haldeman and the campaign had employed numerous "dirty tricks," including doctored photographs to make Nixon's opponent appear "pro-Communist" — shades of his 1946 and 1950 campaigns — as well as the spurious use of "Democratic citizens'" committees. With respect to the latter tactic, a court judgment found it had been "approved by Mr. Nixon personally."

In 1972 Nixon's men had been in power for four years, and to obtain "four more years" they would, as always, do whatever had to be done. Like Vince Lombardi, the football coach who was a presidential idol, they believed that "winning isn't the main thing; it's the only thing."

The President, meanwhile, was conducting his own overt reelection campaign simply by being President, the visible leader of the most powerful nation in the world, personally possessed of the authority and wisdom enabling him to make fundamental change in international relations. By the journey to Peking he signified that American policy toward China had been wrong for twenty-two years, or if not wrong at the beginning, at any rate continued too long.

Peking's reasons for accepting detente went beyond the obvious one of confounding Moscow and ending its own "capitalist encirclement." It could better hope for improved relations from a conservative administration which had broken with the past than from Democrats who might still fear accusations of appeasement. The withdrawal from Vietnam showed, moreover, that the United States, for all its military might, lacked clearly defined political goals. The war had proved it could not work its will on Asia. It could therefore be talked with. The American President became a welcome guest.

It may have nonplussed Maoists all over the world to see the great revolutionary hope of mankind, as they regarded China, breaking bread and exchanging toasts with the hated imperialist enemy. Chou En-lai, if typically wary, did not seem embarrassed. He had been trying since Bandung in 1955 to win wider acceptance of the Five Principles of Coexistence. They were now stated in the Sino-American communiqué on Nixon's visit: respect for sovereign and territorial integrity, nonaggression, noninterference in internal affairs, equality, peaceful mutuality. Equality was the real gain for Peking. The Russian failure to acknowledge it had been at the heart of the Sino-Soviet enmity. The matter of Taiwan, though unresolved as long as the United States had a treaty with Chiang, was not permitted to mar the Sino-American accord, for as the communiqué tactfully declared, it could not be challenged that "all Chinese . . . maintain there is but one China and that Taiwan is a part of China."

The red-lettered billboard that greeted the President when he arrived at the Peking airport was there when he left, its message unaltered. "Make trouble, fail; make trouble again, fail again; until their doom: that is the nature of all imperialists and reactionaries of the world; this is a Marxist law and they will never violate it."

Something had changed in the United States, however, besides the regulations covering Chinese imports. After the Peking visit the adjectives chosen most frequently by Americans to describe the Chinese besides "hard-working" were, according to a Gallup Poll, "intelligent," "artistic," "progressive" and "practical." In 1965 they had been "ignorant," "warlike," "sly" and "treacherous." Not the official toasts but television pictures showing thousands of Chinese sweeping up after a snowfall were accounted the most salient impression of "the week that changed the world," as the President called it.

Whether Nixon got in Peking any indication of help in persuading Hanoi to resume the broken-off secret peace talks was one of the many things that remained undisclosed about his visit. In the New Hampshire primary campaign Senator Muskie, in the absence of any progress at the formal talks in Paris, proposed the perennial alternative to a negotiated settlement, the fixing of a withdrawal date in return for an exchange of prisoners. White House, cabinet and Republican party spokesmen all berated him for giving aid and comfort to the enemy.

Pending any eventual agreement, the sustained American bombing over the years, whatever it failed to accomplish, had driven millions of South Vietnamese from NLF or contested areas to those held by the Saigon government. Thieu's control was more extensive than ever before, and in anticipation of the war's end and what it might bring, he had like Diem and Nhu a decade before begun to form his own political organization, the Democracy party, compelling military officers, province chiefs, village heads and police officials to join. As with Diem, politics was in the hands of a brother, Nguyen Van Khieu. Diem's police had arrested many opposition politicians; Thieu's did also. The South Vietnamese President at the same time was given emergency powers by the National Assembly, though against considerable opposition in the Senate.

If Thieu held more territory than before in South Vietnam the Communists had won more in Cambodia and Laos. In one encounter with insurgents a whole Cambodian brigade deserted in a body, officers and men, changed into civilian clothes and scattered across the border into South Vietnam, abandoning their weapons. In Laos the long-secret CIA base at Long Tieng was put out of action by Communist artillery barrage and infantry onslaught, and 30,000 troops fled, most of them Meo tribesmen.

Hanoi had plans for its own territorial gains in South Vietnam also. Just as they had done at Tet in 1968, with major effect on the American presidential election, so in 1972 on the eve of Easter, North Vietnam and the NLF struck out in a broad and powerful offensive, seeking to shatter the dream of Vietnamization as Tet had ended Americanization. The Tet uprising had been largely an internal one by NLF units in more than a score of cities. The Easter offensive was largely North Vietnamese, a frontal assault across the Demilitarized Zone and from Cambodia into the central highlands, while NLF units operated in the interior, especially in the Mekong Delta. The boasted American electronic system, set up to catch the very sound of breathing on the Ho Chi Minh trail, failed to detect the buildup of hundreds of Soviet-supplied tanks across the DMZ. Virtually all of Hanoi's twenty divisions were out of their own country, in the general action.

President Nixon reacted sharply and angrily to the North Vietnamese action. The Easter offensive ended all remaining restrictions on American bombing above the 17th parallel. The Air Force command was freed to hit industrial as well as military targets, and B-52's dropped thirty to forty tons of bombs each. Hanoi and Haiphong were rescheduled for "military targets," which meant civilian casualties, and a Soviet ship was hit in Haiphong harbor. North Vietnam's vital system of dikes, like the Dutch a barrier against disaster by inundation, was reported damaged despite Pentagon disavowals. As always before, one result of more bombing was more American prisoners. Before the Easter offensive 1,618 airmen were listed as captured or missing, and these figures were being added to almost daily. By the end of the year they would be nearly 2,000.

Full-fledged air war was waged not only against North Vietnam and its Laotian supply lines but in support of ARVN forces in South Vietnam. All through the war the United States had never been able to engage North Vietnamese forces in divisional strength or to win a set-piece battle by superior strength and firepower. Now after all but 70,000 American troops had departed, Hanoi had opened a main-force conventional armored assault against the South Vietnamese army. Even in the week before the offensive began, ARVN suffered 445 dead and more than 1,000 wounded, the highest casualty toll in nine months. Thieu still cheerfully declared that South Vietnam was prepared to take the same rate for as long as ten years if necessary. It was how the NLF had once talked.

The intensified bombing of North Vietnam was in a sense a hidden war, like the one in Laos. It could not be reported except peripherally. Hanoi announced some of its alleged effects and Saigon and Washington denied them. Visiting Americans were taken to inspect some bomb damage, but its true extent or the number of casualties remained a secret of war.

The air assault in South Vietnam, and its devastating effect on towns and cities was, to the contrary, visible to all. North Vietnamese tanks, artillery and infantry had attacked in the South Vietnamese border province, Quang Tri; in the highlands at Kontum and Anloc; along the Cambodian border; toward Hue and Danang on the coast, and along main highways. ARVN, receiving the full impact of pitched battle for the first time, held in some places but failed to hold in others. In Quang Tri the Third Division broke and fled in utter rout, and the North Vietnamese took Quang Tri city, the provincial capital, to hold it for more than four months. The North Vietnamese captured some towns without a fight. To recover or try to recover them, American air power smashed at the towns on a vast and furious scale. They were destroyed, not to be saved but to be denied.

A passing incident in the Easter offensive occurred at My Lai. Four years after the massacre the two villages destroyed by Charlie Company and since rebuilt were destroyed again with twenty-one others, as the result of an NLF sweep across Batangan peninsula. The method of destruction was typical. The South Vietnamese guarding the fortified villages fled, leaving their weapons, when an NLF unit called for their surrender from the woods. The insurgents then "liberated" My Lai by tearing down the gates and left without any shooting or damage. Twenty-four safe hours later the South Vietnamese returned in armored personnel carriers and called in artillery and air strikes. For the second time My Lai was left in ruins by "friendly forces," ending a two-year program of "pacification."

The American hit on the Soviet ship in Haiphong harbor, though it injured several crew members, passed with only a pro forma protest from

Moscow. Then the President took the step that his predecessor had avoided. In direct challenge to the Soviet Union, which was bringing Hanoi most of the outside supplies it received, American planes criss-crossed the sea entrances to Haiphong and sowed them with mines at every depth, eight thousand in the coastal ports, and three thousand more in inland waters.

The mining constituted a blockade, which under international law is accounted an act of war. Nixon furthermore openly charged the Soviet Union with responsibility for the North Vietnamese offensive because it had provided the tanks, artillery and other heavy equipment. In his television speech, however, hidden beneath the tough talk were two American proposals which served as the carrot to the stick. One was for a cease-fire, tied to an agreed date for final American withdrawal. The other was affirmation of the principle that the Vietnamese should settle their own political future.

After his return from Peking and as he prepared to visit Moscow, Nixon appeared to be raising the stakes in Haiphong harbor as he had in Cambodia in 1970 and in Laos in 1971. He might, it seemed, have imperiled the summit at the Kremlin and the SALT agreement already worked out for signature there. His supporters cheered him for in effect spitting into the Russian eye. But Moscow had that eye fixed firmly on the coming summit and was apparently willing to accept damage to its own ships, not to mention its prestige, for the sake of an initial nuclear arms limitation, a Berlin agreement leading to a European security conference, and increased trade and other economic and scientific interchange with the United States. If such an attitude dismayed Hanoi it is possible that Moscow, like Washington, had become surfeited with the Vietnam War and the demands it made. Not only had bad harvests necessitated large Soviet grain purchases abroad, but an economy which could not summon up enough productivity had to look to the West for technology and even for capital investment, loans and credits, and joint enterprises to develop natural resources like oil and gas. Whatever revolutionary movements Moscow in theory favored around the world, her own state interests came first.

Washington waited for Soviet reaction to the mining of Haiphong and the prevailing feeling was that the President's trip to Moscow would at least be postponed, if not canceled as Lyndon Johnson's had been by the invasion of Czechoslovakia in 1968. Nothing happened. As the bombs fell on North Vietnam and Soviet vessels were excluded from Haiphong, Ambassador Anatoly Dobrynin and Trade Minister Nikolai Patolichev were photographed chatting amiably with President Nixon in the White House. There was no need to hold one's breath any longer. The summit would take place on schedule.

The mining of Haiphong harbor sent Nixon's rating up sharply in the national index of "confidence" in his "handling" of the war, from 56 percent to 67 percent. The poll showed that 60 percent of Americans believed he was "doing everything he [could] to end the war." The White House reported a flood of letters and telegrams approving the mining in a ratio of 5 to 1. As usually happened after a presidential action, the "public reaction" had to a large extent been organized on the administration's behalf on the local level, but this time it was not the Repubican National Committee or various state committees that did the organizing. The Committee for the Reelection of the President had become the carburetor and spark plugs in the "engineering of consent." Besides stirring up White House mail, it paid for an ad in the New York *Times* supporting the mining of Haiphong, without bothering to tell those whose names it used where the ad originated or who paid for it.

Money is the high-octane fuel of any political campaign, but in 1972 fund-raising by the presidential committee, functioning across the street from the White House at 1701 Pennsylvania Avenue, not only reached an unprecedented level of amassment, some $60 million, but wrought a qualitative change in the political process. The Committee to Reelect, as it was familiarly called, was in fact the President's own personal apparatus, both in terms of his responsibility for it and because it was interwoven with the White House and the executive branch of the government. By its separation of President from party, to the obvious unhappiness of the Republican National Committee and the Republican congressional and gubernatorial candidates, it dealt a blow to the traditional party system and in effect created two distinct 1972 elections. One was a presidential plebiscite, in the manner of de Gaulle, or going back into French history, Louis Napoleon; the other, the routine matter of filling seats on Capitol Hill and in various state houses.

In this personal presidential campaign, with the White House as the source of all authority and favor, the committee wallowed in funds. Long before John Mitchell took it over, while he was still Attorney General, he and Secretary of Commerce Maurice Stans had engaged in campaign planning and had drawn up the budgets for campaign spending, while the President's personal attorney, Herbert Kalmbach, another veteran of the 1962 California campaign, solicited funds from corporations — though such corporate donations were illegal — including those engaged in government litigation or seeking preferential treatment, as well as wealthy individuals craving to be ambassadors. The flow of contributions, many of them in cold cash, was speeded by a new law making April 7 the deadline for receiving funds which did not have to be identified. By April 7 more than $10 million of undisclosed origin had been received.

Perhaps the most important contribution, for its effect on future events, came from Robert L. Vesco, a New Jersey financier whose affairs were being looked into by the Securities and Exchange Commission. After donating $200,000 Vesco found it possible with Attorney General Mitchell's sympathetic interest to get a more friendly discussion of his problems with the government.

Just before the April 7 deadline the Nixon campaign treasurer, Hugh W. Sloan, Jr., gave $350,000 in cash of the unreported funds to the White House supposedly for political polls, while Gordon Liddy received $199,000. The latter's plan to "bug" Democratic National Committee headquarters had gone forward at another strategy meeting — this time at the Florida White House a few days after Mitchell left the Justice Department for the Committee to Reelect — and the clandestine machinery of "consent" was in full operation. It had already vexed the New Hampshire and Florida primaries with petty "dirty tricks" — a forged letter charging Muskie with an ethnic slight to French Canadians, false charges of lewd behavior against Humphrey and Jackson, "whispered" telephone calls to stir racial hostility, the mysterious cancellation of arrangements for Democratic meetings, and the infiltration of local campaign organizations, among others.

The Grand Design of espionage and subversion would seem, in retrospect, to have been completely unnecessary. As the other script for 1972 unfolded in full public view, Richard Nixon had in all probability already won reelection, six months before Polling Day, two months before a Democratic nominee had been chosen; won it by the mining of Haiphong and the successful challenge to the Soviet Union.

A plaque reading "Richard Nixon slept here" will never mark the historic site and occasion, but as the American flag flew over the Kremlin for seven days in May, at the same time that American bombs fell on North Vietnam, it was evident to all that the Vietnam War had entered its final phase, whatever difficulties still lay ahead. It was also clear, if only to historians, that once again, as in the Cuban missile crisis of 1962, world peace rested less on American power or good will than on Soviet accommodation, or at least Soviet appreciation of its own national interests.

This did not mean Soviet want of wariness, or an end to global rivalry, or an ideological cease-fire. Nor did it mean any lessening of the American burden of defense, though Nixon returned with the first SALT agreement on nuclear weapons, freezing their number and limiting antiballistic missiles. Secretary of Defense Laird at once let it be known that the Pentagon could not support the SALT agreement unless it received a record $85.9 billion defense budget for new weapons. Nixon was only too willing to agree, if in fact it was not his plan to begin with. Indeed, it was said, the Russians expected the United States to keep arming, as they themselves would, and both sides to improve their missiles qualitatively. This would make possible further agreements on limitation. The SALT agreement in fact recalled the 1963 treaty banning nuclear tests in the atmosphere, which led to more and larger underground tests, produced the multiple warhead, and started a new round in the nuclear competition.

After Nixon's visit to Moscow, Soviet President Podgorny made a trip to Hanoi to explain matters and urge acceptance of a cease-fire. Chou En-lai had also gone to Hanoi, after Nixon's visit to Peking, to pledge continued support "whatever you do." That meant primarily ending the war.

Hanoi eventually conceded that Nixon's May 8 speech announcing the mining of Haiphong could be read as evidence of American willingness to return to the 1954 Geneva agreement, the violation of which, it held, began the war. That could be explored, as well as the offer of a fixed American withdrawal date. Thus the May 8 announcement led directly to the October 8 preliminary cease-fire agreement. Some would attribute the outcome to the mining, others to the American negotiating concession.

Henry Kissinger in any case followed his missions to Peking and Moscow with another one to Paris, to resume the secret talks with Le Duc Tho, and then to Saigon, to tell President Thieu that the time had come to make a settlement. The man in Saigon, his future suddenly uncertain, clung to the views his American allies had abandoned. He still insisted on his "four No's" and restated his own peace plan: "We have to kill the Communists to the last man!" Hanoi was by contrast conciliatory, no longer insisting that Thieu had to step down as a precondition to settlement. Time would take care of that. Meanwhile, in anticipation of a cease-fire, the North Vietnamese were winning more ground in South Vietnam. Though willing to resume the negotiations, they had no intention of halting their offensive, any more than the Americans had of stopping the bombing for the sake of talks. Besides gaining and holding as much territory as it could, Hanoi was intent on mauling ARVN as destructively as possible, to cripple the Thieu regime.

The mining of Haiphong and the continuing American air offensive in both North and South Vietnam intensified the end-the-war feeling in the United States. The Senate Foreign Relations Committee voted to cut off all Vietnam funds by December 31, contingent on the return of American prisoners. Antiwar demonstrations broke out again in the large cities and on many campuses, accompanied by acts of "civil disobedience" which provoked clashes with police, drew tear gas, and resulted in thousands of arrests. A march of thirty thousand in New York City shouted "Out Now!" Leading figures of the art, theater and literary worlds were jailed at an end-the-war rally on the grounds of the Capitol in Washington. A bomb went off in the Pentagon after telephoned notice from the Weathermen. Despite the size, apparent spontaneity, and strong feelings of the many demonstrations, however, they were not the headline-seizing, trauma-causing, politically polarized occasions some of their predecessors had been in the earlier years. For all the bombing, for all the ferocity of the Easter offensive and the counterferocity against it, the war was too close to ending for much more passion. Or so it seemed in May.

The campus demonstrations, the first since the student strike after Kent State, were not a repetition of 1970, much less of 1968. They were smaller, and despite their sporadic brushes with the police, apparently reflective of a deeper feeling of uncertainty and anxiety, than of anger or resentment. The scholastic trend, as one college bookstore noted, citing its more popular titles, was toward Human Development and Spiritual Growth, and included a large interest in Buddhism, Zen, the *Bhagavad-Gita*, the *I Ching*, Yoga and Occultism.

Campus dissent was most marked, as usual, in the East, especially at Harvard and Columbia. The editorial boards of eight Ivy League colleges joined in a call for a one-day student strike, and the presidents of the eight colleges added their protest of the bombing. The strike proved to be decidedly a minority affair. Having paid their expensive tuition, most students wanted tutelage. At Columbia the radical activists who sought to rouse the entire campus numbered only 150 in a student body of 15,000. Without leadership or fervor, they commanded neither any appreciable following nor the television cameras. In their sparse numbers, Columbia radicals sat down in college buildings and proclaimed "possession." No police were called. The administration issued no edicts. The faculty solidly opposed the sit-in. The strike of the few was abruptly ended by the many: students ousted students. Classes had continued without a halt.

SDS was heard from again, protesting the bombing, but it too had diffused its energies and shifted its targets. In convention at Harvard Law School as the North Vietnamese offensive began, SDS was primarily concerned with racism. The middle-class students who sat as delegates, neatly dressed and with short hair, did not condemn generals or politicians but sociologists like Arthur Jensen and Edward Banfield, who believed blacks were inherently less intelligent than whites. American youth, even the wilder spirits, had become "realistic," turning from violence not merely on philosophical grounds but because violence meant head-busting and arrests requiring bail money and court appearances. Confrontation with the police had lost whatever symbolic meaning it had. The youth of the Seventies appeared to have no dogma and no personality cult, and to have decided that the war would end when it ended.

As the Easter offensive went into its second month, calculations showed that a ton of bombs had been dropped on Indochina for every minute of the Nixon administration. The B-52's, chauffeured by skilled young technicians, went out in waves over both North and South Vietnam, blowing huge craters in the terrain below. From heights of 30,000 to 50,000 feet the air strikes came without warning. The big machines fixed their targets by radar and dropped their bombs without seeing where they fell. In the long slow flight from Guam the crews ate TV dinners and blueberry pies from the commissary, warmed up in galley ovens. The six men of a B-52 crew, remote from the reality of the war, acted as an extension of the computer which governed their plane. They constituted the most detached and impersonal operation in the history of warfare. The triumph of technology was complete, confirmed by the fact that American ground troops in Vietnam, now 69,000, were outnumbered by Air Force personnel for the first time.

The Americans on the ground were no longer fighting, however. It was North Vietnamese against South Vietnamese, and at the beginning the former had scored significantly. After Quang Tri city fell to them, Kontum was surrounded and Anloc besieged. The revolutionary troops drove toward Hue and South Vietnamese military collapse in the northern provinces seemed inevitable. Lack of leadership was the primary failing. After a dozen years of American tutorship ARVN was still run in too many cases by political or nepotistic favoritism. So plain was the debacle that the general in charge was relieved, arrested, and tried for cowardice. Even under the best leadership, the motivation and morale of South Vietnamese young men, thrown into a war which never ceased, were no match for the North Vietnamese and NLF soldiers. American air power was. At every point where the North Vietnamese had succeeded heavy loads of bombs shattered their ranks and the towns and villages they had seized. Long streams of refugees fled the bombs and napalm, not northward, but southward.

ARVN received the full force of the North Vietnamese onslaught, as Hanoi had planned, but with American air power the offensive was slowed, and then gradually halted and rolled back. The head-on conflict was only one part of the revolutionary strategy, however. As South Vietnamese units were brought in from their bases to reinforce Kontum and Anloc, the irregulars of the NLF were able to assert control in many areas in the Mekong Delta and other locales considered "safe." Behind the guns the Provisional Revolutionary Government dug itself into position, in leopard-spot pattern throughout South Vietnam, to await the cease-fire.

The North Vietnamese and the NLF paid a heavy price in casualties to demonstrate that Vietnamization had not been successful, but President Nixon saw matters otherwise. The offensive proved Vietnamization had succeeded, he said, because without South Vietnamese ground forces American air power alone could not have beaten it back. The argument was persuasive to many Americans, who were waiting for the war to end and believed the President was doing all he could to end it. Beneath the national surface however, a feeling of discomfort had begun to spread, in contemplation of what things might be like when peace did return.

Disillusion over ten years of Vietnam, the approaching conclusion of the lunar program, cutbacks in the aerospace industry, and the curtailment of federal funds for science underlined the recovery from the spree which the Soviet sputnik had touched off fifteen years before. Skepticism about science and technology was a countermovement perhaps as overdone as the scientific movement itself had been, and the postwar prospects of American industry were affected by it. Japan complained about the dumping of cheap and often shoddy American goods, as the United States had once complained about cheap Japanese goods. American multinational corporations meanwhile produced more and more goods in Japan for sale in the home country — electronic equipment, typewriters, cameras and other precision work in which the United States no longer excelled.

The American psyche, desensitized by violence in Vietnam and inured to violence at home, turned to the romantic celebration of violence for even more of its entertainment. The sentimental saga of the Mafia, the best-selling novel *The Godfather*, transformed to the screen, opened in New York City in five first-run movie houses simultaneously, and rapidly became so popular throughout the country that it broke all box-office and profit records. Its slaughter was after all done in the context of the Family, in exemplification of such admirable traits as Honor, Loyalty and Discipline. How much more American could one be?

The American Association of Suicidology reported a rapidly rising rate among the young in its particular field of interest, while the American Psychiatric Association warned of the time bombs planted in the society by the hidden problems with which so many veterans returned from Vietnam.

The case of the Harrisburg Seven, pressed by the government for the sake of J. Edgar Hoover's credibility, collapsed when a jury in conservative Pennsylvania Dutch country failed to agree that Father Philip Berrigan, Sister Elizabeth McAlister and their friends had conspired to "kidnap" Henry Kissinger and blow up Washington's municipal heating system. It did find the priest and the nun guilty of smuggling "contraband" into a prison, in the form of their letters, a verdict reduced on appeal. Meanwhile, a few weeks after the Harrisburg trial, Hoover himself, the only director the FBI had known, died after forty-seven years of unlegislated power.

At what amounted to a state funeral, in the Capitol rotunda, Hoover's greatest public admirer, the President, pronounced the official encomium of the archetypal crime-buster. The White House had in fact broken with the stern old autocrat for rejecting the 1970 Internal Intelligence Plan and refusing any FBI role in the illegal aspects of the Ellsberg investigation, but though importuned by Ehrlichman and Mitchell, the "law and order" President had been unable to bring himself to discharge a presumed public idol. As Hoover's body lay in state in the Capitol, Daniel Ellsberg and others taking part in an antiwar rally outside were set on by a group of Cubans from Miami, under instruction of the "special investigators" who had, for the White House, supplanted the FBI.

While Philip Berrigan was standing trial, his brother Daniel was freed from Danbury on parole, and vowed to continue his anti-Vietnam activity because the war was "still the first fact of life." The Catholic Ultra-Resistance he returned to had run down. It had never been the formidable threat that Hoover had imagined. The Berrigans considered themselves, as Daniel put it, among the few "just men" on whom "God . . . still settles," a small and intimate group, perhaps a clique, hardly a full-blown political conspiracy. Their actions seemed more symbolistic, perhaps naive, than anything else. After Hoover's death, at any rate, the government decided that no more inconvenience was to be expected from the Berrigans by releasing Philip also. Any influence they could have on other Catholics, it may have been reasoned, could not compete with the appeal for Catholic votes made by President Nixon in his firm public opposition to abortion and his support of federal aid to parochial schools, the Supreme Court to the contrary notwithstanding.

The Catholicism the Berrigans found after their time in prison had undergone institutional changes. Seminaries were closing down in all parts of the country, and enrollment had dropped in many others. Young priests left their orders for secular jobs and even marriage. Students for the priesthood wore long hair and beads, dressed in blue jeans and dungarees, hung up psychedelic decorations and listened to rock music, in a new "life-style" replacing the monastic regime of dawn prayers, Gregorian chant, and semicloistered discipline. Even at St. Patrick's things were different. The Cardinal Archbishop, Terence Cooke, Cardinal Spellman's successor in the New York archdiocese and as Military Vicar, had finally come out against the war, or at least against its continuation. A group of nuns prostrated themselves inside the Cathedral to protest the war, and the American Catholic Coalition for Peace, including six bishops, called the Vietnam conflict "immoral."

In the secular world one trial overlapped another, one government setback succeeded another. As the Harrisburg case ended, Angela Davis faced a jury in San Jose, California, for complicity in the attempted courtroom delivery at San Rafael two years before, and the all-white panel stupefied law-and-order advocates when it found her not guilty of murder, kidnapping, or conspiracy. She did not feel that the acquittal proved the fairness of the American judicial system; she should not have been tried at all, she declared. Blacks, not many of whom were Communists like her, rejoiced at the Davis acquittal, as they had at the acquittal of the Harlem Black Panthers and the dismissal of charges against Bobby Seale.

The Angela Davis verdict seemed further proof of the jury rebellion that was taking place throughout the country. The tough talk of the administration, the relentless prosecutors, special grand juries, FBI provocateurs, police undercover agents, and wholesale fanciful conspiracies had piled up in a huge legalistic compost heap. Members of the Davis jury explained that they had encountered a reasonable doubt about the government's case, but the doubt was larger than the trial itself, it was evident, extending to the very intentions of the government and the good faith of the "System."

After the series of courtroom rejections the administration received its heaviest blow, preventing it from seeking retrials, when the Supreme Court unanimously outlawed wiretapping in cases of domestic "national security" without court order based on specific need. Attorney General Mitchell and his assistants had arrogated both the right and the power to act in such fashion from the first days of the Nixon administration, and the President had authorized wiretaps on his own officials.

The Supreme Court's denial of the Attorney General's assumed powers no longer publicly concerned John Mitchell, now serving as campaign director at the Committee for the Reelection of the President. Two days before the tribunal's decision, however, a "third-rate burglary," as the White House labeled it in dismissal, took place at the Democratic National Committee headquarters involving just such surveillance, and its ramifications would affect not only Mitchell but the President himself.

There was other evidence, besides the mistrials and acquittals, that "law and order," however strong as a campaign appeal, fell somewhat short in practice. Police Commissioner Frank Rizzo of Philadelphia, a leading exponent of "treat 'em rough" tactics, had been elected mayor of the onetime City of Brotherly Love, with its large black population, and he identified himself with the Nixon reelection campaign and was invited to the White House as warranty for Nixon's continuing pledge to "clean up" crime. Meanwhile crime had increased under Mayor Rizzo even more than under Police Commissioner Rizzo. His Honor continued to talk tough, demand the death penalty, and assail "permissive" judges.

More reasoned attempts to resolve urban problems were not successful, either. Multiracial New York City, with a relatively enlightened approach to social realities like poverty and welfare, could not get at the core of its ills. So much had drugs become one of them that the city resorted to putting thirty-two thousand addicts on its relief rolls as "disabled," thus threatening the breakdown of the already swollen welfare system. The rationale was that public money, paid out to control the habit of the addicts, kept other citizens from being robbed.

Urban problems were complicated and the fragile structure of racial relations shaken in many places when the national leadership challenged further desegregation, especially in the matter of school bussing. Not only were antibussing forces in the North encouraged, as in Pontiac, but the President's attitude as he entered his reelection campaign discouraged those in the South who had finally become reconciled to the law and were introducing the necessary remedial measures.

Bussing received its first electoral test in the Florida primary on March 14 but it was not a clear-cut one. While 71 percent of the voters opposed bussing, even more expressed themselves in favor of equal education for all, though unlike the Supreme Court, they presumably still meant equal but separate. As to their presidential preference, Florida Democrats chose George Wallace, who this time was not planning a third-party campaign. The Alabama Governor won 42 percent of the votes, with Humphrey, Jackson and Muskie far behind and George McGovern, who supported bussing while the others either opposed it or evaded the issue, receiving a meager 6 percent. After the Florida primary President Nixon advocated a "moratorium" on the bussing question, to woo the Wallace supporters. In this form was found the unspoken issue of the 1972 election, what the Kerner Commission had put its finger on, racism. "The issue ain't the bus, it's us," one prominent black leader declared.

Black political power had increased in the South. Going into the 1972 elections, 829 blacks held offices in eleven southern states. Mississippi, the most reluctant, accounted for 128 of these, more than any other state. Even George Wallace, by order of the Supreme Court, had to name blacks to 25 percent of the positions in the Alabama state police. Birmingham was a striking example of how things had changed since it was the center of the civil rights conflict a decade before. The four-hundred-man local police force included twenty-four blacks, and the police chief appeared weekly on a black radio station, talking about crime and drugs, and taking complaints about police conduct. The nine-member city council included two blacks, elected with the aid of white votes, one of them an NAACP attorney whose home had been bombed three times in the Sixties. Black and white civic leaders breakfasted together weekly. Birmingham, in short, had become much like any other American city.

Nixon was not interested in black votes, in South or North. The average American, the polltakers informed him, was "un-black, un-young and un-poor." That was the constituency he addressed, to provide him with the majority he had failed to win in 1968.

The 1972 election campaign derived its historical significance less as a contest between the two political parties — especially since Nixon was seeking to put himself above party — than from the Democratic primaries and national convention. They brought into action, on behalf of George McGovern, the advocates of a New Politics in a coalition intended to replace Roosevelt's of forty years before. McGovern's tireless enthusiasts canvased for new votes from enfranchised youth, blacks and other minorities, and various "liberation" movements. The South Dakota minister's son was portrayed in the role of St. George in combat with the Dragon of bossism, cynicism and materialism, struggling for the soul of the Democratic party. McGovern carried an evangelical message of American spiritual restoration while his advisers — like all advisers — made deals and raised funds. Some of them were veterans of the victorious practical politics of the 1960 Kennedy campaign.

A tide flowed in the 1972 Democratic primaries against the old political machines and familiar candidates. Hubert Humphrey's Politics of Joy, ill founded in 1968, had given way to the equally inutile Politics of Opportunism. McGovern and Wallace, capitalizing on discontent, offered radical change, or what sounded like it, and in the primaries McGovern won the largest number of convention delegates and Wallace the biggest popular vote. The calculated centrism of Edmund Muskie rapidly arrived nowhere in particular, since that was where it was aimed. The man from Maine dropped out when his position as "front runner" was not confirmed by the voters. His own neighboring state of New Hampshire, in the very first primary, gave him 46.4 percent against McGovern's surprising 37 percent, attained on a position of rapid withdrawal from Vietnam and reduced defense spending. Muskie's fortunes began to go downhill with a public appearance in New Hampshire in which he was brought to tears when responding to an opposition newspaper's attack. This was based, as it turned out, on one of the Nixon campaign's "dirty tricks," a forged letter alleging Muskie had used the term "Canuck" to disparage French Canadians. How much effect the fraud, taken from the secret scenario for the 1972 campaign, had on the New Hampshire result was not known. In the public scenario President Nixon, having returned from China a week before, received 68 percent of the Republican vote in the Granite State.

Not to be anticipated in any election script, the President also gained by a grisly note injected into the campaign, reminiscent of 1968, when George Wallace on the day before the important Maryland primary in May was shot down from the midst of a cheering crowd in a shopping center in a Washington suburb. He was not fatally wounded, as Robert Kennedy had been, but his legs were paralyzed, and though he declared he would continue to campaign, and went to the convention in July, it was clear that the American electoral process had again been grievously blemished.

Wallace's would-be assassin, Arthur Bremer, a twenty-one-year-old white unemployed busboy, did not have anything against the Alabama Governor either politically or personally. He pulled the trigger, his diary showed, to gain notoriety and self-gratification. He had in fact set out with the idea of killing President Nixon. Instead he helped insure the President's reelection. The added Wallace vote gave Nixon his 1972 landslide.

Self-evidently, Wallace's followers, nominally Democrats in the primaries, could never support McGovern, though both men were widely regarded as "anti-Establishment" figures. There was no common ground
between a McGovernite who opposed the war and heavy defense spending
and favored a broader welfare program, and a Wallaceite who opposed
bussing, welfare and "pointy-headed intellectuals," and favored Vietnamization. Matters were not made easier for McGovern when his friend and
next-door neighbor Hubert Humphrey pictured him as a dangerous radical,
as Humphrey himself had once been considered by many. McGovern belied the charge by every detail of his manner and style. Despite the fresh
blood he had attracted into electioneering, his method was still the old
politics of ringing doorbells and forming alliances. His economics, if mud-
dled, were not Marxist, whether he proposed to give every American $1,000,
or all poor families $4,000; conservative economists like Milton Friedman
had advocated a form of guaranteed income; so had Richard Nixon in his
discarded Family Assistance Plan. Humphrey's charges and McGovern's
economic confusion had their effect in California, where an expected 20
percent McGovern margin was reduced to about 5 percent, but even so,
from the Golden Gate the road lay open to Miami Beach.

By the time of the California primary the McGovern movement had
amassed a clear majority of convention delegates. The McGovern campaign was not entirely based on devotion, as the McCarthy campaign of
1968 had been. The principal motivation seemed to be the acceptable
alternative it offered to many young people who not long before had been
"turned off." McGovern's twenty-one-year-old "campaign manager" and
twenty-seven-year-old "political director" were resolved to show themselves
as politically astute as the old pros, or the hard-boiled "media advisers."
Not only were they engaged in politics within the "System," they intended
to take over, and make over the "System."

Both party conventions were to be held in Miami Beach, protected by
its drawbridges from the mainland. The Florida resort city was where
Nixon had been nominated in 1968 but it was not his first choice for 1972.
That was San Diego, in his own homeland of California conservatism,
and convenient to the San Clemente White House. The place where all
good admirals go when they retire was proud of its thriving tourist trade,
but also not eager for a political charivari bound to attract malcontents,
Yippies, marijuana fiends, blacks and Chicanos. A glimpse into the Nixon
administration's workings through what came to be known as the "ITT
affair" helped clinch San Diegan reluctance. The International Telephone
and Telegraph Corporation, one of the nation's great conglomerates, had
among other acquisitions taken over the Hartford Fire Insurance Company
in the biggest merger in American financial history. A Senate committee,
in the midst of the primary campaign, having learned of an ITT offer to

contribute $400,000 to bring the Republican convention to San Diego — where one of its subsidiaries was opening a new hotel — raised the question whether this was connected with a subsequent antitrust settlement by the Justice Department, including approval of the insurance merger. The site of the convention was moved to Miami Beach. And three weeks before the Democratic convention more campaign material was provided, when five men with burglar tools, surgical gloves, a camera, electronic equipment and a walkie-talkie transmitter were discovered in the Watergate Building offices of the Democratic National Committee in Washington, and arrested at gunpoint. Their leader was identified as James W. McCord, Jr., a veteran of both the FBI and the CIA who had become security chief for the Committee for the Reelection of the President. The four others were Miami Cubans, all of them previously employed by the CIA, and two of whom as it later developed had broken into the offices of Daniel Ellsberg's psychiatrist nine months before. In charge in both cases were the White House "vigilante squad" members, Howard Hunt and Gordon Liddy. The lurid conspiracy of espionage, subversion and political misprision which formed the secret scenario for the 1972 campaign had surfaced. Hunt and Liddy were also at the Watergate and had escaped, but the former's name and telephone number, and the notation "W. House," were found in a notebook in the hotel room of one of the burglars. Found too were $100 bills amounting to $5,300, which came from the $199,000 given to Liddy for campaign expenses, including money which had been "laundered" through Mexican and Miami banks after originating as a campaign contribution from a Houston oilman.

The Watergate complex of office building, hotel, and luxury apartment house — its tenants included Nixon cabinet members and several senators — got its name from its location, beyond the Lincoln Memorial where the Potomac River flows around an island and is crossed by the bridge to Arlington National Cemetery. It was the site of an old ceremonial landing stage. Until the buildings were erected, Watergate meant the confluence of the river and the outdoor auditorium beside it, where free summer band concerts were given. It came to mean the 1972 labyrinth of campaign practices, as well as the cover-up attempt at high levels reminiscent of My Lai and the secret bombing of Cambodia.

The news of the Watergate burglary reached President Nixon as he basked in the sun of Key Biscayne, two weeks after his triumphant return from Moscow. Though minimized by the White House press secretary and disavowed by the President himself — "This kind of action has no place whatever in our governmental process. . . . The White House had no involvement whatever in this particular incident" — the arrests touched off something like panic in the White House recesses. John Dean, the presidential counsel, ordered Hunt's safe opened in the office building next door and removed the documents in it, while the FBI took the gun, several holsters, camera and electronic plugs it also contained. A week later Dean gave the documents to the new acting FBI director, L. Patrick Gray, and suggested that as "political dynamite" they should "never see the light of day." Gray kept them at home for awhile, then burned them. They included Hunt's forged diplomatic cable linking John Kennedy to Diem's murder. Dean also tried to get the CIA to pretend responsibility for the Watergate burglary by furnishing bail and legal fees for the arrested men, while the President's two principal aides, Haldeman and Ehrlichman, asked the CIA to block the FBI's investigation of the "laundered" campaign money, on the ground that it might compromise CIA interests in Mexico. Both requests were refused.

At the Committee to Reelect, Gordon Liddy, having fled the Watergate, destroyed a large pile of secret papers in the giant shredder and prepared to weather any storm by the approved CIA method of stonewall silence. When he refused to answer FBI questions he was summarily dismissed by John Mitchell. Three days later the campaign director himself resigned abruptly, citing his wife's objections, made known in telephone calls to reporters, to "the dirty things that go on." But while no longer officially attached to either administration or committee, Mitchell remained heavily and closely involved with both, and held scores of meetings with their principal figures in July and August, giving rise to suspicions that he might be supervising the "containment" of the Watergate matter. Before "resigning" he at any rate authorized the committee's payment of the "legal expenses" of the arrested men, and Herbert Kalmbach, the President's personal attorney, and later Fred La Rue, a White House political adviser, paid out funds eventually amounting to $450,000.

Martha Mitchell's discovery that "politics is a dirty business" did not surprise those Americans who had always "known" it. The impression encouraged by the White House and by scoffing Republicans was that Watergate was a "caper," one of the games that politicians of both parties customarily play in seeking an advantage over their opponents. Who could be disturbed by such pranks even if some Democrat or editorial writer called them "dirty tricks"?

McGovern's preconvention speeches and interviews raised questions about the ITT affair and the Watergate "caper," but stirred no particular concern. His Democratic rivals, still hoping to prevent his nomination, pressed him into fumbling explanations of his economic policies and his plans for reducing defense spending. His own chief interest, as he moved toward Miami Beach, was still Vietnam, though his staff complained that it was making him a "one-issue" candidate.

That issue, moreover, was being blunted by the continuing American withdrawal. Two weeks before the Democratic convention, with the troop level down to 49,000, President Nixon announced a further reduction of 10,000 by September 1, and at the same time revealed that draftees would no longer be sent to Vietnam, whatever residual force remained, unless they volunteered. The intensive bombing went on, with new records being set daily, but it did not seem to trouble too many Americans.

For the day ultimately dawned in Danang, seven years and five months after the Marines landed there, when the last American ground troops in Vietnam stood down. Returning from their final patrol, 240 GI's of the Third Battalion, Twenty-first Infantry, Americal Division, were greeted with a South Vietnamese artillery salute and a Sousa march by the band. They left for home a few days later, without ceremony. The same day 3,000 tons of bombs were dropped on North Vietnam, another new record for the war. The departure of the last American ground combat unit — an armed helicopter squadron remained — was barely noticed in the United States. The Washington *Post* gave the news two paragraphs on page 20.

When the big American base at Long Binh was closed down, where 50,000 troops had been stationed and nine divisions supplied and kept in battle, where ten years of planning had sent men into combat all over Vietnam, all the places fought for in the headlines and won — Dakto, Iadrang, Anlao, A Shau Valley, Benhet, My Lai, War Zones C and D, the Michelin rubber plantation, Hiepduc, Khe Sanh — were under control of the North Vietnamese or the NLF.

One reason the "wind-down" in Vietnam was not more news at home was domestic politics, arriving at its initial climax of the presidential year, the nominating conventions of the two parties. The Democrats came first, and unusually early by design, in order to give them extra time for the most difficult accomplishment in the electoral process, the unseating of an incumbent President. George McGovern, though he had won only a quarter of all the primary votes cast, had gathered enough delegate strength to appear assured of first-ballot nomination. A large measure of thanks could go to the new party rules — he had been instrumental in reforming them — which opened the convention unprecedentedly to new kinds of delegates, especially young people, women and blacks.

Besides his eager supporters as assets for the campaign against Nixon, McGovern had what would seem to be pertinent issues — the continuing war, the continuing inflation and unemployment, the administration's coziness with Big Business and its preference for defense spending over social welfare legislation. Above all there was the apparent deep American desire for change, as expressed in the opinion polls. These showed that the number of Americans who felt "alienated" had increased from 40 percent to 47 percent in the single year past. Sizable majorities believed that "the rich get richer" and that what they themselves thought was not given much account by the government. The greatest disaffection was among blacks, low-income groups, the least educated, people over sixty, union members, and big-city dwellers. Nearly all these discontents could be classified as urban, and McGovern and his managers envisioned an electoral victory founded on the populous states of the East and West, while the Republicans took the rural areas. There seemed to be no doubt that the country wanted change. The question was, how much, what kind, and how badly?

While McGovern was fighting his way to Miami Beach, state by state, the Republican primaries had been easily won popularity contests for Richard Nixon, with token opposition from the small liberal antiwar wing of Representative Paul McCloskey of California, and the disillusioned right wing led by Representative John Ashbrook of Ohio. If the President had already virtually been guaranteed reelection with his trips to Peking and Moscow, capped by the unchallenged mining of Haiphong, the Democrats lost the election at their convention, as Nixon himself thought.

Miami Beach was the first national party assemblage for 80 percent of the Democratic delegates. Those who had been outside the hall in Chicago in 1968 were this time inside and not merely symbolically. The new McGovern coalition was in full control of the proceedings, and therefore felt able to indulge a demonstration of democracy at work in its most untrammeled form. It was dramatic, to be sure, but as it turned out, distasteful to millions of television-viewing Americans.

A generation before, in 1948, Hubert Humphrey had led a convention revolt against the party establishment on the civil rights issue, forcing the southern "Dixiecrats" to walk out, while at the same time Henry Wallace and his supporters split off on the left, protesting the Cold War. Hubert Humphrey was now the symbol of party regularity. He and other leading Democrats were opposed by newer forces. The Roosevelt combination of big-city bosses, southerners, labor chieftains, and "ethnics" had been superseded by those who wanted to establish McGovernment. At Chicago in 1968, when Abe Ribicoff of Connecticut nominated George McGovern in forlorn hope and remarked upon the "Gestapo" actions of the police, the convention host Mayor Daley rose to shout obscenities, as any lip-reader could plainly see on television. At Miami Beach Senator Ribicoff nominated McGovern again and Daley was not even in the hall, having been unseated with his delegation for violating the party reform rules fashioned by the McGovern commission. In 1968 Representative Wayne Hays of Ohio had made a speech reviling long-haired kids; in 1972 they were in the hall, and Hays was not.

Most unthinkable, Abbie Hoffman and Jerry Rubin strolled about the Miami Beach convention hall as "media representatives," and in the balloting Rubin even received one vote for Vice-President. The Yippies, whose presidential "candidate" in 1968 was Pigasus, had switched to McGovern, to his considerable annoyance, since this encouraged Humphrey's charges of radicalism. McGovern's Kennedy-trained aides suspected a leftist conspiracy to discredit the "System" among youth by engineering Humphrey's nomination through radical support of McGovern. Actually the Yippies were too busy enjoying themselves to engage in plots or plague the police. Hoffman and Rubin had decided that the latter were not all Pigs, many being "exploited members of the working class" and "scapegoats for the power establishment." The Yippies ate watermelon in Flamingo Park with Miami Beach's transplanted senior citizens, their connotative and in some cases their actual grandparents. Hoffman and Rubin made it clear that the original instructions to youth to hate their parents did not apply to the parents' parents. Only the "Crazies" in their unreconstructed way were trying to raise a ruckus for ruckus' sake at Miami Beach, but there were no riots, no tear gas, no broken heads. After the election, in fact, the Yippies "expelled" Rubin and Hoffman for preventing "necessary" demonstrations and failing to share their lecture fees. They were excommunicated for "becoming more like the ruling class in their old age," which was thirty-four and thirty-five respectively.

The most active nondelegates at the convention were the last vestiges of the SDS. They forced a confrontation with McGovern in his hotel lobby, protesting the latest version of his "peace plan," which involved retention of an American force in Thailand during withdrawal from Vietnam. The South Dakotan held his ground and SDS departed. Inside the hall planks were being adopted in favor of tax reform, against corporate privilege, for the breakup of monopolies, and for a quick end to the war. Legalized abortion and "freedom" for homosexuality were debated, but the New Politics drew the line at making them party doctrine.

The New Politics, in fact, could more and more be seen as the Old Math, based on traditional electoral arithmetic. The Roosevelt coalition had been a congeries of interests, largely economic, often incompatible, with the common purpose of seeking mutual benefit from their combined vote. The McGovern coalition seemed rather an amalgamation of ideas. Some economic interests were involved, but others like abortion, women's "liberation" and the legalization of marijuana were social or psychosocial. The common purpose was greater participation in the civic processes. Politics was the means by which all would be achieved, but personal relationships were equally important. The 1972 Democratic convention may have been less a political occasion than a rather large encounter group. Unfriendly observers pointed to the relative affluence, higher education and liberal leanings of a large number of delegates to say that they constituted a new elite, not truly representative of the Democratic party with its grass roots and working-class sympathies. Of those seated, 38 percent were women, 14 percent blacks, and 13 percent aged under twenty-five, while

95 percent had one year of college or more. There were even 30 Indian delegates and 117 acknowledged "gays."

Despite the broadsides of criticism and the painful workings of the convention as maximally shown by the television cameras, the fact remained that as a result of Chicago, four more years of war and antiwar protest, and the new social currents and whirlpools, the Democratic party had opened itself and thereby the American political structure to renovation. How long it would take to absorb the new political and social elements created by the Sixties remained to be seen, but that it would be done eventually to some degree seemed certain. For 1972 the top campaign priority for the Democrats was the massive registration of new voters.

Humphrey and others of the Old Guard questioned whether the convention had to be a faithful mirror image of the pluralistic society, as called for by the McGovern rules or their interpretation. A new kind of quota system was discerned in the make-up of delegations in conformity with population ratios. McGovernites explained that these were quotas designed to include new groups, not exclude them.

The energy at work in the convention hall, the seriousness and intenseness with which the new delegates carried on the debates, caucuses, nominating and seconding — to the point where McGovern had to delay his acceptance speech until 3 A.M., long past television prime time, and address a sleeping nation — were plainly visible, but many who witnessed the televised proceedings regarded what they saw as radical, and dangerously volatile. In reality a first-ballot McGovern nomination was speedily achieved by parliamentary maneuver so skillful and pragmatic as to blur the distinction between old and New Politics. The McGovern party reform commission had proposed the end of unit rule in state delegations, but California had not followed the recommendation. At the convention McGovern claimed and won all 271 California votes, under unit rule, in violation of his own precepts. Similarly, the Daley delegation from Illinois, unseated for improper selection procedure, was replaced by a McGovern delegation chosen in the same improper way.

While McGovern was being nominated for President, and Thomas Eagleton, a personable young senator from Missouri for Vice-President — as it turned out, he would not remain on the ticket for very long — American bombs continued to fall on North Vietnam. A few days earlier a South Vietnamese student in the United States, Nguyen Thai Binh, twenty-four, had carried out an act of faith like the Buddhist monks who had immolated themselves in the early Sixties. Binh was studying fisheries management at the University of Washington on an American scholarship, and with six other Vietnamese students had demonstrated against the war. When their scholarships were canceled at the request of the Thieu government the six others, knowing they would be punished when they returned home, fought their expulsion. Binh used his plane ticket. As his flight to Saigon left Manila he showed the stewardess a knife and a silver foil package he said contained a bomb, and demanded that the pilot fly to Hanoi. The plane landed at Saigon as scheduled and an American passenger, a retired San Francisco policeman working for the Thieu regime, shot the young Vietnamese five times. The pilot kicked the frail body out of the plane. Student Nguyen Thai Binh was back home. The tin foil he dropped contained two lemons.

American students displayed the last remnants of their antiwar feelings in less dramatic fashion. A survey by the J. D. Rockefeller III Fund reported that only 30 percent of them would fight "to protect our national interests." In 1968, at the height of campus turbulence, the number had been 54 percent. Now only 29 percent would fight "to contain the Communists," by comparison with 45 percent in 1968. The 1972 college commencements offered another undramatic contrast with those of 1968. A million students became alumni without walkouts, demonstrations or the booing of speakers. Commencement orations as of yore emphasized the values of hard work, patience and respect for the "System." If the rhetoric was traditional again, the style of many commencements was less formal than ever before. Not many caps and gowns were worn, and simple graduation ceremonies were held in small separate groups, even as picnics. Restraint did not mean apathy or resignation. Dr. Willard Dalrymple of Princeton University thought that youth could afford forbearance because it had won its "revolution." The negative aspects would be forgotten, he believed — its scruffiness, coarse language, sex freedoms, drugs, interest in the occult, mindless music, disrespect for the past — while the positive results endured, in the form of a new candor, tolerance for diversity, more acute sensibility, political alertness, and reaffirmation of a belief in the individual.

Some of the phenomena of the earlier youth "consciousness" had certainly faded. Most of the commune "families" of the Sixties foundered on ineptitude, lack of common interests and beliefs, insufficient funds, drugs, dysentery, and absence of purpose. The Whole Earth Catalog had ceased publication for want of readers. Human nature being what it is, the communes had found that free loaders were more plentiful than free spirits. The discovery that soap was as good as detergents, that candles could be made at home to replace electricity, and heat provided by kitchen stoves, was the opposite of revolutionary. Going communal, whether in the city or on Cold Comfort Farm, was not much of an affront to the "System" and living on welfare or government food stamps was not independence.

The other runaways of 1968, to Haight-Ashbury and the East Village, had gone back home, and many of the blacks who had come north to the

Promised Land were leaving its crowded ghettos, dangerous streets, poverty, unemployment, crime and drugs, and returning to Georgia, Alabama and Mississippi. They felt more "at home" there, the visible signs of discrimination had to a noticeable extent been removed, and new industry in the South offered jobs.

Blacks in the colleges had broadened their perspectives as well as increased their numbers. Black Studies had slipped away and the Black Student Union dissolved on many campuses. Where it survived it had become reformist. Some college blacks supported Nixon, and for that matter George Wallace. Black Power had become less a revolutionary slogan than a college diploma and a position in a bank. The redistribution of wealth would not come about by looting but by entering the white business world. Floyd McKissick, former head of the Congress for Racial Equality, one of the fire-eaters of black nationalism, was suddenly a successful "black capitalist" in real estate and a Nixon supporter.

Black indignation had also been diverted — some might say sublimated — by the increasing number and popularity of black films. A few of them, by black directors, were "serious," reflecting "the black experience" in urban settings, the rural South and personal relationships. Then, just as capitalistic publishers had sold books by and about young revolutionaries, so the white movie studios turned out black films for black audiences with the same content of violence, crime and sex that white films had found profitable. Most of them catered in addition to flagrant racism, portraying whites overcome by the cleverness, contempt, strength and skill of their heroes — creating what some blacks called the myth of "Super-Nigger" — more than amply compensating for the amused condescension with which Stepin Fetchit and other black actors had been treated in the white films of the Thirties.

Because of the growing market represented by the black middle class, as much as any awakened social conscience or pressures from equal rights or civil liberties groups, television had also introduced not only black programs but black commercials. Some black TV programs, shown in the "Sunday ghetto" of viewing time once occupied by white "cultural" subjects and documentaries, engaged in serious discussion of black problems — of construction worker, parent, drug addict, intellectual — but the level seldom rose above the low one of white discussion programs.

Black "access" to the mass media, the appearance of black TV reporters and news anchormen, the black-financed housing project in economically dislocated Newark, the congressional "black caucus" and the first National Black Political Convention, the Nixon administration's boast that more than a score of blacks were employed in the Executive offices, only emphasized the reality of continuing widespread racial discrimination. Blacks still tried without great success to gain admission to the craft unions.

Northern whites fought school bussing while indignantly denying racist motives. Some of the scenes in the Canarsie section of Brooklyn, as whites prevented black students from entering a school to which they had been bussed, recalled Little Rock fifteen years before.

Unlike the Democratic convention, where they had numbered nearly five hundred, black faces were few at what many Democrats scornfully viewed as the Republican "coronation" in Miami Beach a month later, at which Nixon and Agnew were renominated. Richard Nixon's Middle Americans served as the cast in a deftly managed television production which for that very reason — in contrast to the turbulent, emotional any-thing-can-happen atmosphere of the Democrats — did not make very dra-matic viewing. No dissension was evident on the floor, and when four antiwar veterans made their appearance, one in a wheelchair, large Amer-ican flags were neatly flung in front of them to hide them from the cameras.

At the Democratic convention youthful delegates had participated in the caucuses and all floor business. At the Republican several hundred young people, brought in by the National Committee, sat in the public galleries and applauded on command, as studio audiences do. Instead of trying to broaden their party by bringing in new members, the Republicans voted down proposed reforms, let conservatives retain control, and adopted the strategy of becoming a "new majority" by enlisting disaffected Demo-crats instead.

Many hundreds of young people were also outside Convention Hall, not sunbathing in Flamingo Park as the Democratic "nondelegates" had done, but trying to disrupt or delay the Republican convention schedules by impeding traffic or harassing arriving delegates. Their efforts were un-successful. They did not disturb the convention and did not get on tele-vision either, and although twelve hundred of them were arrested, no mem-ory of Chicago was evoked. The more cynical among the Democrats sus-pected that some of the rowdy phalanxes might have been hired by the Republicans themselves to supply dramatic counterpoint to the sedate convention. Nothing could be proved but the suspicion was not far-fetched. Provocation was implicit in the situation. Not only did the Committee to Reelect expect convention disturbances — to find out more about them was one of the purported reasons for the Watergate burglary — but its informa-tion came directly from the government. By the good offices of Assistant Attorney General Robert Mardian, who like Mitchell had moved over to the committee, James McCord was given access to reports of the Justice Department's Internal Security Division about anticipated violence. They came in many instances from FBI informers who had infiltrated various groups — among them the Vietnam Veterans Against the War and even the Weathermen — with the thought to provoke them into illegal action.

Threats of disruption could therefore be regarded as in a sense self-fulfilling. Nor did disruptive action actually have to take place. A few days before the Republican convention seven members of the Vietnam Veterans and a sympathizer were indicted in Florida for alleged disruptive intentions. They never got to Miami Beach but they would be tried anyway, and eventually acquitted, as the Gainesville Eight.

The Justice Department's unsanctioned aid to a political and highly partisan enterprise was short-circuited by McCord's arrest at the Watergate, both facts having afforded further proof that in the nervous world of professional "security" there was no distinction between legality and illegality, and the end justified the means. By his own account McCord indeed believed that the illegal was made legal by Attorney General Mitchell's evident approval of the committee's industrious design for espionage and sabotage, and behind Mitchell the White House's.

The FBI's use of agents provocateurs had flourished under J. Edgar Hoover — in addition to the Harrisburg Seven trial, based on the Berrigan-McAlister letters intercepted by an informer, there was the case of twenty-eight persons, ultimately acquitted, who were arrested in Camden, New Jersey, for breaking into draft board offices and destroying files with tools and means of entry given them by an FBI informer — but whatever might be said about the deceased director and his ideology or methods, his services to the White House and Congress were at least nonpartisan and professional, making the crucial differentiation between state and administration. His successor, L. Patrick Gray, undertook campaign speeches on behalf of Nixon's reelection.

The tone of the campaign was set in the President's acceptance of his renomination at a convention at which only one delegate vote was cast against him, for Representative McCloskey. The triumphant oration, intended to rise above party politics in its appeal for One America, made it plain that Nixon's One America was For Americans Only, and that all who did not vote for him were to be considered un-American. The theme would run, an anti-Red thread, through all the fall's electioneering, Nixon's last hurrah sounding exactly like his first in 1946, seeking to discredit his opponent by constant attack and innuendo. There was this difference, that in 1972, as a President engaged in global moving and shaking, he did not have to carry out an active personal campaign, but limited his public appearances to those he could call "nonpolitical," while cabinet members and other stand-ins made the running against McGovern.

Nixon was aided by the fact, as post-convention polls showed, that most Americans believed he had kept the promise made in the same Miami Beach hall four years before "to bring an honorable end to the war in Vietnam." The piecemeal withdrawal of troops and the continued bombing during negotiations were preferred across the nation to McGovern's campaign pledge of unilateral withdrawal within ninety days of his inauguration.

The campaign was for McGovern ill fated from its beginning. The advantage of the early convention was lost, and much more, when his running mate, Senator Eagleton, verified newspaper reports that he had several times been hospitalized for fits of depression, and acknowledged that he had not told McGovern when asked if there were any "skeletons in the closet." McGovern's "1,000 percent" endorsement of Eagleton, quickly followed by his decision to ask the Senator to step down, in response to demands from old-line Democrats and leading pro-McGovern newspapers, created a picture of indecisiveness, of softness succeeded by harshness, and offended many of the candidate's youthful followers, as well as Americans who had undergone psychiatric treatment without any detriment to their capabilities. The Democratic National Committee replaced Eagleton with R. Sargent Shriver, a link to the Kennedys by marriage, and as some saw it, a surrogate for Edward Kennedy, who did not want to run himself, at least not in 1972 and certainly not for Vice-President.

If the Eagleton "affair" detracted from the McGovern-Shriver candidacy, it might have been supposed that the Watergate "affair" would aid it. Eventually seven persons, the five arrested and the two leaders of the foray, Hunt and Liddy, who had fled the scene, were indicted for conspiracy to carry out political espionage. But John Mitchell's successor as Attorney General, Richard G. Kleindienst, regarded the case as a narrow one restricted to burglary and wiretapping, without entering into wider questions of motive and conduct in the name of "political intelligence."

The Justice Department's undisguised reluctance to get to the top of things defeated its own purpose. Under Hoover the FBI had frequently leaked news intended to be damaging to those, like Martin Luther King, with whom the director was annoyed. Now some in the FBI, and soon others on the prosecutors' staff, the Committee to Reelect, and even in the White House, leaked news that could not but be damaging to those who they believed were impeding or subverting the Watergate investigation. Day after day the Washington *Post* and other newspapers told the story, with its intimations of conspiracy, obstruction of justice, violation of campaign laws, and perjury.

The President himself was compelled to speak up, saying "categorically" that "no one in this Administration, presently employed, was involved in this very bizarre incident. . . . We're doing all we can to investigate the incident, not cover it up." No longer "presently employed" in the administration, John Mitchell, in a deposition in a civil suit filed by the Democratic National Committee as a result of the burglary, denied he was present at any meeting where "bugging" was discussed, and "I'll swear to that." Secretly, meanwhile, McCord and the others caught in the Watergate, as well as their lawyers, received funds from the Committee to Reelect and advice from Howard Hunt to plead guilty, remain silent, go to prison, and eventually be freed by Executive clemency.

The Watergate allegations were followed by others against the administration in news media with revitalized investigative instincts. The billion-dollar sale of American grain to the Soviet Unon, one of the results of the Nixon visit to Moscow, brought the accusation that large profits had been made by exporters through inside advance information. The Soviet grain sale, reducing American supplies — it amounted to one-fourth the entire wheat crop — also helped raise domestic food prices. In another case, an increase in milk-price supports was approved by the administration after dairy organizations made generous contributions to the Republican campaign.

Somehow the Watergate and other disclosures failed to rub off on the Nixon administration in its reelection drive. The President studiously ignored McGovern's remarks alleging venality — the Senator charged that the administration was "the most corrupt in history" — and kept the news media at a distance, thus preventing questioning, as he appeared at "non-political" occasions against such television backdrops as the Statue of Liberty and Independence Hall. At formal dinners newsmen were privileged to listen to him in another room, on closed-circuit television.

McGovern found himself in effect campaigning against himself, defending himself against previous statements or positions, while Nixon, who had made truly major reversals in his thinking, was accepted as a pragmatist. McGovern's principal issue, the Vietnam War, was defused by Kissinger's negotiations with the North Vietnamese and the continuing expectation of a cease-fire.

Since the President was holding himself above politics, the news media turned their camera eyes on McGovern and the opposition to him within his own party. Sizable blocs of Democratic voters were in the process of defection from the "wild radicals" in control; John Connally, the former Governor of Texas and former Secretary of the Treasury in the Republican administration, had formed "Democrats for Nixon"; organized labor was split as the result of George Meany's professed "neutrality," and various elements and personalities were in constant conflict behind the scenes of McGovern's campaign apparatus. Such news coverage, with its thoroughly negative yield for McGovern, amounted to a partiality previously unknown in modern political campaigns. On the nation's editorial pages, moreover, Nixon was supported by 753 of the 1,054 daily newspapers, representing 77.4 percent of the total circulation, and McGovern by only 56 dailies with a mere 7.7 percent of the circulation.

This overwhelming press support was given despite the Nixon administration's patent threat to the First Amendment, as shown by prior censorship of the Pentagon Papers; by subpoenas, citation and jailing of reporters for refusing to reveal their sources; by the numerous conspiracy trials, and the extensive wiretapping and civilian surveillance. The Chicago *Tribune* contributed $1,000 to the defense fund for Peter Bridge, imprisoned in Newark for refusing to tell a grand jury how he got a story about municipal corruption, but it wholeheartedly endorsed Nixon.

Most foreign newspapers also seemed to prefer the known to the unknown, if only in terms of the continuity of American policy, however unpredictable it might be. The Soviet press, while passing kind to McGovern, favored Nixon because Soviet-American relations came ahead of all else, and he had broken bread in the Kremlin. Moscow correspondents in Washington ignored the Watergate affair as well as the journey to Peking. McGovern's campaign against war, wealth and unemployment, which Nixon's surrogates viewed as anticapitalist propaganda, was to the Russians of less moment than the American wheat or visions of trade sugarplums. It was ironic to recall that in 1963 Nixon had condemned the mere thought of selling the Russians wheat as "harming the cause of freedom." "Why should we pull them out of their trouble and make Communism look better?" he had asked.

However it may have been particularized — in terms of race, at home; in terms of "peace" abroad — the paramount concern of the 1972 campaign was containment: the end of the attempted containment of Communism around the world, and the further containment of social change domestically. Behind the scenes, the White House believed it had already succeeded in "containing" the Watergate affair, limiting it to the seven men indicted for the "third-rate burglary."

The essence of the electoral campaign was Nixon's promise of gradual "change that works," while McGovern's supporters wanted a swifter pace and deeper purpose. Americans had made their desire for change known in every opinion poll, but they did not mean "too radical" change, or change at their expense, as they feared, in favor of the blacks, the "liberation" movements, and other "permissiveness." Enough was enough. In the first presidential election of the Seventies the events of the previous decade, which had acted as catalysts of change, in the end produced resistance to change. The antibodies overwhelmed the fever.

Richard Nixon was reelected on November 7 with 61 percent of the total popular vote. Only the single state of Massachusetts and the District of Columbia gave electoral support to McGovern. Yet the sweeping Nixon victory was something less than a positive mandate.

The "new American majority" Nixon had achieved was not a Republican majority. He was the first President to have an opposition Congress in both terms. The Democrats in fact won two additional seats in the Senate and gave it an increased liberal flavor despite the continuing authority of conservative southerners as committee chairmen. Several Republican stalwarts were defeated in such states as Iowa, Colorado, Maine and Delaware, and the President was blamed by many in his party for failing to support them for the sake of his own personal victory. In the House of Representatives three new members were added to the Black Caucus, to make sixteen.

The split ticket was more widely voted in 1972 than ever before, giving new form to the constitutional theory of checks and balances. What amounted to two separate elections, the presidential and the congressional, had opposite results. The President, with his emphasis on foreign policy and the war, had been elected above party, as he desired, and without debating the issues despite all McGovern's efforts. Some observers thought they detected the firming of a presidential system, like de Gaulle's, and thus a significant change in the traditional American system of three nominally equal branches of power. On the other hand, in electing a Democratic Congress with many young and vigorous new members, the nation may have acted subconsciously to protect and insure the survival of the system. Richard Nixon read the results his own way. After the election he moved gradually but inexorably to extend presidential authority in the domestic sphere as in the foreign. The conflict over presidential powers and prerogatives was being honed to cutting edge.

What the President had overlooked in his gratification over the huge vote of November 7 was the nonvote. The true election majority consisted of that abstention plus the anti-Nixon vote. Only 54.5 percent of the eligible electorate cast ballots; 39 million Americans did not register, and 24 million more, though registered, failed to vote. The absentees included newly enfranchised youth, who had been thought to be panting to cast ballots. Instead, their voting proportion was even smaller than the general average, only 49 percent of the eligible.

The wholesale abstention, whether the result of apathy or of conscious repugnance for both candidates, confirmed the uncertainty expressed by the indices of American hopes and fears. The relatively small turnout continued the downward trend in voting shown since 1960. Despite the record campaign expenditures, the registration rallies, the emotion involved in such questions as bussing, and the "clearest choice" of the century, 65 million Americans still did not care enough for the democratic process to take part in it. After all the politicization, depoliticization seemed to be the result.

McGovern had obviously failed in the political equivalent of a Billy Graham crusade — contributing to the failure by his own indecision, equivocation and compromise — but he had perhaps paved the way for future change and lessened the impact of future shock, by his stand against massive defense spending — when weapons become weapons systems the costs accelerate — against corporate excesses, and for tax revision, income redistribution, and a more open society. The Democratic party might be recaptured by those who considered themselves of the center — including many who had become "Democrats for Nixon" — but the center would have moved to the left, as a result of the McGovern campaign.

Yet the establishment of the "new American majority" and the overwhelming repudiation of the candidate who had raised questions about the bombing and the war, civil liberties and the Bill of Rights, political corruption and the concentration of Executive power, showed that for all their professed alienation middle-class Americans — or at least those who voted — would let nothing override affluence, comfort and the Horatio Alger myth.

By election time Americans had apparently disposed of the Vietnam War, throwing it away as part of the waste of an industrial society with an ever-increasing Gross National Product. Like cars and appliances, the lives and money spent in Southeast Asia were expendable. The best to hope for was that they would be stored in the national memory bank.

The war was not so easily discarded in terms of Vietnam itself. Five months to the day since the mining of Haiphong harbor Henry Kissinger and Le Duc Tho had on October 8 agreed upon a cease-fire, Hanoi having made it possible by abruptly changing its firm position that a military truce and a political settlement were inseparable. After the many months of stubborn deadlock, and while the fighting and bombing savagely continued, the North Vietnamese now demanded that the war end literally two weeks from next Thursday, or October 26. The October 8 agreement was to be kept secret until President Thieu could signify his acceptance, but if all went well Richard Nixon would have what he called "peace with honor" by Election Day.

The departure of American combat troops, the slowing down of its long offensive, and the pressure of the Soviet Union all contributed to North Vietnam's altered view. In the end it was not Hanoi but Saigon which still sought to win at the negotiating table what it had not been able to win on the battlefield: the acceptance of its unchallenged sovereignty in South Vietnam and the withdrawal of the 135,000 North Vietnamese troops there.

Nguyen Van Thieu had long anticipated the day when the United States would have to leave, and like Ngo Dinh Diem seventeen years before, in order to obtain the strongest possible political base, he had abolished elections in South Vietnam's villages and hamlets. The heads of these small units were again appointed by the province chiefs, all military men chosen by Thieu himself. Withdrawing their troops, the Americans could no longer insist on even the façade of democracy. Thieu made no attempt to gloss over his actions. Democracy was "difficult," he declared, and South Vietnam was not yet ready for it. A cease-fire would mean the return to political competition with the revolutionary forces, and the military man's instinct was against any democratic social change to meet the challenge. South Vietnam's "lost revolution" was irretrievable.

Before abolishing local elections, Thieu tightened his press censorship still more, and by decree he also hardened penalties for various crimes and made the death sentence applicable to more of them. He had proclaimed martial law, because of the North Vietnamese offensive, and received emergency powers from an unwilling Assembly. These enabled him to arrest 15,000 more Communist "sympathizers" and it was soon being widely reported that they were being tortured in "reeducation centers." The United States, which had trained and financially supported the national police, called the arrests an internal matter, the State Department declaring, after twenty years of contrary practice, that Washington could not "interject" itself into Saigon's affairs. In short order two more American-tutored Asian countries dissolved what little of the democratic patina they possessed. President Ferdinand Marcos invoked martial law in the Philippines, with many arrests, a purge of the civil service, and press censorship, on the familiar grounds of a "Communist" plot to overthrow the government. In South Korea, where 40,000 American troops were still maintained, President Park also resorted to martial law, to insure himself a constitutionally forbidden fourth term, in order to deal with the new and perhaps precarious situation caused by a sudden political thaw in North Korea, corresponding to that between the two Germanys.

It could be said in fairness to Thieu that he reestablished strong-man rule against the disruption and loss of authority caused by the war, and intensified by American withdrawal. The war had "fragged" South Vietnamese society, uprooted a generation, and destroyed much of the country's agricultural fundament by creating forced urbanization without the required industrial skills. There was also no doubt that a good many of the elected village chiefs had either been NLF sympathizers or accepted the reality of circumstances in which the guerrillas ruled at least by night.

While taking strong measures in foreknowledge of American departure, Thieu did his best to keep the Americans for a while longer. He made speeches calling for the "destruction" of North Vietnam, implicitly by the United States, instead of negotiations, and expressed fears that South Vietnam could not long survive without it. ARVN could not fight without the American air and artillery support on which it depended.

In the four years of the Nixon administration the South Vietnamese had lost more than in the preceding four years when the war was in escalation. They had suffered more dead in the four Nixon years than the United States had in the entire war, and had incurred 500,000 civilian casualties in addition. Vietnamization meant also that for the week preceding September 21 MACV could announce that there had been no American combat deaths in Vietnam, the first such casualty-free period since the Marines landed in March 1965. In November came a week in which no American deaths at all occurred, in combat or by accident. Further to dismiss the war as an American political issue, President Nixon had announced the end of conscription, in favor of an all-volunteer army in 1973.

The United States Senate took note of the pre-cease-fire political developments in South Vietnam by condemning the Thieu regime for its suppression of democracy. Then it rejected an amendment which would have cut off further funds for Vietnam, and approved a $1.8 billion military aid bill, thus reversing in September an antiwar amendment passed in July. The House similarly voted down any limitation of the war by statute. It was the end of any antiwar posturing by the Ninety-second Congress. In the final analysis it had proved unwilling to challenge presidential authority lest this entail responsibility which it did not really want to assume. It had accepted the role of a separate but unequal branch of the national government. Bogged down in its rules and procedure, dominated by its aged chairmen, wrapped up in committee secrecy, Congress would not even say, as it had dared say at the end of the Mexican War, that the United States had won a conflict "unnecessarily and unconstitutionally begun by the President of the United States," in that instance James K. Polk.

The truth was that the United States had not won in Vietnam under the cease-fire terms worked out by Henry Kissinger. Hanoi had yielded in accepting the separation of truce from political settlement, and in dropping its demand for what Nixon termed the "overthrow" of Thieu by American action. The United States on the other hand had accepted conditions which Saigon saw as leading to ultimate NLF control of the country. A cease-fire in place allowed North Vietnamese troops to hold what they had in South Vietnam, instead of withdrawing mutually with the Americans. The Provisional Revolutionary Government in effect received American acquiescence.

Hanoi had not "won" the war either; that is, it had not taken over in Saigon. But it had stood off the world's greatest military power for years, and finally exacted a settlement. It had an army in position in South Vietnam and controlled territory with at least a million people. That could be reckoned as only the beginning. The United States had, moreover, offered reparations, called reconstruction aid, to both Vietnams.

The Kissinger-Tho agreement of October 8 came four years to the day after Nixon's campaign speech denying "another chance" to those who had failed to make peace in their own four years in office. Because of objections from Thieu, and perhaps from Nixon himself after he had become aware of the implications, the United States delayed signature of the agreement. Radio Hanoi then lifted the secrecy from the negotiations, and revealed the cease-fire agreement which Thieu's rejection, it said, had made the United States break.

The charge that Nixon had allowed Thieu to exercise a veto brought the public announcement from Kissinger that an agreement was indeed "in sight," arrived at "with considerable difficulties and with considerable anguish," that the Vietnam War was "drawing to a conclusion," that in short, "peace is at hand." All that was required, he said, was another bargaining session of a few days, to adjust details and obtain clarification of some already agreed points. The President's negotiator misspoke himself. The points to be "clarified" were the vital issues of the peace, as they had been from the beginning. Besides, the revealed details of the agreement gave George McGovern a new lease on the Vietnam issue in the last days of the campaign. It was no better a conclusion than could have been had when Nixon took office in 1969, he declared, and those who agreed with him included some who, like Averell Harriman, had conducted the original Paris talks for the Johnson administration.

As with so much else in the campaign, the electorate apparently did not care about the specifications of the cease-fire. Any doubts about the terms or their earlier availability were overcome by the consolation of the war's long-promised termination. The administration could say that at least it had obtained an agreed settlement and thus "peace with honor," whereas McGovern would have withdrawn from Vietnam unilaterally, if elected, and without assurance of the release of American prisoners.

Yet by the same token Nixon would never be free of the possible accusation of history that his four years of war were unnecessary. For how many deaths, American, South Vietnamese and North Vietnamese, would the separation of a cease-fire from a political settlement compensate? How many destroyed South Vietnamese villages and North Vietnamese "military targets" was an eventual Saigon coalition instead of an immediate one worth? How many bombs had it taken to keep Thieu in office for the "decent interval" that the Nixon-Kissinger formula required? How, above all, could it be said that Vietnamization had succeeded, except that after years of American involvement the withdrawal of American troops would allow both Vietnams to proceed with the solution of their differences that had been so long suspended?

If the things agreed to at the end of 1972 had been agreed at the beginning of 1969 the United States would have been spared not only four years of soul-wracking travail but 20,000 dead and 50,000 wounded, and South Vietnam an admitted 80,000 dead (the actual number was probably higher), 240,000 wounded, 165,000 civilian dead and 400,000 wounded, and 1,850,000 refugees.

President Thieu's objections might add to the dead by delaying the cease-fire. He could not prevent it. He utilized the pause before the final act of agreement to speed the preparations for the struggle that would continue after the shooting officially stopped. Government propaganda teams were sent into the villages as they had not been since the forgotten days of "revolutionary development." Thieu's new Democracy party, with its levied membership, besought the remaining older political groupings to join with it in competition with the PRG political apparatus that the Phoenix program had not been able to eliminate. The result was called the Popular Front for Peace and Self-determination.

On the military side the pause before the final agreement served the important purpose of a wholesale arms delivery to ARVN by the United States, including planes of all categories, artillery, rifles and ammunition, in an emergency airlift recalling that which relieved Berlin in 1948. It could be presumed that the North Vietnamese were receiving similar deliveries to their positions in the South.

Another round in the Paris peace talks produced another deadlock. The North Vietnamese charged that the United States, under Thieu's influence, had presented numerous new demands. When Hanoi made counterdemands a recess was called and Kissinger, returning home, blamed the other side for changing its position and refusing to bargain "seriously."

In the United States, though the final signatures had not yet been affixed and there would be further "considerable anguish" before they were, the perceived end of the longest, most frustrating, most unpopular, most divisive war in American history, was accepted by 65 percent of those asked in a Harris Poll as a "fair compromise," while 13 percent felt the outcome was an American defeat. No cheers were to be expected, no parades, no feeling of a job well done, or a too-manifest sense of release, in view of the problems the conflict had created to add to those it had failed to solve. Foremost was that of Executive authority. Congress had not been able, if it ever intended, to contest the President's war-making power, and the conflict was ending as it had begun and had been continued, by White House fiat. The Senate was not required to give "advice and consent" to the Executive agreement which substituted for a treaty. As one Senate constitutionalist believed, an illegal war was illegally terminated.

On the domestic side the issue of presidential versus congressional authority had grown to involve the ultimate power of the purse strings. Inflation and the huge budgetary deficits led the President to demand control of the limits of federal spending, and to exercise a veto on congressional appropriations by refusing to expend funds which the legislators allocated. For Richard Nixon power over the budget meant the reduction of appropriations for education, social services, and on urban and ecological problems, but not those for defense. He vetoed an anti–water pollution bill to which the administration had pledged itself because he found it too costly. The $24.6 billion it called for was about what the space-moon program had cost. When Congress passed the bill over the veto the President countered with notice that he would spend only half the authorized money.

The controversy over budget control was carried into the new Ninety-third Congress and the second Nixon term, as was the controversy over "law and order." That cry had become somewhat muffled and the "Support Your Local Police" bumper stickers somewhat frayed, at accumulating evidence not limited to New York City, of police graft, acceptance of bribes, and connivance with the Mafia and the narcotics traffic. In New York, in an "inside job," police stole $73 million worth of heroin that was being held as evidence in the property clerk's office. In many cities civilian patrols went into the streets at night to supplement inadequate police protection, while the police themselves, demanding more men and more pay, took part in "job actions" amounting to illegal strikes. The President's answer to those who pointed out that toughness had not reduced crime was to propose more toughness, including the reintroduction of the death penalty for assassination, treason, kidnapping and air-hijacking. He coupled this with scorn for "soft-headed judges" and the "permissive philosophy" that sees social injustice breeding crime.

At the time of Nixon's reelection, more students were at college and more was being spent on the quest for "universal higher education" — a contradiction in terms — than ever before. By the end of 1972 the American learning establishment was turning out thirty thousand new Ph.D.'s a year. The 1970 Census revealed the quantitative increase in education. Of adults aged twenty-five or over, 75.2 percent had had at least a high school education, as compared with 39.6 percent in 1940. Those who had finished high school plus some college numbered 34.9 percent, as compared with 14.7 percent three decades before, while a college education or more had been attained by 12 percent as compared with 4.6 percent.

At the end of 1972 eight years had passed since the Berkeley "free speech" insurrection, and no discernible campus political activism was to be seen, except on behalf of local or limited causes. There had in fact been a return to the awareness that education was more than participation in current events. Some notable changes had been effected, though not entirely for the better in terms of a broad general education. Required courses had disappeared in many colleges, the traditional arts and sciences curriculum abandoned, written exams and grades abolished. Students were increasingly told to "design" their own courses. Not a few educators advocated an end to all formal study, and to classrooms, holding that "true education" came from life and from social mix.

The campus drug crisis seemed to have abated. Marijuana and hashish were widely used, but hard drugs had become few, if only because of high prices. The Consumers Union followed the American Bar Association, the American Medical Association, and other "Establishment" groups in advocating the end or lessening of legal restrictions on marijuana, as unenforceable. The man who had helped inaugurate American youth's drug experience ten years before, Timothy Leary, came to the end of his long psychedelic trip also. Forced to leave Switzerland after a brief stay as tourist, his claim to political sanctuary denied, he had wound up in Kabul, Afghanistan, one of the ports of call on the Ocean of Joy. Federal narcotics agents brought him home to face not only escape charges but a new indictment for drug-smuggling. He went back to the prison farm with a further sentence added to his original one, and was put to work in the garden.

Stokely Carmichael also returned to America, after three years in Africa, to fill what he regarded as a vacuum in black leadership, and to seek black unity through a new All-African Peoples Revolutionary Party. It seemed a case of too little and too late. Too much had happened in his absence. SNCC no longer existed, the Black Panthers had gone respectable, the Brown Berets were deactivated, the Young Lords of East Harlem were organizing unions instead of "revolutionary" demonstrations. Bobby Seale was a candidate for mayor of Oakland, where the Panthers had begun, and Erika Huggins, his codefendant in the New Haven trial, was an elected member of the Berkeley Development Council. Imamu Amiri Baraka, despite his conversion to Islam, was building a "New Ark" in Newark in the form of middle-income housing. Huey Newton went to church and Panthers passed the collection plate. Eldridge Cleaver had outstayed his welcome in Algiers and was seeking asylum in France. In their two years in Algeria the Panthers had experienced increasingly strained relations with a revolutionary government that, like those in Moscow and Peking, had found accommodation with the colonial-imperialists and was negotiating a large liquid-gas deal with the United States. Matters were brought to a head when the Algerian police seized $1.5 million in cash brought in for the Panthers by two sets of plane hijackers and returned it to the airlines, despite Cleaver's pleas.

The hijackers' writ also ran out in Cuba. Fidel Castro had become tired of receiving murderers, bank robbers and other criminals as political refugees. Many of the sixty Americans who had fled to Havana for haven found it in jail or the cane fields. Like Boumedienne of Algeria, Castro now saw benefit in improved relations with the United States, and began them with an antihijacking agreement.

Moscow and Peking, the ideological and historical opponents, were rivals also for American favor, the Russians especially having come to a carefully pondered decision in which Nixon's sweeping reelection was the pivotal element. The huge American wheat deal was made necessary by a Soviet crop failure, but this was only part of the general economic misfortune which had befallen the workers' state, after more than a half-century of planning in the name of socialism. Instead of the scheduled growth in national income of 6 percent only 4 percent had been achieved in 1971, making necessary a 50 percent reduction in the planned increases of consumer goods. Harking back, in effect, to Lenin's New Economic Policy of a half-century before, Brezhnev's Politburo had evidently come to the conclusion that future economic development was more surely achieved in cooperation than in competition with Western technology and finance. The American wheat purchase opened the Soviet door to the prospect of capital investment from abroad, credits, loans, joint industrial enterprises with American and Japanese firms, and the sale of Soviet bonds in the snakepit of capitalism, Wall Street. The president of the New York Stock Exchange was feted in Moscow, the Rockefellers' Chase Manhattan Bank opened an office on Karl Marx Square, and Pepsi-Cola, which Vice-President Nixon had persuaded Soviet leaders to taste timorously in his "kitchen cabinet" visit in 1959, was given a franchise in exchange for the increased export of vodka to the United States. One cost of Soviet-American detente was the Kremlin's increased repression of dissident intellectuals. It would reach culmination in the expulsion of the Nobel Prize novelist Alexander Solzhenitsyn. Thaw abroad did not mean relaxation at home.

With international relations becoming more stabilized by the ending of the Vietnam intervention, the moves toward European security, the nuclear arms limitations, and the rapprochement between the two Germanys, domestic economic considerations seemed likely to become the principal concern of the second Nixon administration, however much the foreign policy–minded President might want to apply himself to his and Kissinger's new world order. Inflation, budgetary deficits, the value of the dollar, and consumer complaints daily became larger problems as the Gross National Product which served as the index of affluence steadily increased.

But the peace upon which the return to other priorities depended was delayed. Two months after Henry Kissinger had reported it "at hand," no American troops or prisoners had come home for Christmas, as had been hoped. The Nativity was celebrated, instead, by the resumption of bombing against North Vietnam, at levels of intensity and sustainment never before achieved in the history of warfare. The statistics of sorties, strikes and targets became meaningless as hour after hour wave after wave of B-52 bombers spread their destruction across the countryside. From Thailand and distant Guam they struck deliberately at Hanoi and Haiphong, this time without resort to semantics. This time also the North Vietnamese were prepared. One B-52 after another was shot down, seventeen in all, by Soviet-supplied SAM missiles.

The bombing was ordered by President Nixon after the United States abruptly broke off the Paris talks between Kissinger and Le Duc Tho. They had stretched into fifteen sessions instead of the two or three confidently foreseen by the White House adviser. The stumbling block was, as it had always been, whether Vietnam was one state or two. Thieu demanded full sovereignty over all South Vietnamese territory, including that held by North Vietnamese and NLF troops.

Possibly, Kissinger explained about the new rupture, Hanoi after long years of war preferred its continuation to the greater uncertainties of peace. The same might be said of the Thieu government. Both Hanoi and Saigon could want a postponement of the cease-fire to become the better prepared for it. It could not be doubted, as experience had taught since Yalta, that negotiating with Communists was difficult. They were suspicious of the West no matter how much state interests took over from ideology. They apparently believed that if terms were arrived at which the other side could accept — as the United States had originally done — they must by definition be ill-advised for the Communist side. They pressed for all the smallest points, and beyond.

Did the Gordian knot in Paris, however, warrant the kind of bombing campaign — rejected by Lyndon Johnson during his years in office — that Richard Nixon had commanded? The American air assault, against "military targets" in a country which Intelligence had declared to have no worthwhile military targets, devastated residential areas, hit hospitals, foreign embassies and ships, and shook the American POW compound, the "Hanoi Hilton." The unlimited aerial campaign could be measured against Nixon's pledge of five months before: "We are not going to bomb civilian targets in the North. We are not using the great power that could finish North Vietnam in an afternoon, and we will not." It might take several afternoons.

The new Australian government — after more than two decades, Labor regimes had replaced Conservative in both Australia and New Zealand — protested the American bombing, which began December 18 and with the single respite of Christmas Day continued until December 30. Sweden came to the verge of a diplomatic breach with the United States over its Prime Minister's condemnation of the bombing. The Canadian Parliament took the unprecedented step of officially rebuking a foreign government. Some of America's European allies, including Chancellor Brandt, sent private messages to the White House expressing consternation. Students demonstrated in Bonn and Amsterdam. The Pope was distressed. In the United States, though the death rained from the skies did not visibly disturb most Americans in their record Christmas shopping, congressional sentiment for ending the war by cutting off funds was rekindled. The Military Vicar, Cardinal Cooke, decided not to visit troops in Southeast Asia for Christmas. In Thailand Bob Hope's jokes at the B-52 base at Utapao were not uproarious as the bombers went out and came back, leaving planes and captured and dead pilots behind. One B-52 pilot on the day after Christmas refused to fly any more missions. Captain Michael Heck of Chula Vista, California, a holder of the DFC and Air Medal with twenty-two clusters, won in 175 missions and three tours of Vietnam duty, was the first flying officer to fail to obey combat orders, though several had been grounded for "fear of flight." He was ready to go to prison, he said. "I can live with that easier than I can taking part in the war." A court-martial was decided against, and he was discharged "less than honorably."

The B-52 crews which came from distant Guam returned there shaken. They had been shot at over North Vietnam by whole salvos of missiles, the equal in number of their own "sticks" of dropped bombs. The cool young technicians who were used to operating with impunity at 30,000 feet had been jolted back to reality. Brought down after peace had been declared "at hand," new POW's were paraded before cameras and microphones in Hanoi. Some Americans at home admitted to reporters they were "almost glad" that the B-52's had been shot down, so much did they resent the unexplained bombing.

The Russians and Chinese both gave lip protest to the bombing, and Leonid Brezhnev let it be known that his scheduled 1973 visit to the United States still depended on an end to the war. But again, as with the mining of Haiphong, Moscow and Peking did not let their concern for their small ally jeopardize their competing relations with the United States. In an earlier time they might have created a diversion in Berlin, or Quemoy and Matsu, even the Middle East or Zanzibar. There were no longer any East-West flash points, and as if to emphasize the passing of the era which had been ruled by the doctrine that bore his name, Harry Truman had died in Kansas City at the age of eighty-eight.

The Twelve Days of Christmas Bombing dismayed many Americans because, apart from the violence of the action itself, they gave evidence that the President, more than ever after his reelection, planned to act as a Consensus of One. He did not consult with others on vital decisions and he consulted with Henry Kissinger only to the point of brooking no dissent. He ignored Congress and his cabinet, and taunted the news media, through his press secretary, with admonitions against hampering delicate international explorations by criticism. The President was virtually unaccountable.

The Vice-President also apparently deemed himself a law unto himself, in his own fashion. Spiro Agnew had celebrated Christmas by receiving his regular cash payment from Maryland contractors, as he had done throughout his four-year term. At the same time a grand jury had been impaneled in Baltimore County to inquire into kickbacks received by the Democrats who had succeeded him there. Agnew was not perturbed. The investigation was in the hands of a Republican United States Attorney, who was the brother of a United States senator and a Nixon loyalist. The Vice-President felt safe.

The new Congress convened in the new year, aroused by the actions taken during its recess, though by now the bombing had been reduced again when Hanoi agreed to resume the Paris talks. Republicans as well as Democrats on Capitol Hill threatened resolutions to end the war if the

President did not, but any test was held off pending the return to diplomacy. Having failed to eventuate by Election Day, the cease-fire agreement was expected by Inaugural Day. If that was the target date, it was missed by not very much. The talks began again on January 8 on a frosty note. The obvious question was whether their resumption was due to the damage inflicted upon North Vietnam, or as some felt, whether Nixon had not in effect bombed himself back to the negotiating table, since it was the United States that had broken off the talks, while Hanoi had said it was ready to meet again at any time. Those who supported the bombing were still able to believe that, like Hiroshima and Nagasaki, it had accomplished its purpose of ending the war.

The cease-fire negotiators, at least, were not concerned with how they came to find themselves back in Paris. It was enough they were there, and the icy surface thawed quickly. This time Hanoi accepted Thieu's demand that the Demilitarized Zone be reinstated as a boundary line, within the meaning of the 1954 Geneva agreement. To this extent South Vietnam preserved its claim to sovereignty and separate entity.

On the same day that the Paris talks reopened, January 8, the Watergate trial began in a federal court in Washington. Daily revelations in the Washington *Post* had piled up after the indictment of the seven defendants in September, but since the majority of the pro-Nixon press throughout the country had paid scant attention to the accumulating details, the White House appeared confident that the matter could be confined to its narrowest dimensions, those of a "third-rate burglary." Any other intimation, said the President's press secretary, was hearsay, insinuation and "character assassination." The Committee to Reelect declared that to put the burglary into any larger context was "not only fiction but a collection of absurd lies." The White House again publicly denied its own involvement in "sabotage, spying or espionage." Jeb Stuart Magruder, who had been the deputy campaign director, said, "When this is all over you'll know that there were only seven people who knew about Watergate, and they are the seven indicted by the Grand Jury." He had striven to this end by his own testimony before that body of citizens.

Of the seven, the four Cuban-Americans from the large Miami community of anti-Castro exiles had taken their arrest stoically, as part of the risk they were prepared to incur for the "liberation" of Cuba. They had entered Watergate at the solicitation of the man they had known as "Eduardo" in the Bay of Pigs adventure — E. Howard Hunt. The object, they were told, was to look for documents showing that Fidel Castro had contributed to Democratic campaign funds. They found none.

As the trial approached, the committee's security chief somberly contemplated his prospects. He was "different from the others," McCord told friends. The balding, respectable, almost prim family man, who had

achieved his own "consultation" agency after twenty-five years of appreci-
ated service in the FBI and CIA, who was active in his Maryland suburban
community and church, and taught a course in industrial and retail security at a local college, had seen his position and career thrown away in a few
moments by a venture he had been dubious about to begin with. Apart
from the taint of common criminality he faced long imprisonment.

The CIA code was, if caught by the "enemy," to keep silent, take the
consequences, and be assured of help from "friends." After the indictment
the federal prosecutors had made McCord a customary offer, that he plead
guilty on one count of the seven against him, give state's evidence, and receive leniency. This would still mean jail, however, and McCord had no
intention of being confined. He devised a plan for freedom that could have
come from one of Howard Hunt's novels, telephoning the Israeli and
Chilean embassies, identifying himself as a Watergate defendant, and requesting visas, thus implying he planned to flee the country. The rest should
be easy. Since "sensitive" diplomatic missions were by common knowledge
"bugged" by their friendly host government, McCord would demand that
the prosecution disclose all wiretap material concerning him, and the government, to avoid embarrassment by admission of its eavesdropping, would
quickly drop the case against him.

The scheme failed. The government denied any record of the conversations. In another setback McCord's motion for a mistrial was rejected after
Hunt suddenly pleaded guilty and the four Cuban-Americans followed
suit. Meanwhile McCord had been receiving offers from John Dean, the
White House counsel, through an intermediary, of Executive clemency if
he too would change his plea. He did not credit them and continued to
demand his freedom. His grievances against the White House peaked when
Jeb Magruder took the witness stand and denied any previous knowledge
of the burglary he had discussed in planning meetings.

Magruder committed his later acknowledged perjury amid his busy
new duties as executive director of the Nixon Inaugural Committee, deep in
arrangements for the most elaborate installation festivities ever held. The
Watergate trial was still in progress when the President took the oath of
office for the second time, the only fly in the sweet-smelling ceremonial
ointment being the fact that the cease-fire finally arrived at in Paris required so much drafting that it would not be ready by January 20. The
President had, however, halted all war action against North Vietnam on
January 15, and Kissinger and Le Duc Tho would initial the agreement on
January 23, three days after his new term had begun.

Nixon's second inaugural in 1973 was in a historical sense a parallel to
Lincoln's in 1865. Again the country was emerging from a bloodletting
civil war — though in this case a Vietnamese civil war, as Kissinger at last
publicly acknowledged — which had torn apart the American political,

social and spiritual fabric. For a time Nixon was reported taking Lincoln as his model, since he almost always could find someone to emulate. It was the occasion again to "bind up the nation's wounds" so painfully inflicted and self-inflicted. But Lincoln had also called for "malice toward none; with charity for all," in order to achieve "a just and lasting peace, among ourselves" as well as "with all nations." The Lincoln theme was dropped. As Nixon stood on the Capitol portico, his hand raised, 150 congressmen were absent in boycott of the ceremony, and 75,000 antiwar demonstrators at the Washington Monument and other patriotic sites took part in what was in effect a memorial for all the protests and parades of the preceding decade.

Spiro Agnew was also sworn in again that day. He had begun to hear rumors that the grand jury in Baltimore County was looking into his affairs, but he reflected confidence and serenity, as always, when he took his oath of office.

What might have been a Lincoln-like Nixon second inaugural had instead the pre-Depression flavor and sentiments of Calvin Coolidge's inaugural in 1925, stressing individual self-reliance and limited governmental responsibility. Nixon used Kennedy's 1961 pledge of engagement to promise governmental disengagement at home and abroad. "Let each of us ask not just what Government will do for me, but what I can do for myself." He did not attempt to bind up the wounds, but would let history judge of America's greatness and good intentions. The inaugural motif was America the Beautiful, symbolizing national self-satisfaction.

The most specific repudiation of obligation was in the field of foreign affairs. "The time has passed when America will make every other nation's conflict our own, or make every other nation's future our responsibility, or presume to tell the people of other nations how to manage their own affairs." The Washington correspondent of the Hungarian news agency called the speech the first explicit American recognition of "peaceful coexistence." Moscow and Peking, it was to be presumed, found it similarly to their liking.

Two days after the inaugural, and as Kissinger arrived in Paris on the last of the twenty-four negotiating journeys since his commutation ticket was punched in August 1969, Nixon's predecessor in the Presidency died of a heart attack at his Texas ranch. A few hours before, Lyndon Johnson had been notified by the White House of the imminence of the cease-fire, and his energetic life must have ended with mixed feelings: relief that the war which had been his albatross and the malediction of his administration had finally ground to its end; and envy, perhaps bitterness, that it had been ended by a luckier man whom he had never much valued, a man in the process of dismantling the Johnsonian positive contribution to American history — the aims and agencies of the Great Society, including the other war, against poverty, which he had also been unable to win.

Lyndon Johnson was the overcomer, the overreacher, brought down, some thought, by hubris, the causative element in classical tragedy. The Texan's critics included those who believed he should not have embarked upon full-scale military operations in Vietnam, and those who believed he had not done what was required there to insure "victory." In the end Johnson's own words had to be applied to his administration. "It isn't hard to do what is right," he said. "The hardest thing for a President is to know what is right." He had not known.

The day after Johnson's death Kissinger returned from Paris. The cease-fire agreement had been concluded, and President Nixon was able, with unconcealed satisfaction, to tell the nation that "peace with honor" had been duly achieved as promised. The truce would go into effect after its formal signing four days later, and this time, unlike Geneva in 1954, the United States would be a full and convenanted party to the agreement. The President pledged strict adherence to it.

The whys and wherefores of the cease-fire might be argued, but the assay of it for most Americans was that, sixty days after the second Nixon inaugural, all American forces and prisoners would be out of Vietnam, and the American intervention there officially over. With it would go the PX's, the black market, the barbecue pits, the swimming pools, the barber shops, the commissaries, the slot machines, and other alien amenities. The Vietnamese villages which had sprung up around American bases remained desolately and without reason when the bases closed. Debris, rubble and empty beer cans were Ozymandias' monument.

The end of the war for Americans did not mean peace for the Vietnamese. Political conflict would certainly continue, and actual fighting in fact went on between the two sides long after the cease-fire — with 10,000 estimated dead in the first month and a toll of 60,000 in the ensuing year — while American bombing was maintained in Laos and Cambodia pending the formal cessation of action there.

"The last man to die in Vietnam hasn't been born yet," the cynical in Paris said of the cease-fire. Nationality was not specified. From bitter experience it was said in Vietnam that peace would come only when all Vietnamese were dead. A good start to that end had already been made. Nobody could really know, but the North Vietnamese and NLF dead in South Vietnam were estimated at 925,000, with 130,000 dead or disabled in the 1972 offensive alone. The South Vietnamese counted their own military dead at 185,000, plus 415,000 civilians. In the 1972 offensive the official South Vietnamese figures were 36,000 dead and 90,000 wounded, and a million new refugees. ARVN was so damaged and demoralized that Thieu had had to replace eleven of his thirteen division commanders. Without the support of enormous and instantaneous American air power ARVN might well have been destroyed.

Who then could claim victory in Vietnam? Having achieved "peace with honor" — as was believed by 58 percent of those asked in a Gallup Poll two days after the cease-fire — the United States was theoretically able to do so, though many Americans saw only a belated use of the Aiken formula proposed six years before that the war simply be declared "won" as the troops left. Failing all else, as the President made clear, the United States could equate "victory" with the safe return of its prisoners from Hanoi. The principal American objective, to crush a revolutionary movement, had assuredly not been realized.

Both North and South Vietnam were able to find victory in more particular terms, Saigon because Hanoi had not succeeded in displacing the Thieu regime, and because Thieu had obtained Nixon's reassurance that for the United States his was "the sole legitimate government of South Vietnam"; Hanoi if only because it had retrieved the 1954 Geneva agreement and had not had to withdraw its troops from South Vietnam mutually with the Americans. The National Liberation Front, above all, could lay claim to victory for having in effect created a third Vietnam. As any diplomat could point out, the "sole legitimate government of South Vietnam" was not the sole government in South Vietnam. The Provisional Revolutionary Government was recognized by some thirty other states.

When they began their war against the French in 1946 the revolutionary forces of Ho Chi Minh had nothing except their slogans, some captured arms, and a burning nationalism directed at the expulsion of foreign power. In 1954 at Geneva they had received sanctioned sovereignty over virtually half of Vietnam. They began to fight for the remainder of it in 1960, and now they had part of that remainder — they held one-fourth the area of Thieu's "sole legitimate" domain — able to spread their ideology as well as carry out all administrative functions. More than that, after the cease-fire and in violation of it, supplies and many more men, not only soldiers but civilians, poured across the Demilitarized Zone and down the Ho Chi Minh trail, into the territories held by the PRG. The reinforcement, Hanoi explained, was to counter the massive infusion of arms made by the United States into South Vietnam during the pause in negotiations. The North Vietnamese supplies included tanks, antiaircraft guns, heavy artillery, and missiles of various kinds, and the Khe Sanh landing strip so long ago abandoned by the U.S. Marines became the airfield for the new revolutionary areas in what had been South Vietnam's border region.

In Laos and Cambodia indigenous revolutionary forces aided by the North Vietnamese had also greatly increased territorial control. When a Laotian cease-fire was declared a month after that in Vietnam the Pathet Lao not only held more land and people than ever before — half the area and one-third the population of three million — but had made a major political gain over the 1962 agreement. Instead of the previous tripartite coalition of leftists, rightists and neutralists, the new government was bipartite, half Pathet Lao and the other half rightists and neutralists together, and Communist troops and police were allowed positions in the two capitals, Vientiane and Luang Prabang, which were declared "neutralized."

There was no cease-fire in Cambodia, where the anti–Lon Nol forces held half the country and nearly half the seven million people. The vacuum caused by the overthrow of Prince Sihanouk had never been filled, but though the exiled ruler tried three times through Chou En-lai to obtain a meeting with Henry Kissinger, he was rebuffed — later acknowledged a serious American error — and the United States continued its aid to the Lon Nol regime, which the war, authoritarianism, incompetence and corruption had made intensely unpopular. President Nixon saw it as "probably the best investment in foreign assistance that the United States has made in my lifetime," but it did not help matters any more than the continuing American bombing. The daily B-52 attacks instead stirred Congress to its boldest challenge of the President's powers. It could no longer be said that the bombing protected the lives of American troops, and all the American prisoners were being returned. Though congressional appropriations had constituted support of the undeclared Vietnam War, as several courts had ruled, the cease-fire had cleaned the slate, and there was no sanction for the bombing of Cambodia.

The day after he announced it, Nixon conceded that the peace was a "fragile" one. To add to the uneasiness and acerbity of his relations with the new Congress, he made no secret of his domestic intentions for his second term. In his first four years he had not been able, if he had wanted to, to carry out his pledge to "bring us together." With China and Russia he had opened channels of communication and accommodation. He had agreed to a cease-fire with Hanoi. But he had not made peace at home. His second term, it was clear, would be one of continued national division. While calling for reduced federal spending, he increased the proposed defense budget and sought the discard or diminution of social programs, such as the Office of Economic Opportunity, the Job Corps, Model Cities slum rehabilitation, and aid for education, science and health. He proposed increasing the cost of Medicare to the elderly, and decreasing grants to students, farmers, veterans, small businessmen, the unemployed, and the mentally ill. To Richard Nixon these were "special interests."

Many of the Great Society agencies had undeniably failed, and it was common sense to remove them as a surgeon removes a diseased appendix. The risk was that more vital organs might be injured in the surgery upon social services, and their transplanting from federal to local responsibility. Admittedly, also, many problems had not only not been solved by the Great Society programs, but new problems created in the attempt. Money, it had been discovered, did not automatically buy solutions. Social engineering was not quite the same as hydraulic, electrical or civil engineering. But could poverty, unemployment, crime and bad housing be alleviated by being designated local problems instead of national concerns?

The economy was expanding and industrial earnings rising when the war ended. The Gross National Product had increased 6.5 percent in 1972, the biggest gain since the mid-Sixties. Inflation, however, and the accumulated deficits at home caused by accumulated dollars abroad made a hollowness of abundance. Fourteen months after the devaluation of the dollar, intended to restore monetary stability, it was necessary to devalue again by another 10 percent, while continuing to hope for the best. The new crisis was precipitated by the premature lifting of domestic economic controls, and inflation-caused drainage of confidence took the form of a world flight from the dollar and soaring prices for gold. Congress had given the President power to impose controls, and with it the power to remove them, but the distressing results of the administration's actions were an inevitable bone of contention.

The Watergate trial and its aftermath created another front in the conflict between the Executive and Legislative branches, which was the broadest and most important of all; for apart from its own substance the Watergate affair served as the translation, a kind of political Rosetta stone, for all the other passages at arms — war powers, impoundment, budget control, Executive Privilege, centralization of authority and decentralization of responsibility. These were legal and constitutional as well as political questions, either too intricate and technical for general understanding, or shrugged off as partisan. When Watergate ceased to be a "third-rate burglary" and became the symbol for a broad range of official misdemeanor, a nation case-hardened by My Lai and the Pentagon Papers, reared to believe "politics is dirty," finally began to appreciate its significance: that presidential rule had been extended as never before, to the subversion of the fundamental political assumptions.

Ten days after Nixon's second inaugural the Watergate trial ended with the swift conviction by the jury of the two defendants who had not pleaded guilty, Gordon Liddy and James McCord. Judge John Sirica, displeased by the trial's lack of scope and initiative — in its conspiracy cases against radicals the Department of Justice had by contrast inquired minutely into motives, movements and associations — suggested to the accused that it was not too late to talk to the grand jury. To make his intention plain he imposed long prison terms on the five who had pleaded guilty but kept the sentences provisional, dependent on the extent of aid given to any juridical or congressional inquiry. He postponed the sentencing of McCord and Liddy, to afford them time for reflection. The judge, a conservative Republican, had won the nickname "Maximum John" for his usual severity.

As the frustrating trial ended, Judge Sirica declared that Congress might well wish to examine the background of the Watergate affair, since the Department of Justice had not. A week later the Senate unanimously voted an investigation, and Senator Sam Ervin, Jr., a North Carolina Democrat, a septuagenarian, a former judge and a constitutional expert — his devotion to the First and Fourth Amendments surpassed that to the Fourteenth and Fifteenth, to judge by his voting record — was named chairman of a select committee to scrutinize all aspects of the 1972 presidential election campaign. Eighteen years earlier Ervin had been the junior member of the select committee which recommended censure for Senator Joe McCarthy. This time the senatorial sights were perforce fixed on the White House.

Three days before he and Liddy were to be sentencd, McCord wrote Judge Sirica from the District of Columbia jail asserting that "political pressure" had been used to obtain silence and the guilty pleas, and that perjury had been committed and other persons were implicated, in the Watergate affair. At the same time John Dean was warning Nixon of "a cancer growing on the Presidency," and, according to the White House counsel, telling the President of the payments to Hunt and the others, now grown into blackmail, and of the possible involvement of "higher-ups." By ironic coincidence the White House was at the time immersed in a far-reaching plan for revision of the federal criminal code, and the President in a message to Congress had urged action "without pity" against law-breakers.

Judge Sirica read McCord's letter in a crowded courtroom struck into silence. The Watergate had burst, loosing the flood. McCord was summoned before the revitalized grand jury. Dean and Magruder were questioned by the federal prosecutors. The White House issued several denials of any prior knowledge of Watergate but the President in a television appearance finally acknowledged "major developments" in the case, while Ron Ziegler, the press secretary, characterized all the denials as "inoperative." John Mitchell admitted, after long maintaining the opposite, that he had indeed participated in conversations about the "bugging." Attorney General Kleindienst disqualified himself from the Watergate investigation because so many of his friends were involved, and soon resigned. Dean announced that he would not be made a scapegoat, and prepared his story for the Senate committee.

Whoever had taken part in the Watergate affair and to whatever extent, Richard Nixon learned on April 15 that the cover-up had failed. The evening before, he had attended the annual dinner of the White House Correspondents' Association but left early, before an award was made to Bob Woodward and Carl Bernstein, the two youthful Washington *Post* reporters who for nearly a year, with headline after shocking headline, had been covering the Watergate story. Attorney General Kleindienst stayed late at the dinner, and returned home to be informed of Dean's and

Magruder's testimony to the prosecutors about the concealment and the implication of "higher-ups." The next day, Palm Sunday, Kleindienst attended the White House prayer-breakfast, the President's favorite form of devotions, and after it he broke the dolorous news.

In true Euripidean fashion, misfortune had swept down upon Richard Nixon as he stood on the pinnacle of exultation. He had won "peace with honor," and within the stipulated sixty days after the cease-fire all American prisoners of war had returned from North Vietnam to their homes and families. These reunions, with cheers and tears commingled, took the place of any victory parades, although March 29 was in effect VV-Day, as the President proclaimed the end of the war.

It was not entirely over. The American command in Vietnam was terminated after eleven years, but it merely moved to adjoining Thailand, where 50,000 Americans remained, and from which the bombing of Cambodia continued daily. When the Senate Foreign Relations Committee raised the question of constitutional authority, the administration described the bombing as "cease-fire activity." The senators did not accept the explanation. A new dispute had crystallized, though temporarily overshadowed by the return of the prisoners.

Operation Homecoming was in its unfolding on the nation's television screens another example of presidential stagecraft. As the 566 men stepped off their planes, one by one, their senior officers made strikingly similar speeches to the theme of "God bless America and the commander-in-chief." Some of the prisoners charged they had been tortured, and many had undoubtedly been harshly treated, although prison conditions had improved after Henry Kissinger and Le Duc Tho began to talk in 1969. If there was any evidence of "brainwashing" among the released men it had not been done by the North Vietnamese, for all their methods of "re-education," but came from lifelong indoctrination in American ways of thought.

With the return of the prisoners, the long and harrowing war had its American heroes. They were for the most part members of an elite corps, career officers who had been automatically promoted while in captivity and had considerable back pay waiting. They were men who had fought the war by dropping bombs at designated points that were no different to them than points for turning or changing altitude. They had endured the years of captivity through organization and discipline under their senior officers. Despite the tight order in the prison camps of North Vietnam, however, a generation gap existed. Prisoners ranged in age from the late forties to the early twenties, and not all the younger men were so sure that the war was right or necessary. The newest captives, those of the Christmas Bombing of 1972, were especially indignant over the futility of what they had been ordered to do, as they viewed it. Unmistakable differences of opinion were evident in prison between various groups, but after release "amnesty" was tacitly granted to the dissenters by the Pentagon and was observed until an Air Force colonel, shot down in Laos, filed charges of misconduct against five Army and three Marine Corps enlisted men who had been captured in ground combat in South Vietnam and marched all the way to Hanoi. The men were accused of aiding the enemy, but after one of them committed suicide, the charges against the others were dropped.

While the returned prisoners were feted, and offered jobs, cars and vacations, those at the other end of the war's spectrum, the draft resisters and deserters, came under the dictum the President had applied to all criminals: that they be treated "without pity." Several members of Congress introduced amnesty measures but they touched no chord at the White House. Those who had broken the law, the President firmly declared, would have to take the consequences if they wished to return. Amnesty would be unfair to those who had served, and to the families which had borne loss. "You cannot admit these people died for nothing," explained Senator Hugh Scott, the Republican minority leader, after seeing the President.

Beyond legal or emotional arguments there were deeper reasons for a rejection of amnesty, having to do with the much-evaded question of the right and wrong of the war. Thousands of young men had ruined or tarnished their lives, by accepted standards, for their early recognition of what a majority of Americans later came to realize: that Vietnam was a "wrong" war in any pragmatic sense, however justified some might still think it. Any public controversy over amnesty meant the revival of old animosities. The issue was left to lie.

The liberated prisoners should have been those best able to see the changes that had taken place at home in the Vietnam decade. They had in a sense been frozen in time, with values that many other Americans had meanwhile relegated to the past. One reason for the emotional welcome they received may have been a widespread feeling of recapture of that past, if only fleetingly. A difficult readjustment was forecast for many of them as they rejoined wives and children who had learned to live without them. There were divorces and separations, and soon after the return the first POW suicide. Some of them may have felt resentment for their long confinement, and others guilt, both for what they had done and because friends had been killed. Such personal problems did not constitute a major social crisis. There were, after all, tens of thousands finding it difficult to readjust among the nearly three million veterans, mostly conscripts, who had done their time in Vietnam.

The inner meaning of Operation Homecoming, if it could have been realized by those who were part of it, was that they had returned to a different country, made so to a large extent by the war and its impact. They were given summarized news accounts of their missing years; were surprised by long hair, short skirts and high prices, and were greeted by a new language, new car models, new ice cream flavors, and a Gomorrah of pornography. There was a New Politics, new technology, new music, new race relations, up to a point, and new social "permissiveness." These were the outward manifestations of change. The returned prisoners could also see and appreciate, if they but would — perhaps the only Americans truly able to do so — the change in the nation's heart and marrow wrought by the traumatic events of the Sixties. They did not have to wait long to learn of some of the things that had happened to their country in their absence, as the seven members of the Senate Select Committee opened hearings on Watergate and the 1972 election campaign.

In the same mammoth Senate Caucus Room where fifty years before the Teapot Dome oil-field leasing scandal had been examined, where nineteen years before Joe McCarthy had destroyed himself in his conflict with the Army and his senatorial colleagues, the highest proceedings in the land were once again convoked — what might be called the Grand Inquest.

Constitutionally it is for the courts to judge men under law, but there are other rituals which go more deeply to the sensibilities of an open, democratic society, and lead to judgments as powerful and effective as any in jurisprudence. Only when a majority public opinion had decided after the Army-McCarthy hearings that the Wisconsin Senator had used "improper tactics" did the Senate find itself able to vote censure, and that public opinion was crystallized by the daily exposure on television to the Senator's methods, and the insight into his intentions. In the same way the Select Committee on Presidential Campaign Activities set itself to ascertain whatever facts it could, under broader rules than were permitted in court and with far more extensive range. As the Watergate trial of the seven burglars had shown, the whole truth was not always derived from formal legalistic procedure, with its canons of evidence, its plea bargaining, and seriatim appeals. What the Senate could do and the courts could not was to explore matters not covered by statute. Specific criminal charges were the province of the United States Attorneys. The senators, Richard Nixon's political peers, could lay bare to public judgment the manner and methods of his governance, indeed if truth be told, the morality of his administration and the propriety of his own conduct. What the Supreme Court had refused to do — pass upon the powers of the Presidency by passing upon the constitutionality of the Vietnam War — the Senate could essay in its own way by scrutinizing the extent to which presidential power had been carried and the uses to which it had been put. Implicit in any judgment on Watergate would be a judgment on Vietnam, for the one had led inevitably to the other, and both had involved the exercise of power unaccountably, covertly and even illegally. Both represented the operation of a presidential system rather than the tripartite system of the Constitution. Whatever was or was not done in correction, it was the duty of the Grand Inquest to make error known.

The very fact that it had been summoned indicated that somehow the "System" had gone wrong. Accretion of presidential power did not have to imply seizure of power. It had come about by the domestic application of the boundless prerogatives employed in war and Cold War, and contributing to it had been congressional default and public disinterest, deference, perhaps irresponsibility. The nation itself was therefore being judged, while at the same time, ambiguously, it sat as jury in what has been called "trial by television." The universal medium would do again what it did best, the live transmission of historic national occasions, in this case functioning as a channel of education, teaching Americans how government had come to work outside the civics textbooks. Television not only communicated the news but was part of the news, and helped create it. Statements were made on television and instantly reacted to on television. Arguments were presented, admissions elicited, explanations offered before the cameras and for the viewers' benefit. The impact was immeasurable; in its special technical way television was the most overpowering news medium ever known. In the more traditional meaning of the term, however, that a news medium is concerned with the ascertainment of facts, their assemblage and the conclusions to be drawn from them, television had not distinguished itself before the Watergate burst. The mirror it had held up to society reflected mainly the headlines of the Washington *Post* and a few other newspapers and magazines which had done their investigative reporting against every possible obstacle, from official scorn to public suspicions. Television had become the principal source of "news" for most Americans, but the continuing story of Watergate with its grave implications demonstrated how limited its First Amendment credentials were. The newspapers had exposed. Only then did television disseminate.

There are even more serious, because more subtle, inhibitions on television as a news medium than lack of editorial initiative or courage. As the Senate Watergate hearings began, it had been nineteen years since the Army-McCarthy hearings with their chilling fascination, and Americans had seen in their living rooms countless court dramas in the Perry Mason vein and episodes of *Mission Impossible* without end. Since Guatemala, the U-2 affair, and the Bay of Pigs they had acquired an infinite awareness and perhaps acceptance of clandestine operations. They had become jaded, and at the same time less able than they once might have been to tell the differences between reality and "entertainment," so well had television done its work upon them. When Senator Lowell Weicker of Connecticut, one of the Select Committee, spoke in his opening remarks of the "acts of men who almost stole America" was he to be taken seriously, or was this a line from a late, late TV movie? Moreover, by being "immediate," television was also ephemeral. Would Watergate fade out, too, after its allotted thirteen or twenty-six weeks?

The answer at first seemed affirmative. Engrossing spectacle though the Senate hearings were, apart from their obvious significance, many Americans as so often before availed themselves of their right not to know. Complaints from those who missed their daytime soap operas and game shows led the three commercial networks to break precedent and agree to rotate their coverage, abandoning their jealous competitiveness. But as CBS, NBC and ABC opted for business much as usual, Public Television, the fourth network, attained a new level of national civic service with uninterrupted live coverage of thirty-seven full days of the hearings and complete replay in evening prime time. The Watergate television story more than matched *As the World Turns* and *Return to Peyton Place* in intricacy of plot, number of subplots, tangled motives, devious relationships, strange quirks of character, and singular behavior. At the end of the ten weeks of the first phase of hearings the audience ratings were at the top of daytime viewing on the commercial networks also.

The Senate committee began its long, painstaking inquiry two months after James McCord sent his letter to Judge Sirica, and fresh disclosures had filled the interim. The Watergate case had crossed paths openly with the Pentagon Papers case. The Ellsberg-Russo trial had plodded for tedious weeks through the intricacies of governmental classification when John Dean revealed to the Watergate prosecutors the burglary of Ellsberg's psychiatrist's office in 1971. The government's wiretaps of 1969 and 1970 against news leaks also came to light, including those which heard Ellsberg. When the government could not produce the wiretap records or authorization Ellsberg succeeded where McCord had failed. On the eighty-ninth day of the trial the Pentagon Papers case was dismissed, as Judge William Matthew Byrne put it, because of "improper Government conduct shielded so long from view." The dismissal did not vindicate the two defendants and it foreclosed any immediate chance of resolving the intrusion of the Executive into the judicial process. The intrusion had in fact continued during the trial itself to a point normally inconceivable, for Judge Byrne had been summoned to nearby San Clemente and was offered the directorship of the FBI, which was being vacated by the ineptitude of L. Patrick Gray.

The surprise ending in Los Angeles came the day after a New York grand jury indicted John Mitchell and Maurice Stans, the twin bulwarks of Nixon's original cabinet, for perjury, conspiracy to obstruct justice, and conspiracy to defraud the government, in connection with the $200,000 Vesco contribution to the President's reelection campaign. A few hours later, in Washington, the House of Representatives for the first time in the long history of the Indochina war voted against the administration, defeating a measure which would have transferred other Pentagon funds to the bombing of Cambodia. Since the amount was small and the money accessible from earlier grants, the House suspected a "Little Tonkin Gulf Resolution." In short order the Senate Appropriations Committee, which had supported all the administration's Vietnam moves, voted unanimously to refuse any additional funds for Cambodia and Laos, and the full Senate followed suit. Both Houses had thus said no to the President even as commander-in-chief. From Guam, meanwhile, a dozen B-52 pilots had written to their senators and congressmen protesting the continuing bombing of Cambodia. Several of them were grounded because of their opposition.

The President was beset on all sides, it appeared, and he had cleared decks to confront the situation which threatened his assumed invincibility. Two weeks after his first television appearance, when he had given the impression of joining the Watergate inquiry because he had failed to halt it, he addressed the nation again. Accepting responsibility for what he described as an excess of zeal by loyal subordinates, he announced the resignation of Haldeman, Ehrlichman and Attorney General Kleindienst, and the dismissal of John Dean. He parted from his close associates with regret, he said, and called Haldeman and Ehrlichman "two of the finest public servants it has been my privilege to know," which must have been how Shakespeare's Richard III regarded Catesby and Ratcliff. A bust of Lincoln flanked the President on one side as he spoke, a picture of his family on the other, and he ended his words with "God bless America, and God bless each and every one of you." Many who saw and heard him were reminded of the similarly emotional 1952 "Checkers" appeal which had retained him his place on Eisenhower's presidential ticket. This time it was different. Three days after the President's speech the public opinion returns were in, and 40 percent of those polled said they believed that he had not told the truth, and 50 percent that he had taken part in the cover-up.

The Senate hearings began on the same day Henry Kissinger met again with Le Duc Tho in Paris, trying to repair the ineffective cease-fire in Vietnam and to find some solution for Cambodia following the glaring failure to do so in January. Watergate obviously did not aid his bargaining position. It had not only shocked most of the rest of the world but cast doubt on the future effectiveness of Nixon leadership. But help came for the President from his newest friends. Leonid Brezhnev, visiting West Germany, dismissed the matter offhandedly — "The United States still stands," he said — and was soon himself in Washington and San Clemente to seek American technology, investment and industrial aid. John Dean's testimony before the Senate committee was delayed for a week in deference to the Soviet-American summit, and as American bombs fell heavily on Cambodia daily, as they had fallen on North Vietnam when Nixon visited Moscow, the President and Brezhnev signed a pledge not to use force or the threat of force against each other, or other countries.

David K. E. Bruce, the doyen of American diplomatists, arrived in Peking, meanwhile, to establish a "liaison office" which was in effect an American embassy. More than eighty countries were now represented in the Chinese capital and a considerable concession was made in receiving the representative of the only one that still recognized Taipei also. When Huang Chen arrived in Washington to open his "liaison office" he was immediately and warmly welcomed at the White House without the usual protocol delay.

The pattern of world relations had manifestly changed. Lenin's "locomotive of history" had made a sharp turn. Though they all took part in the twelve-nation conference held in Paris to endorse the Vietnam cease-fire, the Big Four of World War II and after — the United States, the Soviet Union, Britain and France — no longer disposed of the world's affairs. A new Big Five — the United States, the Soviet Union, China, Japan and western Europe — would, in Henry Kissinger's plans, create a new balance.

The design had some obvious shortcomings. The Five, unlike Metternich's Concert of Powers, were not only unequal but still engaged in acute political, economic and even military rivalry. No reconciliation seemed possible between the Russians and the Chinese. They were adversaries in the Third World, and confronted each other armed across their own border. Moreover, when Chou En-lai assailed the "Superpowers," as he so frequently did, he meant the Americans as well as the Russians, in spite of the Spirit of the Forbidden City. Though Japan's economic relations with the United States were put under considerable stress by questions of trade and currency, the Japanese could not avoid both Russian and Chinese suspicions of serving as surrogates for "American imperialism." Nor did the future seem any more tranquil. The American pledge to Peking to break with Taiwan could conceivably put Chiang Kai-shek's successors within Moscow's fold to prevent Peking's reclamation of the island. It was certainly evident that as a result of the Vietnam War and Hanoi's expansion, Moscow had gained prestige in Asia.

Kissinger's global concept derived from Metternich, in spirit at least. The Austrian statesman's purpose had also been to achieve "a generation of peace" and his nineteenth-century Concert of Europe represented the restoration of conservatism after the Napoleonic upheaval. Now, in the final quarter of the twentieth century, the great political revolutions having run their course — as Kissinger evidently believed — why could not the two great Communist powers join the three capitalist powers in a condominium based essentially on status quo conservatism? Ideologies no longer seemed to be important in the relations among nations. To translate the concept from wishful thinking to actuality, to transform the secret diplomacy of the Vietnam era into the open joint consideration of the world's diverse problems, Kissinger became Secretary of State in title as well as in substance. He pledged a nonpartisan foreign policy — which he distinguished from a bipartisan one — and solicited the advice and consent of Congress.

Nixon and Kissinger had altered the possibilities of the future. But while they concerned themselves with the world balance of power, Watergate had been rearranging the balance of power between the Presidency and the Congress. Would America's international influence, authority and prestige also be affected by the political erosion around the White House?

Within a week after the Senate hearings began, the President gave further shaky ground. As the price for confirmation of a new Attorney General, Elliot Richardson, he grudgingly accepted a special prosecutor to take charge of the criminal aspects of the case, Archibald Cox of the Harvard Law School, who had been the Solicitor General under Kennedy and Johnson. Giving notice that he would not resign but would try to ride out the storm, Nixon at the same time confirmed the 1969 wiretaps that had begun the covert White House operations, the 1970 Domestic Intelligence Plan he had approved and J. Edgar Hoover had blocked, and the 1971 "Special Investigations Unit," and conceded there might have been "unethical as well as illegal activities" in the 1972 campaign. His justification for all these things was "national security." The presidential reply was characteristic. Patriotism had always been the first refuge of Richard Nixon.

The Senate hearings of 1973 were compared by the President's supporters — who argued that Watergate, if a crime, was a "victimless" one, and not much more than standard practice in American politics — to Joe McCarthy's political witch-hunt of the Fifties, which as they may have forgotten, many of them favored. There was a fundamental difference. The McCarthyites investigated thoughts and speech, and in effect tried and convicted many Americans not charged with criminal activities. The Ervin Committee investigated the allegation of grave statutory offenses, possibly implicating the President. Its proceedings were flavored by the chairman's moral homilies and quotations from the King James Version of the Bible.

A parade of former cabinet officers and White House aides; officials of the FBI, the CIA and the Department of Justice; consultants, advisers, undercover operatives and campaign functionaries, provided an abundance of testimony which though often conflicting and confusing showed that there had been subversion of the democratic process in the 1972 election. The young men who appeared as witnesses — neat, clean, soft-spoken, respectful, of the kind some parents would have pointed out for admiration to their own shaggy and argumentative sons — put their loyalty to Richard Nixon above legality. If they ever had any qualms, they also had the example of their elders in the administration, their suborners. John Ehrlichman told the senators he would hesitate to draw the line anywhere, even at murder, for the furtherance of "national security."

The inescapable conflict over Executive Privilege was provoked by the President himself with the disclosure that he had in 1970 installed secret recording devices in his offices and telephones, ostensibly in the service of historical record. These had preserved the conversations which could confirm or refute John Dean's allegations of the President's early knowledge of the concealment conspiracy, and specifically his receptiveness to the payment of hush money and the granting of Executive clemency to the imprisoned Watergate burglars. The President defied the subpoenas of both the Senate committee and the Special Prosecutor for the tape recordings, interposing the issue of constitutionality before that of criminality. The case entered the courts, and the man who collected "firsts" as Franklin D. Roosevelt had collected stamps had established another precedent. He became "the respondent President" in suits filed "in the name of the United States." In 1807 Thomas Jefferson had refused a court subpoena for himself and documents relating to the treason trial of Aaron Burr, but in the end he submitted the papers and averted a showdown.

Similarly Richard Nixon, after he had decided not to take the matter of Executive Privilege to the Supreme Court, avoided citation for contempt of the lower courts by eventually and reluctantly yielding the White House tape recordings as he had been ordered to do. Only then was it revealed that two of the most important presidential conversations had not been recorded — that with John Mitchell three days after the Watergate break-in, and one with John Dean after the latter's disclosures to the prosecutors — and that the essential portions of a third conversation, one with Haldeman that related to a "public relations" offensive to blunt the impact of Watergate — in short, the cover-up — had been somehow erased, while other passages were incomprehensible. The extravaganza of the White House tapes inflicted further serious damage to presidential credibility.

In the Watergate case, whether or not the President was personally involved, it was at any rate evident that the things done by his men were things they believed he wanted done. If he did not know about them it may have been because he did not want to know. As the occupant of the White House he was nevertheless responsible.

During the hearings the word impeachment was made thinkable by a resolution introduced in the House by Representative Paul McCloskey, the man who had obtained the lone non-Nixon vote at the Republican convention, and various formulas for presidential resignation were also broached on editorial pages. A more formal motion to impeach the President "of high crimes and misdemeanors,'" introduced by Representative Robert Drinan, Massachusetts Democrat and Jesuit priest, did not rest on

Watergate but among other matters cited the impoundment of funds voted by Congress, the administration's war on the news media, and the large sums expended for the improvement of the President's homes in San Clemente and Key Biscayne.

Some Americans, especially those who opposed Nixon's foreign policy initiatives, may have regarded his impeachment or resignation tolerable, if it should ever come, because he would be succeeded by their true favorite, Spiro Agnew. But the Vice-President, though "clean" as regards Watergate, had also come under suspicion of wrongdoing, in the Maryland investigation having to do with state contracts when he was Baltimore County executive and later Governor.

Seizing the initiative, and to forestall indictment, Agnew in effect volunteered for impeachment, asking Congress to sit in judgment on his case. The House leadership refused to contravene the courts, and as the grand jury began to hear the evidence against him, Agnew not only tried to halt the proceedings by charging that its action against a sitting Vice-President was unconstitutional, but began suit against four newspapers, two television networks, and two newsmagazines for disseminating allegedly prejudicial leaks. He thus ended his incumbency as he had begun it, in diversionary embroilment with the news media. The leaks apparently came for the most part from his own attorneys and even the White House. But behind the scenes Agnew was engaged in plea bargaining with the Justice Department and thus in effect with the White House, to which he represented acute and added embarrassment. To great applause the Vice-President told a meeting of Republican women in Los Angeles, "If indicted, I will not resign," and repeated it for emphasis. This was not a promise to fight for vindication, as his followers believed, but notice to the White House that if not indicted he would resign, provided he did not have to go to prison. The bargain was struck. The Vice-President came to court in Baltimore, pleaded nolo contendere to one count of tax evasion for 1967 (the year deliberately chosen because it was before his election on the Nixon ticket) and was let off with a fine and three years of unsupervised probation. Legally he was now a convicted felon, and the Justice Department published a lengthy compendium of specifications of bribery and extortion.

Well on his way to the Republican presidential nomination in 1976, Agnew had been eliminated as a factor in American politics. His conservative supporters, betrayed by their paladin — their auto bumpers had read "Spiro is my hero" — sought solace in the hope that the message had not been vitiated by the untrustworthiness of the medium. The thirty-ninth Vice-President was the first to leave his high office in disgrace. The principal public reaction seemed to be one of disappointment that he had not gone to jail. Yet Agnew's offenses, familiar in politics, were dwarfed by the immensity of those bruited against the man who still sat in the White House, and who had twice chosen him for Vice-President.

By the date of Agnew's resignation, besides the seven original Watergate convictions, there had been fifteen resignations from the Nixon administration, four indictments, three pleas of guilty, numerous resorts to the Fifth Amendment, and the suicide of a congressman who had received covert campaign funds. Investigations were being conducted by two separate grand juries in Washington, four Senate committees, a House committee and the General Accounting Office, and three civil suits were in progress. In Los Angeles, Ehrlichman, Liddy and two other former White House aides were indicted for the Ellsberg case burglary.

The principal item in Representative Drinan's bill of particulars for impeachment was not any domestic "high crimes and misdemeanors," but a matter which the Senate was studiously considering: the unrevealed bombing of Cambodia for fourteen months before the 1970 invasion, and the deliberately falsified official reports which concealed it. Congress was at the same time perturbed by the continuing heavy daily bombing of Cambodia since the Vietnam cease-fire in January, and after Nixon had vetoed the congressional refusal to provide further funds, the Senate attached an end-the-bombing amendment to the key appropriations bill by which the government could keep functioning. Finally brought to bay, the President agreed to end all American action in Cambodia, and thus in Indochina, on August 15.

Nixon did not conceal his resentment and anger at the historic if belated action, and blamed Congress in advance for whatever dire might happen in Indochina, but on the appointed day, though the B-52's pounded away until the very last hour, the greatest sustained aerial bombardment in the history of warfare, carried out against all four parts of Indochina since 1964, did indeed come to a halt. It had unloosed 7.4 million tons of bombs — though "only" one million on North Vietnam — more than 2,000 American airmen had been killed, more than 1,200 were missing, and 3,700 planes had been lost.

The bombing of Cambodia concluded with 160 consecutive days of heavy attack, amounting to 36,000 sorties in which 250,000 tons were dropped. Yet when it was over, Phnom Penh was virtually encircled, its provisions brought in under fire by road and river, and 80 percent of Cambodia was held by the Khmer Rouge. The way seemed open for the return of Prince Sihanouk, who was prepared, he said, to help the Khmer Rouge "rule over a Communist Cambodia," though with no love for his revolutionary partners. If Cambodia represented the Nixon Doctrine "in its purest form," as the President had once stated, it had been a disaster for American policy.

With the bombing ended, Nixon sought also to put Watergate behind him and the nation. As to the blame for the White House climate which produced Watergate, "I accept it all," he declared. He deliberately did not present a definitive refutation of the testimony heard by the Senate committee, or try to answer many of the questions and contentions, but in television speech, written statement and rare news conference he reasserted his innocence and appealed to Americans to "get on" with the country's "urgent business." He stood then at 31 percent in public approval of his Presidency, matching Truman's end-of-term rating twenty years before and lower than Lyndon Johnson's when he withdrew in 1968. At Nixon's second inaugural, seven months before, he had enjoyed 68 percent approval. As he began to try to work his way back, the Manchester *Guardian* asked the question for everyone: "Can a leopard change its spots?"

The answer appeared to be no. The extended public controversy over the submission of the White House tapes, and the probing by the Special Prosecutor's office into the President's finances and friendships, culminated in the abrupt dismissal of Archibald Cox on orders of the "commander-in-chief." This in turn brought the pained resignation of Attorney General Richardson and his deputy, William Ruckelshaus. Their presence in the Justice Department had been the warranty for an unimpeded investigation.

Nothing so vividly illustrated Nixon's isolation in the White House and the confoundedness with which much of the nation was increasingly regarding him as what some called his dementia pro Cox. Public dismay raised what the White House itself described as a "firestorm" of protest, with 250,000 telegrams, a record number, descending upon the Capitol, and demands for impeachment from the American Civil Liberties Union, the AFL-CIO, numerous bar associations, and the deans of thirty-six law schools. In the House of Representatives some forty resolutions for impeachment or inquiry were introduced, and finally, after indecision, reluctance and delay, the congressional process of determining whether a bill of impeachment should be drawn up was begun. It was only the second such occasion in American history. The President's popularity fell to a new Gallup Poll low of 27 percent. (Congress, however, was rated even lower.) The pro-Nixon press deserted him. Not only the New York *Times* but the Detroit *News* and the Denver *Post* said he should resign. The "hard-hats," whom he had cultivated, turned against him, various polls showed. Even if no formal impeachment were to result, it was evident that in the court of public opinion Richard Nixon was being tried for gross breach of public trust, and found guilty by many.

The President sought desperately to repair matters. To replace Agnew he chose a veteran legislator, Representative Gerald Ford of Michigan, the House minority leader, and for the first time Congress instead of the electorate installed the man who would be a heartbeat — or perhaps an impeachment, a resignation, or a declaration of physical or nervous incapacitation — away from the Presidency. Ford was an archconservative, plodding and pedestrian, but he was at least reckoned honest and, reassuring to Republican congressmen seeking reelection, not above party. However, Ford's safe House seat, which he had held for twenty-five years and which had been in Republican possession since 1910, was won by a Democrat in the subsequent by-election, presaging widespread bad news for the GOP at the regular congressional polls in November.

Nixon also appointed a new Attorney General, Senator William B. Saxbe of Ohio, and a new Special Prosecutor, Leon Jaworski of Texas, and promised the latter the same plenary powers he had supposedly given Cox. The President made disclosures of various of his transactions that had come under scrutiny, including his real estate dealings and his income tax returns, the latter revealing that he had availed himself of many loopholes and had taken large deductions. He undertook a series of public appearances to emphasize his determination not to resign, and in the process brought the American Presidency to its moral nadir, some thought, with his televised affirmation, "I'm not a crook." The implication was that such a disavowal had become necessary.

But Nixon's real hopes for finishing out his term rested upon the nature of the Presidency itself, and its indispensable authority in matters of great moment. For emergency piled upon emergency, foreign and domestic, to demand strong executive action, and Nixon was able to demonstrate that, even if not to everybody's satisfaction, he could act decisively and as he himself put it, "keep cool."

Thus, in the midst of the Agnew contingency, four days before the Vice-President's abrupt resignation, the new Soviet-American detente was shaken by another outbreak of war in the Middle East. Arab forces from Egypt and Syria opened a two-front attack on Israel, across the Suez Canal into Sinai and upon the Golan Heights, trying to regain some of their territory lost in the Six-Day War of 1967. This time the conflict lasted eighteen days and its significance lay not only in an unexpected Arab fighting spirit but in their skilled use of the modern weapons which the Russians had plentifully provided. The attack, begun on the solemn Jewish Day of Atonement, Yom Kippur, was eventually contained by the Israelis; indeed, they surrounded an Egyptian army corps after themselves crossing the canal and taking new Egyptian soil. The Kremlin, attempting to save the situation for its clients, proposed joint Soviet-American intervention to end the hostilities, and failing that, indicated it might act alone. The United States responded with a worldwide alert of its armed forces. A possible Great Power confrontation was avoided when the United States and the Soviet Union joined in support of a United Nations cease-fire resolution. But so low had presidential credibility shrunk that the alert aroused widespread suspicion as a possible diversion from Watergate, suspicion which Secretary Kissinger attributed to the successive presidential "crises of authority."

The Mid-East conflict shook the world balance Kissinger was trying to establish, not only because Soviet-American rivalry there could threaten detente, but because it reduced western Europe to separate nationalisms competing for oil favors from the Arabs, while Japan, its economic existence dependent on imported fuel, was weakened by reduced supplies.

The crisis had its welcome amends for the embattled President. Kissinger engaged in more personal shuttle diplomacy, seeking Arab-Israeli disengagement, and Nixon projected trips to the Middle East, to Europe, and for a second time to Russia, to preserve the image of the indispensable world statesman.

The Mid-East War stimulated a domestic American emergency also. The Arab oil-producing states, to discourage American support of Israel, imposed an embargo on their exports. These represented only a minor portion of the American oil supply, but the Arab action finally precipitated an energy crisis which had been long in the making. Its true causes were the profligate habits of an affluent society and the restrictive practices of the oil industry. As the government acted to reduce the use of fuel, dimming Christmas lights, curtailing air and highway travel, and "browning out" the cities, television screens continued to burn brightly with their commercials for automobiles and ever newer and more frivolous appliances. But with layoffs in the auto and aviation industries, with multiplying fears of major unemployment and recession in 1974, and with inflation inexorably increasing, the Yuletide was for many Americans a gloomy one.

For some it had its compensations. Judge "Maximum John" Sirica, formally sentencing six of the original Watergate defendants — Gordon Liddy had remained defiantly silent in prison — rewarded them for their aid to the various inquiries with minimum terms, allowing early parole. At the same time Donald Segretti, who had pleaded guilty to campaign "dirty tricks," began a six-month sentence. He was followed by Egil Krogh of "the plumbers," the first White House aide to go to jail; Krogh had also pleaded guilty.

Then, on March 1, 1974, as John Mitchell and Maurice Stans went on trial in New York in the Vesco case — the first such proceedings against former cabinet officers since the Harding era — came the climax of the Washington grand jury's year-long inquiry into the cover-up of the Watergate affair. Eighteen months after indicting the seven Watergate burglars, the panel of twenty-three average citizens returned indictments against seven alleged higher-ups. They included the four men who had been the closest presidential advisers — Mitchell, Haldeman, Ehrlichman and Charles W. Colson, Nixon's former special counsel — as well as former Assistant Attorney General Robert Mardian; Kenneth Parkinson, attorney for the Committee to Reelect; and Gordon Strachan, Haldeman's aide, who had served as liaison between the White House and the committee. All were charged with conspiracy, and other allegations of obstruction of justice and perjury were apportioned among them. "Deceit, craft, trickery and dishonest means" were ascribed.

The grand jury did not indict Richard Nixon; it had been told that such an action was not tenable. But it had asked the President to testify before it, and he had refused to do so. Now it sent Judge Sirica a sealed report relating to the President, and asked that it be passed to the House Judiciary Committee, which was considering the question whether impeachment required a criminal offense. Meanwhile, the open indictment charged Haldeman, the President's former chief of staff, with perjury in testifying that Nixon had demurred at the payment of hush money to the Watergate burglars. Thus it implicitly upheld John Dean's story that the President had approved.

The long-awaited findings by the grand jury brought the count against the Nixon administration to a score of persons indicted, several of them more than once; nine others who had pleaded guilty, five of whom had turned state's evidence, the latest being Herbert Kalmbach, the President's personal attorney and fund-raiser; and seven corporations and their executives, fined for making illegal campaign contributions. The Watergate cover-up indictments would be followed by others in the ITT, milk-price, and other campaign-financing cases.

Each new Watergate development brought an increase in public sentiment for a constitutional showdown. Even some of the President's loyal supporters challenged the House committee, "Impeach him or get off his back." But the impeachment process was intrinsically a protracted one, made further so by the President's employment of delay, the fourth dimension of defense. He and his lawyers also professed to regard impeachment as a conventional adversary process, demanding proof of criminal activity, permitting briefs and cross-examination, rather than a constitutional quest for truth. Above all, Richard Nixon sought to erase any distinction between himself as President and the Presidency as an institution and the bulwark of the Republic.

At any rate, Congress had to decide whether to sit in judgment on the Chief Executive. It had already done so to some extent by ending the bombing of Cambodia in August 1973. Then, on the first anniversary of Nixon's "landslide" election victory Congress had passed over his angry veto a bill defining presidential war powers. Under it the outbreak of hostilities must be reported to Congress within forty-eight hours, and they must be ended within sixty days if congressional authority to continue them is not granted. Some liberals thought the measure gave the President a prerogative for starting war which the Constitution did not, and it was generally agreed that Congress would find it difficult, as with Vietnam, to stop a war to which troops had been committed. But unsatisfactory as it was, the bill represented at least a token redemption of Congress's powers as an equal arm of government, the necessity for which Vietnam and Watergate had pointed to. By the pendulum of American history, Executive and Legislature seem to have alternated in authority, but the restoration of the Congress should not imply the ability, even if it had the desire, to exercise alone the ultimate decisions, in Walter Lippmann's phrase, of "war and peace, security and solvency, order and insurrection." Congressional redress should mean shared and balanced powers, not the mutually exclusive sort Nixon had tried to assert. To the extent that Executive Privilege has been a largely undefined area and presidential powers vague, assumed and "inherent," Watergate could lead to a much-needed constitutional resolution. It is in fact not only appropriate and necessary but perhaps fortunate that as the nation arrives at its bicentenary Americans should be contemplating the strengths and weaknesses of their political system, now one of the oldest on earth. It is a time to distinguish between power and authority, in both internal and international relations, and to recall the words of Richard Nixon in the 1968 campaign: "The people have a right to know why. The President has responsibility to tell them, to lay out all the facts. . . . Only through an open, candid dialogue with the people can a President maintain his trust and leadership."

Constitutional interpretation aside — and the original intention was certainly not the installation of a President-king — the remedies for unaccountable and unshared power, as exposed by Vietnam and Watergate, would seem self-evident. They suggest constraint through statutory limitations on surveillance and secrecy, more congressional overseership of quasi-independent agencies, and greater public answerability by Executive personnel. Some form of public financing of elections has become mandatory, for the original Corrupt Practices Act appears to have been more conducive than preventive. Even a new constitutional convention was proposed as a fitting observance of the bicentenary.

To prevent or arrest the spread of gangrene in the body politic from the wounds of Vietnam and Watergate requires more than first aid, however. A blood transfusion is needed in the political process, freer and more open elections and wider participation in them and in the definition of the issues they address. A proposal to return to the civics of the textbooks risks being called simplistic. Vietnam and Watergate may indeed have encouraged further cynicism toward political practice. One of the key witnesses before the Senate committee, Gordon Strachan, former White House aide, gave to young people wóndering about public service his advice to "stay away." Exactly the opposite is imperative, not antipolitics and nonpolitics but more politics. "Staying away" permitted presidential power to accumulate and decay. The people must verify that they want moral leadership, instead of only administrative management or the protection of their penates and prejudices. While Americans may no longer much believe in the old institutions, "they still believe in the old values," as James Reston has put it, and yearn for principled guidance out of their frustration and impotence.

The Grand Inquest, then, seemed to offer the opportunity for a gigantic catharsis, signifying the restitution of the "System" which had been corroded and corrupted. The very fact that Watergate could be brought to book, it was said, demonstrated that despite its weaknesses the "System" had "worked." But the escape from what might have happened, and what Americans not very long ago believed "can't happen here," had been a narrow one. The men who "almost stole America" had done so without excessive hindrance. A few judges, a few undaunted reporters and editors, some conscientious civil servants, a minority of congressmen, a handful of private citizens like those of Common Cause and Nader's Raiders, were the geese on Capitoline Hill who had awakened the garrison.

What some, more radical interpreters saw as a putsch, a conspiratorial attempt to take total control of a government — with secret police methods, illegal use of government agencies, extortion of funds, invocation of national security, defiance of legislature and courts, and congenital falsehood — had failed also because of the Nixon administration's own incompetence, pettiness and hollowness. But in this view the formula for American fascism had been devised; it *could* happen here.

There could be no cause for congratulation if the nation returned to the complacency of its old habits, if punishment of the subverters of the "System" were to suffice for reform of the "System" itself. After two hundred years of American political experience eternal vigilance was still the price of liberty, and "so deepe a wound," in the phrase of Euphues, "cannot be healed with so light a playster."

Hundreds who stood through the Watergate hearings — a new kind of Washington tourist in the summer of 1973 — were young, disenchanted and skeptical, both fascinated and repelled by what they heard. The Sixties had seen the emergence of American youth into a new regard of itself and the nation. With violence, confusion, arrogance and idealism, youth had challenged the order of things. Now, by other means, the challenge had to be pursued and made politically productive.

It would help that some of the objective factors in the national divisiveness seemed to have moderated. The war and bombing were over. Racial militance had been more usefully channeled. The nation's third city, Los Angeles, had elected a black mayor and so had Detroit and even Atlanta, which regarded itself as the symbol of the New South. College tumult had been muted. The Center for the Study of Violence, mass and urban, at Brandeis University closed down as no longer needed. The long series of conspiracy trials had petered out. Father Philip Berrigan and Sister Elizabeth McAlister had married. So had Tom Hayden and the antiwar activist-actress Jane Fonda. Rennie Davis, of the Chicago Seven and May Day, had become a follower of the "Perfect Master," a teen-age Indian guru. David Rockefeller had been feted in Moscow and Peking, John D. Rockefeller III had written *The Second American Revolution*, and the American Communist party had issued open membership cards for the first time since 1948. At Watkins Glen, New York, not far from Woodstock geographically but four years and an eon later, 600,000 young people attended a rock concert which was not political, not a protest or anti- or countercultural, but "just a party." Everywhere the contagion of drug abuse seemed gradually to be lessening. Even long hair was being trimmed back in the barbershops of the nation.

If America had not yet been brought together, perhaps it was not so much apart as it had for some years been, and this despite its continued restiveness and sense of unfulfillment, despite the President's natural instincts and calculated talents for the politics of polarization. Whatever issues may have lost divisiveness, the divisiveness of Nixon himself would, after Watergate, remain.

But its tenure was constitutionally limited. The elections of 1976, following two Presidencies which had lost their way, held forth the principal lever of popular power, that of the voting booth, for application to the fulcrum of democracy to restore responsive, fair and effective government. That would be less a matter of political party than of presidential integrity. Johnson and Nixon had amply verified the essential axiom of Euripides that Character is Destiny.

The thirteen colonies became the United States of America in 1776, and the date of the next presidential election therefore has an enhanced significance. The Bicentennial, after Vietnamization and after Watergate, given a cease-fire within Americans as well as between them, could mark another historical epoch, the beginning of Re-Americanization. For democracy is not inherently stable, and unless America becomes more democratic it runs the risk, as the events of the past decade have shown, of becoming less so.

POSTSCRIPT

The "decent interval" Henry Kissinger yearned for between his prize-winning "peace with honor" and the inevitable in Vietnam proved to be two years. It was not long enough to avoid the mortification from failure of thirty years of American policy there under six Presidents.

The forces of North Vietnam and the Provisional Revolutionary Government, having consolidated their positions inside South Vietnam, in March

1975 increased pressure in the Central Highlands and captured the provincial capital of Ban Me Thuot. President Thieu attempted a general strategic withdrawal, but the uncoordinated retreat turned into a rout and his disorganized troops abandoned large stores of American arms as they fled. Communist divisions rolled to the seacoast, took the big cities of Hue, Danang and Nha Trang virtually without battle, and in three weeks possessed three-fourths of the country. The now outnumbered ARVN fought desperately on the approaches to Saigon but as a military noose tightened around the capital Thieu resigned and General "Big" Minh surrendered on April 30. The way was open to "nation building" by the Vietnamese themselves and eventual reunification. The American presence was foreclosed, in a mass exodus with Vietnamese retainers and other refugees. Saigon was renamed Ho Chi Minh City.

In Cambodia, ravaged by five years of fighting after the American "incursion of 1970, the end came equally swiftly and decisively. Marshal Lon Nol took refuge in Hawaii, and on April 17 Pnom Penh surrendered to the Khmer Rouge. The American Embassy was evacuated.

Cambodia had been declared "the Nixon Doctrine in its purest form," but the political precept barely survived its promulgator. Richard Nixon gave history the last of his Presidential "firsts" by resigning his office on August 9, 1974, to avoid impeachment and removal for obstruction of justice and abuse of power in the Watergate conspiracy, as revealed by the White House tapes. Gerald Ford became the 38th President and Nelson Rockefeller, former Governor of New York, his unelected Vice-President.

The new Chief Executive, received on a tide of good will, quickly vitiated much of it with the abrupt "full, free and absolute" Presidential pardon of his predecessor, in brooding self-exile in San Clemente. More than a score of Nixon's associates had however been branded guilty of varied felonies and misdemeanors, and the key Watergate cover-up trial resulted in the New Year's Day conviction of Haldeman, Ehrlichman and Mitchell. The latter had been previously acquitted with Stans in the Vesco affair, but Stans then pleaded guilty to a campaign fund violation.

Generally relieved, if saddened and discomfited, by the outcome both of Watergate and in Vietnam, Americans occupied themselves with the problems of recession, unemployment and inflation. But the debacle in southeast Asia, and Thieu's farewell charges of broken American promises, created concern in the Administration for American "credibility" and "commitments" around the world. The Kissinger balance-of-power structure had also been severely shaken in the Middle East, the Mediterranean and western Europe — a left-wing military regime had taken power in Portugal — and though still preeminent in military and economic might, "the United States is no longer awesome," Defense Secretary James R. Schlesinger lamented, thirty years after Hiroshima.

So, as the official pageantry of the Bicentennial began, the time had come for re-evaluation as well as celebration, for the contemplation of not only whence America had come but where America was going, not only what America had been but what America would be.

BIBLIOGRAPHY

———

Abel, Elie. *The Missile Crisis*. Philadelphia, Lippincott, 1966.
Ambrose, Stephen E. *Rise to Globalism*. Baltimore, Penguin, 1970.
Arlen, Michael J. *Living-Room War*. New York, Viking, 1969.
Ashmore, Harry S., and William C. Baggs. *Mission to Hanoi*. New York, Putnam's, 1968.
Avorn, Jerry L. *Up Against the Ivy Wall*. New York, Atheneum, 1968.
Barber, James David. *The Presidential Character*. Englewood Cliffs, N.J., Prentice-Hall, 1972.
Bator, Victor. *Vietnam: A Diplomatic Tragedy*. London, Faber and Faber, 1967.
Becker, Howard S., ed. *Campus Power Struggle*. New York, Aldine, 1970.
Berrigan, Daniel. *Night Flight to Hanoi*. New York, Perennial Library, 1968.
Bodard, Lucien. *The Quicksand War: Prelude to Vietnam*. Boston, Atlantic–Little, Brown, 1967.
Brandon, Henry. *Anatomy of Error*. Boston, Gambit, 1969.
Bunting, Josiah. *The Lionheads*. New York, Braziller, 1972.
Casey, William Van Etten, and Philip Nobile, eds. *The Berrigans*. New York, Avon, 1971.
Chen, King C. *Vietnam and China 1938–54*. Princeton, Princeton University Press, 1969.
Chi, Hoang Van. *From Colonialism to Communism*. London, Pall Mall, 1964.
Chomsky, Noam. *American Power and the New Mandarins*. New York, Random House, Vintage, 1969.
———. *At War with Asia*. New York, Random House, Vintage, 1970.
Clubb, O. Edmund. *China and Russia: The "Great Game."* New York, Columbia University Press, 1971.
Cook, Fred J. *The Corrupted Land*. New York, Macmillan, 1966.
Cooper, Chester L. *The Lost Crusade*. New York, Dodd, Mead, 1970.
Corson, William R. *The Betrayal*. New York, Norton, 1968.
Cox Commission Report. *Crisis at Columbia*. New York, Vintage, 1968.

Critchfield, Richard. *The Long Charade: Political Subversion in the Vietnam War.* New York, Harcourt, Brace & World, 1968.
Demaris, Ovid. *America the Violent.* Baltimore, Penguin, 1970.
Devillers, Philippe, and Jean Lacouture. *End of a War.* Translated by Alexander Lieven and Adam Roberts. New York, Praeger, 1969.
Dooley, Agnes W. *Promises to Keep.* New York, Farrar, Straus, 1962.
Dooley, Thomas A. *Deliver Us from Evil.* New York, Farrar, Straus and Giroux, 1956.
Duncanson, Dennis J. *Government and Revolution in Vietnam.* New York, Oxford University Press, 1968.
Ellsberg, Daniel. *Papers on the War.* New York, Simon and Schuster, 1972.
Fair, Charles. *From the Jaws of Victory.* New York, Simon and Schuster, 1971.
Fall, Bernard. *Hell in a Very Small Place.* Philadelphia, Lippincott, 1966.
———. *Last Reflections on a War.* Garden City, N.Y., Doubleday, 1967.
———. *The Two Viet-Nams: A Political and Military Analysis.* 2d rev. ed. New York, Praeger, 1967.
Fall, Bernard, ed. *Ho Chi Minh on Revolution.* New York, Praeger, 1967.
Ferber, Michael, and Staughton Lynd. *The Resistance.* Boston, Beacon, 1971.
Firestone, Ross, ed. *Getting Busted.* New York, Douglas, 1970.
FitzGerald, Frances. *Fire in the Lake.* Boston, Atlantic–Little, Brown, 1972.
Friedman, Edward, and Mark Selden, eds. *America's Asia: Dissenting Essays on Asian-American Relations.* New York, Random House, Vintage, 1971.
Galbraith, John Kenneth. *Ambassador's Journal.* Boston, Houghton Mifflin, 1969.
Gallagher, Teresa. *Give Joy to My Youth.* New York, Farrar, Straus and Giroux, 1965.
Gannon, Robert I. *The Cardinal Spellman Story.* New York, Doubleday, 1962.
Getlein, Frank. *Playing Soldier.* New York, Holt, Rinehart and Winston, 1971.
Glasser, Ronald J. *365 Days.* New York, Braziller, 1971.
Goldman, Eric F. *The Tragedy of Lyndon Johnson.* New York, Knopf, 1968.
Goulden, Joseph C. *Truth Is the First Casualty.* Chicago, Rand McNally, 1969.
Goulding, Phil G. *Confirm or Deny.* New York, Harper & Row, 1970.
Graff, Henry F. *The Tuesday Cabinet.* Englewood Cliffs, N.J., Prentice-Hall, 1970.
Graham, Frank, Jr. *Since Silent Spring.* Boston, Houghton Mifflin, 1969.
Greene, Graham. *The Quiet American.* New York, Viking, 1956.
Griffith, William E. *The Sino-Soviet Rift.* London, Allen and Unwin, 1964.
Gruening, Ernest, and Herbert W. Beaser. *Vietnam Folly.* Washington, National Press, 1968.
Gurtov, Melvin. *The First Vietnam Crisis.* New York, Columbia University Press, 1967.
Halberstam, David. *The Making of a Quagmire.* New York, Random House, 1965.
———. *Ho.* New York, Random House, Vintage, 1971.
———. *The Best and the Brightest.* New York, Random House, 1972.
Hammer, Richard. *One Morning in the War.* New York, Coward-McCann, 1970.
———. *The Court-Martial of Lt. Calley.* New York, Coward-McCann & Geoghegan, 1971.
Harriman, W. Averell. *America and Russia in a Changing World.* New York, Doubleday, 1971.
Harrington, Michael. *The Other America.* New York, Macmillan, 1962.
Harvey, Frank. *Air War — Vietnam.* New York, Bantam, 1967.
Heren, Louis. *No Hail, No Farewell.* New York, Harper & Row, 1970.
Higgins, Marguerite. *Our Vietnam Nightmare.* New York, Harper & Row, 1965.
Hilsman, Roger. *To Move a Nation.* Garden City, N.Y., Doubleday, 1967.
Hoopes, Townsend. *The Limits of Intervention.* New York, McKay, 1969.
Horowitz, David. *From Yalta to Vietnam.* Harmondsworth, England, Penguin, 1967.
———. *The Free World Colossus.* New York, Hill and Wang, 1971.
Johnson, Lyndon Baines. *The Vantage Point.* New York, Holt, Rinehart and Winston, 1971.
Johnson, Sam Houston. *My Brother Lyndon.* New York, Cowles, 1970.
Kahin, George M., and John W. Lewis. *The United States in Vietnam.* New York, Dial, 1967.

Kalb, Marvin, and Elie Abel. *Roots of Involvement*. New York, Norton, 1971.
Katzman, Allen, ed. *Our Time*. New York, Dial, 1972.
Kissinger, Henry A. *The Necessity for Choice*. New York, Harper, 1961.
Kornbluth, Jesse, ed. *Notes from the New Underground*. New York, Viking, 1968.
Krause, Patricia A., ed. *Anatomy of an Undeclared War*. New York, International Universities Press, 1972.
Kunen, James Simon. *Standard Operating Procedure*. New York, Avon, 1971.
Lacouture, Jean. *Vietnam: Between Two Truces*. Translated by Konrad Kellen and Joel Carmichael. New York, Random House, Vintage, 1966.
————. *Ho Chi Minh: A Political Biography*. Translated by Peter Wiles. New York, Random House, Vintage, 1968.
Lansdale, Edward Geary. *In the Midst of Wars*. New York, Harper & Row, 1972.
Leames, Lawrence. *The Paper Revolutionaries*. New York, Simon and Schuster, 1972.
Leary, Timothy. *Jail Notes*. New York, Douglas, 1970.
Lederer, William J. *Our Own Worst Enemy*. New York, Norton, 1968.
Lederer, William J., and Eugene Burdick. *The Ugly American*. New York, Norton, 1958.
Lippmann, Walter. *Conversations with Walter Lippmann*. Boston, Atlantic–Little, Brown, 1965.
McAlister, John T., Jr., and Paul Mus. *The Vietnamese and Their Revolution*. New York, Harper & Row, 1970.
McCarthy, Mary. *Vietnam*. New York, Harcourt, Brace & World, 1967.
Manning, Robert, and Michael Janeway, eds. *Who We Are*. Boston, Atlantic–Little, Brown, 1969.
Mecklin, John. *Mission in Torment*. Garden City, N.Y., Doubleday, 1965.
Miller, Michael V., and Susan Gilmore, eds. *Revolution at Berkeley*. New York, Dial, 1965.
Mungo, Raymond. *Famous Long Ago*. Boston, Beacon, 1970.
Oberdorfer, Don. *Tet!* New York, Doubleday, 1971.
Pentagon Papers, The. Senator Gravel edition, 5 vols. Boston, Beacon, 1972.
Pfeffer, Richard M., ed. *No More Vietnams?: The War and the Future of American Foreign Policy*. New York, Harper & Row, 1968.
Pike, Douglas. *Viet Cong: The Organization and Techniques of the National Liberation Front of South Vietnam*. Cambridge, MIT Press, 1966.
Polner, Murray. *No Victory Parades*. New York, Holt, Rinehart and Winston, 1971.
Powers, Thomas. *Diana: The Making of a Terrorist*. Boston, Houghton Mifflin, 1971.
Powledge, Fred. *Black Power/White Resistance*. New York, Clarion, 1971.
Quinn, Edward, and Paul J. Dolan. *The Sense of the 60's*. New York, Free Press, 1968.
Rader, Dotson. *I Ain't Marchin' Anymore!* New York, McKay, 1969.
Ramparts, Editors of. *Two, Three . . . Many Vietnams*. San Francisco, Canfield, 1971.
Randle, Robert F. *Geneva 1954*. Princeton, Princeton University Press, 1969.
Reedy, George E. *The Twilight of the Presidency*. Cleveland, World, 1970.
Rigg, Robert B. *How to Stay Alive in Vietnam*. Harrisburg, Pa., Stackpole, 1966.
Rostow, Eugene V. *Peace in the Balance*. New York, Simon and Schuster, 1972.
Russell, Bertrand. *War Crimes in Vietnam*. New York, Monthly Review, 1967.
Sainteny, Jean. *Ho Chi Minh and His Vietnam*. Chicago, Cowles, 1972.
Salisbury, Harrison E. *Behind the Lines — Hanoi*. New York, Harper & Row, 1967.
Schoenbrun, David. *Vietnam: How We Got In, How to Get Out*. New York, Atheneum, 1968.
Shaplen, Robert. *The Lost Revolution: The U.S. in Vietnam, 1946–1966*. Rev. ed. New York, Harper & Row, Colophon, 1966.
Smith, R. Harris. *OSS*. Berkeley, University of California Press, 1972.
Standard, William L. *Aggression: Our Asian Disaster*. New York, Random House, 1971.
Steel, Ronald. *Imperialists and Other Heroes*. New York, Random House, 1971.
Stickney, John. *Streets, Actions, Alternatives, Raps*. New York, Putnam's, 1971.
Swanberg, W. A. *Luce and His Empire*. New York, Scribner, 1972.
Sweezy, Paul M., Leo Huberman, and Harry Magdoff. *Vietnam: The Endless War*. New York, Monthly Review, 1970.

Taylor, Maxwell D. *Responsibility and Response*. New York, Harper & Row, 1967.
Taylor, Telford. *Nuremberg and Vietnam: An American Tragedy*. Chicago, Quadrangle, 1970.
Trewhitt, Henry L. *McNamara*. New York, Harper & Row, 1971.
Ungar, Sanford J. *The Papers and the Papers*. New York, Dutton, 1972.
United States Army. *Area Handbook for Vietnam*. Washington, 1962.
Warner, Denis. *The Last Confucian*. New York, Macmillan, 1963.
Warth, Robert D. *Soviet Russia in World Politics*. London, Vision, 1963.
Weintal, Edward, and Charles Bartlett. *Facing the Brink*. New York, Scribner, 1967.
White, Ralph K. *Nobody Wanted War*. New York, Doubleday, Anchor, 1970.
Williams, John A. *The King God Didn't Save*. New York, Coward-McCann, 1970.
Windchy, Eugene G. *Tonkin Gulf*. Garden City, N.Y., Doubleday, 1971.
Yarmolinsky, Adam. *The Military Establishment*. New York, Harper & Row, 1971.

INDEX